Tolley's Discrimination in Employment Handbook

by

members of the Employment Department, Baker & McKenzie LLP

and

members of Blackstone Chambers

edited by Sarah Gregory, (Partner), and Paul Harrison, (Of Counsel), Baker and McKenzie LLP

with a foreword by Anthony Lester QC

LexisNexis®

Members of the LexisNexis Group worldwide

United Kingdom	LexisNexis, a Division of Reed Elsevier (UK) Ltd, Halsbury House, 35 Chancery Lane, London WC2A 1EL, and London House, 20–22 East London Street, Edinburgh EH7 4BQ
Australia	LexisNexis Butterworths, Chatswood, New South Wales
Austria	LexisNexis Verlag ARD Orac GmbH & Co KG, Vienna
Benelux	LexisNexis Benelux, Amsterdam
Canada	LexisNexis Canada, Markham, Ontario
China	LexisNexis China, Beijing and Shanghai
France	LexisNexis SA, Paris
Germany	LexisNexis Deutschland GmbH, Munster
Hong Kong	LexisNexis Hong Kong, Hong Kong
India	LexisNexis India, New Delhi
Italy	Giuffrè Editore, Milan
Japan	LexisNexis Japan, Tokyo
Malaysia	Malayan Law Journal Sdn Bhd, Kuala Lumpur
New Zealand	LexisNexis NZ Ltd, Wellington
Poland	Wydawnictwo Prawnicze LexisNexis Sp, Warsaw
Singapore	LexisNexis Singapore, Singapore
South Africa	LexisNexis Butterworths, Durban
USA	LexisNexis, Dayton, Ohio

Published by LexisNexis

A CIP Catalogue record for this book is available from the British Library.

ISBN 13: 9780754538851

Printed in Great Britain by Hobbs the Printers Ltd, Totton, Hampshire
Visit LexisNexis at www.lexisnexis.co.uk

List of contributors

Members of Baker & Mckenzie LLP

Eleanor Babiker, LLB (Hons), solicitor - Race Discrimination (6)

Mitchell Bell, LLB (Hons), solicitor – Race Discrimination (6)

Danielle Brouard, LLB (Hons), solicitor – Sexual Orientation (9)

Zoe Christoforides, MA (Hons) (Cantab), solicitor – Disability Discrimination (3)

Katherine Coleman, BA (Hons), solicitor – Sex Discrimination (8)

Lily Collyer, BA (Hons), solicitor – Common Concepts (1)

Victoria Costella, LLB (Hons), solicitor – Race Discrimination (6)

Lorren Crabbe, BA (Hons), solicitor – Common Concepts (1)

Sarah Cramp, MA (Hons) (Cantab), solicitor – Sex Discrimination (8)

Tessa Cranfield, BA (Hons) (Oxon), solicitor – Common Concepts (1)

Romaana Dookhun, MA (Cantab), solicitor – Common Concepts (1)

Daniel Ellis, BA (Hons) (Oxon), solicitor – Gender Reassignment (4)

John Evason, LLB (Hons), solicitor – Sexual Orientation (9)

Chris Garrett, LLB (Hons), solicitor – Disability Discrimination (3)

Sarah Gregory, LLB (Hons), solicitor – Religion and Belief (7)

Paul Harrison, BA (Hons) (Oxon), solicitor – Age Discrimination (2); Disability Discrimination (3)

Clare Horvath, BA (Hons), solicitor – Fixed-Term and Part-Time Workers (10)

Tom Kerr Williams, BA (Hons) (Oxon), solicitor – Religion and Belief (7)

Monica Kurnatowska, LLB (Hons), solicitor – Common Concepts (1)

Colin Leckey, MA (Oxon), solicitor – Sex Discrimination (8)

Ana-Maria Norbury, MA (Cantab), solicitor – Sex Discrimination (8)

Joanne Pairman, LLB (Hons), solicitor – Common Concepts (1)

Yvonne Payne, BA (Hons) (Oxon), solicitor – Age Discrimination (2)

Stephen Ratcliffe, MA (Cantab), solicitor – Equal Pay (11)

Kim Sartin, LLB (Hons), solicitor – Common Concepts (1)

Andrew Sutton, BA (Hons), solicitor – Disability Discrimination (3)

Mandy Tang, LLB (Hons), solicitor – Equal Pay (11)

List of contributors

Hilary Wilde, BA (Hons), solicitor – Fixed-Term and Part-Time Workers (10)

Julia Wilson, MA LLB (Hons), solicitor – Common Concepts (1)

Members of Blackstone Chambers

Tom Cleaver, BA Hons (Cantab) barrister – Common Concepts (1)

Tom Croxford, MA (Cantab) barrister – Common Concepts (1)

Paul Goulding QC, MA (Oxon) (Cantab), barrister – Age Discrimination (2)

Diya Sen Gupta, MA (Cantab), barrister – Sex Discrimination (8)

Ivan Hare, LLB (Hons) (London), BCL (Oxon), LMM (Harvard), MA (Cantab), barrister – Race Discrimination (6)

Tristan Jones, MA (Cantab); MPA (Harvard), barrister – Disability Discrimination (3)

David Lowe, MA (Cantab) BCL (Oxon) – Marital Status and Civil Partnership (5); Sexual Orientation (9)

Christopher McCrudden, Professor of Human Rights and Equality Law, Queen's University, Belfast, Barrister (Blackstone Chambers) – Religion and Belief (7)

Tom Mountford, BA (Hons) (Oxon), DipLaw (City, London), barrister – Common Concepts (1)

Jane Mulcahy, BA (Hons) London, barrister – Fixed-Term and Part-Time Workers (10)

Emily Neill, BA (Oxon), Certificat Supérieur de Droit Français (Université de Paris II), BCL (Oxon), barrister – Common Concepts (1)

Simon Pritchard, MChem (Oxon) barrister – Marital Status and Civil Partnership (5); Sexual Orientation (9)

Tom Richards, BA (Hons), DipLaw, barrister – Age Discrimination (2)

Iain Steele, MA (Cantab), BCL (Oxon), barrister – Equal Pay (11)

Sarah Wilkinson, BA (Hons) (Oxon), DPhil (Oxon), MA (Oxon), barrister – Common Concepts (1); Gender Reassignment (4)

Foreword by Lord Lester of Herne Hill QC

Lord Lester QC is a practising barrister at Blackstone Chambers and a Liberal Democrat life peer. As Special Adviser to the Home Secretary (Roy Jenkins) between 1974 and 1976, he developed policy on what became the Sex Discrimination Act 1975 and the Race Relations Act 1976. His Private Member's Bills have resulted in the enactment of Human Rights Act 1978, the Civil Partnership Act 2004, the Forced marriage (Civil Protection) Act 2007, and the Equality Act 2010.

In my preface to the first edition of this book, I looked forward to the day when the recommendations of the Independent Review of the Enforcement of UK Anti-Discrimination Legislation, *Equality: A New Framework,* by Professor Sir Robert Hepple QC, Mary Coussey, and Tufyal Choudhury, published in July 2000 ('the *Hepple Report*') would provide the basis for a comprehensive, coherent and accessible Equality Act. That day has at last come.

The *Hepple Report* was followed by the *Discrimination Law Review: A Framework for Fairness: Proposals for a Single Equality Bill for Great Britain*, published in June 2007. The passage of Labour government's Equality Bill was protracted, but the *Equality Act 2010* ('the Act') received Royal Assent on 24 April 2010, on the eve of the general election in May 2010. The main provisions of the Equality Act 2010 came into force on 1 October 2010. It is the most innovative and radical equality legislation in the common law world.

The Act is important for public and private law practitioners alike, and affects most areas of current law. It provides for equal treatment without direct or indirect discrimination in employment, housing, education and the provision of public services. It gives new protection to the fundamental right to equal treatment without discrimination anchored in Article 14 of the European Convention on Human Rights and EU equality legislation.

The Act clarifies and extends the concepts of discrimination, harassment and victimisation and applies them across nine protected characteristics: age, disability, gender reassignment, marriage and civil partnership, pregnancy and maternity, race, religion or belief, sex and sexual orientation. The Act

- extends the circumstances in which a person is protected against discrimination, harassment or victimisation because of a protected characteristic;
- extends the circumstances in which a person is protected against discrimination by allowing people to make a claim if they are directly discriminated against because of a combination of two relevant protected characteristics;
- allows an employer or service provider or other organisation to take positive action so as to enable existing or potential employees or customers to overcome or minimise a disadvantage arising from a protected characteristic;
- extends the permission for political parties to use women-only shortlists for election candidates to 2030;
- enables an employment tribunal to make a recommendation to a respondent who has lost a discrimination claim to take certain steps to remedy matters not just for the benefit of the individual claimant (who may have already left the organisation concerned) but also the wider workforce;
- amends family property law to remove discriminatory provisions and provides additional statutory property rights for civil partners in England and Wales so as to enable the United Kingdom to ratify Protocol 7 to the European Convention on Human Rights;
- amends the Civil Partnership Act 2004 to remove the prohibition on civil partnerships being registered in religious premises.

- empowers the government to enact appropriate harmonising provisions in response to any future EU imposed equality obligations (notably for a Council Directive on implementing the principle of equal treatment between persons irrespective of religion or belief, disability, age or sexual orientation {SEC(2008) 2180} {SEC(2008) 2181} forwarded to the EU Council on 8 July 2008.

The provisions on the public sector equality duty (ss 149–157), and s 159 (positive action in recruitment and promotion) will come into force on 6 April 2011. Draft regulations setting out what the specific duties supporting the public sector duty will require public bodies to do, and to which of the public bodies listed in Schedule 19 to the Act they will apply, have been published. The government will soon finalise the draft Regulations and lay them before Parliament for debate to come into effect on 6 April 2011. A draft order amending Schedule 19 will also be laid to come into force on that date. Guides are available on the web on the public sector duty and on positive action in recruitment and promotion; http://www.equalities.gov.uk/pdf/Public%20Sector%20Equality%20Duty%20guide.pdf and http://www.equalities.gov.uk/pdf/Positive%20Action%20in%20Recruitment%20and%20Promotion%20Guide%201.pdf.

The government will not bring into effect s 1 of the Act, which would have imposed a vague and unenforceable duty on public bodies to consider socio-economic disadvantage when carrying out their public functions.

The Explanatory Notes published with the Act provide lucid guidance on the structure and content of the new Act, and are available on the government's legislation web-pages; http://www.legislation.gov.uk/ukpga/2010/15/notes/contents.

The Act defines nine protected characteristics: age, disability, gender reassignment, marriage or civil partnership, pregnancy and maternity, race (including colour, nationality and ethnic or national origins), religion or belief, sex and sexual orientation. Powers are conferred to enable caste discrimination to be made unlawful as part of the definition of unlawful racial discrimination.

The Act defines the types of conduct which are prohibited (direct discrimination, indirect discrimination, victimisation and harassment) which apply (with limited exceptions) to all the protected characteristics. The particular issues faced by the disabled are reflected in a definition of direct discrimination which acknowledges that disabled people need to be protected but not necessarily by being treated in exactly the same way as those who are not disabled. The duty to make reasonable adjustments for the disabled remains and the concept of indirect discrimination is extended to disability for the first time.

European law will continue to influence the interpretation of the Act[1]. Apart from European Union law, the European Court of Human Rights has recently recognised that Article 14 of the Convention applies not only in areas covered by other Convention rights, but also where the State has voluntarily decided to provide additional rights: see *JM v United Kingdom* Application no. 37060/06, 28 September 2010, paragraph 45.

The pre-existing public sector equality duty applied only to race, sex and disability. It now applies to the other protected characteristics and has three elements:

- the elimination of discrimination, harassment, victimisation and any other conduct prohibited by the Act;
- the advancement of equality of opportunity between persons who share a relevant characteristic and persons who do not share it;

---

[1] Council Directive 2000/43/EC implementing the principle of equal treatment between persons irrespective of racial or ethnic origin; Council Directive 2000/78/EC establishing a general framework for equal treatment in employment and occupation; Council Directive 2004/113/EC implementing the principle of equal treatment between men and women in the access and supply of goods and services; and European Parliament and Council Directive 2006/54/EC on the implementation of the principle of equal opportunities and equal treatment between men and women in matters of employment and occupation (recast).

- fostering good relations between persons who share a relevant characteristic and persons who do not share it.

This duty is only enforceable by judicial review and the effective exercise of the Equality and Human Rights Commission's ('EHRC;) strategic enforcement role will be essential. The Act provides a mechanism whereby the EHRC can issue a compliance notice and if the public authority in question fails to comply with it, the EHRC may then seek a court order requiring the authorities to comply.

The EHRC, created by the *Equality Act 2006*, came into operation in October 2007. The EHRC brought together the three existing British equality commissions—the Equal Opportunities Commission (EOC), the Disability Rights Commission (DRC), and the Commission for Racial Equality (CRE)—and was the first statutory body in Great Britain charged with the protection and promotion of human rights. (The Northern Ireland Human Rights Commission, in existence since March 1999, was created by the *Northern Ireland Act 1998, s 68,* in compliance with a commitment made by the UK Government in the Belfast (Good Friday) Agreement of 10 April 1998).

The EHRC has issued statutory Codes of Practice which inform the application of the Act:

- a Code of Practice on Equal Pay;
- a Code of Practice on Employment;
- a Code of Practice on Services, Public Functions and Associations.

The Codes were issued by the EHRC on 26 January, paving the way for them to be brought into force. It is anticipated that they will be brought into force by a separate Order in late February 2011.

Much will depend upon the knowledge and skill of discrimination practitioners and the judiciary in translating the Act's legal principles and rules into practical reality, not only in the interests of their clients but in the wider public interest. The detailed chapters which follow provide guidance for legal practitioners and public and private bodies.

Anthony Lester QC

Contents

Contents

List of abbreviations

General

AAL	=	Additional adoption leave
ACAS	=	Advisory, Conciliation and Arbitration Service
All ER	=	All England Law Reports, 1942–date
AML	=	Additional maternity leave
BMA	=	British Medical Association
BNP	=	British National Party
CA	=	Court of Appeal
CEHR	=	Commission for Equality and Human Rights
CIPD	=	Chartered Institute for Personnel and Development
CML	=	Compulsory maternity leave
CRE	=	Commission for Racial Equality
DBERR	=	Department for Business, Enterprise and Regulatory Reform
DRC	=	Disability Rights Commission
EAT	=	Employment Appeal Tribunal
ECHR	=	European Convention on Human Rights
ECJ	=	European Court of Justice
EEC	=	European Economic Community
EHRC	=	Equality and Human Rights Commission
EOC	=	Equal Opportunities Commission
ET	=	Employment tribunal
ETS	=	Employment Tribunal Service
EWC	=	Expected week of childbirth
EWCA	=	England and Wales Court of Appeal
GMF	=	genuine material factor
GOQ	=	genuine occupational qualification
GOR	=	genuine occupational requirement
IRLR	=	Industrial Relations Law Reports
JES	=	job evaluation study
KIT	=	keeping in touch (days)
LIFO	=	Last in, first out
NMW	=	National minimum wage
OML	=	Ordinary maternity leave
PRP	=	performance-related pay
QB	=	Queen's Bench Division
SAP	=	Statutory adoption pay
SGO	=	Special guardianship order
SMP	=	Statutory maternity pay
SOCA	=	Serious Organised Crime Agency
SPP	=	Statutory paternity pay
SSAT	=	Social Security Appeals Tribunal
TUPE	=	Transfer of Undertakings (Protection of Employment)

Legislation

AR 2006	=	Employment Equality (Age) Regulations 2006 (SI 2006/1031)
CDA 1998	=	Crime and Disorder Act 1998
CPA 2004	=	Civil Partnerships Act 2004
DDA 1995	=	Disability Discrimination Act 1995
DPA 1998	=	Data Protection Act 1998
DPEA	=	Disabled Persons (Employment) Acts 1944 and 1958
DRCA 1999	=	Disability Rights Commission Act 1999
EA 2002	=	Employment Act 2002

List of abbreviations

EA(SO) Regs 2007	=	Equality Act (Sexual Orientation) Regulations 2007 (SI 2007/1263)
EqA 2006	=	Equality Act 2006
EqA 2010	=	Equality Act 2010
EqPA 1970	=	Equal Pay Act 1970
ERA 1996	=	Employment Rights Act 1996
FTR 2002	=	Fixed-term Employees (Prevention of Less Favourable Treatment) Regulations 2002 (SI 2002/2034)
GRA 2004	=	Gender Recognition Act 2004
HFEA 1990	=	Human Fertilisation and Embryology Act 1990
HRA 1998	=	Human Rights Act 1998
MPL Regs	=	Maternity and Parental Leave etc Regulations 1999
PHA 1997	=	Protection from Harassment Act 1997
PTWR 2000	=	Part-time (Prevention of Less Favourable Treatment) Regulations 2000 (SI 2000/1551)
RBR 2003	=	Employment Equality (Religion or Belief) Regulations 2003 (SI 2003/1660)
RRA 1976	=	Race Relations Act 1976
SSCBA 1992	=	Social Security Contributions and Benefits Act 1992
SDA 1975	=	Sex Discrimination Act 19875
SOR 2003	=	Employment Equality (Sexual Orientation) Regulations 2003 (SI 2003/1661)
WTR 1998	=	Working Time Regulations 1998

Table of Statutes

References in the right-hand column are to division and paragraph number. Paragraph references printed in **bold** type indicate where the Statute is set out in part or in full.

T

W

Table of Statutory Instruments

References in the right-hand column are to division and paragraph number. Paragraph references printed in **bold** type indicate where the Statutory Instrument is set out in part or in full.

Table of Statutory Instruments

Table of European Legislation

References in the right-hand column are to division and paragraph number. Paragraph references printed in **bold** type indicate where the Legislation is set out in part or in full.

Primary Legislation

Treaties and Agreements

Conventions

Secondary Legislation

Directives

Regulations

Recommendations

Table of Cases

A

Table of Cases

B

Table of Cases

C

D

F

G

Table of Cases

H

I

J

K

L

M

N

O

Table of Cases

P

Q

R

S

T

X

Y

Z

Decisions of the European Court of Justice are listed below numerically. These decisions are also included in the preceding alphabetical list.

Table of Cases

1 Common concepts

1.1 INTRODUCTION

Under UK law there is no general prohibition against discrimination. Instead, UK legislation makes discrimination on certain grounds and in certain fields unlawful. Since 1 October 2010, the principal piece of legislation dealing with discrimination is the *Equality Act 2010* ('*EqA 2010*').

The main aims of the *EqA 2010* are to consolidate, simplify and harmonise existing UK discrimination legislation and 'to strengthen the law to support progress on equality'. As such, in addition to harmonising key definitions to iron out inconsistencies and addressing important recent case law, such as the decisions in *Lewisham London Borough Council v Malcolm* [2008] UKHL 43, [2008] 1 AC 1399, [2008] 4 All ER 525 (disability-related discrimination) and *Coleman v EBR Attridge Law LLP* [2010] 1 CMLR 846, [2010] ICR 242, EAT (associative discrimination in the context of disability), the *EqA 2010* has also introduced a number of new discrimination protections.

The *EqA 2010* brings together the various strands of pre-existing discrimination protection covering: age; disability; gender reassignment; marriage and civil partnership; pregnancy and maternity; race; religion or belief; sex; and sexual orientation ('protected characteristics') (*EqA 2010, s 4*). It extends beyond the employment sphere, imposing a specific equality duty on public bodies (*EqA 2010, s 149*) and prohibiting discrimination in the provision of goods and services (*EqA 2010, s 29*). Both the public sector equality duty and discrimination in the provision of goods and services are outside the scope of this book.

The *EqA 2010* is supplemented by a set of Explanatory Notes ('*Explanatory Notes to the EqA 2010*'). The Equality and Human Rights Commission ('EHRC') has also published three statutory Codes of Practice, governing employment; equal pay; and services, public functions and associations (as to which, see **1.7**); together with separate non-statutory guidance ('Guidance'). At the time of publication, both the Codes and Guidance had been finalised (although the Codes remain subject to parliamentary approval).

1.2 UK discrimination legislation prior to October 2010

Prior to *EqA 2010* coming into force, there were several principal pieces of legislation which made up UK discrimination law, listed below. All of this legislation, with the exception of the *Part Time Workers (Prevention of Less Favourable Treatment) Regulations 2000 (SI 2000/1551)* ('*PTWR 2000*'), the *Fixed-term Employees (Prevention of Less Favourable Treatment) Regulations 2002 (SI 2002/2034)* ('*FTR 2002*') and *Schedules 6 and 8* to the *Employment Equality (Age) Regulations 2006 (SI 2006/1031)* ('*AR 2006*') (duty to consider working beyond retirement), has now been replaced in its entirety by *EqA 2010*:

(a) the *Equal Pay Act 1970* ('*EqPA 1970*') gave a man or a woman a right to the same contractual pay and benefits as a person of the opposite sex in the same employment, where the man and the woman are doing like work, work rated as equivalent, or work of equal value;

(b) the *Sex Discrimination Act 1975* ('*SDA 1975*') prohibited discrimination on the grounds of gender in employment, education, the provision of goods, facilities and services, the disposal and management of premises and in the exercise of public functions. It also prohibited discrimination on the grounds of pregnancy in employment related fields and some forms of discrimination on the grounds of marital or civil partnership status. *SDA 1975* did not cover discrimination in relation to pay or pensions;

(c) the *Race Relations Act 1976* ('*RRA 1976*') prohibited discrimination on racial grounds in employment, education, the provision of goods, facilities and services, the disposal and management of premises and in the exercise of public functions;

(d) the *Disability Discrimination Act 1995* ('*DDA 1995*') prohibited discrimination against disabled persons in employment, education, the provision of goods, facilities and services, the disposal and management of premises and in the exercise of public functions;

(e) the *PTWR 2000* give part-time workers the right not to be treated less favourably than full-time workers;

(f) the *FTR 2002* make it unlawful to treat fixed-term employees less favourably than comparable permanent employees and limit the use of successive fixed-term contracts;

(g) the *Employment Equality (Sexual Orientation) Regulations 2003 (SI 2003/1661)* ('*SOR 2003*') prohibited discrimination on the grounds of sexual orientation in employment and vocational training;

(h) the *Employment Equality (Religion or Belief) Regulations 2003 (SI 2003/1660)* ('*RBR 2003*') prohibited discrimination on the grounds of religion or belief in employment and vocational training;

(i) the *Equality Act 2006, Part 2* ('*EqA 2006*') prohibited discrimination on the grounds of religion or belief in the provision of education, goods, facilities and services, the disposal and management of premises and in the exercise of public functions;

(j) the *AR 2006* prohibited discrimination on the grounds of age in employment and vocational training. There was no corresponding legislation in relation to goods and services, premises or public functions;

(k) the *Equality Act (Sexual Orientation) Regulations 2007 (SI 2007/1263)* ('*EA(SO) Regs 2007*') prohibited discrimination on the grounds of sexual orientation in the provision of education, goods, facilities and services, the disposal and management of premises and in the exercise of public functions.

1.3 The Human Rights Act

The *Human Rights Act 1998* ('*HRA 1998*') gives effect in the UK to the *European Convention on Human Rights* ('*ECHR*') and enables individuals to enforce the rights contained in *HRA 1998, Sch 1* in the UK either directly, in the case of public authorities, or indirectly through obligations on courts, tribunals and public authorities to give effect to Convention rights. In the discrimination context, the most important Convention rights contained in *Sch 1* are the right to respect for private and family life (*Article 8*), the rights to freedom of thought, conscience and religion (*Article 9*), freedom of expression (*Article 10*) and (but only in conjunction with one or more other Convention rights) the prohibition of discrimination (*Article 14*). These rights are not absolute rights; each is restricted or qualified.

HRA 1998 also requires UK primary and subordinate legislation to be construed in a way which is compatible with Convention rights.

1.4 The Equality Act 2010

Overview

As noted above, the main aims of the *EqA 2010* are to consolidate, simplify and harmonise existing UK discrimination legislation and 'to strengthen the law to support progress on equality'. The format of the legislation is completely new. The *EqA 2010* is arranged by topic, rather than protected characteristic, and the drafting focuses on equality in various spheres, including the workplace.

The vast majority of the *EqA 2010* came into force on 1 October 2010. Deferred provisions are discussed further below. Key changes include:

— harmonised definitions for direct and indirect discrimination, harassment and victimisation (see **1.45**, **1.73**, **1.87** and **1.99**);

— extension of protection against discrimination by association and perception, bringing the law into line with the ECJ decision in *Coleman v Attridge Law: C-303/06* [2008] ECR I-5603, [2008] All ER (EC) 1105 (see **1.53–1.56**);

— extension of the concept of indirect discrimination to disability and gender reassignment (see **3.68–3.74** and **4.11**);

— the introduction of a new form of disability discrimination—'discrimination arising from disability'—intended to reverse the effect of the House of Lords decision in *Malcolm* (see **3.61–3.67**);

— the introduction of the right to take positive action in recruitment and promotion (see **1.160**);

— limitations on making health or disability-related enquiries of job applicants (see **3.99–3.103**);

— a new protection rendering unenforceable any rule or provision preventing employees from discussing their pay with colleagues for the purpose of identifying an element of discrimination (see **1.109**);

— the extension of the power for tribunals to make recommendations following a successful claim for discrimination (see **1.181**);

— the introduction of a new right enabling an employee to bring a direct sex discrimination claim 'in relation to contractual pay' where there is no real comparator for the purposes of an equal pay claim (see **1.70** and **8.40**).

1.5 *Deferred provisions*

The *EqA 2010* came into force on 1 October 2010, with the following exceptions:

— combined discrimination: the right for claimants to bring a claim for direct discrimination on two combined protected characteristics. These provisions were expected to come into force in April 2011, although the government has not committed to this date;

— gender pay gap reporting: the obligation for employers with more than 250 employees to publish information about the gender pay gap in their workforce. The government has indicated that it will not implement this provision in the immediate future, preferring to work with employers on developing a voluntary approach;

— positive action: the right for employers to take certain steps to encourage individuals who are disadvantaged or are under-represented as a result of their membership of a protected group. A general right to take positive action under *EqA 2010, s 158* was brought into force on 1 October 2010. An additional right to prefer certain candidates on recruitment or promotion, under *EqA 2010, s 159* will come into force on 6 April 2011 (see **1.96–1.105**);

— *EqA 2010* enables legislation to be passed to expressly cover caste as a protected characteristic. The previous government's view was that caste is covered within the definition of 'race' but this power gives the right to amend the law should this assumption prove to be incorrect. The extent of caste prejudice in the UK was the subject of further research by the National Institute of Economic and Social Research, the findings of which may also influence the approach taken.

Although outside the scope of this book, note that age protection in the provision of goods, facilities, services, premises and public functions is anticipated to come into force in April 2012.

1.6 *Transitional provisions*

The transitional provisions for *EqA 2010* are set out in the *Equality Act 2010 (Commencement No 4, Savings, Consequential, Transitional, Transitory, and Incidental Provisions and Revocation) Order 2010 (SI 2010/2337)* ('*the Commencement Order*'). The pre-*EqA 2010* legislation will apply to any discriminatory acts occurring before 1 October 2010 and the *EqA 2010* to acts occurring after that date. Where there is a discriminatory course of conduct straddling 1 October 2010, *Article 7* of the *Commencement Order* states that the enforcement provisions of the *EqA 2010* will apply where:

(i) an act which was unlawful under pre-*EqA 2010* legislation is carried out before 1 October 2010;

(ii) that act continues on or after 1 October 2010 and is also unlawful under the *EqA 2010.*

In these cases an employee will therefore have to show that discrimination is unlawful both under the old and new legislation, although only the enforcement provisions of *EqA 2010* will apply. This generally should not cause difficulties, since the *EqA 2010* introduces few fundamental changes. However, where new protections have been introduced under *EqA 2010* (see for example the amended tests in respect of disability discrimination (see **3.11**) and the 'three strikes' rule for harassment (see **1.95**)) it is understood that these will only apply in respect of acts which took place after 1 October 2010.

The *Commencement Order* clarifies that, for the purposes of victimisation, bringing proceedings under the pre-*EqA 2010* legislation or doing anything for the purposes of or in connection with pre-*EqA 2010* legislation will amount to a protected act.

1.7 Codes of Practice

The EHRC has produced three Codes of Practice covering: employment; equal pay; and services, public functions and associations. These Codes take the place of the Codes of Practice produced by the previous equality bodies which covered equal pay, sex, race and disability, each of which was specific to a single strand of discrimination protection. The power to issue codes of practice itself is created by *EqA 2006, s 14*, as amended by *EqA 2010, s 211(1), Sch 26.*

As with the previous Codes of Practice, failure on the part of any person to observe any provision of a Code of Practice is not of itself unlawful: the Codes do not impose legal obligations, nor are they an authoritative statement of the law. However, the contents of the Codes are admissible in evidence in an employment tribunal or court, and the tribunals and courts must take into account any part of the Codes that appears to them relevant to any case (*EqA 2006, s 15(4)*).

STOP PRESS: The final Statutory Codes of Practice were issued by the EHRC on 26 January 2011 and came into force on 6 April 2011. The codes issued under the previous discrimination legislation were revoked from the same date, although they will continue to apply to proceedings arising from alleged contraventions of the previous discrimination legislation and in certain other cases (see *The Former Equality Commissions' Codes of Practice (Employment, Equal Pay, and Rights of Access for Disabled Persons) (Revocation) Order 2011 (SI 2011/776)*).

1.8 Non-statutory guidance

The EHRC has also produced seven sets of non-statutory guidance documents for employers, and six sets of guidance for workers. Although this guidance in itself does not have legal effect and would not be referred to by tribunals, its purpose is to provide practical guidance on the EHRC Codes of Practice (see 1.7). Following the guidance is intended to help an employer comply with the EHRC Codes of Practice and so failure to comply with the guidance is likely to mean a breach of the Code, which can be taken into account in tribunal proceedings.

There are separate sets of guidance for employers and workers. The guidance focuses on different issues that arise in the employment relationship, as follows:

(1) recruiting/applying for a job;

(2) working hours, flexible working and time off;

(3) pay and benefits;

(4) career development—training, development, promotion and transfer;

(5) managing people/being managed;

(6) dismissal, redundancy, retirement and post-employment;

(7) (a guide specific to employers only): good equality practice: equality policies, equality training and monitoring.

The EHRC has also produced specific guidance for service providers, service users and education providers, which are outside the scope of this book.

1.9 Northern Ireland

Apart from a few provisions (largely relating to offshore work) *EqA 2010* does not apply to Northern Ireland. Therefore, in relation to Northern Ireland the position will, for the most part, remain as it was prior to October 2010.

DDA 1995 extends to Northern Ireland, and continues to do so even though it has been repealed in relation to England and Wales. While *SDA 1975, RRA 1976, SOR 2003, RBR 2003* and *AR 2006* do not, there are comparable legislative provisions in Northern Ireland.

There are two areas of Northern Irish employment law which are substantially different from the law in the rest of the UK.

The first concerns the detailed provisions requiring employers of more than ten people in Northern Ireland to maintain detailed information in relation to the religious background and sex of job applicants and employees for monitoring purposes and to register and file an annual return to the Equality Commission of Northern Ireland.

The second area is the obligation in Northern Ireland which requires public authorities to have due regard to the need to promote equality of opportunity between people of different religious beliefs and political opinions, race and age and between disabled and non-disabled people, and people with dependents and people without.

1.10 Scope of this book

This book covers only those provisions of UK discrimination legislation which relate to employment and related fields. It does not cover discrimination in the provision of goods and services.

Principles and concepts which are common to all or most of the UK discrimination legislation are discussed in this chapter. Those which are not, and those which require specific consideration in different contexts, are covered in the chapters which follow.

The derivation of the UK legislation and, where applicable, its EU sources is detailed in the following chapters.

1.11 *Sources of further information*

Further information is available from:

— ACAS: Rights at work: equality and discrimination, available at: http://www.acas.org.uk/CHttpHandler.ashx?id=2856#x00026;p=0

— ACAS: Guidance entitled 'The Equality Act – What's new for employers?', available at http://www.acas.org.uk/CHttpHandler.ashx?id=2833#x00026;p=0

— European Commission: Commission Recommendation of 27 November 1991 on the protection of the dignity of women and men at work (92/131/EEC), available at http://eur-lex.europa.eu/LexUriServ/LexUriServ.do?uri=CELEX:31992H0131:EN:HTML

— EHRC: The Equality and Human Rights Commission's Non-statutory Guidance for employers, available at http://www.equalityhumanrights.com/legislative-framework/equality-bill/equality-act-2010-guidance/

— EHRC: The Equality and Human Rights Commission's Non-statutory Guidance for workers, available at www.equalityhumanrights.com/legislative-framework/equality-bill/equality-act-2010-guidance/

— EHRC: The Equality and Human Rights Commission's Non-statutory Guidance for service providers, available at http://www.equalityhumanrights.com/legislative-framework/equality-bill/equality-act-2010-guidance/

— EHRC: The Equality and Human Rights Commission's Non-statutory Guidance for service users, available at http://www.equalityhumanrights.com/legislative-framework/equality-bill/equality-act-2010-guidance/

— CIPD: Guidance entitled Discrimination, available at http://www.cipd.co.uk/EmploymentLaw/FAQ/_Discrimination/Discrimination?NRMODE

— — CIPD: Guidance entitled Equality Act 2010, available at http://www.cipd.co.uk/subjects/dvsequl/general/equality-act-2010?NRMODE.

1.12 COMMON CONCEPTS

Scope of protection

EU law

Council Directive 2000/78/EC ('the *Framework Directive*'), establishing a general framework for equal treatment in employment and occupation, provides at *Article 3* (Scope) that:

> '1 Within the limits of the areas of competence conferred on the Community, this Directive shall apply to all persons, as regards both the public and private sectors, including public bodies, in relation to:
>
> (a) conditions for access to employment, to self-employment or to occupation, including selection criteria and recruitment conditions, whatever the branch of activity and at all levels of the professional hierarchy, including promotion;
>
> (b) access to all types and to all levels of vocational guidance, vocational training, advanced vocational training and retraining, including practical work experience;

(c) employment and working conditions, including dismissals and pay;
(d) membership of, and involvement in, an organisation of workers or employers, or any organisation whose members carry on a particular profession, including the benefits provided for by such organisations.'

Council Directive 2000/43/EC ('the *Race Directive*') in respect of discrimination based on racial or ethnic origin contains a virtually identical provision (*Article 3*). *Council Directive 2006/54/EC* ('the *Equal Treatment Directive*'), implementing the principle of equal treatment between men and women in matters of employment and occupation, sets out a slightly different scope at *Article 1* (Purpose):

> 'The purpose of this Directive is to ensure the implementation of the principle of equal opportunities and equal treatment of men and women in matters of employment and occupation.
>
> To that end, it contains provisions to implement the principle of equal treatment in relation to:
>
> (a) access to employment, including promotion, and to vocational training;
> (b) working conditions, including pay;
> (c) occupational social security schemes.'

1.13 *UK law*

It is unlawful for an employer to discriminate, directly or indirectly:

(a) in the arrangements he makes for deciding who should be offered employment;

(b) in the terms on which he offers employment; or

(c) by not offering employment (*EqA 2010, s 39(1)*).

Section 39(1) effectively replicates the pre-October 2010 legislation, which can be found at *SDA 1975, s 6(1); RRA 1976, s 4(1); DDA 1995, s 4(1),(2); RBR 2003, reg 6(1); SOR 2003, reg 6(1); AR 2006, reg 7(1)*. The case law interpreting these previous provisions will therefore continue to be relevant to the interpretation of *s 39(1)*.

Once a person is in employment, it is also unlawful for an employer to discriminate against him:

(d) in the terms of employment which he affords him;

(e) in the way it affords him access to opportunities for promotion, transfer or training, or to any other benefit, facility or service, or by not affording him with such access; or

(f) by dismissing him or subjecting him to any other detriment.

(*EqA 2010, s 39(2)*).

This sub-section also replicates the pre-October 2010 legislation (*SDA 1975, s 6(2); RRA 1976, s 4(2); DDA 1995 s 4(2); RBR 2003, reg 6(2); SOR 2003, reg 6(2); AR 2006, reg 7(2)*) and therefore case law interpreting this earlier legislation will also continue to be relevant.

The 'detriment' suffered in the case of opportunities for promotion, training, transfer or other benefits is simply the lack of access to the opportunity; the employee, for example, would not need to demonstrate that he would have been successful in his application.

Dismissal includes the failure to renew a fixed-term contract (*EqA 2010, s 39(7)(a)*; reflecting previous case law, for example *Metropolitan Police Comr v Harley* [2001] ICR 927, [2001] IRLR 263, EAT), constructive dismissal (*EqA 2010 s 39(7)(b)*; again reflecting previous case law, for example *Derby Specialist Fabrication Ltd v Burton* [2001] 2 All ER 840, [2001] IRLR 69, EAT) and compulsory retirement.

1.14 *Detriment*

The House of Lords has considered the meaning of 'detriment' in two key cases which remain relevant to *EqA 2010*. In *Chief Constable of West Yorkshire Police v Khan* [2001] UKHL 48, [2001] 1 WLR 1947, [2001] ICR 1065 and *Shamoon v Chief Constable of the Royal Ulster Constabulary* [2003] UKHL 11, [2003] 2 All ER 26, [2003] ICR 337, the House of Lords upheld earlier judgments of the Court of Appeal in *Ministry of Defence v Jeremiah* [1980] QB 87, [1979] IRLR 436 and *De Souza v Automobile Association* [1986] ICR 514, [1986] IRLR 103, which stated that 'detriment' is established if a reasonable worker would or might take the view that he had been disadvantaged in the circumstances in which he had to work.

The test is, in part, objective, so an unjustified sense of grievance is not sufficient to establish a detriment (*Barclays Bank plc v Kapur (No 2)* [1995] IRLR 87, CA). While the existence of a detriment is viewed from the standpoint of the alleged victim, that view must be justified. For this reason, the EAT dismissed a complaint from an employee who complained that colleagues keeping records of his actions amounted to an act of race discrimination, where no action had been taken as a consequence of those records (*Bayode v Chief Constable of Derbyshire EAT 2008 WL 2148158*).The fact that an employee is unaware of the detriment at the time is not a defence (*Garry v Ealing London Borough Council* [2001] EWCA Civ 1282, [2001] IRLR 681). It was held in *Shamoon* that it was not necessary to demonstrate physical disadvantage or financial loss. More recently in *Olasehinde v Panther Securities plc* (*EAT 2008 WL 2821555*) the EAT held that making false and unreasonable accusations against an employee, even where they did not result in disciplinary action, could amount to a detriment.

An employee does not suffer a 'detriment' if he is denied a benefit which is not provided to others in the same grade of employment. In *Clymo v Wandsworth London Borough Council* [1989] 2 CMLR 577, [1989] ICR 250, the EAT held that Mrs Clymo was not subjected to a detriment when she was refused permission to job share, as no one else in her grade was entitled to do so. In *Relaxion Group plc v Rhys-Harper* [2003] UKHL 33, [2003] 4 All ER 1113, [2003] ICR 867, the House of Lords held that failure to provide a non-contractual benefit will not normally be a 'detriment' unless it is one which is normally provided to others in comparable circumstances.

Where the detriment suffered is sufficiently 'trivial' it may not amount to discrimination (*Peake v Automotive Products Ltd* [1978] QB 233, [1978] 1 All ER 106, where women were allowed to leave work five minutes before their male colleagues to avoid a crush and, more recently, *Khan v Direct Line Insurance plc* (22 November 2005, unreported), ET, where an alternative to a sales incentive of a bottle of wine was not offered to a Muslim).

Detriment may include any aspect of the role, such as work scheduling (both breaks during the working day: *Mayuuf v Governing Body of Bishop Challoner Catholic Collegiate School* (21 December 2005, unreported), ET, and rota-setting: *Estorninho v Zoran Jokic t/a Zorans Delicatessen* (18 August 2006, unreported), ET); the way in which discipline and grievances are handled (*Dresdner Kleinwort Wasserstein Ltd v Adebago* [2005] IRLR 514); taking away responsibility for conducting staff appraisals (*Shamoon*); carrying out security checks only on employees of a particular colour (*BL Cars Ltd v Brown* [1983] ICR 143, [1983] IRLR 193, EAT); and the requirement to work voluntary overtime in less pleasant conditions, even when compensated by an extra payment (*Ministry of Defence v Jeremiah* [1980] QB 87, [1979] 3 All ER 833, [1980] ICR 13); together with the withholding of benefits properly due, such as a reference (*Khan v Chief Constable of West Yorkshire Police* [2001] UKHL 48, [2001] 4 All ER 834, [2001] 1 WLR 1947), pay rise or promotion. Only benefits offered by the employer which an employee enjoys by virtue of his employment, rather than benefits which he enjoys because they are also made available to members of the public at large, are covered.

De Souza v Automobile Association [1986] ICR 514, [1986] IRLR 103, CA, where a racist comment made about an employee by her manager to another manager did not amount to a detriment, is probably no longer good law where the comment made is sufficiently offensive, even if an isolated incident (*Whitehead v Brighton Marine Palace and Pier Co Ltd: C-3102595/04* (5 May 2005, unreported), where a one-off but very offensive remark made to a third party constituted harassment).

1.15 Who is protected?

UK discrimination law protects a wide range of individuals within various fields, including in employment, occupation and vocational training. In the employment sphere, it covers employees, contract workers, job applicants, partners and office-holders, amongst others (see **1.15–1.40**).

1.16 *Employees*

Discrimination protection extends to those who are in 'employment', who are applying for 'employment' and, where there is sufficient connection, after such a relationship has come to an end (*EqA 2010, ss 39, 108)* (see **1.35**).

'Employment' in *EqA 2010, s 83(2)(a)* is defined as:

> 'employment under a contract of employment, a contract of apprenticeship or a contract personally to do work'.

This is a broad definition and one which is significantly wider than the definition for purposes of rights under the *Employment Rights Act 1996* ('*ERA 1996*'). It will encompass both 'employees' and 'workers' (as defined under *ERA 1996, s 230(1), (3)*). It will also cover the genuinely self-employed carrying out a business on their own account, provided the individual has undertaken to execute any work or labour personally (rather than employing others to do it); and the obligation to execute work or labour personally is the 'dominant purpose of the contract' (*Mirror Group Newspapers Ltd v Gunning* [1986] 1 WLR 546, [1986] ICR 145, [1986] IRLR 27).

Individuals engaged under a contract of apprenticeship also fall within the definition of those in 'employment' for the purposes of *EqA 2010*. Contracts of apprenticeship are generally fixed-term contracts whose primary purpose is training. Apprenticeships can either arise under common law (*Flett v Matheson* [2006] EWCA Civ 53, [2006] ICR 673, [2006] IRLR 277where a labourer's contract had become a contract of apprenticeship because of training commitments given by his employer) or via an express contract of training or apprenticeship. This includes the modern apprenticeship model, which is a contract between an employer, a trainee and a training provider.

Volunteers, however, are unlikely to fall within its scope. In *X v Mid-Sussex Citizens Advice Bureau* [2009] EWCA Civ 340, the claimant, a volunteer, argued that she should be protected from discrimination on grounds of disability on the basis her role was an 'occupation' for purposes of the *Framework Directive* and that the definition of employment contained in *DDA 1995* ('employment under a contract of service or apprenticeship or a contract personally to do any work') was deficient in this respect. Based on the fact there was no binding contract, and in any event 'occupation' under the *Framework Directive* was only relevant to initial access to employment, the Court of Appeal held that a volunteer in her circumstances was not protected.

There is no requirement for a minimum qualifying period of service in respect of the protection afforded by the legislation.

Prior to October 2010, the definition of 'employment' varied slightly in different contexts (*SDA 1975, s 82(1); RRA 1976, s 78(1); RBR 2003, reg 2(3); SOR 2003, reg 2(3); AR 2006, reg 2(2*); *DDA 1995, s 68(1)*), but was still very wide:

> 'employment under a contract of service or apprenticeship or a contract personally to [execute any work or labour] (*SDA 1975, RRA 1976*) [do any work] (*RBR 2003, SOR 2003, AR 2006, DDA 1995*)'.

The change in definition pre- and post-October 2010 does not appear to have been intended to change the legal meaning of 'employment'. There is no reference to such an intention in either the *Explanatory Notes to the EqA 2010* or the *ECHR Employment Code*. The case law prior to *EqA 2010* governing employment status can therefore be expected to continue to apply when considering who is an employee or worker. A full consideration of employment status is outside the scope of this book.

1.17 *Contract workers/principals*

It is unlawful for a principal (the end user who contracts with another person for the supply of contract workers) to discriminate against those workers in the work he provides to them (*EqA 2010, s 41* which effectively replicates the preceding legislation: *SDA 1975, s 9; RRA 1976, s 7; DDA 1995, s 4B; RBR 2003, reg 8; SOR 2003, reg 8; AR 2006, reg 9*). The principal is treated as if it were the employer for purposes of the non-discrimination provisions in *EqA 2010*, extending the protection, for example, to a prohibition on harassment and victimisation.

The duty to make reasonable adjustments applies to both the principal and the employer of a contract worker (*EqA 2010, s 41(4)*). *EqA 2010, Sch 8* governs the relationship between their duties. The employer is under a duty to make reasonable adjustments where the contract worker is likely to be substantially disadvantaged by:

(i) a provision, criterion or practice applied by or on behalf of all or most of the principals to whom the contract worker is or might be supplied, and where the disadvantage is the same or similar in the case of each of those principals (*EqA 2010, Sch 8, para 5(3)*);

(ii) a physical feature of the premises occupied by each of the principals to whom the contract worker is or might be supplied, and where the disadvantage is the same or similar in the case of each of those principals (*EqA 2010, Sch 8, para 5(4)*);

(iii) the non-provision of an auxiliary aid which would likely put the contract worker at a substantial disadvantage that would be the same or similar in the case of each of the principals to whom the contract worker is or might be supplied (*EqA 2010, Sch 8, para 5(5)*).

The principal has similar duties to those of the employer but does not have to make any adjustment which the employer should make (*EqA 2010, Sch 8, para 6(2)*). The *EHRC Employment Code* provides a number of examples of the application of the duties of the employer and principal (*paras 11.0–11.14*).

There is no requirement that the principal 'control' the worker for the protection to apply. An employee of an arms-length management company set up by a city council was able to bring a claim against the council, regardless of its lack of control, due to the closeness of the relationship between the contracting council and management company (*Woodhouse v Leeds City Council* [2010] IRLR 625, [2010] IRLR 625). Employees of concessionaires in a department store who were required to have 'store approval' from the department store, which included complying with the store's dress code, were likewise able to bring claims for race discrimination (*Harrods Ltd v Remick* [1998] 1 All ER 52, [1998] ICR 156, [1997] IRLR 583) as was a contractor who was harassed by a customer (*O'Shea (CJ) Construction Ltd v Bassi* [1998] ICR 1130, EAT).

EqA 2010, s 41(5)(b) reflects the principle in *Abbey Life Assurance Co Ltd v Tansell* [2000] IRLR 387, CA that there does not need to be a direct contractual relationship between the employer and the principal. In that case the Court of Appeal confirmed that where a worker provides their services to an end user via both an employment agency and their own personal company, they will still be deemed to be a contract worker with protection against discrimination by that end user. The only requirement is that the worker is supplied under a contract between the end user and a third party; there is no requirement that the end user and the personal company directly contract.

In addition to the general protection from discrimination detailed above, with effect from 1 October 2011, agency workers (ie those engaged by an employment agency to work under the supervision and direction of a hirer) will have the right to 'equal treatment' in respect of certain basic working and employment conditions, including pay, once they have completed 12 weeks on assignment with an end user (*Agency Workers Regulations 2010, SI 2010/93, reg 5*).

'Pay' for these purposes includes any sums that the hirer would normally pay if the agency worker had been hired directly as an employee or worker to do the particular role in question, including wages and salary, fees, commission, holiday pay and overtime (*reg 6(2)*). However, it excludes certain payments, such as occupational sick pay and occupational maternity, adoption and paternity pay (*reg 6(3)*). See also **8.69**, **8.81**, **8.96** and **8.107**.

1.18 *Job applicants*

An employer must not discriminate against or victimise a person:

(a) in the arrangements he makes for deciding to whom to offer employment (*EqA 2010, s 39(1)(a), (3)(a)*);

(b) as to the terms on which he offers the person employment (*EqA 2010, s 39(1)(b), (3)(b)*);

(c) by not offering the person employment (*EqA 2010, s 39(1)(c), (3)(c)*).

Those provisions effectively replace *SDA 1975, s 6(1); RRA 1976, s 4(1); DDA 1995, s 4(1); RBR 2003, reg 6(1); SOR 2003, reg 6(1), and AR 2006, reg 7(1)*.

However, in respect of the protection in *s 39(1)(c)* and *s 39(3)(c)*, the language of *EqA 2010* is wider than that of the legislation which it replaces, which used the phrase '*refusing or deliberately omitting to offer employment*'. Neither the *Explanatory Notes to EqA 2010*, nor the *ECHR Employment Code* explain what, if anything, was intended by the widened wording (a change which is also found, amongst other places, in the provisions on partnerships and trade organisations).

Liability can be established under any one of the grounds set out above. The word 'arrangements' will be construed widely and will include matters such as advertisements for jobs, the application process and the interview stage (*EHRC Employment Code, para 10.8*). Thus, for example, the Court of Appeal has held that an arbitration agreement constitutes 'arrangements' which may restrict the class of those to whom the parties are able to offer employment, falling within *RBR 2003, reg 6(1)* (*Hashwani v Jivraj* [2010] EWCA Civ 712, [2011] 1 All ER 50, [2010] IRLR 797) and it is sufficient to prove that an interview was conducted in a discriminatory manner, without showing that the interview arrangements were discriminatory (*Nagarajan v London Regional Transport* [2000] 1 AC 501, [1999] 4 All ER 65, [1999] ICR 877, both cases above approving *Brennan v JH Dewhurst Ltd* [1984] ICR 52, [1983] IRLR 357, EAT). If the employer has made discriminatory arrangements for recruitment, a claim may be made even if the post was not filled for other reasons (*Roadburg v Lothian Regional Council* [1976] IRLR 283).

'Word of mouth' recruitment may be indirectly discriminatory (*Coker v Lord Chancellor* [2001] EWCA Civ 1756, [2002] ICR 321, [2002] IRLR 80 (see 'Methods of recruitment' at **1.38**).

The terms on which a job is offered may be indirectly discriminatory. In *Meade-Hill and National Union of Civil and Public Servants v British Council* [1996] 1 All ER 79, [1995] ICR 847, [1995] IRLR 478 a mobility clause requiring the employee to relocate to anywhere in the UK was held to discriminate on grounds of sex and marital status against a woman because a greater proportion of women are secondary earners and their husbands cannot move with them.

Under *EqA 2010, s 40(1)* (which replaces *SDA 1975, s 6(2A); RRA 1976, s 4(2A); DDA 1995, s 4(3); RBR 2003, reg 5(1); SOR 2003, reg 5(1)* and *AR 2006, reg 6(1))* it is unlawful for an employer to harass a person who has applied to him for employment (see 'Harassment' at **1.86** ff).

Under the pre-*EqA 2010* legislation, certain of the strands made it an offence to publish an advertisement indicating an intention to discriminate, enforceable only by the EHRC (*SDA 1975, s 38(5); RRA 1976, s 29(5)* and *DDA 1995, s 16B(2B)*). The *EqA 2010* no longer contains a separate provision for advertising. Instead, the publishing of a discriminatory advert is intended to be covered within direct discrimination itself and will be actionable by individuals, as well as potentially subject to enforcement action by the EHRC (*EqA 2010, Sch 26* preserves the EHRC's enforcement powers under *EqA 2006*).

The *EHRC Employment Code* gives the example of an employer who stated in an advert 'that Gypsies and Travellers need not apply', which it is said would amount to actionable discrimination by a Gypsy or Traveller who might reasonably have applied for the job were it not for this statement (see *EHRC Employment Code, paras 3.12, 3.32* and *16.19–16.29*). This is intended to reflect the ECJ decision in *Centrum voor gelijkheid van kansen en voor racismebestrijding v Firma Feryn NV: C-54/07* [2008] ECR I-5187, [2008] IRLR 732, which concerned a company which stated publicly that it would not accept job applications from certain minority groups.

However, it is not entirely clear under EqA 2010 how a potential claimant would show less favourable treatment in these circumstances. Following the Centrum case it may be sufficient to show that the language of the advertisement would have deterred applications from individuals with a certain protected characteristic, reflecting the Race Discrimination Directive (Directive 2000/43/EC), meaning it is no longer necessary to show that the claimant's application may have been successful. However, a claimant will still need to show that he himself was deterred from applying when he would otherwise have done so. This reflects the principle in *Keane v Investigo* UKEAT/0389/09/SM under AR 2006, that a 'professional litigant' who submits job applications for purposes of securing a settlement rather than with any intention of taking up a role will have suffered no detriment when they are rejected.

EqA 2010 introduces two new protections relevant to job applicants. First, *s 60(1)* prohibits an employer from asking about an applicant's health before offering work to that applicant or including them in a pool of successful candidates to be offered a job when a suitable position arises, unless one of the exceptions specified in *s 60(6)* applies. Those include, amongst others, questions to establish whether reasonable adjustments should be made to the assessment process; questions to establish if an applicant can carry out a function intrinsic to the work concerned; and questions posed as part of diversity monitoring. Only the ECHR can take action to enforce breach of the prohibition (*EqA 2010, s 60(2), s 120(8)*). However, an unsuccessful claimant claiming disability discrimination can rely on the asking of a prohibited question to reverse the burden of proof in subsequent discrimination proceedings (*EqA 2010, s 60(3)–(5)*).Second, *EqA 2010, s 159* (*Positive action: recruitment and promotion*) will permit from April 2011, an employer to take a protected characteristic into consideration when deciding whom to recruit, where people having the characteristic are at a disadvantage or under-represented (see **1.154**ff).

1.19 *Partnerships*

Insofar as a worker is employed by a partnership he will receive precisely the same protection against discrimination as if he were employed by a limited company or an individual (see **1.16**).

As a matter of partnership law, however, a partner is not an employee of a partnership, but rather a principal within it. For a definition of 'partnership', and for the incidents and liabilities of partnerships in general, see Lindley and Banks, *Partnership* (19th edn, 2010). *EqA 2010* therefore makes specific provision for partners. This protection can be summarised as follows.

It is unlawful for a firm to discriminate against a partner:

(a) as to the terms on which they are a partner;

(b) in the way in which the firm affords the partner access, or by not affording the partner access, to opportunities for promotion, transfer or training or for receiving any other benefit, facility or service;

(c) by expelling the partner;

(d) by subjecting the partner to any other detriment (*EqA 2010, s 44(2)*).

There is protection for those who are prospective partners, in the requirement that a firm or proposed firm not discriminate against a person:

(a) in the arrangements it makes for deciding to whom to offer a position as a partner;

(b) as to the terms on which it offers the person a position as a partner;

(c) by not offering the person a position as a partner (*EqA 2010, s 44(1)*).

The protection extends to a prohibition on harassment, victimisation, and the duty to make reasonable adjustments (*EqA 2010, s 44(3)–(7)*). *Section 45* places those same obligations on limited liability partnerships ('LLPs'). Persons proposing to form themselves into a partnership or incorporate an LLP (a 'proposed firm' or 'proposed LLP' under *s 46(3)* and *46(5)*) come within the scope of the relevant obligations. In the case of limited partnerships, the obligations only apply in relation to those partners who are involved with the operation of the firm ('general partners' within the meaning of the *Limited Partnerships Act 1907* (*EqA 2010, s 44(8)*). Former partners will be protected under *EqA 2010, s 108* (*Relationships that have ended*).

EqA 2010 largely replicates the preceding legislation (*RRA 1976, s 10; SDA 1975, s 11; DDA 1995, ss 6A, s 6C(1); SOR 2003, reg 14; RBR 2003, reg 14; AR 2006, reg 17*). However, there are three main points to note about the position under *EqA 2010* compared to the legislation it replaces.

First, *EqA 2010* removes two anomalous exceptions in relation to discrimination on ground of race in the context of partnerships, which arose from *RRA 1976*. They were that:

(a) a partnership of fewer than six members could not be liable for direct discrimination on grounds of nationality or colour (*RRA 1976, s 10(1), (1A)*); and

(b) a partnership of fewer than six members could not be liable for indirect discrimination at all.

Second, in certain respects the wording of *EqA 2010* is wider than that of the preceding legislation. For example, the phrase '*refuse or deliberately omit to offer*' is replaced by the wider '*not offering*' or '*not affording*'. Neither the *Explanatory Notes to EqA 2010* nor the

ECHR Employment Code explain what, if anything, is intended by the wider wording, rather (aside from the removal of the anomalies in race discrimination) *EqA 2010* is said to replicate that previous legislation. Arguably, the new wording removes the requirement that there be some intent behind the omission or refusal which can be construed from the removal of the word 'deliberately'.

Third, the definition of 'expulsion' has been widened to include, in the case of a partner of a firm, termination of the person's position as a result of the dissolution of the partnership. This reflects the development in case law which ensured protection for persons in two-member partnerships which have, by reason of an expulsion, technically ceased to exist (*Dave v Robinska* [2003] ICR 1248, [2003] NLJR 921, EAT).

As in the employment context, it is possible for partnerships to rely on the occupational requirement exception in respect of partners.

1.20 *Trade organisations*

Insofar as a worker is employed by a trade organisation, he will receive precisely the same protection against discrimination as if he were employed by a limited company or an individual (see **1.16**). However, if a member of a trade organisation wishes to make a claim of discrimination, he will have to rely on the specific provisions laid out in *EqA 2010, s 57.*

A trade organisation is defined as:

(a) an organisation of workers;

(b) an organisation of employers; or

(c) any other organisation whose members carry on a particular trade or profession for the purposes of which the organisation exists (*EqA 2010, s 57(7)*).

This replicates the definition in the preceding legislation (*SDA 1975, s 12(1); RRA 1976, s 14(1); DDA 1995, s 13(1); SOR 2003, reg 15(4); RBR 2003, reg 15(4); AR 2006, reg 18(4)*). This is a broad definition. Whilst the most obvious organisations included are trade unions, the phrase 'organisation of workers' would appear to include, for instance, a factory football team, or an office hobby club.

The phrase 'trade organisation' has also been held to be wide enough to include organisations whose membership include the self-employed (*National Federation of Self-Employed and Small Businesses Ltd v Philpott* [1997] ICR 518, [1997] IRLR 340, EAT), and organisations of professional persons such as doctors (*Sadek v Medical Protection Society* [2004] EWCA Civ 865, [2005] IRLR 57; *Dr C Wagunyanya v Medical Defence Union Services Ltd* UKEAT/0270/06/LA).

A trade organisation must not discriminate against a person:

(a) in the arrangements it makes for deciding to whom to offer membership of the organisation;

(b) as to the terms on which it is prepared to admit a person as a member;

(c) by not accepting a person's application for membership (*EqA 2010, s 57(1)*).

As for present members, a trade organisation must not discriminate against a member:

(a) in the way it affords them access, or by not affording them access, to opportunities for receiving a benefit, facility or service;

(b) by depriving them of membership;

(c) by varying the terms on which they are a member;

(d) by subjecting them to any other detriment (*EqA 2010, s 57(2)*).

For both present and prospective members, there is protection against harassment (*EqA 2010, s 57(3)*) and victimisation (*s 57(4) and (5)*). The duty to make reasonable adjustments also applies (*s 57(6)*).

EqA 2010 largely replicates the protection afforded by the legislation it replaces. However, there is an extension of the protection of prospective members, to cover the arrangements made for determining to whom membership should be offered, which was not included under the previous discrimination legislation. Given the wide interpretation given to the term 'arrangements', confirmed in recent case law (see **1.18** above), that change significantly extends the obligations of trade associations.

By reason of *EqA 2010, s 108*, former members will be protected if the discrimination arises out of and is closely connected to the relationship of membership which used to exist. This appears to alter the position as it was under the previous legislation. In *Diakou v Islington Unison 'A' Branch* [1997] ICR 121, the EAT held that any detriment alleged must have been suffered at the time the claimant was a member of the trade organisation, because there was a specified list of acts which were unlawful as against non-members listed in *RRA 1976, s 11(2)*.

Where a trade organisation is found liable for unlawful discrimination under the provisions outlined above, it is possible for individual office-holders or members within the organisation also to be personally liable if they knowingly help the organisation to discriminate (*EqA 2010, s 112(1)*). There will be a defence if the member can establish that they reasonably relied on a statement by the trade organisation that the act for which the help was given was not unlawful under *EqA 2010* (*EqA 2010, s 112(2)*). In this respect *EqA 2010* effectively replicates previous legislation on aiding unlawful acts (*SDA 1975, s 42; RRA 1976, s 33; DDA 1995, s 57; SOR 2003, reg 23; RBR 2003, reg 23; AR 2006, reg 26*) (see 'Aiding Discrimination' at **1.62**).

1.21 *Vocational training providers*

EqA 2010 prohibits discrimination on all protected grounds by vocational training providers and others providing employment services ('employment service-providers') (*EqA 2010, s 55*).

EqA 2010, s 56(2) defines the provision of an employment service insofar as relevant to vocational training as including the provision of, or making arrangements for, the provision of vocational training or guidance. However, it does not include training or guidance in schools, or to students at universities or further and higher education institutions, which are addressed at *EqA 2010, Part 6* (*EqA 2010, s 56(4), (5)*).

Work experience placements and training for employment are expressly included within the meaning of 'vocational training', as is careers guidance (*EqA 2010, s 56(2)(g) and 56(2)(6)*). This is a broad definition and one which differs from that contained under *SDA 1975, s 82(1)*. However the earlier definition was itself broad in scope and had been held to include everything from work experience (*Lana v Positive Action Training in Housing (London) Ltd* [2001] IRLR 501) to formal professional training (*Fletcher v Blackpool Fylde and Wyre Hospitals NHS Trust* [2005] ICR 1458, EAT).

An employment service provider must not discriminate against a person:

(a) in the arrangements it makes for selecting persons to whom to provide, or to whom to offer to provide, the service;

(b) as to the terms on which the service-provider offers to provide the service;

(c) by not offering to provide the service to the person;

In relation to users of the employment service, the service-provider must not discriminate against a person:

(a) as to the terms on which the service is provided;

(b) by not providing the service;

(c) by terminating the provision of the service; or

(d) by subjecting the person to any other detriment (*EqA 2010, s 55(1), (2)*).

Protection from harassment and victimisation also extends to both users and prospective users of employment-services (*EqA 2010, s 55(3), (4), (5)*). In relation to employment-service providers more generally, see **1.36–1.40**.

Disability

1.22 A duty to make reasonable adjustments is expressly conferred on an employment service-provider except in the provision of a vocational service (*EqA 2010, s 55(6)*). In all other respects, under *EqA 2010* the prohibitions against discrimination, harassment and victimisation in the context of vocational training are now the same for disability as for other protected characteristics.

1.23 *Qualifications bodies*

Authorities or bodies which can confer an authorisation or qualification which is needed for, or facilitates engagement in, a particular profession or trade must not discriminate against an individual:

(a) in the arrangements it makes for deciding upon whom to confer a relevant qualification;

(b) as to the terms on which it is prepared to confer a relevant qualification; or

(c) by not conferring a relevant qualification (*EqA 2010, s 53(1)*).

In relation to those upon whom the qualifications body has already conferred a relevant qualification, it likewise must not discriminate:

(a) by withdrawing the qualification or varying the terms on which it is held; or

(b) by subjecting the person to any other detriment (*EqA 2010, s 53(2)*).

Protection from harassment and victimisation extends equally to those seeking a relevant qualification and those who already possess such a qualification (*EqA 2010, s 53(3), (4), (5)*).

EqA 2010 largely replicates the preceding legislation (*SDA 1975, s 13; RRA 1976, s 12; SOR 2003, reg 16; RBR 2003, reg 16; AR 2006, reg 19; DDA 1995, s 31AA*). However, in certain respects the wording of *EqA 2010* is wider than that of the preceding legislation. For example, the phrase 'refuse or deliberately omitting to grant [the relevant qualification]' (*SDA 1975, s 13(1)(b)*) is replaced by the wider 'not conferring'. Neither the *Explanatory Notes to the EqA 2010* nor the *ECHR Employment Code* explain what, if anything, is intended by the wider wording. Arguably, (as in the case of Partnerships, see **1.19**) it removes the requirement that there be some intent behind the omission or refusal.

The *EqA 2010, s 53(6)* also imposes a duty to make reasonable adjustments on a qualifications body. No liability for disability discrimination exists, however, where a qualifications body applies a 'competence standard' to a disabled person unless it constitutes indirect discrimination under *EqA 2010, s 19* (*EqA 2010, s 53(7)*). 'Competence standard' is defined as an academic, medical or other standard applied for the purpose of determining whether or not a person has a particular level of competence or ability (*EqA 2010, s 54(6)*).

'Qualification'

1.24 Under *EqA 2010, s 54(3)*, a relevant qualification is defined as an 'authorisation, qualification, recognition, registration, enrolment, approval or certification which is needed for, or facilitates engagement in, a particular trade or profession.' Whilst not identical, this is a similar formulation to that contained under the previous legislation (see *SDA 1975, s 13(3)(a)*). Case law considering the wording in the previous legislation is therefore still likely to be relevant.

In this context, the word 'qualification' has been found to imply some status conferred on a person in relation to his work which is either necessary or advantageous to the lawful carrying on of that work (*Loughran & Kelly v Northern Ireland Housing Executive* [1999] 1 AC 428, [1998] 3 WLR 735, [1998] ICR 828, cf *Hashwani v Jivraj* [2010] EWCA Civ 712, [2011] 1 All ER 50, [2010] IRLR 797 on the appointment of arbitrators falling within the *RBR 2003*).

'Qualifying body'/'qualifications body'

1.25 The question of what is a 'qualifying body' (the term used in *SDA 1975* and *RRA 1976*) or 'qualifications body' (the term which now applies under *EqA 2010* and which applied under *DDA 1995, SOR 2003, RBR 2003* and *AR 2006*) has attracted a significant body of case law. The leading cases are three Court of Appeal decisions:

(a) in *Tattari v Private Patients Plan Ltd* [1998] ICR 106, [1997] IRLR 586, CA, the Court of Appeal considered the question whether a commercial provider of medical and health insurance was a 'qualifying body' insofar as it stipulated that particular qualifications were necessary in order for doctors to be included on its list of specialist practitioners. The court held that it was not, since the insurance provider was not in itself authorised or empowered to confer a qualification or permission;

(b) in *McDonagh and Triesman v Ali* [2002] EWCA Civ 93, [2002] ICR 1026, [2002] IRLR 489, the Court of Appeal held that the Labour Party, in selecting a candidate for local government elections, was not a qualifying body, thereby overturning previous EAT decisions to the contrary (*Sawyer v Ahsan* [2000] ICR 1, [1999] IRLR 609, EAT; *Jepson and Dyas-Elliott v Labour Party* [1996] IRLR 116, EAT). (Note, however, that the *Sex Discrimination (Election Candidates) Act 2002* amended the *SDA 1975* by adding *s 42A* which provides an exception for action taken by political parties in the selection of candidates for parliamentary, European Parliament, Scottish Parliament, National Assembly for Wales and local government elections, for the purpose of reducing inequality in the numbers of members of the body concerned.) *McDonagh* was applied and approved in *Carter v Ahsan (No 1)* [2005] ICR 1817 (CA) and [2008] 1 AC 696 [2008] ICR 22 (HL);

(c) in *Patterson v Legal Services Commission* [2003] EWCA Civ 1558, [2004] ICR 312, [2004] IRLR 153 the Court of Appeal distinguished *Tattari* and *Triesman*, and held that the Legal Services Commission, in its role of awarding legal aid franchises to solicitors, *was* a qualifications body, since it was assessing the solicitor's suitability to perform the work and conferring 'some sort of status' on her, as well as selecting a person to perform services on its behalf.

In line with the relatively strict approach taken by the Court of Appeal in the *Tattari* and *Triesman* cases, the EAT also decided in the case of *Arthur v A-G* [1999] ICR 631 EAT that an appointer of magistrates was not a qualifying body for the purposes of *RRA 1976*.

The *Explanatory Notes to the EqA 2010* give some examples of qualifications bodies: Public Carriage Office, British Horseracing Authority, General Medical Council. The definition of a qualifications body is also designed to catch any body which confers a diploma on people pursuing a particular trade (eg plumbers) even if the diploma is not strictly necessary to pursue a career in that trade but shows that the person has reached a certain standard (*para 191*). These examples are consistent with the *Tattari* and *Triesman* approach which will continue to be relevant under the *EqA 2010*.

EqA 2010 expressly excludes schools, institutions of further and higher education and authorities conferring A Levels and GCSEs from the definition of a qualifications body (*EqA 2010, s 54(4)*).

'Facilitates'

1.26 In *British Judo Association v Petty* [1981] ICR 660, [1981] IRLR 484, the EAT held that the word 'facilitates' covers all cases where the qualification in fact facilitates employment, whether or not it is intended by the authority or body which confers the authorisation so to do. It was not necessary to show detriment or loss. See also *Hardwick v Football Association* EAT/1036/97 and *Igboaka v Royal College of Pathologists* [2010] Med LR 78, EAT.

Appeals

1.27 Where there is a statutory right of appeal, or proceedings in the nature of an appeal, against a particular act, a complaint cannot be made to a tribunal concerning a qualifications body (*EqA 2010, s 120(7)*: formerly under *SDA 1975, s 63(2); RRA 1976, s 54(2); DDA 1995, s 17A(1A); SOR 2003, reg 28(2)(a); RBR 2003, reg 28(2)(a); AR 2006, reg 36(2)(a)*). See *British Medical Association v Chaudhary and linked applications* [2003] EWCA Civ 645, [2003] ICR 1510; *Bari v General Medical Council* UKEATPA/0660/05/LA; *Khan v General Medical Council* [1996] ICR 1032, [1996] IRLR 646, CA; *R v Department of Health, ex p Ghandi* [1991] 4 All ER 547, [1991] 1 WLR 1053, [1991] ICR 805.

1.28 *Crown employment*

The discrimination laws bind the Crown and apply to Crown employment, and to House of Commons and House of Lords staff (*EqA 2010, s 83(2)(b)–(d), (5)–(9)*; formerly under *SDA 1975, ss 85–85B; RRA 1976, ss 75–75B; DDA 1995, ss 64–65; RBR 2003, regs 36–38; SOR 2003, regs 36–38; AR 2006, regs 44–46*). Ministers of the Crown are excluded (*EqA 2010, Sch 3, Part 1, para 2*).

1.29 *Police*

Although the holding of an office, including the position of cadet, within the police is not 'employment' for the purposes of *ERA 1996*, the discrimination laws deem the holding of such office to be 'employment' for their own purposes (*EqA 2010, s 42(1)*: formerly *SDA 1975, s 17; RRA 1976, ss 76A–76B; RBR 2003, reg 11; SOR 2003, reg 11; AR 2006, reg 13*). Constables seconded to the Serious Organised Crime Agency, the Scottish Police Services Authority and the Scottish Crime and Drugs Enforcement Agency are also considered to be employed by the relevant body (*EqA 2010, s 42(5), (6)*).

A new subsection *17(1A)* was inserted into the *SDA 1975* in 2003 and a new *s 76A* into the *RRA 1976* to confirm that Chief Officers of police are vicariously liable for the acts and omissions of police officers as employers, reversing the effect of *Chief Constable of Bedfordshire Police v Liversidge* [2002] EWCA Civ 894, [2002] ICR 1135, [2002] ICRLR 651. This remains the position under *EqA 2010* (*EqA 2010, s 42(1)(a)*). Proceedings should therefore be brought against the Chief Constable and/or the police authority and individual officers who have discriminated.

Chief Officers of police may be directly liable for management decisions on matters such as recruitment and postings (*Hendricks v Metropolitan Police Comr* [2002] EWCA Civ 1686, [2003] 1 All ER 654, [2003] ICR 530 endorsing *Chief Constable of Cumbria v McGlennon* [2002] ICR 1156, [2002] All ER (D) 231 (Jul), EAT).

EqA 2010 removes the requirement to pay out of police funds compensation and related costs arising from the personal liability of chief officers or chief constables in Scotland for acts which are unlawful under *EqA 2010*. Such liability will instead be dealt with under the *Police Act 1996* and the *Police (Scotland) Act 1967* as for all other police officers (*Explanatory Notes to the EqA 2010, para 156*).

1.30 *Armed forces*

Members of the armed forces are in the service of the Crown (*EqA 2010, s 83(3)*). They are therefore subject to and protected by discrimination laws (see **1.28** above), with the following exceptions.

The armed forces must not do anything that constitutes discrimination, harassment or victimisation in exercising their public functions (*EqA 2010, s 29(6)*) but this prohibition does not apply in relation to age, disability, gender reassignment or sex discrimination if the action taken is for the purpose of ensuring the combat effectiveness of the armed forces (*EqA 2010, Sch 2, Part 1, para 4*). In any event, the *s 29(6)* duty is not yet in force for the purposes of age discrimination (*EqA 2010 (Commencement No 4, Savings, Consequential. Transitional, Transitory and Incidental Provisions and Revocation) Order 2010 (SI 2010/2317), Article 2(3)(a)*).

There is a total exemption from liability for disability or age discrimination relating to service in the armed forces (*EqA 2010, Sch 9, Part 1, para 4(3)*: formerly *DDA 1995, s 64(7); AR 2006, reg 44(2)*).

The exemption under *SDA 1975* in respect of sex discrimination where an act is done to ensure 'combat effectiveness' (*SDA 1975, s 85(4)*), has been narrowed under *EqA 2010* so that there is no liability for offering employment, not offering employment or affording access to training and promotion where a requirement is imposed that the person in question be a man or not be a transsexual person if the imposition of that requirement 'is a proportionate means of ensuring the combat effectiveness of the armed forces' (*EqA 2010, Sch 9, Part 1, para 4*. See also *Explanatory Notes to the EqA 2010, para 808*).

Internal complaints procedures must be invoked before a claim to the ET is made (*EqA 2010, s 121*: formerly *SDA 1975, s 85(9B)–(9E); RRA 1976, s 75(8)–(9B); RBR 2003, reg 36(7)–(10); SOR 2003, reg 36(7)–(10)*) (see 'Sanctions, Remedies and Enforcement' at **1.169**).

In *Sirdar v Army Board and Secretary of State for Defence: C-273/97* [1999] ECR I–7403, [2000] ICR 130, the ECJ rejected the submission that matters relating to national security fell outside EU anti-discrimination provisions, but held that exclusion of women from special combat units such as the Royal Marines may be justified under the *Equal Treatment Directive, Article 2(2)*, which exempts occupational activities for which the sex of the worker is a determining factor.

1.31 *Office-holders*

The discrimination laws apply to persons who are not (or might not be) 'employees', but are rather private or public 'office-holders' (*EqA 2010, ss 49, 50*: formerly *SDA 1975, ss 10A–10B; RRA 1976, s 76ZA; DDA 1995, ss 4C–4F; RBR 2003, reg 10; SOR 2003, reg 10; AR 2006, reg 12*). Protection for office-holders was introduced following the broadening of the application of the principle of equal treatment in the *Treaty on European Union* ('*EC Treaty*'), *Article 141(3)* and *Directive 2002/73/EC, Article 3* beyond 'employment' to 'self-employment and occupation'. Those appointed, recommended or approved by central government are included. Elected and appointed members of central or local government are expressly excluded. Under *EqA 2010*, protection for office-holders applies where other work provisions do not ie if the office-holder is also an employee, they are protected by the provisions dealing with employment (*Explanatory Notes to the EqA 2010, paras 172–176*). The duty to make reasonable adjustments (*EqA 2010, ss 49(9), 50(11)*) and duties not to harass (*EqA 2010, s 49(4), (7)* and *s 50(4), (8)*) or victimise (*EqA 2010, s 49(5), (8)* and *s 50(5), (9)*) are extended to a person who has the power to make an appointment to a private or public office and to a relevant person as defined in *EqA 2010, s 52(6)*.

The particular case of employment judges (known, prior to 1 December 2007, as employment tribunal chairmen) has given rise to considerable dispute:

(a) in *Perceval-Price v Department of Economic Development* [2000] NI 141, [2000] IRLR 380, NI CA it was held that tribunal chairmen claiming discrimination in connection with pension rights were 'workers' in 'employment' within the meaning of *Article 119* of the *EC Treaty* and the *Directives*, even though they were excluded from the NI equal pay and sex discrimination legislation as holders of a statutory office. The Court of Appeal disapplied domestic law because of the conflict with EU law, following *Marshall v Southampton and South West Hampshire Area Health Authority (Teaching): 154/84* [1984] QB 401, [1986] IRLR 140. This was only possible because the defendant was an 'emanation of the State';

(b) in *Christie v Department for Constitutional Affairs* [2007] ICR 1553, (2007) Times, 4 September, EAT the EAT more recently rejected a similar challenge to the statutory exclusion brought by a part-time tribunal chairman under the *PTWR 2000* and the *Part-time Workers Framework Directive (97/81/EC)*. The EAT held, relying on *Wippel v Peek & Cloppenburg Gmbh & Co KG: C-313/02* [2004] ECR I-9483, [2005] IRLR 211: (1) that there was no autonomous meaning of 'worker' in EU law; (2) under the *Framework Directive*, Member States had a discretion to determine how 'worker' and 'employment' should be defined; (3) alternatively, the *PTWR 2000* clearly excluded holders of a statutory office, and therefore could not be read compatibly with the *Directive*, and could not be disapplied. *Christie* was applied in *O'Brien v Department of Constitutional Affairs* [2008] EWCA Civ 1448, [2008] 2 CMLR 389, [2009] ICR 593 in relation to Recorders.

1.32 *Barristers and advocates*

It is unlawful for a barrister, barrister's clerk, advocate or advocate's clerk to discriminate on the basis of any protected characteristic in relation to:

(a) arrangements for offering pupillage or tenancy;

(b) the terms on which pupillage or tenancy is offered;

(c) not offering pupillage or tenancy;

(d) the terms applicable to a pupil or tenant;

(e) access to opportunities for training or gaining experience, and benefits, facilities or services;

(f) termination of pupillage; or pressure to leave chambers;

(g) any other detriment.

(*EqA 2010, ss 47, 48*: formerly *SDA 1975, s 35A(1), (2); RRA 1976, ss 26A, 26B; DDA 1995, s 7A; SOR 2003, regs 12, 13; RBR 2003, regs 12, 13; AR 2006, regs 15, 16.*)

Harassment and victimisation of pupils and tenants is also prohibited (*EqA 2010, s 47(3)–(5)*). The duty to make reasonable adjustments now applies to a barrister (*EqA 2010, s 47(7)*).

Furthermore, it is unlawful for any person to discriminate against a barrister on any protected ground in the giving, withholding or acceptance of instructions (*EqA 2010, s 48*: formerly *SDA 1975, s 35A(3); RRA 1976, s 26A(3); DDA 1995, s 7A(4); SOR 2003, reg 12(4); RBR 2003, reg 12(4); AR 2006, reg 15(4)*).

1.33 *Work-seekers dealing with employment service-providers*

Under *EqA 2010, s 55(1)(b)*, workers supplied by employment agencies will enjoy protection against discrimination, harassment and victimisation by the principal to whom they provide services as a 'contract worker' (see **1.17**) and against the agency which supplies them (see Employment Service-Providers **1.36**). Individuals using the services of an agency to look for work, receive vocational training or careers guidance are also protected against discrimination, harassment and victimisation by that service-provider (see **1.36**).

Further information

1.34 Further information is available from:

— BERR: Agency Workers: know your rights, available at: http://webarchive.nationalarchives.gov.uk/+/http://www.berr.gov.uk/files/file49917.pdf

1.35 *Former employees*

An individual is protected against certain discriminatory acts where the detriment complained of 'arises out of or is closely connected to' a previous relationship which falls within one of the protected categories outlined above (*EqA 2010, s 108(1)*; see **1.16–1.33**). The acts covered are direct or indirect discrimination, harassment and the duty to make reasonable adjustments. Examples of typical acts which would be sufficiently connected to the previous relationship would include failure to pay expenses or commission, or a dispute relating to pensions entitlement. Where an employee has commenced proceedings or has raised a grievance as a precursor to submitting a claim, employers can face a difficult choice between creating disclosable documentation that may prejudice their defence in the litigation, and having a victimisation claim added to the previous grounds as a result of their failure to progress the grievance, or give a reference (see 'Victimisation' at **1.98** ff).

EqA 2010, s 108(1) replicates the pre-October 2010 legislation (see *SDA 1975, ss 20A, 35C; RRA 1976, s 27A; DDA 1995, s 16A; RBR 2003, reg 21; SOR 2003, reg 21; AR 2006, reg 24*). It also closes a lacuna under the *RRA 1976* which meant that claimants alleging discrimination on grounds of colour or nationality had to rely on the test in *Relaxion Group plc v Rhys-Harper* [2003] UKHL 33, [2003] 4 All ER 1113, [2003] ICR 867 instead of the statutory protection.

However, there is an apparent omission in the *EqA 2010* in respect of the most common type of post-termination discrimination complained of, victimisation. This can occur where an individual is treated less favourably, for example a reference denied or outstanding pay withheld, because they have raised a complaint of discrimination (whether by way of informal complaint, statutory grievance or litigation) (see, for example, *Coote v Granada Hospitality Ltd: C-185/97* [1998] ECR I-5199, [1998] All ER (EC) 865, [1998] 3 CMLR 958). *EqA 2010, s 108(7)* expressly excludes former employees from protection against victimisation, apparently based on a misunderstanding, as set out in the explanatory notes, that post-termination victimisation is covered under the separate victimisation provisions of *EqA 2010*. (Because victimisation is no longer defined as discrimination under *EqA 2010* there is no conflict between *s 108(7)* and *s 108(1)*, which states that discrimination protection generally applies to former employees.) See 'Victimisation' at **1.98** for details of the test which will apply until this apparent omission in the *EqA 2010* is rectified.

1.36 *Employment service-providers*

EqA 2010 consolidates protection of work seekers against 'employment service-providers'. *EqA 2010, ss 55–56* bring together the scope of the pre-October 2010 legislation which covered employment agencies and vocational training (see *SDA 1975, ss 14–15; RRA 1976, ss 13–14; DDA 1995, s 21A; RBR 2003, regs 17–18; SOR 2003, regs 17–18; AR 2006, regs 20–21*). 'Provision of an employment service' is defined in *EqA 2010, s 56(2)* and includes work-finding services, the supply of workers, the provision of vocational training and guidance and general careers advice services. It excludes training and guidance covered elsewhere in *EqA 2010* (for example apprentices and trainees who are categorised as employees (see **1.16**)). The definition also excludes school and further education institutions which are covered separately, and which are outside the scope of this work.

Individuals who use the services of employment service-providers (including employment agencies) are protected against discrimination:

(a) in the arrangements the service-provider makes for selecting persons to whom services are provided;

(b) in the terms on which the service-provider offers to provide any of its services;

(c) by the service-provider not providing any of its services;

(d) by the service-provider terminating the provision of the service or by subjecting a person to whom the service is provided to any detriment; or

(e) by the service-provider harassing or victimising any work-seeker (*EqA 2010, s 55(1)–(5)*).

Employment service-providers are also under an obligation to make reasonable adjustments, except in relation to the provision of a vocational service (*s 55(6)*).

Employment service-providers, in particular employment agencies and employment businesses, can also be liable where they knowingly aid the end user's act of unlawful discrimination under the provisions on aiding discrimination (*EqA 2010, s 112*, see **1.62**). They can also be liable where they carry out an act that breaches *EqA 2010* on instructions from a principal, unless reasonably relying on an assurance that this would not be unlawful (*EqA 2010, s 110*).This is likely to result in an apportionment of liability between the agent and the principal, as the principal will also be liable where they have authorised or instructed the service-provider to discriminate (*EqA 2010, s 111*, see **1.60–1.61**).

Focusing on employment agencies and businesses, the following are specific areas of the recruitment process where they may be exposed to liability.

Accepting client instructions

1.37 To establish a defence against a claim that they 'knowingly aided' the unlawful acts of their clients under *s 112* (see **1.62**), agencies should seek a written assurance from the client that the instructions are not unlawful. Even with the benefit of such a statement, it must still be reasonable for the agency to rely on it in order to accept the client's instructions, and so it would be well advised either to take its own legal advice or to seek a written legal opinion from the client where it believes instructions may not be lawful. However, to be liable, the agency must have foreseen that discrimination was a probable outcome of the client's instructions: a reasonable suspicion that it might take place was not enough (*Hallam v Avery* [2001] UKHL 15, [2001] 1 WLR 655). Merely allowing an environment to exist where the unlawful act may occur does not amount to knowingly aiding (*Okerago v May & Baker Ltd (t/a Sanofi-Aventis Pharma)* UKEAT/0278/09/ZT, [2010] IRLR 394, [2010] All ER (D) 79 (Mar), EAT. Foreseeability is crucial—if the agency does not know of the unlawful act before or at the time it occurs, *s 112* cannot not be made out (*May*).

Where the client knowingly or recklessly makes a false or misleading statement that the instructions are not unlawful, and the agency relies on this, the client is liable to a fine (*EqA 2010, s 112(3)*). However, the agency itself may still be liable. The safest course for the agency is to obtain an indemnity in respect of liability arising out of the client providing discriminatory instructions, but this does not address the reputational issues of an agency being found to have discriminated both in respect of potential candidates and clients.

Clearly, where it would be lawful for the client not to employ or engage the candidate, the instructions will not be discriminatory and so the agency will bear no liability. Lawfulness in this context is not limited to Occupational Requirements ('ORs') (see *EqA 2010, Sch 9, Part 1, para 5* and **1.110** and **1.145** ff).

Methods of recruitment

1.38 Executive search firms typically do not use advertisements to carry out recruitment for their clients in the private sector, although they are generally required to do so for public sector bodies, who—with effect from April 2011—have a duty to promote equality of opportunity (outside the scope of this book). Recruitment by way of contacting specific targeted individuals involves a more limited pool of potential candidates, both in terms of number and the protected characteristics they share (such as age and race). This argument was considered by the Court of Appeal in relation to a former Lord Chancellor's recruitment of a personal acquaintance as special adviser, where it found no disproportionate impact on the claimants on the basis that the correct pool of comparators was made up of individuals known to the Lord Chancellor, which was a legitimate requirement of the role (*Coker v Lord Chancellor* [2001] EWCA Civ 1756, [2002] ICR 321, [2002] IRLR 80). In that case, the pool of comparators comprised solely the successful candidate, who satisfied the requirement of being known to the Lord Chancellor whilst also having the other necessary skills. The Court of Appeal nonetheless stated that recruitment from a pool of those known to the employer or by 'word of mouth' was not best practice in accordance with the EOC and CRE Codes and could result in unlawful discrimination. Similar guidance is given in the *EHRC Employment Code* (*para 16.20*). This is more likely to be the case where an employer does not impose a requirement that it personally knows the candidate, but instead relies on head-hunting or recruitment through personal contacts where, in contrast to the *Coker* case, it is likely that a wider group of candidates could meet its requirements and so disproportionate impact on a group protected under the statutes would be shown.

Selection

1.39 An employment agency may interview candidates, either to consider whether to accept them for job-seeking services, to compile a shortlist or even to select the successful candidate on behalf of its client. In doing so the same obligations apply to it as to the prospective employer, namely to avoid unlawful discrimination in the way the recruitment process is operated. This encompasses all steps in the recruitment process, from arrangements for interview (see in particular **3.75** with regard to reasonable adjustments), establishing non-discriminatory job criteria (see for example, **2.51** and **2.53** with respect to the setting of requirements for minimum age or experience), ensuring consistent selection processes and assessment of all candidates (Britannia Products Ltd, Brooke Street Bureau (Bradford) and Network Industrial Recruitment, CRE formal investigation, 1994) and avoiding asking questions or making comments that give rise to an inference of unlawful discrimination (*Saunders v Richmond-upon-Thames London Borough Council* [1978] ICR 75, [1977] IRLR 362, EAT.

The agency should also consider, and refer to its client, any questions raised by candidates with regard to adjustments to the role where refusal may potentially give rise to indirect discrimination (see for example **3.75** with regard to reasonable adjustments such as working hours or location, provision or modification of equipment and changes to job duties, and **8.37**, **8.144** ff and **2.51** and **2.53** with regard to changes to working hours or location to accommodate caring responsibilities).

Agencies should also be mindful of the prohibition on asking candidates for information about their health until they have effectively already succeeded in their application (*EqA 2010, s 60*). See **3.99** on pre-employment health checks.

Terms of supply

1.40 Employment businesses, which supply temporary workers, continue to be under a duty not to discriminate throughout the term of the contract (and potentially beyond; see **1.35**). Again, the pre-October 2010 case law will continue to apply: an employment agency breached the *SDA 1975* as a result of its failure to carry out a risk assessment when placing a pregnant work-seeker with a client (*Brocklebank v Silveira* UKEAT/571/05), and when it failed to allow a worker to return to the temporary post which she had occupied following her return from maternity leave (*BP Chemicals Ltd v Gillick* [1995] IRLR 128, EAT).

1.41 **Jurisdiction**

Limitation period

Under *EqA 2010, s 120(1)* an employment tribunal has jurisdiction over complaints relating to work (*EqA 2010, Part 5*), as well as claims arising out of a work-related relationship that has ended (*s 108*) and claims for instructing, causing or inducing discrimination (*s 111*) or aiding contraventions (*s 112*) relating to work.

Claimants must present their claim within three months from the date of the act to which the complaint relates, or such other period as the tribunal thinks just and equitable (*EqA 2010, s 123(1)*). There is an exception to that rule in armed forces cases where the period is extended to six months to allow use of an internal complaints procedure (*ss 121, 123(2)*) and in relation to equal pay claims (*s 129(3)*).

EqA 2010, s 123(3) deals with time starting to run in cases of: (a) continuing discrimination; and (b) discrimination by omission.

As to (a), conduct extending over a period is to be treated as done at the end of the period. The *Explanatory Notes to EqA 2010* consider *s 123* to replicate the effect of the preceding legislation (see *SDA 1975, s 76(6); RRA 1976, s 68(7); DDA 1995, Sch 3, para 3(3); RBR 2003, reg 34(4); SOR 2003, reg 34(4); AR 2006, reg 42(4)*). Note, however, there is some difference in wording. The preceding legislation used 'act' where *EqA 2010* uses 'conduct'. The effect, if any, of that change will remain to be seen. Arguably, 'conduct' imports the idea that the behaviour may not be just one isolated act, removing the possible contradiction in the concept of an 'act extending over a period' which existed in the former legislation.

Case law under previous legislation held that the application of a consistent policy or practice was 'an act extending over a period' in *East and North Hertfordshire NHS Trust v Dr A Fernando* UKEAT/0727/04/DM; but contrast *Rovenska v General Medical Council* [1998] ICR 85, [1997] IRLR 367, CA, where a series of rejected applications for registration were each discrete acts. The guidance of Mummery LJ in *Hendricks v Metropolitan Police Commissioner* [2002] EWCA Civ 1686, [2003] All ER 654, [2003] ICR 530 was that:

> 'The focus should be on the substance of the complaints that [the respondent] was responsible for an ongoing situation or a continuing state of affairs in which [the protected group] were treated less favourably. The question is whether that is "an act extending over a period" as distinct from a succession of unconnected or isolated specific acts, for which time would begin to run from the date when each specific act was committed'.

Hendricks has been cited by the EAT as the best guide to the correct approach to continuing discrimination (*Allen v The Secretary of State for Work and Pensions (Jobcentre Plus)* UKEAT/0498/08/DM, 19 January 2010).

As to (b), failure to do something is to be treated as occurring when the person in question decided on it. This replicates the preceding legislation. Accordingly, case law construing the term 'decided' will likely remain authoritative. In *Swithland Motors plc v Clarke* [1994] ICR 231, [1994] IRLR 275 the EAT interpreted that term (as it appeared in *SDA 1975 s 76(6)*) as meaning:

'"decided at a time and in circumstances when [the respondent] was in a position to implement that decision" and not "decided on the hypothetical basis that he will implement the decision when and if circumstances arise in which he is able to do so"'.

The tribunal's discretion to extend the three-month time limit in *EqA 2010, s 123(1)(b)* also replicates the provisions of the pre-*EqA 2010* legislation. Circumstances in which it has been held 'just and equitable' to extend time include:

(1) where the claimant's adviser realised they had a right of action as a result of subsequent publication of a judicial decision (*British Coal Corpn v Keeble* [1997] IRLR 336);

(2) where the claimant only became aware of facts that would found a complaint after expiry of the usual time limit (*Afolabi v Southwark London Borough Council* [2003] EWCA Civ 15, [2003] ICR 800, [2003] IRLR 220). A tribunal will have to address the question of whether a claimant's ignorance was and remained reasonable (*Perth and Kinross Council v Townsley* UKEATS/0010/10/BI, 17 August 2010). Where the claimant was a university lecturer surrounded by colleagues well versed in employment law, it was not just and reasonable to extend time on the basis of a misunderstanding that the *SDA 1975* did not apply to men (*University of Westminster v Dr G N Bailey OBE* UKEAT/0345/09/JOJ, 22 September 2009);

(3) where an applicant's lawyers mistakenly failed to comply with the time limit (*Virdi v Metropolitan Police Comr* [2007] IRLR 24, [2006] All ER (D) 214 (Oct), EAT, applied by the EAT in *Benjamin-Cole v Great Ormond Street Hospital for Sick Children NHS Trust* (2010) UKEAT/0356/09/DA, [2010] All ER (D) 73 (Feb)). However, *Virdi* and *Benjamin-Cole* were exceptional cases and are therefore exceptions to the general rule that tribunals will not exercise their discretion to extend time where the mistake is the fault of the adviser;

(4) where the applicant reasonably waited for the outcome of an internal grievance, having been advised to do so (*Marks & Spencer plc v Williams-Ryan* [2005] EWCA Civ 470, [2005] ICR 1293, [2005] IRLR 562) (in respect of the normally stricter test under *ERA 1996, s 111*). However, delay pending resolution of an internal grievance procedure is not sufficient ground in itself for extending time, rather is but one factor to be taken into account (*Apelogun-Gabriels v Lambeth London Borough Council* [2001] EWCA Civ 1853, [2002] ICR 713, [2002] IRLR 116 at para [16]; *University of Westminster v Dr G N Bailey OBE* at para [22]);

An active decision by a claimant to delay is likely to mean the tribunal will refuse to extend time (*Hutchinson v Westward Television Ltd* [1977] ICR 279, [1977] IRLR 69).

The *ECHR Employment Code* at *para 15.31* sets out a list of particular factors to which a tribunal will have regard when considering whether to exercise its 'just and equitable' discretion.

Equal pay claims are generally subject to a six-month time limit (*EqA 2010, s 129(3)*). However, the High Court in *Abdulla v Birmingham City Council* [2010] EWHC 3303 (QB), [2011] IRLR 309 has recently confirmed that an employee may bring an equal pay claim in the civil courts, thereby benefiting from a six-year limitation period (see 'Equal Pay' at **11.43**).

Claims of discrimination relating to services, public functions, premises, education and associations (*EqA 2010, Parts 3, 4, 6, and 7*) can be brought in the county court (the sheriff court, in Scotland) under *EqA 2010, s 114*. Those claims will benefit from the six month time limit contained in *EqA 2010, s 118*.

1.42 *Territorial scope*

Pre October 2010 position

Before the *EqA 2010* came into force, all discrimination legislation (except certain strands of discrimination under the *RRA 1976* (see **6.60**) made it unlawful for an employer to discriminate against an individual in relation to employment by it 'at an establishment in Great Britain'.

Employment was to be regarded as being 'at an establishment in Great Britain' if the employee:

(a) worked wholly or partly in Great Britain; or

(b) worked wholly outside Great Britain and the following additional conditions were satisfied:

   (i) the employer has a place of business at an establishment in Great Britain;

   (ii) work was done for purposes of that business carried out in Great Britain; and

   (iii) the individual in question was ordinarily resident in Great Britain either when he applied for or was offered employment, or at any time during the employment

(*SDA 1974, s 10; RRA 1976, s 8; DDA 1995, s 68; RBR 2003, reg 9; SOR 2003, reg 9; AR 2006, reg 10.*)

In effect, at the material time the employee must have been working partly in Great Britain or working for the benefit of an establishment here, and in the latter case must have been ordinarily resident here at some point during recruitment or employment. *Williams v The University of Nottingham* UKEAT/0124/07/RN held that whether work was done 'for the purposes of the employer's business carried on at its establishment in Great Britain' was the same question as that considered by the House of Lords in *Lawson v Serco Ltd* [2006] UKHL 3, [2006] 1 All ER 823, [2006] IRLR 289 in an unfair dismissal claim, ie whether work was done 'for the purposes of a business carried on in Great Britain'.

The EAT confirmed in the case of *Neary v Service Children's Education* (2010) UKEAT/0101/10/DA, [2010] ICR 1083, [2010] IRLR 1030 that the phrase 'ordinary residence' should be given the same meaning as in UK tax legislation. It summarised the applicable principles as follows: (1) the phrase is to be given its ordinary and natural meaning; (2) 'ordinary residence' refers to a person's abode in a particular place or country which he has adopted voluntarily and for settled purposes (including, for example, the purposes of employment, education or family reasons) as part of the regular order of his life, whether of short or long duration; (3) a person can be ordinarily resident in two countries at once; and (4) it is wrong to look for the employee's permanent base or centre adopted for general purposes, ie his 'real home'.

The individual's entire period of employment is taken into account in assessing his place of work, rather than just the period in which the acts of discrimination took place (*Saggar v Ministry of Defence* [2005] EWCA Civ 413, [2005] ICR 1073, [2005] IRLR 618). This period is assessed at the time of the discrimination. In *Tradition Securities and Futures SA v X* [2009] ICR 88, [2008] IRLR 934, EAT the EAT held that two employees could not bring claims in respect of acts that occurred while employed in France; at the time of the alleged discrimination, they worked wholly outside Great Britain, and therefore their claims were limited to further acts taking place after they had relocated to Great Britain.

Where an employee is based abroad but visits Great Britain, he may have been entitled to protection under the pre-*EqA 2010* legislation if the visits were for essential work purposes and were not *de minimis (Ministry of Defence v Gandiya* [2004] ICR 1708, where one day's required attendance in the UK and two voluntary visits related to the role were insufficient to establish employment in the UK). In *Mak v British Airways plc* (2010) UKEAT/0055/09/SM, [2010] All ER (D) 162 (Jan), however, the EAT upheld a decision of the employment tribunal that airline cabin crew based in Hong Kong could bring employment tribunal claims under the sex, race and disability discrimination legislation. The claimants were of Chinese nationality, worked under employment contracts governed by Hong Kong law, and began their flights at their base in Hong Kong. The lead claimant flew around 28 'flight cycles' between Hong Kong and London each year. The time spent in Great Britain was calculated to be approximately 5% of working time. In deciding that the claimants worked partly in Great Britain, the tribunal took into account both the amount of time spent in Great Britain, and the significance of the relevant duties undertaken there, which were described by the EAT as integral to the role. The decision is currently on appeal to the Court of Appeal.

The territorial scope of the pre-*EqA 2010* discrimination legislation was further extended by the case of *Wallis v Ministry of Defence* (2010) UKEAT/0546/08, [2010] ICR 1301, [2010] IRLR 1035 (applying the decisions of the Court of Appeal in *Duncombe v Secretary of State for Children, Schools and Families* [2009] EWCA Civ 1355, [2010] IRLR 331 which, in turn, reaffirmed the principles set out in the EAT decision in *Bleuse v MTB Transport Ltd* [2008] ICR 488, [2008] IRLR 264) so that individuals working wholly outside the UK (but within the EU) were able to avail themselves of protections under the *SDA 1975* where their contracts of employment were governed by English law (for a fuller discussion of the '*Bleuse*' principle see **1.43** below).

The rules will, however, be disapplied where they are in conflict with *Article 48* of the *EC Treaty* relating to free movement of workers (*Bossa v Nordstress Ltd* [1998] ICR 694, [1998] IRLR 284, where an Italian national was entitled to claim in the employment tribunal for discrimination against him by an Italian employer whilst he was resident in the UK).

This test continues to apply for acts committed before October 2010

Position from October 2010

1.43 Unlike the previous single strand legislation, the *EqA 2010* does not include any express territorial limitation and it will therefore be left to tribunals to determine who can, in practice, bring a claim. *Paragraph 15* of the *Explanatory Notes to the EqA 2010* states:

> 'As far as territorial application is concerned, in relation to Part 5 (work) and following the precedent of the Employment Rights Act 1996, the Act leaves it to tribunals to determine whether the law applies, depending for example on the connection between the employment relationship and Great Britain'.

We do not yet know how, in practice, tribunals will approach the question of whether there is a sufficient connection with Great Britain. The *EHRC Employment Code* suggests that a tribunal may consider such matters as: 'where the employee lives and works, where the employer is established, what laws govern the employment relationship in other respects, where tax is paid, and other matters it considers appropriate' (*para 10.71*). All of these are likely to be relevant, but do not necessarily provide an easy answer.

Tribunals might simply continue to apply the pre-October 2010 'establishment in Great Britain' test set out above. However, the repeal of that test suggests that Parliament may have intended a change of approach.

Alternatively, the reference in the Explanatory Notes to *ERA 1996* might suggest that tribunals will adopt the approach in *Lawson v Serco* [2006] UKHL 3, [2006] 1 All ER 823, [2006] IRLR 289, in which Lord Hoffmann identified (in relation to unfair dismissal) three main categories of employees, namely:

(a) employees who ordinarily work in Great Britain at the time of the relevant act (in that case, dismissal);

(b) peripatetic employees, where the relevant issue is to consider where the employee is based. The House of Lords confirmed that in deciding the employee's base, the factors referred to in the earlier case of *Todd v British Midland Airways Ltd* [1978] ICR 959, [1978] IRLR 370, CA are likely to be relevant. These include not only what is stated in the employee's contract, but also his physical base/HQ or where his travels begin and end (normally the key consideration), where he lives, where he is paid and in what currency, and where he pays National Insurance;

(c) expatriates, ie employees working and based abroad. These employees will only be regarded as working in Great Britain for the purposes of unfair dismissal protection in exceptional circumstances. Lord Hoffmann considered that it was not enough that the employee was recruited in Britain by a British employer, and suggested that 'something more' is needed, but that examples of expatriate employees who could bring claims might include:

    (i) employees working for a British employer operating within a British extra-territorial political or social enclave in a foreign country;

    (ii) employees posted abroad by a British employer for the purposes of a business carried on in Great Britain, such as a foreign correspondent of a British newspaper.

Lord Hoffmann did not regard these examples of expatriates as closed, and considered that there may be other examples of individuals who could claim based on the same principles. In practice, however, (with notable exceptions such as *Duncombe* and *Wallis* mentioned below), subsequent decisions have tended to apply these principles relatively narrowly. If this approach is followed for the *EqA 2010*, therefore, it is likely to lead to a more limited extraterritorial effect than applied previously under the establishment in Great Britain test.

A third possible approach is that adopted in the working time case *Bleuse v MTB Transport Ltd* [2008] ICR 488, [2008] IRLR 264, EAT. The case concerned a German lorry driver who lived in Germany and worked on the continent, but was employed by an English company, under an English law contract. The EAT held that the employee had rights under the *WTR 1998* which could be enforced in an English employment tribunal. The EAT commented that:

> 'Where either English law is the proper law of the contract, or where it provides the body of mandatory rules applicable to the employment relationship by virtue of Article 6(2) of the Rome Convention, an English court properly exercising jurisdiction must seek to give effect to directly effective rights derived from a Community Directive by construing the relevant English statute, if possible, in a way which is compatible with the right conferred'.

The EAT went on to say:

> 'The scope of the provision must be extended to give effect to the directly effective rights under Community law. That law operates as part of the system of domestic law and must be given effect accordingly . . . if this were not done it would mean that the principle of effectiveness would not be satisfied: there would be no effective remedy for a breach of the Community right.'

The Rome Convention, to which the EAT referred, has since been replaced by the *Rome I Regulation* (for contracts entered into after 18 December 2009). *Rome I* gives the parties freedom to choose the governing law of an employment contract, but in the absence of a choice, *Article 8* provides:

> '2 . . . the contract shall be governed by the law of the country in which or, failing that, from which the employee habitually carries out his work in performance of the

contract. The country where the work is habitually carried out shall not be deemed to have changed if he is temporarily employed in another country.

3 Where the law applicable cannot be determined pursuant to paragraph 2, the contract shall be governed by the law of the country where the place of business through which the employee was engaged is situated.

4 Where it appears from the circumstances as a whole that the contract is more closely connected with a country other than that indicated in paragraphs 2 or 3, the law of that other country shall apply.'

In other words, broadly speaking, English law will apply if England is the 'effective centre of his working activities and where or from which he performed the essential part of his duties' (*Rutten v Cross Medical Ltd: C-383/95* [1997] ECR I-57, [1997] ICR 715 and *Weber v Universal Ogden Services Ltd: C-37/00* [2002] QB 1189, [2002] ECR I-2013, [2002] ICR 979) or, if that does not provide the answer, where the employer is based here. Either result can be overridden if there is a closer connection with another country.

Rome I also specifies that where the parties have chosen the governing law, the employee cannot be deprived of the benefit of so called 'mandatory rules' that would have been applicable in the absence of a choice. Mandatory rules are those laws which cannot be derogated from by contract and include discrimination legislation.

If *Bleuse* is correct, and is applied to determine claims under the *EqA 2010*, it would mean:

(a) employees working under English law contracts have the benefit of rights granted by the *EqA 2010*, whether they are working in Great Britain or overseas;

(b) employees whose contracts do not include an express choice of law also have the benefit of rights granted by the *EqA 2010*, if the employment tribunal decides that English law applies based on the fact that they habitually work in England or Wales, or (if they do not habitually work in one place) were hired by an employer based in England, or in either case, because the employment has in any event the closest connection with England;

(c) employees whose contracts specify a law other than English law will still have the benefit of rights under the *EqA 2010* if English law would have applied in the absence of an express choice.

There have been some criticisms of the decision in *Bleuse*:

(a) the case involved a private sector employer, whereas the *Working Time Directive* is not directly effective other than against emanations of the State;

(b) the EAT appeared to link the question of direct effect and the principle of effectiveness (ie the need for an effective remedy), whereas the latter does not depend on there being direct effect. In *Duncombe*, the Court of Appeal focused on the effectiveness principle, noting ' there is an obligation on the part of the member state to make rights under the Directive effective by providing an effective domestic law forum for enforcement. That can be done by modification, if necessary, to the extra-territorial or other limitations, which are otherwise a barrier to the enforcement of the EC right';

(c) *reg 1(2)* of the *WTR 1998* expressly provides that '[t]hese Regulations extend to Great Britain only';

(d) if the *Bleuse* principle is correct, it suggests that where English law applies, all EU-derived statutory employment protection would apply, regardless of where the employee worked (or where the employer is based): this would include most of our health and safety legislation, as well as a raft of other statutory provisions which implement EU law.

Nevertheless, despite these criticisms, the decision in *Bleuse* was approved by the Court of Appeal in *Duncombe v Secretary of State for Children, Schools and Families* [2009] EWCA Civ 1355, [2010] ICR 815. In the recent decision of the EAT in *Wallis v Ministry of Defence* (2010) UKEAT/0546/08, [2010] ICR 1301, [2010] IRLR 1035, the same principle was applied to modify the 'establishment in Great Britain' test under the *SDA 1975*.

Wallis involved claims by two women married to service personnel working at NATO bases in the Netherlands and Belgium. The women were employed to work in international schools established at the bases. They were recruited while overseas under a policy which encouraged the employment of dependants of service personnel. They did not work in Great Britain at all, and on the face of the *SDA 1975*, could not bring sex discrimination claims in the English employment tribunal. However their contracts were governed by English law. The employment tribunal applied the *Bleuse* principle and allowed the women to bring their claims under the *SDA* 1975. The decision was upheld by the EAT.

In relation to the objection identified at (d), the claimants in *Bleuse, Duncombe* and *Wallis* all worked in the EU. It remains unclear whether the *Bleuse* principle applies only to those working in the EU, or whether it applies regardless of the place of work. In *Wallis* the EAT appeared to be influenced by the question whether the employee had rights under the Directive in question. The EAT stated that:

> 'it is clear that the premise of Elias P's reasoning in *Bleuse*, albeit unspoken, was that the Working Time Directive necessarily required member states to accord the rights conferred by it to all employees working (at least within the EU) under contracts of which their law was the proper law or the applicable law under Article 6(2) of the Rome Convention.'

However while the suggestion that the employee must be working in the EU to benefit may appear attractive, not least because the employer must have been aware of the risk EU law would apply, the legal basis for any such limitation is not completely clear. It would also involve the tribunal in the practical question of deciding whether the test was satisfied at the time of the alleged discrimination, and raises difficult questions as to what period should be considered: should it be the period of the complaint, or the whole of the employment (as in the pre-*EqA 2010* case of *Saggar v MOD*, where the employee was found to work partly in Great Britain based on the period before his overseas posting, even though the alleged discrimination occurred while he was posted abroad). A limitation of the *Bleuse* principle to EU-based employees would also raise difficult questions in the case of peripatetic employees, such as those based in the EU but working elsewhere, those based outside the EU but working from time to time in the EU, and those who had been working in the EU but were no longer doing so when the discrimination occurred.

Given the endorsement in *Duncombe*, and the specific application to the *SDA 1975* in *Wallis*, the *Bleuse* principle may be the most likely candidate to fill the gap. However pending a determinative authority on the *EqA 2010* itself, which may take some time, the issue will remain open to argument. *Bleuse* does not, however, fully address the position of workers covered by the *Posted Workers Directive*, and this is considered further below.

The above comments relate to England and Wales. In relation to employees with contracts governed by the law of Scotland or Northern Ireland, or who work in Scotland or Northern Ireland, the position is similarly unclear. *Bleuse* and *Duncombe* are not binding on Scottish and Northern Irish tribunals, although they may well be persuasive

Practitioners should also note that, whatever the appropriate test for deciding territorial scope of the legislation, a claimant will also have to establish that the employment tribunal has jurisdiction. In *Bleuse, Duncombe* and *Wallis*, the EAT did not have to consider the question of jurisdiction, as the employer had a place of business here. However, this will not always be the case. In *Pervez v Macquarie Bank Ltd* (2010) UKEAT/0246/10/CEA, [2011]

ICR 266, [2011] IRLR 284, EAT, the EAT concluded that an employee seconded from a Hong Kong based company, which did not have a place of business in the UK, to work for a UK company in the same group on a long-term basis, could bring claims for discrimination and unfair dismissal. The company could be said to be 'carrying on business' in England and Wales for the purpose of establishing jurisdiction under the *Employment Tribunals (Constitution and Rules of Procedure) Regulations 2004 (SI 2004/1861)* on the basis of the secondment alone.

Posted workers

1.44 The *Posted Workers Directive* ('*PWD*') requires EU Member States to provide certain minimum protections for employees who are temporarily posted to their jurisdiction from overseas, including protection under EU derived anti-discrimination legislation.

Pre-October 2010, the UK discrimination legislation did not deal expressly with posted workers, but they were covered by the 'establishment in Great Britain' test by virtue of the fact that they worked partly in Great Britain.

Post-1 October 2010, there is still no express provision in the *EqA 2010* for posted workers. If the tribunals apply the *Bleuse* principle in standard cases (see above), this will not be adequate to cover posted workers with foreign law contracts, since the parties will not have chosen English law, and as the habitual place of work is likely to be the overseas country, English law mandatory rules will not apply either. As tribunals are obliged to construe English statutes in such a way as to be consistent with EU directives, it is likely that tribunals will conclude workers who are entitled to the protection of the *PWD* have a sufficient connection to be entitled to the protection of the *EqA 2010* regardless of the law applicable to their contracts of employment. In this respect, although *Articles 1.1* and *1.3* seem to contemplate that *PWD* applies only to employers established in the EU, *Article 1.4* also provides that '[u]ndertakings established in a non-Member State must not be given more favourable treatment than undertakings established in a Member State'.

Consequently it may be that posted workers will benefit from the *EqA 2010* regardless of their country of origin; otherwise, if the protection were to be limited to EU-based employees, this is likely to be regarded as treating non EU-employers more favourably.

1.45 DIRECT DISCRIMINATION

Introduction

EU law

Council Directive 2000/78/EC ('the *Framework Directive*'), establishing a general framework for equal treatment in employment and occupation, provides that:

> 'direct discrimination shall be taken to occur where one person is treated less favourably than another is, has been or would be treated in a comparable situation, on any of the grounds referred to in Article 1' (*Article 2.2(a)*).

Council Directive 2006/54/EC ('the *Equal Treatment Directive*'), implementing the principle of equal treatment between men and women in matters of employment and occupation, contains a virtually identical provision (*Article 1(a)*), as does *Council Directive 2000/43/EC* ('the *Race Directive*') in respect of discrimination based on racial or ethnic origin (*Article 2.2(a)*).

1.46 *UK law*

The statutory definition of 'direct discrimination' is the same for all protected characteristics (with one significant exception):

> 'A person (A) discriminates against another (B) if, because of a protected characteristic, A treats B less favourably than A treats or would treat others.'

(*EqA 2010, s 13(1)*)

The exception is pregnancy and maternity. In this case direct discrimination occurs where a person treats a woman *unfavourably* because of pregnancy or childbirth (*EqA 2010, s 18(2)*, see **8.16**). No comparator is required in these cases.

Prior to October 2010, the statutory definition of direct discrimination on the grounds of sex, race, disability, religion or belief and sexual orientation was:

> 'A discriminates against B when A treats B less favourably than he treats or would treat another, and does so on a prohibited ground.'

(*SDA 1975, ss 1(1)(a), 2(1), 3(1)(a), 3A(1)(a), 3A(1)(b); RRA 1976, s 1(1)(a); DDA 1995, s 3A(5); RBR 2003, reg 3(1)(a); SOR 2003, reg 3(1)(a).*)

Direct discrimination because of age is distinct from other strands, in that A will not unlawfully discriminate against B if A can objectively justify the discrimination by demonstrating that it was a proportionate means of achieving a legitimate aim (*EqA 2010, s 13(2)*) (see **2.16**ff). This was also the case under the preceding legislation (*AR 2006, reg 3(1)(a)*). The defence of justification is not available for direct discrimination because of any other protected characteristic.

The expressed intention behind the change to the definition in the *EqA 2010* was to simplify, rather than to change, the legal meaning, with one significant exception (*Explanatory Notes to the EqA 2010, note 61*): cases of associative discrimination and discrimination based on perception are now covered (see **1.53–1.56**).

Concerns were raised during consultation that the wording 'because of' could be read as requiring conscious motivation or intent to discriminate (see **1.51**). Although tribunal judgments will be needed to confirm the position, Mr Justice Underhill in a decision of the EAT in *Ahmed v Amnesty International* [2009] ICR 1450, [2009] IRLR 884, EAT stated that 'because of' could be used as a synonym for 'on grounds of' provided this did not go so far as to 'import a causation or 'but for' test'. The decision was cited in a subsequent decision of the EAT (*Johal v EHRC* 2010 WL 2937469), and is expected to provide useful guidance to tribunals as they interpret the new *EqA 2010* definition.

Note that more favourable treatment of a disabled person does not amount to discrimination against a non-disabled person (*EqA 2010, s 13(3)*) (see **3.43**). In a similar vein, special treatment of women in connection with pregnancy and childbirth does not amount to discrimination against a man (*EqA 2010, s 13(4)(b)*) (see **8.16**).

EqA 2010 contains a provision permitting claims of direct discrimination on the basis of two protected characteristics in combination (*EqA 2010, s 14*) (see 'combined discrimination' **1.57**). However, this section is not yet in force. It was originally anticipated to take effect from April 2011 but, at the time of writing, the government has not committed to this date.

The test which the tribunal will usually apply to determine whether direct discrimination has occurred is to consider whether the two key elements of the statutory definition are met: has there been less favourable treatment and, if so, was that treatment because of a protected characteristic? In other words, what was the reason for the treatment in question?

Although it is useful for the tribunal to ask the two questions sequentially, there is scope for a tribunal to consider these as one issue, where the less favourable treatment cannot be determined without first examining the reasons for the treatment.

The facts of cases are not always capable of division into neat sub-headings and sequential analysis may give rise to problems where, for example, it is the appropriate comparator which is in question. For these reasons, as the House of Lords found in *Shamoon v*

Chief Constable of the Royal Ulster Constabulary [2003] UKHL 11, [2003] 2 All ER 26, [2003] ICR 33, in determining whether there has been direct discrimination, if the statutory test is treated as two parts, rather than one question, problems may arise, per Lord Nicholls, paras 7 and 8: 'Sometimes the less favourable treatment issue cannot be resolved without, at the same time, deciding the reason why issue. The two issues are intertwined'. In reality, this is how evidence will be presented at a tribunal. *Shamoon* was followed in *Brown v Croydon London Borough Council* [2006] All ER (D) 320 (May). Elias LJ indicated that 'it is not necessary for a tribunal, in each and every case, specifically to identify the two-stage process'.

1.47 Less favourable treatment

The comparator must be someone whose relevant circumstances are the same or not materially different from B's circumstances. These circumstances will be those considered by A in treating B in the way that he did, discounting the alleged discriminatory factor (*Shamoon*). In reality, it may be difficult to identify a real comparator possessing the same characteristics and so, often, B will identify several people who provide useful evidence of how A might have treated a real comparator. These comparators are often referred to as 'evidential' comparators. For a discussion of comparators see **1.63–1.71**, but in many cases, focusing on the correct comparator will reveal the reason for the treatment and so the elements of the claim are inextricably linked.

In many cases less favourable treatment will be easy to identify. Significantly, the discriminatory reason need not be the sole or even the principal reason for A's behaviour, but must be an important factor (see *Owen and Briggs v James* [1982] ICR 6184, [1982] IRLR 502, CA and *Nagarajan v London Regional Transport* [2000] 1 AC 501, [1999] IRLR 572, HL, *EHRC Employment Code, para 3.11*). Obvious behaviour, such as failing to promote, depriving someone of a pay rise, or dismissal, will be caught, as may be less obvious treatment, such as discouraging an employee or treating others preferentially.

Less favourable treatment must have occurred. Although the statutory test for direct discrimination considers how the employer treats or would treat a comparator, it does require B *to have suffered* the less favourable treatment. An employer does not discriminate if B can only argue that A *would* have treated him less favourably. In *Baldwin v Brighton and Hove City Council* [2007] ICR 680, [2007] IRLR 232, EAT, B was a transsexual. B argued that unlawful discrimination took place when he perceived that, if he attended an interview, he would be less favourably treated by a clergyman whom he believed to be a transphobe. The EAT acknowledged this argument could only succeed if B's manager had knowledge of B's gender reassignment and, with that in mind, had selected this interviewer. But the interviewer did not treat B any less favourably than an actual or hypothetical comparator simply by agreeing to join the interview panel. In *Ladele v London Borough of Islington* [2009] EWCA Civ 1357, [2010] 1 WLR 955 the Court of Appeal decided that a Christian registrar had not been directly discriminated against under *RBR 2003* when she was required to carry out the same duties as colleagues who did not share her beliefs, and was not afforded special treatment to exempt her from duties to which she objected because of her faith. See also **7.16**.

It is not necessary for a tribunal to examine the consequences of the less favourable treatment, or determine whether objectively B is worse off because of it. In *Chief Constable of West Yorkshire Police v Khan* [2001] UKHL 48, [2001] 1 WLR 1947, [2001] ICR 1065, HL the West Yorkshire Police refused to give K a reference, and K claimed race discrimination. The West Yorkshire Police argued that the reference they would give would have been poor and therefore not helpful to K. The House of Lords held that the tribunal need not consider the consequences of a reference which might, when given, be unhelpful to K. What mattered was that K 'would have preferred not to have been treated differently' from others. The bar is therefore relatively low.

An employer cannot defend less favourable treatment by arguing that the overall benefits offered to the employee compensate for any less favourable treatment (*Ministry of Defence v Jeremiah* [1980] QB 87, [1979] 3 All ER 833, [1979] 3 WLR 857, [1980] ICR 13, CA): where men were paid an enhanced overtime rate to undertake 'dirty work' there was still less favourable treatment on the grounds of sex. It was a detriment to the men to be required to do dirty work which the women were not.

1.48 *Unreasonable or poor treatment distinguished from less favourable treatment*

The test in *Shamoon* requires a comparison; it is not enough to show unfavourable treatment. A's treatment of B will not be unlawful discrimination if it is not less favourable than the way he treats or would treat others. To determine whether it is less favourable, B must identify a real or hypothetical comparator (C) and show that A did or would treat B less favourably than C (see **1.63** ff).

A will not discriminate simply because his behaviour is unreasonable. The complainant will not prove less favourable treatment simply by comparing the treatment with that of a reasonable employer: an employer's unreasonableness does not mean that an employee has been treated less favourably (*Glasgow City Council v Zafar* [1998] ICR 120, [1997] IRLR 229). The extent to which unreasonable behaviour may be relevant in drawing inferences of discrimination was considered by the Court of Appeal in *Bahl v Law Society* [2004] EWCA 1070, [2004] IRLR 799, and *Wong v Igen Ltd (Equal Opportunities Commission intervening) and conjoined cases* [2005] EWCA Civ 142, [2005] ICR 931, [2005] IRLR 258.

If A can show that he treats all employees equally badly he may escape liability for discrimination. This argument was successfully run in *Madarassy v Nomura International plc* [2007] EWCA Civ 33, [2007] ICR 867, [2007] IRLR 246, para 93, in which M complained that her manager intimidated and threatened her. The tribunal found on the evidence that he treated all staff this way, regardless of gender, and the Court of Appeal observed, '[t]his was the culture of this workplace. It might be horrible, but it was not sexist'.

There are limits to this 'defence'. A may need to adduce evidence of universally bad treatment (*Anya v University of Oxford* [2001] EWCA Civ 405, [2001] ICR 847, [2001] IRLR 377, para 14). Further, the courts have considered the circumstances in which a tribunal may draw inferences where there is no explanation for the unreasonable treatment. In *Bahl* the Court of Appeal confirmed that unreasonable behaviour alone will not create an inference of discrimination, but the absence of an alternative explanation may do so (para 101). In *Igen*, the Court of Appeal acknowledged that a tribunal may draw such inferences in these circumstances, but nevertheless cautioned against drawing them too readily (para 76).

An employer does not discriminate if it fails to provide an advantage in circumstances where it does not offer that advantage to other employees (*Clymo v Wandsworth London Borough Council* [1989] 2 CMLR 577, [1989] ICR 250). In *Clymo*, a female employee argued she was treated less favourably when after the birth of her child her application for a job-share was refused. The employer did not offer job-sharing to anyone of her grade, and consequently the EAT held she did not suffer a detriment.

An employer does not discriminate simply because it treats two employees differently. For instance, where an employer introduced a dress code which required its employees to dress in a smart and conventional way, but the dress code requirements for male and female employees were not the same, there was no less favourable treatment (*Smith v Safeway plc* [1996] ICR 868, [1996] IRLR 456, CA).

Whether the treatment is regarded as less favourable is essentially an objective consideration although, inevitably, depending on the nature of the alleged less favourable treatment, subjective elements do come into it. *Khan* is an illustration of this, as (although outside the employment sphere) is *Birmingham City Council v Equal Opportunities Commission* [1989] AC 1155, [1989] 2 WLR 520, [1989] IRLR 173, where the House of Lords took into consideration the subjective preference of parents to send their girls to grammar schools. There were more single sex boys' schools than girls' schools in the relevant area. The House of Lords held that it was not necessary for B to prove objectively that grammar schools were better than non-selective schools to demonstrate less favourable treatment, rather that girls had fewer opportunities to attend grammar schools than boys.

1.49 *The reason for the less favourable treatment*

To establish whether there has been less favourable treatment one must look at the reasons for that treatment.

Where B can show he has suffered less favourable treatment by A, compared with an actual or hypothetical comparator, C, his claim for direct discrimination will not succeed if that treatment was not because of a protected characteristic (age; disability; gender reassignment; marriage and civil partnership; race; religion or belief; sex; or sexual orientation: (*EqA 2010, ss 4, 13(1)*). The tribunal must consider *why* B was treated less favourably. A different approach applies in respect of the protected characteristic of pregnancy and maternity, where the test is one of 'unfavourable treatment' (*EqA 2010, s 18(2)*) (see **8.59**).

'But for' test or 'reasons why'

1.50 The orthodox test for establishing the reason for the treatment is one of *classic causation*, ie for the tribunal to ask whether, 'but for' B's particular characteristic (ie his age, sex, race, etc) the less favourable treatment would have occurred. The 'but for' test was approved by the House of Lords in *James v Eastleigh Borough Council* [1990] 2 AC 751, [1990] ICR 554, HL. The Council gave women over 60 free access to the swimming pool while charging men full price until they were 65; the Council argued that the reason for the policy was that men did not reach pensionable age until 65. The House of Lords found that these reasons were irrelevant: J was able to show that 'but for' his sex, a man between the ages of 60 and 65 would not have had to pay for access to the swimming pool, and this was discriminatory. The 'but for' test excludes an examination of motive or intention.

In *O'Neill v Governors of St Thomas More RCVA Upper School* [1996] IRLR 372, [1997] ICR 33, EAT, the guidance given was that the tribunal should adopt a simple, commonsense approach, asking what was the 'effective and predominant cause' or 'real and efficient cause' of the treatment complained of.

More recently, the tribunals have moved away from the 'but for' test in favour of the 'reasons why' test, which involves the tribunal in a consideration of A's conscious or subconscious reasons for treating B less favourably.

One reason for this trend away from the 'but for' test is that it may not in fact reveal the reason for the treatment. In *Shamoon*, S was a Chief Inspector who had certain responsibilities under the appraisal process as a counselling officer. Complaints were made about the way she conducted the appraisals, and her counselling role was withdrawn. S complained that she had been treated less favourably than two male Chief Inspectors.

The House of Lords said that the tribunal must enquire why the claimant received the less favourable treatment noting that 'save in obvious cases, answering the crucial question will call for some consideration of the mental process of the alleged discriminator'. This reflects the shift in the burden of proof (see **1.128** ff) and is a more sophisticated approach than the application of the 'but for' test. It can, however, on first sight create confusion as the older authorities are peppered with references to the fact that the employer's intention or motivation should be irrelevant. The authors believe, however, that in *Shamoon* the House of Lords does not advocate that it is relevant to consider whether the employer intended to discriminate—a lack of intention would indeed be irrelevant if the impact was to discriminate—but to examine the underlying reasons for the less favourable treatment.

The problem is illustrated by *B v A* [2007] IRLR 576, EAT, in which a solicitor, B, had a relationship with a female personal assistant, A. When the affair ended, A was dismissed. The tribunal concluded that the dismissal would not have occurred but for the fact that A was a woman. However, the EAT upheld B's appeal and found that the issue was not merely one of 'but for' causation. It held that the test has a subjective element, and a court must ask itself why, as a matter of fact, the alleged discriminator acted the way he did. The 'but for' test revealed nothing about the motives of B.

See also *Martin v Lancehawk Ltd t/a European Telecom Solutions* [2004] All ER (D) 400 (Mar) (approved in *Igen*), in which the employer's male managing director had an affair with a female employee, M. The tribunal concluded that the reason for the dismissal was the breakdown in the relationship and not her gender. She argued that if she had not been female she would not have been dismissed. The EAT found that the 'but for' test is sometimes inappropriate—the hypothetical comparator proffered by M was a heterosexual male with whom the managing director did not have an affair. However, this did not explain *why* M had been dismissed. The EAT held if there were an appropriate comparator in this case (and the EAT noted that there might not) it would be a hypothetical male employee with whom the managing director had an affair, following which the male employee was dismissed. On the facts before the EAT there was no evidence that the managing director would treat the hypothetical comparator any differently. In any event, M's sex was not the motivating factor behind her dismissal, but it was the affair which had led to a breakdown in the relationship, and the managing director to hold that the employee was untrustworthy.

The EAT decision in *Orr v Milton Keynes Council* [2009] WL 3643812 applied similar principles. There an employee was dismissed as a result of his 'gross insubordination and unprofessional conduct' in two incidents, in one of which his manager made a racist remark. A 'but for' test, considering whether Mr Orr would still have been dismissed had the manager not made the racist remark, was insufficient. The correct test was to ask *why* Mr Orr was dismissed, which was his own conduct in the two incidents (albeit one of those incidents should be disregarded for disciplinary purposes because of the racial element). As the other incident alone amounted to gross misconduct, the dismissal was fair and not an act of race discrimination.

In the light of *Shamoon*, *Khan* and *Igen*, it seems that there will be limited circumstances where the 'but for' test will now be applied. This is more so since the shift in the burden of proof following implementation of *Directive 97/80/EC* (see **1.128** ff) as tribunals increasingly look for and/or receive from the employer an explanation for the conduct complained of at an initial stage of the proceedings.

No requirement for discriminatory motivation or intent

1.51 As stated above, although the recent trend is to consider the reasons why less favourable treatment occurred, this was motivated by a concern that the 'but for' test could lead to a finding of direct discrimination where there was no discriminatory *reason* for the treatment. Prior to October 2010 however, there was clearly no requirement for a tribunal to find a discriminatory *motive* or *intent* for the less favourable treatment to constitute direct discrimination, if the reasons why A acted in the way he did lead to a finding of discrimination (*R v Secretary of State for Education and Science, ex p Keating (1985)* 84 LGR 469; *Glasgow City Council v Zafar* [1998] ICR 20, HL; *Nagarajan v London Regional Transport* [1999] ICR 877, HL; *English v Thomas Sanderson Blinds Ltd* [2008] EWCA Civ 1421, [2009] 2 All ER 468). The courts have recognised that there will be limited circumstances when A acknowledges that the reason for the treatment was an individual's sex or race, etc. In so far as it can, the tribunal must consider what subconscious motivation can be inferred from the evidence before it. Where the employer has good and non-discriminatory motives for their actions, however, it may be that they will avoid a breach of the implied term of trust and confidence and so will not be liable for constructive unfair dismissal in these circumstances (*Ahmed v Amnesty International* [2009] ICR 1450, [2009] IRLR 884, EAT).

The use of the phrase 'because of' in the direct discrimination definition in *EqA 2010, s 13(1)*, which came into force in October 2010, did raise some concerns that it implied a need for discriminatory motivation or intent, contrary to the earlier case law. However, as discussed above (see **1.46**), the government did not intend to change the meaning of the definition in this way and it seems likely that tribunals will continue to follow the principles in *Zafar* and *Nagarajan*.

Protected characteristic need not be the only reason for discrimination

1.52 The protected characteristic need not be the sole or main reason for the less favourable treatment. It might be one of several reasons, although the discriminatory reason must be a significant cause of the unlawful discrimination (*Nagarajan*, in which Lord Nicholls said, at para 886: 'decisions are frequently reached for more than one reason. Discrimination may be on racial grounds even though it is not the sole ground for the decision . . . If racial grounds or protected acts had a significant influence on the outcome, discrimination is made out').

The statutory burden of proof provisions mean, strictly, that, 'it is necessary for the employer to prove, on the balance of probabilities that the treatment was in no sense whatsoever on the grounds of sex, since 'no discrimination whatsoever' is compatible with the Burden of Proof Directive' (per Judge Ansell at para 25, *Barton v Investec Henderson Crosthwaite Securities Ltd* [2003] ICR 1205, [2003] IRLR 332, EAT). The Court of Appeal in *Igen*, while approving this (and rejecting the modification suggested by HH Judge McMullen in *Chamberlin Solicitors v Emokpae* [2004] ICR 1476, [2004] IRLR 592, that the respondent need only prove that the treatment was 'significantly influenced by' grounds of [sex]—as in *Nagarajan*) stated that, ' . . . we doubt if Lord Nicholls' wording is in substance different from the 'no discrimination whatsoever' formula. A "significant" influence is an influence which is more than trivial. We find it hard to believe that the principle of equal treatment would be breached by the merely trivial' (per Peter Gibson LJ at para 37).

1.53 Discrimination by association or perception

The new definition of direct discrimination at *EqA 2010, s 13(1)* provides that A will discriminate against B if, because of a protected characteristic, A treats B less favourably than A treats or would treat others. This form of wording is intended to cover associative discrimination and discrimination based on perception within the provisions on direct discrimination and harassment (but not indirect discrimination).

Although the intention was to extend protection across all the strands, there are practical difficulties which may limit the application of *s 13(1)* both to associative discrimination and to discrimination by perception, which are discussed below.

In addition, the protection has two exceptions. First, in the case of marriage and civil partnership, the victim (B) must be the person who is married or is a civil partner (*EqA 2010, s 13(5)*) for discrimination by association or perception to be unlawful. In relation to associative age discrimination, there is also an exception relating to the provision of child care to a particular age group (*EqA 2010, Sch 9, Part 2, para 15*, see **2.47**).

1.54 *Associative discrimination*

In relation to the new definition of direct discrimination, the *Explanatory Notes to EqA 2010* state:

> 'The definition is broad enough to cover cases where the less favourable treatment is because of the victim's association with someone who has that characteristic (for example, is disabled)'

(*Explanatory Notes to the EqA 2010, note 59*).

The wording of *EqA 2010* is broad enough to protect an employee penalised for refusing to discriminate against a third party based on that third party's protected characteristic (reflecting the authorities, see *Showboat Entertainment Centre Ltd v Owens* [1984] 1 All ER 836, [1984] 1 WLR 384, EAT and *Weathersfield Ltd (t/a Van & Truck Rentals) v Sargent* [1998] ICR 198). Protection would also now be available to the employee in each of these scenarios under *EqA 2010, s 111(5)* (see 'Instructing, causing and inducing' at **1.60**). But contrast *Redfearn v Serco Ltd (t/a West Yorkshire Transport Service)* [2005] IRLR 744 where the Court of Appeal held that despite the fact there were racial considerations behind the dismissal of a BNP member, he was not dismissed on 'racial grounds'.

EqA 2010 also now prohibits associative direct discrimination across all strands (save marriage and civil partnership as set out above and, arguably, pregnancy and maternity (see further below)). Prior to *EqA 2010*, the courts had attempted to interpret UK legislation to this effect. In *EBR Attridge LLP v Coleman (No 2)* (UKEAT/0071/09) this required the EAT to effectively re-write *DDA 1995*. The case had been referred to the ECJ, which held that it was not necessary under the *Framework Directive* for a victim of harassment to be disabled, because the Directive required the unwanted conduct to be 'based on' a disability (*Coleman v Attridge Law: C-303/06* [2007] ICR 654). Since the *DDA 1995* specified that harassment had to be 'for a reason which relates *to the disabled person's* disability', the ECJ held that the *DDA 1995* did not fully implement the Directive. The employment tribunal (and subsequently the EAT) held that words could be read into the *DDA 1995*, to enable a non-disabled person to bring a claim where he/she was harassed 'for a reason which relates to the disability *of another person*'.

UK legislation implementing the *Framework Directive* was more easily interpreted to prohibit harassment based on the victim's association with another, for example under *RBR 2003* (*Saini v All Saints Haque Centre, Bungay and Paul* UKEAT/0227/08) and *SOR 2003* (*English v Thomas Sanderson Blinds Ltd* [2008] EWCA Civ 1421, [2009] IRLR 206, [2009] 2 All ER 468).

Although not expressly excluded under *EqA 2010, s 13*, the *EHRC Employment Code* states that discrimination by association on grounds of pregnancy or maternity will not be unlawful under the associative discrimination provisions. This is consistent with the fact that *EqA 2010, s 25* states that pregnancy and maternity discrimination is discrimination under *ss 17 or 18*, and does not include *s 13* as for the other protected categories. The *EHRC Employment Code* states, however, that in these circumstances the worker may have a sex discrimination claim (at *para 3.18*).

This approach is consistent with the pre-*EqA 2010* EAT decision in *Kulikaoskas v MacDuff Shellfish* 4 October 2010, EAT, in which the EAT refused to allow a pregnancy associative discrimination claim under *SDA 1975*. The EAT also expressed the view that it was unclear whether the claim would have succeeded if brought under *EqA 2010*. This is questionable. The EAT's decision was based on the fact that pregnancy protection stems from the *Pregnant Workers' Directive* and the *Equal Treatment Directive*, rather than the *Framework Directive* which was relevant in *Coleman v Attridge*, a case brought under *DDA 1995*. The purpose of *EqA 2010* is, however, to consolidate the law rather than to implement any of the Directives, and so this should not be relevant. This issue may be tested in the context of requests for leave and pay under the right to additional paternity leave which applies in respect of babies born after 3 April 2011. See **8.60**.

Also controversial is the former government's position that parents and carers would be protected by the new rules on association, stating that: 'an employer could not refuse to promote a member of staff just because he cares for an older relative'. It is, however, questionable whether the legislation would have this effect. In this example, is the refusal to promote because the employee has caring responsibilities, or because of the age of the person that the employee cares for? The former explanation is more likely to apply, and therefore on the face of the legislation such a refusal would be lawful: the employer's action would only be unlawful where: (i) it is motivated by the age (or disability, or other protected characteristic) of the relative, rather than because the employee cares for them; and (ii) the employer cannot show the refusal is objectively justified. The facts of *Coleman* were unusual in relating to direct discrimination and harassment, and it would seem unusual that an employer would target an employee because of the particular characteristics of the person they care for (which would be unlawful under *EqA 2010*), rather than because of the general impact of their caring duties on the employer's business (which would not, even if incapable of objective justification).

Note also that for an associative discrimination claim to succeed, the claimant will need to identify a comparator. If an employer is equally inflexible in the face of all requests for flexible working, direct discrimination could not be made out (see 'Comparators' at **1.63** ff).

As such, protection against associative discrimination may be of limited application to carers notwithstanding the former government's intention.

1.55 *Discrimination by perception*

The definition of direct discrimination under *EqA 2010* is intended to capture discrimination where the victim, or someone associated with them, is wrongly thought to have a relevant protected characteristic. The *Explanatory Notes to EqA 2010* imply that protection against discrimination based on perception is limited to the characteristics of the victim himself ('[t]he definition is broad enough to cover cases where the victim is wrongly thought to have [that characteristic]'), but the wording of *EqA 2010, s 13* in fact also covers discrimination based on the perceived characteristic of someone associated with the claimant, and the *EHRC Employment Code* gives examples to support this interpretation.

It is not yet clear what a claimant will need to demonstrate in order to succeed in a claim for discrimination by perception and the *Explanatory Notes* and *EHRC Employment Code* do not assist. Taking disability as an example, does the claimant have to show:

(a) that the respondent believed the claimant had a medical condition that, as a matter of fact, satisfied the definition of disability in *EqA 2010*; or

(b) that the respondent believed the claimant had a medical condition that the respondent perceived to be a disability (even if it was not); or

(c) simply that the respondent's treatment of the claimant was motivated by their medical condition, which would be a very significant widening of the protection in this field.

Aside from the issue of the correct legal test, there is also potentially a significant evidential hurdle in establishing the respondent's motivation in these circumstances. In a case that pre-dated EqA 2010, *J v DLA Piper UK LLP* (2010) UKEAT/0263/09/RN, [2010] ICR 1052, [2010] IRLR 936, the EAT considered whether the *DDA 1995* covered discrimination based on a perception that an employee was disabled and identified difficult issues that will be relevant to *EqA 2010, s 13*:

> 'The concept of "perceived disability" presents issues different from those presented by the question whether a person (either a claimant or a person with whom he or she is "associated") is in fact disabled. What the putative discriminator perceives will not always be clearly identifiable as "disability". If the perceived disability is, say, blindness, there may be no problem: a blind person is necessarily disabled. But many physical or mental conditions which may attract adverse treatment do not necessarily amount to disabilities, either because they are not necessarily sufficiently serious or because they are not necessarily long-term. If a manager discriminates against an

> employee because he believes her to have a broken leg, or because he believes her to be "depressed", the question whether the effects of the perceived injury, or of the perceived depression, are likely to last more or less than twelve months may never enter his thinking, consciously or unconsciously (nor indeed, in the case of perceived "depression", may it be clear what he understands by the term). In such a case, on what basis can he be said to be discriminating "on the ground of" the employee's—perceived—disability?'

Similar issues might apply to claims of discrimination based on a perception of gender for purposes of gender reassignment, or to religion and belief, amongst other characteristics.

There also remains a question whether the situation addressed by the Court of Appeal in *English v Thomas Sanderson Blinds Ltd* [2008] EWCA Civ 1421 is squarely covered by *EqA 2010*. In the *English* case, an employee taunted using homophobic insults but who was known not to be gay, was found to be protected by the *SOR 2003*. The claim was brought under the *SOR 2003* which prohibited discrimination 'on grounds of' sexual orientation. The Court of Appeal held (by a majority) that the form of the discrimination in this case was related to sexual orientation because the victim was 'perceived to have stereotypical characteristics associated with homosexuals' or at least that 'his fellow employees thought it was funny to taunt a man they knew to be heterosexual with being homosexual'. The court held that it was irrelevant that the discrimination was not motivated by a perception, even if incorrect, of the victim's circumstances.

EqA 2010, s 13(1) prohibits discrimination 'because of protected characteristic', which is similar wording to that of the previous *SOR 2003*. Although the *English* case remains good authority post-*EqA 2010*, Laws LJ's dissenting judgment that the harassment in that case was not motivated by sexual orientation, but was merely the form it took and so was not prohibited under *SOR 2003*, would seem to have some force. It could be argued that it is for this reason that *EqA 2010, s 26(2)* specifically replicates the broader prohibition under *SDA 1975* by prohibiting 'unwanted conduct of a sexual nature'. An earlier draft of the *EHRC Employment Code* gave the *English* scenario as an example of conduct that would be prohibited under *EqA 2010* but this has now been removed. Whilst it may have been the intention to prohibit this form of conduct, arguably *EqA 2010* does not address the potential lacuna here.

1.56 Stereotypical assumptions

Stereotypical assumptions relating to a protected characteristic can constitute direct discrimination. This was demonstrated in the case law prior to October 2010: '[t]he words "on the grounds of" also cover cases where the reason for discrimination was a generalised assumption that people of a particular sex, marital status or race possess or lack certain characteristics . . . ' (*Horsey v Dyfed County Council* [1982] ICR 755, [1982] IRLR 395, and reiterated in the *EHRC Employment Code, para 16.43*).

The fact that a stereotypical assumption contains an element of truth, or that it was at some time in the past true, does not alter this. (In *European Roma Rights Centre v Immigration Officer at Prague Airport (United Nations High Commissioner for Refugees intervening)* [2004] UKHL 55, [2005] 2 AC 1, [2005] 1 All ER 527, Baroness Hale said (at para 74), 'The individual should not be assumed to hold the characteristics which the supplier associates with the group, whether or not most members of the group do indeed have such characteristics . . . ').

1.57 COMBINED DISCRIMINATION

EqA 2010 contains a new provision enabling an employee to bring a discrimination claim on two combined protected grounds, for example where an older woman was treated less favourably than a younger woman or an older man would have been (*EqA 2010, s 14*). This addresses a perceived difficulty under existing legislation on the basis that the employee must show that the reason for the discriminatory conduct was the relevant protected characteristic, which may not be the case where there are two such reasons. In practice it is unclear how widely used this new provision will be, given that in a single strand claim it is only necessary for the claimant to show that the protected ground is a 'significant cause' (rather than the sole or main cause) for the treatment complained of (*Nagarajan*). In practice, tribunals have already proved willing to accept what are effectively dual discrimination claims on the basis of a single strand claim (see for example *Khan v Ghafoor ta/ Go Go Real Estate*, unreported, where a claim of discrimination where a non-practising Muslim woman was penalised for not wearing a headscarf was upheld on grounds of single strand religious discrimination and sex discrimination).

Note that the provision was not implemented on 1 October 2010 and the government has not committed to a specific date for its introduction. The *EHRC Employment Code* states that the government is considering how the combined discrimination provisions can be best implemented for business and the public sector respectively, and so it does not discuss these provisions. However, an earlier draft of the *EHRC Employment Code* did provide guidance on combined discrimination, and this is discussed below.

The relevant section of the *EqA 2010*, once implemented, is as follows:

> 'A person (A) discriminates against another (B) if, because of a combination of two relevant protected characteristics, A treats B less favourably than A treats or would treat a person who does not share either of those characteristics' (*EqA 2010, s 14(1)*).

Only two characteristics can be used; claims based on more than two characteristics are not permitted. The provision also covers only direct discrimination; the combined discrimination provision is not relevant to indirect discrimination or harassment.

Significantly, *s 14(1)* only applies to *relevant* protected characteristics. These are listed in *s 14(2)*: age; disability; gender reassignment; race; religion or belief; sex; and sexual orientation. Combined discrimination claims cannot be brought where marriage and civil partnership or pregnancy and maternity are one of the grounds complained of, however it may be that in reality these claims could be brought as sex discrimination. In any event, either claim could still be brought as a single strand discrimination claim in parallel with a combined discrimination claim.

For the purposes of combined discrimination, disability is treated as a single characteristic. Therefore, even where B has more than one condition arising out of the same disability, or more than one disability, for example, visual impairment and HIV, B cannot bring a combined discrimination claim. In this situation, the claimant should bring a single strand claim (or claims) for direct disability discrimination (*Draft EHRC Employment Code, para 3.33*).

EqA 2010 specifically provides that B need not show that the less favourable treatment is a result of *each* characteristic taken separately (*EqA 2010, s 14(3)*). This implies that the claimant would need to effectively prove a single strand claim based on at least one of the two characteristics in order to succeed, however this does not appear to be the intention. The previous draft of the *EHRC Employment Code* stated that the claimant should show that the *combination* of the two characteristics was an effective cause of the treatment (*para 3.36*). The *Explanatory Notes to the EqA 2010* envisage claimants bringing combined discrimination claims where they will not succeed with a single strand claim (*notes 66, 68*). In practice, claimants are likely to plead combined discrimination in the alternative to single characteristic claims which may make hearings longer and more complicated.

1.58 Defences

A combined discrimination claim will not succeed where an exception or justification applies to *either* of the protected characteristics relied upon (*EqA 2010, s 14(4)*). This sits rather uncomfortably with *s 14(3)*, as it seems to imply that a claimant must effectively be able to make out direct discrimination on each of the characteristics as mentioned above (a direct contradiction of *s 14(3)* and *note 66 of Explanatory Notes to the EqA 2010*). However, it should be assumed that *s 14(3)* is correct, and that *s 14(4)* should be interpreted to mean that the defences which would apply to a single strand claim will also apply to a combined discrimination claim. Another technical drafting issue is that ORs do not fall within the defence set out in *s 14(4)*, because *s 14(4)* applies where the treatment would otherwise amount to direct discrimination, whereas an OR is still categorised as discrimination, albeit it is lawful. Again, this will be for the tribunals to interpret if *EqA 2010, s 14* is implemented in its current form.

Note that the previous draft of the *EHRC Employment Code* stated that if discrimination could be proved because of two different protected characteristics separately (ie the claimant could bring two separate claims), then a claim of combined discrimination would not be made out (*para 3.37*). Whilst *s 14* does not expressly support this, *s 14(1)* states that discrimination will take place where there is 'a combination of two relevant protected characteristics'. This arguably allows tribunals to interpret the provision in accordance with the intention as set out in the *Explanatory Notes to the EqA 2010*, which is that *s 14* is intended to protect against discrimination resulting from the combination of the two factors, where a single strand claim would not succeed.

1.59 Comparators

EqA 2010, s 14(1) states that the appropriate comparator will be someone who does not have either of the relevant characteristics, for example, a black woman could be compared with a white man. Hypothetical comparators can be constructed, for which purpose it may be relevant to look at the treatment of two actual comparators who in each case lack one of the two protected characteristics on which the combined discrimination claim is based. For example, in the case of a black woman claiming dual race and sex discrimination, the two individuals from whom a hypothetical comparison would be drawn would be a white woman and a black man.

Note that such a comparison in isolation does not prove combined discrimination. For example, comparing a black woman with a white man might point to dual race and sex discrimination, but it could equally point to just race discrimination or just sex discrimination. In order to establish that combined discrimination had occurred, it would strictly be necessary to examine the treatment of (in this example) white women and black men too.

The draft *EHRC Employment Code* did not seem to envisage this three-stage comparison being made in every case. *Paragraph 3.40* of the draft Code stated that it may be simpler to concentrate on the reason for the treatment, and focuses on 'prejudice' or 'assumptions' that are based on the combination of characteristics (stereotypes based on dual characteristics are also referred to in *Explanatory Notes to the EqA 2010, note 68*). Nonetheless, combined discrimination claims and defences are likely to be complicated by multiple comparisons.

Whether a claim of combined discrimination can be brought may also depend on the identity of the claimant. For example, an employer favours older men in its organisation, which seems at first glance to be a clear case of combined discrimination. However, the persons who are discriminated against in this organisation would be older women, younger men and younger women. It seems that only younger women would be able to bring a claim of combined discrimination: a claimant who was a older woman would have to bring a claim of sex discrimination only, while a younger man would have to bring a claim of age discrimination only.

EqA 2010, s 24(2) provides that the characteristics of the alleged discriminator are irrelevant in assessing whether combined discrimination has taken place. The explanatory notes make clear that this is the case whether the discriminator shares one or both of the relevant characteristics. This new provision reflects the existing legal position, as case law has confirmed that an individual who shares the relevant protected characteristic with their victim can still be liable for discrimination, however of the pre-October 2010 legislation only *RBR 2003* expressly provided that it was no defence to a claim of direct discrimination that the alleged discriminator shared the same religion or belief as the victim.

1.60 INSTRUCTING, CAUSING OR INDUCING DISCRIMINATION

EU law

Council Directive 2006/54/EC ('the *Equal Treatment Directive*') implementing the principle of equal treatment between men and women in matters of employment and occupation provides that:

> 'For the purposes of this Directive, discrimination includes:
>
> . . .
>
> (b) instruction to discriminate against persons on grounds of sex; . . . ' (*Article 2*).

Council Directive 2000/78/EC ('the *Framework Directive*'), establishing a general framework for equal treatment in employment and occupation contains a virtually identical provision (*Article 2.4*), as does *Council Directive 2000/43/EC* ('the *Race Directive*') in respect of discrimination based on racial or ethnic origin (*Article 2.4*).

1.61 UK law

It is unlawful for a person ('A') to instruct, cause or induce someone ('B') to discriminate against, harass or victimise another person ('C'), or to attempt to do so (*EqA 2010, s 111*). A claim can be brought by the 'victim' of the discrimination (C), the person who was instructed to carry out the discrimination (B), if they are subjected to a detriment as a result of A's conduct, and also by the EHRC. Liability will arise whether or not the person instructed to carry out the discrimination in fact goes on to do so. However, A and B must be in a relationship where discrimination, harassment or victimisation is prohibited (see **1.16–1.36**).

The statutory right of the person instructed to carry out the discrimination to bring a claim is largely new, however it reflects the existing common law position (see *Weathersfield Ltd (t/a Van & Truck Rentals) v Sargent* [1999] ICR 425, [1999] IRLR 94, CA). The *AR 2006* right of action to individuals penalised for refusing to comply with or complaining about unlawful instructions in respect of age is now reflected in the separate victimisation provisions (see 'Victimisation' at **1.98** ff). The provision allowing the intended 'victim' to bring proceedings, even where the instruction is not carried out (provided he suffers detriment), is entirely new, and the *Explanatory Notes to the EqA 2010* state that the intention is to ensure greater clarity about the protection under current legislation.

The *EHRC Employment Code* emphasises that 'inducement' to discriminate 'may amount to no more than persuasion', and may not involve any direct benefit or loss for the person being influenced (*para 9.18*).

1.62 AIDING DISCRIMINATION

It is unlawful for a person (A) to knowingly help someone (B) to carry out an act which is unlawful under *EqA 2010, s 112(1)*. In contrast with the liability provisions under *EqA 2010, ss 110(1), 111(1)* (see refer to 'Instructing, Causing or Inducing discrimination' at

1.60), A is only liable where B has actually committed an act which breaches *EqA 2010*. The help given will be unlawful even if it is not substantial or productive, so long as it is not negligible (*EHRC Employment Code, para 9.27*).

A will not be liable unless he knows that B's act is likely to result in an unlawful act, even if that was not the intention of either A or B (*EHRC Employment Code, para 9.28*). Knowledge here is likely to reflect the pre-October 2010 case law, which was that it was not necessary for A to have intended or even to have thought that the act was likely to result in a discriminatory outcome. It was enough that A could have foreseen that discrimination was a probable outcome, albeit he may not have specifically addressed his mind to it (*Allaway v Reilly* [2007] IRLR 864, a case under the *SDA 1975*).

A will not be liable if he or she reasonably relies on a statement by B that the act was not unlawful (*EqA 2010, s 112(2)*). What is reasonable will depend on all the circumstances, including the nature of the act and how obviously discriminatory it is, B's level of authority and A's knowledge (*EHRC Employment Code, para 9.29*). As with *EqA 2010, s 110* (liability of employers and principals) (see 'vicarious liability' at **1.163** ff) it is an offence for B to tell A that the act was not unlawful where that statement is false or misleading, where he does so either knowingly or recklessly.

An example given by the *EHRC Employment Code* is where a clerical worker helps a manager to discriminate against male candidates by letting him know the gender of applicants for a role (*EHRC Employment Code, paras 9.27–9.28*). The example does not, however, shed light on the trickier question of the threshold to establish A's knowledge that the request was likely to result in an act of discrimination. Despite the statement in the *EHRC Employment Code* that B's intention is not relevant here, motivation is likely to be a key evidential point as to whether A was on notice that the likely outcome of the act would be unlawful. The Court of Appeal judgment in *Bird v Sylvester* [2007] EWCA Civ 1052, [2008] ICR 208, [2008] IRLR 232 remains relevant: in this case a law firm was held not to be liable for victimisation based on a letter they had written to a client's employee threatening disciplinary action, because they had merely advised the client and had not themselves taken the decision to threaten action. The court held, however, that an agent in this scenario could potentially be liable if they actively promote a certain course of action, rather than limiting their role to giving objective advice and executing instructions received.

Individuals or companies who provide resourcing services to third parties, for example recruitment consultants, employment businesses and outsourced service providers, will want written confirmation from that third party that the actions required of them do not breach the *EqA 2010*.

For liability of employees and agents and liability of employers and principals for acts of employees and agents, see **1.164** ff.

1.63 COMPARATORS

Introduction

The legal concept of discrimination has at its heart the task of *comparison*. The discrimination law of the United Kingdom does not prohibit the unfair or unreasonable treatment of minorities *per se*. Indeed, as Lord Browne-Wilkinson observed in *Zafar v Glasgow City Council* [1998] ICR 120, [1998] IRLR 36, HL, the fact that an employer (or other alleged discriminator) has acted unreasonably in its treatment of an alleged victim of discrimination is technically irrelevant (see also *Madarassy v Nomura International plc* [2007] EWCA Civ 33, [2007] ICR 867, [2007] IRLR 246, para 93). While unreasonable conduct cannot found an inference of discrimination, if there is no explanation for the unreasonable treatment, the absence of an explanation (rather than the unreasonable treatment itself) may found an inference of discrimination: *Bahl v Law Society* [2004] EWCA Civ 1070, [2004] IRLR 799. Nonetheless, the question—subject to limited exceptions discussed in **1.64** below—is always whether the alleged victim has or has not been treated *less favourably* than someone else, on a prohibited ground.

That comparison is central to discrimination is evident from the definitions of discrimination found in the *EqA 2010*. By *s 13(1)*, direct discrimination is described as arising where '[a] person (A) discriminates against another (B) if, because of a protected characteristic, A treats B less favourably than A treats or would treat others'. Likewise, the concept of indirect discrimination is defined in terms of a comparison requiring, *inter alia*, a provision, practice or criterion which puts or would put persons with whom B shares a relevant protected characteristic at a particular disadvantage when compared with persons with whom B does not share it (*EqA 2010, s 19(2)(b)*).

The 'someone else' or 'other', actual or hypothetical, with whom a claimant in a discrimination case compares his treatment, is known as a 'comparator'. The task of identifying actual or hypothetical comparators, and comparing their treatment with that of the alleged victim, is a central task in any direct discrimination case. Indeed, as the House of Lords observed in *Shamoon v Chief Constable of the Ulster Constabulary* [2003] UKHL 11, [2003] 2 All ER 26, [2003] ICR 337, the question whether a particular person is or is not a proper comparator can often be determinative of the outcome of a case.

1.64 Circumstances in which a comparator is not necessary

Pursuant to *EqA 2010*, there are five exceptions to the general requirement that a comparator is always necessary.

First, a comparator is not required where the complaint is that an employer has segregated workers because of race (*EqA 2010, s 13(5)*).

Second, pursuant to *EqA 2010, s 15(1)*, a comparator is not required where the complaint is that A has treated B unfavourably because of something arising in consequence of B's disability, and A cannot show that the treatment is a proportionate means of achieving a legitimate aim. This section reverses the effect of the House of Lords decision in *Lewisham London Borough Council v Malcolm* [2008] UKHL 43, [2008] 1 AC 1399 and is discussed further in **DISABILITY DISCRIMINATION (3)**.

Third, no comparator is required where the complaint is in respect of discrimination because of pregnancy or a pregnancy-related illness (*EqA 2010, s 18(2)*). As with disability discrimination, unfavourable treatment because of pregnancy or because of an illness suffered as a result of the pregnancy will suffice; it is not necessary to show less favourable treatment by reference to a comparator.

Fourth, unfavourable treatment suffices to show discrimination where a woman is on compulsory maternity leave or is exercising or seeking to exercise, or has exercised or sought to exercise, the right to ordinary or additional maternity leave (*EqA 2010, s 18(7)*).

Fifth, victimisation does not require a comparator. The worker need only show that they have experienced a detriment because they have done a protected act or because the employer believes (rightly or wrongly) that they have done or intend to do a protected act: *EqA 2010, s 27(1)*.

1.65 The statutory definition of 'comparator'

The statutory definition of the characteristics required for someone to be a proper comparator, actual or hypothetical, for the purposes of a discrimination case has been amended by the *EqA 2010*. *EqA 2010, s 23(1)* requires that:

> 'On a comparison of cases for the purposes of sections 13, 14, or 19, there must be no material difference between the circumstances relating to each case'.

Sections 13, 14 and 19 refer to direct discrimination, combined discrimination and indirect discrimination respectively. *Section 14* (combined discrimination) is not yet in force.

This definition has replaced that contained in the previous legislation. The relevant provision in the *RRA 1976, s 3(4)* (which was materially mirrored in all the other discrimination statutes), provided as follows:

> 'A comparison of the case of a person of a particular racial group with that of a person not of that group under *s 1(1)* or *1A* must be such that the relevant circumstances in the one case are the same, or not materially different, in the other'.

(*SDA 1975, s 5(3); DDA 1995, s 3A(5); RBR 2003, reg 3(3); SOR 2003, reg 3(3)* and *AR 2006, reg 3(2)*)

The definition in *EqA 2010, s 23(1)* is expanded in *s 23(2)–(3)*. *EqA 2010, s 23(2)* provides that the circumstances relating to a case include a person's abilities if, on a comparison for the purposes of direct discrimination (*s 13*), the protected characteristic is disability (or in the case of combined discrimination in *s 14*, one of the protected characteristics is disability) see further discussion in **Disability discrimination (3)**. Meanwhile, *EqA 2010, s 23(3)* provides that if the protected characteristic is sexual orientation, the fact that one person is a civil partner while another is married is not a material difference between the circumstances relating to each case.

1.66 *'Material difference between the circumstances'*

The *Explanatory Notes to the EqA 2010* explain, at *para 91*, that *s 23(1)* requires that like must be compared with like. Thus, the treatment of the claimant must be compared with that of an actual or hypothetical person—the comparator—who does not share the same protected characteristic as the claimant (or in the case of combined discrimination, either of the protected characteristics in the combination), but who is or is assumed to be in not materially different circumstances from the claimant.

By way of guidance, the following examples are given in the *Explanatory Notes to the EqA 2010, para 93*:

— a blind woman claims she was not shortlisted for a job involving computers because the employer wrongly assumed that blind people cannot use them. An appropriate comparator is a person who is not blind—it could be a non-disabled person or someone with a different disability—but who has the same ability to do the job as the claimant.

— a Muslim employee is put at a disadvantage by his employer's practice of not allowing requests for time off work on Fridays. The comparison that must be made is in terms of the impact of that practice on non-Muslim employees in similar circumstances to whom it is (or might be) applied.

In the context of combined discrimination, the appropriate comparator for a black woman complaining of discrimination on the grounds of race and sex would be a white man.

It is not clear if the reference to 'circumstances' in *EqA 2010, s 23(1)* rather than 'relevant circumstances' as in the previous statutory formulation could entail a stricter test for determining an appropriate comparator. The *Explanatory Notes to the EqA 2010* indicate that *s 23* 'replicates similar provisions in previous legislation', but accommodates the new concept of combined discrimination. Consequently, it would appear that the existing case law regarding the 'circumstances' to be considered still applies.

The former statutory formula ' . . . such that the relevant circumstances in the one case are the same, or not materially different, in the other' was considered in detail in the decision of the House of Lords in *Shamoon* (see **1.46**). The ratio, in short, of their Lordships' decision was that the 'relevant circumstances' which cannot be 'materially different' if someone is to constitute a proper comparator are:

(a) all those circumstances that *were* taken into account when the allegedly discriminatory decision was made (aside of course from the prohibited grounds); and

(b) all those circumstances that *would have been* taken into account if the alleged comparator had been in the position of the alleged victim.

The importance of the second category of relevant circumstances identified above was illustrated by the particular facts of the *Shamoon* case itself. In that case, a female police officer argued that she had been discriminated against on ground of her sex because she had had the task of performing staff appraisals taken away from her after a complaint was made against her. She compared herself with two male police officers of the same rank who continued to perform such appraisals. However, it was held that those male police officers were *not* proper comparators, because: (i) neither had had a complaint made about them; and (ii) both worked in a different department. Those two circumstances *would have been* taken into account had those men been in the claimant's position and were therefore, to put the House of Lords' decision in terms of the statute, 'relevant circumstances' which were 'materially different'.

In *Nelson v Newry and Mourne District Council* [2009] NICA 24, [2009] IRLR 548, NI CA, it was found that a male employee had not been treated less favourably than a female employee after being demoted by the local authority for taking bedding plants from her for personal use (and the female employee was treated less harshly). The court found that the allegations of discrimination had to be considered in the context of all the surrounding evidence; and given that Nelson had been the instigator and had engaged in subsequent dishonesty, the difference between Nelson and his colleague were such that a local authority could reasonably have concluded that they were not in a comparable position demanding equal disciplinary treatment.

The characteristics of a comparator are not subject to any further limitation than that in *s 23(1)*. Accordingly, where that test is met, comparison is possible with employees in associated companies, as opposed to the same company: *EqA 2010, s 79(4)* (see **1.68**).

1.67 *Discriminatory different circumstances*

A significant problem is posed when an alleged discriminator seeks to rely, in an attempt to argue that a nominated comparator is not a proper one, on an allegedly materially different 'circumstance' which is *in itself* discriminatory. The two leading cases in this area do not speak with one voice by any means:

(a) *James v Eastleigh Borough Council* [1990] 2 AC 751, [1990] IRLR 288, HL. The respondent Council permitted free access to a swimming pool for women at the age of 60, but for men at the age of 65. The respondent argued that the reason for this distinction was the difference in 'pensionable age', ie the age at which men and women received state pensions, and therefore the difference in treatment was not 'on ground of sex'. The House of Lords rejected this argument, holding that it is impossible to defend a discriminatory act as not being 'on ground of sex' when it is based on a statutory scheme which *itself* discriminates on ground of sex. At least one way of understanding the *James* case would be that a person (in that case a woman aged 60 to 64) cannot be prohibited from being a legitimate comparator by virtue of a circumstance (in that case pensionable age) which is in itself discriminatory.

(b) *Dhatt v McDonalds Hamburgers Ltd* [1991] 3 All ER 692, [1991] 1 WLR 527, [1991] ICR 238, CA. The applicant was of Indian nationality and, under the *Immigration Act 1971*, was entitled to live and work in the United Kingdom without restriction or need for a work permit. He was given a job but was dismissed for failing to provide evidence of his right to work. He complained that he had been unlawfully discriminated against on the ground of his race by comparison with citizens of Member States of the European Economic Community ('EEC citizens'), who were not required to produce evidence of their entitlement to work. The Court of Appeal, however, held that EEC citizens were *not* proper comparators within the meaning of *RRA 1976, s 3(4)*, since Parliament, by giving a right of freedom to work in the United Kingdom to British and EEC citizens, had distinguished between them and nationals of other states so that a comparison between the applicant and those groups was not a comparison of like with like. In other words, the Court of Appeal held that the difference in treatment between EEC citizens and non-EEC citizens was a 'relevant circumstance' that was 'materially different'.

It is often argued that the *Dhatt* decision is incompatible with the *James* decision and therefore wrong. This is a jurisprudentially difficult argument, since: (i) the Court of Appeal in *Dhatt* both considered and distinguished the *James* decision; and (ii) the *Dhatt* decision has since been followed by the EAT, in *Ice Hockey Super League Ltd v Henry* EAT/1167/99/0203.

The basis for the Court of Appeal's distinction between the facts of the *Dhatt* and *James* cases was that in *Dhatt*, nationality was a relevant circumstance ' . . . because Parliament itself recognises and seeks to enforce by reference to nationality a general division between those who by reason of their nationality are free to work and those who require permission' (per Neill LJ at 535), whereas in *James*, Parliament had *not* in any way enacted 'that concessions granted by local authorities on the ground of age should depend on the attainment of pensionable age' (per Neill LJ at 534), and therefore 'pensionable status' could not be a materially relevant circumstance since it was in itself discriminatory. Although it is difficult to find any basis for this distinction in the discrimination legislation, it is nevertheless conceptually tenable.

Until a further appellate case resolves the tension between the *James* and *Dhatt* cases, therefore, the law would appear to be that it *is* possible to rely on a materially different circumstance which is in itself discriminatory but *only* where the difference in treatment itself arises directly from legislation.

1.68 *Comparisons in the context of sex equality and terms of employment*

EqA 2010, s 79 sets out the requirements for a 'comparator' in the context of claim based on lack of sex equality in employment terms. If A is employed, B is regarded as a comparator if B is employed by A's employer or by an associate of A's employer, and A and B work at the same establishment (*EqA 2010, s 79(3)*). Employers are associated employers if one is a company of which the other has control, directly or indirectly, or if both are companies of which a third person has control, directly or indirectly: *EqA 2010, s 79(9)*.

If A and B do not work at the same establishment, B can still be regarded as a comparator where common terms apply at the establishments (either generally or as between A and B): *EqA 2010, s 79(4)*. If work is not done at an establishment, it is treated as done at the establishment with which it has the closest connection: *EqA 2010, s 80(3)*. The case law regarding common terms and conditions applying at different establishments has been considered in a number of cases under similar provisions in the *EqPA 1970* and will continue to be relevant (see EQUAL PAY **(11)**).

There is no requirement in a claim regarding employment terms for the employee to establish contemporaneous employment with her chosen comparator: *Macarthys Ltd v Smith* [1981] QB 180, CA. This position is now codified in *EqA 2010, s 64(2)*. In the *Macarthys* case, at issue was comparison with a predecessor; the language in *EqA 2010, s 64(2)* is, however, sufficiently broad to suggest that comparison with a successor would also be permitted.

On the question of hypothetical comparators in the context of sex equality and employment terms, see **1.70** below.

1.69 *Comparisons where own membership of protected class not relied on*

A further difficulty with the comparative exercise arises where a claimant alleges associative discrimination on ground of *someone else's* membership of a protected class. Where such a claim is brought, the comparative exercise can be modified.

Prior to the *EqA 2010*, a claim of associative discrimination was available in respect of: *RRA 1976*, which prohibited discrimination 'on racial grounds'; *RBR, reg 3(1)(a)*, which referred to less favourable treatment on grounds of the religion or belief of someone other than the respondent; *SOR 2003, reg 3(1)* which protected employees from less favourable treatment 'on grounds of sexual orientation'; *DDA 1995*, following the case of *EBR Attridge Law v Coleman (No 2)*, in which the EAT 'read in' a new *sub-s 3A(5A)* addressing less favourable treatment 'by reason of the disability of another person'; but not *SDA 1975, s 1(2)(a)* which only protected an employee against less favourable treatment 'on ground of her sex'; *SDA 1975, s 3(1)(a)* in respect of marital status; *SDA 1975, s 2A(1)* in respect of gender reassignment; *SDA 1975, s 3A* in respect of pregnancy and maternity; and not *AR 2006, reg 3(1)(a)* which refers to less favourable treatment on grounds of 'B's age' (see **1.54**).

However, the *EqA 2010, s 13* extends the scope of associative discrimination to all of the protected grounds, except 'marriage and civil partnership' as, pursuant to *s 13(4)*, a claim may only be brought on this ground where the person less favourably treated is married or a civil partner.

The leading case on the comparative exercise in the context of associative discrimination is still *Showboat Entertainment Centre Ltd v Owens* [1984] 1 All ER 836, [1984] 1 WLR 384, EAT, in which a white manager was dismissed for refusing to obey an instruction to exclude all black customers from an entertainment centre. The respondent argued that it was necessary to compare how it treated the applicant with the way in which it would have treated another manager who also refused to carry out the instruction. The EAT robustly rejected this argument, holding that (emphasis added):

> 'Although one has to compare like with like, in judging whether there has been discrimination you have to compare the treatment actually meted out with the treatment which would have been afforded to a man having all the same characteristics as the complainant except his race *or his attitude to race*. Only by excluding *matters of race* can you discover whether the differential treatment was on racial grounds. Thus, the correct comparison in this case would be between the applicant and another manager who did not refuse to obey the unlawful racialist instructions'.

It would therefore appear that where a person is treated less favourably on ground of someone else's membership of a protected class, the court must exclude that person's 'attitude to' members of that protected class when assessing whether an actual or hypothetical comparator is a proper one. Further (obiter) examples of the application of the principle were given in:

(i) the decision of the House of Lords in *Applin v Race Relations Board* [1975] AC 259, HL at 289–290, in which Lord Simon observed that the dismissal of a white employee by a white employer for marrying a black person was plainly within the 'mischief' which the *RRA 1976* was intended to address; and

(ii) the decision of the Court of Appeal in the same case (*Race Relations Board v Applin* [1973] QB 815, CA at 828a–e), in which Lord Denning MR observed that a white publican who refused to admit or serve a white customer on the ground that she was accompanied by a black person would be liable in principle for race discrimination. In both of these cases, the judges approached the matter on the basis that the correct comparison was with someone who had *not* married a black person and/or was *not* accompanied by a black person.

This approach presented the Court of Appeal in the subsequent case of *Redfearn v Serco Ltd* [2006] EWCA Civ 659, [2006] ICR 1367 with some difficulty. In that case, Mr Redfearn, who was white, had been employed by Serco as a bus driver and escort for people with disabilities. A local newspaper identified him as a British National Party (BNP) candidate in forthcoming local elections. The BNP sought the restoration of Britain as a predominantly white nation. Mr Redfearn was elected as a BNP councillor and was subsequently summarily dismissed by Serco on the basis that his employment would present a risk to the health and safety of its employees and passengers and would jeopardise Serco's reputation. Mr Redfearn, relying heavily on the *Showboat* case, argued that he had been treated less favourably on ground of race because Serco had employed a race-based criterion in his dismissal. The Court of Appeal firmly rejected this argument, and in doing so significantly narrowed the ambit of the ratio in the *Showboat* case. The relevant passage of the judgment of Mummery LJ reads as follows:

> '**44** The essence of *Showboat* is that an employee who refuses to implement his employer's racially discriminatory policy is entitled to be protected from less favourable treatment under the 1976 Act. The use of the employee to implement the employer's racially discriminatory policy means that "racial grounds" operate directly in the less favourable treatment of the employee, whether the race or colour in question is that of the employee or that of a third party. Mr Bowers' proposition goes far wider so as to embrace cases in which the employer, far from seeking to implement a racially discriminatory policy contrary to the policy of the 1976 Act, is acting to eliminate race discrimination in accordance with the policy of the 1976 Act. According to Mr Bowers (subject to his points on causation and remedy) the employee would be entitled to receive the same protection under the 1976 Act from unfavourable treatment, such as dismissal, however racially discriminatory he was towards third parties contrary to his employer's instructions.
>
> **45** Mr Bowers' proposition turns the ratio of *Showboat* and the policy of the race relations legislation upside down. It would mean that any less favourable treatment brought about because of concern about the racist views or conduct of a person in a multi-ethnic workplace would constitute race discrimination. The ratio of *Showboat* is that the racially discriminatory employer is liable "on racial grounds" for the less favourable treatment of those who refuse to implement his policy or are affected by his policy. It does not apply so as to make the employer, who is not pursuing a policy of race discrimination or who is pursuing a policy of anti-race discrimination, liable for race discrimination.
>
> **46** In this case it is true that the circumstances in which the decision to dismiss Mr Redfearn was taken included racial considerations, namely the fact that Serco's customers were mainly Asian and that a significant percentage of the workforce was Asian. Racial considerations were relevant to Serco's decision to dismiss Mr Redfearn, but that does not mean that it is right to characterise Serco's dismissal of Mr Redfearn as being "on racial grounds". It is a non sequitur to argue that he was dismissed "on racial grounds" because the circumstances leading up to his dismissal included a relevant racial consideration, such as the race of fellow employees and customers and the policies of the BNP on racial matters. Mr Redfearn was no more dismissed "on racial grounds" than an employee who is dismissed for racially abusing his employer, a fellow employee or a valued customer. Any other result would be incompatible with the purpose of the 1976 Act to promote equal treatment of persons irrespective of race by making it unlawful to discriminate against a person on the grounds of race.'

Redfearn was followed in *HM Prison Service v Potter* UKEAT/0457/06/1411, EAT, in respect of a Prison Service policy which precluded the employment of individuals who were members of any political organisation with a racist philosophy. However, it was held that the tribunal was entitled to examine whether the policy gave rise to direct or indirect discrimination on the basis of the claimant's complaint that it had only been applied to white organisations.

In *English v Thomas Sanderson Blinds Ltd* [2008] EWCA Civ 1421, [2009] 2 All ER 468, [2009] IRLR 206, the Court of Appeal regarded *Showboat* and *Redfearn* as indicating that the statutory intent should be determinative of the reach of associative discrimination. The court concluded that there had been a breach of *SOR 2003, reg 5* where homophobic banter had been directed at a man who: (i) was not gay, (ii) was not perceived or assumed to be so by his tormentors; and (iii) accepted that they did not believe him to be gay. What was required was that the claimant's or someone else's sexual orientation, whether real or supposed, should have been the basis of harassment directed at him or her.

1.70 *Hypothetical comparators*

It is important to note that—apart from in equal pay cases which are considered further below—a claimant is not obliged to name an actual comparator in order to have a viable discrimination case. Where there is no actual comparator who meets the statutory requirements, a tribunal or court is instead obliged to consider what would have happened to a hypothetical comparator (*Balamoody v UK Central Council for Nursing, Midwifery and Health Visiting* [2001] EWCA Civ 2097, [2002] ICR 646, [2002] IRLR 288 at [54]). This remains the case pursuant to *EqA 2010: s 13(1)* (referring to direct discrimination arising if A treats B less favourably than A treats or *would treat* others); *s 19(2)(a)* (referring to indirect discrimination arising where A applies, or *would apply* a provision, criterion or practice to persons with whom B does not share the relevant characteristic) (see also **1.72ff**).

The hypothetical comparator is *not* required to be ' . . . a clone of the applicant in every respect (including personality and personal characteristics) except that he or she is of a different race' (or other protected characteristic) (*Madden v Preferred Technical Group CHA Ltd* [2004] EWCA Civ 1178, [2005] IRLR 46 per Wall LJ, [87]). Rather, as with an actual comparator, the only requirement is that the relevant circumstances of the hypothetical comparator should not be materially different.

In considering whether a hypothetical comparator has been treated less favourably than a claimant, there are two (not necessarily alternative) approaches that a tribunal can adopt.

The first approach is to consider the alleged discriminator's treatment of other actual persons who are not proper comparators within the meaning of the discrimination statutes ('evidential comparators'). From the treatment of these people it is said to be possible to infer how the hypothetical comparator would have been treated. The leading case is *Chief Constable of West Yorkshire v Vento* [2001] IRLR 124, EAT, in which the EAT approved a process by which a tribunal had used four persons who were not actual comparators ' . . . as if building blocks in the construction of the neighbourhood in which the hypothetical male officer was to be found' (at [15]). The *Vento* case was approved by the Court of Appeal in *Balamoody* (cited above). See also *Shamoon* at **1.46** and **1.66** per Lord Scott at [109].

The second approach has become known as the 'reason why' approach. Why was the claimant treated in the fashion he was treated? This was the approach recommended by the House of Lords in the *Shamoon* case. The relevant passage of the speech of Lord Bingham ([7]–[12]) provides:

> ' . . . employment tribunals may sometimes be able to avoid arid and confusing disputes about the identification of the appropriate comparator by concentrating primarily on why the claimant was treated as she was. Was it on the proscribed ground which is the foundation of the application? That will call for an examination of all the facts of the case. Or was it for some other reason? If the latter, the application fails. If the former, there will be usually be no difficulty in deciding

> whether the treatment, afforded to the claimant on the proscribed ground, was less favourable than was or would have been afforded to others'.

In the light of subsequent cases, such as *Chief Constable of West Yorkshire Police v Khan* [2001] UKHL 48, [2001] 1 WLR 1947, [2001] ICR 1065 and *Wong v Igen Ltd* [2005] IRLR 258 it seems that the 'reason why' approach is, in hypothetical comparator cases, preferable. The artificiality of the hypothetical exercise is kept to a minimum if the tribunal starts by asking itself, on the basis of all the evidence before it, whether a claimant would have been treated any differently but for their membership of a protected class. This can include even disregarding the burden of proof provisions and adopting a one-stage approach by ' . . . acting on the assumption that the burden may have shifted to the respondent and then considering the explanation put forward by the respondent' (*Madarassy v Nomura International plc* [2007] EWCA Civ 33, [2007] ICR 867, [2007] IRLR 246, [81]).

The 'reason why' approach has been applied to cases of victimisation as well as discrimination (*Cartamundi UK Ltd v Worboyes* UKEAT/0096/09/CEA).

In the context of equal pay, *EqA 2010* requires an actual rather than a hypothetical comparator before a sex equality clause or rule can operate. However, where there is no actual comparator, *EqA 2010, s 71* permits a claim of direct discrimination on grounds of sex (whether alone or combined with another potential characteristic in a combined discrimination claim) to be brought in a situation where an equality clause would not operate because there is no comparator doing equal work. The *Explanatory Notes to EqA 2010, s 71* provide as follows (at *para 246*):

> 'An employer tells a female employee "I would pay you more if you were a man" or tells a black female employee "I would pay you more if you were a white man". In the absence of any male comparator the woman cannot bring a claim for breach of an equality clause but she can bring a claim of direct sex discrimination or dual discrimination (combining sex and race) against the employer.'

EqA 2010, s 71 entails an important departure from the previous position and reduces the impact of the inability to use a hypothetical comparator when bringing a claim regarding equality of terms. (See **11.10**.)

1.71 *Illegitimate hypotheses*

The hypothetical approach does, however, have an important limitation, namely that the tribunal or court must not hypothesise as to what might have happened to the claimant or some other person in an admittedly different situation which seems, in a broad sense, comparable. In particular, it is generally not appropriate for tribunals to consider 'mirror image' scenarios whereby, for instance, a female applying for a job at a male-dominated employer would be compared with a male applying for a job at a female-dominated employer. The tribunal must not be dragged into considering apparent converses of the facts before it. The task of a tribunal or court is to consider the case before it. The point can be illustrated by reference to three cases in particular:

(a) *Chief Constable of West Yorkshire Police v Khan* [2001] UKHL 48, [2001] 1 WLR 1947, [2001] ICR 1065. The claimant, Sergeant Khan, started proceedings in an employment tribunal alleging racial discrimination against his employer. He then asked for a reference, which request was refused. Mr Khan argued that his request had been refused because of his protected act. The Chief Constable argued that the court ought to compare Mr Khan with a hypothetical police officer who: (i) had not lodged the proceedings; and instead (ii) had brought proceedings against the Chief Constable on some other ground, such as libel or wrongful dismissal. The House of Lords comprehensively rejected the second half of this submission, holding that the statute called for a simple comparison between the treatment given to Sergeant Khan and the treatment which would have been given to a police officer who had not done a protected act. It was not appropriate to speculate as to what might have happened had Sergeant Khan made some other complaint.

(b) *Smyth v Croft Inns Ltd* [1995] NI 292, [1996] IRLR 84, NICA. S, a Roman Catholic, was employed as a barman in a pub with Protestant customers in a loyalist area of Belfast. A message was delivered to the pub saying that S should be advised not to be in the bar in the following week. The employers took no action. S, believing that his life was at risk, resigned and claimed that he had been discriminated against on grounds of religious belief in that he had been constructively dismissed. The Court of Appeal in Northern Ireland held that the relevant comparison was *not* a hypothetical Protestant barman working in a Catholic bar in a nationalist area, but rather simply between S and a hypothetical Protestant barman working in the *same bar*.

(c) *Grieg v Community Industry* [1979] ICR 356, [1979] IRLR 158, EAT. The applicant, a woman, was refused work in a painting and decorating department as she would be the only woman in a team of men and that would cause an 'unacceptable imbalance in the group's composition'. The EAT held (at [1979] ICR 356, 361) that ' . . . the relevant employment to consider is not some hypothetical employment with the personnel concerned totally different, but is the employment for which the applicant applied', and that it was therefore irrelevant to speculate what might have happened had the claimant been a man applying for a job in an all-woman department. Something of the flavour of this case can be detected from the fact that the EAT was also required to reject a submission to the effect that, if it was ' . . . in the applicant's best interests that she should not be offered the job', then there would be no discrimination at all (at [1979] ICR 356, 360).

The one caveat to the above is that whilst a hypothetical 'mirror image' comparison is not appropriate for determining whether there has been less favourable treatment, such a comparison *can* be legitimate as a way for a court or tribunal to determine what the real reason for the treatment in question was. See the *Showboat* and *Madarassy* cases cited above.

1.72 INDIRECT DISCRIMINATION

Introduction

EU law

Council Directive 2006/54/EC ('the *Equal Treatment Directive*') on the implementation of the principle of equal opportunities and equal treatment of men and women in matters of employment provides:

> 'indirect discrimination [occurs] where an apparently neutral provision, criterion or practice would put persons of one sex at a particular disadvantage compared with persons of the other sex, unless that provision, criterion or practice is objectively justified by a legitimate aim and the means of achieving that aim are appropriate and necessary'
>
> (*Article 2(1)(b)*)

Similar provisions exist in *Council Directive 2000/43/EC* ('the *Race Directive*'), *Article 2(1)(b)* and *Council Directive 2000/78/EC* ('the *Framework Directive*'), *Article 2(2)(b)*. Although not identical, the essential elements of: (i) a provision, criterion or practice; (ii) particular disadvantage; and (iii) objective justification, are mirrored in all the above.

1.73 *UK law*

EqA 2010 introduced a new universal definition of indirect discrimination covering age, disability, gender reassignment, marriage and civil partnership, race, religion or belief, sex and sexual orientation:

> '(1) A person (A) discriminates against another (B) if A applies to B a provision, criterion or practice which is discriminatory in relation to a relevant protected characteristic of B's.

(2) For the purposes of subsection (1), a provision, criterion or practice is discriminatory in relation to a relevant protected characteristic of B's if:
(a) A applies, or would apply, it to persons with whom B does not share the characteristic,
(b) it puts, or would put, persons with whom B shares the characteristic at a particular disadvantage when compared with persons with whom B does not share it,
(c) it puts, or would put, B at that disadvantage, and
(d) A cannot show it to be a proportionate means of achieving a legitimate aim' (*EqA 2010, s 19*).

Despite its new formulation, the essential elements of the definition—that there is a measure that puts a protected group at a disadvantage and that measure cannot be objectively justified—remain the same as in the previous legislation, and therefore much of the pre-*EqA 2010* case law on the interpretation of indirect discrimination provisions will continue to be relevant (for precise formulations of the pre-October 2010 definitions see *SDA 1975, ss 1(2)(b)* and *3(1)(b); RRA 1976, s 1(1A); RBR 2003, reg 3(1)(b); SOR 2003, reg 3(1)(b)) and AR 2006, reg 3(1)(b)*).

1.74 EqA 2010 changes

The *EqA 2010* has changed the landscape of indirect discrimination in three key ways: (1) it applies one definition across all the relevant protected characteristics to ensure uniformity; (2) it extends the concept of indirect discrimination to disability and gender reassignment; and (3) it is no longer necessary for B to suffer the disadvantage—it is now sufficient that B *would suffer* the disadvantage in question (see 'Personal disadvantage' **1.82**). There is no explicit provision in *EqA 2010* for indirect discrimination in the case of pregnancy and maternity, but such cases may constitute indirect sex discrimination (see *EHRC Employment Code at para 4.2*) and note the wide protection for pregnancy and maternity discrimination under *EqA 2010, s 18* (see **Sex discrimination (8)**).

The pre-October 2010 legislation made a distinction between two types of indirect race discrimination: discrimination on the grounds of colour or nationality; and discrimination on the grounds of race and ethnic or national origins. This distinction has been eliminated by *EqA 2010, s 9(1)*, which provides that 'race' includes 'colour, nationality, ethnic or national origins'.

1.75 Meeting the definition of indirect discrimination

'Provision, criterion or practice'

Section 19 of *EqA 2010* requires B to show that A applied a provision, criterion or practice ('PCP') to B; and that A applied, or would apply, it to persons who do not share B's protected characteristic. There is no statutory definition of a PCP. However, the *EHRC's Employment Code, para 4.5*, states that the terms should be widely construed so as to include, for example 'policies, rules, practices, arrangements, criteria, conditions, prerequisites, qualifications or provisions' whether they are formal or informal. The *EHRC Employment Code* goes on to note that a PCP may also include decisions to do something in the future, such as a policy or criterion that has not yet been applied, as well as one-off or discretionary decisions.

The need to identify a PCP was also part of the pre-October 2010 indirect discrimination tests, and as the government intended to extend, rather than change, the protection (see *Explanatory Notes to the EqA 2010, note 81*), the earlier case law will continue to be used to interpret these terms. Such case law includes:

— *Eweida v British Airways plc* [2010] EWCA Civ 80, [2010] ICR 890, [2010] IRLR 322: The EAT considered whether not allowing an employee to wear a cross on a necklace outside her uniform was indirectly discriminatory on the grounds of her

Christian religion. The relevant PCP identified by the tribunal was 'that personal jewellery or items (including any item worn for religious reasons) should be concealed by the uniform unless otherwise expressly permitted by BA';

— *Starmer v British Airways plc* [2005] IRLR 862, [2005] All ER (D) 323 (Jul): The EAT, considering a case where an employee asking to work 50 per cent of her former working hours was offered a reduction to 75 per cent, held that the employer's stipulation that the employee must work 75% of her former hours was a PCP even though it had been a one-off discretionary management decision that only applied to the claimant;

— *ABN Amro Management Services Ltd v Hogben* UKEAT/0266/09: The EAT held that an employer's decision to change its policy and introduce less generous terms as to the payment of bonus to dismissed employees could not, in itself, constitute a PCP;

— in *Ministry of Defence v DeBique* UKEAT/0048/09, the EAT upheld a tribunal decision that an employee had been placed at a disadvantage by a combination of PCPs (a requirement to be available for duty on a '24/7' basis and a restriction on bringing relations from abroad to facilitate childcare).

1.76 *Group disadvantage*

EqA 2010, s 19 also requires B to show that the application by A of the PCP puts or would put him, and others with whom he shares a protected characteristic, at a 'particular disadvantage'. It is necessary to determine the relevant protected group before undertaking a comparison to identify 'particular disadvantage'. It is then for B to demonstrate that he is also put at the 'particular disadvantage' identified.

That there is a disadvantage to a group (ie to 'person*s*', *EqA 2010, s 19(2)(b)*) sharing B's protected characteristic, is an essential element of the test. In *Eweida v British Airways plc* [2010] EWCA Civ 80, [2010] IRLR 322, [2010] ICR 890, the Court of Appeal rejected the argument that an indirect discrimination claim can be based on disadvantage to an individual (cf the duty to make reasonable adjustments in disability discrimination). In this case, the tribunal had found that there was no evidence that anyone but Ms Eweida felt disadvantaged by BA's uniform policy (which required her to conceal a small silver cross beneath her uniform) and so her claim failed.

Sharing a protected characteristic

1.77 In the majority of cases, it will be clear who shares B's protected characteristic for the purposes of establishing the relevant protected group. However, this will not always be the case, with certain protected characteristics presenting more challenges than others. For example, if B brought a claim for indirect disability discrimination, it is difficult to know how similar another's disability must be for B to share the protected characteristic see **3.71**.

Different—but no less significant—challenges may arise in claims for indirect age discrimination (in the context of determining the appropriate 'age group' (*EqA 2010, s 5(1)(b)*) see discussion at **2.14**; and for indirect discrimination because of religion (where there may be different denominations within one religion) (see *Eweida v British Airways plc* [2010] EWCA Civ 80, [2010] IRLR 322, [2010] ICR 890). See *EHRC Employment Code, para 4.16*.

The pool for comparison

1.78 In order to establish particular disadvantage it is necessary to compare the advantaged and disadvantaged groups. Before that comparison can be made, B must first identify the proper pool for comparison, so that a tribunal can assess whether or not those sharing B's characteristic were put at a particular disadvantage. For the purposes of the comparison under *EqA 2010, s 19*, there must be 'no material difference between the circumstances relating to each case' (*EqA 2010, s 23(1)*).

It is for B to advance what he believes to be the appropriate pool. This will depend on the nature of the PCP itself, and those who are affected or potentially affected by the application of the measure in question. The pool can vary greatly in size. For instance, where the measure is national employment legislation, the appropriate pool is likely to be all employed people who can avail themselves of rights under that legislation (*R v Secretary of State for Employment, ex p Seymour-Smith* [2000] 1 All ER 857, [2000] 1 WLR 435; *Rutherford v Secretary of State for Trade and Industry* [2006] UKHL 19, [2006] ICR 785, [2006] IRLR 551), ie the working population of the United Kingdom. Where the measure challenged is applied by one employer to one section of his workforce, the appropriate pool may be the employer's entire workforce, or just that section of it.

Although in the absence of agreement, B must advance what he believes to be the appropriate pool or pools, the tribunal may substitute its own pool if B's choice is not appropriate. The higher courts have generally been unwilling to lay down guidance for establishing the correct pool for comparison, setting out only broad principles.

The Court of Appeal in *Jones v University of Manchester* [1993] ICR 474, [1993] IRLR 218 expressed the view that a broad pool is desirable. Lord Walker in *Rutherford* added that the pool should not be 'narrowed by reference to qualifications or conditions which are not logically relevant' (at para 66) (see also *London Underground Ltd v Edwards (No 2)* [1999] ICR 494 at 508–509, CA; and *Barry v Midland Bank plc* [1999] 3 All ER 974, [1999] 1 WLR 1465, [1999] ICR 859 at 869–870, HL).

However, the pool 'must be one which suitably tests the particular discrimination complained of' (per Sedley LJ in *Grundy v British Airways plc* [2007] EWCA Civ 1020, [2007] All ER (D) 345, para 27). It should therefore not be so narrow that no useful comparison can be made, nor so large that the comparison is no longer of like with like (per Sedley LJ in *Grundy*). Nor should the pool include those 'who have no interest in the advantage or disadvantage in question' (per Baroness Hale of Richmond in *Rutherford*, para 82). This formulation was applied by the Court of Appeal in *Pike v Somerset County Council* [2009] EWCA Civ 808, [2010] ICR 46, [2009] IRLR 870. Mrs Pike was a teacher who retired and then returned to work on a part-time basis. Under the Teachers' Pension Scheme, teachers who retired and returned full-time could rejoin the scheme, but teachers who came back part-time could not. Mrs Pike claimed that this rule had a disproportionate impact on women and was indirectly discriminatory.

When considering disproportionate impact the employment tribunal included in the comparator pool all teachers, including those who had retired and those who had not. There was no disproportionate impact on that basis. The Court of Appeal held that was the wrong pool. The appropriate pool was limited to teachers who had retired and returned to work. Teachers who had not yet retired were neither advantaged nor disadvantaged by the rule: it did not apply to them. The comparator pool for assessing disproportionate impact in indirect discrimination claims should therefore not include individuals who are not potentially impacted by the provision, criterion or practice in question.

Thus, the pool should consist of all those to whom the provision, criterion or practice does or can apply. In a case concerning indirect discrimination on the grounds of sex where the employer applied a policy to all employees that it would not allow employees who were in a partnership (ie an emotional relationship) also to be in a supervisor/subordinate relationship, the complainant identified the wrong pool for comparison when she argued for a pool comprising those people who had partners who were working for the employer (*Faulkner v Chief Constable of Hampshire Constabulary* [2007] UKEAT/0505/05/LA). The EAT held that the appropriate pool should be the whole of the Hampshire Police workforce, as the policy applied to all employees.

However, when the British Medical Association (BMA) refused to support a member's race discrimination claim against a regulatory body, the Court of Appeal, in a decision which has attracted criticism, found that the tribunal had erred in identifying the correct pool as all members of the BMA (*Chaudhary v British Medical Association* [2007] EWCA Civ 788, [2007] IRLR 800, CA). The Court of Appeal held (obiter), in the light of the decision in *Rutherford* that the pool should be limited to those who wanted the benefit in question, ie BMA members who want the advice and support of the BMA for race discrimination claims against specific regulatory bodies. As the BMA would not have supported any such claims there was no comparative disadvantage for any racial group. This decision potentially prevents a claim of indirect discrimination where an organisation decides not to provide a particular service or benefit to anyone.

Selection of the wrong pool will invalidate the finding and consequently the pool selection is often appealed (*London Underground Ltd v Edwards (No 1)* [1995] ICR 574, CA; *University of Manchester v Jones* [1993] ICR 474, CA; *Perera v Civil Service Commission (No 2)* [1983] ICR 428, [1983] IRLR 166, CA). However, it is not the case that there is only one suitable pool in each case; B must advance a legitimate pool for comparison, but a finding of discrimination cannot be challenged solely on the basis that a different, also legitimate, pool would have produced a different result (*Grundy v British Airways plc* [2007] All ER (D) 345, para 31).

Disparate impact

1.79 Once the pool for comparison has been determined, a comparative exercise must be undertaken to demonstrate that the protected group suffers or would suffer a particular disadvantage compared with those others in the pool who do not belong to the group.

The concept of 'particular disadvantage' (or 'disparate impact' as it is sometimes called) is not new; it also formed part of the test for indirect discrimination under the pre-October 2010 legislation. However, it was not defined in the pre-October 2010 legislation, nor is it defined in the *EqA 2010*. *Paragraph 4.9* of the *EHRC Employment Code* states:

> '"Disadvantage" is not defined by the Act. It could include denial of an opportunity or choice, deterrence, rejection or exclusion. The courts have found that "detriment", a similar concept, is something that a reasonable person would complain about—so an unjustified sense of grievance would not qualify. A disadvantage does not have to be quantifiable and the worker does not have to experience actual loss (economic or otherwise). It is enough that the worker can reasonably say that they would have preferred to be treated differently'.

The way in which the comparison exercise is carried out will depend on the circumstances of the case. Before 1995 (and before *EqA 2010* in relation to indirect discrimination on grounds of nationality and colour) the test for indirect discrimination required a claimant to show that the proportion of the disadvantaged group which could comply with a requirement or condition was considerably smaller than the proportion of the advantaged group who could comply. This required a statistical analysis of the proportions of each of the groups who could comply. It may be appropriate in some cases to carry out a formal comparative exercise using statistical evidence. However, this is not required and in some cases, especially where there is inadequate or unreliable information or the numbers of people are too small to allow a statistically significant comparison, other approaches such as the evidence of expert and other witnesses may be used (see *EHRC Employment Code, para 4.13*).

In order to show particular disadvantage it is not necessary to show that a person can or cannot comply with a particular measure: it is sufficient that complying would put them at a disadvantage. Thus arguments such as those in *Sykes v JP Morgan* EAT/279/00 (July 12, 2002, unreported), where a highly paid woman who could afford to employ a nanny was found able (albeit unwilling) to comply with a requirement to work full-time, will be of much less relevance. A critical issue in many cases will not be whether the claimant is in theory able to comply with a particular measure, but the degree of disadvantage he suffers by so doing, whether and how the disadvantage suffered relates to the protected ground, and whether the tribunal considers that the disadvantage suffered merits redress (see also comments of Elias J in the EAT in *Eweida v British Airways plc* [2009] IRLR 78).

Statistics

1.80 Early authorities under the *SDA 1975* and *RRA 1976* typically determined whether a particular protected category had been put at a disadvantage using statistical analysis of the proportions of advantaged and disadvantaged people in the pool. There will, however, be many cases where the disparity of treatment is marginal, and depending on whether the statistical analysis focuses on those who are advantaged or disadvantaged within the pool, the results can lead to starkly different conclusions.

The trend in these early cases was to undertake an 'advantaged-led' analysis, considering the relevant percentages of those in the 'advantaged' groups who could comply with the PCP in question, as a proportion of the whole pool (*R v Secretary of State for Education, ex p Schaffter* [1987] IRLR 53). Take as an example a situation where all employees must have 15 years' employment as a full time-employee with A in order to secure a particular benefit from A, which is potentially indirectly discriminatory on the grounds of sex (or age) as potentially fewer women will be able to satisfy the length of service requirement. The statistical analysis requires an assessment of the percentage of women in the pool that can comply, compared with the percentage of men that can comply. The two percentages are then compared to each other rather than to the whole pool.

More recently, it was recognised that while it could be a useful starting point to look at this percentage (ie that of the advantaged group), it may also be relevant to consider the disadvantaged group (ie those who could not comply with the PCP in question) as a percentage of the whole pool. However, in *Rutherford (No 2)* the Court of Appeal confirmed that the main focus should be on the relative proportions within the advantaged groups (*Rutherford v Secretary of State for Trade and Industry (No 2)* [2004] IRLR 894, CA). This was endorsed by the minority in the House of Lords; the majority preferring to resolve the case by reference to broad principles rather than looking at statistical evidence, and assessing whether the difference indicates a 'particular disadvantage' (*Rutherford v Secretary of State for Trade and Industry (No 2)* [2006] UKHL 19, [2006] ICR 785, HL). This is not to say that there is no place for considering the disadvantaged groups, and it will not be an error of law if a tribunal does not make an advantaged-led analysis (*Grundy v British Airways plc* [2007] All ER (D) 345, para 35). The *EHRC Employment Code* also appears to endorse a more 'disadvantage-led' approach (*paras 4.21–4.22*).

A narrow pool which focuses on the disadvantaged will usually assist the complainant in demonstrating a disparate impact, and it is likely that these arguments will continue to be run (on the basis of Lord Nicholls' judgment in *Seymour-Smith* and Lord Walker of Gestingthorpe (obiter) in *Rutherford*, para 67).

In *R v Secretary of State for Employment, ex p Seymour-Smith* [1999] 2 AC 554, [1997] ICR 447, ECJ, paras 61–62 the ECJ ruled that it is for a national court to determine whether the statistics used are 'relevant and sufficient for the purposes of resolving the case before it'. In particular, the ECJ noted that there will be cases where the statistics illustrate 'purely fortuitous or short-term phenomena'. Statistical data will be open to challenge if it is out of date, or for other reasons distorts the proper comparison.

Where the pool for comparison involves a large workforce, of which the disadvantaged group is a small proportion, it may be appropriate to express the proportions in the disadvantaged group as a ratio of each other (*Barry*, para 36).

In *Coker v Lord Chancellor* [2001] EWCA Civ 1756, [2002] ICR 321, [2002] IRLR 80, the Lord Chancellor had appointed a friend as his special adviser. C claimed she should have been considered for the position. The pool for comparison comprised those who were appropriately qualified for the position of special adviser, and the allegedly discriminatory requirement was that applicants needed to be known personally to the Lord Chancellor. On the facts, nearly the entire pool of comparators was excluded from being considered for appointment (as very few were personally known to the Lord Chancellor). Consequently it was not possible for the requirement to have a disproportionate impact on different groupings within the pool.

Given the difficulties, a flexible approach to the assessment of the disparate impact issue is now favoured, particularly in situations where, on the advantaged-led analysis, the statistics demonstrate a marginal percentage difference between the advantaged groups, and yet there is demonstrable indirect discrimination. In *London Underground Ltd v Edwards (No 2)* [1999] ICR 494, [1998] IRLR 364, CA, a case involving a change to a shift rota system, E, for childcare reasons, could *not* comply with the change to the rota system. London Underground employed 2,023 male train drivers and 21 female drivers; all men could comply with the new rota system and only one female driver (the complainant) could not comply. On pure numbers alone, the fact that only one woman could not comply was not persuasive on the issue of disparate impact. The statistical analysis of those advantaged by the rota system (ie those who could comply with it) showed that 95.2% of women could comply, compared with 100% of men, a disparate impact of 4.8%. The EAT and the Court of Appeal found indirect discrimination. Although the statistical evidence was not necessarily compelling, it was right for the tribunal to focus on the percentage discrepancy between the numbers of male and female operators (demonstrating the job was difficult or unattractive to women), despite the numerical evidence that only one woman could be found unable to comply.

It may be appropriate to consider whether there is an intrinsic risk that someone with a particular characteristic is disadvantaged. In *Chief Constable of Avon and Somerset Constabulary v Chew* [2001] All ER (D) 101 (Sep) a police officer's application to work part-time was rejected because she was unable to comply with the roster shifts cycle. She claimed indirect sex discrimination. The chosen pool for assessing the disparate impact was all police officers in that constabulary. Of the pool of 3,016 police officers, only 11 could not comply with the requirement to work the shift roster: ten women and one man. 99.96% of male officers and 97.7% of female police officers were able to comply. On a pure statistical analysis there was a disparate impact of only 2.26%. The tribunal and EAT found that although a disparate impact of 2.26% was, at face value, insufficient to establish indirect discrimination, the tribunal was entitled to take into other factors, as the requirement to comply with a roster shift cycle was intrinsically more likely to impact on women more than men because women tend to have the main childcare responsibility. Relying on the ECJ decisions in *O'Flynn v Adjudication Officer: C-237/94* [1996] ECR I-2617, [1996] All ER (EC) 541, [1996] 3 CMLR 103 and *Seymour-Smith*, the EAT found that a rigid statistical analysis will not always suffice to reveal underlying indirect discrimination.

National statistics

1.81 Even where relevant and reliable national statistics are available, a purely mathematical approach may not be appropriate (see *Seymour-Smith* [1999] ICR 447). Expert evidence may be used to displace or call into question the relevance of statistical evidence.

On occasion, a tribunal may take into account matters considered to be of common or general knowledge. For example, in *London Underground v Edwards (No 2)* [1999] ICR 494, [1998] IRLR 364, CA, a tribunal acknowledged that more single parents are female than male. Such assumptions may be challenged, however, if, for example, they are without foundation, are outdated, or are themselves based on stereotypical beliefs (as in *Sinclair, Roche & Temperley v Heard* [2004] IRLR 763, EAT, where the tribunal should not have concluded that because more women than men had responsibility for childcare, fewer high-paid senior women executives could work long hours).

1.82 *Personal disadvantage*

As with a claim of direct discrimination, B will only be able to found a claim of indirect discrimination if he can show that he has suffered (or would suffer) the disadvantage. It is not enough to point to a disadvantage suffered by others who share the protected characteristic. To take an obvious example, a woman who claims that the imposition of a shift system is indirectly discriminatory against women with childcaring responsibilities will not be able to claim indirect discrimination if she does not have childcare responsibilities preventing her from complying.

In addition to covering claimants who are actually put at a particular disadvantage by a PCP, the new definition of indirect discrimination in the *EqA 2010* extends to cover claimants who *would be* put at such a disadvantage. This allows challenges to PCPs which have not yet been applied but which would have a discriminatory effect if they were. While such challenges were possible in relation to race under the pre-October 2010 legislation (*RRA 1976, s 19(2)(c)*), it was not clear if they were possible in relation to any of the other protected characteristics.

Paragraph 4.8 of the *EHRC Employment* Code provides the following example to demonstrate the effect of the new definition:

> 'The contracts for senior buyers at a department store have a mobility clause requiring them to travel at short notice to any part of the world. A female senior buyer with young children considers that the mobility clause puts women at a disadvantage as they are more likely to be the carers of children and so less likely to be able to travel abroad at short notice. She may challenge the mobility clause even though she has not yet been asked to travel abroad at short notice. By contrast, a female manager in customer services at the same store might agree that the mobility clause discriminates against women—but, as she is not a senior buyer, she cannot challenge the clause'.

This new wording will also protect those who are, for example, put off from applying for a job because they know that a PCP would prevent them being successful. However, a claimant will still need to show that he himself was deterred from applying when he would otherwise have done so in order to found an indirect discrimination claim. This reflects the principle in *Keane v Investigo* UKEAT/0389/09/SM (considered under AR 2006), that a 'professional litigant' who submits job applications for purposes of securing a settlement rather than with any intention of taking up a role will have suffered no disadvantage when they are rejected.

1.83 *Justification*

Indirect discrimination is unlawful, even where the discriminatory effect of the PCP is not intentional, unless it can be objectively justified. Justification is also available for cases of direct age discrimination (see **Age discrimination (2)**) and cases of discrimination arising from disability (see **Disability discrimination (3)**).

Where B has demonstrated that a PCP has the requisite disparate impact, the burden of proof shifts to the employer to justify the application of the PCP. To succeed in this, A must show that the PCP is 'a proportionate means of achieving a legitimate aim' (*EqA 2010, s 19(2)(d)*).

The test for objective justification in relation to indirect discrimination under *EqA 2010* is broadly a codification of the decision in *Bilka-Kaufhas GmbH v Weber von Hartz: C-170/84* [1986] ECR 1607, [1986] 2 CMLR 701 and replicates the pre-October 2010 law (other than in relation to nationality or colour where there was an anomaly). Therefore, much of the pre-existing case law (see below) will be relevant when applying *EqA 2010, s 19(2)*, and the *EHRC Employment Code* summarises the position taken in those cases (*paras 4.24–4.32)*.

In all the relevant Directives, the test is that indirect discrimination will occur unless 'that provision, criterion or practice is objectively justified by a legitimate aim and the means of achieving that aim are appropriate and necessary' (*Race Directive, 2000/43/EC, Article 2; Framework Directive 2000/78/EC, Article 2; Equal Treatment Directive 76/207/EC* as amended by *2002/73/EC, Article 2*).

In *Bilka-Kaufhaus* a department store had a policy of requiring employees to have worked full-time in 15 of their 20 years' service in order to qualify for an occupational pension scheme: the rationale was to discourage part-time work, as part-time employees tended to refuse to work less sociable hours at which times the store nevertheless needed staff cover. The policy was indirectly discriminatory to women, but could it be justified? The ECJ held that this was a matter for national courts to determine, and in doing so they should consider whether the measures taken: (i) correspond to a *real need* on the part of the employer; (ii) whether they are *appropriate* with a view to achieving the objectives pursued; and (iii) whether they are *necessary* to that end (para 36).

UK law, as set out in *EqA 2010, s 19(2)(d)*, has shortened this test, replacing 'appropriate and necessary' with 'proportionate'. However, this change is not intended to override the language in the Directives, or the test set out in *Bilka-Kaufhaus*: the government has argued that the terms 'appropriate and necessary' and 'proportionate' can be used interchangeably. Therefore, despite the legislature's literal departure from the EC legislation, its implementation of the justification test reflects the interpretation of the test in European case law (see *EHRC Employment Code, para 4.31*).

Whether the government's view is correct depends on the interpretation of 'necessary'. The government view is that necessity, in European law, does not mean absolute necessity; the principle of proportionality inherently involves a balance between the interests of the employer and the employee and therefore the employer is required to show that its actions were 'reasonably necessary'; see, for example, *Barry*. In any event, the ECJ decisions are clear that whether or not a discriminatory practice can be justified is a matter for the national courts.

In order to demonstrate justification under UK law, an employer therefore has to demonstrate: (1) that it was pursuing a legitimate aim in applying the PCP; and (2) that the measures taken to achieve that aim were proportionate.

Legitimate aims

1.84 The concept of 'legitimate aim' is not defined in *EqA 2010* or the pre-October 2010 legislation. However, adopting the language in *Bilka-Kaufhaus*, the measures taken must correspond to a 'real need' on the part of the employer. The scope of what could constitute a 'legitimate aim' is therefore very broad. The *EHRC Employment Code, paras 4.28–4.29* states:

> 'The aim of the PCP should be legal, should not be discriminatory in itself, and must represent a real, objective consideration. The health, welfare and safety of individuals may qualify as legitimate aims provided that risks are clearly specified and supported by evidence. Although reasonable business needs and economic efficiency may be legitimate aims, an employer solely aiming to reduce costs cannot expect to satisfy the test. For example, the employer cannot simply argue that to discriminate is cheaper than avoiding discrimination.'

In relation to the use of cost, following the case of *Cross v British Airways plc* [2006] EWCA Civ 549, [2006] IRLR 804 it was suggested that, while cost alone could not amount to a legitimate aim, cost considerations could be included along with other factors. This became known as the 'cost plus' rule. However, there is now some doubt about this rule following the case of *Woodcock v Cumbria Primary Care Trust* (2010) UKEAT/0489/09/RN, [2011] ICR 143, [2011] IRLR 119, in which the EAT commented (obiter) that increased cost alone ought to be sufficient to amount to a legitimate aim if it is disproportionate to the discriminatory effect.

The grounds for justification need not have 'consciously and contemporaneously featured in the decision-making process of the employer' (*Starmer v British Airways plc* [2005] IRLR 862, at para 42; *Cadman v Health and Safety Executive* [2005] ICR 1546; *Seldon v Clarkson Wright & Jakes* [2010] EWCA Civ 895; *Hilde Schonheit v Stadt Frankfurt am Main: C-4/02 and C-5/02* [2003] ECR I-12575, [2004] IRLR 983, at 86–87). In *Starmer*, where an employee pilot's application to work part-time hours was refused, the employer was allowed to advance arguments that its refusal was justified on health and safety grounds when the decision to refuse her application at the time had been based on the employer's resourcing requirements.

An employer must not simply assert its reasons but must show evidence of the need for the measure. Thus, an employer will not justify a discriminatory measure by reference to mere generalisations—he must produce cogent factual evidence that demonstrates why the aim he pursues is legitimate and necessary (*Seymour-Smith* [1999] ICR 447, para 76). The tribunal is required to carry out a critical evaluation of the facts (*Redfearn* [2005] IRLR 744 at 59; *Hardys & Hansons plc v Lax* [2005] EWCA Civ 846, [2005] IRLR 726 at 19–34; *Cadman v Health and Safety Executive* [2003] EWCA Civ 1317, [2004] IRLR 971, [2005] ICR 1546 at 31; *Barry v Midland Bank plc* [1999] IRLR 5821, [1999] ICR 859, HL at 587). In *Cadman*, it was argued before the ECJ that pay rates based on length of service (which were found to indirectly discriminate against women) could be justified by generalisations (for instance it is legitimate to reward loyalty, or an experienced worker will usually be more productive at work as he will be more familiar with the employer's business and its clients). The ECJ, following *Seymour-Smith*, found that the proportionality test requires an employer to demonstrate that the practice he adopts, even where based on a legitimate aim, is conceived so as to minimise its disparate impact on the disadvantaged group (*Cadman*, at 58).

Proportionality

1.85 As noted above, the UK legislation expresses justification by reference to 'proportionality' rather than what is 'appropriate' and 'necessary'.

The principle of proportionality requires consideration of whether the objective pursued is sufficient to override the indirect discrimination (*Enderby*). The greater the disparate impact on the disadvantaged group, the stronger the objective justification must be (*Barry*, para 40; *Starmer; Allonby v Accrington and Rossendale College* [12001] EWCA Civ 529, [2001] IRLR 364, paras 26–29; *Hampson v Department of Education and Science* [1989] IRLR 69, [1990] ICR 511, HL).

This balancing exercise requires the tribunal to consider whether the means chosen by the employer are suitable, and whether or not the employer could achieve its aim by other means. This is not to say that the employer must show that the means chosen are the only way to meet that aim (*Seymour-Smith* [2000] ICR 244). In *London Underground Ltd v Edwards* [1995] ICR 574, [1995] IRLR 355, EAT the employer sought to argue before the tribunal and the EAT that the introduction of a new shift roster for its train drivers (which the tribunal, EAT and Court of Appeal found to be indirectly discriminatory to women) was justifiable as it would allow costs savings of £10 million per year. The tribunal (with whom the EAT agreed) took into account the costs savings, and found that provision could have been made for single parents who were disadvantaged by the shift roster without a significant detriment to the savings sought. This approach is consistent with the ECJ's position that budgetary considerations alone cannot justify discrimination on grounds of sex (*Hilde Schönheit v Stadt Frankfurt am Main: C-4/02 and C-5/02* [2003] ECR I-12575, [2004] IRLR 983; *Jorgensen v Foreningen af Speciallaeger* [2000] IRLR 726 ECJ, para 39).

It does not follow that where there is an alternative means of achieving an objective, the employer should always take that route. If the means chosen are proportionate and the aim legitimate, then the employer's practice will be justified (*Redfearn v Serco Ltd (t/a West Yorkshire Transport Service)* [2006] EWCA Civ 659, [2006] ICR 1367; *Allonby*). In *Redfearn* the employer argued that R's presence created a risk. Although ultimately it was not necessary for the Court of Appeal to reach a conclusion on justification, it found that the tribunal's decision (that the dismissal was justified on health and safety grounds) was not perverse simply because it had not considered other non-discriminatory ways in which the employer could achieve its aim.

It is for the tribunal to decide whether a PCP is justifiable. In *Hardys & Hansons plc*, a full-time female employee applied to job-share her current role, her employer refused and she subsequently claimed indirect sex discrimination. Considering the employer's justification arguments, the Court of Appeal found that the tribunal was in such cases required to undertake a very careful, critical analysis of the reasons put forward by the employer, demonstrating such in its own reasoned decision. While acknowledging that the word 'necessary' used in *Bilka-Kaufhaus* is to be qualified by the word 'reasonably', Pill LJ said:

> 'That qualification does not, however, permit the margin of discretion or range of reasonable responses for which the appellants contend. The presence of the word "reasonably" reflects the presence and applicability of the principle of proportionality. The employer does not have to demonstrate that no other proposal is possible. The employer has to show that the proposal, in this case for a full-time appointment, is justified objectively notwithstanding its discriminatory effect. The principle of proportionality requires the tribunal to take into account the reasonable needs of the business. But it has to makes its own judgment, upon a fair and detailed analysis of the working practices and business considerations involved, as to whether the proposal is reasonably necessary. I reject the . . . submission . . . that, when reaching its conclusion, the employment tribunal needs to consider only whether or not it is satisfied that the employer's views are within the range of reasonable responses' (para 32).
>
> 'The power and duty of the employment tribunal to pass judgment on the employer's attempt at justification must be accompanied by a power and duty in the appellate courts to scrutinise carefully the manner in which its decision has been reached.'
>
> (para 34)

1.86 HARASSMENT

Introduction

EU law

Council Directive 2000/78/EC ('the *Framework Directive*') establishing a general framework for equal treatment in employment and occupation provides that:

> 'Harassment shall be deemed to be a form of discrimination . . . when unwanted conduct related to [age, disability, religion or belief or sexual orientation] takes place with the purpose or effect of violating the dignity of a person and of creating an intimidating, hostile, degrading, humiliating or offensive environment . . . .' (*Article 2.3*)

Council Directive 2000/43/EC ('the *Race Directive*'), implementing the principle of equal treatment between persons irrespective of racial or ethnic origin, contains a virtually identical provision (Article 2.3), as does the *Equal Treatment Directive* ('the *ETD*')

76/207/EEC (as amended by *Directive 2006/54/EC, Article 2.1(c)*) in respect of discrimination based on gender. The *ETD* also contains an additional, separate definition of sexual harassment:

> ' . . . where any form of unwanted verbal, non-verbal or physical contact of a sexual nature occurs with the purpose or effect of violating the dignity of a person, in particular when creating an intimidating, hostile, degrading, humiliating or offensive environment' (*Article 2.1(d)*)

Separately, the European Commission has also published a *Code of Practice on measures to combat sexual harassment* which sets out useful guidance on the scope of sexual harassment from a European perspective (see Commission Recommendation of 27 November 1991 on the Protection of the Dignity of Women and Men at Work (92/131/EC)).

1.87 *UK law*

The *EqA 2010* introduced a new universal definition prohibiting harassment related to the protected characteristics of age, disability, gender reassignment, race, religion or belief, sex, and sexual orientation (*EqA 2010, s 26*). Colour and nationality are now specifically covered under race (see *EqA 2010, s 9(1)(a)* and *s 9(1)(b)*). Harassment related to marriage and civil partnership and pregnancy and maternity are not covered within this section (see **1.88** below).

There are three types of harassment, which are now defined in *EqA 2010, s 26* as follows:

'(1) A person (A) harasses another (B) if:
- (a) A engages in unwanted conduct related to a relevant protected characteristic, and
- (b) the conduct has the purpose or effect of:
  - (i) violating that other person's dignity; or
  - (ii) creating an intimidating, hostile, degrading, humiliating or offensive environment for B.

(2) A also harasses B if:
- (a) A engages in unwanted conduct of a sexual nature, and
- (b) the conduct has the purpose or effect referred to in subsection (1)(b).

(3) A also harasses B if:
- (a) A or another person engages in unwanted conduct of sexual nature or that is related to gender reassignment or sex,
- (b) the conduct has the purpose or effect referred to in subsection (1)(b), and
- (c) because of B's rejection or submission to the conduct, A treats B less favourably than A would treat B if B has not rejected or submitted to the conduct.'

EqA 2010 also contains protection against harassment of employees by third parties (*EqA 2010, s 40*): see **1.95**.

Prior to the implementation of *EqA 2010*, the legislation prohibiting harassment was inconsistent and did not afford individuals with equal protection across all of the discrimination strands. Statutory harassment was defined in different ways in different contexts and there remained a number of anomalies (see *SDA 1975, s 4A(1)* and *(3); RRA 1976, s 3A; DDA 1995, s 3B; SOR 2003, reg 5; RBR 2003, reg 5; AR 2006, reg 6*).

EqA 2010 changes

1.88 Harassment is now prohibited where it is 'related to' the protected characteristic across all strands (save marriage and civil partnership, and pregnancy and maternity) (the 'relevant strands').

Under the old regime, the definition differed from strand to strand. Whereas *RRA 1976, RBR 2003, SOR 2003* and *AR 2006* provided that harassment would occur where the unwanted conduct occurred 'on grounds of' the relevant characteristic; the *SDA 1975* required the unwanted conduct to be 'related to' sex, whether that of the complainant or of another person (*SDA 1975, s 4A(1)(a)*, amended from 'on the ground of her sex' by the *Sex Discrimination Act 1975 (Amendment) Regulations 2008* ('the *SDA Regulations 2008*') following challenge by the EOC). In a third variation, *DDA 1995, s 3B* provided that there would be harassment where a disabled person was subject to harassment 'for a reason which relates to the disabled person's disability'.

Under the previous legislation, there were also differences between protection from harassment because of association with a person with a protected characteristic. This has now been standardised. Protection under *EqA 2010* applies to conduct related to 'a relevant protected characteristic' rather than B's own characteristic. This means that protection from harassment based on association or perception now applies across all the relevant strands (see **1.53**).

The *EqA 2010* applies most of the previous protective provisions, which were restricted to certain characteristics under the old harassment legislation, to all of the relevant strands. For example, the provisions on employer liability for third-party harassment—previously only contained under the *SDA 1975*—now apply to all of the relevant strands.

However, not all of the previous protective provisions have been treated in this way. For persons who 'reject' or 'submit to' conduct such as unwanted sexual advances, claims will continue to be restricted to those based on sex or gender reassignment (*EqA 2010, s 26(3)(c)*). The government also announced in its Response to the Consultation (pp 161–176) that the *EqA 2010* would not standardise protection from harassment outside the context of employment law. In particular, *EqA 2010, s 29*, which prohibits harassment in the exercise of public functions or the provision of goods, facilities and services, does not cover religion or belief or sexual orientation (*s 29(8)*).

The *EqA 2010* has also removed an anomaly in relation to race. Under the *RRA 1976*, colour and nationality were not covered under the harassment provisions at all. Colour and nationality are now specifically included within the definition of 'race' (see *EqA 2010, s 9(1)(a), (b)*).

The protected characteristics of marriage and civil partnership and pregnancy and maternity are excluded from the harassment provisions under *EqA 2010, s 26(5)*. However, the *EHRC Employment Code* states that pregnancy and maternity harassment would amount to harassment related to sex, and harassment related to civil partnership would amount to harassment related to sexual orientation (*para 7.5*). See **Sex discrimination (8)** and **Sexual orientation (9)**.

1.89 *Harassment: key elements*

Despite some changes to the definition and scope of harassment protection since the introduction of the *EqA 2010*, the key elements have remained the same, so that the pre-October 2010 case law will continue to apply.

The necessary elements of liability for harassment are threefold:

(1) did the respondent engage in unwanted conduct?;

(2) did the conduct in question

 (a) have the purpose, or

 (b) the effect of either

  (i) violating the claimant's dignity, or

(ii) creating an adverse environment for the claimant; and

(3) was the conduct related to a protected characteristic?

There is still overlap between the questions that arise in relation to each element. The question of whether conduct was 'unwanted' overlaps with the question of whether that conduct created an adverse environment for the claimant. Many acts that are found to create an adverse environment for an employee, will also violate the employee's dignity (see *Dhaliwal v Richmond Pharmacology Ltd* [2009] ICR 724, [2009] IRLR 336, EAT, for an example).

'Unwanted conduct'

1.90 The *EqA 2010* replicates the previous harassment legislation by requiring conduct to be unwanted. Earlier guidance and case law is therefore likely to be relevant in determining what amounts to 'unwanted conduct', as will the new *EHRC Employment Code* and non-statutory Guidance.

A wide range of conduct and behaviours may give rise to a harassment claim. According to the *EHRC Employment Code* unwanted conduct covers a wide range of behaviours including 'spoken or written words or abuse, imagery, graffiti, physical gestures, facial expressions, mimicry, jokes, pranks, acts affecting a person's surroundings or other physical behaviour' (*para 7.7*).

Conduct must also be unwanted, meaning 'unwelcome' or 'uninvited' (*EHRC Employment Code, para 7.8*). However, there is no requirement for an express objection to made to the conduct before it can be considered unwanted. The explanatory notes to *SOR 2003* and *RBR 2003* provided that it would not always be necessary for the complainant to indicate that he finds certain conduct or language unacceptable: '*there may be cases where it will be perfectly clear that offensive remarks about persons . . . are unwanted by those persons*'. There is similar guidance in the *EHRC Employment Code* (*para 7.8*). Conduct can be unwanted, even where the employee has put up with it for years. Neither does the fact that the employee initiated talk of a sexual nature with the harasser, as a coping strategy, mean that the conduct was not unwanted (*Munchkins Restaurant Ltd v Karmazyn* UKEAT/0359/09).

There is also no opportunity for a would-be harasser to 'test the water' to determine another's sensibilities - a one-off incident can constitute harassment, for example, a single incident of 'groping or racial abuse' will be self-evidently unwanted conduct amounting to harassment (see EHRC Guidance for Employers entitled 'What equality law means for you as an employer: managing workers', p 31). See also *Insitu Cleaning v Heads* [1995] IRLR 4 when a proprietor's son called out to a female employee 'hiya big tits', it was readily acknowledged to be:

> 'a form of bullying [which] is not acceptable in the workplace in any circumstances . . . such conduct is likely to create an intimidating, hostile and humiliating work environment for the victim'.

For a series of less serious incidents however, it may be necessary for someone to object to the behaviour for it to be clear that it is unwanted. If the behaviour persists after the perpetrators have been asked to stop, then their behaviour may amount to harassment. An example of a less serious incident may be where the victim overhears dirty jokes, or where he is the subject of thoughtless remarks which cause him offence or distress. In such a situation, it may be necessary for him or her to have indicated at the time (and subsequently) that the conduct is unwanted. In *Steele v Optika Ltd* [1997] 20614/95/ET, a woman who chose to participate in, and appeared to enjoy sexual activity at the time, failed to show that the conduct was unwanted.

Clearly, it will be easier for a claimant to establish that conduct is unwanted if it is obvious that this was or should have been the case: extreme forms of conduct, eg assault or violent and abusive language directed solely at the victim, will readily be recognised as harassment, even if the claimant does not specifically object to the behaviour or complain about it contemporaneously. As the term 'unwanted conduct' was used in the old legislation, guidance from existing case law will still be of assistance.

In *(1) Reed and (2) Bull Information Systems Ltd v Stedman* [1999] IRLR 299, the EAT gave guidance to employment tribunals on what might constitute unwanted behaviour, noting (in a sexual harassment case) that while a woman might appear to be unduly sensitive to what otherwise might be regarded as unexceptional behaviour:

> 'it is for each person to define their own levels of acceptance, the question would be whether by words or conduct she had made clear that she found such conduct unwelcome. It is not necessary to make a public fuss to indicate her disapproval, walking out of the room may be sufficient. Tribunals will be sensitive to the problems that victims may face in dealing with a man, perhaps in a senior position to herself, who will be likely to deny that he was doing anything untoward and may say the victim was over-sensitive . . . '

As it is for each person to define their own levels of what is acceptable conduct, the question is whether by words or conduct a person makes it clear that such conduct is unwelcome. Provided that any reasonable person would understand the victim to be rejecting the conduct of which they were complaining, continuation of the conduct will, generally, be regarded as harassment.

In *Bracebridge Engineering Ltd v Darby* [1990] IRLR 3 two male colleagues indecently assaulted D. She reported this but no action was taken. She resigned and claimed constructive dismissal. The EAT held that a single incident of sexual harassment of this severity would amount to discrimination.

In *Driskell v Peninsula Business Services Ltd* [2000] IRLR 151, EAT, D claimed that her manager, who had a history of making sexually explicit comments and banter, advised her to wear a short skirt and a see-through blouse when he interviewed her for a position. Her complaints about him were investigated but rejected. When the company failed to move him, she refused to work and was consequently dismissed. The EAT held that where there is a series of alleged incidents, a tribunal should not consider the effect of each incident in isolation but should assess the situation only after considering all of the relevant facts. Furthermore, when deciding whether sexual banter amounts to sex discrimination, the sex of the parties involved should be taken into account as sexual comments by a male manager may be more intimidating when directed towards a woman than towards a man.

In *Wadman v Carpenter Farrer Partnership* [1993] IRLR 374, EAT, where W complained of sexual harassment after she was singled out for sexual comments of a personal nature made by male colleagues, the EAT advised tribunals to refer to the European Commission Code of Practice for definitions of sexual harassment, and for the steps employers should take to meet their obligations.

In *Wileman v Minilec Engineering Ltd* [1988] ICR 318, [1988] IRLR 144, EAT, the EAT held that a person may be happy to accept the remarks of A or B in a sexual context, and wholly upset by similar remarks made by C. The latter was regarded as unwanted conduct, whereas the former was not. The EAT reasoned that each individual has the right, if the remarks are regarded by them as offensive, to treat them as harassment.

'Related to' a protected characteristic

1.91 In contrast to the earlier legislation, which referred (in most areas) to unwanted conduct 'on grounds' of certain characteristics, *EqA 2010* uses the phrase 'related to', which is also used in the Directives. The new wording is very broad; the *EHRC Employment Code* notes that this covers both conduct related to the worker's own protected characteristic and situations where there is 'any connection with a protected characteristic' whether or not the worker shares it (*para 7.10*).

The widened scope of the wording contained in *EqA 2010, s 26* therefore covers those persons who receive unwanted conduct because of their association with someone with a protected characteristic, or a perception that either they or that third party have the characteristic (see discrimination by association or perception at **1.94**). The protection also extends to cover anyone legitimately offended by conduct based on one of the protected characteristics, even though they may not share it. As set out in the EHRC's Guidance for Employers, *What equality law means for you as an employer: managing workers'* (*p 29*):

> '[C]onduct may also be harassment where the person on the receiving end of the unwanted behaviour does not have the protected characteristic, are not perceived to have it and are not associated with someone who has it, but they find that the treatment violates their dignity or creates for them an intimidating, hostile, degrading, humiliating or offensive environment'.

The causal link that must be established between the protected characteristic and the offensive conduct is arguably weaker under the *EqA 2010* than it was under the old legislation. Under the old law, harassment (except that related to disability or sex) had to be 'on grounds of' a protected characteristic (see meaning of 'on grounds of' in *Shamoon v Chief Constable of the Royal Ulster Constabulary* [2003] IRLR 285). The old wording meant that tribunals had to look at the motivation for the harasser's conduct, ie the characteristic must have been the reason why the harasser acted as he or she did (although see the majority of the Court of Appeal's decision in *English v Thomas Sanderson Ltd* [2008] EWCA Civ 1421 applying *Nagarajan v London Regional Transport* [1999] IRLR 572 in respect of the definition in the *SOR 2003*) (see discrimination by association or perception at **1.94**).

The inclusion of the words 'related to' in *EqA 2010, s 26*, has arguably shifted the focus away from the motive for carrying out such conduct, to the form the conduct takes, reflecting the approach taken in *English v Thomas Sanderson Ltd*. It is now much easier to envisage a situation in which a person acts in such a way so as to create an offensive environment for a complainant. There is no requirement that the language is aimed at an individual with the protected characteristic, or that the 'harasser' intends their conduct to have that effect. For example, a white worker in an office where most of the other workers are also white finds the habitual racist comments of another member of staff also creates a hostile and intimidating environment for them. Under the old legislation, respondents could have relied on the words 'grounds of' to argue that he or she was not motivated by race. Such defences are unlikely now to be available under the *EqA 2010* (although note Lord Justice Laws' comment at para 26 of his dissenting judgment in *English v Thomas Sanderson Ltd* that it is by no means clear that the phrase 'unwanted conduct related to any of the grounds' in the *Framework Directive* excludes the notion of cause and effect).

As it is easier to establish conduct linked to a protected characteristic under *EqA 2010, s 26*, individuals are able to bring a claim in a wider set of circumstances. This may result in an increase in the number of claims brought.

Purpose or effect

1.92 As stated above, to meet the definition under the *EqA 2010*, the harasser's conduct must either have the purpose or effect of violating the claimant's dignity, or of creating an intimidating, hostile, degrading, humiliating or offensive environment for the victim.

A claim based on 'purpose' will inevitably result in an analysis of the alleged harasser's motive or intention. This may require a tribunal to draw inferences as to what that the true motive or intent actually was, as respondents will likely refrain from admitting to an unlawful purpose. Where this occurs, the burden of proof will shift from the claimant to the respondent. *EqA 2010, s 136*, provides that claimants must first establish sufficient facts, which in the absence of any other explanation, point to a breach of the legislation. If the claimant shows this, the respondent must then show that no breach had occurred. See 'burden of proof' at **1.128ff**.

Despite the amendment of the *SDA 1975* to substitute 'related to' for 'on grounds of', it remains unclear, in the absence of any authority, what must be established to prove 'purpose'. There is no corresponding provision under the old law, and the *EHRC Employment Code* and Guidance are silent on what constitutes 'purpose'. However, one of the few authorities on intention to discriminate in relation to indirect race discrimination may assist (see, generally, **6.18ff**). For example, in *Walker (JH) Ltd v Hussain* [1996] ICR 291, [1996] IRLR 11, the EAT found that 'intention' signified that at the time the relevant act was done, the person both wanted to bring about a state of affairs that constitutes the unfavourable treatment, and also knew that the unfavourable treatment would result from his actions. It is also possible that purpose will be regarded as synonymous with such words as motive and reason (see *Nagarajan v London Regional Transport* [2000] 1 AC 501, [1999] 4 All ER 65, [1999] ICR 877, in the context of a direct discrimination claim).

If the harasser's purpose can be proved and is held to violate the other person's dignity or create an intimidating, hostile, degrading, humiliating or offensive environment, the claimant need go no further: there is no qualifying provision. However, for the claimant to show that the treatment had the effect of violating dignity or creating and offensive environment for him, *EqA 2010, s 26(4)* applies. This confirms the pre-*EqA 2010* case law, namely that the tribunal must take into account not only the perception of the claimant, but also the other circumstances of the case, and whether it was reasonable for the conduct to have so offended (etc) the claimant. Therefore, a tribunal must consider the effect of the conduct from the point of view of the claimant (the subjective element), as well as determining whether it was reasonable for the claimant to consider that the conduct had that requisite effect (the objective element) (see *Richmond Pharmacology v Dhaliwal* [2009] IRLR 336 EAT). The *Explanatory Notes to EqA 2010* note that 'in determining the effect of the unwanted conduct, courts and tribunals will continue to be required to balance competing rights on the facts of a particular case', and gives the example of balancing freedom of expression and academic freedom against the right not to be offended (*para 99*).

The sex of both the complainant and the alleged discriminator will be a factor for the tribunal to consider when determining the effect of certain conduct. Sexual badinage by a heterosexual male to another man cannot be completely equated with the same badinage occurring between that man and a woman. The treatment will not be precisely equal, since in the latter circumstance it is the sex of the alleged discriminator that potentially adds a material element absent as between two heterosexual men (*Driskel v Peninsula Business Services Ltd* [2000] IRLR 151, EAT).

Dignity and working environments

1.93 The *EqA 2010* retains the old test that the conduct must have either the purpose or the effect of: (i) violating B's dignity; or (ii) creating an intimidating, hostile, degrading, humiliating or offensive environment for B. This is therefore wider than the Directives which require both (i) and (ii). The reason for this broader definition when it was first enacted, eg in *RRA 1976*, is that existing case law had already established this greater protection for UK employees.

The two strands of the definition are likely to overlap in practice so that conduct that creates an adverse environment for an individual is also likely to violate their dignity, although the converse will not always be true. There has been relatively little case law on the meaning of the phrases. Whether or not the definition is made out is a question of fact and degree for the tribunal to consider in each case (see, for example, *Richmond Pharmacology v Dhaliwal*).

Harassment based on association or perception

1.94 Pre-*EqA 2010*, it was unclear whether a harassment claim had to be based on conduct directed at the claimant's actual protected characteristic as opposed to a perceived characteristic, or the characteristics of others. It was necessary for the EAT to effectively rewrite the *DDA 1995* in order to provide protection from associative discrimination on grounds of disability following the ECJ's decision in *EBR Attridge LLP v Coleman (No 2)* UKEAT/0071/09. However, *RBR 2003* (*Saini v All Saints Haque Centre, Bungay and Paul* UKEAT/0227/08) and *SOR 2003* (*English v Thomas Sanderson Blinds Ltd* [2008] EWCA Civ 1421, [2009] IRLR 206, [2009] 2 All ER 468) could more easily be interpreted to prohibit harassment based on the victim's association with another.

As noted above, the *EqA 2010* now prohibits harassment based on association and perception (apart from marriage and civil partnership and pregnancy and maternity, although arguably pregnancy and maternity may be covered by sex). See also **1.53–1.56**.

1.95 *Third party harassment*

EqA 2010, s 40 has extended employers' liability for persistent harassment of their employees by third parties to all of the protected characteristics covered by the harassment provisions. Prior to the implementation of *EqA 2010*, claims for third-party harassment were only permissible under the *SDA 1975*. *Section 40* retains the 'three strikes' provision that previously applied under the *SDA 1975* following its amendment under the *SDA Regulations 2008* (*SDA 1975, s 6(2B)*), by providing as follows:

'(1) An employer (A) must not, in relation to employment by A, harass a person (B):
(a) who is an employee of A's;
(b) who has applied to A for employment.
(2) The circumstances in which A is to be treated as harassing B under subsection (1) include those where:
(a) a third party harasses B in the course of B's employment, and
(b) A failed to take such steps as would have been reasonably practicable to prevent the third party from doing so.
(3) Subsection (2) does not apply unless A knows that B has been harassed in the course of B's employment on at least two other occasions by a third party; and it does not matter whether the third party is the same or a different person on each occasion.
(4) A third party is a person other than:
(a) A, or
(b) an employee of A's'.

Employers will be legally responsible where they know that an employee has been harassed on two previous occasions by someone who does not work for the employer, but nevertheless fail to take reasonable steps to protect the worker from further harassment. It will not be a defence to argue that the employee was harassed by a different individual on each occasion. Conversely, and peculiarly, an employer will not be liable where it exposes a succession of employees to harassment by the same third party, provided in each case each employee is exposed no more than twice. *Paragraph 10.21* of the *EHRC Employment Code* gives the following example of how *s 40* will work in practice:

> 'An employer is aware that a female employee working in her bar has been sexually harassed on two separate occasions by different customers. The employer fails to take any action and the employee experiences further harassment by yet another customer. The employer is likely to be liable for the further act of harassment'.

At the time of writing, there has not been any case law on third party harassment under the *SDA 1975*. There is therefore no judicial guidance on what steps will be viewed by a Tribunal as 'reasonably practicable'. However, the *EHRC Employment Code* provides that, 'depending upon the size and resources of an employer', reasonably practical steps might include the following:

— having a policy on harassment;

- notifying third parties that harassment of employees is unlawful and will not be tolerated; for example, by the display of a public notice;
- including a term in all contracts with third parties notifying them of the employer's policy on harassment and requiring them to adhere to it;
- encouraging employees to report any acts of harassment by third parties to enable the employer to support the employee and take appropriate action;
- taking action on every complaint of harassment by a third party (*para 10.24*).

The 'good practice' tips contained in the EHRC's *Guidance for Employers* should also be considered. Recommendations include that employers should not to wait for an employee to make two complaints about harassment before taking action. Instead, employers should deal with every incident of harassment at the time it takes place. Employers should advise employees as to when and how they should report intimidating/hostile conduct, as they may otherwise be deemed to be on notice of harassing conduct where relevant decision-makers have not in fact been informed. Where an employer is aware that potential harassment has taken place, the Guidance advises employers to talk to the person who has harassed their employee to tell them their behaviour was not acceptable (it would be prudent to document that this discussion has taken place). In some cases, the Guidance notes that it may be appropriate to stop the person visiting company premises to make sure staff are protected, although there is no explanation of how this would be done (EHRC *Guidance for Employers* entitled '*What Equality law means for you as an employer: Managing Workers*', p 32). What is reasonable is likely to be assessed by reference to the employer's business, the likelihood of incidents of harassment taking place, and steps taken by other employers in that sector.

The authorities on the vicarious liability of an employer for the actions of an employee may also assist in illustrating what steps may be reasonably practicable for the purposes of *EqA 2010, s 40*, as employers can avoid vicarious liability where they have taken 'reasonable steps' to prevent the conduct from occurring. In *Enterprise Glass Co Ltd v Miles* [1990] ICR 787, EAT, an employee complained to her employer that she was being sexually harassed by a male employee. The employee was reprimanded and was informed that if he did not stop, he would receive a formal written warning. When the behaviour continued, the employee again complained to her employers, but was told to ignore his behaviour. The EAT held that the employer had not taken reasonable steps to prevent the behaviour. In *Balgobin and Francis v Tower Hamlets London Borough Council* [1987] ICR 829, [1987] IRLR 401, [1987] ICR 829, the EAT held that the onus will be discharged if there are no practical steps which the employer can take. However, an employer is likely to need to demonstrate special circumstances to enable it to rely on such a defence.

1.96 *Other relevant legislation*

In addition to claims under the *Human Rights Act 1998, Health and Safety at Work Act 1974, Criminal Justice and Public Order Act 1994* and *Malicious Communications Act 1988*, harassment claims may be made, in appropriate circumstances, under the *Protection from Harassment Act 1997* (*PHA 1997*).

PHA 1997 makes harassment both a civil tort and a criminal offence. Initially introduced to protect victims from stalking, it has been used by complainants in harassment claims. Employers can also be found vicariously liable where the harassment occurs in the course of employment (*Majrowski v Guy's and St Thomas' NHS Trust* [2006] UKHL 34, [2007] 1 AC 224; *S&D Property Investments Ltd v Nisbet* [2009] EWHC 1726 (Ch)).

This route is potentially easier for an employee than a claim under the discrimination legislation: the 'reasonable steps' defence to vicarious liability is not open to the employer; a six-year limitation period applies; and, lastly, there is no need to show the harassment was on protected grounds, such as gender or race. However, the threshold for identifying harassment is reasonably high.

Common concepts

Harassment is not specifically defined under the *PHA 1997*. The focus is on the type of conduct that may constitute harassment. The classic formulation is that set out in the *Majrowski case* by Lord Nicholls:

> 'Courts are well able to recognise the boundary between conduct which is unattractive, even unreasonable, and conduct which is oppressive and unacceptable. To cross the boundary from the regrettable to the unacceptable the gravity of the misconduct must be of an order which would sustain criminal liability under section 2 [of the *PHA 1997*]' (para 30).

Baroness Hale also added her view of what might constitute harassment under the *PHA 1997* in the same case:

> 'All sorts of conduct may amount to harassment. . . . A great deal is left to the wisdom of the courts to draw sensible lines between the ordinary banter and badinage of life and genuinely offensive and unacceptable behaviour' (para 66).

The threshold set out by Lord Nicholls—that conduct be 'oppressive and unacceptable' and of a kind to sustain criminal liability—was applied by the Court of Appeal in the case of *Conn v Sunderland City Council* [2007] EWCA Civ 1492, [2008] IRLR 324. In that case, the court found that a specific incident of unpleasant, bad-tempered conduct (in the form of a threat to damage property) did not cross this boundary, although physical threats addressed to the claimant did. The court also concluded that whether conduct was of a type to cross the boundary identified by Lord Nicholls would depend on the context in which it occurred. What might not be harassment on the factory floor or in the barrack room might be harassment in a hospital ward and vice versa; the touchstone for recognising what was not harassment for the purposes of the *PHA 1997, ss 1 and 3* was whether the conduct was serious enough to justify criminal sanctions.

More recently still, the Court of Appeal in *Veakins v Kier Islington Ltd* [2009] EWCA Civ 1288, [2010] IRLR 132 concluded that, to succeed in a claim under *s 3*, the primary focus should be on whether the conduct is 'oppressive and unreasonable', rather than 'merely unattractive, unreasonable or regrettable' (which had been cited in the Court of Appeal decisions in *Allen v Southwark London Borough Council* [2008] EWCA Civ 1478 and *Ferguson v British Gas Trading Ltd* [2009] EWCA Civ 46, [2009] 3 All ER 304). Again, the Court of Appeal confirmed that the conduct must also be sufficiently serious to support a criminal prosecution under the *PHA 1997, s 2*, although it was of the opinion that this should not be the primary focus.

As the conduct in *Veakins* (including public rebuking of the claimant, requiring her to sign in and out every day, tearing up a letter of complaint from the claimant and asking her questions about her private life), had reduced a usually robust woman to a state of clinic depression, the court considered that such conduct was self-evidently 'oppressive and unacceptable'. In the court's view, it was also conduct that would sustain criminal liability.

However, in an effort to limit the impact of its decision, the Court of Appeal indicated that few workplace cases would be likely to give rise to liability for harassment under the *PHA 1997* and, in the majority of cases, discriminatory misconduct by or on behalf of an employer would be better dealt with in the employment tribunal. In its view, the facts of the case were 'extraordinary'. However, the conduct complained of was not particularly extreme and the comments by the court are therefore unlikely to prevent claimants from relying on this decision to bring claims under the *PHA 1997*.

PHA 1997 prohibits conduct which amounts to harassment or which a person knows or ought to know amounts to harassment of the victim, but only where the harassment takes the form of a course of conduct. Course of conduct is defined as involving conduct on 'at least two occasions' and harassment includes alarming the person or causing distress (*s 7*).

This is different from the position under the *EqA 2010*, in which a single incident can amount to unlawful harassment (except for third-party harassment: see **1.95**). For a discussion of what constitutes a course of conduct, see further *Conn v Sunderland City Council*.

In contrast to harassment under the *EqA 2010* (see **1.86** ff), the behaviour must be 'targeted' at the complainant, not some other person, and must be calculated to cause that person alarm and distress (*Dowson v Northumbria Police (No 1)* [2009] EWHC 907).

The offence is committed where the course of conduct 'amounts' to harassment. The effect on the person being harassed is therefore the relevant consideration and, unlike offences under the *Public Order Act 1986*, intention is irrelevant. The test in the second limb where the person ought to know that it amounts to harassment is an objective one and will be satisfied if a reasonable person in the possession of the same information would think that the course of conduct amounted to harassment. If the harasser can show that the conduct was for the prevention and detection of crime or was reasonable in the circumstances in the case, he will have a defence.

The victim of harassment under *PHA 1997* can bring civil proceedings for damages for any anxiety caused by the harassment and to cover any financial loss which has resulted from the harassment (*s 3*). He can also seek an injunction to stop the harassment (backed by powers of arrest) (*s 3*). These remedies are not available in the employment tribunal.

The severity of the conduct may be reflected in the level of damages awarded. The principles in this context are still evolving. An award for damages for psychiatric injury has been upheld in *Martins v Choudhary* [2007] EWCA Civ 1379, [2008] PIQR Q1. It has been suggested that any award made under the *PHA 1997* is likely to be 'modest': *Majrowski*, [29]; *S&D Property Investments*, [75]. For example, in *S&D Property Investments*, Nicol J referred—for cases not involving psychiatric damage—to the guidelines in *Vento v Chief Constable of West Yorkshire Police* [2002] EWCA Civ 1871, [2003] ICR 318.

Some indication of the quantum of damage under the *PHA 1997* can be gleaned from *Rayment v Ministry of Defence* [2010] EWHC 218 (QB). Here, the employee had a lengthy psychiatric history which she had not disclosed in advance of her employment and was employed in part as a driver. After feeling faint on a driving assignment due to a panic attack, she was certified off sick for several weeks. When she returned to work, she was informed that as she could no longer drive, she would be unable to work as a driver; that she no longer had a job at all; and that she was required to repay one month's salary. She was reinstated following intervention by the army welfare service, however, she made a complaint for discrimination and harassment and was signed off sick again. She then received a formal written warning and after the expiry of the warning, but while she was still sick, she was discharged from her duties on the basis that she had not returned to work. A further complaint was that there had been a failure to remove sexually explicit photographs of women in a restroom.

While the court was satisfied that there had been harassment, it noted that there had been faults on both sides: Rayment was a challenging employee and had she disclosed her pre-existing psychiatric disorder, she would have undergone a health assessment and not have been given drivers' duties. The meeting, written warning and discharge exacerbated her existing depressive illness, leading to period of mild to moderate depression of a few months' duration in respect of each event, while the failure to remove the pornographic photographs caused Rayment some distress.

The court concluded that damages of £5,000 were appropriate in respect of the exacerbation of Rayment's depressive illness as it was a 'blip' and because any continuing symptoms were a manifestation of Rayment's recurrent depression and not attributable to harassment (at [85], [88]). A further £500 was permitted for distress caused by the failure to remove the photographs. Special damages of £1,060 were awarded for travel expenses and complimentary medical treatments following Rayment's return to work.

Penalties on conviction are imprisonment for up to six months and/or a fine of up to £5,000. Where the harasser puts the victim in fear of violence, or where the harasser breaches an injunction, the offence is triable either way. If the harasser is convicted on indictment, the maximum penalty is five years' imprisonment and/or a fine.

A claim under *PHA 1997* must be brought in the county court or High Court: the employment tribunals have no jurisdiction to hear the claim. The time limit for bringing a civil claim under the *PHA 1997* is six years. A complainant might therefore consider taking this action if the time limit under *EqA 2010* has expired.

1.97 *Harassment: sources of further information*

Further information is available from:

- ACAS: The Advisory, Conciliation and Arbitration Service's 'Bullying and harassment at work: a guide for employees', available at http://www.acas.org.uk/index.aspx?articleid=797
- ACAS: 'Bullying and harassment at work: a guide for managers and employers', available at http://www.acas.org.uk/index.aspx?articleid=794
- CIPD: The Chartered Institute of Personnel and Development's Fact Sheet on 'Harassment and Bullying at Work', available at http://www.cipd.co.uk/subjects/dvsequl/harassmt/harrass.htm?IsSrchRes=1
- CIPD: 'Bullying at Work: Beyond Policies to a Culture of Respect', available at http://www.cipd.co.uk/NR/rdonlyres/D9105C52-7FED-42EA-A557-D1785DF6D34F/0/bullyatwork0405.pdf
- Joint guidance implementing the European Social Partner Framework Agreement on Harassment and Violence at Work—Preventing Workplace Harassment and Violence, available at http://www.workplaceharassment.org.uk/wp-content/uploads/2009/11/HRE_100_Guidance_report.pdf

1.98 VICTIMISATION

Introduction

EU law

Council Directive 2000/78/EC ('the *Framework Directive*'), establishing a general framework for equal treatment in employment and occupation provides that:

> 'Member States shall introduce into their legal systems such measures as are necessary to protect employees against dismissal or other adverse treatment by the employer as a reaction to a complaint within the undertaking or to any legal proceedings aimed at enforcing compliance with the principle of equal treatment' (*Article 11*).

Council Directive 2000/43/EC ('the *Race Directive*') contains a similar provision at *Article 9* as does the *Equal Treatment Directive 2006/54/EC* at *Article 24*, which also contains specific protection for employees' representatives.

1.99 *UK law*

The *EqA 2010* contains specific protection against victimisation, prohibiting a person (A) from subjecting an individual (B) to a detriment because B has done or A believes that B has done or may do one of the protected acts specified in the legislation:

— bringing proceedings under the *EqA 2010*;

— giving evidence or information in connection with proceedings under the *EqA 2010*;

— doing anything else for the purposes of or in connection with the *EqA 2010*;

— making an allegation that another person has breached the *EqA 2010* (*EqA 2010, s 27(2)*);

— having a relevant pay discussion with a colleague or former colleague (*EqA 2010, s 77(3)*, see **1.109**).

EqA 2010, s 27 on its face does not expressly include steps taken by an individual in respect of the previous discrimination legislation. It refers only to bringing proceedings, giving evidence or doing any other thing (etc) in connection with 'this Act'. This error was rectified by the *Equality Act 2010 (Commencement No 4, Savings, Consequential, Transitional, Transitory and Incidental Provisions and Revocation) Order 2010 (SI 2010/2317), Article 8*, which expressly extends the victimisation protection to cover the acts described in *s 27* (above) but were done in relation to the previous discrimination legislation.

The protection does not apply to treatment of a person by reason of any allegation made by him, or evidence or information given by him, if the allegation, evidence or information was false and made or given in bad faith (*EqA 2010, s 27(3)*: see **1.102** below).

Under the *EqA 2010*, victimisation is not technically a form of discrimination. It is a separate claim which may be made, and it can succeed independently of, or in addition to, a discrimination claim. It is therefore not necessary to show that the underlying complaint had any merit.

A victimisation claim differs from discrimination in that the proscribed ground is the commission of the protected act. This means that the claimant does not need to show the reason for their treatment is because of one of the protected characteristics (such as race or sex).

In a change from the previous law, under *EqA 2010* there is no requirement to have a comparator. In its response to the consultation on the *EqA 2010*, the government stated that the removal of the requirement for a comparator to show 'less favourable treatment' would allow for the situation where 'the 'victim' suffered an absolute harm, irrespective of how others were treated in the same circumstances'. In practice, the approach to establishing victimisation under *EqA 2010* is now likely to mirror the approach under the *Public Interest Disclosure Act 1998*, with a greater emphasis on causation. The absence of a comparator is unlikely to make a significant difference to the success of claims in practice.

1.100 Victimisation: key elements

An employer will victimise an employee if it subjects the employee to a detriment because the employee has done, or may do, a protected act. However, an employer taking 'honest and reasonable steps' to protect itself in the context of litigation should generally not be liable for victimisation (see **1.106**).

1.101 *Protected acts*

A victimisation claim will fail if the claimant cannot show that his actions amount to a protected act. There are five ways in which a claimant might gain protection. These are where *the victim* has:

(a) *brought proceedings under EqA 2010*: this was also the case under the pre-October 2010 legislation. A distinction may be made between bringing proceedings and their continued existence: see *Chief Constable of West Yorkshire Police v Khan* [2001] UKHL 48 and *St Helens Metropolitan Borough Council v Derbyshire* [2005] EWCA Civ 977, [2006] ICR 90. However, it may be that an employer that acts in connection with ongoing litigation in an honest and reasonable way does not victimise if the employee is not unduly prejudiced or disadvantaged by the acts or by the manner in which they are done (see 'Honest and Reasonable Exception' at **1.106** below);

(b) *given evidence or information in connection with proceedings*: This provision gives protection in connection with proceedings brought under *EqA 2010* against the person victimising (A) or any other person and so is very wide. There must, however, be actual proceedings in existence;

(c) *done any other thing for the purposes of or in connection with EqA 2010*: this is a change from the old law, which required things 'under or by reference to' the pre-existing legislation. However, it is likely to be given a wide interpretation, given the broad interpretation of 'by reference to' under the old law. In *Aziz v Trinity Street Taxis Ltd* [1989] QB 463, [1988] 2 All ER 860, [1988] 3 WLR 79, a case under the *RRA 1976*, the Court of Appeal held 'an act can properly be said to be done by reference to the Act if it is done by reference to the race relations legislation in the broad sense even though the doer does not focus his mind specifically on any provision of the Act';

(d) *made an allegation that A or any other person has contravened EqA 2010*: this also replicates the pre-October 2010 legislation. In *Waters v Metropolitan Police Comr* [19970 ICR 1073, [1997] IRLR 589 a policewoman who had been sexually assaulted off-duty complained that her employers failed to respond to and investigate her complaint and that she had been victimised as a result. The Court of Appeal ruled that *SDA 1975, s 4(1)(d)* only applied where the act was one for which the employer would have been liable. The sexual assault was not committed during the course of employment, the employer was not liable and there was therefore no victimisation;

No actual allegation need have been made (*Fearon v The Chief Constable of Derbyshire* UKEAT/0445/02/RN), and the allegation need not be express (*EqA 2010, s 27(2)(d)*).

(e) *sought, made or received a 'relevant pay disclosure'*: This is a new protected act under provisions intending to increase pay transparency which are set out at *EqA 2010, s 77(4)* (see **1.109**).

Protection will apply where A believes that the victim has done, or may do, a protected act. This is similar to the old law, which referred to A 'knowing or suspecting' that the victim would do a protected act. What is important here is what A believes, not what the victim has done. Here, a much broader approach is likely to be permitted, as under the old law:

> 'It requires a state of mind in the discriminator relating to what the victim has done or intends to do . . . [F]or a protected act to fall within this second category, it is not necessary that it take the form of an allegation, or the doing of anything by reference to the Act'
>
> (*Fearon*).

In this case, where senior police officers formed a view that the applicant was or might be aggrieved by his treatment on account of his race, this provision applied.

1.102 *Good faith*

There is no protection against victimisation if an individual gives false evidence or information, or makes a false allegation, in bad faith (*EqA 2010, s 27(3)*). The *Explanatory Notes to the EqA 2010* give the following example (at *para 103*):

> 'A man with a grudge against his employer knowingly gives false evidence in a colleague's discrimination claim against the employer. He is subsequently dismissed for supporting the claim. His dismissal would not amount to victimisation because of his untrue and malicious evidence.'

In *Raja v National Council for Voluntary Organisations* 43786/96 ET a male employee responded to a sexual harassment allegation made by female colleague by claiming she had sexually harassed him. The tribunal found that the allegation was both false and made in bad faith. He therefore could not benefit from protection against victimisation.

However, if an individual gives evidence, provides information or makes an allegation in good faith, but it subsequently transpires that the allegation is factually wrong, or the subsequent proceedings are unsuccessful, that will still constitute a protected act (*EHRC Employment Code, para 9.14*). It is for the employer to establish bad faith.

1.103 *'Because of' a protected act*

Victimisation only occurs where there is detriment 'because' of a protected act. The *EHRC Employment Code, para 9.10* states that this means that the protected act must be one of the reasons for the treatment, but it need not be the only reason for it. It is likely that tribunals will use the pre-existing case law below to help determine this part of the definition.

Under the pre-October 2010 legislation, victimisation took place where the act complained of took place 'by reason that' the claimant had done a protected act. Following a number of judgments dealing with the meaning of this phrase, Lord Neuberger in *St Helens Metropolitan Borough Council v Derbyshire* [2005] EWCA Civ 977, [2006] ICR 90 (see below) held that 'by reason that' should be read as 'because' (see also *Chief Constable of West Yorkshire Police v Khan* [2001] UKHL 48). Therefore the new test under *EqA 2010* in fact effectively reflects the previous case law.

For further guidance, the case law on causation under the *Public Interest Disclosure Act 1998* ('*PIDA 1998*') is instructive. Under *PIDA 1998*, it is sufficient that protected acts, taken cumulatively, have a 'significant outcome' on the act complained of, even if they are not the sole cause of it (*El-Megrisi v Azad University (IR) in Oxford* [2009] UKEAT 0448/08). Where the reason for the alleged detrimental treatment is the way the employee made their disclosure, rather than the disclosure itself, the *PIDA 1998* protection does not apply (*Evans v Bolton School* [2006] EWCA Civ 1653, [2007] ICR 641. See also on this point the EAT in *Martin v Devonshires Solicitors* (2010) UKEAT/0086/10, [2011] ICR 352 in the context of a victimisation allegation).

1.104 *Conscious or unconscious motivation*

As with direct discrimination, victimisation need not be consciously motivated. If A's reason for subjecting B to a detriment was unconscious, it can still amount to victimisation. This was demonstrated in the case of *Nagarajan v London Regional Transport* [1999] IRLR 572, HL. In this case, a former employee with a long history of bringing race discrimination claims against his employers applied for new employment, was rejected and claimed victimisation against London Regional Transport and a personnel manager.

At first instance, the tribunal inferred that the interviewing panel was consciously or subconsciously influenced by the applicant's history of making claims. The EAT, relying on *Aziz v Trinity Street Taxis Ltd* [1989] QB 463, [1988] 2 All ER 860, [1988] 3 WLR 79, and the Court of Appeal, found that for there to be victimisation, there must be conscious motivation on the part of the respondent: mere knowledge that the claimant had carried out the protected acts did not permit the inference that this affected the decision to treat the claimant less favourably. However, without knowledge of the complaint of discrimination, victimisation could not be made out (*South London Healthcare NHS Trust v Al-Rubeyi* 2010 WL 889463).

By a majority, the House of Lords held that conscious or unconscious motivation on the part of the respondent was sufficient to found a victimisation claim and that the claimant need only establish that the fact that the employee had carried out a protected act was a 'significant influence' on the alleged victimisation. The House of Lords also held that the fact that different employees had been involved in the decision-making process did not preclude a finding of victimisation. Acts carried out by one employee were held to be those of the employer and where one employee does not discriminate or victimise but others do, the employer will still be vicariously liable (see **1.163** ff).

In *Lisk-Carew v Birmingham City Council* [2004] EWCA Civ 565, [2004] 20 LS Gaz R 35 the claimant was dismissed for misconduct (he had 'repeatedly failed to comply with reasonable management direction', 'failed to withdraw unsubstantiated allegations against management and other colleagues' and had been 'offensive and uncooperative towards management'). He brought unfair dismissal, race discrimination and victimisation claims. The tribunal held that the dismissal was fair and there was no direct discrimination. However, it found that allegations the claimant had made had had 'a significant influence on the decision to dismiss even if that influence was subconscious rather than conscious'. The tribunal had also concluded that, with one exception, the allegations made by the claimant had not been both false and made in bad faith and the dismissal had not been by reason of the one allegation which did not pass this test. There was therefore victimisation. The EAT and Court of Appeal upheld the decision.

Nagarajan was considered in light of the (subsequent) *Burden of Proof Directive* in *Wong v Igen Ltd (Equal Opportunities Commission intervening)* [2005] EWCA Civ 142, [2005] ICR 931, [2005] IRLR 258, where Peter Gibson LJ stressed that because EU law principles required the eradication of 'all discrimination whatsoever', 'significant influence' must mean an influence which is more than trivial. In *Villalba v Merrill Lynch & Co Inc* [2007] ICR 469, [2006] IRLR 437 the EAT confirmed that, where proper consideration had been given to the possibility of subconscious prejudice, one particular incident among many others might properly be considered 'not a significant influence' in the decision to dismiss Ms Villalba.

1.105 *Detriment*

A detriment capable of amounting to an act of victimisation can take a variety of forms, and covers both contractual and non-contractual benefits. However it must be motivated by a protected act and has sufficient connection with an existing or former relationship (see **1.107** below). In *St Helens* the House of Lords held that whether a detriment has been suffered should be 'determined primarily from the perspective of the alleged victim', although from the viewpoint of a 'reasonable employee' which introduces an objective element.

A number of cases deal with a former employer's refusal to provide a reference, the negative content of such a reference or other disclosure that the former employee committed a protected act (see *Khan*). Other cases deal with the withholding of benefits that would otherwise have been due to the claimant arising out of the former relationship (*Relaxion Group plc v Rhys-Harper* [2003] UKHL 33, [2003] 4 All ER 1113, [2003] 2 CMLR 1329, [2003] ICR 867), acts of harassment designed to dissuade an employee from continuing with a protected act (*Nicholls v Corin Tech* [2008] UKEAT 0290070403), or (one of the trickiest areas) the conduct of litigation (see *Khan* and *St Helens*, below). Again, referring to the case law under *PIDA 1998*, it is likely that an employer will be vicariously liable for post-termination acts of victimisation against the individual by former colleagues, where sufficiently connected to the former relationship (*Carlisle-Morgan v Cumbria County Council* [2007] IRLR 314).

In *D'Souza v London Borough of Lambeth* (heard as part of the *Relaxion* appeals) the House of Lords held that failure to comply with a reinstatement order cannot be regarded as a benefit arising from the employment relationship for the purposes of the victimisation provisions. However this decision is now questionable in light of the Court of Appeal's decision in *Rank Nemo (DMS) Ltd v Coutinho* [2009] ICR 1296, [2009] IRLR 672 that failure to pay a tribunal award could be actionable as an act of victimisation, as well as a debt, if on the facts the judgment debtor's action was motivated by the fact the claimant had brought a discrimination claim.

1.106 *'Honest and reasonable' exception*

One area in which difficulties frequently arise is where an employee argues that the way in which his employer has responded to litigation (on which they are on opposing sides) is itself unlawful victimisation. However, if the employer's conduct can be considered an 'honest and reasonable' response to the litigation, this will not amount to a detriment for victimisation purposes. The leading case on this exception is the House of Lords decision in *Khan*.

K claimed race discrimination, following a number of unsuccessful applications for promotion. Before the tribunal hearing, he applied to another police force, which asked West Yorkshire Police for references and staff appraisals. West Yorkshire Police refused to supply them, stating that, on legal advice, providing the documents might prejudice their case. K claimed victimisation.

The House of Lords held that K's request was not refused 'by reason that' he brought proceedings, but so that the employer could protect itself from further tribunal claims and preserve its position in the ongoing litigation. The employer and employee were engaged in litigation and an employer acting honestly and reasonably should be able to preserve its position and protect itself from further claims which might arise from the contents of any reference.

The correct comparator in this case was someone who had not done the protected act at all.

As the comparator under the old law was someone who had not done the act at all, the practical difference in establishing victimisation under *EqA 2010*, where no comparator is required, is unlikely to be substantially different from pre-*EqA 2010* cases, although the emphasis will now be more firmly on causation.

Notwithstanding the above, there are limits to the scope of the 'honest and reasonable' conduct of litigation exception. In *IRC v Morgan* [2002] IRLR 776 victimisation was found when, after Miss Morgan brought a race discrimination claim, her employer circulated a memorandum advising her colleagues that as a result of her request for information on alleged comparators, confidential data might become public. The EAT rejected the argument that the memo was not sent by reason that the claimant had brought proceedings, but by reason that the respondents wished to preserve their position in the litigation. The EAT acknowledged the 'honest and reasonable' employer test created by the House of Lords in *Khan*, but held that circulating the memo fell outside this exception.

In *St Helens Metropolitan Borough Council v Derbyshire* [2005] EWCA Civ 977, [2006] ICR 90, school dinner ladies brought equal pay claims and most settled, but some did not. The Council wrote to all staff and to the claimants individually (although they were represented by their union) indicating that if the claims continued and succeeded many redundancies might result. The claimants brought victimisation claims. The Court of Appeal (Mummery LJ dissenting) held that the tribunal had been wrong to find that the *Khan* 'honest and reasonable' test did not apply because here the employer was seeking to persuade the employees to settle their case, whereas in *Khan* the employer was seeking to preserve its position in ongoing litigation. The majority held that while the *Khan* 'honest and reasonable' test had no legislative basis, employers in such situations should be able to encourage employees to settle claims without risking victimisation claims.

The House of Lords ([2007] ICR 841, [2007] IRLR 540) (Lord Neuberger) accepted that the outcome in *Khan* was correct but considered, however, that the 'honest and reasonable' test placed a 'somewhat uncomfortable and unclear meaning' on 'by reason that'. Their Lordships thought that the reasoning in *Khan*, which predated implementation of the *Race Directive* should be reconsidered in the light of, in particular, the ECJ decision in *Coote v Granada Hospitality Ltd: C-185/97* [1998] ECR I-5199, [1998] All ER (EC) 865, [1998] 3 CMLR 958, where it was held that employees should be protected against measures taken 'as a reaction to proceedings brought by the employee'.

The House of Lords preferred that the 'honest and reasonable' test be directed not at 'by reason that', but at the issue of detriment, which must be judged from the viewpoint of the claimant. Thus the integrity of the employer's actions should not be assessed by examining its reasons for taking the action (which in this case was to encourage the employees to settle). Rather the issue was whether the employer did anything which might make a reasonable employee feel unduly pressured, given that litigation will ordinarily cause anxiety, to settle her claim. Lord Neuberger believed that the analysis in *Khan* distorted the meaning of 'by reason that', which should simply be read as 'because'. Baroness Hale referred to the corresponding wording in the *Equal Treatment Directive (76/207/EEC)*, which required consideration whether the employer's behaviour was 'a reaction to' the employees' claims—which in this case it clearly was. On the facts of the case they found that it had been open to the tribunal to find that the letters sent did not satisfy the 'honest and reasonable' employer test and restored the finding of victimisation.

The issue of victimisation claims in the context of ongoing proceedings has more recently been considered by the Court of Appeal in *Bird v Sylvester* [2007] EWCA Civ 1052, [2008] IRLR 232. In this case, the claimant alleged that a proposal made by her employer to settle her claim on payment of part of its costs, coupled with an apology and agreement not to litigate further, together with pursuit of its costs in the Tribunal, amounted to victimisation. The Court of Appeal rejected this aspect of her claim on the basis of the judgement in *St Helens*, that the employer's actions were reasonable in order to protect its interests in the litigation. They however considered it possible that the employer's threat of disciplinary action in connection with the way she had conducted the proceedings might amount to an act of victimisation, and this remains a difficult issue where employment is ongoing.

1.107 Former employees

Other than removing the requirement for a comparator, the government did not intend to change the victimisation protection which existed prior to the *EqA 2010* (*Explanatory Notes to the EqA 2010, note 106*).

However, there is an apparent oversight in *EqA 2010* which excludes former employees from the protection available against discrimination and harassment under *EqA 2010, s 108*. *EqA 2010, s 108(7)* expressly excludes former employees from protection against victimisation, apparently based on a misunderstanding, as set out in the explanatory notes, that post-termination victimisation is covered under the separate victimisation provisions of *EqA 2010*. As the statutory protection in place pre-October 2010 (for example under *SDA 1975, s 20A* and *RRA 1976, s 27A*) no longer exists, former employees will need to rely on case law rather than *EqA 2010* for protection against victimisation, which leaves some uncertainty.

The principle that protection against victimisation should continue after the end of the employment relationship stems from *Coote v Granada Hospitality Ltd: C-185/97* [1998] ECR I-5199, [1998] All ER (EC) 865, [1998] 3 CMLR 958 in which the ECJ held that by virtue of *Article 6* of the *Equal Treatment Directive*, former employees should have the right to complain about victimisation that takes place after their employment ends. This ruling was subsequently applied by the House of Lords in *Relaxion Group plc v Rhys-Harper* [2003] UKHL 33, [2003] 2 CMLR 1329, [2003] ICR 867. The essential question is whether the action complained about is 'sufficiently connected' to the former relationship. This is a question of: (i) the nature of the action (for example, a reference is likely to be seen as a benefit arising as part of the employment relationship if usually provided to other former employees), and (ii) its closeness to the employment relationship, including its proximity in time (see for example *Metropolitan Police Service v Shoebridge* [2004] ICR 1690, where the EAT was not convinced that a dismissal which took place 14 months after a change of employer stemmed from actions of the previous employer). This is arguably a slightly narrower test than *EqA 2010, s 108*, which refers to relevant conduct which 'arises out of and is closely connected to' their former relationship.

Note that where the former employer's actions result in an action by a third party, that may not necessarily break the chain of causation. So, where the content of a reference resulted in a job offer being withdrawn, the former employer shared liability with the prospective employer who had withdrawn the offer based on the reference provided (*Bullimore v Pothecary Witham Weld Solicitors* (2010) UKEAT/0189/10/JOJ, [2011] IRLR 18, see Sanctions at **1.169**).

1.108 Instructing and aiding victimisation

Note that it is also unlawful to instruct, cause or induce a person to victimise another, or to aid someone in victimising another (*EqA 2010, ss 111–112*: see **1.60–1.62**).

1.109 DISCUSSIONS ABOUT PAY

EqA 2010, s 77 renders unenforceable any rule or contractual provision which prevents or restricts employees from: (i) seeking a relevant pay disclosure from a colleague or former colleague; or (ii) making or seeking to make a relevant pay disclosure to anyone (whether a colleague or not). A disclosure is a relevant pay disclosure if the purpose is to enable the person who makes it or the person to whom it is made to establish whether there is 'a connection between pay and having (or not having) a particular protected characteristic' (*EqA 2010, s 77(3)*).

This provision was included in *EqA 2010* with the aim of encouraging transparency as a means of promoting equality. Pay secrecy clauses in themselves are not unenforceable. They will only be unenforceable by virtue of *EqA 2010, s 77* where the pay discussion relates—to some degree at least—to the possibility of discrimination.

Providing, obtaining or seeking pay information for the purpose of identifying a connection between pay and having a protected characteristic is a protected act benefiting from protection from victimisation (*EqA 2010, ss 27, 77(4)*). Action taken by an employer against an employee because of his participation in a relevant pay disclosure will therefore be an act of victimisation (see **1.99**). The *Explanatory Notes to the EqA 2010, note 271* provides the following example:

> 'A female employee thinks she is underpaid compared with a male colleague. She asks him what he is paid, and he tells her. The employer takes disciplinary action against the man as a result. The man can bring a claim of victimisation against the employer for disciplining him'.

The right to make a disclosure was deliberately extended to allow disclosures to non-colleages (eg trade union representatives). However, disclosures of pay details for purposes which are unconnected with identifying a connection between pay and having a related characteristic do not benefit from the protections offered by *EqA 2010, s 77*. As such, it would be possible for an employer to take disciplinary action against an employee where the employee has disclosed pay information to a competitor in breach of a confidentiality obligation without facing a claim for victimisation (*EHRC Employment Code, para 14.12*).

1.110 EXCEPTIONS

There are a number of statutory and other exceptions which exempt particular categories of action from the ambit of discrimination law.

1.111 Statutory exceptions common to two or more strands of discrimination legislation

National security

Discriminatory acts will not be unlawful in relation to any protected characteristic where: (a) they are done for the purpose of safeguarding national security; and (b) it is proportionate to discriminate for that purpose (*EqA 2010, s 192*). This exception replicates the approach in the pre-October 2010 legislation (*SDA 1975, s 52(1)*; *RRA 1976, s 42; DDA 1995, s 59(2A); SOR 2003, reg 24; RBR 2003, reg 24; AR 2006, reg 28*) but makes some changes to the scope and applicability of the exception.

Prior to October 2010, what is now the requirement of *proportionality* was expressed as a requirement of justification ('*justified by that purpose*'). Furthermore, this justification test did not previously apply to sex discrimination (*SDA 1975, s 52(1)*). The application of the national security exception to sex is now subject to the same requirement of proportionality as the other protected characteristics (*EqA 2010, s 192*).

It is possible that *EqA 2010, s 192* will narrow the breadth of the exception in that it only provides that the acts will not contravene the *EqA 2010* rather than that they are not unlawful.

1.112 *Benefits to the public*

As under the pre-October 2010 legislation, the *EqA 2010* provides that an employee will not be able to claim that his employer has discriminated against him in his capacity as employer in the provision of facilities, benefits or services where his employer is concerned with the provision of facilities, benefits or services of the same description to the public at large (whether for profit or not) (*EqA 2010, Sch 9, para 19*, given effect by *EqA 2010, s 83*; largely replicating *SDA 1975, s 6(7); RRA 1976, s 4(4); DDA 1995, s 4(4); SOR 2003, reg 6(4); RBR 2003, reg 6(4); AR 2006, reg 7(6)*). The *EqA 2010* has broadened this exception to cover claims by contract workers, partners of a firm, members of an LLP and persons holding offices or posts which are materially alike as well as by employees (*EqA 2010, Sch 9, para 19(3)–(4)*). Together with employees, these categories of persons are now collectively referred to as 'comparable persons' under the *EqA 2010*.

The exception will not apply if: (a) the provision to the public is materially different from the provision to employees (or other comparable persons); or (b) the provision is regulated by the terms of the employee's (or other comparable person's) contract; or (c) the benefit, facility or service relates to training (*EqA 2010, Sch 9, para 19(3)*).

The exemption might apply, for example, where the owner of a leisure centre allows its workers to use its facilities, or where an employee of a bank takes out a mortgage with his employer. This exception will not, however, prevent a comparable person from bringing a discrimination claim in relation to the provision of services under the *EqA 2010, Pt 3*.

1.113 *Compliance with statutory provision*

The *EqA 2010* provides an exception where a potentially discriminatory act is necessary to comply with statutory provisions (*EqA 2010, Sch 22*, given effect by *s 191*). *Schedule 22* largely replicates the pre-October 2010 provisions in the *DDA 1995* and *AR 2006* (*DDA 1995, s 59; AR 2006, reg 27*) but extends the exception to cover discrimination on the grounds of religion or belief. In addition *Sch 22, para 5(2)* replaces the exceptions in relation to nationality and residence which were previously included in *RRA 1976*. In terms of its application to employment law, this exception varies across the different protected characteristics as follows:

(1) **Disability, religion or belief and age.** In relation to each of these characteristics, *Sch 22* provides an exemption. However, the definition of 'statutory provision' is more extensive in relation to disability and religion or belief. Thus, in respect of

discrimination on the basis of both disability and religion or belief, statutory provision includes the requirements of an enactment and relevant requirements or conditions imposed by, amongst others, a Minister of the Crown, by *virtue* of an enactment. By contrast, in respect of discrimination on the basis of age a statutory provision is only defined to include the requirements of an enactment (*EqA 2010, Sch 22*);

(2) **Race**. The *EqA 2010* replicates the pre-October 2010 position on race/nationality discrimination under the *RRA 1976, s 41(2)*. There is an exemption from discrimination on grounds of nationality (but not race, ethnic or national origins) for something required to be done under an enactment or subordinate legislation. There is also an exemption for indirect discrimination against all strands of discrimination where required by an enactment or subordinate legislation to apply a PCP which relates to someone's place of ordinary residence or the length of time they have been present or resident in or out of the United Kingdom or an area within the UK (*EqA 2010, Sch 23, para 1* which is applicable by virtue of *EqA 2010, s 196*);

(3) **Sexual orientation.** As under the pre-October 2010 legislation there is no exception for compliance with statutory provisions in respect of discrimination on the basis of sexual orientation in the context of employment (*EqA 2010, Sch 22*);

(4) **Sex.** Also reflecting the pre-October 2010 legislation approach, there is no general statutory authority exception in relation to discrimination on the basis of sex in the context of employment, except to the extent that such discriminatory acts are required by statute for the *protection* of women (*EqA 2010, Sch 22, para 2*, which largely replicates the old regime under *SDA 1975, s 41*). Under the *EqA 2010* the relevant statutory regimes providing for the protection of women which fall within this exception are now more specifically identified and the exception has thus been restricted to particular legislation currently in force.

Schedule 22 to the *EqA 2010* also allows for an exception in relation to certain kinds of academic appointment or employment in an educational institution where an instrument of the institution requires the holder of the position to belong to a particular religious order or to be a woman (*EqA 2010, Sch 22, para 3*). It also allows for rules about Crown employment to restrict eligibility on the basis of birth, nationality, descent or residence (*Sch 22, para 5*).

1.114 *Occupational requirements*

See **1.145** ff.

1.115 *Positive action*

See **1.154** ff

1.116 *Sport*

There is an exception which applies to discrimination on the basis of sex in relation to participation in a 'gender-affected activity', which is defined as a sport, game or other competitive activity, in which the physical strength, stamina or physique of one sex would put persons of that sex at a disadvantage compared to average persons of the other sex (*EqA 2010, s 195*). This largely replicates the pre-October 2010 approach under *SDA 1975, s 44*, however this exception has now been made gender neutral so as to apply in cases where the relevant disadvantage may apply to men rather than women, for example in a sport where weight is a disadvantage, and in line with the extension of this exception under the *EqA 2010* to cover 'other competitive activities' as well as sports and games. The exception only applies in respect of individuals who are competing in sporting events. So, for example, discriminating on the basis of sex in choosing a coach would not come within the exception (see *British Judo Association v Petty* [1981] IRLR 484, where *SDA 1975* was held not to apply to a referee).

The *EqA 2010* makes provision for the lawful restriction on the participation of transsexual people in a gender-affected activity where necessary on grounds of fair competition or the safety of competitors (*EqA 2010, s 195(2)*).

The *EqA 2010* largely replicates the pre-October 2010 legislation exception in relation to discrimination on the grounds of nationality, birth place or length of residency in order to select someone to represent a country, place or area in a sport, game or other activity of a competitive nature or where the rules of a competition relating to eligibility to compete in a sport, game or activity require it (*EqA 2010, s 195(5)–(6)*; largely replicating *RRA 1976, s 39*). The *EqA 2010* has extended this exception to cover 'other activities' as well as sports and games (see **6.58**).

1.117 *Armed forces*

The *EqA 2010* substantially replicates the pre-October 2010 legislation armed forces' exception, however it narrows its scope. The exception now only applies to direct discrimination in relation to recruitment and access to training, promotion and transfer opportunities (or receiving other benefits, facilities or services) in the application of a requirement to be a man or not to be a transsexual person. In order to come within the scope of the exception the application of the relevant requirement must be a proportionate means of ensuring the combat effectiveness of the armed forces (*EqA 2010, Sch 9*, given effect by *EqA 2010, s 83*; contrast with the breadth of the application of this exception under the *SDA 1975, s 85(4)*) (see **Sex discrimination (8)**).

None of the employment provisions under the *EqA 2010, Pt 5*, in so far as they relate to age or disability, apply to service in the armed forces (*EqA 2010, Sch 9, para 4(3)* replicating *AR 2006, reg 44(4) and DDA 1995, s 64(7)*) (see **Age discrimination (2)**) and **Disability discrimination (3)**).

1.118 *Charities*

The provision of benefits only to persons who share a protected characteristic in pursuance of a 'charitable instrument' is excluded from the scope of the *EqA 2010* by *s 193* if such provision is a proportionate means of achieving a legitimate aim or it is for the purpose of preventing or compensating for a disadvantage linked to the relevant protected characteristic. The *EqA 2010* has extended this charitable exception to all protected characteristics (except that charitable instruments benefitting a class or persons defined by colour will be read as if it does not specify colour: *EqA 2010, s 194(4)*). See the previous charitable exception under the *SDA 1975, s 43*.

'Charitable instrument' is defined as 'an instrument establishing or governing a charity' (*EqA 2010, s 194(4)*). Note that this differs from the old definitions of a charitable instrument under the *SDA 1975* and the *DDA 1995* which focused on an enactment or instrument being made for/relating to 'charitable purposes' (*SDA 1975, s 43(3); DDA 1995, s 18C(3)*).

The *EqA 2010* has narrowed the charities exception in respect of disability discrimination compared to the previous exception under the *DDA 1995, s 18C*. The second part of the exception in relation to 'acts done by a charity or recognised body in pursuance of any of its charitable purpose', previously contained in the *DDA 1995, s 18C(1)*, has not been replicated in the *EqA 2010*.

The exception is confined to the provision of 'benefits' and, except in relation to disability discrimination, does not allow charities to discriminate in the provision or terms of employment, contract work or employment services (*EqA 2010, s 193(9)*). However, the supported employment exception in relation to disability continues to apply (*EqA 2010, s 193(3)*; see previous provision under *DDA 1995, s 18C(2)*).

1.119 **Specific exceptions**

Sex

See also Sex discrimination (**8**):

- ministers of religion (*EqA 2010, Sch 9, para 2*; largely replicating *SDA 1975, s 19*);
- insurance (*EqA 2010, Sch 9, para 20* (also covers gender reassignment, marriage and civil partnership and pregnancy and maternity discrimination); largely replicating *SDA 1975, s 45*);
- communal accommodation and related benefits (*EqA 2010, Sch 23, para 3*; largely replicating *SDA 1975, s 46*) (this exception extends to discrimination on the basis of gender reassignment, but such discrimination of transsexual persons must be a proportionate means of achieving a legitimate aim);
- the special regime in respect of maternity leave (see the maternity-related pay exception, *EqA 2010, Sch 9, para 17*);
- public authorities (see **8.54**).

There are separate provisions on the selection of political candidates and single sex shortlists (*EqA 2010, s 104*) but these are outside the scope of this work.

Some of the former specific exceptions relating to sex have not been replicated in the *EqA 2010* (police officers: height requirements and uniform allowances (*SDA 1975, s 17*); prison officers: height requirements (*SDA 1975, s 18*)).

1.120 *Race*

See also Race discrimination (**6**):

- training to persons not ordinarily resident in an EEA state, where skills are to be exercised outside Great Britain (relevant to nationality grounds only) (*EqA 2010, Sch 23, para 4*; largely replicating *RRA 1976, s 6*). The purpose of this is to enable people from developing countries to acquire vital skills which may not be available in their country of residence (*Explanatory Notes to the EqA 2010*);
- public authorities (see **6.75**).

Some of the former specific exceptions relating to race have not been replicated in the *EqA 2010*, for example, employment for the purposes of a private household (relevant to nationality grounds only) (*RRA 1976, s 4(3)*). The exception relating to pay for seamen recruited abroad to work on a ship contained in *RRA 1976, s 9* (relevant to nationality ground only) is likewise not replicated in the *EqA 2010*. However, it has been saved temporarily pending the introduction of new regulations to address work on ships, hovercraft and seafarers (see further **6.57**).

1.121 *Disability*

See also Disability discrimination (**3**):

- public authorities (see **3.110**).

1.122 *Religion and belief discrimination*

See also Religion and belief (**7**):

- work of an ethos, nature or context such that being of a particular religion or belief constitutes a proportionate occupational requirement (*EqA 2010, Sch 9, para 3*);
- certain educational appointments (*EqA 2010, Sch 22, paras 3–4*);

- membership or participation in the activities of a religious organisation, though this exception does not cover employment (*EqA 2010, Sch 23, para 2*; outside the scope of this work).

1.123 *Age*

See also AGE DISCRIMINATION (**2**):

- retirement (*EqA 2010, Sch 9, para 8*; replicating *AR 2006, reg 30*, although note the anticipated removal of the default retirement age);
- applicants at or approaching retirement age (*EqA 2010, Sch 9, para 9*);
- national minimum wage (*EqA 2010, Sch 9, paras 11 and 12*; replicating *AR 2006, reg 31*);
- benefits based on length of service (*EqA 2010, Sch 9, para 10*; largely replicating *AR 2006, reg 32*);
- enhanced redundancy payments (*EqA 2010, Sch 9, para 13*; replicating *AR 2006, reg 33*);
- life assurance and retired workers (*EqA 2010, Sch 9, para 14*; replicating *AR 2006, reg 34*);
- providing child care only for children of a certain age (*EqA 2010, Sch 9, para 15*);
- contributions to personal pension schemes (ministerial power to make orders) (*EqA 2010, Sch 9, para 16*).

1.124 *Sexual orientation*

See also SEXUAL ORIENTATION DISCRIMINATION (**9**):

- employment for the purposes of a religious organisation (only applies to a limited range of jobs within a religious organisation) (*EqA 2010, Sch 9, para 2*);
- certain benefits to married people where the right to such benefits accrued prior to the *Civil Partnership Act 2004* entering into force (*EqA 2010, Sch 9, para 18*).

1.125 Excluded persons

The *EqA 2010* will not apply to those who work outside its territorial scope (see **1.4**ff).

1.126 Other defences

State immunity

As a matter of general law, where a claim is brought against a foreign sovereign state or its Head of State, that party is entitled to claim immunity from the jurisdiction of the courts of the United Kingdom (*State Immunity Act 1978, s 1*). This rule also extends to, for example, ambassadors, embassies and ministers.

The case of *Fogarty v United Kingdom (Application 37112/97)* [2002] IRLR 148 demonstrates that state immunity may be available in respect of discrimination claims in some cases. In *Fogarty*, an administrative assistant had successfully claimed discrimination under the *SDA 1975* after being dismissed from her job at the US embassy in London. She brought a further claim alleging victimisation, following the embassy's refusals to re-deploy her. The US Government, however, invoked state immunity and as a result her further claim could not be heard.

Ms Fogarty also argued breach of her right to a fair trial before the European Court of Human Rights, but the European Court found that the imposition of state immunity did not constitute a breach of the *Convention for the Protection of Human Rights and Fundamental Freedoms 1950, Article 6(1)*. However, in *Fogarty* the court emphasised that the proceedings which the claimant sought to bring did not concern the contractual rights of a current embassy employee but related to alleged discrimination in the recruitment process which the court felt might involve sensitive and confidential issues, related to the diplomatic and organisational policy of a foreign State.

By contrast, in *Cudak v Lithuania* (2010) 51 EHRR 15 the ECtHR held that a Lithuanian employee of the Polish embassy in Vilnius's access to the courts had been disproportionately restricted when she was barred from bringing a claim for unfair dismissal in the context of alleged sexual harassment by a member of the diplomatic staff. The ECtHR noted that the 1991 Draft Articles, on which the United Nations Convention on Jurisdictional Immunities of States and their Property 2004 was based, specifically excluded a state's employment contracts with the staff of its diplomatic missions abroad from the operation of state immunity rules, and as the claimant's functions were not closely related to the exercise of governmental authority her case did not come within the exceptions to that exception.

It should be noted that parties can waive state immunity by acts of submission, which include instituting proceedings or intervening in or taking any step in proceedings (except such steps as are necessary to claim immunity) (*State Immunity Act 1978, s 2)*.

1.127 *Illegal contracts/conduct*

As a matter of general law, illegality bars a claim based on a contract which was illegal when it was formed or which became illegal through its performance.

Illegality can in certain circumstances constitute a bar to discrimination, but the threshold for illegality in this context is a high one and the general rules relating to contractual illegality are not determinative. In order for illegality to be an effective bar, it is necessary for the claim to be clearly and inextricably connected with the illegal conduct.

In *Hall v Woolston Hall Leisure Ltd* [2001] ICR 99, an employee claimed that she was dismissed because of her pregnancy, contrary to *SDA 1975, s 6(2)(b)*. The tribunal upheld her claim but the Court of Appeal was subsequently charged with considering whether the claim failed as a result of the illegality of the employment contract. On the facts, the court found that the employee had turned a blind eye to her employer defrauding the Inland Revenue by failing to deduct tax and national insurance. The court stated that, in a discrimination claim relating to a dismissal, the employee must to some extent rely on a contract of employment. However, the employee's complaint was not so closely connected with or inextricably bound up with the employee's acquiescence in her employer's defrauding of the Inland Revenue that to award compensation would be to condone her illegal conduct. Accordingly, the employee was entitled to bring the sex discrimination claim.

By contrast, in a race discrimination case (*Vakante v Addey & Stanhope School* [2004] EWCA Civ 1065, [2004] 4 All ER 1056, [2005] ICR 231), the claim was found to be inextricably linked to the illegality. The employee was a Croatian asylum seeker who had been granted asylum in the UK on terms that he could not take up employment without the consent of the Home Office. He obtained a position as a trainee teacher after misrepresenting his immigration status, and his employer was permitted to rely on the defence of illegality in respect of his dismissal. The court held that to find otherwise would have been to condone the employee's illegal conduct in misrepresenting his immigration status.

1.128 BURDEN OF PROOF

Introduction

The burden of proof is extremely important in discrimination cases. As Mummery LJ stated in *Madarassy v Nomura International plc* [2007] ICR 867, [2007] IRLR 246, para 12:

> 'There is probably no other area of the civil law in which the burden of proof plays a larger part than in discrimination cases . . . Most cases turn on the accumulation of multiple findings of primary fact, from which the court or tribunal is invited to draw an inference of a discriminatory explanation of those facts. It is vital that, as far as possible, the law on the burden of proof applied by the fact-finding body is clear and certain'.

Under UK law, the task of proving a discrimination claim lies initially on the claimant. However, provided the employee can demonstrate what is called a 'prima facie case', the burden will shift to the respondent to prove, on the balance of probabilities, that its treatment of the claimant was not discriminatory. The manner in which, and the circumstances in which, this shift occurs is not always straightforward: *King v Great Britain-China Centre* [1992] ICR 516.

1.129 EU law

On 15 December 1997 the Council of the EU adopted *Directive 97/80/EC* on the burden of proof in cases of discrimination based on sex ('the *Burden of Proof Directive*'). The Directive was adopted under the Social Chapter, which did not cover the United Kingdom at that time. The Directive was subsequently extended to the United Kingdom with effect from 13 July 1998 by *Directive 98/52/EC* (OJ L205, 22 July 1998, p 66).

The *Burden of Proof Directive, Article 4(1)* required the United Kingdom, on or before 22 July 2001, to take any measures necessary to ensure that:

> ' . . . when persons who consider themselves wronged because the principle of equal treatment has not been applied to them establish, before a court or other competent legal authority, facts from which it may be presumed that there has been direct or indirect discrimination, it shall be for the respondent to prove that there has been no breach of the principle of equal treatment'.

Council Directive 2000/78/EC ('*the Framework Directive*'), *Council Directive 2000/43/EC* ('*the Race Directive*') and *Council Directive 2006/54/EC* ('*the Equal Treatment Directive*') all contain identical provisions at *Article 10(1)*, *Article 4(1)* and *Article 19(1)* respectively.

1.130 UK law

The *EqA 2010, s 136* provides for a uniform reversal of the burden of proof in all discrimination claims across all protected characteristics. It applies to all proceedings relating to a contravention of *EqA 2010*, including a breach of an 'equality clause or rule' (defined in *s 212* as the clauses and rules established in relation to sex equality and maternity equality by *ss 66, 67, 73, and 75*).

The substance is contained in *s 136(2) and (3)*:

> '(2) If there are facts from which the court could decide, in the absence of any other explanation, that a person (A) contravened the provision concerned, the court must hold that the contravention occurred.
>
> (3) But subsection (2) does not apply if A shows that A did not contravene the provision'.

'The court' is defined in *s 136(6)* as including an employment tribunal, amongst other tribunals.

The burden of proof test under *EqA 2010* has not changed in any material respect from that contained in the previous legislation, although the language used is slightly different (see *SDA 1975, s 63A; RRA 1976, s 54A; DDA 1995, s 17A(1C); SOR 2003, reg 29; RBR 2003, reg 29*; and *AR 2006, reg 37*). As such, previous case law should continue to apply.

However, *EqA 2010* did remove a number of anomalies. As the *Explanatory Notes to the EqA 2010* make clear, this provision has the effect of extending the statutory reversal of the burden of proof to cases which the old provisions did not cover. As such, claims in respect of race discrimination relating to colour and nationality, victimisation on grounds of race, non-work disability discrimination, and sex discrimination relating to the exercise of public functions, will now benefit from a statutory reversal of the burden of proof.

1.131 The statutory burden of proof

General principles: the two-stage process

Both the old and new provisions contemplate a two-stage process. At stage 1, the claimant is required to prove facts from which the tribunal could conclude, in the absence of an adequate explanation, that the respondent has committed an act of unlawful discrimination. If the claimant is able to satisfy this evidential burden, the evidential burden moves to the respondent for stage 2. At stage 2 the respondent is required to explain the basis of the alleged act and, in particular, to demonstrate that it was not discriminatory.

1.132 *Direct discrimination*

What the claimant needs to prove: Stage 1

This means, in direct discrimination cases, that the claimant will be required to prove, at stage 1, facts from which the tribunal could conclude, in the absence of any other explanation, that:

(a) in circumstances relevant for the purposes of any provision of *EqA 2010* (for example, in relation to employment),

(b) the alleged discriminator has treated the claimant less favourably than he treats or would treat others; and

(c) has done so because of a protected characteristic (see, by analogy, *Igen (Formerly Leeds Careers Guidance) v Wong* [2005] ICR 931, at paras 28 and 29).

This is known as a 'prima facie' case.

What the respondent needs to show: Stage 2

1.133 If the claimant has established the 'prima facie' case, the tribunal must consider whether the respondent has provided sufficient evidence to discharge the burden of proving, on the balance of probabilities, that the treatment of the claimant was 'in no sense whatsoever' because of a protected characteristic (*Barton v Investec Securities Ltd* [2003] ICR 1205).

1.134 *Judicial guidance*

The essential judicial guidance on the application of the statutory burden of proof provisions is contained in the decisions of the Court of Appeal in *Igen v Wong* and *Madarassy v Nomura International plc* [2007] EWCA Civ 33, [2007] ICR 867, [2007] IRLR 246 and by the EAT in *Barton v Investec*. *Madarassy* should be read in conjunction with the decisions of the Court of Appeal in two further cases, heard and decided at the same time, namely *Appiah v Bishop Douglass Roman Catholic High School* [2007] EWCA Civ 10, [2007]

ICR 897, [2007] IRLR 264 and *Brown v London Borough of Croydon* [2007] ICR 909, [2007] IRLR 259. These cases deal with the statutory reversal provisions in the old legislation, but there is no reason to think that they will not apply equally to the new regime.

The 'Barton' guidance

1.135 The most significant early case on the application of the statutory burden of proof provisions in direct discrimination cases was the sex discrimination case of *Barton v Investec Securities Ltd* [2003] ICR 1205. In *Barton* the EAT (Judge Ansell presiding) gave guidance as to how a tribunal should approach the task of applying the statutory burden of proof provisions, as follows:

'(1) Pursuant to section 63A of the Sex Discrimination Act 1975, it is for the Applicant who complains of sex discrimination to prove on the balance of probabilities facts from which the Tribunal could conclude, in the absence of an adequate explanation, that the Respondents have committed an act of discrimination against the Applicant which is unlawful by virtue of Part 2 or which by virtue of section 41 or 42 SDA is to be treated as having been committed against the Applicant. These are referred to below as "such facts".

(2) If the Applicant does not prove such facts he or she will fail.

(3) It is important to bear in mind in deciding whether the Applicant has proved such facts that it is unusual to find direct evidence of sex discrimination. Few employers would be prepared to admit such discrimination, even to themselves. In some cases the discrimination will not be an intention but merely based on the assumption that "he or she would not have fitted in".

(4) In deciding whether the Applicant has proved such facts, it is important to remember that the outcome at this stage of the analysis by the Tribunal will therefore usually depend on what inferences it is proper to draw from the primary facts found by the Tribunal.

(5) It is important to note the word is "could". At this stage the Tribunal does not have to reach a definitive determination that such facts would lead it to the conclusion that there was an act of unlawful discrimination. At this stage a Tribunal is looking at the primary facts proved by the Applicant to see what inferences of secondary fact could be drawn from them.

(6) These inferences can include, in appropriate cases, any inferences that it is just and equitable to draw in accordance with section 74(2)(b) of the Sex Discrimination Act from an evasive or equivocal reply to a questionnaire or any other questions that fall within section 74(2) of the Sex Discrimination Act see *Hinks v Riva Systems* EAT/501/96.

(7) Likewise, the Tribunal must decide whether any provision of any relevant code of practice is relevant and if so, take it into account in determining such facts pursuant to section 56A(10) SDA. This means that inferences may also be drawn from any failure to comply with any relevant code of practice.

(8) Where the applicant has proved facts from which inferences could be drawn that the Respondents have treated the Applicant less favourably on the grounds of sex, then the burden of proof moves to the respondent.

(9) It is then for the respondent to prove that he did not commit, or as the case may be, is not to be treated as having committed that act.

(10) To discharge that burden it is necessary for the respondent to prove, on the balance of probabilities, that the treatment was in no sense whatsoever on the grounds of sex, since "no discrimination whatsoever" is compatible with the Burden of Proof Directive.

(11) That requires a Tribunal to assess not merely whether the respondent has proved an explanation for the facts from which such inferences can be drawn,

but further that it is adequate to discharge the burden of proof on the balance of probabilities that sex was not any part of the reasons for the treatment in question.

(12) Since the facts necessary to prove an explanation would normally be in the possession of the respondent, a Tribunal would normally expect cogent evidence to discharge that burden of proof. In particular the Tribunal will need to examine carefully explanations for failure to deal with the questionnaire procedure and/or code of practice.'

This guidance was subsequently approved, with modifications, by the Court of Appeal in *Igen v Wong* (see below). A tribunal is not required, however, to set out this guidance or to go through it paragraph by paragraph in its decision (*Igen v Wong*, para 16).

Igen v Wong

1.136 *Igen (Formerly Leeds Careers Guidance) v Wong* [2005] ICR 931, and the other cases with which it was joined, concerned sex and race discrimination, although it is clear from the judgment that the Court of Appeal (Peter Gibson LJ, giving the judgment of the court) also had in mind the burden of proof provisions in the other pieces of domestic legislation then in force. According to the Court of Appeal the correct approach to the application of the statutory burden of proof was as follows (references in brackets to paragraphs are to paragraphs of the court's judgment):

(a) the statutory amendments changed the law prior to the introduction of the *Burden of Proof Directive* (as laid down in *King v Great Britain-China Centre* [1992] ICR 516 and *Glasgow City Council v Zafar* [1998] ICR 120), in that, if stage 2 is reached, and the respondent's explanation is inadequate, it is not merely legitimate, but necessary for the employment tribunal to conclude that the complaint should be upheld (para 18);

(b) in applying the burden of proof provisions tribunals must obtain their main guidance from the statutory language itself (para 16);

(c) at stage 1, as set out at **1.132**, the claimant is required to prove facts from which the tribunal could conclude, in the absence of an adequate explanation, that there has been discrimination by the respondent (paras 28 and 29);

(d) in considering what inferences may be drawn from the primary facts, the tribunal must assume that the respondent has no adequate explanation for those facts (paras 21 and 22);

(e) to discharge the burden at stage 2 the respondent is required to prove, on the balance of probabilities, that the treatment established by the claimant at stage 1 was not on the ground of sex, race, etc (Annex).

Case law post-Igen and pre-Madarassy

1.137 Following *Igen v Wong* the EAT considered the effect of *Igen* on a number of occasions. It was evident from these cases that there were a number of practical issues concerning how the burden of proof provisions should operate in practice which had been left unresolved. The most significant decisions were the following: *Network-Rail Infrastructure Ltd v Griffiths-Henry* [2006] IRLR 865, EAT (Elias J) decision of 23 May 2006; *NUT v Watson*, decision of EAT (Elias J) of 13 June 2006; *Li v Atkins & Gregory Ltd*, [2006] All ER (D) 26 (Oct), EAT; *Fox v Rangecroft* [2006] EWCA Civ 1112 of 13 July 2006; *Laing v Manchester City Council* [2006] IRLR 748, EAT (Elias J) of 28 July 2006; and *Fernandez v Office of the Parliamentary Commissioner for Administration and the Health Service Comr*, [2006] All ER (D) 460 (Jul), EAT. These decisions illustrated some of the practical difficulties which tribunals were having with the application of the burden of proof provisions. They were cited with approval by Mummery LJ for the court in *Madarassy v Nomura* (para 14).

In *B v BA* [2006] EWCA Civ 132, [2006] IRLR 471, a case concerning discrimination on the ground of gender reassignment, the Court of Appeal held, importantly, that the approach reflected in *SDA 1975, s 63A* may be relevant at an interlocutory stage as well as at the final hearing. The claimant contended that she had been excluded from consultancy work following her transition from male to female. The respondent successfully resisted disclosure of documents relating to work not allocated to her, on the basis that it was for the claimant to particularise her case. The claimant failed to establish her sex discrimination claim at the final tribunal hearing. Despite the tribunal's decision being upheld by the EAT (HHJ Ansell QC), the respondent's approach was criticised on appeal by Lord Justice Hooper, with whom the other Lords Justices agreed. Allowing the appeal against the dismissal of her claim of sex discrimination, he noted (paras 51–55) that it was important that tribunals bear in mind the objectives of the shifting burden of proof at the pre-hearing, as well as at the hearing, stage: 'employers should not be permitted to escape the provisions of *section 63A* [of *SDA 1975*] by leaving it to the employee to prove her case'. A respondent who fails to make documentary evidence available at a preliminary stage may, therefore, be unable to satisfy stage 2 of the process if the burden shifts.

B v BA exemplifies the difficulties faced by tribunals in dealing with the burden of proof in complex cases, and of balancing the significant cost and burden imposed on a respondent against the overriding objective. One way of dealing with the evidential burden in a complicated case may be by way of preparation by the respondent of a 'Scott' schedule, summarising, for example, work not allocated to the claimant and the reason for the non-allocation: the Court of Appeal in *B v BA* suggested this should have taken place. This approach, however, is not without its own difficulties. At a further appeal by the claimant in *B v BA* against case management orders made by the tribunal managing the proceedings after remission by the Court of Appeal, the EAT (HHJ Burke QC, sitting alone) on 28 June 2007 indicated that, once the claimant had such a schedule, it was legitimate to require her (in effect) to particularise her case through service of a counter-schedule. The EAT commented that:

> 'it is common in many types of litigation where complex issues of fact arise that 1) one party, usually the party bearing the burden of proof, is required to draw up a schedule and to set out its case in brief as to each item on that schedule and 2) thereafter the opposing party is required to set out either on that schedule or in a separate counter schedule its response to each such item. This exercise is a normal and standard aspect of case management in cases appropriate for a schedule . . . It does not involve any reversal of the burden of proof or any injustice to the party required to respond'.

Madarassy v Nomura

1.138 A number of the practical issues raised in the post-*Igen* case law were resolved by the Court of Appeal in *Madarassy v Nomura, Appiah* and *Brown v Croydon*. After approving *Igen v Wong*, Mummery LJ, giving the judgment of the Court, indicated that the value of *Madarassy*, taken together with *Appiah* and *Brown v Croydon*, was in 'showing how the burden of proof should work'. In particular, the court clarified the following important practical issues concerning the operation of the burden of proof (references to paragraphs are to paragraphs of the various judgments of the Court of Appeal):

(a) proof of a difference in status and a detriment at stage 1 is not sufficient to shift the burden to the respondent:

> 'The bare facts of a difference in status and a difference in treatment only indicate a possibility of discrimination. They are not, without more, sufficient material from which a tribunal 'could conclude' that, on the balance of probabilities, the respondent had committed an unlawful act of discrimination'
> (*Madarassy v Nomura*, paragraph 56);

(b) 'could conclude' at stage 1 means that a reasonable tribunal 'could properly conclude' from all the evidence before it. This includes all relevant evidence, including evidence adduced by the respondent. It would include evidence as to whether the act complained of occurred at all; evidence as to any comparators relied on by the claimant; or (controversially) evidence as to the reasons for the less favourable treatment (*Madarassy v Nomura*, paras 57, 67–72; *Appiah*, para 43). So, to adopt one example suggested by Elias J in *Laing v Manchester City Council* (above), if an employer withheld money from a number of employees, one of whom was black, for working to rule, and did not withhold money from those who were not working to rule, it would be open to the employer to adduce evidence at stage 1 that many white employees had also had money withheld. This would not be 'explanation', but 'factual evidence presenting a fuller picture of the material facts and putting the evidence of the claimant in context' (*Laing* (above), para 62);

(c) while there is a distinction between 'fact' and 'explanation', these categories are not hermetically sealed, however, and there is plainly a relationship between them (*Appiah*, para 43, approving *Laing* (above), para 68, in which Elias J noted that 'facts will frequently explain, at least in part, why someone has acted as they have'). It will not always be easy, in the circumstances, to tell when evidence is 'fact' and when it is 'explanation'. So, for example, if an employee complains that she was shouted at by her line manager when pregnant, is the fact that he shouted at everyone in his department, male or female, pregnant or non-pregnant, an 'explanation' for prima facie less favourable treatment, admissible only at stage 2, or 'factual evidence putting the evidence of the claimant into context', admissible at stage 1?

(d) although the application of the statutory burden of proof provisions involves a two-stage process, the tribunal is not required, in practice, to hear the evidence and argument in two stages. It will have heard all the evidence in the case before it embarks on the two-stage analysis. Additionally, although it will generally be good practice to apply the two-stage test there will be cases, particularly where a hypothetical comparator is relied on, where it may be appropriate for the tribunal to move directly to stage 2. Again, however, it is not required to do so (*Brown v Croydon*, para 41; *Madarassy v Nomura*, paras 80–84; applying the reasoning of Lord Nicholls in *Shamoon v Chief Constable of the Royal Ulster Constabulary* [2003] ICR 337, paras 7–12).

Subsequent application

1.139 The EAT (Slade J) confirmed in *Hammonds LLP v Mwitta* UKEAT/0026/10 that the facts at stage 1 must be such that the tribunal could conclude that there *had* been an act of discrimination, not merely that there *could have* been; evidence of a disparity in treatment is not enough if there is no prima facie case that the claimant's race was the reason for her treatment. In *Beck v Canadian Imperial Bank of Commerce* (2010) UKEAT/0141/10/RN, [2011] 2 CMLR 82, however, it was held that the inclusion of the word 'younger' in a briefing to recruit a replacement employee, on advice and surviving several drafts, could in itself be enough to reverse the burden of proof in an age discrimination claim.

Reasonableness

1.140 One issue not fully resolved by the case law is the issue of the extent to which unreasonable behaviour on the part of a respondent will be sufficient to satisfy stage 1 such that explanation from the respondent is required. In *Bahl v Law Society* [2004] EWCA Civ 1070, [2004] NLJR 1292, [2004] IRLR 799, a case decided on facts occurring before the changes to the burden of proof, the Court of Appeal (Peter Gibson LJ, giving the judgment of the court) emphasised that unreasonable treatment does not of itself justify an inference of discrimination, although unexplained unreasonable treatment may justify the drawing of such an inference.

It is not clear whether the reasoning in *Bahl* is affected by the introduction of the statutory burden of proof. *Bahl* was cited with approval by the Court of Appeal in *Madarassy v Nomura* (para 14), although the court was not required to consider its application to the specific facts of the case. The facts of *Igen v Wong* suggest, however, that unreasonable conduct, at least where it is 'strikingly unreasonable' (para 46) may be sufficient to cause the burden of proof to shift. Nevertheless, the Court of Appeal in *Igen v Wong* did caution tribunals generally against 'too readily inferring unlawful discrimination on a prohibited ground merely from unreasonable behaviour where there is no evidence of other discriminatory behaviour on such ground' (para 51).

For a post-*Madarassy* example of unreasonable behaviour being held to satisfy stage 1, see *Birmingham City Council v Samuels* UKEAT/0208/07 (McMullen J).

1.141 *Indirect discrimination and duty to make reasonable adjustments*

The application of the two-stage test appears to have given rise to fewer problems in indirect discrimination cases and cases of alleged failure to make reasonable adjustments for disability. This is, no doubt, because the statutory components of these claims themselves contemplate a multi-stage approach, with the respondent required, where appropriate, to establish justification.

What the claimant needs to prove

1.142 In indirect discrimination cases the claimant is required to prove disparate adverse impact at stage 1 (*Nelson v Carillion Services Ltd* [2003] EWCA Civ 544, [2003] ICR 1256, [2003] IRLR 428) (Simon Brown LJ, with whom the other Lords Justices agreed); *Chaudhary v Secretary of State for Health* [2007] EWCA Civ 789, paras 66, 75 (Mummery LJ, giving the judgment of the court).

In 'reasonable adjustments' cases Elias J has suggested (*Project Management Institute v Latif* [2007] IRLR 579, para 45) that the claimant is required, at stage 1:

(a) to establish the provision, criterion or practice relied on; and

(b) to demonstrate substantial disadvantage.

The burden then shifts to the respondent to show that no adjustment or further adjustment should be made.

Equal pay

1.143 The application of the two-stage test appears, in practice, however, to have given rise to greater problems in the field of equal pay. The claimant must identify the comparator group and produce the statistical evidence to show an appreciable difference in pay for jobs of equal value (*Abbott v Cheshire and Wirral Partnership NHS Trust* [2006] EWCA Civ 523, [2006] ICR 1267, [2006] IRLR 546, para 17 (Keen LJ, with whom the other Lords Justice agreed)). In *Bailey v Home Office* [2005] EWCA Civ 327, [2005] ICR 1057, [2005] IRLR 369 Peter Gibson and Waller LJJ, with both of whom Sir Martin Nourse agreed, doubted whether claimants in equal pay litigation bore the burden of demonstrating that the relevant difference in pay had a disparate adverse impact on women, and, therefore, whether *Carillion* was appropriately applied in this type of case (paras 9, 37). They concluded that, in any event, *EqPA 1970, s 1(3)*—now *EqA 2010, s 69*—did not demand a high threshold for the establishment of disparity. Waller LJ suggested (para 39) that where a difference in pay was established, and statistics seemed to indicate a *possibility* of a disproportionate adverse impact, the burden should shift. In *Armstrong v Newcastle Upon Tyne NHS Hospital Trust* [2005] EWCA Civ 1608, [2006] IRLR 124, however, Arden LJ endorsed *Carillion* and noted that the burden shifted where the figures *demonstrated* a disproportionate adverse impact (para 103).

Pre-employment enquiries about disability and health

1.144 The *EqA 2010* introduces a new protection prohibiting an employer from asking pre-employment health questions, save in limited circumstances (*EqA 2010, s 60(1)*). Asking a prohibited question will not, in itself, amount to actionable discrimination. However, if the employer subsequently does not shortlist the employee for a role, for example, and the applicant subsequently brings a direct disability discrimination claim, the burden of proof will automatically pass to the respondent to show that it did not discriminate. See further **Disability discrimination (3)**.

1.145 OCCUPATIONAL REQUIREMENTS

The *EqA 2010* contains a number of exceptions permitting discrimination that would otherwise be prohibited. One of these is the exception for occupational requirements.

The *EqA 2010* has created a unified occupational requirement exception across all protected characteristics (*EqA 2010, Sch 9, paras 1–6*). *Paragraph 1* is of general application and provides a defence for an employer to a claim of discrimination if he can demonstrate that the requirement to have a particular protected characteristic:

(a) is an occupational requirement,

(b) the application of the requirement is a proportionate means of achieving a legitimate aim, and

(c) the person to whom the employer applies the requirement does not meet it (or the employer has reasonable grounds for not being satisfied that the person meets it) (*EqA 2010, Sch 9, para 1*).

The exception applies to recruitment, opportunity for promotion, training and other benefits during employment, and dismissal. However, it does not apply to the terms and conditions offered or to other types of detriment in employment including, importantly, victimisation and harassment (*EqA 2010, Sch 9, para 1(2)*).

The exception for occupational requirements also extends to contract work, partnerships, office-holders (*EqA 2010, Sch 9, para 1(2)*), to the provision of vocational training (*EqA 2010, Sch 12, para 4*) and to employment service providers (*EqA 2010, Sch 9, para 5*).

This unified exception absorbs the pre-October 2010 law on genuine occupational requirements (GORs) (*RRA 1976, s 4A; SOR 2003, reg 7; RBR 2003, reg 7; AR 2006, reg 8*) and genuine occupational qualifications (GOQs) (*SDA 1975, ss 7–7B; RRA 1976, s 5)*. There is no longer a legal concept of a GOQ under the *EqA 2010*.

The *EqA 2010* has extended the scope of the occupational requirement exception by its application to disability, sex, gender reassignment, colour and nationality. Under the pre-October 2010 legislation there was no GOR exception under the *DDA 1995* and the *SDA 1975* only provided for GOQ, not GOR, exceptions in relation to sex.

1.146 Application of the occupational requirement exception

In certain circumstances, it will be lawful for an employer to require a job applicant or worker to have (or not have) a particular protected characteristic, provided certain conditions are met. In these situations, the employer can seek to rely on the occupational requirement exception.

The occupational requirement exception provides that a person will not contravene the *EqA 2010* in applying a requirement that a person has a particular protected characteristic when: (a) the requirement is an occupational requirement; (b) the application of the requirement is a proportionate means of achieving a legitimate aim; and (c) the person to whom the requirement is applied does not meet the requirement or the person applying the requirement has reasonable grounds for not being satisfied that he meets it (*EqA 2010, Sch 9, para 1(1)*). As with any exception, the *EHRC Employment Code* states that the exception should be interpreted narrowly (*para 13.1*).

An employer should not 'have a blanket policy of applying an occupation requirement exception' and should reassess a role whenever it becomes vacant to determine whether a particular requirement still satisfies the statutory conditions (*EHRC Employment Code, para 13.20*). If an employer fails to comply with the statutory conditions listed above, it is likely to result in a claim for direct discrimination.

1.147 *Occupational requirement*

The pre-October 2010 legislation referred to a 'genuine' occupational qualification or requirement (*SDA 1975, s 7, RRA 1976, s 4A; SOR 2003, reg 7; RBR 2003, reg 7; AR 2006, reg 8*). This language has not been replicated under the *EqA 2010*, nor has the stipulation that the requirement must be a 'genuine *and determining* requirement'. However, the *Explanatory Notes to the EqA 2010* state that the new unified provision was intended to replicate the effect of the pre-existing exceptions (*para 789*). The removal of these words is therefore not likely to have a significant impact: an employer will still need to demonstrate that the occupational requirement is 'genuine' (ie not a sham or a pretext: see *EHRC Employment Code, para 13.7*) and there must be a link between the requirement and the job in question.

The *Explanatory Notes to the EqA 2010* give the following examples where it may be appropriate to rely on the occupational requirement exception:

— the need for authenticity or realism might require someone of a particular race, sex or age for acting roles (for example, a black man to play the part of Othello) or modelling jobs;

— considerations of privacy or decency might require a public changing room or lavatory attendant to be of the same sex as those using the facilities;

— an organisation for deaf people might legitimately employ a deaf person who uses British Sign Language to work as a counsellor to other deaf people whose first or preferred language is BSL.

In *Amnesty International v Ahmed* [2009] IRLR 884 Miss Ahmed, of northern Sudanese ethnic origin, applied for a promotion to the role of 'Sudan researcher' for Amnesty International. Amnesty declined to promote Miss Ahmed as it considered that someone of her ethnic origin would compromise its perceived impartiality (and thus its effectiveness) and would expose Miss Ahmed to safety risks when travelling to Sudan. Miss Ahmed resigned and claimed race discrimination and constructive unfair dismissal. The EAT upheld the tribunal's decision that the non appointment of Miss Ahmed constituted direct discrimination on the grounds of her national/ethnic origins. However, it indicated (although the point was not argued by Amnesty) that a 'genuine occupational requirement' defence may have been available. Whilst this point was not explored in depth, employers facing similar claims should consider relying on *EqA 2010*'s occupational requirement exception when responding to a similar claim.

1.148 *Proportionate means and legitimate aim*

In order to rely on an occupational requirement, an employer must be able to demonstrate that the application of the requirement to have/not have a particular characteristic is a proportionate means of achieving a legitimate aim. These concepts are familiar from objective justification (see **1.83–1.85**).

1.149 *Framework Directive*

In *Wolf v Stadt Frankfurt am Main* the ECJ considered the application of the *Framework Directive, Article 4(1)*, which allows Member States to provide that 'a difference of treatment which is based on a characteristic related to [religion or belief, disability, age or sexual orientation] shall not constitute discrimination where . . . such a characteristic constitutes a genuine and determining occupational requirement, provided that the objective is legitimate and the requirement is proportionate'.

The ECJ held that a maximum recruitment age of 30 for German fire-fighters was lawful under *Article 4(1)*. This was not on the basis that someone over 30 could not do the job, but on the basis that very few officials over 45 could perform fire-fighting activities, and there was a need to ensure that fire-fighters would be able to carry out those duties for a reasonable period after training. The reasoning was that it was a genuine and determining occupational requirement that a fire-fighter have high physical capacities. This is a characteristic related to age. The maximum recruitment age pursued a legitimate objective of maintaining the operational capacity and proper functioning of the fire service. It was proportionate to ensure that the majority of firefighters had the ability to carry out the physically demanding operational duties and to ensure that new recruits would be able to able to carry out those duties for a reasonable period.

This suggests a wide scope for applying the occupational requirement exception. However, the scope of the exception under *Article 4(1)* is wider than under *EqA 2010*, where it is the protected characteristic itself which has to be an occupational requirement, not a characteristic related to the occupational requirement. Therefore the reasoning in Wolf does not apply to the interpretation of the occupational requirements exception under *EqA 2010*.

1.150 *Specific protected characteristics*

In the case of gender reassignment the requirement to have a protected characteristic is to be read as a requirement not to be a transsexual person and in the case of marriage and civil partnership as references to requirements not to be married or in a civil partnership (*EqA 2010, Sch 9, para 1(3)*).

1.151 *Burden of proof*

The *EqA 2010* makes clear that the person seeking to rely on the exception has the burden of proving it (*EqA 2010, Sch 9, para 1(1)*). It is submitted that the tribunals will continue to apply an objective test, where the employer's assessment of the requirements of the job is only one piece of evidence to be taken into account.

1.152 *Job advertisements*

It also seems likely that the advice of the CRE and the EOC under the pre-October 2010 legislation remains good practice, that where an employer, employment agency (or other person able to rely on the exception) believes an occupational requirement applies, the exception should be specified in any job advertisement. This will assist in substantiating the occupational requirement reason in any legal challenge and may also help to avoid the risk that a publisher may refuse to accept the advert (see **1.18**).

1.153 Specific GORs

Specific exceptions also apply in respect of sexual orientation, sex, gender reassignment, marriage and civil partnership in the context of employment for the purposes of an organised religion (*EqA 2010, Sch 9, para 2*; largely replicating *SOR 2003, reg 7* and provisions of the *SDA 1975*) and in the context of work of a particular ethos or nature based on a religion or belief (*EqA 2010, Sch 9, para 3*; largely replicating *RBR 2003, reg 7*). For a further discussion of these provisions see **Gender reassignment (4)**, **Marital status and civil partnership (5)**, **Sex discrimination (8)**, **Disability (3)**, **Sexual orientation (9)** and **Religion and belief (7)**.)

Common concepts

1.154 POSITIVE ACTION

Introduction

Positive action is a limited exemption to the general rule that discrimination is unlawful in the UK, whatever its motivation. Pre-*EqA 2010* legislation has for some time allowed certain specified action to be taken to promote under-represented groups in the workplace, stopping short of actual discrimination in their favour, and these provisions survive into *EqA 2010* and are broadened. Beyond this, a provision of *EqA 2010* which comes into force in April 2011 will permit an employer, for the first time to prefer (in limited circumstances) a candidate with a protected characteristic to a candidate without that characteristic in connection with recruitment or promotion.

1.155 EU law

EU law, under *Directive 2000/43/EC, Article 5, Directive 2000/78/EC, Article 6* and *Directive 2006/54/EC, Article 3*, allows Member States to maintain or adopt measures to prevent or compensate for disadvantages linked to a protected characteristic, 'with a view to ensuring full equality in practice'. *Directives 2000/43/EC* and *2000/78/EC* refer to 'specific' measures, but this does not appear to produce any significant difference from *Directive 2006/54/EC.*

The distinction between lawful positive action and unlawful positive discrimination has been considered by the ECJ in *Kalanke v Freie Hansestadt Bremen: C-450/93* [1995] ECR I–3051, [1996] All ER (EC) 66, [1996] 1 CMLR 175; *Marschall v Land Nordrhein-Westfalen: C-409/95* [1997] ECR I-6363, [1997] All ER (EC) 865, [1998] 1 CMLR 547; *Re Badeck (Landesanwait beim Staatsgerichtshof des Landes Hessen and Heissischer Ministerprasident intervening): C-158/97* [2000] ECR I-1875, [2000] IRLR 432; *Abrahamsson and Anderson v Fogelqvist: C-407/98* [2000] ECR I-5539, [2000] IRLR 732; *Lommers v Minister van Landbouw, Natuurbeheer en Visserij: C-476/99* [2002] ECR I-2891,[2002] IRLR 430.

For instance, in *Lommers* the ECJ held that a Dutch policy offering subsidised childcare to female employees in order to address under-representation was lawful provided that the same facilities were offered to men taking care of children by themselves or in exceptional circumstances. Similarly, in *Badeck*, it was held not to be unlawful to recruit a female candidate in preference to an equally qualified male candidate provided the preference was not automatic and there was some assessment of the specific personal situations of both.

The case law was reviewed in *Briheche v Ministre de l'Interieur* [2004] ECR I-8807 in the context of sex discrimination, the ECJ summarising at [23]:

> 'A measure which is intended to give priority in promotion to women in sectors of the public service must be regarded as compatible with Community law if it does not automatically and unconditionally give priority to women when women and men are equally qualified, and the candidatures are the subject of an objective assessment which takes account of the specific personal situations of all candidates'.

1.156 UK law before Equality Act 2010

Job-related training and encouragement

Before *EqA 2010*, discrimination legislation permitted positive action in relation to 'particular work' in the form of:

(i) providing access to facilities for training to fit a person for that work; and

(ii) encouraging a person 'to take advantage of opportunities for doing that work'.

RRA 1976, s 37 allowed such steps to be taken in favour of persons of a particular racial group where it reasonably appeared to the person taking the steps that, at any time in the 12 months prior to the positive action being taken, the number of persons of that racial group doing the particular work in Great Britain was zero or was small in comparison with the percentage of the population of Great Britain being from that group.

RRA 1976, s 38 permitted an employer to take such steps, in relation to work in his employment at a particular establishment, if the number of people from that group doing that work at that establishment was zero or was small compared with the proportion of employees at that establishment, or of the population of the area where the employer normally recruited for employment there, being from that group.

SDA 1975, ss 47–48 made equivalent provision in relation to sex. *Section 47(3)* specifically allowed training bodies to make special provision to train persons with a special need of such training by virtue of a period spent discharging domestic or family responsibilities to the exclusion of regular full-time employment.

RBR 2003, reg 25, SOR 2003, reg 26, and AR 2006, reg 29 were less specific in setting out the circumstances in which positive action was lawful; all allowed equivalent steps to be taken where it reasonably appeared to the person doing the act that those steps would prevent or compensate for disadvantages linked to the protected characteristic suffered by persons with that characteristic doing the work or likely to take up the work.

RRA 1976, s 35 similarly permitted acts to be done to afford persons of a particular racial group access to facilities or services to 'meet the special needs of persons of that group in regard to their education, training or welfare, or any ancillary benefits'. The Court of Appeal confirmed that the scope of the permissible action did not extend to making offers of employment (*Lambeth London Borough Council v Commission for Racial Equality* [1990] ICR 768, [1990] IRLR 231). This exemption was unqualified by the need to show that the racial group in question was under-represented within the employer's workforce.

1.157 *Other positive action*

Other than the above, the scope for positive action under the old legislation was limited. *RRA 1976, s 36* provided an exemption for the provision of education or training or 'ancillary benefits' where the employer or training provider believes the person will leave Great Britain after the period of employment of training in question.

In addition, however, the provisions concerning discrimination on grounds of disability or maternity/pregnancy made it unlawful to discriminate against people *with* those characteristics, but did not impose a reverse obligation not to discriminate against people *without* them. As such, those provisions could produce effects akin to positive discrimination.

For instance, *DDA 1995, s 4A* required employers to make positive adjustments to accommodate a disabled employee. That duty extended, in limited circumstances, to considering creating a new role where a person could not perform their current role as a result of disability (*Southampton City College v Randall* [2006] IRLR 18). See **Disability discrimination (3)**.

AR 2006 permitted direct discrimination on the grounds of age if it could be justified as a proportionate means of achieving a legitimate end, leaving some doubt about whether a measure amounting to positive action could be justified in this way, or whether the specific inclusion of a provision relating to positive action in *reg 29* had the effect of excluding such arguments.

With regard to pregnancy and maternity, the *Management of Health and Safety at Work Regulations 1999* required (and still require) an employer to take positive steps to protect its pregnant workers, for example by undertaking a risk assessment and making any necessary modifications to her working conditions (see **Sex discrimination (8)**). This may be viewed as treating the pregnant worker more favourably than her non-pregnant colleague, but is an attempt to remove the disadvantage the pregnant employee may otherwise be under, akin to the effect of *DDA 1995* in respect of disabled workers. A similar rationale informs the duty under the *Maternity and Paternity Leave etc Regulations 1999 (SI 1999/3312)* to give preferential treatment to an employee on or returning from maternity leave in a redundancy situation, by appointing her to a vacant role for which she is qualified in preference to a colleague who is also at risk of redundancy, and may be better skilled for the role, but is not on maternity leave (see Sex discrimination (8)).

1.158 Equality Act 2010

EqA 2010 standardises the position across the protected characteristics and enlarges the scope of permissible positive action. It contains two provisions relating to positive action: *s 158*, which allows a person to take action to encourage the advancement of disadvantaged groups, and *s 159*, which with effect from April 2011 will allow a person in certain circumstances to favour a person with a protected characteristic over a person without that characteristic in relation to recruitment or promotion.

Paragraphs 525 and 529 of the *Explanatory Notes to the EqA 2010* state that *s 158* and *s 159* 'extend what is possible to the extent permitted by European law, and apply in relation to all protected characteristics'.

1.159 *Positive action generally: s 158*

EqA 2010, s 158 provides:

'(1) This section applies if a person (P) reasonably thinks that:
   (a) persons who share a protected characteristic suffer a disadvantage connected to the characteristic,
   (b) persons who share a protected characteristic have needs that are different from the needs of persons who do not share it, or
   (c) participation in an activity by persons who share a protected characteristic is disproportionately low.

(2) This Act does not prohibit P from taking any action which is a proportionate means of achieving the aim of:
   (a) enabling or encouraging persons who share the protected characteristic to overcome or minimise that disadvantage,
   (b) meeting those needs, or
   (c) enabling or encouraging persons who share the protected characteristic to participate in that activity.

(3) Regulations may specify action, or descriptions of action, to which subsection (2) does not apply.

(4) This section does not apply to:
   (a) action within section 159(3), or
   (b) anything that is permitted by virtue of section 104.

(5) If section 104(7) is repealed by virtue of section 105, this section will not apply to anything that would have been so permitted but for the repeal.

(6) This section does not enable P to do anything that is prohibited by or under an enactment other than this Act.'

In other words, for a positive action measure to be lawful:

(i) the person implementing the measure must reasonably think that one of the criteria in *s 158(1)* is satisfied;

(ii) the measure must advance one of the three aims listed in *s 158(2)*; and

(iii) the measure must be proportionate to that aim.

Section 158(4) excludes from the scope of the section: (1) matters relating to the selection of candidates by political parties, and (2) positive action falling under *s 159*. *Section 158(5)* clarifies the position in relation to single-sex shortlists, so that if such shortlists are made unlawful by a repeal of *s 104(7)* they will not be permitted under *s 158* instead.

The *Explanatory Notes to the EqA 2010*, at *para 519*, give two examples of permissible positive action:

> 'Having identified that its white male pupils are underperforming at maths, a school could run supplementary maths classes exclusively for them.
>
> An NHS Primary Care Trust identifies that lesbians are less likely to be aware that they are at risk of cervical cancer and less likely to access health services such as national screening programmes. It is also aware that those who do not have children do not know that they are at an increased risk of breast cancer. Knowing this it could decide to establish local awareness campaigns for lesbians on the importance of cancer screening'.

The *EHRC Employment Code*, at *para 12.14*, suggests that the requirement to 'reasonably think' that one of the *s 158(1)* criteria is satisfied does not necessarily require sophisticated statistical data and research, but may simply involve looking at profiles of one's workforce and making enquiries of comparable employers. The Code also makes the point at *12.30* that a positive action measure which continues indefinitely without review may become disproportionate if there is a change in the specific circumstances which justify it.

Because of the limits of this section, employers must be careful that the training or encouragement they provide by way of positive action does not constitute employment or lead automatically to employment. 'On-the-job' training or apprenticeships which amount to employment and not training cannot lawfully form part of an employer's positive action programme.

Section 158 places no *requirement* on any person to minimise a disadvantage or meet a need, so any positive action taken under it is voluntary. Where, however, a person fails to take remedial action even though he knows (or ought to know) that inequalities exist, this may lend support to a discrimination claim arising out of other acts or omissions.

1.160 *Positive action: recruitment and promotion: s 159*

EqA 2010, s 159 permits employers, for the first time, to take positive action measures in the context of recruitment and promotion. 'Recruitment' is defined broadly, so that it includes, for example, offers of partnership, offers of work as a contractor and offers of employment. *Section 159* provides:

> '(1) This section applies if a person (P) reasonably thinks that:
> (a) persons who share a protected characteristic suffer a disadvantage connected to the characteristic, or
> (b) participation in an activity by persons who share a protected characteristic is disproportionately low.
>
> (2) Part 5 (work) does not prohibit P from taking action within subsection (3) with the aim of enabling or encouraging persons who share the protected characteristic to:
> (a) overcome or minimise that disadvantage, or
> (b) participate in that activity.
>
> (3) That action is treating a person (A) more favourably in connection with recruitment or promotion than another person (B) because A has the protected characteristic but B does not.
>
> (4) But subsection (2) applies only if:
> (a) A is as qualified as B to be recruited or promoted,

(b) P does not have a policy of treating persons who share the protected characteristic more favourably in connection with recruitment or promotion than persons who do not share it, and
(c) taking the action in question is a proportionate means of achieving the aim referred to in subsection (2).

(5) 'Recruitment' means a process for deciding whether to:
(a) offer employment to a person,
(b) make contract work available to a contract worker,
(c) offer a person a position as a partner in a firm or proposed firm,
(d) offer a person a position as a member of an LLP or proposed LLP,
(e) offer a person a pupillage or tenancy in barristers' chambers,
(f) take a person as an advocate's devil or offer a person membership of an advocate's stable,
(g) offer a person an appointment to a personal office,
(h) offer a person an appointment to a public office, recommend a person for such an appointment or approve a person's appointment to a public office, or
(i) offer a person a service for finding employment.

(6) This section does not enable P to do anything that is prohibited by or under an enactment other than this Act.'

In other words, if an employer reasonably thinks that a person with a protected characteristic (A) suffers a related disadvantage, or that persons with that characteristic are under-represented in a particular activity, he can treat A more favourably in connection with recruitment or promotion than a person without that characteristic, provided:

(i) A is 'as qualified ' as B to be recruited or promoted;

(ii) there is no policy of treating persons with A's characteristic more favourably than others in recruitment or promotion;

(iii) the more favourable treatment is a proportionate means of enabling persons with A's characteristic to overcome or minimise their disadvantage or participate in the activity in which they are under-represented.

However, if any of those conditions are not satisfied, the employer will have unlawfully discriminated against B by treating A more favourably.

This section appears to be intended to reflect the approach of the ECJ in cases such as *Kalanke v Freie Hansestadt Bremen: C-450/93* [1995] ECR I-3051, [1996] All ER (EC) 66 and *Badeck* [2000] IRLR 432. As such, the requirement in *s 159(4)(b)* that P must not have a policy of treating persons with the protected characteristic more favourably should be understood as requiring that there be no automatic preference in favour of persons with the protected characteristic, and that the individual circumstances should be taken into account.

The phrase 'as qualified' is not defined by the *EqA 2010*, nor does the *EHRC Employment Code* provide any assistance (the provisions on positive action in recruitment and promotion were removed from the Code when *s 159* was not brought into force on 1 October 2010. It remains to be seen whether they will be reinstated). However, government guidance (which is not a statutory code of practice) refers to the notion of two candidates 'of equal merit' and invites employers to take a broad approach to an assessment of the candidates' respective skills and competencies, including their 'overall ability, competence and professional experience together with any relevant formal or academic qualifications, as well as any other qualities required to carry out the particular job' (*Equality Act 2010: What do I need to know? A quick start guide to using positive action in recruitment and promotion*, p 6), rather than an exclusive focus on academic qualifications. This echoes the approach in the draft *EHRC Employment Code* (at *7.20*).

The guidance also provides that higher academic qualifications do not necessarily mean that one candidate is better qualified than another. It gives the example of a male candidate with relevant experience but no academic qualifications being potentially 'of equal merit' to a female candidate who has a relevant degree but little practical experience (at p 7).

When assessing how an employer can show that it '*reasonably thinks*' that there is a group(s) of people with a protected characteristic who are under-represented or who suffer disadvantage, the guidance suggests that the threshold is not high. It states that detailed statistical evidence or research is not required, merely '*some information or evidence*'. The guidance is consistent with the recommendations which appeared in the draft EHRC Employment Code in this regard and in the final *EHRC Employment Code* in relation to *s 158*. Examples given in the guidance include looking at workforce profiles, local or national data eg labour force surveys, making enquires of other comparable employers in the area, and qualitative evidence obtained perhaps from discussions with employees/representatives.

There is no obligation on an employer under *EqA 2010, s 159* to take positive action in the circumstances specified—it is entirely voluntary—and (despite the guidance) there remains uncertainty about how the provisions will apply in practice. Employers who choose to rely on the provisions will face the risk that, if they are found not to fall within the terms of the exception in *s 159*, they will have directly discriminated against the unsuccessful candidate in preferring the successful candidate because of their protected characteristic.

1.161 Codes of Practice

The *EHRC Employment Code*, in *Chapter 12*, gives a number of examples of possible positive action measures under *EqA 2010, s 158*, including shadowing and mentoring schemes, internships and open days, targeted advertising, statements in recruitment advertisements that applications from a particular group are welcomed, training in IT skills, and providing bursaries for training courses. However, as noted above, the provisions on positive action in recruitment and promotion were removed from *EHRC Employment Code* when *s 159* was not brought into force on 1 October 2010. Employers will therefore have to rely on the guidance referred to above. As this is not a statutory code, it does not need to be taken into account by tribunals.

1.162 Forms of treatment analogous to positive action

Since both *EqA 2010* and its predecessor legislation operate so as to render unlawful a number of forms of discrimination in one 'direction' and not the other, this may produce effects akin to positive action. For instance, an employer might discriminate against a person with a disability by failing to make reasonable adjustments, but by making such adjustments does not discriminate against a person for whom no adjustments were necessary. *EqA 2010, s 13(3)* now provides explicitly that there is no direct discrimination against a person (B) who is not disabled simply because A treats a disabled person more favourably than B.

Similarly, *EqA 2010, s 13(6)* provides that, for the purposes of establishing direct discrimination on grounds of sex against a man, no account is to be taken of special treatment afforded to a woman in connection with pregnancy or childbirth.

By *EqA 2010, s 13(4)*, a claim for discrimination because of marriage and civil partnership can only arise where the treatment is because it is B, the claimant, who is married or a civil partner.

In addition, the definition of the protected characteristic of gender reassignment is a 'one-way' definition, although it carries no specific provision along the lines of the above.

The duty to avoid indirect discrimination may also extend to taking positive steps in some circumstances that may be seen as a type of positive action. For instance, to avoid a finding of indirect sex discrimination on the basis that women proportionately bear greater caring responsibilities, an employer will need to accommodate a female employee's flexible working request where this is to allow her to care for a child or dependent relative save where his refusal is objectively justified (see **Sex discrimination (8)**). Where black employees were not represented in senior management, it was indirectly discriminatory on grounds of race to require an applicant for the role of Equal Opportunities Manager to be of senior management grade (*Aina v Employment Service* [2002] DCLD 103D). And to avoid discriminating unlawfully on the grounds of religion or belief, an employer will need to give careful consideration to an observant Christian employee's request not to work Sundays, including rearranging shifts where reasonably practicable (*Copsey v WWB Devon Clays Ltd* [2005] EWCA Civ 932, [2005] ICR 1789, [2005] IRLR 811; (see **Religion and belief (7)**).

1.163 VICARIOUS LIABILITY

Employers can be vicariously liable for acts of discrimination committed by their employees or agents both under UK legislation and at common law.

1.164 Liability for an employee's or agent's acts under EqA 2010

Liability

Previously, the legislation shared common provisions on vicarious liability. Anything done by a person in the course of his employment was treated as if done by both him and his employer, whether or not done with the employer's knowledge and approval (*SDA 1975, s 41; RRA 1976, s 32; DDA 1995, s 58; RBR 2003, reg 22; SOR 2003, reg 22; AR 2006, reg 25*).

These provisions have now been repealed and replaced by *EqA 2010, s 109*, pursuant to which employers and principals are liable for acts of discrimination, harassment and victimisation carried out by their employees in the course of employment or by their agents acting under their authority. It does not matter whether or not the employer or principal knows about or approves of those acts (*s 109(3)*). To give an example, the liability of a principal includes liability for the discriminatory decision of a training provider to terminate a contract (*Lana v Positive Action Training in Housing (London) Ltd* [2001] IRLR 501).

In the employment context, the meaning of 'in the course of employment' is widely construed, relying both on the broad definition of 'employment' under the legislation (see **1.16**) and the fact that the legislation makes clear that an employer will be vicariously liable regardless of whether he condoned or even was aware of the unlawful acts. In the leading case *Jones v Tower Boot Co Ltd* [1997] 2 All ER 406, the Court of Appeal also held that to apply the principle that vicarious liability should not extend to more extreme examples of harassment and discrimination, on the basis they were outside the usual course of employment, would undermine the purpose of the legislation. Not only acts at the workplace, but at work-related social events are covered, for example at post-work drinks and a work leaving party held in a pub (*Chief Constable of Lincolnshire Police v Stubbs* [1999] IRLR 81). Whether the circumstances show that the acts were an extension of employment is largely a question of fact for the tribunal to decide: an offsite 'family fun day' organised by an employer but to which staff were accompanied by family and friends was not an extension of the workplace (*Sidhu v Aerospace Composite Technology Ltd* [2000] EWCA Civ 183, [2000] IRLR 602) and nor were police living quarters (*Waters v Metropolitan Police Comr* [1997] ICR 1073, [1997] IRLR 589).

This test is similar to, but still slightly wider than, the approach taken in respect of common law negligence claims, where an employer will not be liable unless there is a sufficiently close connection between the nature of the employee's job and the unlawful acts carried out by him such that it is fair and just to hold the employer liable (*Lister v Hesley Hall Ltd* [2001] UKHL 22, [2002] 1 AC 215; *Mattis v Pollock (t/a Flamingos Nightclub)* [2003] EWCA Civ

887, [2004] 4 All ER 85, [2003] 1 WLR 2158; *Brink's Global Services Inc v Igrox Ltd* [2010] EWCA Civ 1207, [2011] IRLR 343; *Maga v Roman Catholic Archdiocese of Birmingham* [2010] EWCA Civ 256, [2010] 1 WLR 1441).

1.165 *Defence*

Pursuant to *EqA 2010, s 109(4)*, employers who can show that they took all reasonable steps to prevent their employees from acting unlawfully will not be held liable. This is similar to the pre-October 2010 position, which provided a defence for the employer who 'took such steps as were reasonably practicable to prevent the employee from doing that act or from doing in the course of his employment acts of that description' (*SDA 1975, s 41(3); RRA 1976, s 32(3); DDA 1995, s 58(5); RBR 2003, reg 22(3); SOR 2003, reg 22(3); AR 2006, reg 25(3)*). By virtue of *EqA 2010, s 109(5)*, the defence does not apply to criminal offences under the *EqA 2010*, other than offences under *Part 12* relating to transport for disabled persons.

The courts approach the defence by: (i) identifying whether the employer took any steps to prevent the employee whose acts are complained of from carrying out those acts in the course of his employment; and (ii) considering whether the employer could have taken any further acts which were reasonably practicable (*Canniffe v East Riding of Yorkshire Council* [2000] IRLR 555). The focus is on what the employer had done prior to the occurrence of the act, and not his reaction after its occurrence: *Haringey London Borough Council (Haringey Design Partnership Directorate of Technical and Environmental Services) v Al-Azzawi* (2002) 703 IDS Brief 7, EAT. In *Canniffe*, the EAT (at [14]–[22]) also confirmed that the fact that the acts complained of were so serious that the employee who committed them would have been aware that their conduct was unacceptable without the need for instruction, or that the steps were not realistically likely to succeed, did not of itself mean the employer could rely on the 'reasonable steps' defence, for the policy reasons given by the House of Lords in *Jones v Tower Boot Co*. The fact that those steps were unsuccessful does not, however, mean that the defence will fail, or it would never be relied on: by definition the defence is only needed where an act of discrimination has, in fact, taken place.

The test of reasonable practicality equates to proportionality. It involves a balancing exercise between the extent of the difference the employer's steps are likely to make, and the time, effort and expense of the suggested measures. In *Croft v Royal Mail Group plc* [2003] EWCA Civ 1045, [2003] ICR 1425, [2003] IRLR 592, the court was satisfied that the employer, in briefing staff of a colleague's sex change, reminding them of their duty of non-harassment, and issuing an informal warning when subsequent verbal harassment took place (which had the effect of preventing that harassment), had taken reasonably practicable steps. The tribunal took into account the fact there was no evidence that the employees complained of did not know their acts constituted harassment, and that further education would have been unlikely to have resulted in their accepting the claimant's decision to undergo gender reassignment. In *Caspersz v Ministry of Defence* UKEAT/0599/05/LA the fact that the employer had in place a 'dignity at work' policy which was 'conscientiously implemented' was sufficient to establish the 'reasonable steps' defence. The tribunal and EAT judgments provide little guidance as to what on those facts amounted to 'conscientious implementation', save that the harasser in that case was aware of the policy, the respondent had apologised for a previous potential breach of that policy (where the individual complained of had already left its employment and so could not be disciplined), and that, in relation to the incidents that founded the tribunal complaint, it had promptly investigated and had dismissed the employee who had breached that policy.

Whether reasonable steps have been taken is largely a question of fact to be determined by the tribunal, and as such the case law is somewhat inconsistent. In *Enterprise Glass Co Ltd v Miles* [1990] ICR 787, EAT, an oral warning was insufficient to establish the defence. In *Balgobin v Tower Hamlets London Borough Council* [1987] ICR 829, EAT, the EAT refused to interfere with a decision of the tribunal that notwithstanding the fact that there was no evidence that the employer trained staff on its equal opportunities policy or even brought it to their attention, and that it failed to act on prior complaints before the particular sexual harassment complained of, it had taken 'reasonable steps'. More extensive steps will, however, generally be expected of an employer where he is aware that an employee presents a particular risk, in particular where that employee is in a senior role compared to the complainant (*Canniffe* and *Caspersz*).

In order to rely on this defence, an employer should draw up an equal opportunities policy which complies with the minimal provisions of the Commission Code of Practice (Commission Recommendation number 92/131/EEC) and relevant CRE, EOC, ACAS and EHRC Codes. Employers may wish to include a requirement to act compatibly with equality law in the worker's terms of employment or contract to make it obvious that breaches of equality law will be treated as disciplinary matters or breaches of contract (*EHRC Code on Good Practice: Equality Policies, Equality Training and Monitoring*, p 37). Alternatively, the policy should state that breach may amount to gross misconduct, require employees to report their concerns as to breach of the policy (*Canniffe*) and set out alternative personnel with whom complaints should be raised (to avoid the possibility that the individual named may in fact be the subject of the complaint) (as noted in *Caspersz*). A person of appropriate seniority and character should be given overall responsibility for the policy: the EAT in *Caspersz* noted *obiter* that if evidence had been put to it that the employer had been aware of the character of the harasser in the case at the time it gave him overall responsibility for the employer's equal opportunities policy, it may not have been able to rely on the defence.

Monitoring of the effectiveness of the policy is also advisable (this was expressly not considered so did not form part of the decision to exonerate the employer in *Caspersz*). Employers should demonstrate that they are not simply paying 'lip service' to their obligations by running regular training sessions for staff on the policy, and, most importantly, to consistently investigate and, where appropriate, discipline where either formal or informal complaints of breach of the policy are made. The *EHRC Employment Code* notes that an employer may not be liable if its training on its equal opportunities policy includes annual refreshers, but would be liable regardless of written policies and training if in practice it 'turned a blind eye' to discriminatory practices. It also reinforces previous case law (*Caspersz*) that an employer will be expected to deal effectively with employee complaints in order to be deemed to have taken reasonable steps for purposes of *s 109(4)* (at *paras 10.50–10.53*).

Overall, the correct approach is to identify what steps were taken by the employer, and whether there were any other reasonably practicable steps which would have been likely to be effective. By way of example of the type of conduct that will be regarded as fulfilling the requirement of taking 'all reasonable steps', the *EHRC Employment Code* gives the example of an employer who makes all employees aware of its harassment policy, trains managers in the policy, implements the policy, and then takes disciplinary action against an employee who has made anti-Semitic remarks against a Jewish colleague (*para 10.50*).

In contrast to the position with employers, the 'all reasonable steps' defence is not extended to principals. However, a principal can avoid liability for unlawful discrimination carried out by its agents where the agent has acted without the authority of the principal.

1.166 *Personal liability of employees and agents*

Employees and agents may be personally liable for breaches of the *EqA 2010* where the employer or principal is also liable. The employee/agent can also still be liable even where the employer/principal is able to rely on the 'reasonable steps' defence *(EqA 2010, s 110(2)*) (see **1.165**), confirming the previous case law: *Crofton v Yeboah* [2002] EWCA Civ 794, [2002] IRLR 634).

Furthermore, under *EqA 2010*, an employee or agent can be personally liable for carrying out another person's discriminatory act, even where the employee or agent did not know that the act was unlawful (*EqA 2010, ss 109(1)–(2), 110*). This is a change to the position pre-October 2010, where employees were only liable where they were aware of the unlawfulness of their action which they were instructed to carry out, and generally were only required to pay part or all of an award where their own personal conduct was in some way egregious. To illustrate the new position the *EHRC Employment Code* cites the example of a manager who dismisses an employee because of disability-related absence, who will be liable regardless of the fact she was not aware of an employer's duty to make reasonable adjustments.

The employee/agent or the employer/principal may be able to escape liability, and make the other party entirely responsible for any award, where one of the statutory defences applies.

In the case of employees and agents, they will not be liable under *s 110(1)* where they rely on a statement by the employer or principal that the discriminatory action is not in breach of *EqA 2010*, provided it is reasonable for them to do so *(EqA 2010, s 110(3))*. There are no restrictions on the type of statement which is effective for this purpose. As such, *s 110(3)* can be expected to be relied on in its ordinary sense of including an oral or written comment, however employees and agents concerned about the lawfulness of instructions given to them would be well advised to ask for written confirmation that the actions do not breach *EqA 2010*. Examples might include a manager implementing redundancies who has concerns over the approach to selection stipulated by the company's HR Department. Where the manager is concerned that it may not be reasonable to rely on his employer's assurance, he might ask to see a copy of the employer's legal advice or may ask for a cost contribution to enable him to take his own legal advice.

In the case of employers/principals, an employee will be solely liable where the employer had taken all reasonable steps to prevent their action. The actions that can be taken by employers to avoid liability have already been outlined above at **1.165**. Where neither of these defences applies, the employee/agent and employer/principal will share liability. The case law on apportionment of liability between employee/agent and employer/principal is likely still to be relevant in that it is likely to be linked to responsibility for the damage incurred and culpability, and not to ability to pay (*Rooproy v Rollins-Elliott* [2001] All ER (D) 91 (Jul)).

EqA 2010, s 110(4) and (5) make it an offence, punishable by a fine of (currently) up to £5,000, if an employer or principal knowingly or recklessly makes a false statement about the lawfulness of doing something under the EqA 2010.

It should be noted that these provisions on personal liability do not apply to disability discrimination in schools, which is not actionable against individuals: *EqA 2010, s 110(7)*.

1.167 Liability for an employee's acts under the Protection from Harassment Act 1997

An employer can also be vicariously liable for harassment by its employees in breach of *PHA 1997* where the unlawful act complained of is committed in the course of employment (*Majrowski v Guy's and St Thomas' NHS Trust* [2006] UKHL 34, [2006] 4 All ER 395; *S&D Property Investments Ltd v Nisbet* [2009] EWHC 1726 (Ch)). (See above at **1.96**.)

1.168 Liability for acts of third parties

An employer may also be liable towards its employees where its employees suffer discrimination from third parties in the course of their employment which it was within the employer's power to prevent (*Burton v De Vere Hotels Ltd* [1996] IRLR 596). While this principle has been disapproved by the House of Lords (*Pearce v Governing Body of Mayfield Secondary School* [2003] UKHL 34, [2004] 1 All ER 339, [2003] ICR 937) on the basis that the employer was not motivated by unlawfully discriminatory reasons in failing to protect its employees, *Pearce* no longer applies in the case of harassment.

In the case of harassment, *EqA 2010, s 40(2)* provides that the circumstances in which an employer (A) will be treated as harassing an employee (B) includes those where a third party harasses B in the course of the B's employment and A has failed to take such steps as would have been reasonably practicable to prevent the third party from doing so. However, A will only be liable where A knows that B has been harassed in the course of B's employment on at least two other occasions by a third party; and it does not matter whether the third party is the same or a different person on each occasion. (See further **1.95**.)

1.169 SANCTIONS, REMEDIES AND ENFORCEMENT

Summary

EqA 2010, s 120 provides that an employment tribunal has jurisdiction to determine a complaint brought under *Part 5 (Work)* or *s 108* (relationships that have ended), *s 111* (instructing, causing or inducing contraventions) and *s 112* (aiding contraventions) in relation to *Part 5 (Work)*. *Section 122* of the *EqA 2010* provides that, if it appears to a court that a claim or counter-claim or a question about a non-discrimination rule arising in those proceedings could be more conveniently determined by an employment tribunal, then the court may strike out that claim and/or refer it to an employment tribunal and may stay the court proceedings in the meantime (*EHRC Employment Code, paras 15.14–15.19*).

The time limit for bringing a claim in a work-related case is generally three months starting with the date of the act to which the complaint relates, which period is extendable by the tribunal on just and equitable grounds (*EqA 2010, s 123(1)*). However, there is an exception to that general rule in armed forces cases where the period is extended to six months to allow use of an internal complaints procedure (*EqA 2010, ss 121, 123(2)*) and in relation to equal pay claims (*EqA 2010, s 129(3)*). See further **1.41**.

EqA 2010, s 124 sets out the remedies available in a case brought under *s 120* which preserves the structure of monetary compensation, declarations and recommendations that was available under the old equality legislation (*EqA 2010, s 124(2)*). Reinstatement or re-engagement are not available as remedies (save where a discrimination claim is brought with a successful unfair dismissal claim pursuant to *ERA 1996, ss 114–115*).

The decision as to which remedies are awarded is in the tribunal's discretion. *EqA 2010* does not, however, state that a tribunal must order whichever of the available remedies that it considers to be 'just and equitable' as did the old legislation but it is difficult to imagine that remedies will be selected on any other basis (*SDA 1975, s 65(1); RRA 1976, s 56(1); DDA 1995, s 17A(2); RBR 2003, reg 30(1); SOR 2003, reg 30(1); AR 2006, reg 38(1)*).

In equal pay claims which occur wholly before 1 October 2010 and therefore fall under the *EqPA 1970* rather than the *EqA 2010*, where an equality clause is implied into the contract in successful claims, arrears of remuneration are payable for the six years prior to the date that the claim was received by the tribunal (*EqPA 1970, s 2(1)*).

1.170 Procedure

Compromise agreements

Once the issue of liability is determined, the parties may agree the amount of any financial remedy between themselves under a compromise agreement. *EqA 2010, s 144(4)(b)* introduces the concept of a 'qualifying compromise contract'.

Section 147(3) sets out the new requirements which a compromise agreement must meet to settle a claim under *EqA 2010*. Those conditions broadly replicate the position prior to the *EqA 2010* save in one important respect. *Section 147(5)(d)* appears on its face to preclude a qualified lawyer who is acting for a party to a complaint from advising that party on the compromise agreement and therefore from meeting the requirement in *s 147(3)* that the complainant receive advice from an independent adviser before entering into the compromise agreement. The effect of this would potentially be that compromise agreements could not be used to settle claims arising out of the *EqA 2010*.

The *Explanatory Notes to the EqA 2010* do not suggest that any change to current practice was intended and it is widely considered that this is a drafting error. Different views have been taken, however, as to the correct interpretation of the section, with prominent QCs offering conflicting advice. It is submitted that the better view is that an independent lawyer acting for a potential claimant can be a 'qualified lawyer' for the purposes of *s 147* so that valid compromise agreements can still be executed in the same way as under the old discrimination legislation, and this is the view that the government has expressed. However, until this issue is resolved, practitioners should exercise caution in the use of compromise agreements and should refer to the most recent Law Society Practice Note on the issue. In the meantime, the safest method of entering into a compromise agreement is to make the agreement through ACAS in the COT3 format but sufficient time should be allowed for this process to be pursued.

1.171 *Remedies hearing*

Alternatively, the question of remedy may be decided at a remedies hearing. This may be relatively informal, simply involving submissions on the schedule of loss and counter-schedule of loss. The higher the value of the claim, however, the more formal the proceedings are likely to become, to the extent of requiring directions for the exchange of witness statements, cross-examination, expert evidence and a separately listed hearing. See *Buxton v Equinox Design Ltd* [1999] ICR 269 at [16] per Morison J and *De Keyser v Wilson* [2001] IRLR 324 on expert evidence. A lengthy delay between a liability and remedy hearing will not necessarily preclude a fair hearing of the remedy issue or prevent the tribunal from making an assessment of causation of the losses or injuries claimed (*Abegaze v Shrewsbury College of Arts and Technology* [2009] EWCA Civ 96, [2010] IRLR 238 at [39]–[48] per Elias LJ).

1.172 **Compensation**

Pecuniary loss

An employment tribunal has the power to award compensation under the following 'heads': (1) pecuniary loss (eg loss of earnings/future loss of earnings, including 'stigma' damages for bringing a claim, other financial losses); (2) injury to feelings; (3) personal injury; (4) aggravated damages; and (5) exemplary damages. The following general principles apply:

(a) there is no ceiling to the award that can be made under *EqA 2010*. The statutory cap on unfair dismissal compensation cannot be a cap on compensation for discrimination even if the act of unfair dismissal came after the act of discrimination and the losses claimed were, therefore, arguably attributable to the unfair dismissal rather than the discrimination: *HM Prison Service v Beart* [2005] EWCA Civ 467, [2005] ICR 1206;

(b) pecuniary awards are made according to the tortious measure of civil damages, ie the aim is, so far as possible, to put the claimant in the position he or she would have been in had they not suffered the unlawful act of discrimination (*Ministry of Defence v Cannock* [1994] ICR 918 per Morison J at 517; *Brash-Hall v Getty Images Ltd* [2006] EWCA Civ 531);

In the *EqA 2010*, this is expressed as the amount of compensation that could be awarded by a county court or the sheriff under *s 119* (remedies within the civil courts jurisdiction). Under the old legislation, this principle was expressed as compensation corresponding to any damages that could have been awarded by a county court or a sheriff court to pay to the complainant if the complaint had been brought in a county court, save in respect of compensation for disability discrimination, which is expressed as being calculated by applying the principles to the calculation of damages in claims in tort or (in Scotland) in reparation for breach of statutory duty (*SDA 1975, s 65(1)(b); RRA 1976, s 56(1)(b); DDA 1995, s 17A(2)(b), (3); RBR 2003, reg 30(1)(b); SOR 2003, reg 30(1)(b); AR 2006, reg 38(1)(b)*);

(c) the ordinary rules of mitigation in tort apply; *Kelly v University of Southampton* (2010) UKEAT/0139/10/LA, [2010] AlL ER (D) 91 (Sep), EAT at [17] per Keith J. As such, an individual who is dismissed for a discriminatory reason is expected to take reasonable steps to mitigate his loss, for example, by finding a new job (*EHRC Employment Code, para 15.43*);

(d) employers may be vicariously liable for the acts of their employees (*EqA 2010, s 109*; formerly contained in *SDA 1975, s 41(1); RRA 1976, s 32(1); DDA 1995, s 58(1); RBR 2003, reg 22(1); SOR 2003, reg 22(1); AR 2006, reg 25(1)*);

(e) individual employees against whom a claim is brought may be personally liable to pay compensation, whether or not their employer is vicariously liable. A finding against an individual employee can be made under the provisions for 'aiding unlawful acts' in the old equality legislation and under the provisions liability of employees or agents (*s 110*) or for 'instructing, causing or inducing' (*s 111*) or 'aiding' (*s 112*) contraventions under the *EqA 2010*, see **1.60–1.62** and **1.166**. See *Gilbank v Miles* [2006] ICR 12 at [8] per Pugsley J; *Gbaja-Biamila v DHL International (UK) Ltd* [2000] ICR 730 at [33]–[35] (*EqA 2010, ss 111, 112*; formerly contained in *SDA 1975, s 42; RRA 1976, s 33; DDA 1995, s 57; RBR 2003, reg 23; SOR 2003, reg 23; AR 2006, reg 26*);

(f) where the employer is also liable, liability of employer and employee is joint and several. A tribunal should take into account the considerations set out in *Way v Crouch* [2005] ICR 1362 at [23] if it is considering making a joint and several award;

(g) compensation can be increased or a compensatory award made if an employer fails to implement a recommendation ordered by the tribunal (*EqA 2010, s 124(7); SDA 1975, s 65(3); RRA 1976, s 56(4); DDA 1995, s 17A(5); RBR 2003, reg 30(3); SOR 2003, reg 30(2); AR 2006, reg 38(3)*);

(h) where there has been an unreasonable failure to follow the terms of the ACAS Code on Disciplinary and Grievance Procedures in the context of the complaint before the tribunal, the tribunal has the power to either increase or reduce the compensation (depending upon the party at fault) by up to 25% (Trade Union and Labour Relations (Consolidation) Act 1992 (TULRCA), s 207A, as inserted by the *Employment Act 2008*);

(i) awards for pension and earnings loss relating to a tortious act predating termination of employment are not taxable and are not subject to grossing up. Other awards should be grossed up by taking into account the appropriate marginal tax rates for each part of the award (*Cuerdon v Yorkshire Housing Ltd* (2010) KEAT 0397/09/SM, [2010] All ER (D) 52 (Sep), EAT at [29], per Peter Clark J; see also *Visa International Service Association v Paul* [2004] IRLR 42). It is clear that awards for injury to feelings are non-taxable where the discrimination giving rise to the payment is not related to termination of employment (*Walker v Adams (Inspector of Taxes)* [2003] STC (SCD) 269). Where however, the injury to feelings payment does relate to the termination of employment, the position is less clear;

(j) loss of pension rights should be approached in accordance with the current tribunal guide to Compensation for Loss of Pension Rights (3rd ed, 2003). Two approaches are set out in that guide: the simplified approach and the substantial loss approach.

Guidance as to their application can be found in *Greenhoff v Barnsley Metropolitan Borough Council* [2006] ICR 1514 per Silber J and *Sibbit v Governing Body of St Cuthbert's Catholic Primary School* (2010) UKEAT/0070/10/ZT, [2010] All ER (D) 20 (Sep);

(k) a tribunal award is enforceable as if it were payable under a county court order in England, Wales and Northern Ireland, and as if it were a extract registered decree arbitral bearing a warrant for execution issued by a sheriff court in Scotland (*Tribunals, Courts and Enforcement Act 2007, s 24*).

Successful discrimination claims will often be accompanied by successful claims for unfair dismissal on grounds of discrimination. Complainants will commonly elect to have their compensation assessed under the discrimination provisions because there is no ceiling on the award that can be made (*Lambeth London Borough v D'Souza* [1999] IRLR 240). Further, the recoupment provisions under the *Employment Protection (Recoupment of Jobseeker's Allowance and Income Support) Regulations 1996 (SI 1996/2349)* which apply to compensation for unfair dismissal do not apply to compensation under the discrimination provisions. Receipt of incapacity benefit does not preclude a claimant recovering compensation for loss of earnings (*Sheffield Forgemasters International Ltd v Fox* [2009] ICR 333).

To reflect the tortious measure, losses must flow from the act of discrimination itself. In contrast, under *ERA 1996, s 123(1)*, the tribunal must have regard to the losses sustained by the complainant in consequence of the dismissal in so far as that loss is attributable to the to action taken by the employer. Although, the *s 123(1)* test appears broader, since the decision in *Dunnachie v Kingston-upon-Hull City Council* [2004] UKHL 36, [2005] 1 AC 226 in which it was held, amongst other things, that employees should not receive more than their actual losses as compensation for unfair dismissal, the difference in sums awarded for reasons of causation is likely to be minimal, although the statutory cap on unfair dismissal awards will continue to make a remedy under discrimination legislation more attractive.

In most cases, the following are the most common heads of loss:

(a) the employee's loss of earnings to date of tribunal hearing;

(b) the employee's loss of future earnings;

(c) the employee's expenses in bringing the tribunal claim (other than legal expenses, eg photocopying costs).

The sum awarded may be adjusted to take account of the following factors:

(i) the percentage likelihood of future events occurring. Cumulative percentage chances can be calculated (*Ministry of Defence v Cannock* [1994] ICR 918 and *Ministry of Defence v Bristow* [1996] ICR 544);

(ii) the percentage likelihood that the dismissal or other event from which loss flows would have happened even if there had been no discrimination (*Chagger v Abbey National plc* [2010] EWCA Civ 1202, [2010] ICR 397 at [57]–[60] per Elias LJ);

(iii) a reasonable length of time within which an employee could regain employment (in dismissal cases) subject to the ordinary rules of mitigation. Future loss may be awarded for as long as five years (*Blundell v Governing Body of St Andrew's Catholic Primary School* (2010) UKEAT/0330/09/JOJ, [2010] All ER (D) 68 (Oct) at [24] per Wilkie J or for loss of career and change to another career at a lower salary where the complainant can show that he cannot obtain comparable employment in his former career; cf *Chagger v Abbey National plc* [2009] EWCA Civ 1202, [2010] ICR 397 at [74]–[75] per Elias LJ. See also *Wardle v Credit Agricole Corporate and*

Investment Bank (2010) UKEAT/0535/09/SM, [2010] All ER (D) 77 (Oct)], where an employee was awarded career loss earnings, even though he had already found alternative employment in the same sector. The complainant must take reasonable steps to procure further employment;

(iv) contributory negligence: see *Way v Crouch* [2005] IRLR 603 applying the approach of the *Law Reform (Contributory Negligence) Act 1945* in tort claims to sex discrimination claims;

(v) discount for accelerated receipt in larger award cases (*Bentwood Bros (Manchester) Ltd v Shepherd* [2003] EWCA Civ 380, [2003] ICR 1000);

(vi) the discriminator's motives: this factor, whilst not relevant to a finding of discrimination, may be relevant to an award of compensation. In *Chief Constable of Manchester v Hope* [1999] ICR 338, no compensatory award was made where there was a finding of no discriminatory intent.

1.173 *Indirect discrimination*

There are specific rules governing compensation where unintentional indirect discrimination has occurred. Under *EqA 2010, s 124(4)* and *(5)*, where a claimant succeeds in an indirect discrimination claim but the tribunal is satisfied that the provision, criterion or practice in question was not applied by the employer with the intention of discriminating against the claimant, the tribunal must not make an order for compensation unless it has first considered making a declaration or recommendation. Of course, if the tribunal considers that another remedy is not appropriate in the circumstances, it may make an award of damages. However, it must still have regard to the order set out in *s 124(5)* when considering which remedy to award (see also *EHRC Employment Code, paras 15.44–15.45*).

1.174 *Injury to feelings*

EqA 2010, s 119(4) expressly provides that an award of damages may include compensation for injury to feelings (whether alone, or in conjunction with compensation on any other basis). An individual can therefore receive an award for injury to feelings whether or not they have also suffered any pecuniary loss.

In *Vento v Chief Constable of West Yorkshire Police* [2002] EWCA Civ 1871, [2003] ICR 31, the Court of Appeal set out three bands of awards linked to the degree of seriousness of the discrimination to guide tribunals (known as the *Vento Guidelines* or *Vento bands*). The original bands have now been updated to take account of inflation: *Da'Bell v National Society for the Prevention of Cruelty to Children* [2010] IRLR 19.

The lowest band range is from £600 to £6,000 for less serious cases involving one-off or isolated incidents of unlawful conduct. The middle band range is from £6,000 to £18,000 for serious cases not meriting an award in the highest band (see discussion of middle band cases in *Blundell v Governing Body of St Andrew's Catholic Primary School* (2010) UKEAT/0330/09/JOJ, [2010] All ER (D) 68 (Oct) at [17]–[18] per Wilkie J). The highest band range is from £18,000 to £30,000 for where there has been, for example, a lengthy campaign of discriminatory harassment. It is now rare for awards to be below £600 and, equally, awards above £30,000 are exceptional.

The claimant may recover both injury to feelings and personal injury awards irrespective of what they did or did not know about the motivation of the employer in committing the discriminatory act (*Taylor v XLN Telecom* (2009) UKEAT/0385/09/ZT, [2010] ICR 656 at [9] per Underhill P).

In cases involving more than one type of discrimination, eg race and disability, the tribunal should consider the effect on the complainant of each type separately when deciding on the level of award for injury of feelings although there is no need to apportion specific amounts to each type. The tribunal should then look at the overall award and make any adjustments necessary to ensure that there is no element of double counting; *Al Jumard v Clwyd Leisure* [2008] IRLR 345 at [48]–[50] per Elias P. It is possible that claimants may seek to persuade tribunals to adopt this approach in combined discrimination cases (if and when combined discrimination comes into force (see **1.57**). However, since the point of combined discrimination is to blend two protected characteristics into one, it is unlikely that such an argument would succeed. In practical terms, as was pointed out in *Al Jumard* at [56] per Elias P, separate consideration of each type of discrimination may not in any event result in a higher award than would be made for discrimination of one type alone.

1.175 *Personal injury*

Compensation is also available for personal injury (most commonly psychiatric injury) subject to the ordinary principles for recovery for such a claim in tort:

(a) the injury must flow from the act(s) of discrimination;

(b) employers must take employees as they find them.

It was suggested by Stuart-Smith LJ in *Sheriff v Klyne Tugs (Lowestoft) Ltd* [1999] IRLR 481, CA at [21] that an employee claiming for personal injury in a discrimination case might well wish to obtain a medical report. A tribunal is unlikely properly to conclude that an injury, particularly a psychiatric injury (as opposed to injury to feelings not amounting to a clinical condition), was caused by an act of discrimination in the absence of a medical report.

However, in *Essa v Laing Ltd* [2004] EWCA Civ 02, [2004] ICR 746 per Pill LJ at [34]–[39] it was held that it was not necessary for the injury to be reasonably foreseeable, and was probably sufficient if the injury was a direct consequence of the act(s) of discrimination (note the dissenting view of Rix LJ at [106], approved in *Chagger v Abbey National plc* [2009] EWCA Civ 1202, [2010] ICR 397 at [12] and [56] per Elias LJ).

Compensation may be assessed as the percentage contribution of the unlawful discrimination to the psychiatric injury. The tribunal should ask itself: (1) did the conduct for which the respondent is liable materially contribute to the harm, and if so (2) to what extent should liability for that harm fairly be attributed to the respondent (*Thaine v London School of Economics* (2010) UKEAT/0144/10, [2010] ICR 1422 at [17] and [23], per Keith J).

Awards for both injury to feelings and for psychiatric injury may be awarded in the same case, as in *Vento v The Chief Constable of West Yorkshire Police* [2002] EWCA Civ 1871, [2003] ICR 318, [2003] IRLR 102 in which the award included sums for both psychiatric damage (clinical depression and adjustment disorder) and injury to feelings, although the award for injury to feelings was substantially reduced.

1.176 *Occupational pension schemes*

Additional remedies are available where there has been a contravention of the terms on which someone has become a member of an occupational pension scheme or the terms on which such members are treated (*EqA 2010*, s 126; *EHRC Employment Code, para 15.56*). Specifically, a tribunal may declare that a complainant has the right to be admitted to the scheme if the contravention related to the terms of membership or the tribunal may declare that the complainant has a right to membership of the scheme without discrimination if the complaint relates to treatment. In the latter case, such a declaration may only be made if the compensation is for injured feelings or is awarded where an employer has failed to comply with a tribunal's recommendation (*EqA 2010, s 124(3)*). Both declarations may have retrospective effect (*EqA 2010, s 126(4)(b)*).

1.177 *Stigma damages*

Where an employee finds it more difficult to obtain new work because subsequent employers stigmatise him for having brought proceedings under the equality legislation against a former employer, compensation is recoverable against the former employer even though the loss could be said to arise from the unlawful victimisation of the potential new employers who stigmatise the individual (*Abbey National plc v Chaggar* [2010] ICR 1202 at [89] per Elias LJ). In cases where compensation includes loss of future earnings, it will not generally be necessary to award stigma as a separate head, it will simply be reflected in assessing how long it will be before the employee finds another job. However, there could be an 'exceptional case' where it might be necessary to award compensation specifically by reference to the impact of stigma on future prospects eg where there was no direct financial loss flowing from the discrimination, so that stigma was the only head of loss. In these circumstances, where a specific period of unemployment related to the stigma could not be shown and stigma was only one of the difficulties faced by the claimant, Elias LJ suggested that it might be appropriate to award a 'modest lump sum' by analogy with the approach taken to compensating for the risks of future disadvantage on the labour market in *Smith v Manchester Corpn* [1974] 17 KIR 1. However, in all cases an employee will need to show evidence from which the tribunal can infer that stigma is likely to be playing a part in the difficulties facing the employee looking for new employment (Elias LJ at [99]).

1.178 *Aggravated and exemplary damages*

Aggravated damages are available for discrimination claims in England and Wales and should not be incorporated into an award for injury to feelings (*Scott v IRC* [2004] EWCA Civ 400, [2004] ICR 1410, [2004] IRLR 713). In Scotland, however, aggravated damages are not part of the law of tort and are not recoverable for discrimination claims. However, account may be taken of the way in which an employee was treated in setting the level of an award for injury to feelings. See *Virgo Fidelis Senior School v Boyle* [2004] IRLR 268 and *Ministry of Defence v Fletcher* [2010] IRLR 25 for successful awards of aggravated damages. Aggravated damages may also be awarded for the manner in which a party conducts the remedies hearing (*Blundell v Governing Body of St Andrew's Catholic Primary School* (2010) UKEAT/0330/09/JOJ, [2010] All ER (D) 68 (Oct)).

In theory, exemplary damages are also available for discrimination claims other than equal pay claims, although in very narrow circumstances. Those circumstances are, firstly, where there has been oppressive, arbitrary or unconstitutional action by agents of the government and, secondly, where the tortfeasor's conduct was calculated to make a profit for himself which would exceed any compensation payable to the complainant (*Kuddus v Chief Constable of Leicestershire Constabulary* [2001] UKHL 29, [2002] 2 AC 122). Even in a case where the respondent's conduct was 'oppressive, arbitrary and unconstitutional', its conduct did not cross the high threshold warranting an award of exemplary damages (*Ministry of Defence v Fletcher* [2010] IRLR 25 at [115] per Slade J).

1.179 *Interest*

Simple interest should be added to the net sum of an award pursuant to the *Employment Tribunals (Interest on Awards in Discrimination Cases) Regulations 1996 (SI 1996/2803)* save where the tribunal considers that: (i) there are exceptional circumstances, whether relating to the claim as a whole or to a particular element of the award; and (ii) those circumstances are such that serious injustice would be caused if interest were to be awarded by reference to the periods set out in the regulations. If those circumstances apply, the award of interest is in the tribunal's discretion.

The rate to be applied in England and Wales is that of the Special Investment Account pursuant to the *Court Funds Rules 1987 (SI 1987/821), r 27(1)*.

1.180 *Declaration of rights*

The tribunal may state the rights of the complainant and the respondent in relation to the act to which the complaint relates. Rarely, where the employee is still employed, it may be sufficient remedy for the employer to agree to put right the discriminatory act (*EqA 2010, s 124(2)(a)*; *EHRC Employment Code, para 15.39*).

1.181 *Recommendation for action*

EqA 2010, s 124(3)(b) extends the tribunal's pre-existing powers to make a recommendation that the respondent take, within a specified period:

> 'action appearing to the tribunal to be practicable for the purpose of obviating or reducing the adverse effect of any matter to which the proceedings relate: (a) on the complainant; (b) on any other person'.

Under the previous legislation, the power for tribunals to make a recommendation following a successful claim was limited to steps to reduce the adverse effect of the discrimination *on the claimant* alone. In practice, this power was of limited effect as, in the vast majority of cases, the claimant had already left employment with the respondent. The *EqA 2010* seeks to remedy this limitation, by enabling tribunals to make recommendations benefiting the wider workforce.

Further, the power now extends to any matter to which the complaint relates, not merely to any act of discrimination to which the complaint relates (contrast *EqA 2010, s 124(3)* with *SDA 1975, s 65(1)(c)*).

It is important to note that recommendations are not binding on an employer. The remedy for non-compliance is, as set out above, increasing or substituting a compensatory award (*Nelson v Tyne and Wear Passenger Transport Executive* [1978] ICR 1183) but only in respect of failures to comply with a recommendation which relate to the complainant and not to others (*EqA 2010, s 124(7)*). However, tt is conceivable that, in deciding whether to accept an employer's explanation in a subsequent claim brought by a different employee but on facts which fell within the recommendation, a tribunal would give weight to the fact that an employer had not complied with a recommendation. This is supported by the *EHRC Employment Code* which provides that '[a] failure to comply with a recommendation could also be adduced in evidence in any later cases against the same organisation' (*para 15.54*). There is, however, no freestanding right to bring a claim for failure to comply with a recommendation. Potential claimants can use the questionnaire procedure (see **1.183**) to ask employers whether relevant recommendations have been made in previous cases.

Tribunals have a broad discretion to make recommendations although it has been held not to extend to the recommending of appointments to available jobs for those who have been denied them through discrimination (*Noone v North West Thames Regional Health Authority (No 2)* [1988] IRLR 530) although an employer has been order to notify a complainant of suitable vacancies (*Hazlehurst v Cross Country Trains Ltd* (5 July 2005, ET/1701807/04)). Practicality has to be decided by reference to the effect on the complainant and the discriminator; compare *Fasuyi v Greenwich London Borough Council* EAT/1078/99 per Lindsay J at para 24 with *Leeds Rhinos Rugby Club v Sterling* EAT/267/01 (9 September 2002) at para 6.1 per HH Judge Reid QC. A respondent should not be required, however, to make statements with which they did not agree, however wrongheadedly (*Blundell v Governing Body of St Andrew's Catholic Primary School* (2010) UKEAT/0330/09/JOJ, [2010] All ER (D) 68 (Oct) at [36] per Wilkie J).

Types of recommendation made include training on discrimination issues for those advising on them in the workplace (*Ghali v Transperfect Translations Ltd* (5 Aug 2009, ET/3201752/08)) or training on the duty to make reasonable adjustments for those responsible for dealing with employees returning from sick leave (*Hazlehurst v Cross Country Trains Ltd* (5 July 2005, ET/1701807/04)). Recommendations for training for managers inevitably affect employees other than the complainant and, to that extent, the wider power to recommend under *EqA 2010* may make little practical difference.

Recommendations must not be made in national security proceedings (defined in *EqA 2010, s 125(2))* in relation to a person other than the complainant, however, if the recommendation would affect anything done by the Security Service, the Secret Intelligence Service, GCHQ or a part of the armed forces which is assisting GCHQ.

1.182 *EHRC*

The Equality and Human Rights Commission (initially known as Commission for Equality and Human Rights) or EHRC was established by the *EqA 2006*, replacing the Equal Opportunities Commission, Commission for Racial Equality and Disability Rights Commission. The ECHR's powers to intervene in legal proceedings, instigate investigations and seek remedies are wider than those enjoyed by the bodies it replaces. *EqA 2006, ss 20–32* which set out these powers came into force on 1 October 2007 (see also *EHRC Employment Code, para 15.59*):

(a) the EHRC may investigate if it suspects that a person has committed an unlawful act (*EqA 2006, s 20*);

(b) it may give a notice of unlawful action to a person and require the person to prepare an action plan to avoid repetition of the unlawful act or recommend action to be taken by that person. (*EqA 2006, s 21(1) and (4)*);

(c) it may agree with a person not to investigate or issue a notice if the person undertakes not to commit an unlawful act (*EqA 2006, s 23*);

(d) it may apply to court for an injunction to restrain a person it thinks likely to commit an unlawful act (*EqA 2006, s 24*);

(e) it may bring a complaint to a tribunal or court where unlawful advertising or unlawful pressure to discriminate has occurred (*EqA 2006, s 25(2)*); it may likewise apply to court for an injunction to prevent any, or any further, incident of unlawful advertising or pressure taking place.

(f) it may provide legal assistance to an individual who is a party to legal proceedings relating to the equality enactments (*EqA 2006, s 28*);

(g) it may intervene in any legal proceedings if they are relevant to the EHRC's functions (*EqA 2006, s 30*). See, for example, *Redcar and Cleveland BC v Bainbridge* [2009] ICR 133 (equal pay), *R (on the application of E) v Governing Body of JFS (Secretary of State for Children, Schools and Families, interested parties) (United Synagogue intervening)* [2009] UKSC 15, [2010] 1 AC 278 (ethnic and race discrimination) and *R (on the application of Age UK) v Secretary of State for Business, Innovation & Skills* [2009] EWHC 2336 (Admin), [2010] ICR 260 (compulsory age retirement);

(h) it may assess the extent to which public authorities have complied with duties under the equality legislation (*EqA 2006, s 31*) and issue a compliance notice to a public authority if there has been a failure to comply (*EqA 2006, s 32*).

1.183 **QUESTIONNAIRES**

An individual who believes that he has been discriminated against, victimised or harassed can serve a questionnaire under *EqA 2010, s 138* to elicit further information from the respondent before or shortly after tribunal proceedings have commenced. *EqA 2010, s 138* was intended to replicate the pre-existing procedure (*Explanatory Notes to the EqA 2010, note 458*).

Standard questionnaires and answers forms are provided at *Sch 1* to the *Equality Act 2010 (Obtaining Information) Order 2010 (SI 2010/2194)* but there is no requirement that questions or answers are presented in this form. So, for example, although the specimen questionnaire form does not include a question as to previous tribunal proceedings against the respondent (which was mooted during the consultation on the forms), a complainant could choose to add this question into their own questionnaire. In accordance with the overall aims of *EqA 2010*, the 20 forms which applied pre-October 2010 have now been consolidated into four forms, one set to cover prohibited discrimination and the other set specific to equality of terms.

The purpose of serving the questionnaire is to enable the complainant to assess the merits of his claim and to decide how to conduct the case properly depending on the replies received. A complainant will usually serve the questionnaire before submitting a claim in the employment tribunal. If, after receiving a reply to the first, it appears that further questions need to be asked, the claimant can ask the employment tribunal to grant leave to serve another questionnaire. In *Carrington v Helix Lighting Ltd* [1990] IRLR 6, EAT, the EAT stated, albeit obiter, that '[i]t is a sensible and necessary part of the procedure that after an initial questionnaire an applicant should be able to seek leave, on notice, to administer a further questionnaire.' However, if any questions (either in the first or any subsequent questionnaire) are irrelevant, the respondent may refuse to reply on the grounds that the questions are irrelevant or oppressive and ask the tribunal not to draw inferences from the refusal to respond to such questions.

Provided a questionnaire has been served within the relevant time limits laid down in the legislation (see paragraph below), the questions and the replies will be admissible as evidence, regardless of whether the questionnaire or replies follows the format prescribed by the Secretary of State (*EqA 2010, s 138(3)*). In *Dattani v Chief Constable of West Mercia Police* [2005] IRLR 327, the EAT confirmed that an employer, asked a direct question in writing by an aggrieved person, who failed to respond, or did so evasively, ought to be treated in the same way irrespective of whether a question had been asked under the statutory questionnaire procedure.

The relevant time limit will depend on whether the claimant has submitted his claim form to the employment tribunal and the type of discrimination complained of. In general, if the claimant has not lodged his claim form, a questionnaire can be served on the intended respondent at any time *(Equality Act 2010 (Obtaining Information) Order 2010, Article 5).* The legislation no longer expressly states that all questionnaires must be served within three months of the date of the complained act. If the claim has been presented to the employment tribunal the claimant must serve the questionnaire within 28 days of lodging the claim form (*Equality Act 2010 (Obtaining Information) Order 2010, Article 4*). The employment tribunal has discretion to grant an extension to the time limits stated above. In *Williams v Greater London Citizens Advice Bureaux Service* [1989] ICR 545, the EAT upheld the tribunal's decision not to grant an extension of time to the claimant. The claimant had not given a reason for the delay and had not produced a copy of the proposed questionnaire, and the employment tribunal was entitled to exercise its discretion and refuse leave.

A respondent is not obliged to answer the questions, whether in a specific timeframe, or at all. However, inferences may be drawn by the employment tribunal if it is of the view that the respondent has, without reasonable excuse, failed to reply before the end of eight weeks beginning on the day of service of the questionnaire, or given evasive responses to the questions asked. Such 'reasonable excuses' are limited to those referred in to *EqA 2010, s 138(5)*, which apply where a response to questions might prejudice the respondent in criminal proceedings or impact national security. In *Virdee v ECC Quarries Ltd* [1978] IRLR 295, it was held that one answered question out of nine questions asked constituted an evasive reply. There are detailed rules relating to service of questions and answers set out in *SI 2010/2194* including that they can only be deemed served on a business day and must be sent before 4.30 pm on a particular day to be deemed served on that day.

However, inferences should only be drawn in appropriate cases, and guidance can be found in *Dr C D'Silva v NATFHE (now known as University & College Union)* [2008] IRLR 412. In *D'Silva* the EAT held that failure to answer a questionnaire does not automatically raise a presumption of discrimination. The key question is whether that failure is capable of constituting evidence supporting the inference of discrimination, and if so whether in the light of any explanation supplied it does in fact justify that inference. The EAT noted that in many cases there will be failures in questionnaire responses which are 'reprehensible', but which 'can have no bearing on the reason why' an act occurred.

If the employment tribunal draws an inference that the employer has discriminated etc unlawfully, the burden of proof is reversed and it will be for the employer to show that the less favourable treatment or detriment was not because of or related to the protected characteristic (*EqA 2010, s 136*). In *Dresdner Kleinwort Wasserstein Ltd v Adebayo* [2005] IRLR 514, the EAT confirmed that equivocal or evasive answers to legitimate queries in statutory questionnaires will properly assume a greater significance in cases where the burden of proving that no discrimination has occurred is found to have passed to the employer. In *Barton v Investec Henderson Crosthwaite Securities Ltd* [2003] IRLR 332, EAT, the EAT held that the employment tribunal had erred in failing to draw adverse inferences from the employer's failure to deal properly with the statutory questionnaire procedure. There were a number of serious matters arising out of the failure of the employer to deal properly with the questionnaire procedure and/or to give clear and consistent replies that required the tribunal to draw adverse inferences such that they could conclude, in the absence of an adequate explanation, that an act of discrimination had occurred. Thus, the burden of proof passed to the employer to prove that sex was not a reason for the claimant's less favourable treatment.

2 Age discrimination

2.1 INTRODUCTION

The Equality Act 2010

Council Directive 2000/78/EC establishing a general framework for equal treatment in employment and occupation (the '*Framework Directive*') requires Member States to provide for the prohibition of discrimination on grounds including age.

Before the enactment of *EqA 2010*, the age discrimination aspects of the *Framework Directive* were implemented in the UK by the *Employment Equality (Age) Regulations 2006 (SI 2006/1031)* ('*AR 2006*'), which came into force on 1 October 2006 (apart from provisions in *AR 2006* relating to occupational pensions, which came into force two months later on 1 December 2006).

As of 1 October 2010, *AR 2006* have been superseded by *EqA 2010*, which, as discussed at **1.4**, aims to restate and to harmonise discrimination legislation. Although *EqA 2010* introduces some structural and other significant changes (discussed in the course of this chapter), in substance *EqA 2010*'s age discrimination provisions are broadly similar to those of *AR 2006*. However, the government has announced its intention to phase out the default retirement age from 6 April 2011 (subject to transitional provisions) and this will have a major impact on age discrimination law, which is discussed below at **2.64**.

2.2 The Framework Directive 2000/78/EC

The *Framework Directive* recognises at *Recital 25* that age discrimination is special among the strands of discrimination:

> 'The prohibition of age discrimination is an essential part of meeting the aims set out in the Employment Guidelines [agreed by the European Council at Helsinki on 10 and 11 December 1999] and encouraging diversity in the workforce. However, differences in treatment in connection with age may be justified under certain circumstances and therefore require specific provisions which may vary in accordance with the situation in Member States. It is therefore essential to distinguish between differences in treatment which are justified, in particular by legitimate employment policy, labour market and vocational training objectives, and discrimination which must be prohibited'.

Article 6(1) accordingly allows Member States to provide that differences of treatment on grounds of age shall not constitute discrimination, if:

> 'within the context of national law, they are objectively and reasonably justified by a legitimate aim, including legitimate employment policy, labour market and vocational training objectives, and if the means of achieving that aim are appropriate and necessary'.

AR 2006 were challenged on the basis that they went too far in sanctioning discrimination on age grounds, and thus failed properly to implement the Directive. The challenge, however, failed: *R (on the application of Age UK) v Secretary of State for Business, Innovation & Skills* [2009] EWHC 2336 (Admin), [2009] IRLR 1017, discussed below at **2.18**, **2.34** and **2.64**.

Age discrimination

2.3 Before AR 2006

Before 1 October 2006, discrimination on grounds of age had never, at least as a matter of domestic law, been unlawful in the United Kingdom. In June 1999, the government published a voluntary *Code of Practice on Age Diversity in Employment*, Department of Trade and Industry as part of a broader public awareness campaign entitled *Age Positive*, but there was no legal remedy for those discriminated against on the ground of age.

In the case of *Rutherford v Secretary of State for Trade and Industry (No 2)* [2006] UKHL 19, [2006] 1 ICR 785, an attempt was made to use the EC law on equal pay (*Article 141, EC Treaty*) to mount an indirect challenge to the discriminatory age cap in the unfair dismissal legislation, but despite initial success in the employment tribunal, the challenge failed in the EAT, Court of Appeal and House of Lords.

In *Mangold v Helm: C-144/04* [2006] IRLR 143, however, which involved a challenge to German legislation on the ground that it was age discriminatory, the CJEU appeared to hold that the principle of non-discrimination on grounds of age had to be regarded as a general principle of Community law, and the German court should disapply national legislation conflicting with it, albeit that the time period for the implementation of the *Framework Directive* had not expired in Germany (see *Mangold* especially at [75]–[77]). That is a controversial proposition, analysed and doubted by Mazak AG in his opinion in *Palacios de la Villa v Cortefiel Servicios SA: C-411/05* [2007] IRLR 989 at [78] to [99]; but the CJEU has since referred to *Mangold* with approval (see eg *Seda Kucukdeveci v Swedex GmbH & Co KG: C-555/07* [2010] IRLR 346 [20], [21], [27]), and the case remains binding on a UK court (see *Lloyd-Briden v Worthing College* [2007] 3 CMLR 722, EAT at [19], per Wilkie J).

On that basis, one might have expected that claimants could have based claims involving facts prior to 1 October 2006 (where *AR 2006* did not assist) on a general EC principle against age-discrimination. However, in *Lloyd-Briden* itself, the EAT distinguished *Mangold* on the ground that in that case, the Member State in question (Germany) had enacted age discriminatory legislation during the implementation period, in breach of its implied obligations under the *Framework Directive, Article 18*; Wilkie J at [21] held that the general principle of non-discrimination on grounds of age was only effective where the Member State's obligations under the Directive had been broken—and that was not the case in the UK. Moreover, as Sharpston AG explained in *Bartsch v Bosch und Siemens Hausgerate (BSH) Altersfursorge GmbH: C-427/06* [2008] ECR I-7245 at [89], now that time for implementation of the *Framework Directive* has expired, the 'general principle' identified in *Mangold* will be used to interpret the Directive rather than operating autonomously. It seems highly unlikely that this general principle (characterised by Sharpston AG as the 'general principle of equality of treatment well known in Community law') has anything particular to add to the express terms of the Directive, although it may provide a basis for UK courts to give direct effect to the *Framework Directive* in disputes between private individuals where UK legislation is inconsistent (see *Kücükdeveci*). Thus, while *Mangold* is a problematic case, its impact on age discrimination law in the UK has been limited.

2.4 Authorities and aids to interpretation

Since *EqA 2010* restates in large part the provisions of *AR 2006*, domestic case law on *AR 2006* will be of very great assistance in the interpretation of the age discrimination provisions of *EqA 2010* (although may not be strictly binding: *Farrell v Alexander* [1977] AC 59).

The *Framework Directive* itself and judgments of the CJEU on its interpretation also continue to be crucial to the interpretation of the UK's domestic age discrimination provisions. Since *EqA 2010* implements *Framework Directive*, courts and tribunals must interpret the Act's age discrimination provisions as far as possible in the light of the wording and purpose of the Directive (see *Marleasing SA v La Comercial Internacional de Alimentacion SA: C-106/89* [1990] ECR I-4135).

Some further assistance as to the statutory purpose behind the age discrimination provisions of *AR 2006* (and thus of *EqA 2010* which restates them) may be found in the UK government's consultation documents produced in the course of consultation prior to the creation of *AR 2006*: Equality and Diversity: Age Matters, Department of Trade and Industry, July 2003 ('Age Matters'), and Equality and Diversity: Coming of Age, Department of Trade and Industry, July 2005 ('Coming of Age').

The *EHRC Employment Code* now covers age discrimination and has the status of a statutory code of practice under *EqA 2006* which means is admissible as evidence in proceedings and must be taken into account by a court or tribunal where the court or tribunal considers it to be relevant. The EHRC has also published non-statutory guidance for employers and employees. Where issues are not covered by either the *Code* or the guidance, employment tribunals may well (but are not bound to) have regard to the non-binding *Age and the Workplace*, guidance for employers published by ACAS and available at http ://www.equalityhumanrights.com/advice-and-guidance/information-for -advisers/informal-guidance/.

2.5 THE MEANING OF AGE DISCRIMINATION, HARASSMENT AND VICTIMISATION

Age discrimination in context

Age is a 'protected characteristic' under *EqA 2010, s 4*. 'Age discrimination' is defined by *EqA 2010, s 25(1)* as 'discrimination within *section 13* because of age' and 'discrimination within *section 19* where the relevant protected characteristic is age'. *Sections 13* and *19*, and the provisions defining harassment and victimisation (*ss 26* and *27* respectively), are the same 'harmonised' provisions as apply in the case of other protected characteristics.

However, age discrimination under *EqA 2010* continues to differ fundamentally from other forms of discrimination in two respects.

First, unlawful age discrimination remains narrower in scope than discrimination relating to any other protected ground. This is a result of the additional latitude given by the *Framework Directive* for the objective justification of age discrimination, which is translated in *EqA 2010* into the exceptional justifiability of direct discrimination under *s 13(2)* and into a considerably greater range of exceptions to the prohibition of discrimination than are found in relation to the other protected characteristics (see **2.33**).

The second fundamental difference is conceptual. Age is not a discrete characteristic; a person's age falls somewhere on a continuum: see the observations of Mazak AG in his Opinion in *Palacios de la Villa* at [61] and of Jacobs AG in *Lindorfer* at [84]. On the other hand, sex, race, sexual orientation, and even religion or belief tend to fall relatively easily into discrete categories (disability is the protected characteristic most similar to age so far as concerns the difficulties in precise categorisation: cf the discussion of particular disadvantage in the context of disability at **3.71**).

2.6 Direct discrimination

Under *EqA 2010, s 13(1)*, a person (A) discriminates against another (B) if, because of a protected characteristic, A treats B less favourably than A treats or would treat others. However, *s 13(2)* provides that if the protected characteristic is age, A does not discriminate against B if A can show A's treatment of B to be a proportionate means of achieving a legitimate aim. This scope for the justification of direct discrimination is unique to age among the protected characteristics.

2.7 *Less favourable treatment*

The general concept of less favourable treatment is discussed at **1.47**.

2.8 *'Because of [age]': discrimination by association and perception*

It should be noted that under *EqA 2010* A discriminates against B if A treats B less favourably because of age. It is not necessary that the age be B's age: A may discriminate against B if A treats B less favourably because of the age of a third party ('associative discrimination'). In this respect, *EqA 2010* differs from *AR 2006*, where the predecessor provision to *s 13(1)* and *(2)* (*reg 3(1)*) required treatment 'on grounds of B's age' to constitute direct age discrimination. In adopting a more restrictive definition of age discrimination, *AR 2006* appear to have failed properly to implement the *Framework Directive*, under *Article 2(2)* of which prohibited direct discrimination is defined as less favourable treatment 'on any of the grounds referred to in Article 1' (cf, in relation to disability discrimination, the judgment of the ECJ in *Coleman v Attridge Law: C-303/06* [2008] IRLR 722, discussed at **3.7**). However, it is likely that *AR 2006* would have been read as covering associative discrimination, in the light of the EAT's decision in *Coleman v Attridge Law: C-303/06* that the *DDA 1995* could be read as covering associative discrimination, in order to ensure compliance with the *Framework Directive*.

A redundancy decision taken in order to avoid a person (B) qualifying to take immediate early retirement which they would be eligible to receive on reaching pensionable age fell within the scope of the term 'on grounds of B's age' under *AR 2006, reg 3* (see *Wooster v Mayor and Burgesses of the London Borough of Tower Hamlets* [2009] IRLR 980, EAT at [47]) and will equally constitute treatment 'because of age' under *s 13(1)*.

AR 2006 provided that for the purposes of direct discrimination, B's age included B's apparent age (*reg 3(3)(b)*). No such express provision is made by *EqA 2010*. However, the definition of direct discrimination in *s 13* is intended to be wide enough to covered discrimination based on a mistaken perception that someone has a particular protected characteristic (see *Explanatory Notes* at *para 59* and *EHRC Employment Code* at *Section 3.26*), COMMON CONCEPTS **(1)**.

2.9 *Comparators*

Less favourable treatment is a comparative concept: a claimant must demonstrate less favourable treatment by comparison with some other person. That other person, known as a comparator, may be actual or hypothetical; for a general discussion, see COMMON CONCEPTS **(1)**.

Section 23(1) of the Act provides that on a comparison of cases for the purposes of *ss 13*, *14*, or *19* there must be no material difference between the circumstances relating to each case. Like must be compared with like (compare generally *Shamoon v Chief Constable of the Royal Ulster Constabulary* [2003] ICR 337, [2003] IRLR 285 at [4]; *AR 2006, reg 3(2)* made provision to the same effect).

In some circumstances, the proper comparator in a direct age discrimination case will be easy to identify: where a person is less favourably treated on grounds of having reached a fixed trigger age (for example, if a firm of solicitors compels a partner to retire on his 65th birthday because it insists on partners retiring on reaching 65), the comparator should be aged anything below that age, but otherwise in the same position in all material respects.

The selection of the appropriate comparator has caused some difficulty elsewhere in discrimination law, but the fact that age is not a discrete characteristic (see **2.5**) may create a difficulty peculiar to age discrimination. If a man is treated less favourably because of his sex, it is clear that the appropriate comparator is a woman who is otherwise in the same position in all material respects. However, if a woman aged 60 seeks to show that she has been treated less favourably because she is 'too old', how young the appropriate comparator should be may be a difficult question (a woman aged 59 might have been treated identically, but not a woman age 40; it will not suffice to pick a comparator who is simply 'younger'). In many direct age discrimination cases, apart from those where a particular trigger age is involved, it may be a futile exercise to attempt to identify the appropriate comparator prior to asking whether the claimant has been treated less favourably because of age (cf *Shamoon* at [8], where Lord Nicholls observed that '[s]ometimes the less favourable treatment issue cannot be resolved without, at the same time, deciding the reason why issue', the two issues being 'intertwined').

It is likely that the smaller the difference in age between a claimant and the appropriate comparator, the less plausible will it appear to a tribunal that direct age discrimination is the reason for unfavourable treatment, with a stronger and clearer *prima facie* case required before the burden of proof will be reversed (see eg *ABN AMRO Management Services Ltd v Hogben* (20 November 2009, unreported), EAT at [35]; for the reversal of the burden of proof in discrimination cases, see COMMON CONCEPTS (1)).

2.10 *Justification*

As noted above, direct age discrimination can, exceptionally among the protected grounds, be justified: conduct which is a proportionate means of achieving a legitimate aim does not fall within the definition of direct age discrimination at all. Justification is discussed in detail at **2.16**.

2.11 Combined discrimination

By *EqA 2010, s 14*, which has not been brought into force at the time of writing (see *SI 2010/2317, Article 2(2)*), a person (A) will discriminate against another (B) if, because of a combination of two relevant protected characteristics, A treats B less favourably than A treats or would treat a person who does not share either of those characteristics: *s 14(1)*. The relevant protected characteristics for these purposes include age: *s 14(2)*.

Combined discrimination is discussed generally at **1.57**. Of particular note in the context of age is that, by force of *s 14(4)*, B cannot establish a contravention of *EqA 2010* by virtue of *s 14(1)* if, in reliance on another provision of *EqA 2010* or any other enactment, A shows that A's treatment of *B 'is not direct discrimination because of either or both of the characteristics in the combination'*. Thus if A shows that A's treatment of B is not direct discrimination because of age since the treatment is justified under *s 13(2)*, neither will A's treatment of B amount to combined discrimination.

2.12 Indirect discrimination

Under *EqA 2010, s 19(1)*, A discriminates against B if A applies to B a provision, criterion or practice which is discriminatory in relation to a relevant protected characteristic of B's. *Section 19(2)* provides that a provision, criterion or practice (referred to here as a 'PCP') is discriminatory in relation to a relevant protected characteristic of B's if:

(a) A applies, or would apply, it to persons with whom B does not share the characteristic;

(b) it puts, or would put, persons with whom B shares the characteristic at a particular disadvantage when compared with persons with whom B does not share it;

(c) it puts, or would put, B at that disadvantage, and

(d) A cannot show it to be a proportionate means of achieving a legitimate aim.

Relevant protected characteristics for these purposes include age: *s 19(3)*).

For a discussion of the general principles of indirect discrimination, see **1.72**ff.

Insofar as it concerns indirect age discrimination, *s 19* must be read together with *s 5* of the Act. *Section 5(1)* provides that a reference to a person who has a particular protected characteristic is a reference to a person of a particular age group, and a reference to persons who share a protected characteristic is a reference to persons of the same age group. By *s. 5(2)*, an 'age group' is a group of persons defined by reference to age, whether by reference to a particular age or to a range of ages.

The effect of *s 19(2)* read together with *s 5(1)* is that a PCP is discriminatory in relation to B's age if A applies or would apply it to persons who are not of the same age group as B, it puts or would put persons of B's age group at a particular disadvantage when compared with persons who are not of the same age group, it puts or would put B at that disadvantage, and A cannot show it to be a proportionate means of achieving a legitimate aim (ie justify it). The provisions are thus to the same effect as the old *AR 2006, reg 3(1)(b)*.

2.13 *Provision, criterion or practice*

The language of 'provision, criterion or practice' is common to the European discrimination directives and their implementing UK legislation. What is meant by a 'provision, criterion or practice' is discussed generally at **1.75**.

A *change* in an employer's practice over time, such that one practice is replaced with a new practice, is not in itself a PCP: the law of indirect discrimination is not concerned with differences in the age profile of affected employees before and after a change in practice, but with the differential impact of a particular practice at a particular time (see *ABN AMRO Management Services Ltd v Hogben* (20 November 2009, unreported), EAT at [27]–[29], and *Loxley v BAE Systems Land Systems (Munitions & Ordnance) Ltd* [2008] IRLR 853 at [14]). Note though that the EAT in those cases was not considering the different situation where a new practice is introduced for new employees and operates alongside an old one, eg where a particular benefit is not provided to employees who join after a particular date, but continues to be provided to employees who join before that date.

2.14 *Particular disadvantage*

In order to establish indirect age discrimination under *EqA 2010* it is necessary to show (as it was under *AR 2006*) that persons of the claimant's age group are put at a 'particular disadvantage'.

Under the old statutory test for indirect discrimination, prior to the introduction of the *Framework Directive*'s test of 'particular disadvantage', the House of Lords held that discrimination law did not require the impact to be absolutely identical, but simply prohibited a significant disparity of impact. It seems likely that courts and tribunals will equally interpret 'particular disadvantage' as continuing to require a relative disadvantage which is more than insignificant: so the EAT has held, albeit without argument, that what is required is a disadvantage *'which is more than trivial or insignificant'*: *Pike v Somerset County Council* (3 October 2008, unreported) at [28], per HHJ McMullen QC. For a general discussion see **1.76**; it should be noted, however, that authority on the meaning of 'particular disadvantage' under other discrimination strands may not be of assistance in the context of age discrimination: *Homer v Chief Constable of West Yorkshire* [2010] EWCA Civ 419, [2010] IRLR 619 ('*Homer*'), [35], per Maurice Kay LJ.

The particular disadvantage suffered must be the result of the application of the PCP: a requirement which may be particularly significant in age cases. In *Homer* an older employee argued that he had experienced a particular disadvantage in that he had insufficient time before retirement to acquire a particular benefit from his employer (namely, a pay rise conditional on having a law degree). This argument was rejected by both the EAT and the Court of Appeal, essentially on the ground that insofar as there was a 'disadvantage', it was the result of the claimant's age and the imminence of retirement, not the result of the application of the PCP: see [34] per Maurice Kay LJ, endorsing the reasoning of the EAT (at [2009] IRLR 262 [39]–[41]) and [43], [47] and [49] per Mummery LJ.

It is difficult to imagine similar reasoning being adopted by the courts in relation to other strands of indirect discrimination (for example, that a disadvantage was caused not by a PCP but by the claimant's sex). The court's decision in *Homer* appears to be motivated by an understandable desire to limit the scope of prima facie indirect age discrimination: the introduction of any new benefit by an employer might otherwise be challenged by older employees on the ground that they have less opportunity to enjoy it than younger employees. Whether it is appropriate to use the test of particular disadvantage as a filter in this way (rather than recognising an indirectly discriminatory impact but holding that it is readily justified) is debatable, and may be considered by the Supreme Court, to which the Court of Appeal's decision in *Homer* is under appeal.

2.15 *Age group*

Section 19(2) read with *s 5(1)* requires the effect of a PCP on persons of B's age group to be compared with its effect on persons who are not of B's age group. 'Age group' is defined by *s 5(2)* (as it was under *reg 3(3)(a)*) as a group of persons defined by reference to age, whether by reference to a particular age or a range of ages. The fact that age is a characteristic that falls along a continuum creates a problem: where are the limits of any particular age group to be drawn, and what groups are to be compared? As observed at *para 37* of the *Explanatory Notes to the EqA 2010*:

'• An age group would include "over fifties" or twenty-one year olds.
• A person aged twenty-one does not share the same characteristic of age with "people in their forties". However, a person aged twenty-one and people in their forties can share the characteristic of being in the "under fifty" age range.'

In sex discrimination cases, by contrast, the nature of the relevant characteristic makes matters relatively simple; but as Jacobs AG observed in *Lindorfer v EU Council: C-227/04P* [2007] ECR I-6767, '[s]ex is essentially a binary criterion, whereas age is a point on a scale'. In Figure 1 below, illustrating the adverse effect of a provision on members of a pool of different sexes, there are two columns to be compared. In Figure 2, which illustrates the adverse effect of a provision on members of a pool aged between 18 and 65, there are no columns, but a line.

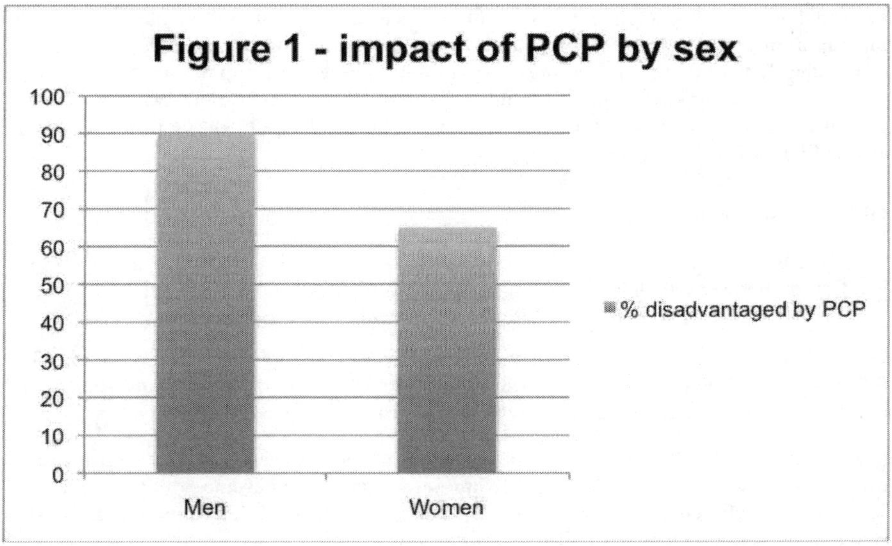

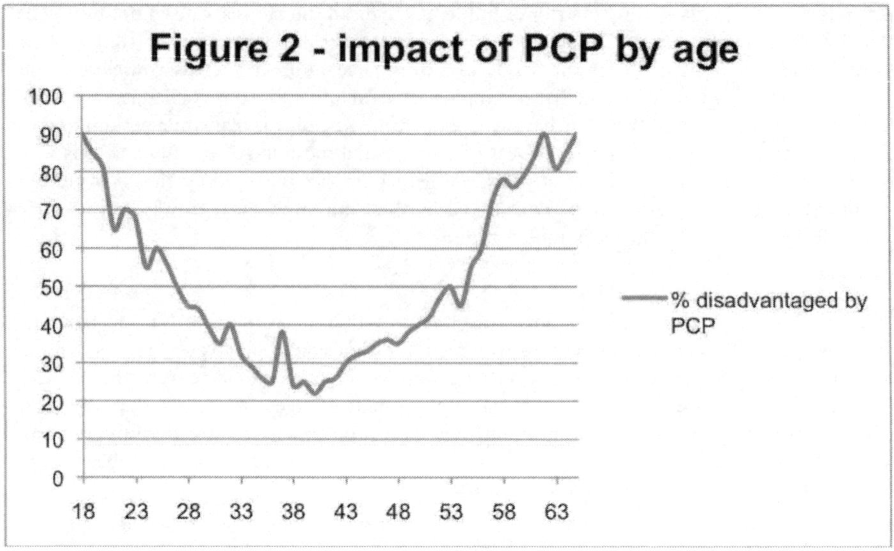

This makes the identification of the age group—the question of where to draw the boundary that marks out the relevant age group from everybody else—particularly important. Indeed, it may be determinative of the question whether there is 'particular disadvantage' at all. In the notional example at Figure 2, if the relevant age group is 40+, there is no real disparity, on average, between the effect of the PCP on that age group and its effect on those not in the age group. If, however, the relevant age group is 58+ plus, members of that group will on average be substantially worse affected by the PCP than persons who are not of that age group.

The EAT has not yet given guidance on the identification of age groups. However, one would expect that it must be for the claimant, in the first instance, to identify the relevant age group, just as it is for the claimant to identify the pool relied on in relation to other protected grounds; but that the tribunal will not necessarily accept that the age group relied on is appropriate: cf *Abbott v Cheshire and Wirral Partnership NHS Trust* [2006] EWCA Civ 523, [2006] ICR 1267 at [17]. In some cases, the appropriate age group may be clear. By way of example, if an employer requires recruits to possess GCSE qualifications (without making allowance for equivalents), there is likely to be a clear cut-off in age of those adversely affected (since GCSE examinations were first sat in 1987).

2.16 Objective justification

As highlighted above, both indirect and, unusually, direct age discrimination are capable of justification under *EqA 2010*, by showing that the provision, criterion or practice, or the less favourable treatment, is a proportionate means of achieving a legitimate aim.

Objective justification of indirect discrimination is discussed generally at **1.83–1.85**. The following discussion considers the justification of direct age discrimination, and features of the justification of indirect discrimination that are special to age.

The justification of direct age discrimination is already the subject of a considerable quantity of case law, and is likely to assume even greater importance once the Default Retirement Age for employees has been phased out, as is due to take place from 6 April 2011 (see the discussion below at **2.64**).

2.17 *Objective justification under the Framework Directive*

Provision for the justification of indirect discrimination is made by the *Framework Directive* itself. The application of a PCP that puts people of a particular age at a particular disadvantage compared with others is excepted from the definition of indirect discrimination in *Article 2(2)(b)* if *'that provision, criterion or practice is objectively justified by a legitimate aim and the means of achieving that aim are appropriate and necessary'*. *Article 2(2)(b)* is now given effect by *EqA 2010, s 19(2)(d)*.

The *Framework Directive* does not make any equivalent provision in respect of direct discrimination. However, *Article 6(1)* permits Member States to provide that differences of treatment on grounds of age (which would otherwise constitute direct discrimination) shall not constitute discrimination if:

> 'within the context of national law, they are objectively and reasonably justified by a legitimate aim, including legitimate employment policy, labour market and vocational training objectives, and if the means of achieving that aim are appropriate and necessary'

and *Article 6(1)* proceeds at sub-paras (a)–(c) to set out a non-exhaustive list of such differences of treatment. This provision is unique to age discrimination.

2.18 *Objective justification of direct age discrimination under AR 2006* and *EqA 2010*

Article 6(1) does not in itself create any justification defence applicable in cases of direct age discrimination. Rather, it has the effect of permitting Member States to create specific exceptions to the prohibition on direct age discrimination where such exceptions are objectively and reasonably justified. Thus, for example, by *AR 2006, reg 32* the United Kingdom created an exception to the prohibition of direct age discrimination in the case of employee benefits based on length of service (now contained in *EqA 2010, Sch 9, para. 10*, discussed further below at **2.36**).

The United Kingdom, however, went further, taking the view that *Article 6(1)* permitted it in effect to create a general justification defence available in all cases where a person can show less favourable treatment on grounds of age to be a proportionate means of achieving a legitimate aim. Thus under *AR 2006, reg 3(1)* the objective justification proviso (that A's conduct would only amount to discrimination if A could not show it to be a proportionate means of achieving a legitimate aim) was applied not only to indirect discrimination but to direct discrimination also. *Section 13(2)* of *EqA 2010* is to the same effect, providing by way of exception to the general definition of direct discrimination that A does not discriminate against B if A can show A's treatment of B to be a proportionate means of achieving a legitimate aim.

The United Kingdom's creation of the objective justification defence for direct discrimination was controversial, and was challenged as incompatible with the *Framework Directive*, principally on the ground that *Article 6(1)* did not permit the creation of a general justification defence, but only of specific and defined exceptions. On a reference from the Administrative Court, the CJEU held that a general and flexible defence of this kind was permissible, but only if its creation could itself be justified by the Member State in accordance with *Article 6*: *Incorporated Trustees of the National Council on Ageing (Age Concern England) v Secretary of State for Business, Enterprise and Regulatory Reform: C-388/07* [2009] ECR I-1569, [2009] IRLR 373. It accordingly fell to the national court to determine whether the defence was justified—and the High Court held that it was, in *R (on the application of Age UK) v Secretary of State for Business, Innovation & Skills* [2009] EWHC 2336, [2009] IRLR 1017. Blake J accepted the UK government's argument that the creation of the defence pursued the legitimate social policy aim of 'preserving the confidence and integrity of the labour market and providing sufficient clarity to the workforce and employers to prevent that confidence being damaged with detrimental consequences to employment and the terms on which employment is offered in the UK' (at [86]) and that—for the time being, at least—the defence was a proportionate means of achieving that objective (see [92]–[94]).

It should be noted that at [96] of his judgment, Blake J stated that 'I consider that any defect in Regulation 3 when drafted can to a certain extent be remedied by the national court reading down and reading in what the emerging ECJ jurisprudence requires to be read in to achieve compatibility', referring to the interpretative principle in *Marleasing SA: C–106/89* [1990] ECR I-4135. The reference to a *Marleasing* construction is potentially confusing, because Blake J did not identify any defect in *reg 3* as drafted. Litigants may seize on this paragraph of the judgment as indicating that Blake J concluded that some special, Community law construction of *reg 3* was required; but it is suggested that the better view is that Blake J simply intended to point out that if future developments in CJEU case law ('emerging ECJ jurisprudence') establish that it is not permissible to allow justification of direct age discrimination in the way the UK has, any defects so emerging could be cured by a *Marleasing* construction, without the need to strike the legislation down.

2.19 *Legitimate aims under EqA 2010, s 13(2)* and social policy

The CJEU in *Age Concern England* made it clear that the sorts of legitimate aims that may be relied upon by Member States under *Article 6* to justify exceptions to the prohibition of direct age discrimination are public interest or social policy aims, in distinction to the usual aims of an individual employer may have (see [46]). But where an employer wishes to rely upon the justification defence under *EqA 2010, s 13(2)*, to what extent must its aims be of a social policy or public interest nature in order to be legitimate?

In *Age UK*, Blake J held at [92] that

> 'there is no reason to believe that in the special context of age discrimination, the kind of business practice reasons that can justify indirect discrimination are fundamentally different from those that can justify direct discrimination'.

However, he proceeded to refer at [97] to 'the individual employer justifying particular practices or treatment in reliance upon [the UK's] social aim', suggesting that it might be necessary for the aims of individual employers to correspond with the UK's social policy objectives in order to qualify as legitimate. In *Seldon v Clarkson, Wright & Jakes* [2010] EWCA Civ 899, [2010] IRLR 865, the Court of Appeal rejected an argument that only social policy objectives could qualify as legitimate aims to justify direct age discrimination under *AR 2006, reg 3(1)* (now *EqA 2010, s 13(2)*), holding it to be sufficient—and necessary—that the aim relied upon should be 'within' or 'consistent with' the social policy objective which justifies *reg 3* ([20]–[22] per Sir Mark Waller).

It is not entirely clear what sorts of legitimate aims will pass or fail the test identified by the Court of Appeal in *Seldon*, not least because the test is formulated in two different ways: an employer's aim might conceivably be 'consistent with' the UK government's social policy objective without falling 'within' that objective. For example, the EAT in *Seldon* ([2009] 3 All ER 435, [2009] IRLR 267) suggested that environmental or charitable objectives could amount to legitimate aims (see [67]), and while such aims are not inconsistent with the UK's social policy objective, it is difficult to see how they fall 'within' it. Permission to appeal the Court of Appeal's judgment is being sought from the Supreme Court; for the present, it is safest to assume that, in order to qualify as legitimate under *s 13(2)*, aims will need at least to have some relation to the social policy objective relied upon by the UK.

2.20 *Identification of legitimate aims under s 13(2)*

Official guidance and consultation documents published in connection with *AR 2006* repeatedly suggested business needs, health and safety, training requirements and the like as examples of legitimate aims which might be relied upon in justification of direct age discrimination: see eg *Impact of the Age Regulations on Pension Schemes* (DTI, December 2006) p 7; *Coming of Age*, p 33; *Age and the Workplace* (ACAS) p 31. Authority for the legitimacy of aims of this broad nature may now be found in domestic case law, which, apart from the possible hurdle set up by *Seldon* (discussed above) has been fairly generous in its recognition of aims as legitimate. Decisions of the CJEU on the justification of exceptions to the prohibition on direct discrimination have also taken a generous approach to the recognition of legitimate aims, and are of assistance in the identification of legitimate aims for the purposes of *s 13(2)*; but the CJEU cases must always be approached with caution, since they involve the justification by Member States of legal exceptions to the prohibition of direct age discrimination, rather than the reliance by private parties on the UK's justification defence (Blake J stated in *Age UK* that private parties relying on the domestic defence would face a *'much more rigorous task'* than Member States relying on *Article 6*: see [97]).

Whether a matter which an employer wishes to rely upon in justification of a discriminatory measure is properly analysed as an aim in itself or a means of achieving an a further aim may be a matter of semantics over which tribunals need not 'cudgel their brains': see *Loxley v BAE Systems Land Systems (Munitions & Ordnance) Ltd* [2008] IRLR 853 at [37] and *Pulham v London Borough of Barking and Dagenham* [2010] ICR 333, [2010] IRLR 184 at [15].

The principal legitimate aims recognised in the age discrimination case law to date are as follows:

Promoting intergenerational fairness. Promoting fairness between various generations of workers was recognised as a legitimate aim in the first major employment tribunal case on justification of direct age discrimination: *Bloxham v Freshfields Bruxhaus Deringer* (9 October 2007, unreported). While the employment tribunal's decision is not authoritative, and indeed the legitimacy of the aim was conceded by the claimant, the proposition that promoting intergenerational fairness must be a legitimate aim for the purposes of *s 13(2)* can hardly be controversial. Further support for the proposition can be found in *Gisela Rosenbladt v Oellerking Gebäudereinigungsges mbH: C-45/09* [2011] IRLR 51 at [45], where the CJEU upheld the legitimacy under *Article 6* of the aim of sharing employment between generations (see too *Petersen v Berunfungsausschuss für Zahnartze fur den Bezirk Westfalen-Lippe: C-341/08* [2010] All ER (EC) 961 at [65]–[68]).

Rewarding long service and protecting older workers. In *Rolls-Royce plc v Unite* [2009] EWCA Civ 387, [2009] IRLR 576 at [95]–[100] the Court of Appeal held that rewarding long service (partly to reward loyalty and partly to achieve a stable workforce in a redundancy process) was a legitimate aim. At the *Article 6* level, the CJEU has recognised the legitimacy of seeking to protect workers with many years of service in an undertaking and to help them to find new employment (*Ingeniørforeningen i Danmark, acting on behalf of Ole Anderson v Region Syddanmark: C-499/08* [2011] 1 CMLR 1140 at [31]).

Creating or improving opportunities for younger (or older) workers. The creation of opportunities for more junior workers was accepted as a legitimate aim in *Seldon*, cited above (in that case the aim was achieved by forcing senior partners in a solicitors' firm to retire after reaching 65). Further support for the legitimacy of the aim may be derived from decisions of the CJEU, which has repeatedly held that the promotion of the integration of young people into the labour market or further education is a legitimate aim for the purpose of *Article 6*: see *Palacios de la Villa v Cortefiel Servicios SA: C-411/05* at [65]; *Hütter v Technische Universität Graz: C-88/08* [2009] All ER (EC) 1129 at [42]; *Petersen v Berunfungsausschuss für den Bezirk Westfalen-Lippe: C-341/08* [2010] All ER (EC) 961 at [74] and *Georgiev v Tehnicheski universitet: C-250/09 and C-268/09* [2011] 2 CMLR 179 at [45]. Cf *Mangold v Helm: C-144/04* [2006] All ER (EC) 383, [2006] IRLR 143 at [60], where the integration into employment of unemployed older workers was equally held to be a legitimate aim capable of justifying an exception to the prohibition on direct age discrimination.

'Congeniality'. In *Seldon*, the firm's rule of compulsory retirement sought among other things to maintain a congenial working atmosphere, by avoiding the need to performance-manage senior partners towards the end of their careers; and this aim too was recognised as legitimate. Whilst the legitimacy of this aim might in some respects be thought surprising (why should the unpleasantness of performance management ever trump the unpleasantness of age discrimination?), it derives support from the decision of the CJEU in *Gisela Rosenbladt v Oellerking Gebäudereinigungsges mbH: C-45/09* [2011] IRLR 51, where the court held at [45] that avoiding the humiliation of termination on grounds of competence could be a legitimate aim of a Member State under *Article 6*.

Avoiding 'windfalls' to employees. In *Loxley v BAE Systems Land Systems (Munitions & Ordnance) Ltd* [2008] IRLR 853 the EAT suggested that it was legitimate under a redundancy scheme to seek to avoid 'windfall' benefits to certain workers, ie benefits which those workers had done nothing to earn; see too *Kraft Foods Ltd v Hastie* (2010) UKEAT/0024/10/ZT, [2010] ICR 1355 at [16] and *Woodcock v Cumbria Primary Care Trust* (2010) UKEAT/0489/09/RN, [2011] ICR 143.

Facilitating workforce planning/ easing the burden on employers. It appears that aims do not need to benefit workers in order to qualify as legitimate. One of the aims held to be legitimate in *Seldon* was the facilitation of workforce planning: by knowing when senior partners would retire, the firm was better able to plan the organisation and development of the workforce. Cf *Seda Kucukdeveci v Swedex GmbH & Co KG: C-555/07* [2010] All ER (EC) 867 at [34], where it was held by the CJEU to be a legitimate aim for a Member State to seek to relieve employers of the burden of lengthy notice periods for younger workers.

Not cost alone? In *Cross v British Airways* [2005] IRLR 423, an indirect sex discrimination case, the EAT surveyed the case law of the CJEU and held that cost alone could never justify indirect discrimination: a need to reduce cost can be put 'into the balance, together with other justifications if there are any' (*Cross* at [72]), but cannot stand alone as a legitimate aim (see generally **Common concepts (1)**). Although the EAT declined to depart from *Cross* in *Redcar and Cleveland Borough Council v Bainbridge* [2008] ICR 249 (see esp [90]), in the recent age discrimination case of *Woodcock v Cumbria Primary Care Trust* [2011] EqLR 4 it has expressed the view, albeit *obiter*, that it should be possible to justify indirect discrimination or direct age discrimination by reference to cost alone: [32]. It remains clear, however, that employers cannot justify a failure to eliminate discrimination by allocating the costs of so doing to a particular budget and declaring that that budget has been exhausted: *Pulham v London Borough of Barking and Dagenham* [2010] ICR 333, [2010] IRLR 184 at [42].

The age discrimination case law of the CJEU contains further examples of aims which would be likely to be upheld by a domestic court as legitimate for the purposes of *s 13(2)*. In *Gergiev v Tehnicheski: C-268/09* (18 November 2010, unreported), the CJEU held at [46] that the aim of fostering an inter-generational mix to promote an exchange of experiences and innovation was upheld as legitimate; and in *Petersen v Berunfungsausschuss für Zahnartze fur den Bezirk Westfalen-Lippe: C-341/08* [2010] All ER (EC) 961 the objective of protecting public health was capable of justifying an exception to the prohibition on age discrimination, by reference to *Article 2(5)* of the *Framework Directive* (the exception for national security, prevention of crime, public health etc). Cf also *Wolf v Stadt Frankfurt am Main: C-299/08* [2010] All ER (EC) 939, discussed below in relation to genuine occupational requirements at **2.32**.

The legitimate aims discussed above are by no means exhaustive, and courts and tribunals appear likely to take a generous approach, subject to the requirements of *Seldon*. However, aims which are themselves tainted by age discrimination will certainly not be legitimate. Thus in *Seldon* itself the employment tribunal rejected one of the aims relied upon by the respondent (maintaining the turnover of partners so that any partner could hope to become senior partner in due course) on the ground that it was tainted by age discrimination: see the judgment of the EAT [2009] 3 All ER 435, [2009] IRLR 267 at [10] and [17].

2.21 *A lower standard for justification of age discrimination?*

Certain comments in Opinions of Advocates General might be interpreted as suggesting that justifying age discrimination may be easier than justifying discrimination of other forms. Thus in *Lindorfer* Jacobs AG stated at [84] to [85] that:

> 'Sex is essentially a binary criterion, whereas age is a point on a scale. Sex discrimination based on actuarial tables is thus an extremely crude form of discrimination, involving very sweeping generalisations, whereas age discrimination may be graduated and may rely on more subtle generalisations.
>
> 'Moreover in law and in society in general, equality of treatment irrespective of sex is at present regarded as a fundamental and overriding principle to be observed and enforced whenever possible, whereas the idea of equal treatment irrespective of age is subject to very numerous qualifications and exceptions . . . '

Sharpston AG did not take issue with Jacobs AG on this point in her Opinion in the same case (given following the judgment in *Mangold*); and Mazak AG expressed a consistent, though more cautious, view in his Opinion in *Palacios de la Villa* at, eg, [62]:

> 'whilst the application of the prohibition of discrimination on grounds of age . . . requires a complex and subtle assessment, age-related distinctions are very common in social and employment policies'.

However, it would be unwise to conclude that a lower standard of objective justification is required in the case of age discrimination. In fact Jacobs AG and Mazak AG both appear to address two distinct issues: the widespread social and political acceptance of direct age discrimination in certain forms, and the difficulty of establishing discrimination due to the nature of age as a characteristic (cf the discussion of 'particular disadvantage' in the context of age and 'age groups', above at **2.14**). While it is recognised in EC law that direct age discrimination may be socially necessary, or even beneficial, it by no means necessarily follows that if an age group can be identified as particularly disadvantaged by the application of a provision, that indirect discrimination ought to be any more readily justifiable than indirect discrimination against, for example, a racial group.

2.22 *No higher standard of objective justification for direct age discrimination*

It was argued in the *Age Concern England/Age UK* litigation that direct age discrimination must require a higher standard of justification than indirect discrimination, not least because *Article 6* of the *Framework Directive* requires exceptions to the prohibition on direct age discrimination to be 'objectively *and reasonably*' justified (whereas the Directive speaks simply of 'objective justification' in relation to indirect discrimination). However, this argument was rejected by the CJEU, which held that what sets *Article 6* justification apart is not the standard of the test but the fact that it involves justification of legislative exceptions by Member States rather than justification of conduct by private individuals; the words 'and reasonably' in *Article 6* were not significant: [65].

There thus appears to be no particular reason why the test for justification of direct age discrimination should be any different to that for indirect discrimination. In *Seldon* [2009] 3 All ER 435, [2009] IRLR 267 the EAT held that tribunals 'must apply the normal principles of legitimate aim and proportionality' ([41]) without any further criterion of exceptionality; the distinction between justification of direct and indirect discrimination lay not in the legal concept, but in practice: it will be harder to justify a directly discriminatory measure as proportionate, because the overall discriminatory effect will be greater ([43]; see too the EAT decisions of *MacCulloch v Imperial Chemical Industries plc* [2008] IRLR 846 at [12], *Pulham v London Borough of Barking and Dagenham* [2010] ICR 333, [2010] IRLR 184 at [15] and *Kraft Foods Ltd v Hastie* (2010) UKEAT/0024/10/ZT, [2010] ICR 1355 at [4(2)]). The Court of Appeal in *Seldon* broadly upheld the EAT's decision, subject to the apparent proviso (discussed above at **2.19**) that in cases of direct age discrimination an employer's legitimate aim must be 'consistent with' or fall 'within' the UK's social policy objective that itself justifies the justification defence. There is further support for the view that the test remains the same whether the discrimination is direct or indirect in the judgment in *Rolls-Royce plc v Unite* [2009] EWCA Civ 387, [2010] WLR 318, where Arden LJ suggested *obiter* at [155] that it would not make any difference on the facts of that case whether the discrimination was direct or indirect, because the same justification analysis would apply.

2.23 *Proportionality*

To establish a defence of justification to an age discrimination claim, whether under *s 13(2)* or *s 19(2)(d)*, a person must establish not only a legitimate aim but that his treatment of the claimant or the provision, criterion or practice applied to the claimant is a proportionate means of achieving that aim. For a general discussion of the principles of proportionality, see **1.85**; see too the summary in *MacCulloch v Imperial Chemical Industries plc* [2008] IRLR 846 at [10]–[11].

There has been considerable discussion of proportionality in domestic age discrimination jurisprudence. CJEU decisions on the justification of exceptions to the prohibition on age discrimination under *Article 6* of the *Framework Directive* must be treated with caution, since they involve justification of measures by Member States, which enjoy a considerably broader margin of discretion under *Article 6* than do individuals under domestic law (see *Age UK* at [97]), but they nonetheless contain helpful guidance on the application of proportionality principles in the context of age discrimination. The following factors emerge from the case law as particularly important.

The need for evidence and the avoidance of stereotyping. In *Seldon* [2009] 3 All ER 435, [2009] IRLR 267 the EAT gave the salutary reminder that while it is not necessary for a tribunal to have *'concrete evidence, neatly weighed, to support each assertion made by the employer'* ([73]), justification requires at least some evidential basis. One of the employment tribunal's conclusions—that a firm's mandatory retirement age of 65 for partners was justified as a means to achieving the legitimate aim of avoiding the unpleasant performance management of partners with declining abilities at the end of their careers—was overturned because there was nothing beyond age-based stereotyping to support the assumption that older partners were indeed more likely to underperform. For further examples of justification defences that have failed for want of sufficient evidence see the employment tribunal cases of *Hampton v Lord Chancellor* [2008] IRLR 258 and *Baker v National Air Traffic Services* ((2009) Times, 27 February); cf *Wolf v Stadt Frankfurt am Main: C-299/08* [2010] All ER (EC) 939 at [41], where the CJEU appeared impressed by the evidence advanced by the German government to the effect that few officials in the fire service older than 45 had sufficient physical capacity to perform the fire-fighting part of their duties.

Coherence and consistency. Some attempted justifications may simply not stand up as a matter of logic. Thus in *Hütter v Technische Universität Graz: C-88/08* [2009] All ER (EC) 1129 the aims relied upon by the Austrian government were each legitimate but were mutually contradictory ([46]); moreover, while one of the aims was to reward professional experience, the measure in question in fact operated to reward workers for the age at which they had acquired that experience ([47]). See also *Seda Kukudeveci v Swedex GmbH & Co KG: C-55/07* [2010] All ER (EC) 867, where the CJEU held that the aim relied upon by the Member State (alleviating the burden on employers by making it easier to dismiss young workers) was legitimate, but that the means by which it sought to achieve that aim (a rule that years of employment prior to the age of 25 did not count towards a statutory minimum notice period based on length of service) was not appropriate for achieving the aim, since it applied to all employees who joined the undertaking before the age of 25, whatever their age at the time of dismissal ([39]–[40]).

Tailored measures. Measures will not pass the proportionality test unless they are properly tailored to the aim which they are supposed to achieve: see *Hütter*, above, and *Petersen v Berufungsausschuss für Zahnärzte für den Bezirk Westfalen-Lippe: C-341/08*

[2010] All ER (EC) 961, where a rule imposing a maximum age on the practice of dentistry was held not to be a proportionate means of achieving the aim of protecting public safety under *Article 2(5)* of the *Framework Directive*, because a significant category of dentists was excepted from the rule altogether ([61]).

Consent and collective negotiation. The fact that a person has agreed to a particular measure (whether personally or by collective negotiation) may be a significant factor in assessing its proportionality: *Seldon* [2010] EWCA Civ 899 at [30] (partner had signed partnership deed containing provision as to mandatory retirement); *Rolls-Royce plc v Unite* [2009] EWCA Civ 387, [2010] 1 WLR 318 at eg [120] (redundancy scheme had been negotiated with union with a view to achieving fairness generally); *Loxley v BAE Systems Land Systems (Munitions & Ordnance) Ltd* [2008] IRLR 853 at [42] (redundancy scheme had been negotiated with trade unions). However, consent is not conclusive, and tribunals must not abdicate the responsibility for carrying out the necessary proportionality exercise; moreover, a consensus may only be relevant if the negotiating parties have actually considered the justifiability of a provision: *Pulham v London Borough of Barking and Dagenham* [2010] ICR 333, [2010] IRLR 184 at [40]–[41]. Consent is likely to be given more weight where the parties have some equality of bargaining power (eg an agreement between an employer and a union or between partners of equal status).

Fairness over time. Age discrimination is unusual in that an age discriminatory provision may be something from which all workers will benefit at some stage in the course of their working lives: the fairness of a scheme over time may thus justify its age discriminatory effect at any particular moment (*Rolls-Royce plc v Unite* [2009] EWCA Civ 387, [2010] 1 WLR 318 at [162]; see too *Bloxham v Freshfields Bruxhaus Deringer* (9 October 2007, unreported).

The proportionality of a directly discriminatory measure may be harder to demonstrate. See the discussion above at **2.22**.

The distinction between rules and their application. Once a particular rule has been justified by an employer (eg a compulsory retirement age), the application of that rule to an individual will usually need little justification: *Seldon* [2010] EWCA Civ 899 at [36]; see also *MacCulloch v Imperial Chemical Industries plc* [2008] IRLR 846 at [34]–[36].

2.24 *Relationship with exemptions*

If a potentially discriminatory measure falls within one of the specific exceptions contained within *EqA 2010, Sch 9, Pt 2* (discussed below at **2.33**), it requires no justification under *s 13(2)* or *s 19(2)(d)*.

The fact that a particular measure falls close to, but outside, one of the statutory exceptions may be relied upon by litigants for forensic purposes (with respondents arguing that its proximity to an exception supports their justification, and claimants arguing that the exception does not cover the measure for good reason). Some (limited) significance has been attached to an analogies with statutory exceptions which do not directly apply to support an objective justification (see eg *MacCulloch* at para 7 and *Seldon v Clarkson Wright & Jakes* at para 83), but proximity to a statutory exception is not of any real legal significance. As emphasised by the CJEU in *Age Concern England* [2009] IRLR 373, justification under *Article 6*, which the UK has relied upon in creating the exceptions, is a different exercise to justification by private individuals.

2.25 Harassment and victimisation

The rules on harassment are now unified for all protected characteristics (including age) in a single provision: *EqA 2010, s 26*, discussed at **1.87**ff. So too are the rules on victimisation at *s 27*, discussed at **1.99**ff. There are no specialised harassment or victimisation rules particular to the protected characteristic of age.

2.26 Discussions about pay

EqA 2010, s 77 makes contractual pay secrecy clauses unenforceable to the extent that they prevent employees from making disclosures about pay which are sought or made for the purpose of finding out whether (or to what extent) any different in pay is related to a protected characteristic. Action taken by an employer as a result of an individual making or seeking to make a relevant pay disclosure, or receiving information disclosed in a relevant pay disclosure, may amount to victimisation. This new provision in the *EqA 2010* applies to all strands of discrimination and is considered further at **Common concepts (1)**.

2.27 Instructing, causing or inducing discrimination

It is unlawful to instruct, cause or induce someone to discriminate against, harass or victimise another person, or to attempt to do so (*EqA 2010, s 111*). A claim can be brought by the 'victim' of the discrimination, the person who was instructed to carry out the discrimination and the EHRC. This is wider than the provision under *AR 2006, reg* 5 which made it unlawful to treat somebody less favourably because they refused to carry out a discriminatory instruction or complained about having received the instruction. The new provision is common to all strands of discrimination and is discussed further at **Common concepts (1)**.

2.28 Liability of employer for employees and agents and aiding discrimination

Where employees commit acts of discrimination against fellow employees, their employer will be liable if the acts were committed during the course of employment (*EqA 2010, s 109(1)*). Employers are also liable for the discriminatory acts of their agents if they are acting with the employer's authority (*s 109(4)*). In each case it is irrelevant whether the employer knew or approved of the acts (*s 109(3)*). However, there is a defence for employers in relation to the acts of their employees (but not agents) if they can show that they took all reasonable steps to prevent the employee from doing the act in question (*s 109(4)*). The employees and agents will also have personal liability for their acts of discrimination (*EqA 2010, s 110*), even if the employer has a defence. Again, this is common to all strands of discrimination. See **1.63–1.68**.

It is also unlawful for an individual to knowingly help another to carry out an act which is unlawful under *EqA 2010, s 112(1)*. (See **Common concepts (1)**.)

2.29 DISCRIMINATION IN EMPLOYMENT

Scope of the prohibition on age discrimination

AR 2006 only applied to employment, occupation and training, like the *Framework Directive* they implemented, and the scope of the prohibition on age discrimination under *EqA 2010* continues to be the most limited among all the protected characteristics.

The rules concerning discrimination in employment, which is the subject of this work, are now set out in the *EqA 2010, Pt 5, Chapter 1* and apply to all protected characteristics. They are subject to the exceptions in *Sch 9*, which include a set of specific exceptions relating to age in *Sch 9, Pt 2*.

The prohibition of age discrimination does not yet extend to the provision of goods and services. *Part 3* of the Act (Services and public functions) is drafted so as to apply to age discrimination (except so far as relating to persons who have not attained the age of 18: *s 28(1)(a)*), but its provisions have not yet been brought into force so far as they concern the protected characteristic of age: see *SI 2010/2317, Article 2(3)(a)*. In its January 2010

Policy Statement, *Equality Bill: Making it work—Ending age discrimination in services and public functions*, the then government stated that it was 'firmly committed to eradicating harmful and unjustifiable age discrimination in the provision of services and public functions' and expressed the intention of bringing the relevant provisions into force in 2012. However, the present coalition government has committed to no such timetable. Its position is that it 'is currently considering further how these provisions can be implemented in the best way for business and others involved': see http://www.equalities.gov.uk/equality_act_2010/faqs_on_commencement_of_the_eq/age_discrimination.aspx.

In July 2008 the European Commission published a draft Directive which would prohibit discrimination because of disability, religion or belief, sexual orientation and age, in access to goods and services, housing, education, social protection, social security and social advantage (COM(2008) 426 final). It remains under negotiation.

Of the remaining principal Parts of the Act, it should be noted that *Part 4* (premises) does not apply to the protected characteristic of age; *Part 6* of the Act (Education) does apply to age, with the exception of *Chapter 1* (Schools); and *Part 7* (Associations) is drafted so as to apply to age but its provisions have not been brought into force insofar as they concern the protected characteristic of age (*SI 2010/2137, Article 2(7)*). The new public sector equality duty provided for by the Act will cover age (see *s 149(7)*) but has not been brought into force. These matters are all, in any event, beyond the scope of this book.

The Act makes provision for the scope of the prohibition on age discrimination to be further restricted by *s 197(1)*, not yet in force, under which a Minister may by order amend the Act to provide that any of the following does not contravene this Act so far as relating to age: (a) specified conduct; (b) anything done for a specified purpose; (c) anything done in pursuance of arrangements of a specified description. However, the power does not extend to *Pt 5* (Work) or *Pt 6, Chapter 2* (further and higher education). As the *Explanatory Notes to the EqA 2010* explain at *para 627*, *s 197* is designed to allow exceptions to be made from the new prohibitions on age discrimination in the provision of services and the exercise of public functions, when those provisions are brought into force in relation to age.

2.30 Protection for applicants and employees

There is now a common definition of employee across all strands of discrimination, which is set out in *EqA 2010, s 83(2)(a)* and is discussed further in **Common concepts (1)**.

The specific rules setting out the scope of protection for applicants and employees against age discrimination in relation to employment, which were contained in *AR 2006, reg 7* have also now harmonised and replaced by *EqA 2010, s 39*, which contains a set of rules applicable to all protected characteristics (see **Common concepts (1)**).

There is also a common provision dealing with discrimination against former employees across all strands of discrimination in *EqA 2010, s 108* (replacing *AR 2006, reg 24*) which makes it unlawful for an employer to discriminate against or harass a former employee contrary to *EqA 2010* where such discrimination or harassment arises out of and is closely connected to the employment relationship (see **Common concepts (1)**).

2.31 Protection outside the employment relationship

In addition to applicants, employees and former employees the following groups of individuals and categories of activity were subject to *AR 2006* protection and are now subject to the protection of the *EqA 2010*: contract workers, office holders, occupational pension schemes, partnerships, barristers and advocates, trade organisations, qualification bodies and employment service providers. The scope of the protection of each category is considered in **Common concepts (1)**.

2.32 General exceptions

Schedule 9 (to which effect is given by *s 83(11)*) contains a series of exceptions to *Part 5:* occupational requirements (*Sch 9, Pt 1*), exceptions relating to age (*Pt 2*) and other exceptions (*Pt 3*). The provisions permitting positive action (falling short of positive discrimination) to promote under-represented groups in the workforce have now been standardised across all strands of discrimination and are set out in *EqA 2010, ss 158* and *159* (see COMMON CONCEPTS (1)).

The specific age exceptions contained in *Sch 9, Pt 2* are discussed in detail below. The general exceptions which are relevant to age are occupational requirements (including armed forces) and provision of services to the public (*Pt 3*). For a general discussion of *Sch 9, Pts 1 and 3* see COMMON CONCEPTS (1). There are, however, two particular points of note concerning the provisions of *Sch 9, Pt 1* in the context of age discrimination.

First, in *Wolf v Stadt Frankfurt am Main: C-299/08* [2010] All ER (EC) 939, the CJEU held that, in the context of recruitment to the German fire-service, the possession of exceptionally high physical fitness could be a 'genuine and determining occupational requirement' relating to age ([42]) for the purposes of justifying discrimination under the *Framework Directive, Article 4(1)*. However, it should be noted that under *Article 4(1)* it is a 'characteristic related to' a protected ground that may be a genuine and determining occupational requirement; only the protected characteristic itself may qualify as an occupational requirement under *Sch 9, para 1*. An employer seeking to rely on *para 1* in the context of age discrimination would have to show that age itself is a requirement of the role (eg, to give the classic example, because a child actor is needed); the argument accepted by the CJEU in *Wolf*—that very few people over a certain age possessed the requisite high physical fitness—would not be enough.

Second, *Sch 9, para 4(3)* provides that *Part 5* of the Act does not apply at all to service in the armed forces so far as it concerns age.

2.33 Exceptions specific to age

Schedule 9, Pt 2 defines an 'age contravention' at *para 7* as a contravention of *Part 5* of the Act so far as relating to age, before setting out a series of exceptional scenarios in which an age contravention will not occur. These are discussed below. The government is consulting over whether, on abolition of the default retirement age, it should introduce further exceptions to clarify when it will be lawful for employers to cease cover, require medical underwriting or pass on additional costs in relation to older employees under group insured benefits and when employees should be treated as good leavers under share schemes. At the time of writing the outcome of the consultation has not been published

2.34 *Retirement*

Schedule 9, para 8(1) provides that it is not an age contravention to dismiss a relevant worker at or over the age of 65 if the reason for the dismissal is retirement. A relevant worker for these purposes is defined by *para 8(2)* as:

(a) an employee within the meaning of the *ERA 1996, s 230(1)*;

(b) a person in Crown employment;

(c) a relevant member of the House of Commons staff; or

(d) a relevant member of the House of Lords staff.

Para 8(3) provides that retirement is a reason for dismissal only if it is a reason for dismissal by virtue of the *ERA 1996, Pt 10*.

There are several points to note:

(a) *para 8(1)* does not apply where an employee is compulsorily retired before the age of 65. Such a retirement dismissal is direct age discrimination which must be justified in the ordinary way, in accordance with *s 13(2)*;

(b) it is necessary to refer to a complex set of provisions contained in the *ERA 1996, Pt 10* (ss *98ZA–98ZF*, discussed in detail below at **2.64**) to determine whether the reason for a dismissal is in fact retirement for the purposes of *para 8(1)*;

(c) the definition of an employee for the purposes of *para 8(1)* is narrower than that used generally in the *EqA 2010, Pt 5*. While an employee in general includes anyone employed under a contract of service or of apprenticeship, under a contract personally to do any work (see *s 83(2)(a)*), the retirement exception applies only to employees within the meaning of *ERA 1996, s 230(1)* (ie individuals who have entered into or work under contract of employment), to people in Crown employment and to relevant members of the House of Lords and House of Commons staff. In particular:

    (i) the retirement exception does not apply to workers who are not employees in the narrower sense;

    (ii) the retirement exception does not apply to partners, or to office holders who do not fall within the definition of Crown employment.

In such cases, the direct discrimination involved in compulsory retirement on grounds of age will have to be justified in the ordinary way, in accordance with *EqA 2010, s 13(2)*.

Para 8 is the direct successor to *AR 2006, reg 30* which contained the retirement exception known as the 'Default Retirement Age' or 'DRA'.

Regulation 30, along with *reg 3*, was challenged in the *Age Concern England/Age UK* case, on the ground that it was incompatible with the *Framework Directive*. The UK government initially contended that the DRA did not fall within the scope of the Directive at all, but by the time the point reached the CJEU on a reference the UK had been forced to concede it in light of the court's intervening judgment in *Palacios de la Villa v Cortefiel Servicios SA: C-411/05* [2007] IRLR 989; and the CJEU held that a provision such as *reg 30* did indeed fall within the Directive's scope: see *Palacios* at [45]–[46] and *R (Age Concern England) v Secretary of State for Business, Enterprise and Regulatory Reform* Case 388/07 [2009] IRLR 373 at [28]. Whether the DRA was justified under the *Framework Directive, Article 6* was a matter for the national court to determine. In *R (Age UK) v Secretary of State for Business, Innovation and Skills* [2009] EWHC 2336 (Admin), [2010] ICR 260, [2009] IRLR 1017), Blake J accepted that the DRA pursued a legitimate aim, namely that a social policy aim 'that may generally be described as maintaining confidence in the labour market' ([103]), and that it was proportionate to use *some* sort of DRA ([109]–[113]), but expressed considerable doubt as to the appropriateness of the use of age 65 for the DRA, observing that the case for advancing the DRA to a higher age than 65 seemed '*compelling*' ([117]). Blake J nonetheless upheld the validity of *reg 30*, but on the sole basis that:

(a) the challenge was a historical one, and the DRA's adoption had not been outside the state's margin of appreciation in 2006 when *AR 2006* were introduced; and

(b) the then government had announced that it would be holding an imminent review of the DRA in 2010: [128]–[129].

The coalition government formed after the May 2010 general election committed to phasing out the DRA altogether (see eg the 29 July 2010 consultation document *Phasing Out the Default Retirement Age*). The impact of this is discussed below at **2.64**.

2.35 *Applicants at or approaching retirement age*

Schedule 9, Pt 2, para 9(1) (replacing *AR 2006, reg 7(4)*) provides that a person does not contravene *s 39(1)(a) or (c)* (broadly, does not commit discrimination by not offering a person employment), so far as relating to age, in a case where the other person: (a) has attained the age limit, or would have attained it before the end of six months beginning with the date on which the application for the employment had to be made, and (b) would, if recruited for the employment, be a relevant worker within the meaning of *para 8*.

Para 9(2) provides that the 'age limit' for the purposes of sub-para (1) is whichever is the greater of: (a) the age of 65, and (b) the normal retirement age in the case of the employment concerned. The 'normal retirement age' is to be construed in accordance with the *ERA 1996, s 98ZH* (for which see **2.80**).

Para 9 will be phased out from 6 April 2011 together with the DRA, although the response to the government's consultation has not been published at the time of writing.

2.36 *Benefits based on length of service*

Para 10 creates a qualified exception to the prohibition against age discrimination in the case of the provision of benefits based on length of service. It is the direct successor to *AR 2006, reg 32* and is intended to replicate its effect (*Explanatory Notes to the EqA 2010, para 832*). In effect, it gives employers an exemption from age discrimination claims where benefits are awarded or increased based on up to five years' service. If employers want to use service above five years *para 10* they can do so if they reasonably believe it fulfils a business need. However, the details of the provision are quite technical.

The drafting is slightly convoluted. *Para 10(1)* provides that it is not an age contravention for a person (A) to put a person (B) at a disadvantage when compared with another (C), in relation to the provision of a benefit, facility or service in so far as the disadvantage is because B has a shorter period of service than C. *Para 10(2)* then provides that if B's period of service exceeds five years, A may rely on sub-para (1) only if A reasonably believes that doing so fulfils a business need.

Para 10(3)–(6) establish a compulsory mechanism for calculating a worker's length of service. A can choose that a person's period of service is either:

(a) the period for which the person has been working for A at or above a level (assessed by reference to the demands made on the person) that A reasonably regards as appropriate for the purposes of *para 10*, or

(b) the period for which the person has been working for A at any level. In this case service will include any period in which the person worked for another employer if that period counts as a period of employment with A under *ERA 1996, s 218* (eg work for an associated employer or a prior to a business transfer), or is treated as a period of employment with A by an enactment pursuant to which the person's employment was transferred to A.

In either case the period for which a person has been working for A must be based on the number of weeks during the whole or part of which the person has worked for A (*para 10(4)*), but A may, if it is reasonable to do so, discount (a) periods of absence and (b) periods that A reasonably regards as related to periods of absence (*para 10(5)*).

Para 10(7) provides that for the purposes of *paragraph 10* the reference to a 'benefit, facility or service' does not include a reference to a benefit, facility or service which may be provided only by virtue of a person's ceasing to work.

'Benefit, facility or service'

2.37 In *Rolls-Royce plc v Unite the Union* [2009] EWCA Civ 387, [2010] 1 WLR 318 the Court of Appeal suggested that 'benefit' in *reg 32* (which was defined by *reg 2* as including a 'facility or service') should be broadly interpreted to include any advantage, such that the awarding of points based on length of service under a redundancy selection scheme amounted to a 'benefit': see [103] per Wall LJ, [135] per Aikens LJ, [165] per Arden LJ. The dicta of Wall and Arden LJJ on this point were strictly *obiter*, as they decided the case on the basis of *reg 3* (justification of direct discrimination) rather than *reg 32*, but it is arguable at least that the interpretation of *reg 32* was central to the reasoning of Aikens LJ (with whom Wall and Arden LJJ agreed on this point) and therefore binding.

Para 10 would thus appear to be very broad in scope, encompassing a broad range of 'advantages' connected with employment, subject only to the exclusion in *para 10(7)* of benefits, facilities or services provided only by virtue of a person's ceasing to work. In particular, redundancy payments, which are covered by *Sch 9, para 13* are excluded (see the *Explanatory Notes to the EqA 2010, para 833*); advantages enjoyed under a redundancy selection scheme are of course enjoyed while employment is continuing, which is why they are not excluded from the paragraph.

The justification for para 10

2.38 The government explained in the *Notes on the Regulations* that the purpose of *para 10's* predecessor provision, reg *32, was* to retain service-related benefits, which it considered were justified under the *Framework Directive, Article 6* by the legitimate aim of:

> 'employment planning, in the sense of being able to attract, retain and reward experienced staff. [Service-related benefits] help maintain workforce stability by rewarding loyalty as distinct from performance and by responding to employees' reasonable expectation that their salary should not remain static' ([113]).

While the courts would in all probability recognise rewarding long service as a legitimate aim capable of justifying the provision under *Article 6* (cf *Ingeniørforeningen i Danmark, acting on behalf of Ole Anderson v Region Syddanmark: C-499/08* [2011] 1 CMLR 1140 at [31]), it may be questioned whether *para 10* is a proportionate means of achieving that aim, particularly because, following the approach in *Rolls-Royce* (discussed above), *para 10(1)* would allow an employer in a redundancy situation to select only employees with five years' service or less for redundancy, as a blanket criterion. The compatibility of *reg 32* with the *Framework Directive* was challenged (in part) in the employment tribunal case of *Harrison v Ministry of Defence* [2010] EqLR 255, but without success; there is no appellate authority on the point.

Reasonable belief under para 10(2)

2.39 If B's service exceeds five years it falls upon the employer or principal to 'top-up', as it were, the government's objective justification: A must reasonably believe that relying upon the length of service exception fulfils a business need. This requirement has both subjective and objective elements. First, A must show that he believes or believed that reliance upon the exception fulfilled a business need. Secondly, he must show that his subjective view was reasonable.

The degree of stringency of the objective test may be open to argument. Outside the context of EC-based discrimination law, a reasonableness requirement might require no more than that the employer's view was a view open to a reasonable employer. Here, however, the context (and particularly the fact that *para 10* must itself be justified under *Article 6* to be compatible with the *Framework Directive*) might tend to require reasonableness informed by proportionality—but proportionality is the standard of the test for the justification of direct or indirect age discrimination under *s 13(2)* and *s 19*, and if a measure can be justified under those provisions, an employer would not need to rely upon *para 10* at all. The *EHRC Employment Code* states that the test is less onerous than the general test of objective justification, but that an employer would still need evidence to support a reasonable belief, which could include information gathered through monitoring, staff attitude surveys or focus groups. It also states that employers would be expected to take the interests of their workers into account and not be motivated solely by financial self-interest.

In *Rolls Royce* Arden LJ at [167] suggested 'provisionally' (and *obiter*) that what is required is that 'the reasonable employer has to show that it has balanced all the relevant considerations', which in that case included the fact that the length of service criterion formed part of the employees' contracts of employments and had been the subject of collective negotiation. It may be that the reasonableness of the procedure adopted by the employer in reaching its conclusion may also be relevant ('the court has an important role to play in scrutinising the conclusion of the employer and the processes by which its conclusion was reached': Arden LJ at [168]). For an example of the approach tribunals may take under *para 10(2)* see the employment tribunal's judgment in *Harrison v Ministry of Defence* [2010] EqLR 255. Arden LJ also expressed the (provisional and obiter) view that the subjective part of the test could be satisfied notwithstanding the fact that by the time of the hearing, the employer's assertion at the hearing was that it did not believe that a length of service criterion which it had agreed with the union in the past fulfilled a reasonable business need. Unusually, in that case it was the union which was arguing that the length of service criterion was lawful and the employer was arguing that it was not.

'Business need'

2.40 *Regulation 32(2)* gave 'encouraging the loyalty or motivation, or rewarding the experience' of the employer's workers as examples of fulfilling a business need. These examples do not appear in *EqA 2010* but were included in the *Explanatory Notes to the EqA 2010* (at *para 829*). The *EHRC Employment Code* gives examples of 'rewarding higher levels of experience, or encouraging loyalty or maintaining the motivation of long-serving staff' (*Section 14.23*) It is submitted that apart from encouraging (or rewarding) loyalty, none of the examples is particularly convincing: length of service based benefits do not motivate except insofar as they reward loyal employees, and a new employee might have just as much experience as a long serving employee (though nonetheless, rewarding experience was accepted as a legitimate expectation in the *Article 141* cases *Handels-og Kontorfunktionaer-ernes Forbund I Danmark v Dansk Arbejdsgiverforening, acting on behalf of Danfoss: C-109/88* [1991] ICR 74 and *Cadman v Health and Safety Executive: C-17/05* [2006] ECR I-9583, [2006] ICR 1623: 'Length of service goes hand in hand with experience', *Cadman*, [35]). While the list is non-exclusive, it may be that further examples of business needs are few and far between. The language of 'business needs' does not accommodate intentions that are laudable but unnecessary.

2.41 *National minimum wage*

Paragraph 11(1) provides that it is not an age contravention for a person to pay a young worker (A) at a lower rate than that at which the person pays an older worker (B) if (a) the hourly rate for the national minimum wage for a person of A's age is lower than that for a person of B's age, and (b) the rate at which A is paid is below the single hourly rate.

A 'young worker' for these purposes is defined by *sub-para (2)* as a person who qualifies for the national minimum wage at a lower rate than the single hourly rate, and an 'older worker' as a person who qualifies for the national minimum wage at a higher rate than that at which the young worker qualifies for it. *Sub-para (3)* provides that the 'single hourly rate' is the rate prescribed under the *National Minimum Wage Act 1998, s 1(3)*.

Paragraph 12(1) provides that it is not an age contravention for a person to pay an apprentice who does not qualify for the national minimum wage at a lower rate than the person pays an apprentice who does.

An apprentice for these purposes is defined by *para 12(2)* as a person who: (a) is employed under a contract of apprenticeship; or (b) is treated as so employed as a result of provision made by virtue of the *National Minimum Wage Act 1998, s 3(2)(a)*.

These provisions are designed to replicate the effect of *AR 2006, reg 31*: see the *Explanatory Notes to the EqA 2010, paras 838 and 840.*

2.42 *Enhanced redundancy payments*

Paragraph 13 is the successor to *AR 2006, reg 33* and creates exceptions concerning the award of 'enhanced redundancy payments' to qualifying employees. The detailed provisions are set out below, but in summary it gives employers an exemption where they operate an enhanced redundancy scheme which mirrors the statutory redundancy scheme but is more generous in one or more of the following ways:

(i) it increases or removes the cap on a week's pay;

(ii) it multiplies the 'appropriate amount' (ie the half, one or one-and-a-half week's pay) allowed for each year of employment by a figure greater than 1;

(iii) it multiplies the total payment (after any increases for (i) and (ii)) by an amount greater than one; and/or

(iv) it provides payments to employees who do not have the two years' qualifying service.

For redundancy payments generally, see **TOLLEY'S EMPLOYMENT HANDBOOK (REDUNDANCY – I)** and for the risk of age discrimination in relation to redundancy schemes which do not fall within the statutory exception, see **2.90**.

Exception for award of enhanced redundancy payments

2.43 *Paragraph 13(1)* provides that it is not an age contravention for a person to give a 'qualifying employee' an enhanced redundancy payment of an amount less than that of an enhanced redundancy payment which the person gives to another qualifying employee, if each amount is calculated on the same basis.

Paragraph 13(2) provides that it is not an age contravention to give enhanced redundancy payments only to those who are qualifying employees by virtue of sub-para *(3)(a) or (b)*, ie employees who meet the requirement to have two years' qualifying service.

Qualifying employees

2.44 A 'qualifying employee' under *para 13(3)* is an employee who:

(a) is entitled to a statutory redundancy payment as a result of *ERA 1996, s 135*, ie is dismissed by reason of redundancy or is laid off, is eligible for a redundancy payment by reason of being laid off or kept on short-time;

(b) agrees to the termination of the employment (eg volunteers for redundancy) in circumstances where the person would, if dismissed, have been entitled to a statutory redundancy payment;

(c) would have been entitled to a statutory redundancy payment but for *ERA 1996, s 155* (which makes entitlement conditional on a minimum of two years' continuous employment); or

(d) agrees to the termination of the employment in circumstances where the person would, if dismissed, have been entitled to a redundancy payment but for the fact that they did not have the minimum two year's continuous employment.

Calculation of enhanced redundancy payments

2.45 *Paragraph 13(4)* defines an enhanced redundancy payment as a payment the amount of which is calculated in accordance with the normal rules for statutory redundancy payments set out in *ERA 1996, s 162(1)–(3)*, but then increased in one or more of the ways permitted by *para 13(5) or (6)*.

The starting point therefore is the calculation of a normal statutory redundancy payment under *ERA 1996, s 162*, which involves calculating the employee's continuous service (reckoning back from the effective date of termination) and allowing 'the appropriate amount', ie:

(a) one and a half weeks' pay for a year of employment in which the employee was not below the age of forty-one;

(b) one week's pay for a year of employment (not within para (a)) in which he was not below the age of twenty-two, and

(c) half a week's pay for each year of employment not within para (a) or (b).

A week's pay for these purposes is subject to the statutory maximum under *ERA 1996, s 227* (£400 as of 1 February 2011) and where an employee has more than 20 years' service, only the last 20 years are taken into account.

Sch 9, para 13(5) then allows an employer (or other person making an enhanced redundancy payment) to modify the above calculation by:

(a) treating a week's pay (which by *para 13(7)* is to be read with *ERA 1996, Pt 14, Chapter 2*, including *s 227*) as not being subject to a maximum amount,

(b) treating a week's pay as being subject to a maximum amount above that specified under *ERA 1996, s 227*; and/or

(c) multiplying the appropriate amount (which by *para 13(7)* has the meaning given in *ERA 1996, s 162*) for each year of employment by a figure of more than one.

Para 13(6) allows an employer (or other person) to apply a multiplier of more than one to the figure yielded by the redundancy payment calculation (whether or not *sub-para (5)* has also been relied upon).

Para 13(8) provides that for the purposes of calculating an enhanced redundancy payment in the case of a person who is a qualifying employee by virtue of *sub-para (3)(b) or (d)*, the reference to 'the relevant date' in *ERA 1996, s 162(1)(a)* (ie the date from which entitlement to a redundancy payment is calculated) is to be read as a reference to the date of termination of employment.

2.46 *Life assurance*

Para 14 creates an exception where a person (A) takes early retirement because of ill health. It provides that it is not an age contravention to provide A with life assurance cover for the period starting when A retires and ending: (a) if there is a normal retirement age, when A attains the normal retirement age; or (b) in any other case, when A attains the age of 65. The normal retirement age in relation to A is the age at which, when A retires, persons holding comparable positions in the same undertaking are normally required to retire: *para 14(3)*.

Para 14 is designed to replicate the effect of *AR 2006, reg 34*: see *Explanatory Notes to the Eqa 2010, para 847*.

2.47 *Child care*

Para 15(1) provides that a person does not contravene a relevant provision (namely *EqA 2010, ss 39(2)(b), 41(1)(c), 44(2)(b), 45(2)(b), 47(2)(b), 48(2)(b), 49(6)(b), 50(6)(b), 57(2)(a) or 58(3)(a)*: see *para 15(2)*) so far as relating to age, only by providing, or making arrangements for or facilitating the provision of, care for children of a particular age group. The 'relevant provision' which is relevant to employees is *s 39(2)(b)*, which makes it unlawful to discriminate against an employee in relation to access to opportunities for promotion, transfer or training or for receiving any other benefit, facility or service.

Para 15 (3) gives a non-exhaustive list of examples of 'facilitating the provision of care for a child':

'(a) paying for some or all of the cost of the provision;
(b) helping a parent of the child to find a suitable person to provide care for the child;
(c) enabling a parent of the child to spend more time providing care for the child or otherwise assisting the parent with respect to the care that the parent provides for the child.'

A child for the purposes of *para 15* is a person who has not attained the age of 17, and a reference to care includes a reference to supervision: see *para 15(4)* and *(5)*.

Para 15 is a new provision, which had no equivalent in *AR 2006*. The *Explanatory Notes* explain that its purpose is to allow employers to continue to offer employees child care facilities based on the age of a child without being open to a challenge of direct discrimination from other employees in light of the decision in *Coleman v Attridge Law: C-303/06* [2008] ECR I-5603 (discussed at **2.8** and **3.7**). The *EHRC Employment Code* indicates that the exception extends to activities which are aimed at '*enabling parents to spend more time on childcare*', which will include flexible working.

2.48 *Personal pensions*

Under *para 16(1)* a Minister of the Crown may by order provide that it is not an age contravention for an employer to maintain or use, with respect to contributions to personal pension schemes, practices, actions or decisions relating to age which are of a specified description. Such excepted practices, actions or decisions have been provided for by the *Equality Act (Age Exceptions for Pension Schemes) Order 2010 (SI 2010/2133)*, discussion of which is outside the scope of this work.

2.49 *Statutory authority*

EqA 2010, Sch 22, para 1(1) provides, in relation to age, that a person (P) does not contravene any of the age discrimination provisions in *EqA 2010, Pts 3–7* (which includes the 'work' provisions in *Pt 5*) if P acts pursuant to a requirement of an enactment.

Thus, for example, it is not unlawful under *EqA 2010* for a publican not to allow an employee under the age of 18 to sell alcohol without supervision (since he is required so to act by the *Licensing Act 2003, s 153*). A further example may be found in the case of *Renfrewshire Council v Martin* (30 April 2008, unreported), EAT, in which it was held that in light of *AR 2006, reg 27* (the predecessor of *Sch 22, para 1(1)* so far as age is concerned) an age discrimination challenge in relation to a failure to appoint the claimant to office could not possibly proceed where legislation disqualified him from that office; the respondent's mindset was irrelevant. Cf *Wooster v Mayor and Burgesses of the London Borough of Tower Hamlets* [2009] IRLR 980, EAT, where it was held, albeit without express reference to *reg 27*, that a claimant for age discrimination could not complain of a failure to act in a way which would have been *ultra vires* his local authority employer.

2.50 DISCRIMINATION IN RECRUITMENT

EqA 2010 contains a limited number of provisions which deal directly with issues arising on the recruitment of employees (all of which were also included in *AR 2006*), as follows:

— the prohibition on unlawful discrimination against or victimisation or harassment of applicants is set out in *EqA 2010, ss 39(1), 39(3) and 40* (previously *AR 2006, reg 7(1)*). It is unlawful to discriminate against applicants in the arrangements made for deciding who should be offered employment, in the terms on which they offer employment or by not offering employment;

- the exception in *EqA 2010, Sch 9, Pt 2, para 9* (previously *AR 2006, regs 7(4) and 7(5)*) permitting the rejection of an applicant who has reached age 65 (or the normal retirement age for the role, if higher) or who will reach this age within six months of the application date (see **2.35** but note that the government proposes to phase this out from 6 April 2011 as part of its plans to abolish the default retirement age);
- the application of an occupational requirement contained in *EqA 2010, Sch 9, para 1(1)* (replacing the 'genuine occupational requirements' provisions in *AR 2006, reg 8*) (see **Common concepts (1)**); and
- the exception for positive action contained in *EqA 2010, s 159*, due to come into force in April 2011 (which replaces and extends the provisions previously included in *AR 2006, reg 29*) (see **Common concepts (1)**).

Discrimination in recruitment can arise at any stage from designing a job or person specification, through to interviewing and selecting the successful candidate. Even where no discrimination actually takes place, inferences of discrimination can be drawn, eg from use of age related language. To minimise the risk of a claim employers should focus throughout on the core requirements of the role. Employers should also ensure that they follow a consistent procedure with all applicants and can explain the reason for excluding candidates at each stage, ideally providing supporting documentation. This will put them in a good position to defend any claims.

Employers can however take some comfort from the decision in *Keane v Investigo* UKEAT/0389/09, in which the EAT considered a claim from an older individual who had applied for multiple roles which were advertised in a way which suggested they were seeking a younger employee. She brought proceedings as soon as it became clear she was not being offered an interview but there was evidence to suggest that she was not really interested in getting the roles and was making the applications purely to be able to bring a claim. The EAT held that she was not actually interested in having the job and so did not suffer a detriment and so her claim failed.

2.51 Job specifications

Including unnecessary or unjustifiable requirements in job specifications can lead to direct or indirect discrimination. The *EHRC Employment Code* gives guidance on preparation of job descriptions and person specifications at *Section 16.4–16.15*. It emphasises that job descriptions should accurately describe the job in question and should not include tasks or duties that workers will not in practice need to perform or will only need to do very rarely.

Employers should ensure that criteria relating to skills or knowledge are not unnecessarily restrictive in specifying particular qualifications that are necessary or desirable, as this can amount to indirect discrimination on grounds of age. For example, the requirement for all applicants to hold 'GCSE maths' will potentially discriminate indirectly against older applicants who may have attended school before GCSEs were introduced. The potential discrimination in this instance could perhaps easily be avoided by broadening the requirement to include qualifications equivalent to GCSE maths. Similarly, the requirement to hold a degree may potentially indirectly discriminate against older applicants who may be less likely to have been to university, due to the recent expansion in higher education. That argument was not raised in *Homer v Chief Constable of West Yorkshire* [2010] EWCA Civ 419, [2010] IRLR 619 (see **2.14**).

Absolute age bars on recruitment (whether maximum or minimum ages) will currently amount to direct discrimination unless they can be objectively justified or fall within one of the statutory exceptions. Maximum age limits are currently permitted if they exclude applicants who are within 6 months of age 65 (or the normal retirement age for the role, if higher) *EqA 2010, Sch 9, Pt 2, para 9* (previously *AR 2006, regs 7(4) and 7(5)*), but the government is proposing to remove this exception with effect from 6 April 2011 (subject to transitional provisions). Where there are statutory restrictions on employing someone of a particular age, an employer will be able to rely on the exception for statutory authority (see **2.49**). Where a statutory exception is not available it is likely to be quite difficult to objectively justify age bars in recruitment, particularly once the default retirement age has been abolished. In *Baker v NATS* 2203501/2007, the tribunal considered a blanket ban against anyone over 35 training to become an air traffic controller. The employment tribunal considered that some of the aims relied upon by NATS were legitimate aims, such as achieving a high success rate in training, having a reasonable period of service post training, providing a sufficient pool of air traffic controllers and ensuring safety. However, there was no evidence that the age bar was necessary to pursue these aims and the age bar was found to be unlawful. The tribunal warned against unconscious discrimination which arises from '*assumptions that are insufficiently considered*'. Contrast the decision of the CJEU in *Wolf* [2010] IRLR 244, in which a maximum recruitment age of 30 for front-line fire-fighting duties were held to be lawful (discussed at **2.86**). For a general discussion of objective justification of direct discrimination see **2.18**. The issues here are also similar to the issues surrounding the justification of mandatory retirement at **2.84**.

Another tricky issue arises with respect to length of experience requirements, which are a common feature of job specifications, for example, the requirement for the successful candidate to have at least 'five years' project management experience'. Such requirements may indirectly discriminate against younger candidates who have been working for a shorter period of time and may be unable to meet the requirement, unless they can be objectively justified. In the light of this risk, an employer should consider if a particular amount of experience is genuinely required for the role, as well as whether there are any alternatives such as listing the *types* of experience required or the level of ability required or complexity of the tasks to be undertaken (which will generally be easier to objectively justify). In appropriate circumstances, employers should be prepared to disapply strict requirements. Similar considerations apply when targeting *less* experienced candidates. In *Rainbow v Milton Keynes Council* 1200104/2007 a tribunal ruled that advertising a teaching vacancy as suitable for 'candidates in the first five years of their career' constituted indirect discrimination and was not justified.

Using age-related language in job descriptions can also lead to inferences of discrimination being drawn and employers should bear in mind that even if these are only for internal purposes or for briefing a recruitment consultant, they will have to be disclosed if an unsuccessful candidate brings a tribunal claim. In *Beck v Canadian Imperial Bank of Commerce* (2010) UKEAT/0141/10/RN, [2011] 2 CMLR 82, a 42-year-old employee was ostensibly dismissed for redundancy but successfully claimed age discrimination. The person specification for the role stipulated that the employer was looking to hire a replacement with a 'younger, entrepreneurial profile'. The use of the word 'younger' was considered sufficient to raise a presumption of discrimination, which the employer failed to rebut. The EAT commented that the person specification was '*the clearest possible evidence of potential age discrimination*'.

2.52 Job titles

As for job advertisements, the terminology used in job titles could lead to an inference being drawn that the employer was seeking candidates within a particular age group. The *EHRC Employment Code* at *Section 16.6* gives the example of a job title of 'office boy' or 'shop girl' both of which suggest a bias towards recruiting younger people (as well as suggesting a bias to candidates of a particular sex). Unsuccessful applicants may look to job titles for evidence that their applications were rejected because of their age (see *Beck* above). Instead of using age-related descriptions within job titles, it is therefore preferable for employers to adopt an objective grading system for all job titles based on the level of the employee within the particular organisation.

2.53 Job advertisements

Including age-related requirements in job advertisements could potentially give rise to claims of direct or indirect discrimination (see **1.18**).

Since the introduction of *AR 2006*, there have been a number of cases looking at the content of employers' job advertisements, and it is apparent that the use of descriptions such as 'young', 'mature', 'senior' and 'dynamic' risk potential applicants concluding that the employer is targeting a particular age range to the exclusion of others. The fact that an employer has used such a description in the context of the advertisement will provide useful evidence to an unsuccessful job applicant who is claiming that age played a role in the decision to reject their application, or to a potential applicant who has been deterred from applying. In *McCoy v James McGregor & Sons Ltd* 00237/07IT, a Northern Ireland industrial tribunal drew adverse inferences from the phrase 'youthful enthusiasm' when concluding that an unsuccessful job applicant had suffered discrimination. See also *EHRC Employment Code* at *Section 16.24*. The key for an employer when preparing an advert is to consider how it will be perceived by the public, regardless of the intent.

2.54 Application forms

Asking all candidates to disclose their age or date or birth as part of a standard application form will not, of itself, constitute unlawful discrimination. The risk of requesting this information at an early stage in the recruitment process is that it could be used by a recruiting manager (consciously or sub-consciously) to discriminate and even where it does not in fact influence a decision, an employment tribunal may be invited to draw an adverse inference about the employer's reasons for requesting this information. In this regard, the risk of asking such questions is similar to the risk asking questions around race, religion, etc. Since the introduction of *AR 2006*, many employers have removed standard questions on age or date of birth from their application forms. Instead, these details are now often requested for the sole purpose of equal opportunities monitoring as part of a detachable equal opportunities monitoring form (see *EHRC Employment Code, Section 16.40)*.

In fact, in the case of age, a candidate's age may well become apparent from other information on an application form, eg dates of previous employment and education. The Employer's Forum on Age (an employers' network dedicated to tackling age discrimination in the workplace) recommends the use of an 'age neutral' application form which separates *all* chronological information into a specific section for HR to review, with the recruiting managers having access only to information relating to the candidates' competencies, such as their skills and abilities for the role. This approach has not to date proved popular, but employers who continue to consider such chronological information as part of the recruitment process should be prepared to explain the rationale for requesting these details if faced with claims of discrimination under *EqA 2010* and to rebut any adverse inferences which may otherwise be drawn.

2.55 Interviews

Employers face various pitfalls during the interview stage due to the unpredictable nature of the discussion which can take place during the course of an interview. Interviewers should be trained to avoid questions which are based on a stereotypical assumption about the candidate's suitability for the role based on his age. Obvious examples are questions addressed to older candidates about their views on reporting to a younger manager, or their ability to learn new skills. In *McCoy* (see **2.53**), the employer was criticised by the Northern Ireland tribunal for questioning a candidate about his 'enthusiasm', 'motivation' and 'drive', given other evidence indicating that the employer had made a link between such attributes and age. Again, the fact that such questions are asked may be used as evidence by an unsuccessful candidate that their age was a reason for them not being offered a role. Age-related comments in an interview could also give rise to a claim for harassment. Ideally, interviewers should be trained to recognise when they are making stereotypical assumptions, should follow a set script of standard questions relating to the job description, apply objective scoring criteria and wherever possible and take careful notes of the interview in case the basis for the recruitment decision comes under scrutiny at a later stage. If feedback is provided to unsuccessful candidates, interviewers should avoid terms like 'over-experienced' and 'over-qualified', which can suggest the employer has made age-related assumptions about how an experienced candidate would cope with a more junior role: see *Lyons v The Leeds Teaching Hospitals NHS Trust*. See also the *EHRC Employment Code, paras 16.57, 16.61–16.62*.

2.56 **Recruitment methods**

The recruitment methods adopted by employers may inadvertently exclude or disadvantage applicants within specific age groups. Recruitment through word of mouth, for example, may disadvantage younger candidates who have not had the opportunity to build a network of contacts. Employers would be well advised to take appropriate steps to ensure that their recruitment methods do not directly or indirectly discriminate against applicants within particular age groups, for example by ensuring job advertisements are placed in a range of publications which target all different age groups and by the inclusion of clear diversity statements in recruitment literature as recommended in the *EHRC Employment Code (para 16.29)*.

Particular attention has been placed on the role of graduate recruitment schemes which are targeted at university leavers, and regarded by many employers as a key tool to attracting talent. The imposition of an age limit for graduate recruits is direct discrimination, whereas the requirement for a recruit to have completed university studies within a particular timeframe is likely to amount to indirect discrimination. Use of the term 'recent graduate' may also imply a younger person. In these cases, it will be difficult to justify the imposition of the requirement. Accordingly, graduate recruitment literature should make it clear that the employer invites applications from candidates of all ages, and the shortlisting and selection decisions should reflect this position. See also *Rainbow* (at **2.51**).

Further *EqA 2010, s 109* (and previously *AR 2006, reg 25(2)*), employers are potentially liable for the acts of their agents, for example the discriminatory practices of a recruitment agency, provided that the agent is acting under the authority of the employer (whether express or implied, and whether previous or subsequent). To address this risk an employer should ensure that the recruiters are award of their equality policy and other relevant policies and seek assurances about the agency's compliance with equal opportunities principles, ideally backed by an appropriate indemnity from the agency for any liability which is incurred.

2.57 **DISCRIMINATION DURING EMPLOYMENT**

Pay and benefits: common potentially discriminatory features

In the context of pay and benefits, there are a number of criteria which historically have often been included in remuneration packages which could, potentially, amount to age discrimination. Many employers have taken steps to remove these since the introduction of

AR 2006. However, age-related provisions are still common and can be accepted and supported by employees in some cases. If employers wish to use these criteria they need to consider whether they fall within any of the specific exemptions included in *EqA 2010* and, if not, whether they can be objectively justified. If discriminatory provisions are included, employees could bring a claim for compensation. Alternatively, where the provisions are contractual, included in a collective agreement or amount to a rule of the undertaking employees could seek to rely on the provisions of *EqA 2010, ss 142–148* (see **2.98**) to argue that the discriminatory provisions are void or unenforceable and seek a declaration to that effect, even without having suffered any loss.

2.58 *Age conditions*

Age has often been included as either a condition for access to a particular benefit or as a criterion in determining the level of benefits to which an employee is entitled. For example, age has frequently been used in determining the level of redundancy payments (see **2.90**). Certain benefits, such as health checks, might only have been made available to older workers. Other benefits, such as life assurance, might only have been available to employees who were members of a pension scheme with minimum and maximum ages for admission. Other commonly used age conditions include providing beneficial treatment under share schemes or bonus schemes to employees who leave service after a particular age, and not providing certain benefits (such as income protection policies) to employees who have passed normal retirement age. All of these provisions will be directly discriminatory unless one of the exemptions applies or the criterion can be objectively justified. In the light of *Coleman v Attridge Law* and the extension of the definition of direct discrimination to cover associative discrimination, age conditions relating to an employee's dependants or family members who potentially benefit under a scheme could also give rise to claims of direct discrimination.

A number of specific exemptions might be relevant. There is a specific exemption for setting pay rates by reference to the age bands used for the purposes of the National Minimum Wage (see *EqA 2010, Sch 9, Pt 2, para 11* and **2.41**). Using age as a criterion for access to training might fall within the exception for positive action where it compensates for age-related disadvantages suffered by actual or potential employees of a particular age or age group (see *EqA 2010, s 158* and Common concepts **(1)**). *EqA 2010, Sch 9, Pt 2, para 15* includes a specific exception for age related child care, which allows employers to continue to limit the provision of child care facilities to children (under 17) of a particular age group (see **2.47**). Age criteria might also fall within the specific exemption for statutory authority (see *EqA 2010, Sch 22, para 1* and **2.49**) where, for example, they are required to be included to take advantage of beneficial tax treatment for a particular benefit scheme. There is also a specific exception in *EqA 2010, Sch 9, Pt 2, para 14* (previously *AR 2006, reg 34*) which permits an employer to stop life assurance cover for workers who have taken early retirement on grounds of ill health when they reach normal retirement age or (if there is none) age 65 (see **2.46**).

Note though that the exception for retirement in *EqA 2010, Sch 9, Pt 2* (see **2.34** ff) only protects employers from claims that *the dismissal* of an employee is discriminatory. If an employee remains in employment after the normal retirement age then any less favourable treatment in relation to the terms and conditions on which his employment is extended or the benefits afforded to him could amount to discrimination. If the government's proposals to remove the default retirement age are implemented, the retirement exception will fall away (see **2.64**). However, the government is consulting over whether, on abolition of the default retirement age, it should introduce further exceptions to clarify when it will be lawful for employers to cease cover, require medical underwriting or pass on additional costs in relation to older employees under group insured benefits and when employees should be treated as good leavers under share schemes. At the time of writing the outcome of the consultation has not been published (see **2.64**).

If no specific exemption applies, an employer will need to prove an objective justification if it wishes to retain an age condition (see **2.16**). In *Swann v GHL Insurance Services UK Ltd* ET/2306281/2007 the employment tribunal held that an employer's flexible benefits scheme was not unlawfully discriminatory, even though the premiums for the private medical component were calculated by reference to age and gender. They held (perhaps surprisingly) that there was no less favourable treatment for older employees, because all employees had the same percentage of salary to spend on flexible benefits, even though medical benefits were more expensive for older employees. They also held that, if this was wrong, the flexible benefits scheme was objectively justified as it was introduced with the aim of improving recruitment and retention and was proportionate, as increased premiums for older employees were based on actuarial factors.

One particular difficulty in the field of pay and benefits is that the cost of providing benefits to all employees on the same basis may well be the only reason for the employer wishing to retain age conditions. Case law suggests that there might be difficulties in relying on cost as an objective justification (see 'Justification' under **1.83**ff and also **2.20**). In particular, an employer seeking to rely on costs justifications will need to produce evidence about the financial impact of removing age conditions. This was made clear in *Pulham v London Borough of Barking and Dagenham* [2010] ICR 333, [2010] IRLR 184, a case on pay protection arrangements in which the EAT noted that tribunals require evidence about the financial background and the discriminatory impact on employees in order to assess the affordability of the employer's chosen approach vis-à-vis any alternative, less discriminatory, options.

The Council in *Pulham* operated a scheme which rewarded loyalty and experience by increasing pay by increments once both a length of service *and* an age criterion were satisfied. The scheme was discontinued after *AR 2006* came into force but pay protection arrangements were brought into effect. At the time, Ms Pulham had achieved the length of service criterion but not the age criterion; it was argued that she had suffered direct discrimination. Helpfully for employers, the EAT held that age discriminatory pay protection arrangements are capable of justification and remitted the case to the tribunal. The tribunal held that the arrangements *were* justified. Contrast the EAT's approach to transitional pay arrangements in the context of sex discrimination (see **11.33**).

2.59 *Length of service*

Length of service has frequently been used as a criterion for eligibility for particular benefits. Insurance schemes (such as private health insurance, permanent health insurance or life insurance) frequently have a 'qualifying period' or 'waiting time' before employees are eligible to join, as do benefits such as enhanced maternity pay, enhanced redundancy payments or a staff discounts.

Length of service requirements also frequently determine the level of benefit to which an employee is entitled. For example, the level of holiday or sick pay to which an employee is entitled may increase with length of service. Similarly, the level of redundancy payment to which an employee is entitled is typically determined by length of service. Pay scales also frequently reward length of service. This will be the case where a pay scale for a particular grade of employee is expressly related to length of service in that grade. It might also arise less directly where employees in a particular post receive annual pay increases without reference to a particular pay scale for a post, so that longer serving employees tend to earn more than more recent joiners.

Using length of service as a criterion, unless one of the exemptions applies or the criterion can be objectively justified, is potentially indirectly discriminatory on grounds of age because it will be more difficult for younger workers to satisfy the length of service criterion than for older workers. The longer the length of service criterion which is applied, the more likely it is that it will put employees in a younger age group at a 'particular disadvantage' so as to require objective justification (see discussion of *MacCulloch v Imperial Chemical Industries plc* in **2.94**).

In *Rolls-Royce v Unite* Aikens LJ (para [141]) expressed the view that length of service criteria might not fall within the indirect discrimination provisions in *AR 2006, reg 3(1)(b)* (now *EqA 2010, s 19*) on the basis that, when comparing the impact of a length of service criterion between one age group and another to see whether one age group was put at a particular disadvantage, all comparators had to be such that their relevant circumstances were the same or not materially different (*reg 3(2)*) and length of service was a relevant criterion. Therefore the comparison was whether employees in one age group was put at a particular disadvantage when compared with employees in other age groups, where all had the same length of service. This argument was referred to in *ABN AMRO Management Services Ltd v Hogben* (para [45] note 6) in contrast to the 'conventional' view that length of service criteria can be indirectly discriminatory. It is submitted that the approach of Aikens LJ is unlikely to be followed. Aikens LJ gave the dissenting judgment in *Rolls-Royce* with the other judges assuming (without deciding) that length of service criteria were potentially indirectly discriminatory. He drew support for his analysis from *reg 32* (the exception for benefits based on length of service), commenting that:

> 'If regulation 32 is intended to deal specifically with the possible discriminatory affect of length of service provisions, then if something fits within that Regulation, there is no need for it fit into regulation 3(1)(a) or (b)'.

In fact, this seems to assume that *reg 32* created liability whereas *reg 32* in fact provided an exemption, which would have been unnecessary unless length of service criteria potentially amounted to indirect discrimination. In principle, regarding the ability to comply with the allegedly discriminatory PCP a relevant material circumstance will always lead to a finding that there has been no discrimination and will not provide a pool which adequately test whether the PCP is discriminatory (see *Pike v Somerset County Council*) and it has long been accepted at a European and UK level that length of service criteria can be indirectly discriminatory on grounds of sex (see eg *R v Secretary of State for Employment, ex p Seymour-Smith and Perez (No 2)* [2000] IRLR 263; [2000] ICR 244, HL) (although see discussion of *Homer* at **2.14** for the possibility of a difference in approach in age discrimination cases).

The first consideration in deciding whether a length of service criterion is unlawful is likely to be *EqA 2010, Sch 9, Pt 2, para 10* (see **2.36**), which provide a specific exemption allowing employers to retain length of service criteria of up to five years in relation to any benefits which they award. The exemption also allows employers to justify length of service criteria of more than five years by reference to a test which is likely to be easier to satisfy than the test of objective justification. However, to rely on the exception an employer will need to comply with the strict provisions of *para 10*, for example as to how length of service is calculated. Also, the exemption does not apply to 'benefits awarded to a worker by virtue of his ceasing to work' (see *reg 32(7), para 10(7)* and **2.36**), although the exception for redundancy payments in *EqA 2010, Sch 9, Pt 2, para 13* may be relevant here (see **2.43**).

Where a 'waiting period' is provided for by statute, eg the qualifying period for statutory maternity pay, an employer will be able to rely on the exception for statutory authority (see **2.49**), although in many cases the provision will be justified by *para 10* (or short enough so as not to have any discriminatory effect) in any event.

Even where an exemption does not apply, an employer may be able to show an objective justification for using length of service in pay and benefits by showing that it amounts to a proportionate means of achieving a legitimate aim (see **2.16**). A number of potentially legitimate aims can be identified.

- *Rewarding experience:* There is no necessary link between length of service and experience; a new recruit might have just as much experience from a previous role as a long serving employee. Nor will experience necessarily enable someone to do a role better, at least after an initial period of training. This will depend on the nature of the role. However, case law is sympathetic to the view that a legitimate aim of including a length of service criterion, particularly in a pay scale, may be to reward experience acquired which better enables a worker to perform his duties. In *Cadman*, the ECJ held, in the context of a complaint of sex discrimination in pay, that this constitutes a legitimate objective of pay policy. It also held, following its earlier decision in *Danfoss*, that as a general rule, use of the criterion of length of service is an appropriate way to achieve that objective, since length of service goes hand in hand with experience, and experience generally enables the worker to perform his duties better. The ECJ therefore held that an employer is free to reward length of service without having to establish the importance it has in the performance of an employee's specific tasks. However, elaborating on its decision in *Danfoss*, the ECJ held that where a worker provides evidence capable of giving rise to serious doubts as to whether recourse to the criterion of length of service was an appropriate way to achieve the aim in question, then the employer would have to show that length of service does in fact go hand in hand with experience and that experience enables the employee to perform his duties better, as regards the job in question.

Age discrimination was not directly considered by the ECJ in *Cadman*. However, the decision that rewarding experience which better enables a worker to perform his duties is a legitimate aim of pay policy seems equally applicable to age discrimination and in *Rolls-Royce* Arden LJ appeared to accept that the reasoning in *Cadman* was equally applicable to age discrimination.

- *Retaining employees:* Another common aim of length of service criteria is staff retention. This may be valued by employers as it reduces recruitment and training costs and retains knowledge and experience within an organisation. Retaining employees (and rewarding loyalty) was identified as a legitimate aim in *MacCulloch v Imperial Chemical Industries plc* [2008] IRLR 846.
- *Rewarding loyalty:* It may be that some benefits, such as long service awards which tend to be relatively modest and awarded after many years' service, do not have much of an effect on retaining employees (unless perhaps as part of a contribution to an overall workplace culture) and are in fact designed to recognise and reward loyalty. Rewarding loyalty was also identified as a legitimate aim in *Rolls-Royce plc v Unite* [2009] EWCA Civ 387 and *MacCulloch*.

In any case, the employer will need to be able to prove the aim of using the length of service criterion and that the criterion does contribute to achieving that aim. Tribunals to date have taken a reasonably benevolent approach to the use of length of service in benefit schemes. Length of service criteria can also be indirectly discriminatory on grounds of sex and so give rise to a claim of sex discrimination or for equal pay, because statistically the length of service of female workers tends to be less than that of male workers. The question of whether it does so will need to be considered separately from whether it amounts to age discrimination. The specific age exemptions do not provide a defence to a claim of indirect sex discrimination and a tribunal may not take the same approach to objective justification for both age and sex discrimination. The outcome in *Pulham* also suggests that tribunals may in some circumstances be more benevolent towards age discrimination than sex discrimination. In considering whether a criterion is a proportionate means of achieving a legitimate aim, the discriminatory effect will need to be taken into account and the discriminatory effect on women may be different from the effect on younger workers in any particular case. See also the comments above in relation to *Cadman*.

Medical criteria

2.60 Access to certain insured benefits, such as health insurance, permanent health insurance, critical illness cover and life insurance will often be subject to passing a health check. Such criteria, unless one of the exemptions apply or the criterion can be objectively justified, may be indirectly discriminatory on grounds of age because it may be more likely that older workers will have difficulty in satisfying the criteria. They may also be directly discriminatory if applied only to older employees, unless objectively justified. Such criteria might also be discriminatory on grounds of disability (see DISABILITY DISCRIMINATION (3)).

2.61 Insured benefits

Employers frequently provide employees with insurance as a benefit, eg life assurance, private health insurance, permanent health insurance, critical illness insurance or travel insurance.

The age discrimination provisions of *EqA 2010* do not currently extend to the provision of goods and services and so insurance providers are not covered (see **2.29** for proposals to the prohibition of extend age discrimination to the provision of services). This means that they can apply age-related criteria, whether in relation to the benefits provided, the employees who they are prepared to cover or the premiums which they will charge. Employers, in choosing the schemes that they offer and the terms of those schemes, could however be liable.

In some schemes, age criteria might be objectively justified by the nature of the benefit or some other legitimate aim. For example, it might be possible to argue that the reason for providing cover under a particular permanent health insurance scheme is to cushion them from the effects of losing their salary and that ceasing benefits after an employee reaches an age where they could draw a full pension, might be objectively justified in the circumstances of a particular scheme. Some support for this argument can be drawn from comments made the EAT in *Loxley v BAE Systems Land Systems (Munitions & Ordnance) Ltd* [2008] IRLR 853 (cf *Ingeniørforeningen i Danmark, acting on behalf of Ole Anderson v Region Syddanmark: C-499/08* [2011] 1 CMLR 1140, see discussion at **2.93**). However, if the age criteria cannot be justified by the nature of the benefit, employers will have to consider whether the benefit can be procured or provided on a non-discriminatory basis.

In some cases, it will be possible to obtain insurance cover which does not contain age-related criteria, but that cover may be more expensive. On the basis of the current authorities it is likely to be difficult to objectively justify retaining age-related criteria on the basis of cost alone (see **1.84**).

In other cases, it may be that particular cover is not available in the market place without age-related restrictions. In those circumstances the only way to provide benefits equally to all staff would be to remove the benefit entirely or to self-insure for older workers. An employer who nevertheless provided the benefit with age-related restrictions could potentially be challenged both in relation to the decision to provide the benefit to some but not all (or the decision to provide the benefit at a higher cost for some) and the decision not to self-insure. In relation to these:

- if there is a good business reason for providing a particular benefit, then it should be possible to objectively justify the decision to continue providing the benefit. The employer would need to identify the 'legitimate aim' which was the reason for providing the particular benefit. The employer would also need to show that the scheme in question was a proportionate means of achieving that aim. That would involve considering alternative ways of achieving the aim and ensuring that any element of discrimination is minimised. It might also be valuable to demonstrate that older employees have some replacement benefit of equivalent value to that provided to younger employees. See the decision of the employment tribunal in *Swann* (**2.58**) for a case where a tribunal accepted that age based insurance premiums were objectively justified. In that case it was accepted that cover was not available on any other basis;
- again, current authorities suggest that it might be difficult to justify not self-insuring because of the cost alone. However, it might be argued that self-insurance in effect requires the employer to provide a benefit of a different nature and so would not be providing equal treatment (indeed it may treat older employees more favourably).

Where an employer provides benefits of a particular kind to the public or a section of the public, which includes its employees, *EqA 2010, Sch 9, Pt 3, para 19* and *AR 2006, reg 7(6)* provide that it will not be liable to those employees for provision of those benefits unless:

(a) the provision differs in a material respect from the provision of the benefits by the employer to his employees; or

(b) the provision of the benefits to the employee in question is regulated by his contract of employment; or

(c) the benefits relate to training.

2.62 Pension schemes

Employers can be liable for discriminatory pension schemes in the same way as other benefits. In addition, trustees and managers of occupational pension schemes have a duty not to discriminate on grounds including age (*EqA 2010, s 61*). There are a wide range of exemptions, which duplicate the provisions of *AR 2006* (see *SI 2010/2133*). *EqA 2010* also sets out special rules in relation to occupational pension schemes including implying a non-discrimination rule, a power for trustees and managers to amend the scheme and special procedural rules and provisions as to remedy in relation to proceedings in the employment tribunal. A detailed consideration of these provisions is outside the scope of this work.

2.63 DISCRIMINATION ON TERMINATION OF EMPLOYMENT

STOP PRESS: The *Employment Equality (Repeal of Retirement Age Provisions) Regulations 2011* will come into force on 6 April 2011. They have the effect of abolishing the default retirement age from 6 April 2011. However, the transitional provisions have the effect that the DRA will continue to apply where an employer has given notice in accordance with *AR 2006, Sch 6, para 2 or para 4* prior to 5 April **and** the employee in question reaches age 65 (or normal retirement age, if higher) on or before 30 September 2011.

The Regulations also replace *EqA 2010, Sch 9, para 14* (life assurance) with a new exception permitting employers to cease providing group risk insured benefits from age 65 (or state pensionable age, when that is higher). The exception does not apply to self-insured schemes, although the government is considering future regulations to cover such schemes.

Following consultation, the government concluded that no exceptions were required in relation to share schemes. It also concluded that a formal statutory code of practice in relation to dealing with retirement and holding retirement discussions would be inappropriate and guidance would be more appropriate (see 'Phasing Out the Default Retirement Age: Government Response to Consultation', January 2011). ACAS has therefore published guidance on 'Working Without the Default Retirement Age', which is available at http://www.acas.org.uk/media/pdf/d/4/Working_wtihout_the_DRA_Employer_guidance_-_MARCH_2011.pdf.

2.64 Retirement: overview

During consultation on *AR 2006* one of the most disputed issues was whether employers should be permitted to force employees to retire. The meaning of retirement is considered below, but the issue in dispute was essentially whether it should be possible for employers to dismiss employees because they had reached a particular age.

Prior to *AR 2006* coming into effect, *ERA 1996, s 109* provided that employees could not claim unfair dismissal if they were dismissed at or after the 'normal retiring age' for their position or, if there was no normal retiring age, age 65. Nor were such employees entitled to a statutory redundancy payment (*ERA 1996, s 156*). This meant that an employer could force employees to retire, on grounds of their age, at or above the normal retiring age or (where there is none) age 65, subject only to complying with any contractual obligations (eg to give notice of dismissal, if the contract did not expire automatically).

Following consultation, the then government decided to continue to provide a 'default retirement age' ('DRA') of 65 in *AR 2006*, allowing employers to force employees to retire at or above age 65 without the need to show objective justification. To do so, employers had to follow a specified retirement procedure which included a right for employees to request to continue working beyond the proposed retirement date. This approach was taken primarily because the government concluded that a significant number of employers used a set retirement age as a necessary part of their workforce planning and also to avoid an adverse impact on the provision of occupational pensions and other work-related benefits (see *Coming of Age*, and also the *Notes on Regulations*). Nevertheless, the then government intended to review whether the default retirement age was still appropriate in 2011.

The legality of the DRA (as set out in then in *AR 2006, regs 30* and *7(4)–(5)* and now in *EqA 2010 Sch 9, Pt 2*) was then challenged in judicial review proceedings brought by Heyday, a branch of Age Concern for England, on the basis that the provisions failed to give effect to the UK's obligations under the *Framework Directive* (*R (on the application of the Incorporated Trustees of the National Council for Ageing (Age Concern for England) v Secretary of State for Business, Enterprise and Regulatory Reform* [2007] EWHC 3090 (Admin) , CO/5485/2006). The High Court referred certain questions to the ECJ, which confirmed (as had, by that stage, been conceded in the light of the decision in *Palacios*) that the provisions of the default retirement age fell within the scope of the *Framework Directive* and so would be unlawful unless the government could show that they were objectively justified under *Article 6(1)*. It was for the High Court to determine the question of objective justification. In *R (Age UK) v Secretary of State for Business, Innovation and Skills* [2009] EWHC 2336, [2009] IRLR 1017 the government sought to objectively justify the DRA primarily by reference to its original aims of workforce planning and avoiding an adverse impact on provision of occupational pension schemes and work place benefits, seen as part of a wider social policy aim of maintaining confidence in the labour market. Blake J accepted that the government's aims could have justified it at the time in introducing a mandatory retirement age, at least in the short term, but expressed some reservations about whether a DRA of 65, as opposed to some higher age, could be justified. Ultimately, he concluded that it could in the light of an announcement by the government that it would bring forward its review of the default retirement age from 2010 to 2011. However, Blake J stated that he did not see how the government could justify retaining a DRA of 65 could be after the review.

Following the review, in July 2010 the new government announced its intention to abolish the default retirement age and associated statutory retirement procedure and published a consultation document 'Phasing out the Default Retirement Age'. The proposal is to phase out the DRA from 6 April 2011, but with transitional provisions allowing employers to continue to retire employees in line with the DRA if the retirement procedure has started before that date, in some circumstances. The government is also consulting about whether further exceptions are needed to clarify when it will be lawful for employers to cease cover, require medical underwriting or pass on additional costs in relation to older employees under group insured benefits and when employees should be treated as good leavers under share schemes. At the time of writing the outcome of the consultation has not been published. The DRA will continue to be relevant prior to its abolition and during any transitional period. The detail of the procedure and its implications is considered further at **2.67–2.82**.

Once the DRA is abolished, employers will only be able to force employees to retire at a particular age if they can show that they have an objective justification for doing so (see below). In addition, retirement will no longer be a potentially fair reason for dismissal. In order to defend an unfair dismissal claim, employers will need to show that they have a fair reason for dismissal being the most likely and follow a fair procedure. This is considered further at **2.83**.

A challenge was also made to the law as it existed before *AR 2006*. In *Lloyd-Briden v Worthing College* [2007] 3 CMLR 722 an employee who was dismissed above the age of 65 before 1 October 2006 attempted to argue, on the basis of *Mangold*, that *ERA 1996, s 109* (which imposed the maximum age for claiming unfair dismissal) should be set aside as being inconsistent with the *Framework Directive* and general principles of EU law. The EAT refused to do so, distinguishing *Mangold* on the basis that in that case the national law in question had been introduced during the transposition period for the directive, whereas *s 109* pre-dated the Directive.

2.65 *Meaning of 'retirement'*

The terms 'retirement' or 'retire' are used in several places in the *EqA 2010, ERA 1996 and AR 2006*, but are not defined. For the purposes of *Sch 9, Pt 2, para 8(1)* (and previously *AR 2006, reg 30*) and unfair dismissal, *ERA 1996, ss 98ZA–98ZF* apply to determine whether the reason for dismissal was retirement. These sections are unusual in that they focus on the procedure followed in relation to a dismissal, rather than the motivation of the employer. However, in other parts of the legislation it is necessary to determine the meaning of 'retirement' without reference to *ERA 1996, ss 98ZA–98ZF*, for example, the duty to notify under *AR 2006, Sch 6, para 2*, the definition of 'normal retirement age' in *ERA 1996, s 98ZH* and in applying *ERA 1996, ss 98ZA–98ZF*, where retirement is not conclusively deemed to be the reason for a dismissal.

To date the retirement procedures have given rise to relatively little case law and the issue does not appear to have been considered by the courts. The most likely interpretation, in the light of the government's justification for introducing the default retirement age provisions is that 'retirement' means termination of employment on grounds of an employee's (old) age. In ordinary usage 'retirement' is often associated with stopping work altogether and/or drawing a pension, but there seems no reason for these elements to be relevant to retirement for the purposes of *AR 2006* and *EqA 2010*.

The term 'retirement' is also used in the *Framework Directive* (eg in *recital 14* and *Article 6(1)(c)*), but again is not defined.

The meaning of retirement in other contexts (eg pension and benefit schemes) will not necessarily be the same as under *AR 2006* and *EqA 2010*. In drafting benefit schemes employers would be well advised to specifically define 'retirement' to avoid uncertainty. In the light of the proposed abolition of the DRA, definitions in benefit schemes and other contexts should be reviewed to ensure that they will still make sense after the abolition of the DRA and that they are still lawful.

2.66 Default retirement age

As set out in **2.64**, the government has announced its proposal to abolish the default retirement age ('DRA') with effect from 6 April 2011, with transitional provisions applying to allow employers to retire employees where the DRA procedure has started before that date. At the time of writing the final proposals and implementing regulations are not available. However, the DRA will continue to be relevant until the transitional period is over.

2.67 *Overview*

The DRA is implemented by various provisions:

- *Sch 9, Pt 2, para 8* (previously *AR 2006, reg 30*) provides a defence against claims of age discrimination in relation to the dismissal of employees at or above age 65 where the reason for dismissal is retirement (see **2.34**);
- *Sch 9, Pt 2, para 9* (previously *AR 2006, reg 7(4)*) provides a defence against claims of age discrimination where an employer refuses to offer employment to an employee whose age is (or would, within six months of the application, be) greater than the employer's normal retirement age or, if none, age 65 (see **2.35**);

- *AR 2006, Sch 6* (which was not repealed by *EqA 2010*) sets out the retirement procedure, including a duty to notify an employee of an intended retirement and a duty to consider a request from an employee to work beyond the intended retirement date (see **2.64**);
- *ERA 1996, ss 109* and *156*, which imposed maximum ages for unfair dismissal and redundancy, were repealed by *AR 2006*, but *ERA 1996, s 98* was amended by *AR 2006* to add 'retirement' as a potentially fair reason for dismissal (see **2.79**);
- *ERA 1996, ss 98ZA–98ZF* apply to determine whether the reason for dismissal is retirement for the purposes of *Sch 9, Pt 2, para 8* and unfair dismissal. These provisions are unusual in that they focus primarily upon the procedure which an employer follows in dismissing an employee, rather than what motivates the employer to dismiss.

The combined effect of the provisions is that, where the DRA applies, if an employer complies with the retirement procedure in relation to an employee who is above a normal retirement age (which, if it is under 65 is objectively justified) or, where there is no normal retirement age, is above age 65, then the dismissal will be deemed to be by reason of retirement. In addition, the dismissal will be fair and it will not give rise to a claim for age discrimination.

It appears to be the case that the dismissal will be by reason of retirement and fair even if the employer actually decided to follow the retirement procedure for a reason unrelated to age, eg because of the employee's performance or a redundancy situation, although this was apparently not the Government's intention and a contrary argument can be made (see **2.81**).

However, following the retirement procedure will not give the employer a defence against a claim based on one of the other strands of discrimination (eg sex, race, disability, sexual orientation, religion or belief) arising out of the dismissal. It also appears that employees will still be entitled to a statutory redundancy payment if the reason why the employer 'retired' them was redundancy. This is because, although *ss 98ZA–98ZF* provide that retirement shall be taken to be the only reason for dismissal in certain circumstances, *ERA 1996, Pt X* (which sets out the entitlement to a redundancy payment) does not refer to *ss 98ZA–98ZF*. Therefore it appears that, for the purposes of establishing entitlement to a redundancy payment, the reason for dismissal will continue to be determined in accordance with the definition of redundancy in *ERA 1996, s 139* and the presumption of redundancy in *ERA 1996, s 163(2)*.

Employees might also have contractual entitlements arising out of their 'retirement' dismissal. This might include payments under benefit schemes such as redundancy or severance schemes. Benefit schemes frequently make special provision for employees who 'retire'. This might be more favourable treatment (eg good leaver status under a benefit scheme) or less favourable treatment (eg exclusion from entitlement to a redundancy payment). The application of such provisions will depend on the interpretation of the terms of the particular benefit scheme. If contractual provisions do not expressly refer to *ss 98ZA–98ZF*, then 'retirement' might be interpreted differently in such schemes, particularly where the schemes were put in place prior to 1 October 2006, when *AR 2006* came into effect. In addition, such provisions could give rise to claims for age discrimination; the exception in *Sch 9, Pt 2, para 8* only provides a defence against claims that the dismissal itself amounts to unlawful age discrimination.

Employees who remain in employment past age 65 (or any other mandatory retirement age which an employer might have) will continue to be protected against discrimination by *EqA 2010* in relation to the terms of their ongoing employment.

2.68 Retirement procedure: the duty to notify and the right to request not to retire

AR 2006, Sch 6 sets out a detailed retirement procedure which must be followed where an employer intends to retire an employee, prior to the abolition of the DRA. There is no definition of 'retire' for these purposes in *AR 2006*, but the most natural interpretation appears to be that the procedure applies where an employer intends to dismiss an employee on grounds of his (old) age. The procedures only apply to 'relevant workers' as narrowly defined in *Sch 9, Pt 2, para 8(2)*. Therefore the procedures do not apply to, eg, partners, non-executive directors or independent contractors.

There are two aspects to the procedure. First, there is a duty on the employer to notify the employee of an intended retirement. Second, there is a right on the part of the employee to request not to retire and the employer has a duty to consider any such request in line with a procedure involving meeting with the employee and giving a right to appeal, where a request is not agreed to. The procedures, and the consequences of failure to comply with them, are very complex. Details of the procedures are set out below, along with the consequences of not following the procedure. The consequences of even a minor failure to comply can be quite severe and employers who wish to rely on the retirement procedure to force employees to retire would be well advised to diarise key dates and have standard documentation to ensure that they comply with the procedure. The ACAS guidance on *AR 2006* includes draft documentation which employers and employees can use in following the procedures. For a discussion of the effect of following the procedure see above at **2.67**.

2.69 *Definitions*

There are two terms which are defined in *AR 2006, Sch 6* which are key to understanding the operation of the retirement procedures.

'Intended date of retirement' is, broadly speaking, the date on which an employer intends to retire an employee, established in accordance with *Sch 6, para 1(2)*. It is used in determining whether an employee has the right to request not to retire (*Sch 6, para 5*; see below). Generally, an employee has the right to make such a request once in relation to each intended date of retirement. It is also used in determining whether retirement is the reason for dismissal under *ERA 1996, ss 98ZA–98ZF*; dismissal before the intended date of retirement will not be by reason of retirement. It is defined in *Sch 6, para 1(2)*:

- where an employer complies with the duty to notify (whether under *Sch 6, para 2* or *para 4*; (see below)), before the employee has made a valid request not to retire, the date specified in the employer's notification is the intended date of retirement;
- where an employer has failed to notify in accordance with *Sch 6, para 2* and before the employer notifies in accordance with *Sch 6, para 4*, the employee, having reasonable grounds for believing that the employer intends to retire him on a certain date, makes a request not to retire which specifies that date, the date so specified will be the intended date of retirement;
- where following notification by an employer or a valid request not to retire, the employer and employee agree an earlier retirement date than that notified, or the employer extends employment by six months or less, in accordance with the right to request procedure, the new termination date replaces the original intended date of retirement (*Sch 6, para 2(d)*). In those circumstances any dismissal can still be fair without the need to repeat the retirement procedure;
- finally, where employment is extended because the employer has not responded to a request not to retire by the termination date (see below) the new date of termination is the intended retirement date (*Sch 6, para 2(e)*).

'Operative date of termination' is the date on which termination of employment by an employer takes effect, save where employment is automatically extended in accordance with *Sch 6, para 10* (see below). It is used in determining whether retirement is the reason for dismissal under *ERA 1996, ss 98ZA–98ZF*. Retirement will not be the reason for dismissal where the operative date of termination is before the normal retirement age or, where there is no normal retirement age, age 65.

Duty to notify

2.70 An employer who intends to retire an employee has a duty to notify the employee in writing of:

- the date on which he intends the employee to retire; and
- the employee's right to request not to retire.

This notification must be given not more than one year but not less than six months before the date on which he intends the employee to retire (*Sch 6, para 2*). This duty to notify applies irrespective of any provisions in an employee's contract or any handbook or policy which set out when an employee can expect to retire.

The duty to notify generally arises on each occasion when an employer intends to retire an employee, so that if an employee's request not to retire is granted, a new notification will have to be given if the employer subsequently wants to retire the employee at a later date. However, there is an exception to the duty to notify where the employer has complied with duty to notify in relation to a particular intended retirement date or the employee has made a valid request not to retire, before the duty to notify was complied with and, in accordance with the right to request procedure, the employer either (i) agrees to a retirement date which is earlier than the original intended retirement date; or (ii) agrees or notifies a new retirement date which is within six months after the original date. In those circumstances, no further duty to notify arises in relation to the revised intended retirement date.

If the employer fails to notify between 12 and six months before the intended date of retirement, the duty to notify continues until the fourteenth day before the 'operative date of termination' (*Sch 6, para 4*).

Right to request not to retire

2.71 An employee has a right to request not to retire on the intended date of retirement. This right arises even if the employer does not comply with its duty to notify, although it appears that an employee can only make a request if he has reasonable grounds for believing that the employer intends to retire him on a certain date. This is because, although it is not expressly stated, it appears that the right to request only arises where there is an intended date of retirement (see *Sch 6, paras 5(1)* and *(4)*). Where an employer has not complied with its duty to notify, there will only be an intended date of retirement if the employee has requested retirement having reasonable grounds for believing that the employer intends to retire him on a particular date (see *Sch 6, para 2(c)*). This might arise where an employee's contract automatically expires at age 65 or where an employee's employment has been extended for a fixed term after the normal retirement age.

There are a number of formal requirements for a request to be valid:

- it must be in writing;
- it must state that it is made under *Sch 6, para 5*;
- it must propose that the employee's employment should continue, following the intended date of retirement: (i) indefinitely, (ii) for a stated period, or (iii) until a stated date.

- if the request is made before the employer has complied with its duty to notify, it must identify the date on which the employee believes the employer intends to retire him.

If the employer has complied with its primary obligation to notify an employee of the right to request between six and 12 months (inclusive) before the intended date of retirement, the request must be made more than three months, but not more than six months, before the intended date of retirement. If the employer has not complied with that duty, the request can be made at any time up to the intended retirement date.

Only one request can be made in relation to any one intended date of retirement.

However, there is no new right to request where the employer has complied with the duty to notify in relation to a particular intended retirement date or the employee has made a valid request not to retire, before the duty to notify was complied with and, in accordance with the right to request procedure, the employer either: (i) agrees to a retirement date which is earlier than the original intended retirement date; or (ii) agrees to or notifies a new retirement date which is within six months after the original date.

The employee's right is to request extended employment on the same terms and conditions, although there is nothing to prevent the parties agreeing different terms for ongoing employment.

Duty to consider

2.72 If a valid request is made, an employer is under a duty to consider the request in accordance with the procedure laid down in *Sch 6, paras 7–9* (see *Sch 6, para 6*). Although there is a duty to consider a request, *AR 2006* do not set out any circumstances in which a request must be accepted. Nor is there a duty on employers to give reasons for refusing a request. The original draft of *AR 2006* provided that a request had to be considered in 'good faith'. These words were dropped from the final version of *AR 2006*. However, in *Ayodele v Compass Group plc* an employment tribunal held that it was a breach of the procedure for an employer not to give genuine consideration to a request not to retire. It is also implicit in *Sch 6, para 7(5)* that any representations which the employee makes in support of a request must be considered. However, it is not entirely clear what this requires and the duty still appears to be a relatively low one. An employer who, despite holding the relevant meetings, never gave any consideration to an employee's request on the basis that it operated a policy of never allowing employees to work beyond their normal retirement age would appear to have failed to comply with the duty as in *Ayodele* (making the dismissal of the employee unfair under *ERA 1996, s 98ZG* (see below). However, there would appear to be nothing to prevent an employer from operating a policy of not allowing employees to work beyond normal retirement age provided it considers whether it should abandon or make an exception to that policy when it receives a request.

Where an employer operates a default retirement age, in considering the approach it takes to requests to work beyond the normal retirement age, it should consider the effect which regularly accepting requests might have on its 'normal retirement age' (see **2.80**). If it regularly allows employees to work beyond 65 but regularly requires them to retire at a later age (eg it allows them to remain on a one-year contract to age 66) then the later age could become a 'normal retirement age' making dismissals at age 65 unfair and unlawful age discrimination (unless objectively justified). Allowing employees to stay on to different ages, depending on their individual circumstances, or allowing them to stay on indefinitely should not have this effect, although it might mean that an employer did not have a 'normal retirement age'.

Although there is no duty to give reasons for refusing a request not to retire, ACAS guidance states that giving reasons may enable the employee to leave with dignity and respect and help an employer to maintain good working relationships with other employees, which it states would be in line with normal good practice recommended by ACAS. In considering whether to give reasons, or at least to document them, an employer should also consider that a retirement dismissal could give rise to a claim for discrimination on grounds other than age, or for a redundancy payment as well as a claim for unfair dismissal on the basis of the failure to consider the request (as set out above). Therefore there may be circumstances in which an employer needs to be able to demonstrate the reason for its decision not agree to a request not to retire.

Meeting

2.73 Where a valid request is made, an employer must hold a meeting within a reasonable period after receiving it (*Sch 6, para 7(1)*). The employer and the employee must take all reasonable steps to attend the meeting (*Sch 6, para 7(2)*).

The duty to hold a meeting does not apply if:

- before the end of the period that is reasonable, the employer and employee agree that the employee's employment will continue either indefinitely or for an agreed period and the employer gives notice to the employee of that and (in the latter case) of the length of the agreed period or the date on which employment will end (*para 7(3)*); or

- it is not practicable to hold a meeting within a period that is reasonable and the employer considers the request and any representations made by the employee (*para 7(4)*).

The employer must give the employee notice of his decision as soon as is reasonably practical after the date of the meeting or, where it was not reasonably practicable to hold a meeting, his consideration of the request. This notice must:

- where the decision is that the employee's employment will continue indefinitely, state that fact;

- where the decision is that the employee's employment will continue for a further period (which may be shorter than the period requested), state that fact and specify the length of the period or the date on which it will end;

- where the decision is to refuse the request (and not allow any extension of employment), confirm that the employer wishes to retire the employee and the date on which the dismissal is to take effect;

- where the decision is to refuse the request (including where the decision is to allow employment to continue for a further period, which is shorter than requested by the employee) inform the employee of his right to appeal;

- be in writing and dated.

(See *Sch 6, para 7(7)–(8)*.)

The notice does not need to state a reason.

If this notification has not been given by the date when the employee's employment would otherwise end, employment might be extended (see below).

Appeals

2.74 An employee is entitled to appeal against a refusal of a request or a decision to allow employment to continue for a further period which is shorter than requested by the employee. To do so the employee must give notice to the employer setting out the grounds of appeal. The notice must be given as soon as is reasonably practicable after the notice giving the employer's decision and must be dated and in writing (*para 8(1)*).

If a notice of appeal is given, the employer must hold a meeting with the employee to discuss an appeal within a reasonable period after the date of the notice of appeal. The employer and employee must take all reasonable steps to attend the meeting. The same exceptions to the duty to hold a meeting apply as in the case of the initial meeting (*para 8(5)–(6)*; and see above).

The employer must give the employee notice of his decision on the appeal as soon as is reasonably practicable after the appeal meeting or, where it was not reasonably practicable to hold a meeting, his consideration of the request. The notice must again be in writing and be dated and must contain the same information as the decision following the initial meeting (see above) except that there is no right to appeal (*para 8(9)–(10)*).

Consequences of failure to comply

2.75 If an employer complies with the duty to notify and the right to request procedure in relation to an employee who is above a normal retirement age (which, if it is less than 65 is objectively justified) or, where there is no normal retirement age, is above age 65, then the dismissal will be by reason of retirement. In those circumstances, the dismissal will be fair and it will not give rise to a claim for age discrimination.

If the employer does not comply with the retirement procedure, then the consequences depend on which duty the employer has failed to comply with.

If an employer does not comply with the duty to notify six to 12 months before the intended date of retirement, then the following consequences apply:

- The employee may present a complaint to an employment tribunal and the tribunal will award compensation of such amount as it considers just and equitable, not exceeding eight weeks' pay (subject to the statutory cap on a weeks' pay under *ERA 1996, s 227*). The complaint must be presented before the end of the period of three months beginning with the last day permitted to the employer for complying with the duty to notify under *para 2* (ie six months before the intended date of retirement) or, if the employee did not then know the intended date of retirement, the first day on which he knew or would have known that date. A tribunal can extend this time limit by such period as it considers reasonable where it is satisfied that it was not reasonably practicable for the complaint to be presented before the end of that period (see *Sch 6, para 11*). In *Todd v Sanquhar Home Ltd* S/116418/07 a Scottish employment tribunal awarded one weeks' pay as compensation where an employer provided only 12 weeks' notification of an intended retirement, but then granted the employees' request to stay on past the retirement date. The breach was one of 'timing only' and the employee had continued in employment and suffered no losses.

- The dismissal will not be automatically deemed to be by reason of retirement under *ERA 1996, ss 98ZA–98ZF*. Whether it will be by reason of retirement will depend, in part, on whether the employer complies with the duty to notify at all and, if so, how long before the intended date of retirement (see *s 98ZF*). If retirement is not the reason for dismissal then the dismissal might be unfair and amount to unlawful age discrimination.

- If the reason for dismissal is retirement and the employer has failed to comply with its duty under *para 4* (ie to notify prior to the fourteenth day before the operative date of termination) then the dismissal will be automatically unfair.

- The employee has additional rights under the right to request procedure. In particular, he may submit a request not to be retired at any point up to the intended date of retirement (otherwise it has to be submitted more than three months before). If the request is submitted before the employer complies with its duty to notify and the employee has reasonable grounds to believe that the employer intends to retire him on a particular date, the employee can define the intended date of retirement. It would then be difficult for the employer to 'retire' the employee before that date.

If the employer does not comply with the duty to notify before the 14th day before the operative date of termination, in accordance with *Sch 6, para 4* then:

- retirement is unlikely to be found to be the reason for dismissal under *ERA 1996, s 98ZF* (see above);
- if retirement is found to be the reason for dismissal, the dismissal will be automatically unfair, under *ERA 1996, s 98ZG* (see above).

If the employer does not comply with any part of the duty to consider procedure then there is no direct claim which an employee can present, but there may be an impact on the reason for the dismissal and its fairness. In particular:

- If an employer has not complied with its duty to notify six to 12 months prior to the intended retirement date, then whether the employer has followed the procedures in *Sch 6, para 7* (holding a meeting to consider a request not to retire and giving a decision) will be taken into account in determining whether the reason for dismissal is retirement (see above).
- If the reason for dismissal is retirement, then the dismissal will be automatically unfair if an employer has not complied with *Sch 6, paras 6–8*. This includes the duty to 'consider' a request as well as the procedural requirements in relation to the initial meeting and decision and the appeal. Therefore even a small technical breach (eg not dating a notification) would appear to make the dismissal unfair.

Early indications from employment tribunals suggest that they will take a very technical approach to the question of whether the parties have followed the retirement procedure (see eg *Gabri v Sun Hydraulics Ltd* ET11301796/2007 and *Holmes v Active Sensors Ltd* ET3100214/2007). However, in practice, the procedures gave rise to relatively little case law.

Correcting a failure to comply

2.76 Where an employer realises that it has failed to comply with the duty to notify within the period six to 12 months before it intends to retire an employee then, given the consequences of failure to comply, it might consider putting back the date on which it intends to retire the employee so as to allow it to give six months' notice, as required by *para 2*. If it does so, it can benefit from the conclusive presumption that retirement is the reason for dismissal, avoiding the adverse consequences referred to above. This will be the case even if the new termination date falls after the employer's normal retirement age. Although note the proposed abolition of the DRA (see **2.64**).

If notice of dismissal has already been given to an employee, or if an employee's employment terminates automatically (under the terms of the contract) when he reaches normal retirement age, then the employee's consent would be required to continue employment. However, where the employee wants to remain in employment this is likely to be forthcoming. Where the employee does not agree to extend employment then, even if a dismissal is technically unfair, the fact that the employee has chosen not to have employment extended could help to reduce any compensation payable.

Where an employer has failed to comply with the duty to notify six to 12 months before termination, but does not wish to extend employment, then it appears that the more closely it complies with its duties, the more likely it is that retirement will be the reason for dismissal.

Right to be accompanied

2.77 Employees have the right to be accompanied at both the initial meeting and the appeal meeting if they 'reasonably' request it (*Sch 6, para 9*). Where such a request is made the employer must permit the employee to be accompanied by a worker of his choice employed by the same employer. The chosen companion is permitted to confer with the employee during the meeting and to address the meeting, but not to answer questions on behalf of the employee. If the chosen companion will not be available at the time proposed for the meeting and the employee proposes an alternative time for the meeting which is within seven days after the original time and is convenient for all parties, the employer must postpone the meeting to that time (*para 9(3)*).

Note that, unlike the right to be accompanied at a disciplinary or grievance hearing under *ERA1999, s 10*, there is no right to be accompanied by a trade union representative unless he is also a worker employed by the same employer.

An employee may present a complaint to an employment tribunal that his employer has failed or threatened to fail to comply with his obligation to allow him to be accompanied, or to postpone a meeting so that he can be accompanied. A complaint must be presented before the end of the period of three months beginning with the date of the failure or threat, or within such further period as the tribunal considers reasonable in a case where it is satisfied that it was not reasonably practicable for the complaint to be presented before the end of that period of three months. Where a tribunal finds that the complaint is well founded it will order the employer to pay compensation of an amount not exceeding two weeks' pay, subject to the statutory cap in *ERA 1996, s 227(1)* (*Sch 6, para 12*).

Employees have the right not to be subjected to any detriment by their employer on the ground that they have exercised their right to be accompanied and any dismissal on that ground will be automatically unfair. Workers have the right not to be subjected to any detriment by their employer by reason of having accompanied or sought to accompany an employee and, where the worker is also an employee, any dismissal of an employee on that ground will be automatically unfair (*Sch 6, para 13*).

Dismissal before request considered

2.78 Where an employer has received a valid request not to retire in relation to a proposed dismissal and the employer has not given notice of its decision in relation to that request in accordance with *para 7(6)* (see above) before the day on which that dismissal would otherwise take effect, the employee's employment is automatically extended until the day after that notice is given (*Sch 6, para 10(1)–(2)*).

The new termination date then becomes the 'intended date of retirement'. It also becomes the 'operative date of termination' for all purposes except that it is disregarded for the purposes of *ERA 1996, ss 98ZA–98ZH* (*para 10(4)*), which determine whether the reason for dismissal is retirement for certain purposes (see **2.81**). This means that, for the purposes of considering whether the operative date of retirement was before the normal retirement age or age 65 under *ss 98ZA–ZH* (which would mean that retirement was deemed not to be the reason for dismissal) the dismissal date originally proposed would be considered, rather than the extended date. Therefore an employer who had sought to dismiss an employee before the normal retirement age or age 65, but where the statutory extension had the effect that employment actually terminated after the normal retirement age or age 65, could not take advantage of that fact to argue that retirement was actually the reason for dismissal.

2.79 Unfair dismissal (under DRA)

AR 2006 repealed the maximum age for bringing an unfair dismissal claim which was contained in *ERA 1996, s 109*, but introduced 'retirement' as a new, potentially fair reason for dismissal, as one of the provisions to introduce a default retirement age, which is currently replicated in *EqA 2010* (see **2.38**). *AR 2006* also inserted new provisions into the *ERA 1996* to determine whether the reason for a dismissal is retirement for these purposes and a new test of fairness which applies only to retirement dismissals (*ss 98ZA–98ZF*). These are set out below, after a consideration of the meaning of 'normal retirement age' in *EqA 2010* and *ERA 1996*. Note that the government has announced that it will abolish the statutory retirement procedure with effect from 6 April 2011 (subject to transitional provisions), together with the associated statutory retirement procedures and 'retirement' as a fair reason for dismissal. The position in relation to unfair dismissal where an employee is dismissed for retirement, after the abolition of the DRA is considered below at **2.88**.

2.80 *Normal retirement age*

The concept of the normal retirement age is key to understanding the provisions of the *ERA 1996* relating to retirement dismissals. 'Normal retirement age' is defined as 'the age at which employees in the employer's undertaking who hold, or have held, the same kind of position as the employee are normally required to retire' (*ERA 1996, s 98ZH*). There is no definition of 'retire' here but the most natural interpretation appears to be termination of employment on grounds of (old) age.

Prior to its repeal, *ERA 1996, s 109* provided that employees could not bring a claim for unfair dismissal if they were above the 'normal retiring age for an employee holding the position of the employee' at the effective date of termination. Although the wording is slightly different, and there was no statutory definition of normal retiring age, it is likely that the test is the same and this is the approach indicated in the *EHRC Employment Code* at *Section 13.30*.

The leading case on the meaning of normal retiring age is *Waite v Government Communications Headquarters* [1983] 2 AC 714, where the House of Lords held that the normal retiring age is the age at which employees in a particular position can reasonably expect to be compelled to retire, unless there is some special reason in a particular case for a different age to apply. The House of Lords held that, where there is a contractual retiring age applicable to all or nearly all the employees holding a particular position, there is a presumption that the contractual retiring age is the normal retiring age. However, that presumption could be rebutted by evidence that there is in practice some higher age at which employees holding the position are regularly retired, and which they have reasonably come to regard as their normal retiring age. The correct approach to what is 'normal' was not merely statistical – the tribunal should ascertain what would be the reasonable expectation or understanding of the employees holding that position at the time of their dismissal. There is conflicting case law on whether a normal retiring age could be lower than the contractual retiring age (compare *Royal and Sun Alliance Group plc v Payne* [2005] IRLR 848 and *Cross v British Airways plc* [2006] EWCA Civ 549, [2006] IRLR 804).

2.81 *Reason for dismissal*

For the purposes of unfair dismissal (*ERA 1996, s 98(3A)*) and the application of the exemption from age discrimination for retirement dismissals (*EqA 2010, Sch 9, Pt 2, para 8*) the question whether the reason for dismissal was retirement is to be determined in accordance with *ERA 1996, ss 98ZA–98ZF*.

The provisions are unusual in that, unlike the general approach in unfair dismissal claims, the focus is not on what motivates the employer to dismiss, but on the procedure. Depending on the age of the employee, the existence of a normal retirement age, the date of termination and the extent to which the retirement procedure has been complied with (see below), there will be one of four conclusions:

(a) **Retirement will be deemed to be the only reason for dismissal and any other reason shall be disregarded.** The test for whether the presumption applies appears to be purely procedural (see below) and so in these circumstances, on the face of it, there is no scope for considering the employer's actual motive. The fact that an employer actually followed the retirement procedure because of the employee's performance or a redundancy procedure is irrelevant. However, in the *Coming of Age* consultation paper the Government stated clearly that if an employer used the retirement procedure and the employee felt that the 'retirement' was for other reasons (eg redundancy or competency) then the employee could challenge the dismissal as unfair. It could be argued though, that an employer's motive should be taken into account in deciding whether retirement is the reason for dismissal. This is because retirement will only be deemed conclusively to be the reason for dismissal if the employer has notified the employee 'in accordance with' *Sch 6, para 2*. The duty to notify applies where an employer 'intends to retire' an employee. It could be argued, therefore, that an employer who does not 'intend to retire' an employee does not notify the employee in accordance with *para 2* so that the presumption of retirement does not arise. However, it is also clear from *Coming of Age* that the purpose of the retirement procedure was to provide employers with a high degree of certainty as to the reason for dismissal, provided they comply with the retirement procedure. If an employer had to establish that it intended to dismiss by reason of retirement, before being able to establish that retirement was deemed to be the reason for dismissal, this whole purpose would be undermined and the procedures would actually make it more difficult to prove that retirement was the reason for dismissal than if motive alone was considered.

(b) **Retirement will be deemed not to be the reason (or a reason) for dismissal.** In these circumstances, it would be open to the employer to try to prove another potentially fair reason for dismissal. In circumstances where the actual reason why the employee was dismissed is because he had reached the employer's retirement age, it is not clear whether the tribunal is required to ignore this reason (in which case there may be no reason for dismissal or a subsidiary reason might become the principal reason) or whether the tribunal must look at the employer's actual motivation (ie the employee reaching normal retirement age) and consider whether it falls into another potentially fair reason (eg some other substantial reason). The former interpretation appears more likely (and is consistent with the position where retirement is deemed to be the only reason for dismissal and other actual motivations are ignored). However, this would mean that the tribunal had to decide what 'retirement' meant in order to exclude that part of the employer's motivation.

(c) **The tribunal must determine the reason (or principal reason) for dismissal having particular regard to the matters set out in *ERA 1996, s 98ZF*.** These are:

- whether or not an employer has notified the employee in accordance with *Sch 6, para 4* (ie complied with the duty to notify more than 14 days before the operative date of termination);
- if so, how long before the notified retirement date the notification was given; and
- whether or not the employer has followed, or sought to follow, the procedures in *Sch 6, para 7* (ie the duty, which arises where an employee has requested not to retire, to hold a meeting (where reasonably practicable) and notify the employee of a decision in relation to his request).

Presumably, the more closely an employer has complied with the retirement procedure, the more likely it is that retirement will be found to be the reason for dismissal. However, *s 98ZF* does not preclude other factors from being taken into account and, indeed, the reference to determining whether retirement is the 'principal' reason suggests that other reasons which motivated the dismissal should be taken into account. However it is not clear how a tribunal should balance the procedural requirements (to which it must have particular regard) with the employer's motive (which may suggest other 'reasons' for the dismissal) or other matters such as the employer's reasons for not following the procedure. For example, will a tribunal disregard clear evidence that an employer's decision to dismiss was based on a redundancy situation or performance concerns, where the employer has complied with the duty to notify almost six months prior to the intended date of retirement and complied with *Sch 6, para 7*. Conversely, if an employer has clearly dismissed the employee because of the employee having reached retirement age but has taken no steps to comply with the procedure, will the tribunal ignore the employer's motive and find that retirement was not the reason for dismissal? A finding that retirement was the reason for dismissal in these circumstances would give the employer a defence against an age discrimination claim (*Sch 9, Pt 2, para 8*) but mean that the dismissal was unfair, applying the test of fairness set out below. It seems likely that a tribunal would take all the circumstances into account, giving particular weight to the degree of compliance with the retirement procedure as evidence that retirement is the reason for dismissal, but not treating this as conclusive in the face of clear evidence to the contrary. However, there has been little case law in this area.

(d) **The tribunal must determine the reason (or principal reason) for dismissal and may have regard to the matters set out in *ERA 1996, s 98ZF*, but need not.** This category is not expressly identified in *ss 98ZA–98ZF*, but is referred to in the *Notes on Regulations*. In these circumstances it appears that a tribunal could have regard to any circumstances which appeared to be relevant, in determining the principal reason for dismissal and would not have to have particular regard (or any regard) to the factors set out in *s 98ZF*.

Which of the above conclusions applies in any particular situation is determined as follows:

No normal retirement age: dismissal before 65 OR Normal retirement age: dismissal before retirement age

Where there is no normal retirement age and the operative date of termination is before the employee is aged 65, the dismissal is not by reason of retirement. This is also the case where there is a normal retirement age and the operative date of termination is before the normal retirement age (even if the operative date of termination is after the employee reaches age 65).

No normal retirement age: dismissal at or after 65 OR Normal retirement age of 65 or above: dismissal at or after retirement age

Where there is no normal retirement age and the operative date of termination falls on or after the date when the employee reaches age 65, or the employee has a normal retirement which is 65 or higher, and the operative date of termination falls on or after the date when the employee reaches the normal retirement age:

- If the employer has notified the employee in accordance with *Sch 6, para 2* (ie complied with the duty to notify six to 12 months before the intended date of retirement) and the employment terminates on the intended date of retirement, retirement will be the (only) reason for dismissal.

- If the employer has notified the employee in accordance with *Sch 6, para 2* and the employment terminates *before* the intended date of retirement, retirement will not be the (or a) reason for dismissal.

- If the employer has not notified the employee in accordance with *Sch 6, para 2* and there is an intended date of retirement (because the employer has notified more than 14 days but less than six months before the operative date of termination in accordance with *Sch 6, para 4* or where the employee has made a valid request not to retire before the duty to notify has been complied with) and the employment terminates *before* the intended date of retirement, retirement will not be the (or a) reason for dismissal.

- In all other cases where the employer has not notified in accordance with *para 2* the tribunal must determine the reason (or principal reason) for dismissal in accordance with *s 98ZF*.

- If the employer notified in accordance with *Sch 6, para 2* but the dismissal takes effect after the intended date of retirement, the *Notes on Regulations* state that the tribunal may (but not must) take the factors referred to in *ERA 1996, s 98ZF* into account in determining the reason for dismissal.

Normal retirement age below 65: dismissal at or after retirement age

Where the employee has a normal retirement age which is below 65 and the operative date of termination falls on or after the date when the employee reaches normal retirement age:

- If the normal retirement age is unlawful under *EqA 2010* (note that the exception in *Sch 9, Pt 2, para 8* does not apply to retirements under the age of 65) then retirement is not the (or a) reason for dismissal. In these circumstances retirement can never be the reason for dismissal (even after an employee reaches age 65).

- If the normal retirement age is lawful (ie because it is objectively justified) then the position is the same as if the normal retirement age were 65 or above (see above).

2.82 *Fairness*

If the reason for dismissal is retirement, then the only factors which are relevant in deciding whether the dismissal is fair are whether the employer has complied with particular requirements of the retirement procedure (*ERA 1996, s 98ZG*). In particular the dismissal will be fair if the employer has complied with all of the following requirements, and unfair if it has not:

- the duty to notify of retirement under *Sch 6, para 4* (which only arises if an employer has not complied with the duty to notify six to12 months prior to the intended date of retirement);

- the right to request procedure set out in *Sch 6, paras 6–8* (including the duty to consider a request not to retire and any appeal against a decision on that request, and compliance with the procedural requirements in relation to the meeting and appeal).

The requirements of *paras 4* and *6–8* are set out in detail above (see **2.44** ff). It appears that any failure to comply, no matter how trivial (eg not dating a notification), will render the dismissal unfair. However, the approach which the tribunal will take to compensation is not clear. At present, where a dismissal is only procedurally unfair, a tribunal will reduce any compensation for unfair dismissal to reflect the chances that a fair dismissal would have occurred had a fair procedure been followed. A retirement dismissal would always be fair if the employer complied with the procedural requirements of the duty to notify more than 14 days before the operative date of termination and followed the right to request procedure. Therefore, arguably, compensation should be limited to any additional time which the employee would have been employed whilst the employer complied with those procedures, unless the tribunal concludes that the employer has failed to comply with its duty to consider and that, had it done so, it would have allowed the employee to continue in employment. Given the apparently wide scope for an employer to reject a request not to retire, it should be relatively easy for an employer to show that it would not have agreed to allow an employee to remain in employment.

2.83 Retirement following abolition of DRA and for non-employees

Where *Sch 9, Pt 2, para 8* does not apply, it is direct age discrimination to 'retire' an individual (ie to dismiss him because of his age), unless an objective justification can be shown. In addition, if the person being retired is an employee, his dismissal could be unfair. This might arise in a number of situations, eg:

- once the DRA has been abolished then, subject to the transitional provisions, all employers will need to show objective justification if they wish to force employees to retire at a particular age;
- the DRA has never applied to individuals who do not fall within the limited definition of 'relevant worker' in *Sch 9, Pt 2, para 8* (see **2.29**), eg partners, directors (as office-holders) and independent contractors;
- where the DRA applies, it will still be necessary to show objective justification:
  - if an employer wishes to adopt a mandatory retirement age of less than 65; or
  - if an employee is dismissed after age 65 or normal retirement age but the reason for dismissal is not 'retirement' within the meaning of *ERA 1996, ss 98ZA–98ZF*.

The scope for employers to show an objective justification for mandatory retirement and to defend unfair dismissal claims is considered below. In practice, this is likely to be difficult for most roles and many employers will choose to operate without mandatory retirement. The issues which this will give rise to, are also considered below.

2.84 *Objective justification*

To show that a mandatory retirement age is objectively justified, an employer (or other body, such as a partnership) which is seeking to justify the provision, must show that it is a proportionate means of achieving a legitimate aim. For a more detailed discussion of the law relating to the objective justification of direct age discrimination see **2.16**.

Employers who seek to retain a mandatory retirement age will always face a degree of risk, because it will be for the tribunal to assess on the facts of the particular case whether the objective justification is made out and the outcome cannot be predicted with certainty in advance. Nor is it clear at this stage, quite how easy it will be. Some assistance can be drawn from CJEU decisions on mandatory retirement and maximum recruitment ages and from UK case law outside the employment context. However, as explained below, both need to be treated with a degree of caution. Overall, although each case will need to be considered on its facts, it seems likely that it will be difficult for most employers to justify a mandatory retirement age in most cases—and certainly difficult to do so across an entire workforce.

CJEU cases

2.85 In general, the CJEU has taken a fairly generous approach to attempts to justify mandatory retirement ages or maximum recruitment ages.

There are a number of cases where it has considered whether retirement provisions permitted by national law in a Member State are objectively justified in accordance with *Framework Directive, Article 6(1)*, ie they pursue a legitimate aim and are an appropriate and necessary means of achieving that aim. It has concluded that Spanish and German laws permitting collective agreements to provide for mandatory retirement can potentially be justified under *Article 6(1)* (*Palacios* and *Rosenbladt v Oellerking GmbH*). It has also held that provisions for mandatory retirement of dentists (*Petersen v Berufungsausschuss fur Zahnarzte fur Bezirk Westfalen-Lippe*) and University professors (*Georgiev v Tehnicheski universitet*) at age 68 can potentially be justified under *Article 6(1)*.

In each of these cases the legitimate aims identified under *Article 6(1)* have included sharing employment opportunities between the generations/providing employment opportunities to younger employees. In addition, in *Georgiev* the CJEU accepted that having a mix of different generations of teaching staff so as to promote an exchange of experiences and innovation and develop the quality of the teaching could be a legitimate aim. In *Rosenbladt*, avoiding humiliation by avoiding the need to dismiss older workers for incapability and workforce planning were also accepted as legitimate aims. When considering the question of proportionality, the CJEU has been influenced by the fact that employees were to some extent protected where they could only be forced to retire if they could draw a pension (*Palacios*, *Rosenbladt* and *Georgiev*) and by the fact that provisions had been agreed between the social partners (*Palacios* and *Rosenbladt*).

The CJEU has also identified scope to justify retirement ages under other provisions of the *Framework Directive*. Thus, in *Petersen* it considered that the retirement age for dentists might potentially be justified under *Article 6(5)* which permits national laws for the protection of health. The CJEU accepted that either the protection of health of patients (it being thought that performance of dentists declines after a particular age) or the need to avoid excessive costs in the national health system (through an excess of dentists) could potentially be aims which justified the age limit in principle. However, on the facts of the case the particular law could not be justified on the basis of protection of health because it did not apply to dentists in private practice and so was not a consistent way to protect patients' health. In *Wolf v Stadt Frankfurt am Main* the CJEU held that a maximum recruitment age of 30 for German firefighters was lawful under the *Framework Directive, Article 4(1)* (occupational requirements). The need for high physical abilities was a genuine and determining occupational requirement for the role. It was accepted that this was a characteristic which was related to age, on the basis of uncontradicted evidence from the German government showing that physical ability declines with age. The provision pursued a legitimate objective of maintaining the operational capacity and proper functioning of the fire service and was proportionate. As explained at **2.27** the occupational requirements test in *EqA 2010* is more restrictively framed and is unlikely to provide a route for justifying retirement ages. However, there seems no reason why the same conclusion could not also have been reached the same conclusion under *Article 6(1)*.

The decisions of the CJEU in this area provide some assistance in identifying potentially legitimate aims for retirement provisions under UK law, but have to be treated with a degree of caution. Firstly, in many of the cases, the CJEU did not decide that the provisions in question were in fact justified, only that they were capable of being justified. It was left to the national courts to decide whether the provisions did in fact achieve the legitimate aims identified and whether they were proportionate. Secondly, the cases involve justification by Member States of provisions of legislation (and also in the case of *Rosenbladt* a national collective agreement). The cases emphasise the broad discretion which Member States (and where appropriate the social partners acting at national level) enjoy in the field of social and employment policy, both in identifying legitimate aims and in deciding how to pursue them. In contrast, employers and partnerships who seek to objectively justify a mandatory retirement age in the UK will be relying on *EqA 2010, s 13(2)*. As Blake J pointed out in *Age UK*:

> 'The social aims that the government relies on are ones in which the states enjoy a wide margin of appreciation. Whereas the individual employer justifying particular

practices or treatment in reliance on that social aim has a much more rigorous task . . .'

(See also the comments of Sir Mark Waller in *Seldon v Clarkson, Wright & Jakes* at para 21 and discussion at **2.16–2.19**.) In addition, the CJEU cases consider whether the social policy aim of the Member State is justified in the context of national law and labour markets. As explained below, the abolition of the DRA marks a shift in the policy of the UK towards retirement.

UK case law

2.86 The case law to date in the UK has tended to take a fairly broad approach to identifying legitimate aims, but has generally taken a fairly strict approach to the question of proportionality. Thus tribunals have found that a mandatory retirement age of 65 for recorders (*Hampton v Lord Chancellor*), a mandatory retirement age of 48 for professional football referees (*Martin v Professional Game Match Officials Ltd*) and maximum recruitment age of 36 for air traffic controllers (*Baker v NATS*) were all unlawful, although legitimate aims had been advanced for each of them.

The leading case in UK law is the decision of the Court of Appeal in *Seldon v Clarkson, Wright & Jakes*, although leave to appeal to the Supreme Court is being sought. That case considered the lawfulness of a retirement age of 65 for partners in a small law firm. The employment tribunal had found that the retirement age was objectively justified. The Court of Appeal confirmed that the three aims identified by the Tribunal were legitimate aims:

— ensuring associates in the law firm were given the opportunity of partnership after a reasonable period;

— facilitating workforce planning by having a realistic aim of when vacancies would arise; and

— limiting the need to expel partners for poor performance and thus contributing to the congenial and supportive culture of the firm.

The court held that the first two aims could potentially justify a retirement age of 65. It rejected the argument that a retirement age of 65 could not be justified because a higher age might have been less discriminatory, even though there was no evidence that a retirement age of, say, 68 would not have achieved the aims identified. The retirement provision was proportionate and the choice of 65 as the DRA in the employment context supported that age as a proportionate cut off. The Court of Appeal also held that although both the rule providing for mandatory retirement and its application in the specific case had to be objectively justified but that if the rule is justified, its application in a particular case will be easy to justify. However, the tribunal had been wrong to find that the last aim ('collegiality') justified a retirement age of 65 because there was no evidence that performance deteriorated at age 65. The case was therefore remitted to the tribunal to reconsider whether this affected the issue of proportionality.

At first sight the case might suggest a reasonably broad scope to justify mandatory retirement. However, there are a number of reasons to be cautious. First one of the factors taken into account in assessing proportionality was the relative equality of bargaining power between the partners who negotiated the retirement provision in the partnership deed. That is a feature which is not generally present in the employment relationship or even in much larger partnerships. Second, it was a relatively unusual working environment. There was no mechanism for performance management of partners and so the need for a congenial culture was easier to show than would be the case for a large employer which frequently manages performance. In addition, the career opportunities in a small partnership may have made the workforce planning arguments more compelling than in a larger organisation with a more diverse career structure and higher turnover of employees at a senior level.

A further reason for caution will arise once the DRA has been abolished. First, in *Seldon* the DRA was directly taken into account in deciding that 65 was a proportionate age to set for mandatory retirement. Second, the removal of the DRA represents a distinct policy shift on the part of the UK government. In its consultation paper 'Phasing out the Default Retirement Age' the government stated that the removal of the DRA was part of a policy of enabling and encouraging people to work for longer. This was perceived to have financial, health and social benefits for individuals and financial benefits for the wider economy, by extending working lives and GDP. In considering whether a mandatory retirement age is justified under *EqA 2010, s 13(2)* a court must have regard to whether it is 'within' or 'consistent with' the government's social policy objective for introducing *s 13(2)* (see above at **2.19** and also *Rosenbladt*). Whilst the government's stated social policy objective for *s 13(2)* (or rather for its predecessor, *AR 2006, reg 3*) was the need to preserve the confidence and integrity of the labour market, tribunals may nevertheless be influenced by the policy behind the removal of the DRA.

Position following abolition of DRA

2.87 Although the existing case law needs to be treated with some caution, it does suggest some objectives which might amount to legitimate aims following the abolition of the DRA, although in each case there may be difficulties showing that a mandatory retirement age is a proportionate means of achieving the aim:

— 'workforce planning' is likely to amount to a legitimate aim. This potentially covers a wide range of situations including making room for new recruits so that there is sufficient new intake to identify talent for recruitment (eg *Hampton, Martin*); being able to predict recruitment needs (*Seldon*); making opportunities for promotion so as to retain employees and provide career progression (*Seldon, Martin*); ensuring a balance of ages so that there are the right number of staff at each level (*Petersen, Martin*) and not a risk of too many employees retiring at one time. However, employers will need to show that a retirement age does really further these aims and that they could not be achieved in a less discriminatory way. Where there is a reasonably high turnover or broad career opportunities, it may be unrealistic to suggest that employees will be retained by the prospect of promotion when somebody retires. There may be sufficient natural turnover to ensure there is room for new recruits, or the possibility of creating turnover by removing poor performers (*Hampton, Martin*). Succession planning might be achievable by having discussions with employees about their intentions. Even if there is a need to adopt a retirement age in relation to some roles within an organisation, it seems unlikely that workforce planning could justify mandatory retirement across all roles in most organisations—particularly given the government's findings that most employers already operate without a mandatory retirement age as explained above;

— dignity/performance: providing a 'dignified exit' for employees, rather than managing them out for poor performance was considered legitimate as a way of maintaining a collegiate environment in *Seldon*. Although the working environment in *Seldon* was unusual in that there was no means of performance managing partners, the Court of Appeal stated that 'it is not just within partnerships that it may be thought better to have a cut-off age rather than force an assessment of a person's falling off in performance as they get older' and 'there is a very great difference between employees or partners who are underperforming but not by reason of age and those who are doing their best but it is no longer good enough because age has caught up with them' suggesting this might have wider scope for justification. In some respects it is surprising to suggest that dismissing a good performer purely because of their age is more dignified than dismissing someone for poor performance, although there is support for this being a legitimate aim in *Rosenbladt*. However, even if this survives as a legitimate aim, it is likely to be difficult to find evidence to justify a particular point a particular retirement age, given the lack of evidence of performance tailing off with age at least for roles which are not physically demanding (see *Seldon* but cf *Wolf* in relation to physical roles). Research into the DRA suggests that in most jobs work performance does not deteriorate with age, at least before age 70 and loss of speed, strength and memory are offset by greater experience, interpersonal skills and motivation;

— health and safety: protecting the health of the public is likely to be a legitimate aim in jobs where employees potentially pose a risk to the public (*Petersen*). However, employers are likely to need to show evidence that performance declines with age, rather than simply making (stereotypical) assumptions, and the evidence for this is limited in most professions (see *Seldon, Baker, Martin* but cf *Wolf*). In addition, it might be difficult to show that the aim could not be achieved by a less discriminatory measure such as regular medicals/performance monitoring (see *Baker, Martin*).

Where employers do wish to retain a mandatory retirement age, the cases demonstrate that they will need to give careful thought to what their aims are and show that they have evidence to support the aims and the particular age chosen. The EAT in *Seldon* stated that it will not always be necessary to have 'concrete evidence, neatly weighed, to support each assertion weighed' and tribunals can use their common sense and knowledge of human nature. However, substantive evidence will certainly be an advantage and employers need to avoid stereotypical assumptions. In addition, employers will need to show that they have considered alternatives with an open mind (*Baker v NATS*). Agreeing a retirement age with a trade union or employee representatives can be helpful in showing proportionality (see **2.23**), as could linking retirement to pension entitlement (*Palacios, Rosenbladt*) and having scope to consider allowing employees to stay on in exceptional cases. Retirement provisions will also need to be kept under review as the need for a retirement age may change over time.

2.88 *Unfair dismissal*

In addition to the need to show that a dismissal is objectively justified, employers who wish to operate a mandatory retirement age for their employees may face unfair dismissal claims. For employees to whom the DRA applies, this needs to be considered in the light of the applicable retirement procedures which apply (see **2.79**). However, when the DRA is abolished, the government is also proposing to abolish the retirement procedure and the right to request working beyond retirement and to remove retirement as a potentially fair reason for dismissal.

Therefore, following the removal of the DRA, to defend an unfair dismissal claim, employers will need to show that they had a potentially fair reason for dismissal and that and it must be reasonable to dismiss for that reason. The potentially fair reason which is most likely to be applicable is 'some other substantial reason' under *ERA1996, s 98(1)(b)*. It seems likely that an aim which amounts to a legitimate aim for the purposes of objective justification, will also be a substantial reason for dismissal. However, whether it will justify dismissal in a particular case, will depend on whether it is reasonable to dismiss for that reason in the light of equity and the substantial merits of the case and this is likely to involve a consideration of the reasonableness of the retirement age and whether an exception should be made to it in a particular case. It will also require a fair procedure to be followed.

As regards the procedure, the government is proposing to remove the current retirement procedure when the DRA is abolished. In one case an employment tribunal has held that the ACAS Code on Disciplinary and Grievance procedures applies to dismissals for 'some other substantial reasons' because (unlike dismissals for redundancy or non-renewal of fixed-term contracts) they are not expressly excluded from the Code (*Cummings v Siemens Communications Ltd*). However, the decision is only at tribunal level and so is not binding and the reasoning is questionable. The ACAS Code only expressly applies to disciplinary and grievance situations: there are other circumstances (eg dismissal because of a genuine illness or injury) which are not expressly excluded from the Code, but where it is clear from the ACAS Guide that Code is not intended to apply. It seems more likely that the Code should only apply to dismissals for conduct (including poor performance).

Assuming the Code does not apply, and in the absence of further guidance from ACAS, it seems likely that a fair procedure will involve giving employees advance notification of their proposed retirement, consulting with them before retirement and considering any request for continued working (and doing so consistently with other employees in similar circumstances). Employers may also decide to allow an appeal and give employees the right to be accompanied, although this is not necessarily required to make the dismissals fair if the ACAS Code does not apply; what is required will depend on what is reasonable in the circumstances.

2.89 *Operating without mandatory retirement*

The government's research into the DRA found that, prior to its abolition, only 32% of establishments (employing 45% of employees) operated a mandatory retirement age (see Employment Relations Occasional Paper: Review of Default Retirement Age: Summary of Research Evidence). Given the likely difficulty in justifying a mandatory retirement age following the abolition of the DRA it is likely that many more employers will move away from mandatory retirement.

Clearly, if employees wish to retire there will be nothing to stop them giving notice to terminate their employment in the normal way. However, employees may be keen to know what their options are for retirement before they make a final decision and employers may also want to know what an employee's plans are. One of the issues raised in the government's consultation paper is whether there should be additional guidance or a statutory code of practice that would encourage employers and employees to have a mutually beneficial dialogue about an employees retirement plans. The response to the consultation is not available at the time of writing.

Where employees choose not to retire, they will continue to be protected against discrimination on grounds of age. In dealing with older employees employers will need to treat them consistently with younger employees and avoid making unjustified assumptions about their intentions and their abilities eg that an older employee will not be interested in training or new job opportunities or will not be able to get to grips with new technology. However, the government is consulting about whether further exceptions to the age discrimination provisions of *EqA 2010* are needed to clarify when it will be lawful for employers to cease cover, require medical underwriting or pass on additional costs in relation to older employees under group insured benefits and when employees should be treated as good leavers under share schemes.

Of course, operating without a mandatory retirement age does not mean that an employer cannot dismiss older employees or has to accept lower standards of conduct or performance. Employers will still be able to dismiss employees for the potentially fair reasons which apply to all employees, eg for conduct, capability, redundancy or some other substantial reason. A concern that some employers have expressed in relation to older employees is that their performance will drop off. In fact, the government research in relation to the DRA concluded that the evidence suggests that in most cases work performance does not deteriorate up to age 70 at least in non-physical roles (and see also comments in *Seldon* and the High Court decision in the *Age UK* case). However, if the performance of an older employee does decline or their health declines in a way which affects their ability to do the job, this can be addressed as it would be for a younger employee and will potentially provide the basis for a fair dismissal for capability. In operating performance management procedures, employers should not simply assume that performance issues in older workers are related to age and/or that they will not be able to improve. Equally, employers would be well advised to apply their performance management processes consistently and not, for example, to overlook declining performance in older workers in the expectation that they will soon choose to retire. In dealing with older employees who have health problems, employers will need to bear in mind that employees may also be protected by disability discrimination legislation (see **3.11ff**).

Another issue for employers who do not operate mandatory retirement will be to consider whether to offer flexible working to older employees and what flexibility to allow employees under the company pension scheme. The government research into the DRA (see above) indicated that the number of employees who would be interested in working beyond 65 increased significantly with the prospect of flexible working. The government has announced a proposal to extend the right to request flexible working to cover all employees in the future as part of its equality strategy, although details are not available at the time of writing.

2.90 **Redundancy schemes**

Statutory redundancy pay

The statutory redundancy payments scheme, originally introduced in 1965, historically contained a number of age-related aspects. These included differentiating between three age bands (under 21, 21 to 40, and 41 and over) when calculating redundancy pay, discounting service below the age of 18, imposing an age limit of 65 on the entitlement to redundancy pay and tapering the value of the redundancy payment for employees aged 64. As part of the *Age Matters* consultation, the government initially proposed a broad range of changes to the scheme, including the removal of the age band 'multipliers' and also the abolition of the upper and lower age limits on the entitlement to redundancy pay. The government revised its position on the age band multipliers when publishing the final draft of *AR 2006* in March 2006, announcing that the retention of multipliers which favoured workers as they became older could be objectively justified under the EU's *Equal Treatment Framework Directive* on the basis that older workers were more likely to become long-term unemployed and also experience a substantial fall in earnings in any future employment (see the written statement to Parliament from Mr Gerry Sutcliffe, Parliamentary Under-Secretary of State for Trade and Industry dated 2 March 2006).

The changes to the statutory redundancy payment scheme introduced on 1 October 2006 were therefore limited to the removal of the lower and upper age limits on the entitlement to receive redundancy pay, and the elimination of the tapering of redundancy payments for employees aged between 64 and 65. Other potentially discriminatory aspects of the scheme such as calculating redundancy pay according to each employee's length of service, limiting the relevant period of service to 20 years and applying the age band multipliers have all been retained. An employer who makes redundancy payments to its employees in accordance with the statutory scheme set out in *ERA 1996, Pt XI* should be exempt from claims of age discrimination by virtue of the statutory authority exception set out in *EqA 2010, Sch 22, para 1* (previously *AR 2006, reg 27(1)*) (see **2.49**) and/or *Sch 9, Pt 2, para 13* (previously *AR 2006, reg 33*) (see **2.43**).

2.91 *Enhanced redundancy schemes*

EqA 2010, Sch 9, Pt 2, para 13 (replicating *AR 2006, reg 33)* provides a specific exemption for enhanced redundancy schemes which closely mirror the calculation used in the statutory redundancy scheme (see **2.42**). However, when *AR 2006* came into effect, many employers operated redundancy schemes which calculated payments by reference to age and/or length of service and so were potentially discriminatory. In many cases these had been in place for a long time and were popular with the workforce and the unions and, in some cases, contractual. Eliminating age-related elements would either have involved increased costs for employers or some (usually older) workers receiving lower payments. Therefore many employers have retained such schemes, which will be unlawful unless they can be objectively justified.

Age-based payments

2.92 In *MacCulloch v Imperial Chemical Industries plc* [2008] IRLR 846 the EAT considered the lawfulness of a historic redundancy scheme where the size of redundancy payments varied very substantially depending on age and length of service. The EAT held that the scheme had the legitimate aims of encouraging and rewarding loyalty, reflecting the fact that older workers would be more vulnerable in the workplace if made redundant and retaining a popular scheme which made it easier to manage change that encouraged older workers to leave thereby encouraging turnover. The EAT held that the tribunal had been entitled to draw on its own experience to conclude that older workers will find it more difficult to find work than younger workers. The EAT accepted that it was appropriate to look at the scheme as a whole, rather than its application to an individual, in considering what the aims of the scheme were. It was also necessary to consider the scheme as a whole when considering whether the scheme is proportionate, given the impact on the individual employee. The fact that the scheme rules were fixed and did not vary with individual circumstances was a feature of the scheme which had to be justified, but in practice this would not be difficult because transparency and equality of treatment were important principles in their own right. However, the EAT held that the tribunal had not properly considered the question of proportionality and in particular the large differences between payments under the scheme. The case was remitted to the tribunal which concluded that the scheme was a proportionate means of achieving the legitimate aims.

The *MacCulloch* case is helpful for employers who have retained historic redundancy schemes at least where they are supported by employees/unions. The tribunal, when the case returned to it, did not focus in detail on how particular payments related to particular ages and the need to pursue the legitimate aims identified. It focused on the fact that attempts to change the scheme had been rejected by the workforce and one of the aims of the scheme (which it identified in slightly different terms from those considered by the EAT) was to have a peaceful workforce and allow the employer to manage change and have good industrial relations (see also the reasoning in *Rolls-Royce v Unite*). The fact that the government retains the statutory redundancy payment scheme, which increases with age and length of service (see above) also lends legitimacy to the practice. Where schemes are agreed with trade unions or employee representatives, this will be helpful in showing proportionality and reducing the practical risk of a challenge (see **2.23**). However, each case depends on its facts and it remains to be seen whether, as age discrimination legislation becomes more embedded and the labour market changes, eg with growing youth unemployment and removal of the DRA, the acceptance of such schemes and the assumptions on which they are based will be open to challenge.

Caps and tapers

2.93 Another common traditional feature of redundancy schemes is to provide for payments to be taper as an employee approaches retirement or to be capped at a level to ensure that an employee never receives more than the salary they would have earned between the date of their redundancy and their retirement date. This feature was removed from the statutory redundancy scheme when *AR 2006* was introduced (see above) and is potentially directly discriminatory. However, in *Kraft Foods Ltd v Hastie* (2010) UKEAT/0024/10/ZT, [2010] ICR 1355 the EAT held that the general purpose of redundancy schemes was to compensate redundant employees for the loss of earnings which they would have received had they remained in employment and concluded that it was legitimate to cap redundancy payments at the amount the employee would have earned up to the age at which they could be required to retire to avoid them receiving a 'windfall'. That was the case even though the employer in that case sometimes allowed employees to remain in employment past their normal retirement age. However, following the abolition of the default retirement age (see **2.64**) many employers will not have a mandatory retirement age and the reasoning in *Kraft* will no longer be applicable to those employers.

In *Loxley v BAE Systems Land Systems (Munitions & Ordnance) Ltd* [2008] IRLR 853 the EAT suggested that the fact that an employee was entitled to an immediate pension might justify excluding them from a redundancy payment (and tapering payments as someone approaches that point) even where that was not the age at which they could be required to retire. This was not based on a windfall argument, but on the fact that one of the aims of a redundancy scheme is to cushion workers from the effects of losing their income and this might not be required, at least to the same extent, where an employee was entitled to an immediate pension payment. The EAT noted that whether this was the case would depend on a consideration of the pension and redundancy schemes in each case. In contrast the CJEU in *Ingeniørforeningen i Danmark, acting on behalf of Ole Anderson v Region Syddanmark: C-499/08* held that it was unlawful age discrimination to deprive employees of a service related severance payment on the grounds that they were entitled to draw a pension. The aim of the payment was to facilitate a move to new employment and on this basis the CJEU held it would be legitimate to exclude employees who chose to retire in order to avoid double compensation. However, it was not proportionate to exclude employees who wished to continue to work and not draw their pension as this could force them to draw their pension early and thus receive a lower amount. This does not preclude the possibility of justifying caps and tapers in redundancy schemes, but each case will need to be considered in the light of the particular schemes and their aims.

Length of service

2.94 Many employers, whilst eliminating age factors from the calculation of redundancy payments, have retained service related payments. The exception for the provision of certain benefits based on length of service (as set out in *Sch 9, Pt 2, para 10* (previously *AR 2006, reg 32*); see **2.36**) does not apply to redundancy payments as a consequence of *para 10(7)*, which specifically excludes from the scope of this exception benefits awarded by virtue of an employee ceasing his employment. Therefore redundancy payments based on length of service alone will potentially amount to indirect discrimination. In *MacCulloch* the tribunal had initially not reached a conclusion on whether the scheme (which took account of length of service up to 10 years) could have been indirectly discriminatory. The EAT agreed that it was not necessary to determine this since if the scheme was objectively justified this would provide a defence to both direct and indirect discrimination. It accepted that taking 10 years' service into account could further the legitimate aim of rewarding loyalty. It observed though that if it was necessary to decide the indirect discrimination point the tribunal would have to address the question whether the claimant did suffer on grounds of age as a result of the application of the 10 years' service criterion which, it said, might depend on the ages at which employees were typically recruited into the business. When the case was remitted to the tribunal it found that the claimant, as a 37-year-old employee, was not disadvantaged by the 10-year length of service criterion. For a more general discussion of service related benefits see **2.59** ff.

2.95 *Redundancy criteria*

EqA 2010 does not contain specific provisions dealing with the criteria used by employers when selecting employees for redundancy. Clearly, any selection which is based on the ages of the employees will amount to direct discrimination and objective justification is likely to prove difficult.

The use of length of service in the form or 'last in first out' ('LIFO') is likely to disadvantage younger employees who are likely to have shorter periods of service and could therefore constitute indirect discrimination. The *ACAS Guidance* on the *AR 2006* suggested that any use of length of service in any selection criteria was likely to be age discriminatory. However, in *Rolls-Royce plc v Unite* [2009] EWCA Civ 387, [2010] 1 WLR 318 the majority of the Court of Appeal held that the use of length of service as one of a number of criteria for selection for redundancy contained in a collective agreement was objectively justified (and potentially fell within the exemption in *Sch 9, Pt 2, para 10* (previously *AR 2006, reg 32*) see above at **2.36**). The legitimate aim, identified by Wall LJ was 'the reward of loyalty, and the overall desirability of achieving a stable workforce in the context of a fair process of redundancy selection'. Arden LJ, who was the other judge in the majority focused more on the benefits of having an agreed method of implementing redundancies to avoid workplace disputes.

It was clearly important in that case that length of service was only one of many criteria and was neither determinative nor definitive of selection and there were comments which suggest that using length of service as the sole criterion would not have been proportionate. It was also significant in that case that the criterion was agreed with the trade union. Indeed, unusually, it was the trade union which was arguing that that the criterion was lawful and the employer was contesting this. The union also gave evidence that the use of length of service was supported by younger employees. Therefore it cannot be assumed that use of length of service will always be justified, each case will need to be considered on its facts. The *EHRC Employment Code* reflects the *Rolls Royce* decision, noting that LIFO may amount to indirect age, sex or race discrimination but that used as one criterion among many within a fair selection criterion, length of service could be a proportionate means of achieving a legitimate aim of rewarding loyalty and creating a stable workforce (*Section 19.14–19.15*).

2.96 Notice periods

The statutory minimum periods of notice required to terminate employment (as set out in *ERA 1996, s 86*) increase according to the employee's length of service. The calculation of notice based on length of service will potentially amount to indirect discrimination against younger employees who are likely to have shorter periods of service. However, the provision of statutory minimum notice is likely to fall within the general exception for acts done with statutory authority set out in *EqA 2010, Sch 22, para 1* (previously *AR 2006, reg 27*), so that any resulting discrimination is deemed lawful.

Of course, many employers provide for contractual notice periods which are more generous than the statutory minima. It is unclear whether contractual notice periods fall within the scope of the exception for certain service related benefits set out in *Sch 9, Pt 2, para 10* (previously *AR 2006, reg 32*) (see **2.22**) on the basis that the definition of 'benefits' for these purposes excludes benefits provided by virtue of an employee ceasing employment (*para 10(7)*). The wide definition of 'benefits' adopted in *Rolls-Royce plc v Unite* [2009] EWCA Civ387, [2010] 1 WLR 318 (see **2.37**) could support the argument that a right to remain in employment for longer (ie have a longer notice period) would be a 'benefit' falling within *para 10*. However, the *EHRC Employment Code* states that the exception does not apply to service related termination payments and, at least where the employer has an established practice of making a payment in lieu of notice, this is arguably what a service related notice period amounts to. Therefore, an employer which wishes to have notice periods increasing with service (other than in line with the statutory minimum) may need to be able to show that to do is objectively justified.

2.97 DISCRIMINATION FOLLOWING THE END OF EMPLOYMENT

EqA 2010, s 108 (and previously *AR 2006, reg 24*) sets out specific provisions dealing with relationships which have come to an end, including employment relationships. Accordingly, it is unlawful for an employer to discriminate against or harass a former employee contrary to *EqA 2010* where such discrimination or harassment arises out of and is closely connected to the employment relationship. For example, it would be unlawful to refuse to provide a reference, or to provide an unfavourable reference, to a former employee on the grounds of their age.

However, there is an unintended gap in the protection for former employees from victimisation. *EqA 2010, 108(7)* expressly excludes victimisation. This was done on the basis that the provisions on victimisation would make express provision for former employees. However, *EqA 2010* fails to do so (see COMMON CONCEPTS **(1)**).

2.98 VALIDITY OF DISCRIMINATORY TERMS

EqA 2010, ss 142–148 contain various provisions relating to the validity of contracts (*ss 142–144*), collective agreements and rules of undertaking (*ss 145–148*). Under *s 142* a contractual term which constitutes, promotes or provides for treatment of a party to the contract in question which is unlawful under *EqA 2010* will be enforceable only on the part of the 'victim' of the discrimination. Pursuant to *s 143*, a county court or sheriff court has the power to remove or modify a provision rendered unenforceable under *s 142*.

Section 145(1) provides that a term of a collective agreement will be void in so far as it constitutes, promotes or provides for treatment which is unlawful under *EqA 2010*. *Section 145(2)* provides that 'rules of undertakings' (being employers' rules applicable to employees or prospective employees and rules imposed by trade organisations and qualifications bodies) are unenforceable where they would constitute, promote or provide for treatment which is unlawful under *EqA 2010*. The employment tribunal has the power to declare that a term is void or rule is unenforceable further to *s 146(3)* on the application of an employee or member within certain criteria set out in *ss 146(2), 146(5)* and *146(6)*. These provisions could affect the enforceability of mandatory retirement provisions, age-related benefits or other terms which are incorporated into collective agreements, such as enhanced redundancy formulas or redundancy selection criteria. These provisions replace similar provisions previously contained in *AR 2006, reg 45* and *Sch 5*.

2.99 ENFORCEMENT

Jurisdiction of employment tribunals

EqA 2010, s 136 (previously *AR 2006, reg 37*) provides for the jurisdiction of the employment tribunals to hear any complaint based on unlawful discrimination, harassment and victimisation in the employment context.

Further details relating to the jurisdiction of the employment tribunals in discrimination claims can be found at **1.24**.

2.100 Burden of proof

EqA 2010, s 160 sets out provisions relating to the burden of proof in cases which appear before the employment tribunals, which mirror the provisions previously found in previously *AR 2006, reg 36*.

In summary terms, *s 160* provides that once a complainant had proven facts from which a tribunal could conclude, in the absence of any other explanation, that discrimination or harassment has taken place, the tribunal must uphold the complaint unless the respondent proves to the contrary.

Further details relating to the burden of proof in employment tribunal claims can be found at **1.128ff**.

2.101 Questionnaires

EqA 2010, s 138 (replacing *AR 2006, reg 41*) provides for a questionnaire procedure. As in *AR 2006*, the purpose of the questionnaire procedure is to enable the aggrieved person to obtain information which may assist with pursuing a claim under *EqA 2010*.

Further details relating to the questionnaire procedure can be found at **1.183**.

2.102 Remedies

EqA 2010, s 124 (previously *AR 2006, reg* 36) sets out the remedies open to an employment tribunal if it considers that a complaint under *EqA 2010* is well founded. As in the pre-*EqA 2010* legislation, these include a declaration based on its findings and an award of compensation as the tribunal determines is just and equitable (including compensation for loss of past and future earnings, and injury to feelings). In addition, the *EqA 2010* extended the tribunals' power to make recommendations, so that as well as making recommendations for the benefit of the individual claimant, such recommendations can now be made for the benefit of any other person (*s 124(3)*).

Further details relating to the remedies open to an employment tribunal can be found at **1.169**ff.

The remedies related to a breach of the pensions provisions in *EqA 2010* are dealt with separately in *s 126* (previously in *AR 2006, Pt 1, Sch 2, para 6*).

2.103 Time limits

The provisions relating to time limits for pursuing a claim before the employment tribunals mirror the provisions in the pre-*EqA 2010* legislation and are set out in *EqA 2010, s 123* (previously *AR 2006, reg 41*). A complaint to a tribunal must be brought within a period of three months from the date that the act was committed, subject to the tribunal's discretion to hear a complaint which is out of time if it considers that it is just and equitable to do so. Specific provisions relating to continuing acts are set out in *s 123(3)*.

Further details relating to the time limits for pursuing tribunal claims can be found at **1.41**.

3 Disability discrimination

3.1 INTRODUCTION

Position before 2 December 1996

Prior to 2 December 1996, there was no specific anti-discrimination legislation which prohibited employment-related discrimination against disabled people.

Measures such as the *Disabled Persons (Employment) Acts* ('*DPEA*') *1944* and *1958* established a system under which employers with more than 20 employees had to employ a quota of registered disabled people (usually at least three per cent of the employer's workforce) and reserved certain occupations for disabled workers. The quota system included criminal sanctions, but overall was not very effective because it was rarely enforced and it did not afford disabled people any individual rights.

The failure of the quota system to provide an effective means of protection meant that between 1979 and 1993 there were various attempts to introduce more comprehensive legislation aimed at preventing disability discrimination. These included a number of private members' bills, all of which failed.

3.2 Development of the Disability Discrimination Act 1995

The *Disability Discrimination Act 1995* ('*DDA 1995*') was the result of a government initiative in response to a campaign both inside and outside Parliament for equality and greater protection for disabled people. A consultation document entitled 'Government Measures to Tackle Discrimination Against Disabled People' was issued in July 1994. This was followed by a White Paper, 'Ending Discrimination Against Disabled People', and a Disability Bill (published in January 1995) committing the government to addressing, amongst other things, disability-related discrimination in employment. This Disability Bill became *DDA 1995*, receiving Royal Assent on 8 November 1995. *DDA 1995* repealed the *DPEA* and the quota system and in its place established a framework, supplemented by secondary legislation, for targeting discrimination faced by disabled persons in employment, access to goods, facilities and services, and the purchase or renting of property.

The employment provisions of *DDA 1995, Part II* came into force on 2 December 1996 and were significantly amended over time. The majority of the changes were made from 1 October 2004 by the *Disability Discrimination Act 1995 (Amendment) Regulations 2003 (SI 2003/1673)* ('*2003 Regulations*'), which implemented the changes needed to make *DDA 1995* consistent with the EC Equal Treatment Framework Directive 2000/78/EC ('*Framework Directive*') (see COMMON CONCEPTS (1)). Additional changes were made in 2005 by the *Disability Discrimination Act 2005* ('*DDA 2005*') to general concepts, such as the definition of disability.

3.3 Equality Act 2010

On 1 October 2010 the *Equality Act 2010 ('EqA 2010')* came into force and repealed the *DDA 1995*. It applies to all acts or omissions from 1 October 2010 and any acts carried out before 1 October 2010 which were unlawful under *DDA 1995* and which continue on or after 1 October 2010 (see *Equality Act 2010 (Commencement No 4, Savings, Consequential, Transitional, Transitory and Incidental Provisions and Revocation) Order 2010, SI 2010/2317*). *EqA 2010* consolidated and harmonised much of the existing discrimination legislation (see

COMMON CONCEPTS (1)), but it also strengthened it. It made significant changes in relation to disability discrimination. In particular it extended the concept of indirect discrimination to disability, and introduced a new form of discrimination: discrimination arising from a disability, in place of the concept of disability-related discrimination (see **3.61**). *EqA 2010* also made some changes to the definition of disability (see **3.11**) and the duty to make reasonable adjustments (see **3.75**), although these are likely to be less significant in practice.

3.4 Disability Rights Commission

The Disability Rights Commission (DRC) was an independent statutory body set up to oversee the operation of *DDA 1995*, and to promote equality of opportunity for disabled people. The DRC was established under the *Disability Rights Commission Act 1999* ('*DRCA 1999*'). Under *DRCA 1999, s 2(1)* the DRC had the following four general duties:

(a) to work towards the elimination of discrimination against and harassment of disabled persons;

(b) to promote the equalisation of opportunities for disabled persons;

(c) to take such steps as it considered appropriate with a view to encouraging good practice in the treatment of disabled persons;

(d) to keep the working of *DDA 1995* and *DRCA 1999* under review.

Like the Equal Opportunities Commission (EOC) and the Commission for Racial Equality (CRE), the DRC had a number of specific powers, relating to areas including research, the provision of assistance to individual complainants and enforcement, enabling it to carry out its general duties.

3.5 Equality and Human Rights Commission

From 1 October 2007, the EHRC took over the work of the DRC, and the *DRCA 1999* was repealed in its entirety. The EHRC derives its powers from *Equality Act 2006* ('*EqA 2006*'). Insofar as the EHRC's duties in respect of equality and diversity groups relate to disability matters, these duties are delegated to a disability decision-making committee (*EqA 2006, Sch 1, Part 5)*. The disability committee is empowered, among other things, to monitor the law, give information and advice, offer legal assistance and conciliation and institute judicial reviews. These duties will be delegated to the disability committee for at least five years, at the end of which period the EHRC will review its activities and will recommend to the Secretary of State how long the committee should continue in existence.

3.6 Codes of Practice

In carrying out its duties under the *EqA 2006*, the EHRC has a range of general and enforcement powers (see FOREWORD). These powers include the power to issue statutory Codes of Practice. In relation to disability discrimination in the employment context, the EHRC initially inherited the DRC Code of Practice: Employment and Occupation (2004) ('*DRC Code*'). With the commencement of *EqA 2010*, the EHRC will replace the *DRC Code* with the *Employment Statutory Code of Practice ('EHRC Employment Code')*, a single document that covers all forms of discrimination, including disability. The *EHRC Employment Code* sets out practical guidance on how to prevent discrimination against disabled people in employment or when seeking employment. It also contains guidance on the law, which is designed to help employers, tribunals and others understand and apply the provisions of *EqA 2010* (see further *EqA 2006, ss 14* and *15*).

The *EHRC Employment Code* will be a key aid to the interpretation of *EqA 2010* for employers and their advisors. A failure to comply with the *EHRC Employment Code* does not of itself give rise to liability in civil or criminal proceedings, but its provisions may be used in evidence and must be taken into account by courts and tribunals if relevant to a question in proceedings (*EqA 2006, s 15(4)*). The EHRC has also published non-statutory guidance for employers and workers (see **Common concepts (1)**).

3.7 SCOPE

Comparison between disability and other protected characteristics

In many ways the *EqA 2010* provisions on disability are similar to those relating to other protected characteristics, such as the types of job applicants, employees and contract workers who are covered, and the circumstances in which employers can be liable for unlawful discrimination. (Generally, see **Common concepts (1)**.) However, in other ways the protections relating to disability are unique.

First, the disability provisions differ from the other discrimination strands in the type of protection they provide. As well as protection from direct and indirect discrimination, harassment and victimisation, there is also a duty to make reasonable adjustments (*s 20*), and, by virtue of *s 15*, 'discrimination arising from a disability' is now also unlawful. These two latter types of discrimination only apply to disability; they are not found in relation to any other protected characteristic (see **3.75** and **3.61**).

In addition, rather than providing protection to all from discrimination if it is because of the protected characteristic of 'disability', the discrimination provisions as they relate to disability are asymmetric in the way they operate and, unless the claim is for victimisation, only prohibit discrimination against persons who have, or have had, a disability which meets the definition in *EqA 2010*. Direct discrimination against non-disabled people is expressly permitted (*EqA 2010, s 13(3)*). It follows that more favourable treatment of disabled persons is not prohibited by *EqA 2010*, although such treatment is not *required* except in the case of the duty to make reasonable adjustments. However, in some circumstances employees who do not themselves have a disability will be protected. This will arise in the case of discrimination by perception or association.

In common with other protected characteristics, direct discrimination or harassment based on association with a disability is unlawful (see: **Common concepts (1)**). The prohibition on discrimination based on association follows the ECJ's ruling in *Coleman v Attridge Law: C-303/06* [2008] IRLR 722. This made it clear that the *Equal Treatment Framework Directive* prohibits discrimination against, and harassment of, a person who is not disabled but is the primary carer of a disabled child, provided that the reason for the treatment in question is (the child's) disability. The EAT took an expansive view of that ruling, and held that the *DDA 1995* should be read with the addition of a new *s 3A(5)* and *3B(3)*. The effect of the new words was to prohibit discrimination and/or harassment where the behaviour in question is by reason of the disability of the claimant, or 'any person', without any need to prove an association between the claimant and the disabled person whose disability is the reason for the treatment.

EqA 2010 is also intended to cover direct discrimination and harassment on the basis of perception, ie discrimination against someone who is perceived to have one of the protected characteristics but does not. This will have the effect of extending disability discrimination protection to people who do not have a disability as defined in the *EqA 2010*, although there are practical difficulties in applying this test in the disability context (see **common concepts (1)**) and the EAT decisions in *J v DLA Piper* and *Aitken v Commissioner of Police of the Metropolis* suggest that discrimination based on perception might not have been unlawful under *DDA 1995*.

Disability discrimination

3.8 Protected categories

Even if a person meets the definition of a disabled person, in order to bring a claim of direct or indirect discrimination, discrimination arising from a disability or breach of a duty to make reasonable adjustments (or a harassment or victimisation claim), they must also show that they fall into a category which is protected under *EqA 2010*, which are currently:

(a) job applicants and employees (*ss 39–40*, replacing *DDA 1995, ss 4–4A*);

(b) contract workers (*s 41*, replacing *DDA 1995, s 4B*);

(c) police officers and other office-holders (*ss 42–43*, *49–52*, replacing *DDA 1995, ss 4C–4F*);

(d) members or prospective members of occupational pension schemes (*ss 61–63*, replacing *DDA 1995, ss 4G–4K*);

(e) partners or prospective partners in a partnership (*ss 44–46*, replacing *DDA 1995, ss 6A–6C*);

(f) barristers, advocates and pupils (*ss 47–48*, replacing *DDA 1995, ss 7A–7D*);

(g) members or applicants for membership of trade organisations (*s 57*, replacing *DDA 1995, ss 13–14*);

(h) holders or applicants for professional or trade qualifications (*ss 53–54*, replacing *DDA 1995, ss 14A–14B*);

(i) those receiving or seeking services against employment service-providers (*ss 55–56*, replacing *DDA 1995, ss 14C–14D*);

(j) members of locally electable authorities such as a county council (*ss 58–59*, replacing *DDA 1995, ss 15A–15C*).

This chapter will only consider in detail the position of job applicants and employees under *ss 39–40*. (See **3.113** for a summary of the provisions which are applicable to other individuals and categories of activity. A full analysis of these provisions is, however, outside of the scope of this work.)

3.9 Employment

The prohibition on discrimination in employment is contained in *EqA 2010, Part 5*. *EqA 2010, s 83(2)* defines employment as 'employment under a contract of employment, a contract of apprenticeship or a contract personally to do work' (and goes on to cover Crown employment and employment as a relevant member of the Houses of Parliament). See COMMON CONCEPTS **(1)**) and **3.102** ff for details of the scope of liability of employers and principals towards job applicants and employees before, during and after employment under *EqA 2010*.

3.10 Exceptions and special cases

EqA 2010, Part 5 applies to all private employers irrespective of their size. Prior to 1 October 2004, employers with fewer than 15 employees were exempt from the disability discrimination legislation (then *DDA 1995*). However, this exemption was repealed by the *2003 Regulations*. The *2003 Regulations* also extended the protection of *DDA 1995* to previously excluded Crown employments such as the police, fire fighters, and prison officers. For the most part, *EqA 2010* now applies to the Crown and to Crown employment in the same way as it applies to private employers. There are, however, still some specific circumstances where the employment and occupation provisions either do not apply (such as where the conduct in question is done for the purpose of ensuring the combat effectiveness of the armed forces—*EqA 2010, Sch 3, Part 1, para 4*), or where the legislation makes special provision, for example in relation to contract workers (see COMMON CONCEPTS (1) on exceptions and special cases).

3.11 MEANING OF DISABILITY AND DISABLED PERSON

General

The concept of a disability is defined by the *EqA 2010*. As stated above, the disability provisions of *EqA 2010* only prohibit discrimination and harassment because of or arising from disability, within the meaning of the legislation. Note though that direct discrimination and harassment because of an association with someone who has a disability or because someone is perceived to have a disability is also unlawful under *EqA 2010* (see **3.7**).

It is not enough to be unwell or disabled in a general sense (at least unless they are perceived to be disabled). In order to claim protection under these provisions the disability must fall within the meaning of *EqA 2010, s 6(1)*, which provides that:

> 'A person (P) has a disability if—
>
> (a) P has a physical or mental impairment, and
>
> (b) the impairment has a substantial and long-term adverse effect on P's ability to carry out normal day-to-day activities.'.

This definition is similar to that under the previous legislation (*DDA 1995, s 1(1)*), with one significant change—it is no longer necessary to consider a defined list of capacities when determining whether a person is disabled (see **3.23**). Given the similarity, it is therefore likely that much of the pre-*EqA 2010* case law will be still relevant to the disability definition under *EqA 2010*.

As a practical point to note, once either the respondent concedes that the claimant is disabled, or the claimant makes an informed concession that they are not disabled, the tribunal is not entitled to then examine whether or not the claimant is in fact disabled (*Bowers v William Hill Organisation Ltd* EAT 0046/09 and *London Borough of Redbridge v Baynes* EAT 0293/09).

In *EqA 2010* references to a person who has a particular protected characteristic are to be interpreted, in disability cases, as references to persons with a particular disability and references to persons who share a protected characteristic are to be interpreted as references to persons who have the same disability (*s 6(3)*).

3.12 *Present and past disabilities*

EqA 2010, s 6(2) provides that a disabled person is a person who has a disability. It is, thus, clear that *EqA 2010* protects those who have a disability at the time of any alleged discrimination, but provision is also made protecting those who have had a disability within the meaning of *EqA 2010* in the past (*s 6(4)* and *Sch 1, Part 1, para 9*).

3.13 *Definition of disability under Framework Directive 2000/78/EC*

The approach of the UK legislation, that mere sickness is not a disability, is consistent with the approach taken by the ECJ in relation to the meaning of the concept under the *Framework Directive.* In *Navas v Eurest Colectividades SA: C-13/05* [2006] ECR I-6467, [2006] IRLR 706 the ECJ considered whether a person dismissed by their employer because of sickness was protected by the disability provisions of the *Framework Directive*. The ECJ held that such a person was not protected because for the purposes of the *Framework*

Directive, the concept of disability refers to a limitation which results from physical, mental or psychological impairments, which hinders the participation of the person concerned in their professional life (which is somewhat different from *EqA 2010*, which focuses on the concept of 'normal day-to-day activities' rather than employment activities (see **3.25**)), and which is likely to last for a long time.

3.14 *The medical model*

The definition in *EqA 2010, s 6(1)* (and previously in *DDA 1995, s 1(1)*) uses what can be described as a medical model to define a disabled person as someone with a certain condition or certain limitations on their ability to carry out normal day-to-day activities. Whether a claimant meets this definition is a question of fact for a tribunal to assess (*Vicary v British Telecommunications plc* [1999] IRLR 680; *Abadeh v British Telecommunications plc* [2001] IRLR 23). In *Goodwin v Patent Office* [1999] IRLR 4 the EAT stressed that because it is a piece of social legislation, tribunals should adopt a purposive approach to the language of *DDA 1995*. This will include the definition of disability, and means that in practice tribunals should interpret the language of the legislation (now *EqA 2010*) to give effect to the stated or presumed intention of Parliament behind the legislation (for example to facilitate the full participation of disabled people in employment and routes into employment) and construe the legislation to extend, rather than restrict, protection. Following the implementation of the *Framework Directive*, tribunals are also obliged (where appropriate) to construe *EqA 2010* purposively to give effect to European law.

In *Goodwin*, the EAT also said that the language used in *DDA 1995* should be given its 'ordinary and natural meaning'. Further, in *Ekpe v Metropolitan Police Comr* [2001] IRLR 605, the EAT said that whether a claimant is disabled within the meaning of the *DDA 1995* is a threshold provision, and that it should be viewed in that light (because meeting the definition does not mean that a claimant is automatically entitled to a remedy). However, despite this holding, and despite the requirement to take a purposive approach, in practice tribunals sometimes took a very technical approach to the definition of disability under *DDA 1995*. This made *DDA 1995* more difficult for claimants to use, because unless they could prove that they were disabled within the precise terms of *DDA 1995*, the tribunal would not go on to consider the actual allegations of discrimination. Failure to establish a disability was the single most common reason for claims under the *DDA 1995* to be dismissed. The *EqA 2010* has removed one hurdle for claimants by repealing the statutory list of capacities (see **3.23**).

3.15 *The social model*

The medical nature of the definition in *DDA 1995, s 1(1)* and the problem this sometimes posed for claimants, led the DRC to recommend that the definition of disability should be changed so as to be based on what is known as a 'social model', based on the identification of disabling barriers (for example, in the workplace) and providing protection against discrimination on the grounds of 'impairment' (broadly defined), regardless of the level or type of impairment. However, this approach was not adopted in *EqA 2010* and the government rejected calls from the DRC for a fundamental overhaul of the definition of disability.

3.16 *Meaning of disability in other legislation*

The definition in *EqA 2010, s 6(1)* is specific to the Act. This means that the fact that a person may satisfy the definition of disability in another statute or that they receive, or qualify for, a disability-related benefit does not automatically lead to the conclusion that they are disabled under *EqA 2010* (unless (potentially) they were registered as disabled under *DPEA* (see below)). Equally, the fact that a person does not satisfy the definition of a disabled person under other legislation does not mean that they will not qualify for protection under *EqA 2010*. *DDA 1995, s 68* dealt with these points expressly in connection with mental impairments and the *Mental Health Act 1983*: for discussion of the interaction between the two statutory regimes see *McDougall v Richmond Adult Community College* [2007] IRLR 771. *DDA 1995, s 68* has not been expressly replicated in *EqA 2010*, however the principle remains the same.

In *Hill v Clacton Family Trust Ltd* [2005] EWCA Civ 1456, [2005] All ER (D) 170 (Oct) the Court of Appeal held that the fact that a person was awarded disability living allowance by a Social Security Appeals Tribunal (SSAT) in relation to post-traumatic stress disorder was not definitive evidence that she was disabled for the purposes of *DDA 1995*. The Court of Appeal said there was no rule or principle of law that a tribunal is bound to follow SSAT decisions, and that it is for the tribunal to make up its own mind when deciding whether a person had suffered mental impairment for the purposes of *DDA 1995* (see also *McDougall*). However, if an employer is aware that a person is considered to be disabled for other purposes (eg that they qualify for a disability benefit), that employer may be put on notice that the person could be disabled under *DDA 1995* (*Department for Work and Pensions v Hall* UKEAT/0012/05/DA). This guidance is likely to be followed in relation to *EqA 2010*.

The only circumstance where qualifying as disabled under other legislation is determinative is where a person was registered as disabled under *DPEA* at certain times. If a person's name appeared on the register of disabled persons under *DPEA* on both 12 January 1995 and 2 December 1996, they were treated as disabled under *DDA 1995* for a three-year period starting on 2 December 1996, and therefore to have had a past disability during that period (*DDA 1995, Sch 1, para 7*). Although there is no equivalent provision in *EqA 2010*, this provision was saved from being revoked by the *EqA 2010* by *Equality Act 2010 (Commencement No 4, Savings, Consequential, Transitional, Transitory and Incidental Provisions and Revocation) Order 2010, SI 2010/2317, reg 19(d))*.

3.17 *Burden of proof*

The onus has always been on claimants to prove that they meet the definition of a disabled person under *DDA 1995* (*Kapadia v Lambeth London Borough Council* [2000] IRLR 699), and to produce any necessary supporting expert evidence. This remains the case under *EqA 2010*.

When considering whether a claimant is disabled within the meaning of *DDA 1995* in *Goodwin* (see **3.14**), the EAT held that tribunals should consider the evidence by reference to the following conditions:

(a) Does the claimant have an impairment which is either mental or physical?

(b) Does the impairment have an effect on the claimant's ability to carry out normal day-to-day activities in one of the respects set out in *DDA 1995, Sch 1 para 4(1)*, and does it have an adverse effect?

(c) Is the adverse effect (upon the claimant's ability) substantial?

(d) Is the adverse effect (upon the claimant's ability) long-term?

The *Goodwin* conditions remain a useful checklist under *EqA 2010*, although there is now no need to consider whether normal day-to-day activities are affected 'in one of the respects set out in *DDA 1995, Sch 1 para 4(1)*' as this provision has not been replicated in *EqA 2010* (see **3.23**).

3.18 The meaning of impairment

Guidance

Neither *EqA 2010* nor *DDA 1995* defines the term 'impairment' or contains an exhaustive list of conditions qualifying as impairments. However, some assistance is given in the form of statutory guidance, which tribunals are obliged to take into account where relevant (*EqA*

2010, s 6(5) and *Sch 1, Part 2*; previously *DDA 1995, s 3(3)*). 'Guidance on matters to be taken into account in determining questions relating to the definition of disability' was first published after the *DDA 1995* was introduced. This was then updated with effect from 1 May 2006 ('*DDA Guidance*'), with the old guidance continuing to apply to proceedings where it is alleged that a person unlawfully discriminated contrary to *DDA 1995* before 1 May 2006. The revised *DDA Guidance* applies to all claims relating to discrimination on or after 1 May 2006 and will continue to apply until new guidance is introduced under the *EqA 2010*.

The Office for Disability Issues, at the time of writing, has produced draft Guidance on matters to be taken into account in determining questions relating to the definition of disability under the *EqA 2010* ('*EqA Guidance*') and is preparing the final version. The draft Guidance reflects the simplification of the definition of disability under *EqA 2010* by removal of the statutory list of capacities and also case law developments since the *DDA Guidance* was prepared. The current intention is that the Guidance be finalised and in force from April 2011. The *EHRC Employment Code* also provides some guidance on the meaning of disability (and gives examples of what an impairment might be) at *Appendix 1*.

As 'impairment' was used in the definition of disability under *DDA 1995*, and the government did not intend to change the meaning of 'impairment' in *EqA 2010* (see *Explanatory Notes to the EqA 2010, note 682)*, case law on 'impairment' under the old law is still likely to be relevant. In *McNicol v Balfour Beatty Rail Maintenance Ltd* [2002] EWCA Civ 1074, [2002] ICR 1498 the Court of Appeal held that the term 'impairment' bears its 'ordinary and natural meaning' and said that when considering whether a claimant has a physical or mental impairment:

> 'The essential question in each case is whether, on sensible interpretation of the relevant evidence, including the expert medical evidence and reasonable inferences which can be made from all the evidence, the applicant can be fairly be described as having a physical or mental impairment.'

In answering this question in *Paterson v Metropolitan Police Comr* [2007] IRLR 763 the EAT said that tribunals must read *DDA 1995, s 1(1)* in a way which gives effect to the ECJ decision in *Navas* (see **3.13**), that the concept of disability refers to a limitation which results from physical, mental or psychological impairments which hinders the participation of the person concerned in professional life.

The EAT has held that someone has a physical impairment if they have 'something wrong with them physically' (*College of Ripon & York St John v Hobbs* [2002] IRLR 185). This is a low threshold test which applies equally to mental impairments. This means that the focus of the impairment limb of the definition is simply on whether the claimant has a condition that has a negative impact on them either physically or mentally. The severity of the impairment is dealt with by the requirement that it must have a substantial and long-term adverse effect. As a result, in many cases there will not be a dispute about whether a claimant has an impairment, but rather on whether it has the requisite effects on their ability to carry out normal day-to-day activities.

A disability can arise from a wide range of impairments, some of which may be visible and easy to identify, and others which may not be so immediately obvious. The *EHRC Employment Code* notes that 'impairment' covers physical and mental impairments, including sensory impairments and learning disabilities (*Appendix 1*). The *DDA Guidance* and the draft *EqA Guidance* state that it may not always be possible, and nor is it necessary, to categorise an impairment as either a physical or mental impairment. The underlying cause of the impairment may be hard to establish.

The *DDA Guidance* (para A6) contained examples of some conditions which may qualify as impairments including:

(a) sensory impairments, such as those affecting sight or hearing;

(b) impairments with fluctuating or recurring effects such as rheumatoid arthritis, ME/chronic fatigue syndrome, depression and epilepsy;

(c) progressive impairments, such a motor neurone disease, forms of dementia and muscular dystrophy;

(d) organ specific impairments, including respiratory conditions such as asthma, thrombosis and heart disease;

(e) developmental impairments, such as autistic spectrum disorders and dyslexia;

(f) mental health conditions and mental illnesses, such as depression and schizophrenia;

(g) impairments produced by injury to the body or brain.

This list is repeated in the draft *EqA Guidance* and is extended to refer to fibromyalgia, stroke, dyspraxia, eating disorders, bipolar affective disorders, obsessive compulsive disorders, personality disorders, some self-harming behaviour and learning difficulties.

3.19 *Deemed disabilities*

As under the *DDA 1995*, a number of conditions are deemed to be disabilities under *EqA 2010, s 6(1)*. These are:

(a) cancer, HIV and multiple sclerosis (*Sch 1, Part 1, para* 6 replacing *DDA 1995, Sch 1, para 6A*);

(b) blindness, sight impairment or partial sightedness (where the person is certified as such by a consultant ophthalmologist) (*The Equality Act 2010 (Disability) Regulations 2010 (SI 2010/2128), reg 7* ('*Disability Regulations*'), replacing the *Disability Discrimination (Blind and Partially Sighted Persons) Regulations 1996 (SI 2003/712)*)

(c) severe disfigurements (save for those consisting of tattoos that have not been removed or body piercings used for decorative or other non-medical purposes (see **3.20**)) (*Sch 1 para 3* and *Disability Regulations, reg 5*, replacing *Disability Discrimination (Meaning of Disability) Regulations 1996 (SI 1996/1455) (the 'Meaning Regulations'*).

3.20 *Excluded conditions*

The *Disability Regulations* also exclude certain conditions from *EqA 2010* by deeming that they are not impairments, replicating provisions which were previously contained in the *Meaning Regulations.* The excluded conditions are:

(a) addiction to alcohol, nicotine or any other substance (unless as a result of administration of medically prescribed drugs or other medical treatment);

(b) a tendency to set fires;

(c) a tendency to steal;

(d) a tendency to physical or sexual abuse of other persons;

(e) exhibitionism;

(f) voyeurism; and

(g) seasonal allergic rhinitis (eg hay fever), except where it aggravates the effect of another condition.

Additionally, certain disfigurements (tattoos which have not been removed and body piercings used for decorative or other non-medical purposes, including any object attached through the piercing for the same purposes) are excluded from the definition of an impairment because they are deemed not to have a substantial adverse effect on a person's ability to carry out normal day-to-day activities (*Disability Regulations, reg 5*).

EqA 2010 is concerned with the effect of impairments rather than their cause (see **3.21**), so a claimant can have a disability even if their impairment was caused by an excluded condition (see *DDA Guidance, para A8*, replicated in the draft *EqA Guidance, para A8* and *Power v Panasonic UK Ltd* [2003] IRLR 151). This means that the fact that a claimant has an excluded condition will not prevent them from being disabled under *EqA 2010* if they have another legitimate impairment that meets the definition in the Act. For example, someone who has paranoid schizophrenia which manifests itself as a tendency to physical abuse of other persons might have a disability on the basis of their schizophrenia (*Murray v Newham Citizens Advice Bureau Ltd* [2003] IRLR 340) and someone whose depression has been caused by alcohol abuse might have a disability on the basis of their depression (*Power*).

In cases where a claimant has both a legitimate impairment and an excluded condition it may be difficult to ascertain whether any potentially unlawful discrimination was the result of the impairment or the excluded condition. In *Murray*, the EAT resolved this by finding that only 'free-standing' conditions were excluded by the *Meaning Regulations* and that the exclusion did not apply to conditions which are the consequences of a recognised disability. However, in *Edmund Nuttall Ltd v Butterfield* [2005] IRLR 751 a different division of the EAT said that it did not find this distinction helpful. In *Nuttall* the EAT said that the critical question is one of causation and, applying the same approach taken in other discrimination jurisdictions, held that the tribunal should ask itself whether the legitimate impairment was an 'effective cause' of the less favourable treatment (*O'Neill v (1) Governors of St Thomas More RCVA Upper School (2) Bedfordshire County Council* [1996] IRLR 372).

Applying *Nuttall*, if the legitimate impairment is the effective cause of the less favourable treatment then, subject to any defences available under *EqA 2010* unlawful discrimination will be made out even if the excluded condition also formed part of the employer's reason for the treatment. It is only if the effective cause for the less favourable treatment was the excluded condition that the claim would fail. In a case involving reasonable adjustments, this approach would mean that the employer would only be under an obligation to make adjustments to prevent a provision, criterion or practice or physical feature of premises or failure to provide an auxiliary aid from placing the claimant at a substantial disadvantage in so far as the disadvantage results from a legitimate impairment, rather than an excluded condition. These distinctions will often be difficult to draw, particularly where the legitimate impairment and the excluded condition are causally related.

The most recent decision on this issue is the High Court's decision in *Governing Body of X Endowed Primary School v Special Educational Needs and Disability Tribunal* [2009] EWHC 1842 (Admin), [2009] IRLR 1007 in the education context. The court considered both *Murray* and *Nuttall* and agreed with the conclusion in *Nuttall* that the excluded conditions in the *Meaning Regulations* also covered the symptoms or manifestations of an underlying impairment. The court held that a pupil suffering from Attention Deficit Hyperactivity Disorder ('ADHD') who was excluded from the school after he assaulted a teacher was not entitled to have a reasonable adjustment made in relation to his tendency to physical abuse of other persons (an excluded condition), even though that tendency stemmed from his ADHD (a legitimate impairment). However, on the facts of the case there had been a failure to make reasonable adjustments in relation to the underlying ADHD, even excluding the tendency to physical abuse.

The Draft *EqA Guidance* follows the High Court's decision, and states that '*the exclusions also apply where these tendencies arise as a consequence of, or a manifestation of, an impairment that constitutes a disability for the purposes of the Act*'. It gives an example of a young man with

ADHD which manifests itself in a number of ways including exhibitionism and states that he is not entitled to protection of *EqA 2010* in relation to any discrimination he experiences as a consequence of his exhibitionism.

The balance of authority therefore favours the approach in *Nuttall*, although there is still no binding authority on the point at Court of Appeal level.

3.21 Physical impairment: cause and effect

In some cases, it will be obvious whether a claimant has a physical impairment. However, difficulties can arise when a claimant has physical symptoms, but is unable to show that they are caused by an identifiable condition or disease. Similarly, some physical conditions may give rise to a mental impairment. In *Rugamer v Sony Music Entertainment UK Ltd; McNicol v Balfour Beatty Rail Maintenance Ltd* [2001] IRLR 644 both claimants claimed to have physical impairments, but there was no evidence that their pain had a physical cause. It was accepted that pain can have a psychological rather than a physical cause, but neither claimant had claimed to have a mental impairment. The EAT said that they were not disabled because the correct approach was to focus on the cause rather than the effect of an impairment and a mental condition which causes pain was not a physical impairment.

The EAT took a different approach on similar facts in *Hobbs* (see **3.18**). There was evidence that the claimant's mobility problems were caused by symptoms including muscle cramps and twitching, but there was no proof that these problems were caused by a physical condition. Again, the claimant had not claimed that she had a mental impairment. The EAT nevertheless held that the claimant had a physical impairment because there was no need to distinguish between the cause of an impairment on one hand and the evidence of the effects of that impairment on the other. The Court of Appeal endorsed this approach on appeal in *McNicol* and held that it is not necessary to consider how an impairment has been caused (see Court of Appeal decision in *McNicol v Balfour Beatty Rail Maintenance Ltd* [2002] IRLR 71; *Millar v IRC* [2006] IRLR 112; *DDA Guidance and* draft *EqA Guidance*, *para A8* and *EHRC Employment Code, Appendix 1*). The *DDA* and draft *EqA Guidance* also state that it is not necessary to categorise a condition as being either physical or mental and note that the underlying cause of the impairment may be hard to establish. All of these cases are good examples of the need for claimants to be clear about the nature of the impairment they are relying on (or if there is any doubt to plead that they have both a physical and a mental impairment).

3.22 Mental impairment

Historically, one of the most difficult aspects of *DDA 1995* was its application to mental impairments. Up until 5 December 2005, *DDA 1995, Sch 1, para 1(1)* provided that a mental impairment included an impairment resulting from or consisting of a mental illness only if the illness is a 'clinically well-recognised illness'.

There was no equivalent requirement that physical impairments had to be clinically well-recognised. This is why prior to 5 December 2005 it was important, in cases like *McNicol* (see **3.21**), for the courts to decide whether the claimant had a physical or mental impairment. (For an example of how this worked in practice, see *Morgan v Staffordshire University* [2002] IRLR 190.) This formulation put the focus in claims involving mental illnesses on proving that the claimant had a clinically well-recognised condition rather than simply whether they had a condition which had a negative impact on them mentally.

DDA 1995, s 18(2) removed this requirement from *DDA 1995* from 5 December 2005, and this is replicated in *EqA 2010*. This change means that rather than finding a clinically well-recognised categorisation for mental illnesses, the focus is on establishing the effect the illness is having on the claimant's ability to carry out normal day-to-day activities. The EAT in *J v DLA Piper UK LLP* (2010) UKEAT/0263/09/RN, [2010] ICR 1052, [2010] IRLR 936 confirmed that, although it remained good practice for tribunals to assess the questions of impairment and adverse effect separately, where there is a dispute about the existence of an impairment (as there may well be in cases where a mental impairment is alleged), it will make sense for the tribunal to start making findings about whether the claimant's ability to carry out normal day-to-day activities is adversely affected (on a long-term basis) and to consider the question of impairment in the light of those findings.

The removal of the 'medically-recognised' requirement meant that more employees with mental impairments were able to satisfy the definition of disability for the purposes of *DDA 1995* (and will continue to do so under *EqA 2010*). However, even prior to December 2005, *Dunham v Ashford Windows* [2005] IRLR 608 had already established that mental impairments which did not result from or consist of a mental illness could fall within the definition of a disability without the clinically well-recognised requirement needing to be addressed. *Dunham* claimed he was disabled as a result of the generalised effect his learning difficulties had on a number of skills rather than a specific effect on one skill area (as would be the case, for example, with dyslexia and reading). The EAT nevertheless agreed that he was disabled, and in doing so effectively widened the scope *DDA 1995* in relation to people with generalised learning difficulties; this is expressly addressed in *EHRC Employment Code, Appendix 1*. Note, however, that the EAT said that claimants are unlikely to establish that they have this type of mental impairment solely on the basis of difficulties at school or because they were less intelligent than average. The EAT stressed that claimants would still need to produce expert evidence as to the nature and degree of the impairment on which they were relying (see **3.37**).

A recurring difficulty for practitioners and tribunals is assessing the extent to which a claimant's low mood and anxiety can be classed as a mental impairment. In *J v DLA Piper* the EAT considered the difference between clinical depression (which, it held, was unquestionably an impairment) and a reaction to adverse circumstances (which would not be an impairment), both of which could result in the same symptoms of low mood and anxiety. The EAT recognised that the distinction could be difficult to draw in borderline cases, but held that the 'long term' effect requirement would almost always distinguish between cases of clinical depression and cases where there was 'simply a reaction to adverse circumstances'.

3.23 Ability to carry out normal day-to-day activities

Under *DDA 1995* an impairment only affected normal day-to-day activities if it affected one or more of the capacities listed in *DDA 1995, Sch 1, para 4(1)*. These were:

(a) mobility;

(b) manual dexterity;

(c) physical co-ordination;

(d) continence;

(e) ability to lift, carry or otherwise move everyday objects;

(f) speech, hearing or eyesight;

(g) memory or ability to concentrate, learn or understand; or

(h) perception of the risk of physical danger.

This list of capacities was removed under the *EqA 2010* definition, the government taking the view that it was an unnecessary barrier which served little or no purpose. The government noted in its response to the consultation on the Equality Bill that there was evidence that it could be harder for people with a mental health condition to demonstrate their impairment's effect on one of these capacities. The focus now is simply on the effect in general.

3.24 *Day-to-day activities*

EqA 2010 (like *DDA 1995*) does not define what is or is not a day-to-day activity. This is a question of fact for the tribunal to consider, using their basic common sense, rather than a matter for medical experts (*Vicary*; see **3.14**). However, the *DRC Guidance*, draft *EqA Guidance* and the *EHRC Employment Code* do provide some further assistance. The *DRC* and *draft EqA Guidance* state that state that, in general, day-to-day activities are things people do on a regular or daily basis such as shopping, reading and writing, having a conversation or using the telephone, watching television, getting washed and dressed, preparing and eating food, carrying out household tasks and taking part in social activities. The *EHRC Employment Code* refers to activities carried out on a fairly regular or frequent basis such as:

> 'walking, driving, using public transport, cooking, eating, lifting and carrying everyday objects, typing, writing (and taking exams), going to the toilet, talking, listening to conversations or music, reading, taking part in normal social interaction or forming social relationships, nourishing and caring for one's self'.

The *EHRC Employment Code* also notes that the term includes 'activities which are relevant to working life' (*Appendix 1*).

In *Paterson* (see **3.18**), the EAT had to decide whether participation in high pressure examinations was a normal day-to-day activity. That case involved an employee with dyslexia who argued that his impairment placed him at a substantial disadvantage compared to his non-dyslexic peers when undertaking examinations as part of his employer's promotion process. The EAT held that carrying out an assessment or examination is a normal day-to-day activity, as is the act of reading and comprehension. This was their conclusion under domestic law but was reinforced by the fact that domestic law had to be read consistently with ECJ case law which requires that day-to-day activities should be interpreted as encompassing activities which are relevant to participation in professional life (*Navas*; see **3.13**). Exams and professional activities are expressly dealt with in the *EHRC Employment Code* (see above). However, some elements of some jobs will clearly not amount to day-to-day activities.

3.25 *Normal*

In *Goodwin* (see **3.14**) the EAT stated that:

> 'a normal day-to-day activity is best left unspecified: easily recognised but defined with difficulty.'

The *EHRC Employment Code*, however, does provide some clarification by noting that the term refers to activities which are 'carried out by most men or most women', and does not include tasks which are only normal for a particular group of people, such as playing a musical instrument or sport to a professional standard (*Appendix 1*). The *DDA Guidance* (*para D5*) and the draft *EqA Guidance (paras D3 and D4)* stress that the term should be given its ordinary everyday meaning. It is relevant to look at how far an activity is normal for a large number of people and carried out on a daily or frequent and fairly regular basis, but this does not mean that it has to be regularly carried out by a majority of people or by both sexes. In *Ekpe* (see **3.14**), the tribunal had held that wearing rollers and putting make-up on were not normal day-to-day activities because they are carried out almost exclusively by women. The EAT disagreed, on the basis that this reasoning would exclude anything done by women but not men or vice versa as not being normal. It held that what is 'normal' is best understood as anything that is not abnormal or unusual, or particular to the claimant or a particular group of people defined by reference to some singular characteristic (apart from their gender).

The concept of a normal day-to-day activity therefore does not include highly specialised activities such as a particular hobby or any particular form of work. This is because there is no particular form of work or hobby that is normal for most people. However, whilst some jobs and pastimes might involve unusual or specialist skills, many will also still involve normal day-to-day activities such as sitting down, standing up, walking, and using everyday objects such as a keyboard. The fact that these activities are carried out during the course of a claimant's work or of a specialist pastime will not prevent their ability to do them, and the way they are performed, being relevant for the purposes of assessing whether they are disabled (*Law Hospital NHS Trust v Rush* [2001] IRLR 611, *DDA Guidance, paras D7–D9; draft EqA Guidance, paras D5–D7* and *EHRC Employment Code, Appendix 1*).

The effects of a person's working environment or of another location where a specialist activity is being carried out will also be relevant when determining the effect of an impairment. In *Cruickshank v VAW Motorcast* [2002] IRLR 24 the claimant's asthma was caused and exacerbated by exposure to fumes when he was at work. However, the tribunal decided that he was not disabled because he showed no symptoms when he was not at work. The EAT held that it was not appropriate to confine the evaluation for the purposes of *DDA 1995* to the extent to which a claimant is disabled in a normal day-to-day environment. If a claimant shows symptoms whilst they are at work which affect their ability to carry out normal day-to-day activities then those symptoms will not be discounted just because the nature of their work is specialist or unusual. In a similar vein, the EAT in *Chief Constable of Dumfries & Galloway v Adams* [2009] ICR 1034, [2009] IRLR 612 considered that working during the night could be a normal day-to-day activity. The claimant only struggled to complete activities such as walking up stairs when he worked a night shift, and did not suffer similar problems when working during the day. The EAT held that night shift working is common in the United Kingdom and the 'very ordinary physical activities' that the claimant struggled with during his night shift were normal day-to-day activities. These decisions may raise the (surprising) possibility that a person may be disabled for the purposes of some jobs but not others.

3.26 Substantial adverse effect

To meet the definition of disability under *EqA 2010*, the adverse effect must be substantial. Under *EqA 2010, s 212* 'substantial' is defined as meaning 'more than minor or trivial'. The *EHRC Employment Code, Appendix 1* (mirroring the *DDA Guidance* and draft *EqA Guidance, para B1*) states that:

> 'A substantial adverse effect is something which is more than a minor or trivial effect. The requirement that an effect must be substantial reflects the general understanding of disability as a limitation going beyond the normal differences in ability which might exist among people.'

In *Paterson* (see **3.18**), the EAT interpreted this to mean that a substantial adverse effect is one that falls outside the normal range of effects to be expected from a cross-section of the population. However, when assessing whether an impairment has a substantial adverse effect, the tribunal must not draw comparisons between the performance of the claimant and that of the population at large. The relevant comparison is between the way in which the individual carries out the activity in question and the way they would carry it out if they were not impaired. If that difference is more than the kind of difference one might expect in a cross-section of the population, then the effects are substantial.

Deemed disabilities (see **3.19**), progressive conditions (see **3.30**) and conditions with recurring effects (see **3.35**) are treated as if they have a substantial adverse effect without the need to satisfy all the requirements of *EqA 2010, s 6(1)*.

When considering whether there is a substantial adverse effect in other cases, the *EHRC Employment Code* states that account should also be taken of where a person avoids doing things because of an impairment, and notes that an impairment may not directly prevent someone from carrying out one or more normal day-to-day activities, but may still have a substantial adverse long term effect on how they carry out those activities—for example, where the employee suffers pain or fatigue when carrying out the activity (*Appendix 1*).

The *DDA Guidance* (*paras B1 to B15*) and the draft *EqA Guidance* set out a number of factors which are relevant to considering whether there is a substantial adverse effect in other cases. These are:

(a) the time taken to carry out an activity;

(b) the way in which an activity is carried out;

(c) the cumulative effects of an impairment;

(d) the effects of behaviour (including coping strategies and medical advice);

(e) the effects of the environment;

(f) the effects of medical treatment (see **3.27**).

The *DDA Guidance* also contained some examples (*paras D15–D27*) of the types of impact it might be reasonable to regard as having a substantial adverse effect. However, these examples were not to be used as a checklist (*Leonard v Southern Derbyshire Chamber of Commerce* [2001] IRLR 19), they were illustrative and non-exhaustive. The draft *EqA Guidance* has an Appendix which also contains a list of factors which would be reasonable to regard as having a substantial adverse effect on normal day-to-day activities as well as, helpfully, a list of factors which would not be reasonable to regard as having a substantial adverse effect on normal day-to-day activities.

Again, it is not for a medical expert to tell the tribunal whether an impairment has or has had a substantial adverse effect on a claimant's ability to carry out normal day-to-day activities. This is a matter on which the tribunal must decide (*Vicary* and *Abadeh*; see **3.14**). In *Goodwin* (see **3.14**), the EAT gave some important guidance on how tribunals should carry out this assessment. Mr Goodwin, a paranoid schizophrenic, was dismissed after complaints about his behaviour which included auditory hallucinations (hearing voices), and thought broadcasting (when he imagined that other people could access his thoughts). All of these problems had an adverse effect on Mr Goodwin's ability to concentrate for any sustained period. Mr Goodwin, however, was able to care for himself at home, travel to and from work and carry out his work when he was there. As a result, the tribunal decided that the effect on his ability to concentrate was not substantial. The EAT held that this was the wrong approach and said that when assessing the effect of an impairment on normal day-to-day activities tribunals should focus on the effect that it has on the things a claimant either cannot do or can only do with difficulty, rather than on the things they can do. Where there are still many things that a claimant can do (as in *Goodwin*), this avoids the tribunal concluding that the adverse effect of an impairment cannot be substantial. A similar approach was taken in *Leonard*, where the EAT stressed that it was inappropriate for a tribunal to take examples of what a claimant can do and weigh these in the balance against what they cannot do. The fact that a person can carry out certain activities does not mean their ability to do other activities has not been impaired (see also *Paterson*).

3.27 *Medical treatment*

A particular issue is whether claimants whose impairments are subject to treatment or correction can still claim protection under *EqA 2010*. *EqA 2010, Sch 1, Part 1, para 5(1)* provides that where an impairment would be likely to have a substantial adverse effect on the ability of the person concerned to carry out normal day-to-day activities, but for the fact that measures are being taken to correct it, the impairment is to be treated as having that substantial adverse effect (ie the effect it would have if no corrective measures were being taken). *Sch 1, para 5(2)* states that the term 'measures':

> 'includes, in particular medical treatment and the use of a prosthesis or other aid.'

These provisions replicate *DDA 1995, Sch 1, para 6*. Neither *EqA 2010* nor *DDA 1995* define what will constitute medical treatment, nor what is or is not a 'prosthesis or other aid', but case law suggests that these are broad categories which are not just limited to medication and medical aids. Under the *DDA 1995*, measures included surgical plates and pins (*Carden v Pickerings Europe Ltd* [2005] IRLR 720), counselling with a consultant clinical psychologist (*Kapadia v Lambeth London Borough Council*; see **3.17**) and psychotherapy (*Woodrup v Southwark London Borough Council* [2002] EWCA Civ 1716, [2003] IRLR 111 and Abadeh; see **3.14**), but did not include household objects used to mitigate the effects of a disability, such as the use of an automatic can opener where a claimant has a physical impairment which has a substantial adverse effect on their manual dexterity (*Vicary*; see **3.14**).

In *Goodwin* (see **3.14**), the EAT held that in applying *DDA 1995, Sch 1, para 6(1)*, tribunals should examine how the claimant's abilities have actually been affected at the material time (see **3.36**) whilst on medication, and then consider what effects they think the impairment would have had but for the fact that such measures are being taken: these are then the 'deduced effects'. The question is whether the actual and deduced effects of the impairment on the claimant's ability to carry out normal day-to-day activities are substantial and adverse. In practice, this means that the beneficial effects of corrective measures should be ignored when considering whether an impairment has a substantial adverse effect. For example, the question of whether a person who wears a hearing aid is disabled is to be considered by reference to what their level of hearing would be without that aid.

The approach to corrective measures and medical treatment under *DDA 1995, Sch 1, para 6(1)* (now *EqA 2010, Sch 1, Part 1, para 5(2)*) has been described as a 'peculiarly benign doctrine' (*Woodrup*) and, as a consequence, claimants who wish to rely on these provisions must have relevant expert evidence to support their claim (see **3.37**).

The provisions on deduced effects in *EqA 2010, Sch 1, para 5(1)*, do not apply to the use of spectacles or contact lenses in relation to an impairment to a person's sight (*para 5(3)(a)*). Therefore, sight impairments which are or could be corrected with glasses or contact lenses will not be taken into account in considering whether someone is disabled. Further, *para 5(1)* only applies to continuing medical treatment, ie measures that 'are being taken'. It does not apply to medical treatment that has ended.

3.28 *Coping strategies*

The *DDA Guidance* (*paras B7–B9*) recognised that there are coping strategies which can prevent or mitigate adverse effects so that they are no longer substantial. It also emphasises that where a person avoids doing things which, for example, would cause pain, fatigue or substantial social embarrassment, it would not be reasonable to conclude that a person who employed such an avoidance strategy was, as a result, not a disabled person. The draft *EqA Guidance* contains similar provisions on this point.

Under *DDA 1995* coping strategies were not treated in the same way as continuing medical treatment (*Vicary*, *Leonard* and *Commissioner of Police of the Metropolis v G S Virdi* UKEAT/0338/06). Whether a tribunal took account of coping strategies depended on the extent to which it was reasonable to expect a person to rely on such strategies. The possibility that coping strategies may cease to work in certain circumstances was also taken into account. This case law would seem equally applicable under *EqA 2010*.

3.29 *Severe disfigurements*

Under *EqA 2010, Sch 1, para 3(1)* (replacing *DDA 1995, Sch 1 para 3(1)*), a severe disfigurement will be treated as having a substantial adverse effect on a person's ability to carry out normal day-to-day activities. However, under *Disability Regulations, reg 5*, tattoos that have not been removed and body piercings for decorative or other non-medical purposes (including any object attached through the piercing for such purposes) are excluded from being so treated.

3.30 *Progressive conditions*

EqA 2010, Sch 1, Part 1, para 8(1)–(2) provides that where:

'(a) [a person] P has a progressive condition,

(b) as a result of that condition, P has an impairment which has (or had) an effect on P's ability to carry out normal day-to-day activities, but

(c) that effect is not (or was not) a substantial adverse effect.

(2) P is to be taken to have an impairment which has a substantial adverse effect if the condition is likely to result in P having such an impairment.'

This provision is similar to *DDA 1995, Sch 1, para 8(1)*, and protects those with progressive conditions which are likely to worsen progressively over time, but whose effect is not a substantial adverse effect when symptoms first appear.

In *Kirton v Tetrosyl Ltd* [2003] EWCA Civ 619, [2003] IRLR 353 the Court of Appeal considered the meaning of the requirement in *DDA 1995, para 8(1)(b)* that the impairment must arise as the result of the progressive condition. The claimant developed urinary incontinence as a result of treatment for prostate cancer (under *DDA 1995* cancer was treated as a progressive condition, and was not a deemed disability until 2005). However, his claim that his urinary incontinence was a disability failed because the tribunal and the EAT held that *para 8(1)(b)* did not apply. The EAT held that for *para 8(1)* to apply, the effect on normal day-to-day activities had to result from the claimant's cancer and not the surgery. The Court of Appeal overruled this decision and held that an impairment will result from a progressive condition if it follows from the condition in the ordinary course of events, even if it is not directly caused by the condition. The claimant's surgery was a standard response to prostate cancer, and so his urinary incontinence was a disability by virtue of *para 8(1)*. (Note that cancer is a deemed disability in its own right under *EqA 2010, Sch 1, Part 1, para 6.*)

3.31 *Asymptomatic progressive conditions*

To rely on *EqA 2010, Sch 1, Part 1, para 8* (and formerly *DDA 1995, Sch 1, para 8(1)*), claimants have to show not only that they have a progressive condition, and that it has, or has had, an effect on their ability to carry out normal day-to-day activities; they must also show that it is likely that, at some stage in the future, the condition will have a substantial adverse effect on their ability to carry out normal day-to-day activities.

This can be done by reference to medical evidence of the likely prognosis and/or statistical evidence (*Mowat-Brown v University of Surrey* [2002] IRLR 235). In *Mowat-Brown* the claimant had multiple sclerosis, but the medical evidence was that some years after first being diagnosed he had very few symptoms and that there were: 'grounds for optimism about his future'. In the light of this evidence the EAT held that it was not possible to conclude that the requirements of *DDA 1995, Sch 1, para 8(1)* had been satisfied. It is important to note, however, that this decision predates the House of Lords decision in *Boyle v SCA Packaging Ltd (Equality and Human Rights Commission intervening)* [2009] UKHL 37, [2009] 4 All ER 1181, which held that 'likely' in the context of the *DDA 1995* did not mean 'more likely than not', but rather whether or not something might well happen. If *Mowat-Brown* were to be decided under the *EqA 2010*, then the application of a lower threshold of 'likely' may well have given a different result.

3.32 *Deemed disabilty*

Cases like *Mowat-Brown* led to calls for *DDA 1995* to be amended to provide more protection for those with asymptomatic progressive conditions such as multiple sclerosis. *DDA 2005* inserted *Sch 1, para 6A(1)* into *DDA 1995*, which provided that a person who has cancer, HIV infection or multiple sclerosis is deemed to be disabled from the point of diagnosis. This is replicated in *EqA 2010, Sch 1, Part 1, para 6*, but it does not apply to all progressive conditions. For example, someone with motor neurone disease or muscular dystrophy would still have to satisfy the requirements of *para 8* if at the material time their condition did not have a substantial adverse effect on their ability to carry out normal day-to-day activities. This approach was taken because other progressive conditions which are not covered by *EqA 2010, Sch 1, Part 1, para 6* (formerly *DDA 1995, Sch 1, para 6A(1)*) are identified when the symptoms show, so it was felt that it was not necessary to include them in a list of asymptomatic conditions.

EqA 2010, Sch 1, Part 1, para 8(3) provides that regulations can be made to provide that particular conditions are, or are not, progressive.

DDA 1995, Sch 1, para 6A(2) contained a power for new regulations to be introduced to exclude certain types of cancer from being covered by *Sch 1, para 6A(1)*. It had been intended that this power would be used to exclude people with what were considered to be 'minor', easily treatable forms of cancer (such as some skin cancers) from the deemed disability provisions. However, there was considerable criticism of this approach and this power has not been carried over into *EqA 2010*.

3.33 Long term

Under *EqA 2010, Sch 1, Part 1, para 2(1)* (as under *DDA 1995, Sch 1, para 2(1)*) an impairment will have a long-term effect only if:

(a) it has lasted at least 12 months;

(b) it is likely to last for at least 12 months;

(c) it is likely to last for the rest of the life of the person affected.

This mirrors the position under the *DDA 1995*. In *Patel v (1) Oldham MBC (2) Rushcroft School* EAT/0225/09 the EAT considered whether or not tribunals could have regard to the effect of linked conditions when looking at whether or not an impairment was long term. It held that in looking at whether or not the adverse effect was 'long term', the effect of an illness or condition likely to develop, or which has developed from another illness or condition, forms part of the assessment of whether the effect of the original impairment is likely to last or has lasted at least 12 months.

3.34 *Past disabilities*

In relation to past disabilities, *EqA 2010 Sch 1, para 9* provides that a question of whether a person had a disability at a particular time is to be determined as if the provisions of (or made under) *EqA* 2010 were in force both when the act complained of was done and at the time when it is claimed that the person had the disability. This is the case even if a claimant is relying on having had a past disability before *EqA 2010* came into force.

Under *DDA 1995, Sch 2, para 5* the normal definition of 'long term' was amended in relation to past disabilities by providing that a past substantial adverse effect will have been long-term if it either:

(a) lasted for at least 12 months; or

(b) occurred and recurred over a period covering at least 12 months.

The effect of this was that in determining whether someone had had a past disability where the adverse effect did not last for a continuous 12-month period, the question was not whether the effect had been likely to recur, but whether it had in fact recurred. There appears to be no equivalent provision to this in *EqA 2010*. However, the draft *EqA Guidance* suggests that the position under *EqA 2010* is the same (see *section C5*) and it is clear from the *Explanatory Notes to the EqA 2010* on s 6 and Sch 1 that the government was not seeking to make a change to the law in this respect.

3.35 *Recurring effects*

EqA 2010 also makes specific provision for impairments with recurring or fluctuating effects. *EqA 2010, Sch 1, Part 1, para 2(2)* provides that:

> 'If an impairment ceases to have a substantial effect on a person's ability to carry out normal day-to-day activities, it is to be treated as continuing to have that effect if that effect is likely to recur.'

This replaced similar provisions in *DDA 1995, Sch 1, para 2(2)*. The effect of the provision is that the substantial adverse effect does not have to be continuous throughout the relevant period. Even if the impairment has ceased to have a substantial adverse effect it will be treated as continuing for as long as its substantial adverse effect is likely to recur. This means that conditions with effects that can recur or where effects can be sporadic, such as rheumatoid arthritis and epilepsy, as well as mental health conditions such as schizophrenia, bipolar effective disorder and certain types of depression can still be 'long-term' for the purposes of the *EqA 2010* if they are likely to recur. In this context, something is 'likely' if it 'might well' recur (*EHRC Employment Code, Appendix 1*) or 'could well happen' (draft *EqA Guidance*). This is a departure from the *DDA Guidance*, which used the phrase 'more probable than not' (*DDA Guidance, para C2*), and reflects the new position taken by the House of Lords in *Boyle v SCA Packaging Ltd (Equality and Human Rights Commission intervening)* [2009] UKHL 37, [2009] 4 All ER 1181. In *Swift v Chief Constable of Wiltshire Constabulary* [2004] IRLR 540, the EAT said that when considering *DDA 1995, Sch 1, para 2(2)* the tribunal should ask itself the following questions:

(a) Was there at some stage an impairment which had a substantial adverse effect on the claimant's ability to carry out normal day-to-day activities?

(b) Did the impairment cease to have a substantial adverse effect on the claimant's ability to carry out normal day-to-day activities, and if so when?

(c) What was the substantial adverse effect?

(d) Is that substantial adverse effect likely to recur?

The question for the tribunal is whether the substantial adverse effect is likely to recur, not whether the impairment is likely to recur. Unlike progressive conditions, the likely future effect must be the same as the earlier effect. However, there is no time limit on the recurrence. As long as a substantial adverse effect is likely to recur once in a person's lifetime, it will be treated as ongoing. This approach is likely to be used under *EqA 2010*.

Under the *DDA 1995*, where a past disability had ceased to have a substantial adverse effect on a person's ability to carry out normal day-to-day activities, it was treated as continuing to have that substantial adverse effect if the effect had in fact recurred. However, there does not appear to be an equivalent provision under the *EqA 2010* (see **3.34**).

3.36 *The material time*

There had been some divergence at EAT level about the point in time at which the existence of a disability, including whether an effect is long-term or likely to recur, must be assessed. In *Greenwood v British Airways plc* [1999] IRLR 600 the EAT held that this assessment should take place based on what is known at the time of the hearing, not at the time of the alleged discriminatory act. In contrast, in *Latchman v Reed Business Information Ltd* [2002] ICR 1453 a different division of the EAT expressly disapproved this aspect of *Greenwood* and held that this assessment should take place based on what is known at the date of the alleged discrimination. The EAT reached the same conclusion in *Cruickshank*. In *McDougall v Richmond Adult Community College* [2007] IRLR 771 the EAT declined to follow *Latchman* and expressly approved the decision in *Greenwood*, holding that whether an impairment had a long-term adverse effect should be determined on the basis of the facts known at the time of the hearing.

However, the Court of Appeal clarified the position in its judgment in *McDougall* on the material time for assessing whether an effect is long-term or likely to recur, and has reversed the EAT's decision (*Richmond Adult Community College v McDougall* [2008] EWCA Civ 4). The Court of Appeal found that a tribunal should decide whether a disability is long-term or likely to recur on the basis of the facts at the time of the discriminatory act, not on the basis of the facts known at the hearing. Pill LJ stated (at para 24):

> 'The central purpose of the [*DDA 1995*] is to prevent discriminatory decisions and to provide sanctions if such decisions are made. Whether an employer has committed such a wrong must, in my judgment, be judged on the basis of the evidence available at the time of the decision complained of.'

In deciding this, the Court of Appeal followed Elias J's interpretation of the guidance in *Spence*. In *Croal v Network Rail Infrastructure Ltd* UKEAT/0506/07 the EAT, in the light of the Court of Appeal's decision, confirmed that when considering whether or not the long-term effect of the relevant impairment was likely to last for at least 12 months, the tribunal should not look at whether or not the impairment did in fact last for at least 12 months (with the benefit of hindsight), but rather the assessment should be made at the date of the discriminatory act alleged.

3.37 PRACTICAL ISSUES RELATING TO THE DEFINITION OF DISABILITY

Obtaining expert evidence in cases where disability is in dispute

Medical evidence

The medical nature of the definition of disability means that in cases where disability is in dispute, the evidence of a medical expert will be crucial for both sides. Tribunals are often presented with conflicting medical evidence. It is therefore important that tribunals attach the correct weight to that evidence and are clear about their role and that of the medical expert. It is particularly important that tribunals consider the evidence and know what evidence they can accept and what evidence they can reject. Guidance from pre-*EqA 2010* cases will be helpful in this regard.

Tribunals have to consider all of the medical evidence presented to them and unless they have a good reason for doing so, they should not disregard uncontested medical evidence (*Kapadia*; see **3.17**). It is appropriate for medical reports to deal with the diagnosis of the impairment, any observations of the claimant carrying out day-to-day activities and the ease with which a claimant is able to perform those functions, together with any relevant opinion as to prognosis and the effect of medication. However, although many practitioners will offer an opinion on whether a claimant has a disability within the meaning of *EqA 2010*, this a legal question for the tribunal, and one which cannot be delegated to the medical experts (*Vicary* and *Abadeh*; see **3.14**). In limited circumstances it may also be permissible for a tribunal to disagree with medical evidence. An example of this was *McKechnie Plastics Components v Grant* UKEAT 0284/08, where the EAT found that the tribunal was entitled to reject the findings of the joint medical expert instructed in the case and to conclude instead that, on the basis of the factual evidence before the tribunal, the claimant was in fact disabled within the meaning of *DDA 1995*.

Finally, it is worth noting that medical evidence does not necessarily need to be given by a specialist practitioner. In *J v DLA Piper UK LLP* (2010) UKEAT/0263/09/RN, [2010] ICR 1052, [2010] IRLR 936 the EAT criticised the employment tribunal for disregarding a GP's opinion on the claimant's medical condition. The EAT acknowledged that the evidence of a general practitioner would, all other things being equal, have less weight than that of a specialist, but stated it should still be taken into account when the evidence of a specialist is not available or is inconclusive.

3.38 *Evidence from other experts*

Expert evidence need not always be obtained from a medical practitioner. In *Dunham* (see **3.22**), the EAT held that the evidence adduced to establish the nature of the claimant's learning difficulties could be provided by a suitably qualified psychologist, and need not come from a qualified medical practitioner. The EAT said that what was important was that there should be evidence from a suitably qualified expert who could speak, on the basis of his experience and expertise, as to the relevant condition. However, this decision contrasts sharply with *Hill* (see **3.16**), where the Court of Appeal placed much greater weight on the evidence of the medically qualified experts than the evidence of a psychotherapist.

3.39 *Instructing experts to obtain medical advice*

In *De Keyser Ltd v Wilson* [2001] IRLR 324, the EAT gave some guidance on how expert evidence should be collected in tribunal cases. The guidelines provide the following advice to parties considering obtaining medical evidence:

(a) not to assume that the tribunal will be willing to hear expert evidence. The opportunity should be taken to explore with the tribunal chairman (now employment judge), either at a case management discussion or in correspondence, whether expert evidence is likely to be admitted at the main hearing;

(b) both parties should jointly instruct the same expert unless there are special circumstances in which one party is already committed to using its own expert;

(c) the parties need to agree responsibility for payment of a jointly instructed expert's fees and disbursements;

(d) even if a joint expert is not appointed, an expert report will carry more evidential weight if the contents of the letter of instruction to the expert have been commented on and, preferably, agreed by the other side;

(e) a letter of instruction should:

  (i) contain the questions which the expert has to advise on;

  (ii) state what facts are agreed by the parties and what facts are in dispute;

  (iii) emphasise that the expert's overriding duty is to the tribunal rather than to any party;

  (iv) state what aspects of the case the expert is required to advise on; and

  (v) not be partisan,

(f) to speed matters up, the tribunal can give directions where a joint expert is to be instructed; these might include the date by which the identity of the expert and letter of instruction must be agreed, and a date for production of the expert's report;

(g) where separate experts are instructed, a timetable should be agreed between the parties or fixed by the tribunal. The timetable should include a date for exchange of experts' reports and a date for a without prejudice meeting of the experts with a view to them producing a schedule of agreed issues and points of dispute between the experts.

3.40 MEANING OF DISABILITY DISCRIMINATION IN THE EMPLOYMENT FIELD

Despite the differences between the types of discrimination prohibited by the *DDA 1995* and those prohibited by the *EqA 2010* there is also considerable overlap between the two statutes. The *DDA 1995* does not apply to acts occurring or continuing after 1 October 2010, but the substantive provisions of both Acts are considered below and where possible they are considered together below.

Disability discrimination

Pursuant to the *2003 Regulations*, amendments were made to *DDA 1995* to ensure that it complied with the *Framework Directive.* Those amendments took effect on 1 October 2004. References in this Chapter to *DDA 1995* are to the amended provisions in force after that date. In summary, from 1 October 2004, *DDA 1995* prohibited three types of discrimination (other than victimisation and harassment), namely:

(a) direct discrimination: that is, less favourable treatment amounting to direct discrimination falling within *DDA 1995, s 3A(5)*. Such discrimination could not be justified (*DDA 1995, s 3A(4)*);

(b) disability-related discrimination: that is, less favourable treatment amounting to disability discrimination falling within *DDA 1995, s 3A(1)*. Such discrimination *could* be justified (*DDA 1995, s 3A(1)(b), (3)*) but only if it did not also amount to direct discrimination within *DDA 1995, s 3A(5)*. It should be noted that the term 'disability-related discrimination' is *not* used in the *DDA 1995* itself; it is merely a convenient shorthand for less favourable treatment not amounting to direct discrimination;

(c) failure to make reasonable adjustments.

As is set out further below, the House of Lords' decision in *Malcolm* significantly narrowed the reach of disability-related discrimination. The *EqA 2010* therefore effectively abolished the concept. Since October 2010, *EqA 2010* prohibited four types of discrimination (other than victimisation and harassment), namely:

(a) direct discrimination within *EqA 2010, s 13*. Such discrimination cannot be justified;

(b) discrimination arising from disability within *EqA 2010, s 15*. Such discrimination can be justified if it is a proportionate means of achieving a legitimate aim;

(c) indirect discrimination within *EqA 2010, s 19*. Such discrimination can be justified if it is a proportionate means of achieving a legitimate aim;

(d) failure to make reasonable adjustments within *EqA 2010, s 20*.

Given the overlap between some of the *DDA 1995* concepts and *EqA 2010* concepts, it is sensible to consider the two statutes in tandem where possible. This Chapter therefore addresses the various types of disability discrimination in the following order:

(a) direct discrimination (relevant to both *DDA 1995* and *EqA 2010*);

(b) disability-related discrimination (relevant only to *DDA 1995*);

(c) discrimination arising from disability (relevant only to *EqA 2010*);

(d) indirect discrimination (relevant only to *EqA 2010*);

(e) failure to make reasonable adjustments (relevant to both *DDA 1995* and *EqA 2010*).

3.41 Direct discrimination under DDA 1995 and EqA 2010

Under the *DDA 1995*, direct discrimination was defined as occurring where 'on the ground of the disabled person's disability [an employer] treats the disabled person less favourably than he treats or would treat a person not having that particular disability whose relevant circumstances including his abilities are the same as, or not materially different from, those of the disabled person' (*DDA 1995, s 3A(5)*).

Under the *EqA 2010*, direct discrimination occurs where, 'because of' a disability, an employer treats a person less favourably than he treats or would treat others (*EqA 2010, s 13*). As under the *DDA 1995*, when comparing cases for the purposes of *EqA 2010, s 13*, there must be no material difference between the circumstances relating to each case, including a person's abilities (*EqA 2010, s 23*) (see **3.47** below).

For a general discussion of the meaning of direct discrimination under *EqA 2010*, see **1.46**. It has also been suggested that the term 'because of' in the *EqA 2010* may be a synonym for 'on grounds of' in *DDA 1995*, such that the two concepts are very similar.

3.42 *No justification for direct discrimination*

There is, in general, no possibility of justification for direct discrimination (but see exceptions in relation to occupational requirements (*EqA 2010, Sch 9, para (1)*), complying with statutory provisions (*s 191*) and safeguarding national security (*s 192*). See **3.124–3.127** and **1.145**, **1.113** and **1.111**.

3.43 *No prohibition of discrimination against non-disabled persons*

It is not unlawful to discriminate by treating disabled persons more favourably than non-disabled persons (see *DDA 1995, s 3A(5)* and *EqA 2010, s 13(3)*). It is, thus, entirely lawful for an employer to advertise for, or to recruit or promote, a disabled employee (or an employee having a particular disability) in preference to a non-disabled employee. (Note that while *DDA 1995* and *EqA 2010 permit* more favourable treatment of disabled employees, they do not *require* such treatment, save in the particular case of the duty to make reasonable adjustments.)

3.44 *Less favourable treatment and the reason for the treatment*

For a discussion of what constitutes less favourable treatment, and how to identify the reason for the treatment, see **1.47** and **1.49**ff.

3.45 *Discrimination by association or perception*

The new definition of direct discrimination at *EqA 2010, s 13(1)* prohibits associative discrimination (that is, direct discrimination against B because of B's association with a disabled person) and also perceptive discrimination (that is, direct discrimination against B because of a perception that B is disabled). It is also likely to prohibit discrimination against B because B is associated with a person who is perceived to have a disability (or, similarly, because of a perception that B is associated with a disabled person).

DDA 1995 did not, on its face, prohibit associative discrimination, but it had to be read in such a way as to prohibit associative discrimination following the EAT decision in *EBR Attridge LLP v Coleman (No 2)* UKEAT/0071/09. The EAT has suggested that *DDA 1995* did not need to be read in such a way as to cover perceptive discrimination: *Aitken v Commissioner of Police of the Metropolis* UKEAT/0226/09. See also *J v DLA Piper UK LLP* (2010) UKEAT/0263/09/RN, [2010] ICR 1052, [2010] IRLR 936.

These issues are discussed in more detail at **1.53**.

3.46 *Direct discrimination and stereotypical assumptions*

It follows from the definition of direct discrimination (under both the *DDA 1995* and the *EqA 2010*) that if less favourable treatment occurs because of the employer's generalised or stereotypical assumptions about the disability or its effects, that is likely to be direct discrimination (see *EHRC Employment Code*, *section 3.15*). This is because an employer would not normally make such assumptions about a non-disabled person, but would instead consider his individual abilities.

The *DRC Code* gave the example of a blind woman who is not shortlisted for a job involving computers because the employer wrongly assumes that blind people cannot use them, without making any attempt to consider the individual circumstances and abilities of the applicant. The employer has treated the blind applicant less favourably than others by not shortlisting her; and that treatment is 'on the ground of' her disability because it would not have been assumed that a non-disabled person was unable to use a computer (*DRC Code of Practice*, box after *section 4.8*). This was apparently also the result in *Tudor v Spen* ET/2404211/05, where the claimant was dismissed from her job as an animal nursing assistant after she had a stroke and became blind. Her employer assumed, without seeking any advice, that there was no point in continuing to employ the claimant after her stroke. This was a case properly categorised as direct disability discrimination because the employer had made assumptions, on the ground of the claimant's disability, about her ability to do the job, and such assumptions would not have been made about a non-disabled person. See also *Aylott v Stockton-on-Tees Borough Council* [2010] EWCA Civ 910, [2010] IRLR 994.

That this is the correct approach is underlined by, for example, *SDA 1975* case law holding that the making of generalised assumptions about women may amount to direct sex discrimination. See, for example, *Horsey v Dyfed County Council* [1982] IRLR 395, [1982] ICR 775, EAT, where the assumption by an employer that a wife would follow her husband to his place of work (rather than the husband moving to the wife's place of work) amounted to direct sex discrimination. The EAT stated that the employer 'must look at the particular circumstances of that case and not [act] on the basis of any general assumption'. See **8.39**. It follows that some pre-October 2004 cases such as *Surrey Police v Marshall* [2002] IRLR 843, EAT would or might be differently decided under the new direct discrimination provisions. In *Marshall*, the employer, in refusing the applicant employment as a fingerprints recognition officer in the police force, had acted on the basis of medical opinion about bipolar affective disorder *in general* rather than on a risk assessment or expert opinion based on the applicant's own particular circumstances. Such a decision might well now amount to direct disability discrimination (and, as such, incapable of justification).

The fact that a stereotypical assumption contains an element of truth, or that it was at some time in the past true, does not alter this. See **1.56**.

3.47 *Identification of comparator*

In determining whether direct discrimination has occurred, it will often be crucial to identify the correct comparator. In most cases of direct disability discrimination, the comparator will be a person who does not have the particular disability in question. However, caution is required and the task is not always straightforward, especially in cases of associative or perceptive discrimination. These issues are discussed at **1.63–1.71**.

A particular issue arises in disability discrimination cases which does not arise in the context of other discrimination strands. That is, the comparator must be a person who does not have the claimant's particular disability. But it must also be a person whose circumstances, *including his abilities*, are the same as, or not materially different from, those of the disabled person (see *DDA 1995, s 3A(5)* and *EqA 2010, s 23*). The difficulties arise when one of the claimant's relevant abilities is compromised because of his disability. To take an extreme example: should a blind person who is denied a job as a bus driver because he cannot see be compared to: (a) a sighted person; (b) a person with a visual impairment falling short of a disability but which nevertheless renders him unable to do the job; or (c) another blind person?

The law on this topic remains unclear:

(a) The 'blind bus driver' example is addressed in the *DRC Code* at *section 4.20*. It is said that the suitable comparison would be a person with a visual impairment falling short of the applicant's disability, but which nevertheless falls below the minimum level which is necessary to do the job safely.

(b) Similarly, the *EHRC Employment Code*, in the box after *section 3.30*, gives an example of a disabled man with arthritis who can type at 30 words per minute and who applies for an administrative job which includes typing, but is rejected on the grounds that his typing is too slow. It states that the correct comparator in a claim for direct discrimination would be a person without arthritis who has the same typing speed with the same accuracy rate. This also suggests that the comparator should have the same abilities to do the job as the disabled person, even if those abilities are themselves compromised by the disability. Indeed the Code expressly states that the comparator is someone who has the same abilities or skills as the disabled person 'regardless of whether those abilities or skills arise from the disability itself'.

(c) The same approach was taken in *High Quality Lifestyles v Watts*, in which the claimant was dismissed from his employment as a support worker for people with learning difficulties on the basis that he was HIV positive and that there was a risk of transmission of his condition to service users (who might scratch or bite him, drawing blood). The EAT held that the correct comparator was an employee who had an attribute (other than being HIV positive) carrying 'the same risk of causing to others illness or injury of the same gravity, here serious and possibly fatal'. The case was remitted to the employment tribunal to consider whether such a comparator would have been dismissed. (Note, however, that the outcome of the case may have been affected by the claimant's concession that the appropriate comparator was a person at risk of transmitting a life-threatening disease: judgment, para 38.) This also suggests that the comparator should have the same abilities to do the job as the disabled person, even if those abilities are themselves compromised by the disability.

(d) On the other hand, in the tribunal case of *Tudor v Spen* ET/2404211/05, where the claimant was dismissed from her job as an animal nursing assistant after she had a stroke and became blind, the relevant comparator was said to be someone who was off work for a period with a broken leg, but not someone who had lost their sight.

(e) In *Aylott v Stockton-on-Tees Borough Council* [2010] EWCA Civ 910, [2010] IRLR 994 the Court of Appeal held that, in a direct discrimination claim under the *DDA 1995*, the circumstances of the hypothetical comparator should not include the claimant's particular behavioural and performance difficulties, since those stemmed from his disability (see judgment para 47). This appears to mean that the disabled person should be compared to a hypothetical comparator with the same abilities as the disabled person, except for those abilities which are affected by the disabled person's disability.

The approach suggested in the codes, and in *High Quality Lifestyles v Watts*, has been criticised by some practitioners on the basis that it is artificial to compare a disabled person to someone who, whilst not having their particular disability, nevertheless suffers from the same impairments insofar as those impairments affect the disabled person's ability to do the job. But the alternative approach, of excluding from the comparison all of the disabled person's abilities where they are caused by his disability, is also unsatisfactory: it would mean, for example, that refusing to employ a blind person as a bus driver would be direct discrimination and incapable of justification. This area of the law therefore remains uncertain.

3.48 *Direct discrimination and knowledge of disability*

The House of Lords in *Malcolm* held that there could not be an unlawful act of discrimination under the *DDA 1995* unless the employer had actual or constructive knowledge of the disability. However, it has long been thought that there may also be direct discrimination where the act in question is obviously liable to be discriminatory, and it is arguable that *Malcolm* endorses that view (see eg para 162). To take an example given in the *DRC Code* (box after *section 4.11*), suppose that an employer were to advertise an internal promotion stating that people with a history of mental illness need not apply; and that a disabled employee otherwise eligible for the promotion had a history of schizophrenia of which the employer was unaware. The employee would, notwithstanding the employer's lack of knowledge, have a good claim for direct disability discrimination in relation to the loss of promotion opportunities: the appropriate comparator would be an employee with comparable abilities but not having a history of mental illness, and such an employee would not have been automatically excluded from eligibility.

The *EHRC Employment Code* states at *section 3.11* that the words 'because of' in the *EqA 2010* have the same meaning as the words 'on grounds of' in the *DDA 1995*. The degree of knowledge which is required for direct discrimination under *EqA 2010* is therefore likely to be the same as that under *DDA 1995*.

3.49 *Direct discrimination and reasonable adjustments*

One issue which was addressed in the *DRC Code*, but which is not considered in the *EHRC Employment Code*, is the impact of any reasonable adjustments which were, or ought to have been, made in relation to a disabled person who complains of less favourable treatment. The *DRC Code* says, at *section 4.22*, that the position under the *DDA 1995* was as follows:

(a) in considering a direct discrimination claim, the disabled person and his abilities must be considered *as they in fact were* at the time of the alleged act of discrimination;

(b) if there were particular reasonable adjustments which an employer was required to make, but in fact failed to make, in considering a direct discrimination claim, the disabled person's abilities are nevertheless to be considered as they in fact were and not as they might have been had adjustments been made. An example was given of a disabled person who applies for a typing job, but is not allowed to use her own adapted keyboard (even though the employer ought reasonably to have allowed this). She carries out a typing test at a speed of 30 words per minute (wpm). The proper comparator was said to be a non-disabled candidate with a speed of 30 wpm;

(c) in contrast, if an employer did in fact make adjustments enhancing the disabled person's performance, the disabled person is to be considered on the basis of those enhancements and not as he would or might have been without the benefit of the adjustments. For example, if a disabled person applies for a job and is allowed to use her adapted keyboard, and therefore completes a typing test with a speed of 50 wpm, the proper comparator is said to be a non-disabled candidate with a speed of 50 wpm.

The job applicant in example (b) above would obviously have a claim for failure to make reasonable adjustments. She may also have claims for discrimination arising from disability and indirect discrimination. But on the analysis proposed by the *DRC Code*, her claim for direct discrimination would only succeed if she could show that a comparator applicant with a typing speed of 30 wpm would have been treated more favourably. In contrast, the applicant in example (c) above would have a good claim for direct discrimination if she could show that a comparator applicant with a typing speed of 50 wpm would have been treated more favourably.

In light of the decision in *Aylott v Stockton-on-Tees Borough Council* (discussed at **3.47**), the law in this area is currently unclear and it may be arguable that the applicant's typing speed should not be attributed to the comparator in any event.

3.50 *Direct discrimination required by legislation*

Problems may arise where disability discrimination is considered to be required by legislation. The issue would arise where legislation other than *DDA 1995* or *EqA 2010* (for example, legislation prohibiting insulin-dependent diabetics from piloting ships) was considered to require less favourable treatment of disabled persons on the ground of their disability (often on the basis of a 'blanket ban'). Careful thought will be required in such cases:

(a) it will first be necessary to be clear that the legislation in question does in fact *require* the less favourable treatment in question (rather than, say, merely permitting such treatment). *DDA 1995, s 59(1)* and *EqA 2010, ss 191 and 192* are (even as a matter of domestic law) likely to be narrowly construed: see eg *Hampson v Department of Education and Science* [1990] ICR 511, HL (which deals with the equivalent provisions of *RRA 1976*); and see **1.113**. It is important not to assume that the legislation requires a particular result without a careful check. For a practical example (albeit pre-dating the coming into force of the *2003 Regulations*) see *Lane Group plc v Farmiloe* UKEAT/0352/03/DA, which concerned the application of health and safety legislation on the use of personal protective equipment, in particular protective shoes, to a disabled employee with psoriasis;

(b) it will be necessary to consider whether any reasonable adjustments could be made to avoid the impact of the conflicting legislation (see eg Lane Group v Farmiloe, above, at 41), failing which, the employer will at least be liable for failure to make reasonable adjustments;

(c) in the case where the employer is an 'emanation of the state' for EU law purposes, it will (further) be necessary to consider whether the legislation relied upon complies with the requirement of *Article 2(5)* of the *Framework Directive*, which requires such measures to be 'necessary in a democratic society'—a proportionality test—pursuant to a number of aims, including health (which would include health and safety). If the legislation does not fulfil the test in *Article 2(5)*, the employee may be able to rely upon directly effective *Framework Directive* rights to disapply the necessary legislation. In the light of the decision of the ECJ in *Seda Kucukdevici v Swedex GmbH & Co KG: C-555/07* [2010] All ER (EC) 867 employees of purely private sector employers may also be able to disapply the necessary legislation on the basis that the Framework Directive gives expression to a general principle of EU law.

3.51 *Combined discrimination*

EqA 2010 also contains a new provision enabling an employee to bring a discrimination claim on two (but no more than two) combined protected grounds, although the provision was not implemented on 1 October 2010 and will certainly not be implemented before April 2011. (See COMMON CONCEPTS **(1)**.)

3.52 Disability-related discrimination under DDA 1995

'Disability-related discrimination' is the expression used to denote discrimination which fell within *DDA 1995, s 3A(1)*. As set out above, the *EqA 2010* effectively abolished the concept. This section considers the law as it was prior to *EqA 2010* coming into effect on 1 October 2010. This will be relevant to any claims which are continuing under the *DDA 1995* and also explains the context in which the Labour Government decided to abolish disability-related discrimination and introduce indirect discrimination and discrimination arising from disability. However, as is explained below, there are differences between disability-related discrimination and discrimination arising from disability, and case law on the meaning of disability-related discrimination cannot be directly applied when considering discrimination under *EqA 2010*.

Disability-related discrimination occurred where (paraphrasing *DDA 1995, s 3A(1)*):

(a) for a reason which relates to the disabled person's disability, a person treats the disabled person less favourably than he treats or would treat others to whom that reason does not apply; and

(b) he cannot show that the treatment in question is justified (as to which, see *DDA 1995, s 3A(3), (4)*).

Disability discrimination

Until the decision of the House of Lords in *Malcolm*, it was widely thought that there were important distinctions between direct discrimination, discussed above, and disability-related discrimination. *Malcolm*, however, drastically reduced the scope of disability-related discrimination, making it virtually indistinguishable from direct discrimination.

Disability-related discrimination is a concept which existed only under the *DDA 1995*: it should not be pleaded or relied on for any case falling under the *EqA 2010*.

3.53 *The Malcolm* decision

Malcolm was a decision in a housing context, but the relevant statutory provisions were essentially identical to the employment provisions of the *DDA 1995*, and the *Malcolm* decision therefore also applies to employment proceedings: eg *Aylott v Stockton-on-Tees Borough Council*.

Mr Malcolm was a tenant in local authority accommodation who suffered from schizophrenia. He sublet the premises in breach of the tenancy agreement, which led to the Council taking steps to evict him. Mr Malcolm's case was that his schizophrenia had played a part in his decision to sublet his flat, and that the Council was therefore treating him less favourably for a reason which relates to his disability.

The Court of Appeal applied the law in a way which was consistent with the earlier authorities. First, it held that the 'reason' for the Council's conduct was the fact that Mr Malcolm had sublet his flat. Second, that reason was 'a reason which relates to [Mr Malcolm's] disability'. Third (although this was discussed only briefly in the Court of Appeal), when deciding whether the Council had treated Mr Malcolm less favourably than it 'treats or would treat others to whom that reason does not or would not apply' it would be necessary to compare the treatment of Mr Malcolm to the treatment of a person who had not sublet his flat. Applying that approach, it was clear that the Council would not have evicted a person who had not sublet his flat, and it would therefore follow that the Council had discriminated against Mr Malcolm (in the housing context, the scope for justifying disability-related discrimination was more limited than in the employment context and so a justification defence was not available to the Council on the facts of the case).

The House of Lords overturned the Court of Appeal decision, holding that:

(a) the 'reason' for the Council's conduct was the fact that Mr Malcolm had sublet his flat. However, that reason did not 'relate to' Mr Malcolm's disability;

(b) alternatively, the proper comparison for the purposes of deciding whether there was less favourable treatment was with tenants without a mental disability who sublet a flat;

(c) in order for there to be disability-related discrimination, the alleged discriminator must have knowledge, or imputed knowledge, of the disability.

Each of these is addressed in more detail below.

3.54 *What is a disability-related reason?*

The first step is to identify 'the reason'. If there is more than one reason, or if there is a dispute between the parties over the reason, 'the task of the court is to ascertain the *real reason* for the treatment, the reason which operates on the mind of the alleged discriminator. This may not be the reason given, and may not be the only reason, but the test is an objective one': Lord Bingham in *Malcolm*, para 9.

The second step is to establish whether the reason 'relates to' the disabled person's disability. The proper test is somewhat unclear in the light of *Malcolm*, although it seems clear that there must be some sort of causal connection between 'the reason' and the disability. Lord Bingham said that the expression 'relates to' denotes 'some connection, not necessarily close, between the reason and the disability' (*Malcolm* para 10). Lord Neuberger said that the words 'relate to' 'suggest that a relatively loose or indirect connection between the reason and the disability would suffice' (*Malcolm* para 169).

The lack of clarity regarding the proper test may be illustrated by the result in *Malcolm*. Although all of their Lordships concurred that 'the reason' (the fact that Mr Malcolm had sublet his flat) did not 'relate to' his disability, they reached their conclusions for different reasons. Lord Bingham held that 'the reason' for the Council's conduct was a housing management decision which had 'nothing whatever to do with [Mr Malcolm's] mental disability' (para 11). Lord Scott held that 'the reason' could not 'relate to' Mr Malcolm's disability because the disability played no 'motivating part' in the Council's decision to evict him (para 29). Baroness Hale, Lord Brown and Lord Neuberger all considered that as a matter of fact Mr Malcolm's illness played no part in his decision to sublet, and that it followed that 'the reason' for the Council's conduct was also not related to his disability (paras 93, 117, 173). Baroness Hale indicated, however, that had the subletting been causally related to the illness then 'the reason' for the Council's conduct would have 'related to' Mr Malcolm's disability provided that his illness was or should have been 'present in [the Council's] mind' when it took the relevant decisions (paras 91–92). Lord Neuberger similarly indicated that, had the subletting been causally related to the illness, 'the reason' for the Council's conduct would have been sufficiently connected with the disability that it could be said to 'relate to' it (paras 169–171).

3.55 *Less favourable treatment*

For consideration of what is meant by 'less favourable treatment', see **1.47** and **1.49**ff.

3.56 *Identification of comparator*

Prior to the *Malcolm* decision, it was thought that the correct comparator for deciding whether a disabled person had been treated less favourably for the purposes of disability-related discrimination was a person (who may or may not be disabled) to whom the identified 'reason' does not apply. In *Malcolm*, that would mean the comparator would be a person who had not sublet his flat. Or, to use the famous example of a blind person who is denied entry to a restaurant because he has a dog with him, the comparator would be a person without a dog.

The House of Lords in *Malcolm* held instead that the proper comparator is a non-disabled person in otherwise comparable circumstances. In *Malcolm*, that meant a tenant without a mental disability who sublet a flat. Or, to use the example of the blind man denied entry to a restaurant because of his dog, the comparator would be a sighted person with a dog. This was a crucial departure from earlier authority, with the House of Lords expressly overruling the longstanding Court of Appeal decision in *Clark v Novacold Ltd*.

3.57 *Employer's state of mind*

Their Lordships were unanimous in *Malcolm* in holding that, in order for there to be disability-related discrimination, the alleged discriminator must have knowledge of, or imputed knowledge of, the disability (paras 18, 28, 86, 161). Baroness Hale remarked that it is not, however, necessary for the alleged discriminator to know that the impairment amounts to a disability in law (para 86). Lord Neuberger suggested that, if an act is 'inherently discriminatory', it may be unlawful even if the alleged discriminator has no reason to know of the particular disability (para 161).

3.58 *Justification*

It is sometimes said that *Malcolm* effectively abolished disability-related discrimination. It is certainly true that in practice most cases of disability-related discrimination would also amount to direct discrimination. Given that direct discrimination cannot be justified, any employee alleging discrimination under *DDA 1995* would be well-advised to focus on direct discrimination.

Disability-related discrimination was justified if, but only if, the reason for the treatment was both material to the circumstances of the particular case and substantial (*DDA1995, s 3A(3)*)—although such treatment could not be justified in a case where there had been a failure to make reasonable adjustments unless it would have been justified even if the employer had complied with that duty (*s 3A(6)*; see below).

While *DDA 1995* imposed no explicit overarching test of 'reasonableness' (compare, in the context of unfair dismissal, *Employment Rights Act 1996, s 98(4)*), it was established (cf the reservations expressed by Sedley LJ in *Collins v Royal National Theatre Board Ltd* [2004] EWCA Civ 144, [2004] 2 All ER 851 at 25 and *O'Hanlon* at 98) that the test for justification does nevertheless involved something akin to the 'range of reasonable responses' test in unfair dismissal law (*Jones v Post Office* [2001] EWCA Civ 558, [2001] IRLR 384; *Williams v J Walter Thompson Group Ltd* [2005] EWCA Civ 133, [2005] IRLR 376). Thus:

(a) the use of the word 'material' meant that there must be a 'reasonably strong connection between the employer's reason and the circumstances of the individual case' (*Jones*, per Arden LJ at 37); and

(b) 'if credible arguments exist to support the employer's decision, the employment tribunal may not hold that the reason for the discrimination is not substantial. If, however, the employer's reason is outside the band of responses which a reasonable employer might have adopted, the reason would not be substantial' (*Jones*, loc cit).

3.59 *Justification and reasonable adjustments*

Justification of less favourable treatment was not, however, established in a case where there had been a failure to make reasonable adjustments unless such justification would have been established even if the reasonable adjustments duty had been complied with (*s 3A(6)*). See further *Jangra v Gate Gourmet, London Ltd* EAT/608/01 (23 October 2002). In *Meikle v Nottinghamshire County Council* [2004] EWCA Civ 859, [2004] IRLR 703, the claimant (an employee with a disability affecting her vision) was placed on half pay under her employer's sick leave policy after a certain period of absence on sick leave. The Court of Appeal held that the employer's failure to make reasonable adjustments (eg by providing enlarged written materials and by reducing contact hours) had prolonged the claimant's absence. Had the adjustments been made, the claimant would not have been absent for long enough to be put on half pay. Therefore, the less favourable treatment (the half pay) could not be justified under what is now *DDA 1995, s 3A(6)*.

Notwithstanding the link between justification and reasonable adjustments, it is important to appreciate that a claim for disability-related discrimination and a claim for breach of the reasonable adjustments duty each existed as free-standing claims. A failure to comply with the reasonable adjustments duty is 'discrimination' (*DDA 1995, s 3A(2)*) and there is no need to plead or establish any other type of discrimination (eg direct discrimination or disability-related discrimination) in order to succeed in such a claim. Similarly, it was perfectly possible under *DDA 1995* to bring a claim for less favourable treatment without pleading or proving a reasonable adjustments claim.

3.60 *Justification in practice*

Questions about justification commonly arose in the areas set out below, before the decision in *Malcolm*. These situations could now potentially give rise to claims for discrimination arising from disability (and potentially indirect discrimination and failure to make reasonable adjustments). However, the case law on justification of disability-related discrimination needs to be treated with caution in such claims, because the test of justification for discrimination arising from disability and for indirect discrimination is different and might well prove be a more difficult test to satisfy. Therefore, although the case law in this area may be helpful to consider in dealing with situations arising after 1 October 2010, it cannot be relied on directly.

(a) *Absence/sick leave*. If an employee is less favourably treated (eg by being dismissed) pursuant to an absence policy, and his absence is disability-related, then this may fulfil the 'material and substantial' justification test. *DDA 1995* did not impose an absolute obligation on an employer to refrain from dismissing an employee who is absent on grounds of ill health due to disability: see *Royal Liverpool Children's NHS Trust v Dunsby* UKEAT/0426/05/LA (1 December 2005) at 16 (where the EAT recognised, at 17, that it is rare for a sickness absence procedure to require disability-related absences to be disregarded, and that the question of whether an employer acts unlawfully in taking such absences into account will depend on whether there is 'material and substantial' justification). Justification could be established provided that:

 (i) the employer had properly considered the employee's individual circumstances and had then properly applied the relevant provisions of the policy thereto. (If he had not done these things, there is a risk that the reason for the treatment would not be 'material' in the *Jones* sense);

 (ii) the decision to subject the employee to the treatment in question was within the range of reasonable responses in the circumstances and/or the reason for the treatment 'carries real weight' (otherwise the reason might not be 'substantial');

 (iii) the employer had considered whether the relevant policy places the employee at a substantial disadvantage in comparison with non-disabled persons and, if so, had considered whether to make any reasonable adjustments to it to prevent it from having that effect—and had made any such adjustments. (If he had not done so, he may have failed to comply with his *s 4A* reasonable adjustments duty—in which case, as set out above, he would be unable to rely on the *s 3A* justification defence unless the dismissal would have been justified even if the adjustments had been made—see *s 3A(6)*). This was generally the most difficult area in practice. If persons with a particular disability are likely to have substantially more sickness absence than persons without that disability, then the reasonable adjustments duty is likely to come into play. Ultimately, the question for the tribunal will then be whether it is reasonable for the employer to refuse to modify a policy in a particular case.

This last point was considered, in relation to a claim for full pay while on disability-related sick leave, in *O'Hanlon*. In that case, the EAT ([2006] IRLR 840 at 67 ff) held that it would be a 'very rare case indeed' where an adjustment to an agreed sick pay scheme would be required, although the EAT did not rule out the possibility that such an adjustment could be required in 'exceptional circumstances'. In the Court of Appeal, Hooper LJ (giving the leading judgment) saw 'much force' in the EAT's approach on the point (at 57). Sedley LJ held that collectively agreed pay structures for a very large establishment (while not in principle beyond the reach of the *DDA 1995*) were 'not ready candidates for individual variation' (at 99); and that while it would not be permissible or justified to construct a scheme operating arbitrarily to the disadvantage of the disabled, 'any unplanned discriminatory aspect may well be justified on the ground that such exceptions as can fairly be made in favour of disabled employees are already programmed into the scheme'. See also *Khan v Royal Mail Group* UKEAT/0480/06/DA (5 December 2007) and *Gibson Shipbrokers Ltd v Staples* UKEAT/0263/07 (18 September 2007), both cases where the EAT briefly considered the *O'Hanlon* principle.

(b) *Health and safety concerns*. The key here is that the employer should avoid stereotypical assumptions that a disabled person represents a risk to health and safety (for example because he is in a wheelchair or suffers from a medical condition such as diabetes or epilepsy). If the employer makes such an assumption, and treats the employee less favourably as a result, he risks being liable to claims for both direct discrimination (see above) and disability-related discrimination (because there may well be no 'reasonably strong connection' between the employer's reason and the individual circumstances).

3.61 Discrimination arising from disability under the EqA 2010

In light of the difficulties posed by the *Malcolm* case, the *EqA 2010* has effectively abolished the old category of 'disability-related discrimination'. The government's initial response to the *Malcolm* decision was to propose to extend indirect discrimination to cover disability. However, following consultation, the government concluded that this would not be adequate and that a specific provision was required which emulated disability-related discrimination. They therefore introduced the concept of 'discrimination arising from disability' in *EqA 2010, s 15* (see the explanation of the Solicitor General at the Committee Stage of the passage of the Equality Bill at PBC Deb (Equality Bill), 16 June 2009, c 275). However, the concept of discrimination arising from disability is not intended to simply re-create the position in relation to disability-related discrimination as it was before the *Malcolm* decision, in particular because there is a different justification test which the government intended to be a stricter test (Equality Bill—Government Response to Consultation, July 2008 at para 11.26). The *Explanatory Notes to the EqA 2010, s 15* state that following *Malcolm* the section is 'aimed at re-establishing an appropriate balance between enabling a disabled person to make out a case of experiencing a detriment which arises because of his or her disability, and providing an opportunity for an employer or other person to defend the treatment.'

Discrimination arising from disability occurs where (paraphrasing *EqA 2010, s 15*):

(a) because of something arising in consequence of the disabled person's disability, a person treats the disabled person unfavourably; and

(b) he cannot show that the treatment in question is a proportionate means of achieving a legitimate aim.

3.62 *Discrimination arising from disability and indirect discrimination*

It is important to note that, while there are likely to be significant overlaps between cases of discrimination arising from disability and cases of indirect discrimination, the two concepts are very different. For example, indirect discrimination includes an element of group disadvantage, while discrimination arising from disability may be established if a single disabled person has been unfavourably treated.

However, it is likely that many cases of discrimination arising from disability could be reformulated as cases of indirect discrimination or a failure to make reasonable adjustments. Suppose, for example, that an employee is dismissed because (in consequence of her disability) she is unable to comply with her employer's requirement that she works full-time, 40 hours per week. That employee will (subject to justification) have a good claim for discrimination arising from disability (see below). In indirect discrimination terms, the employer will have applied to her an apparently neutral provision, criterion or practice (the 40 hours per week requirement) applying equally to persons who do not have her particular disability, but which may well put persons with her particular disability at a particular disadvantage compared with others. Subject to the test of justification, the employee would also have a claim for indirect discrimination. The employer would also be under a duty to make any reasonable adjustments to the provision, criterion or practice as the 40 hour week requirement will put her at substantial disadvantage compared with non disabled employees, and so the claim could also be formulated as claim for a breach of that duty.

One situation where a claim for indirect discrimination could succeed but a claim for discrimination arising from disability would fail is when the employer did not know and could not reasonably be expected to know that the employee was disabled (see **3.67** and **3.74**).

In addition, indirect discrimination can arise where an employer 'would apply' a provision, criterion or practice which 'would put' persons with a particular disability at a particular disability and 'would put' the claimant at that disadvantage, whereas a claim for a discrimination arising from disability requires that the employee is actually treated unfavourably.

3.63 *Discrimination by association or perception*

Under *EqA 2010, s 15* discrimination arising from disability arises where a person treats a disabled person unfavourably because of something arising in consequence of that person's disability. There is therefore no scope, at least on a literal reading of the statute, for it to cover discrimination by association or perception.

3.64 *Unfavourable treatment*

There is no definition of 'unfavourable treatment' in the *EqA 2010*. The *EHRC Employment Code* suggests at *section 5.7* that the expression means that the disabled person 'must have been put at a disadvantage', and that the disadvantage may be obvious (for example, being refused a job), or it may not.

The use of the term 'unfavourable' in place of 'less favourable' seems to be an attempt to make it clear that no comparator is required. The *EHRC Employment Code* also states at *section 5.6* that there is no need to use a comparator in deciding whether a person has been treated unfavourably. In particular, there is no need to compare the treatment of the disabled person to the treatment of another person (whether real or hypothetical). For example, the *EHRC Employment Code* states that in deciding whether the dismissal of a disabled worker for disability-related sickness absence amounts to discrimination arising from disability, it is irrelevant whether or not other workers would have been dismissed for having the same or similar length of absence. It is sufficient that there has been unfavourable treatment (the dismissal). The decision to dismiss her will be discrimination arising from disability if the employer cannot objectively justify it.

However, the fact that there is no need to use a comparator does not mean that it will never be helpful or relevant to do so. Identifying a comparator may help to determine whether there has been unfavourable treatment, eg looked at in isolation payment of a discretionary bonus is not obviously unfavourable treatment, but the position may look different if comparator employees have received a much larger bonus.

In practice, it may be difficult to decide whether particular treatment is 'unfavourable' or not. It seems likely that tribunals will treat the term 'unfavourable in a similar way to the more familiar concept of 'detriment' which requires that 'a reasonable worker would or might take the view that he or she had been disadvantaged' (see COMMON CONCEPTS **(1)**). The concept of unfavourable treatment is also used in the context of pregnancy and maternity discrimination in *EqA 2010, s 18* (see SEX DISCRIMINATION **(8)**).

3.65 *Because of something arising in consequence of disability*

In deciding whether the unfavourable treatment was because of something arising in consequence of the disabled person's disability, the first step will be to identify why the person was treated unfavourably. This may not be a straightforward question, especially if there were various reasons for the treatment. It is likely that, in identifying why a person was treated unfavourably, tribunals will adopt the same approach as is applied when establishing the reason for less favourable treatment in direct discrimination cases: see **1.49**.

The second step will be to establish whether the thing which led to the unfavourable treatment *arose in consequence of* the person's disability. The *EHRC Employment Code* states at *section 5.9* that the consequences of a disability 'include anything which is the result, effect or outcome of a disabled person's disability'. The *Code* also gives the example of a woman who is disciplined for losing her temper at work, but whose behaviour was a result of severe pain caused by cancer. The disciplinary action would be unfavourable treatment because of something which arises in consequence of her disability, namely her loss of temper.

Circumstances which commonly gave rise to a claim of disability-related discrimination, before *Malcolm* are now likely to amount to unfavourable treatment because of something arising in consequence of disability. For example, dismissal of an employee for a disability-related period of sickness absence is likely to amount to unfavourable treatment (dismissal) because of something (absence) arising in consequence of the employee's disability (see example in the *EHRC Employment Code* at *section 5.3*).

3.66 *Justification*

Discrimination arising from disability may be justified if the employer can show that the treatment is a proportionate means of achieving a legitimate aim. This is a new test in disability discrimination law, but it is a well-established test in other spheres. The proper approach to the test is discussed at **1.83**ff. The *EHRC Employment Code* states at *section 5.12* that the employer must produce evidence to support their assertion that the treatment is justified and not rely on mere generalisations.

Note that this is a different test from the test for justification in relation to disability-related discrimination under *DDA 1995* and so case law on justification for disability-related discrimination will not be directly applicable. The test applied in relation to disability-related discrimination was akin to a 'range of reasonable responses' test (see para **3.58**) which gave employers a relatively broad discretion in deciding how to proceed, although this flexibility was limited to some extent by the fact that treatment could only be justified if it would have been justified had any reasonable adjustments been made. The objective justification test which now applies is a stricter test and brings with it the question of the extent to which costs can be relied on as a justification (see **Common concepts (1)**). However, the cases on disability-related discrimination may still be of some assistance, even if the precise balancing exercise to be carried out is not the same. In particular, it seems likely that the policy which lay behind some of the tribunal decisions will still be relevant eg the approach to claims to extend sick pay as they in *O'Hanlon* and the acceptance that it is possible to justify dismissal for disability-related absence, in an appropriate case (see para **3.60**).

In contrast to the position in relation to disability-related discrimination under *DDA 1995*, there is no specific link under *EqA 2010* between a consideration of objective justification and the duty to make reasonable adjustments. However, the *EHRC Employment Code* states at *section 5.21* that 'if an employer has failed to make a reasonable adjustment which would have prevented or minimised the unfavourable treatment, it will be very difficult for them to show that the treatment was objectively justified.'

3.67 *Employer's knowledge*

There will not be discrimination arising from disability if the employer did not know, and could not reasonably have been expected to know, that the disabled person had the disability (*EqA 2010, s 15(2)*).

There is a certain ambiguity in *s 15(2)* in that it is unclear whether, in order to commit discrimination arising from disability, the employer must know, or reasonably be expected to know: (a) that the disabled person suffers from an impairment, regardless of whether the impairment meets the legal definition of 'disability'; or (b) that the disabled person suffers from an impairment which meets the legal definition of 'disability'.

The *EHRC Employment Code* states that employers must do all they reasonably can be expected to do to find out if a worker has a disability (*para 5.15*). It also states that if an employer's agent or employee (such as an occupational health adviser or a HR officer) knows, in that capacity, of a worker's or applicant's or potential applicant's disability, the employer will not usually be able to claim that they do not know of the disability. The case law in relation to reasonable adjustments is likely to be relevant here (see *para 3.77*).

3.68 Indirect discrimination under EqA 2010

Extension of indirect discrimination to disability and overlap with duty to make reasonable adjustments

Another important innovation of the *EqA 2010* is the extension of the law on indirect discrimination to cover disability. Under the *Framework Directive*, Member States could choose between prohibiting indirect discrimination in relation to disability and imposing a duty to make reasonable adjustments (*Framework Directive, Article 2(2)(b)*). The UK chose to rely on the duty to make reasonable adjustments under *DDA 1995* to comply with the Directive. In its initial consultation on what became the *EqA 2010*, the government proposed that it would not extend indirect discrimination to disability discrimination, considering that the duty to make reasonable adjustments provided sufficient protection (*A Framework for Fairness: Proposals for a Single Equality Bill for Great Britain*, paras 1.3–1.35). However, the government changed its position and decided to extend the scope of indirect discrimination to disability as its initial response to the *Malcolm* decision, which narrowed the scope of disability-related discrimination. The government subsequently consulted stakeholders and concluded that indirect discrimination was not adequate to address the effects of the *Malcolm* decision and it introduced the concept of discrimination arising from disability (see **3.60**). However, it retained the proposal to extend indirect discrimination to disability.

The concept of indirect discrimination overlaps significantly with the duty to make reasonable adjustments. Both concepts address situations where a neutral 'provision, criterion or practice' ('PCP') puts a disabled person at a disadvantage. However, unlike indirect discrimination, there is no requirement to establish group disadvantage, to succeed in a claim for a breach of the duty to make reasonable adjustments. In *Eweida v British Airways plc* [2010] EWCA Civ 80, Sedley LJ stated, when considering the requirement for group disadvantage in an indirect discrimination claim under *RBR 2003:*

> 'If you look at section 4A of the Disability Discrimination Act 1995 as amended, you see how Parliament provides for indirect discrimination against a single individual: it defines it as arising when a provision, criterion or practice, or any other physical feature of premises, "places the individual concerned at a substantial disadvantage in comparison with persons who are not disabled"'.

At first sight therefore, the two concepts address the same issue, but the duty to make reasonable adjustments is likely to be easier to establish as it does not require an employee to show group disadvantage. However, there are some differences between the concepts in addition to the requirement to show group disadvantage:

(a) A duty to make reasonable adjustments arises where an employee is placed at a 'substantial disadvantage' compared with people who are not disabled, whereas to succeed in a claim for indirect discrimination an employee must show that they have suffered a 'particular disadvantage' compared with people who do not have their particular disability. However, the tests for particular disadvantage and substantial disadvantage are both a relatively low threshold (see **3.81** and **3.69**) and it seems likely that an individual disadvantage which is sufficient to establish a claim for indirect discrimination will also be sufficient to establish a reasonable adjustments claim.

(b) The duty to make reasonable adjustments requires employers to make adjustments which are 'reasonable'. In the case of indirect discrimination, a PCP will need to be changed to avoid a particular disadvantage unless the employer can show that the PCP is objectively justified. It may be that this imposes a slightly higher hurdle for the employee bringing a reasonable adjustments claim, eg it would appear to be open to an employer to rely on costs alone to justify not making a reasonable adjustment, but current case law suggests that this is not possible when considering the objective justification test in indirect discrimination (see **Common concepts (1)**). Note though, that if there are circumstances where an adjustments would not be 'reasonable' but an employer could not establish objective justification (so an indirect discrimination claim might succeed), the employee might be able to succeed in a claim for disability-related discrimination, if no group disadvantage can be established.

(c) There is no knowledge requirement in relation to indirect discrimination (see **3.74**) whereas a duty to make reasonable actual or constructive knowledge of the disability (see **3.79**). In this respect, indirect discrimination is wider than a duty to make reasonable adjustments.

(d) Indirect discrimination can arise where an employer 'would apply' a PCP which 'would put' persons with a particular disability at a particular disability and 'would put' the claimant at that disadvantage, whereas a claim for a duty to make reasonable adjustments requires that the employee is actually put at a substantial disadvantage.

3.69 *Definition of indirect discrimination*

The *EqA 2010, s 19* now prohibits indirect discrimination on the basis of various protected characteristics, including disability:

> '(1) A person (A) discriminates against another (B) if A applies to B a provision, criterion or practice which is discriminatory in relation to a relevant protected characteristic of B's.
>
> (2) For the purposes of subsection (1), a provision, criterion or practice is discriminatory in relation to a relevant protected characteristic of B's if:
>
> (a) A applies, or would apply, it to persons with whom B does not share the characteristic,
>
> (b) it puts, or would put, persons with whom B shares the characteristic at a particular disadvantage when compared with persons with whom B does not share it,
>
> (c) it puts, or would put, B at that disadvantage, and
>
> (d) A cannot show it to be a proportionate means of achieving a legitimate aim'.

As this is the same test for all of the protected characteristics, it is discussed at **1.73ff**.

EqA 2010, s 6(3) provides that in relation to disability, a reference to a person with a person who has particular characteristic is a reference to a person with a particular disability and a reference to persons who share a particular characteristic is a reference to persons who have 'the same disability'.

3.70 *Provision, criterion or practice*

The *EHRC Employment Code* notes at *section 4.5* that there is no definition of 'provision, criterion or practice' in the *EqA 2010* but that it 'should be construed widely so as to include, for example, any formal or informal policies, rules, practices, arrangements, criteria, conditions, prerequisites, qualifications or provisions.' This wide approach is consistent with that taken under earlier legislation: see **1.75**.

In the context of disability discrimination, examples of a relevant provision, criterion or practice might be:

(a) a requirement that all workers in a particular office should work quietly (whereas a disabled person may wish to use voice recognition software to control her computer);

(b) a policy requiring staff to arrive at work by a particular time in the morning (whereas a disabled person may need to arrive later to avoid rush-hour traffic so that he can access public transport with his wheelchair);

(c) a prohibition on working from home.

3.71 *Particular disadvantage*

There is no definition of 'disadvantage' in the *EqA 2010*. It has been suggested that a disadvantage does not have to be quantifiable and that it is enough if the worker can reasonably say they would have preferred to be treated differently (*EHRC Employment Code, section 4.9*).

In deciding whether there is (or would be) a 'particular disadvantage', a comparative exercise is required to consider the impact of the provision, criterion or practice on those who share the relevant protected characteristic compared to the rest of the comparison 'pool'. The law relating to the proper identification of the 'pool' and whether there is (or would be) a disparate impact between those who share the characteristic and those who do not is discussed at **1.78**.

The comparison exercise is likely to give rise to particular difficulties in the context of disability. In a case of sex discrimination, the task involves, first, identifying the pool (broadly speaking, those people who are affected by the provision, criterion or practice), and second, considering the impact of the provision, criterion or practice on men compared to women. What is not clear is how this second step will work in a disability discrimination case. In particular:

In the disability context, the comparison is between persons who share the employee's particular disability (*EqA 2010, s 6(3)(b)*) and others (whether disabled or not) who do not have that particular disability, but whose circumstances are not materially different (*EqA 2010, s 23(1)*). However, unlike in a case of direct disability discrimination, there is no requirement that the comparator's circumstances should include the person's abilities (*EqA 2010, s 23(2)*). The question is, how should one define a person's 'particular disability' for the purposes of *EqA 2010, s 6(3)(b)*? Take for example a person with multiple sclerosis which causes a visual impairment. There are three possibilities:

(a) one might say that his 'particular disability' is multiple sclerosis. This would be consistent with *EqA 2010, Sch 6, para 6(1)*, which says that multiple sclerosis is a disability. If this approach is correct, it would follow that one should consider the impact of the provision, criterion or practice on persons with multiple sclerosis compared to its impact on persons without multiple sclerosis. The problem with such an approach is, of course, that not every person with multiple sclerosis will have a visual impairment; and on the other hand, many people without multiple sclerosis do have visual impairments. This approach is therefore open to the criticism that it fails to properly focus on the particular impairment. Furthermore, whilst the approach might work if the disabled person has an identifiable condition (such as multiple sclerosis) it will be more problematic where a person has complex and/or interrelated disabilities, or where their disability does not fit into any easily identifiable category;

(b) the second possibility would therefore be to focus on the person's impairment, and to say that his 'particular disability' is a visual impairment. This gives rise to the question of what degree of visual impairment would be sufficient for a person to fall within the disabled employee's pool. For example, the pool might include people who have no sight at all, as well as those who occasionally experience blurred vision;

(c) the third possibility would be to focus even more narrowly on the employee's particular impairment, and to say that his 'particular disability' is a visual impairment of a particular type and severity. This is the approach proposed by the *EHRC Employment Code*, which says at *section 4.16* that: 'It is important to be clear which protected characteristic is relevant. In relation to disability, this would not be disabled people as a whole but people with a particular disability—for example, with an equivalent level of visual impairment.'

It seems likely that the third approach is the correct one. However, it should be noted that if the person's impairment is very narrowly defined then it may be very easy to show that there is a 'particular disadvantage'. For example, assume that a disabled person who occasionally becomes very tired during working hours and needs to take time off work complains about a rule which prevents her from doing so. If the comparison group is defined narrowly as 'disabled people who occasionally become very tired during working hours' then (assuming one can identify a sufficiently large group of persons with that particular disability) the group will obviously be at a 'particular disadvantage'.

A further unresolved question, which arises in connection with all strands of discrimination, is how widely one should look when identifying the disadvantaged group (ie the group of persons sharing the claimant's particular disability, who the claimant says would be put at a particular disadvantage compared to persons who do not share that particular disability). This issue is related to the question of the meaning of 'particular disability' because the narrower the definition of 'particular disability,' the less likely it is that other persons will fall within the claimant's group; and the wider the claimant will therefore want the group to be.

The Court of Appeal discussed the question of the width of the disadvantaged group in *Eweida v British Airways plc* [2010] EWCA Civ 80 (in the context of religion and belief discrimination). Sedley LJ suggested at para 18 that, in identifying the group, there were three possibilities: a subset of the employer's workforce, society at large, or an intermediate group comprising the employer's workforce but deemed to include some others with the claimant's protected characteristic. He went on to identify difficulties with each of these possibilities. The difficulty with the narrower approach (focusing on the employer's workforce) was said to be that it might exclude the solitary individual from the protection of the law. However, as Sedley LJ observed, that result is avoided in disability discrimination law (under the *EqA 2010*, by the provisions on reasonable adjustments and on discrimination arising from disability). Tribunals may, therefore, be minded to adopt a narrow approach to the width of the disadvantaged group in disability discrimination cases.

3.72 *Personal disadvantage*

A person will only succeed in an indirect discrimination claim if he can show that the provision, criterion or practice puts or would put him at the particular disadvantage: see **1.82**. It is not enough for him to show that he is a member of the protected group. Take for example a workplace rule banning dogs. If a blind man were to challenge the rule, it would be relatively easy to show that it placed blind people as a group at a particular disadvantage, since blind people are much more likely to need to travel to work with a dog. But if the particular blind man in question does not use or ever intend to use a guide dog, it will be very difficult for him to show that he has suffered a personal disadvantage.

The repeated use of the word 'would' in *EqA 2010, s 19* (as in, 'would apply' and 'would put') demonstrates that the Act is intended to cover not only provisions, criteria and practices which have been applied, but also those which have not yet been applied but which, if they were applied, would be discriminatory.

3.73 *Justification*

Indirect discrimination may be justified if the employer can show that the treatment is a proportionate means of achieving a legitimate aim. This is a new test in disability discrimination law, but it is a well-established test in other spheres. The proper approach to the test is discussed at **1.83ff**. The *EHRC Employment Code* states at *section 4.26* that the employer must produce evidence to support their assertion that the treatment is justified and not rely on mere generalisations.

3.74 *Employer's knowledge*

It is not necessary, for indirect discrimination to occur, for the employer to know that any particular individual has a disability, or to know that the provision, criterion or practice may be indirectly discriminatory. To that extent, the employer's state of mind is irrelevant in deciding whether indirect discrimination has occurred, and wise employers will be pro-active in identifying practices which may inadvertently be indirectly discriminatory.

This is slightly surprising, given the government's conscious decision to include knowledge requirements in relation to discrimination arising from disability and reasonable adjustments. However, where the tribunal is satisfied that the provision, criterion or practice was not applied with the intention of discriminating against the complainant, it must not order compensation without first considering whether to make a declaration or recommendation (*EqA 2010, s 124*). This provides a limited discretion to the tribunal to avoid awarding compensation, although tribunals are likely to award compensation if the discrimination was or should have been obvious to an employer, even if it was unintentional.

3.75 **Duty to make reasonable adjustments under DDA 1995 and EqA 2010**

The duty to make reasonable adjustments is a unique feature of disability legislation, requiring as it does that disabled employees should (in certain circumstances) be treated more favourably than their non-disabled counterparts (see *DDA 1995, s 18D(1)* and eg *Archibald v Fife Council* [2004] UKHL 32, [2004] IRLR 651 per Baroness Hale at 57); cf other 'strands' of discrimination law where such 'positive discrimination' is not required.

The duty to make reasonable adjustments existed in the *DDA 1995* and, is included in very similar terms, in the *EqA 2010*. There are, however, important differences between the two statutes, which are explained below.

The duty is set out, in relation to employers, in *EqA 2010, ss 20, 39* and *Sch 8* and was previously set out in *DDA 1995, s 4A*. In both statutes it requires that where either: (a) a provision, criterion or practice applied by or on behalf of an employer; or (b) any physical feature of premises occupied by the employer, places the disabled person concerned at a substantial disadvantage in comparison with persons who are not disabled, the employer should take such steps as it is reasonable for him to have to take in order to prevent the provision, criterion or practice (or, as the case may be, the physical feature), from 'having that effect' (in the language of the *DDA 1995*) or to 'avoid the disadvantage' (in the language of the *EqA 2010*). The *EqA 2010* introduces a third requirement, namely (c) a requirement, where a disabled person would, but for the provision of an auxiliary aid, be put at a substantial disadvantage in comparison with persons who are not disabled, to take such steps as it is reasonable to have to take to provide the auxiliary aid. In practice, this is unlikely to amount to an extension of the duty under the *DDA 1995* (see **3.82**).

The duty to make reasonable adjustments to PCPs and to provide auxiliary aids applies both in deciding to whom to offer employment and in employment. The duty to make reasonable adjustments to premises applies only in relation to employment (*Sch 8, para 4*). The duty is owed to anyone who is or has notified the employer that he may be an applicant for employment and to employees (*Sch 8, para 5*)

The EAT has given schematic guidance as to the course to be steered by a tribunal prior to a finding of a breach of the reasonable adjustments duty (*Smiths Detection v Berriman* UKEAT/0712/04/0908, updated in *Rowan v Environment Agency* [2008] ICR 218, [2008] IRLR 20). This guidance was set out in relation to reasonable adjustments claims under the *DDA 1995*, but is also likely to apply, with any relevant modifications, to the *EqA 2010*. In short, a tribunal considering a reasonable adjustments claim must identify:

(a) the provision, criterion or practice applied by or on behalf of an employer; or

(b) the physical feature of premises occupied by the employer; or

(c) the identity of non-disabled comparators (where appropriate); and

(d) the nature and extent of the substantial disadvantage suffered by the claimant.

The most obvious modification to this guidance in light of the *EqA 2010* would be the insertion of a step after subparagraph (b) above to require the tribunal to identify, in an auxiliary aid case, the auxiliary aid.

3.76 *Preliminary considerations*

In considering the duty it is necessary to bear in mind a number of preliminary points:

(a) *Failure to make adjustments is discrimination.* A failure by an employer to comply with a duty to make reasonable adjustments is disability discrimination by that employer (*EqA 2010, s 25(2)(d)*, which replaced *DDA 1995, s 3A(2)*). There is no need to prove any additional discriminatory act by the employer. Thus, there is no need to prove that there has additionally been direct discrimination, indirect discrimination or discrimination arising from disability (or, previously, disability-related discrimination under *DDA 1995*). A reasonable adjustments claim is free-standing. (But note that a breach of the duty to make reasonable adjustments is not otherwise actionable (eg it is not actionable as a breach of statutory duty): *EqA 2010, s 21(3)*, which replaced *DDA 1995, s 18B(6)*.)

(b) *Duty to make adjustments in order to prevent disadvantageous effect.* The duty is not simply a duty to make such adjustments as are reasonable in all the circumstances, but a duty to take such steps as are reasonable in those circumstances in order to prevent the provision, criterion or practice (or, as the case may be, the physical feature or lack of auxiliary aid) from having the effect of placing the disabled person concerned at a substantial disadvantage (*EqA 2010, s 20*, previously *DDA 1995, s 4A(1)*).

(c) *Supplementary provision about reasonable adjustments.* It is important to note that *DDA 1995, s 18B* made supplementary provision about the reasonable adjustments duty on employers in *DDA 1995, s 4A* (and about the corresponding reasonable adjustments duties elsewhere in Part 2 DDA 1995—see eg *s 4B(4)*, *(5)* (contract workers); *s 4E* (office-holders); *s 4H* (occupational pension schemes) etc). In particular, *DDA 1995, s 18B* set out factors to which regard is to be had in determining whether it is reasonable for a person to have to take a particular step (*s 18B(1)*); gave examples of steps which may need to be taken in order to comply with a reasonable adjustments duty (*s 18B(2)*); and made provision about the alteration of premises (*s 18B(3)–(5)*). *EqA 2010, s 22* provides for regulations to make similar provision in relation to the *EqA 2010*, although no such regulations have yet been passed. However, guidance is provided in the *EHRC Employment Code* (see Chapter 6) and was previously provided in the *DRC Code (Chapter 5)*.

3.77 *To whom is the duty owed?*

Under the *DDA 1995*, the duty to make reasonable adjustments was owed to 'the disabled person concerned' as defined in *DDA 1995, s 4A(2)* (and not to disabled persons generally). In the case of a provision, criterion or practice for determining to whom employment should be offered, the duty was owed to 'any person who is, or has notified the employer that he may be, an applicant for that employment'; in any other case, the duty is owed to a disabled person who is an applicant for the employment concerned or an employee of the employer concerned.

Under the *EqA 2010*, the duty to make reasonable adjustments is owed to the 'interested disabled person' as defined in *EqA 2010, Sch 8* (and not to disabled persons generally). In the case of a decision regarding to whom employment should be offered, the duty is owed to 'a person who is, or has notified [the employer] that the person may be, an applicant for the employment'; in any other case, the duty is owed to a disabled person who is an applicant for the employment concerned or an employee of the employer concerned.

3.78 *No anticipatory duty to make adjustments*

It follows that there is no 'anticipatory' duty upon an employer to make reasonable adjustments – that is, there is no duty to make such adjustments in anticipation of the possibility that a person with a particular disability may apply for a job or may become an employee of the employer. There is no duty to make adjustments to a role to remedy a substantial disadvantage to a theoretical potential candidate who is disabled before that candidate has applied for the job (or notified the employer that he may do so) (and see *Difolco v NTL Group* [2006] EWCA Civ 1508, 150 Sol Jo LB 1393, at 13). Nor is there any duty on an employer to invest in equipment (such as computer voice-recognition software) or to make adjustments to premises (eg installing wheelchair ramps) in anticipation of the possibility that a person with a particular disability may apply for a job or join its staff. The initial consultation on the *EqA 2010* canvassed the possibility of introducing an anticipatory duty to make reasonable adjustments in the employment context but rejected the idea (*The Equality Bill—Government Response to Consultation* at paras 11.48–11.50).

However, it should be kept in mind that where an employer is also a service-provider, it will (in respect of service provision) be subject to the 'anticipatory' duty to make adjustments under *EqA 2010, s 29* and *Sch 2* (previously *DDA 1995, s 21*). The two types of duty will overlap where there is an overlap between service-provision and employment (for example, if an employer has an office for its employees to which members of the public have access; or if a service-provider employer provides the same material on an intranet site for employees and on an internet site for its customers). Similar overlaps may occur where the employer is a public authority subject to the duty to make adjustments in *EqA 2010, s 29(7)(b)* (previously *DDA 1995, s 21E*).

3.79 *Employer's knowledge*

Under *DDA 1995* no duty to make reasonable adjustments was imposed in relation to a disabled person if the employer did not know, and could not reasonably be expected to know:

(a) in the case of an applicant or potential applicant, that the disabled person concerned is, or may be, an applicant for the employment (*DDA 1995, s 4A(3)(a)*); or

(b) in any case that that person has a disability and is likely to be placed at a comparative substantial disadvantage (*DDA 1995, s 4A(3)(b)*).

The replacement provisions in *EqA 2010* are contained in *Sch 8* and state that an employer is not subject to a duty to make a reasonable adjustment if it does not know and could not reasonably be expected to know:

(a) in the case of an applicant or potential applicant, that an interested disabled person is or may be an applicant for the work in question (*para 20(1)(a)*);

(b) in any other case referred to in this Part of this Schedule, that an interested disabled person has a disability and is likely to be placed at the disadvantage (which gives rise to the duty to make the adjustment) (*para 20(1)(b)*).

According to the *Explanatory Notes to the EqA 2010*, the intention was the provisions of *EqA 2010, Sch 8* simply replaced provisions in *DDA 1995* which were to similar effect and therefore it does not appear that there was any intention to change the law on this point. The *EHRC Employment Code* also suggests that this is the case (*paras 6.17–6.19*). However, there appears to be a problem with the drafting of *EqA 2010, Sch 8, para 20* which may have the effect of limiting the knowledge requirement. The first issue is that *para 20(1)(b)* applies to any 'other' case, ie it does not appear to apply in the case of an applicant or potential applicant (covered by *sub-para (a)*). The second issue is that *sub-para (b)* applies to other cases referred to '*in this Part of this Schedule*', but in fact *Part 3 of Schedule 8* does not refer to any other cases. It may be that this should be a reference to *Schedule 8* as a whole or to *Part 5* of the Act (Work) which incorporates *Schedule 8* and that tribunals will be prepared to correct what appears to be a drafting slip.

Case law under the *DDA 1995* established that the effect of these provisions was that the duty to make reasonable adjustments will not arise if an employer does not and could not reasonably be expected to know *either* that the person has a disability *or* that he is likely to be placed at a comparative substantial disadvantage: see *Alam v Secretary of State for the Department for Work and Pensions* [2010] ICR 665, [2010] IRLR 283 which departed from an earlier decision in *Grey v Eastern and Coastal Kent plc* [2009] IRLR 429.

As to the question of whether an employer could 'reasonably be expected' to know that a particular person has a disability, see the *DRC Code of Practice, section 5.12* and the *EHRC Employment Code, section 6.19*. In *Department for Work and Pensions v Hall* UKEAT 0012/05/3108, the EAT described the question of constructive knowledge as one of 'pure fact', refusing to interfere with the employment tribunal's conclusion that there was such knowledge in a case where the claimant: (i) had declined to provide any information about disability or long-term health conditions on a health declaration form; (ii) had refused permission for the employer to contact her doctor; (iii) thereafter behaved at work in a 'disruptive and volatile' manner involving 'both verbal altercations and minor physical contact'.

One particular issue which may arise for employers is the provision by employees or applicants of medical information to the employer's occupational health advisor. In general, it seems that where such information is provided to such an advisor and the advisor is an agent or employee of the employer, such knowledge will be imputed to the employer (*DRC Code of Practice*, section 5.15, *EHRC Employment Code, section 6.21* and *Hammersmith and Fulham London Borough Council v Farnsworth* [2000] IRLR 691, EAT). Particular difficulties will arise if the employee has not given consent to the information being passed on to the employer: in some circumstances, the *DRC Code* suggested that a line manager may find him- or herself in the situation of making adjustments without knowing precisely why they are needed. In order to avoid this, employers may wish to ensure that it is made clear to applicants and employees that information will need to be shared for discrimination law purposes to the extent necessary to allow adjustments to be made. This will raise data protection issues, as to which, see the Employment Practices Code on Data Protection (Information Commissioner, June 2005), Part 4 (information about workers' health), and particularly the good practice recommendations on occupational health schemes. The *EHRC Employment Code* states that information will not be imputed or attributed to the employer if it is gained by a person providing services to the employee, independently of the employer, even if the employer arranged for the services to be provided.

3.80 *'Provision, criterion or practice'*

As set out above, the duty to make adjustments arises where a 'provision, criterion or practice' places the disabled person concerned at a comparative substantial disadvantage. The term 'provision, criterion or practice' has been used in a number of EC discrimination law directives, the first occasion being in the *Burden of Proof Directive (97/80/EC)* (definition of indirect sex discrimination, *Article 2(2)*). Case law suggests that a broad approach should be taken to the scope of a 'provision, criterion or practice'—so that the reasonable adjustments duty can extend even to adjusting the essential requirements of a job, or to creating a new job.

In *Archibald v Fife Council* [2004] UKHL 32, [2004] IRLR 651, the claimant had been employed by the respondent as a road sweeper, but became physically disabled to the extent that she could not carry out her duties. The only suitable alternative employment, in sedentary office work, was at a slightly higher grade and the respondent required her to go through a competitive interview process. The claimant did so, but was unsuccessful in applying for more than 100 alternative posts. She claimed that the respondent's duty extended to adjusting the competitive interview requirement (so as to transfer her to a post at the slightly higher grade without an interview). The House of Lords held that it was an implied condition or 'arrangement' (the precursor to a 'provision, criterion or practice', formerly in *DDA 1995, s 6(1)(a)*) of the claimant's employment that: (i) she should at all times be physically fit to do her job as a road sweeper; (ii) if she was physically unable to do that job she was liable to be dismissed. The employer's duty (to prevent these 'arrangements' from placing the claimant at a substantial comparative disadvantage) could therefore extend (if reasonable) to transferring the claimant to a vacant clerical post at the higher grade (and salary).

This broad approach to the reasonable adjustments duty can also be seen in *Southampton City College v Randall* [2006] IRLR 18, where the EAT held (at 22) that the *DDA 1995* provisions about reasonable adjustments did not (as a matter of law) preclude the creation of a new post in substitution for an existing post from being a reasonable adjustment.

It seems likely, however, that one limitation on this broad approach is that the courts will continue to require a provision, criterion or practice to be job-related, as did the EAT in *Kenny v Hampshire Constabulary* [1998] ICR 27, EAT: in that case, the applicant needed assistance when going to the toilet. The EAT held that 'arrangements' (old *DDA 1995, s 6(1)(a)*) must be job-related and that, therefore, the duty did not extend to attending to an employee's personal needs.

3.81 *Physical features of premises occupied by the employer*

As set out above, the duty to make adjustments also arises where a physical feature of premises occupied by the employer places the disabled person concerned at a comparative substantial disadvantage. In the *DDA 1995*, the emphasis on premises *occupied by the employer* was clear from the duty to make adjustments at *DDA 1995, s 4A(1)(b)*. In the *EqA 2010*, the emphasis on premises *occupied by the employer* is apparent from reading *EqA 2010, s 20(4)* together with *Sch 8, para 2(2)(b)*.

By *EqA 2010 s 20(10)* (previously *DDA 1995, s 18D(2)*), 'physical feature' includes any of the following:

(a) any feature arising from the design or construction of a building;

(b) any feature of any approach to, exit from, or access to a building;

(c) any fixtures, fittings, furnishings, furniture, equipment or material (or, under the *EqA 2010*, any chattels) in or on premises; and

(d) any other physical element or quality. *DDA 1995, s 18D(2)* limited this final category to 'any other physical element or quality of any land comprised in the premises', whereas *EqA 2010, s 20(10)* refers simply to 'any other physical element or quality'. It therefore appears that *EqA 2010* applies to any other physical element or quality of the land *or any buildings on the premises.*

DDA 1995, s 18D(2) stated expressly that a feature will be a 'physical feature' whether it is permanent or temporary. There is no similar provision in the *EqA 2010*, although it seems likely that a temporary feature would still constitute a 'physical feature' for the purposes of the *EqA 2010*.

This would therefore seem to be a broad definition. According to a list, stated to be non-exhaustive, given at *DRC Code of Practice, section 5.10*, and in the *EHRC Employment Code, section 6.12*, physical features will include 'steps, stairways, kerbs, exterior surfaces and paving, parking areas, building entrances and exits (including emergency escape routes), internal and external doors, gates, toilet and washing facilities, lighting and ventilation, lifts and escalators, floor coverings, signs, furniture, and temporary or movable items'.

Where an employer occupies premises under a lease preventing that employer from making particular alterations to premises in order to comply with the reasonable adjustments duty, provision is made in *EqA 2010, Sch 21, para 3* (previously *DDA 1995, s 18A*) about the seeking of consent from the lessor, such consent not to be unreasonably withheld. Provision is also made for cases where a binding obligation other than a lease (eg a mortgage or restrictive covenant) prevents a building being altered (*EqA 2010, Sch 21, para 2*, previously *DDA 1995, s 18B(3)*). For further detail, reference should be made to *Appendix 3* of the *EHRC Employment Code* and Chapter 12 of the *DRC Code of Practice*.

3.82 *Auxiliary aid*

Under the *EqA 2010* (but not the *DDA 1995*) the duty to make adjustments also arises where the absence of an auxiliary aid places the disabled person concerned at a comparative substantial disadvantage. The duty is to take such steps as it is reasonable to have to take to provide the auxiliary aid. The *EHRC Employment Code* states at section 6.13 that an auxiliary aid is 'something which provides support or assistance to a disabled person'. The *Code* gives as examples the provision of specialist equipment such as an adapted keyboard or text to speech software.

An 'auxiliary aid' includes an 'auxiliary service': *EqA 2010, s 20(11)*. The *EHRC Employment Code* states at section 6.13 that the term may therefore cover such things as the provision of a sign language interpreter or a support worker for a disabled worker.

There was no reference to auxiliary aids under the employment provisions of the *DDA 1995*. However, the change was introduced to harmonise the position in the employment sphere with the position in other areas, such as goods and services, in relation to which *DDA 1995* explicitly referred to auxiliary aids. It is unlikely to amount to an extension of the law in practice since the under the *DDA 1995* a failure to provide an auxiliary aid could amount to a failure to adjust a PCP or a physical feature of premises and the *DRC Code* included examples of reasonable adjustments such as acquiring or modifying equipment and providing a reader or interpreter. The *Explanatory Notes to the EqA 2010, s 20* state at para 86 that the new definition 'reflects current practice by applying the third requirement [auxiliary aids] explicitly to employment.

3.83 *Substantial disadvantage*

The duty to make adjustments arises only where the provision, criterion or practice or physical feature (or, under the *EqA 2010*, the lack of an auxiliary aid) places the disabled person concerned at a 'substantial disadvantage' by comparison with persons who are not disabled (as to the required comparison, see below.)

The *EqA 2010, s 212* defines 'substantial' as 'more than minor or trivial'. The *DDA 1995* did not contain a definition of 'substantial' but the *DRC Code of Practice* also suggested (*section 5.11*) that a disadvantage is 'substantial' if it is merely 'more than minor or trivial'. It is necessary for an employment tribunal considering a reasonable adjustments claim to identify 'the nature and extent of the substantial disadvantage' suffered by the claimant, bearing in mind that identifying this disadvantage may involve considering the cumulative effect of both 'arrangements' and 'physical features' (ie looking at the overall picture) (*Smiths Detection v Berriman* UKEAT 0712/04/CK).

3.84 *Comparators*

The provision, criterion or practice, or physical feature or (under the *EqA 2010*) the lack of an auxiliary aid) must place the disabled person concerned at a substantial disadvantage 'in comparison with persons who are not disabled'. In reasonable adjustments cases, the comparator should normally be readily identifiable by reference to the disadvantage caused by the relevant arrangements (*Smith v Churchills Stairlifts plc* [2005] EWCA Civ 1220, [2006] ICR 524; *Archibald v Fife Council* [2004] UKHL 32, [2004] IRLR 651). In practice, once the substantial disadvantage has been identified, the identification of a comparator is unlikely to be a significant additional hurdle.

In *Smith* itself, the 'arrangements' at issue were the requirement to carry a full-sized (and heavy) radiator cabinet and/or the fact that the offer of a place on a sales training course was subject to the condition of being able to carry such a cabinet. The claimant was unable to lift the cabinet. The tribunal found as a fact that a majority of the population would have difficulty carrying it any distance and lifting it into a car as required. However, the majority of candidates on the training course were able to lift the cabinet. The disadvantage to the claimant was that he was rejected from the course because of his inability to lift the cabinet. The Court of Appeal held (at para 40) that the proper comparators (identified by reference to the disadvantage) were the six successful candidates who were able to comply with the lifting requirement and/or the nine people who were admitted to the course. The arrangements as a whole clearly placed the claimant at a substantial disadvantage in comparison with these comparators, so the requirement of comparative substantial disadvantage was made out.

The issue was also considered by the EAT in *Fareham College Corpn v Walters* [2009] IRLR 991 in the context of a claim by an employee who had been dismissed following a period of disability-related sick leave and brought a claim for failure to make reasonable adjustments under *DDA 1995*. The EAT held that the comparison exercise required was a general comparative exercise involving a class of non-disabled comparators. Unlike cases of direct discrimination, it was not necessary to identify a comparator whose circumstances were the same as the disabled person. The appropriate comparators were employees who were fit to attend work, not those who had had a similar period of absence for a non-disability-related reason. This approach is mirrored in the *EHRC Employment Code* at *section 6.16*.

3.85 *Adjustments required—examples*

The *EqA 2010* gives limited guidance on what may constitute a reasonable adjustment:

(a) under *s 20(6)*, in cases which relate to the provision of information, the steps which it is reasonable for the employer to take include steps for ensuring that the information is provided in an accessible format;

(b) under *s 20(9)*, in cases relating to physical features, reasonable steps may include removing or altering the physical feature, or providing a means of avoiding it.

In contrast, the *DDA 1995, s 18B(2)* set out a lengthy list of 'examples of steps which [an employer] may need to take in relation to a disabled person in order to comply with a duty to make reasonable adjustments'. This list of examples may still provide helpful guidance in a case under the *EqA 2010* and is now included in the *EHRC Employment Code* (see *section 6.33*):

(a) making adjustments to premises;

(b) allocating some of the disabled person's duties to another person;

(c) transferring him to fill an existing vacancy. (Note that (i) 'transfer' may, subject to reasonableness, include a promotion—*Archibald v Fife Council* [2004] UKHL 32, [2004] IRLR 651 (see **3.80**); (ii) the duty may, again depending on the facts and upon what is reasonable, extend to requiring the creation of a new post in substitution for an existing post—*Southampton City College v Randall* [2006] IRLR 18 at 22, see **3.80**); (iii) the duty may also cover swapping the role of a disabled employee with that of another employee—*Chief Constable of South Yorkshire Police v Jelic* UKEAT/0491/09/CEA.

(d) altering his hours of working or training;

(e) assigning him to a different place of work or training;

(f) allowing him to be absent during working or training hours for rehabilitation, assessment or treatment;

(g) giving, or arranging for, training or mentoring (whether for the disabled person or any other person);

(h) acquiring or modifying equipment;

(i) modifying instructions or reference manuals;

(j) modifying procedures for testing or assessment;

(k) providing a reader or interpreter;

(l) providing supervision or other support.

The *EHRC Employment Code* makes the common sense point (*section 6.34*) that it may sometimes be necessary for an employer to take a combination of steps (previously set out in the *DRC Code* at *section 5.19*). The *EHRC Employment Code* also (at *section 6.33*) identifies the following as other steps which might be required by the reasonable adjustments duty:

- allowing a disabled employee to take a period of disability leave;
- participating in supported employment schemes, such as Workstep;
- employing a support worker to assist a disabled employee;
- modifying disciplinary or grievance procedures;
- adjusting redundancy selection criteria;
- modifying performance-related pay arrangements. (As to the position in relation to sick pay, see *O'Hanlon v Commissioners for HM Revenue & Customs Cmrs* [2007] EWCA Civ 283, [2007] ICR 1359; and **3.92**.)

The *DRC Code* included the following two further examples which are omitted from the *EHRC Employment Code:*

- conducting a proper assessment of what reasonable adjustments may be required. This appears to be an incorrect statement of the law: see the discussion of *Tarbuck v Sainsbury's Supermarkets* [2006] IRLR 664, EAT; *Spence v Intype Libra* UKEAT 0617/06/JOJ and related cases; see **3.88**;
- permitting flexible working. As to homeworking, see *Environment Agency v* : in the circumstances of that case, the EAT expressed doubts as to whether a period of homeworking could constitute a reasonable adjustment;

3.86 *Adjustments to policies and procedures*

The duty to make reasonable adjustments can extend to include the making (in appropriate cases) of adjustments to policies and procedures (eg absence policies or disciplinary procedures) placing a disabled employee at a comparative substantial disadvantage. So, for example, a job applicant with a particular disability who is refused a job because of an employer's policy of making health clearance decisions based on the report of an expert who has not examined the applicant in person might bring a claim for failure to comply with the reasonable adjustments duty on the basis that the employer should have adjusted its policy (by arranging for the expert to examine her in person before reaching a decision): compare *Surrey Police v Marshall* [2002] IRLR 843, EAT, where the original tribunal had found that the reasonable adjustments duty had not arisen and there was no cross-appeal on the point. An adjustment to a dismissal procedure was required by the EAT in *Rothwell v Pelikan Hardcopy Scotland Ltd* [2006] IRLR 24, where it was held (at 23–25) that consultation with the claimant prior to the decision to dismiss would have been a reasonable adjustment (although the EAT in that case did not specify the arrangements or the comparative substantial disadvantage caused thereby). And adjustments to ill health absence procedures were discussed in *O'Hanlon v Commissioners for HM Revenue & Customs*; see **3.92**).

3.87 *Adjustments to 'core' requirements of the job*

The duty to make adjustments extends to the terms, conditions and arrangements relating to the essential functions of a disabled person's employment (as well as to more peripheral matters): see *Archibald v Fife Council* [2004] UKHL 32, [2004] IRLR 651 at 41 (see **3.80**), where the House of Lords identified the following as 'arrangements' placing the employee at a comparative substantial disadvantage and thus potentially requiring adjustment:

(a) the requirement that the employee should at all times be physically fit to do her job as a road sweeper;

(b) the fact that if she was physically unable to do the job she was employed to do she was liable to be dismissed.

Compare *Paterson*, where the EAT held that, in the special circumstances of this case, where a standard akin to a competence standard was required to be met by a probationary police officer, the employer was not required to make reasonable adjustments to certain 'irreducible minimum requirements' of the position.

3.88 *Failure to assess or consult on reasonable adjustments*

There is conflicting case law on the question of whether the reasonable adjustments duty imposes a free-standing duty to assess whether adjustments are necessary or to consult with the employee or obtain information (including medical reports) from him in order to inform the process of considering adjustments. The better (and most recent) view is that a failure to carry out such assessment or consultation is not in itself a breach of the reasonable adjustments duty: *Spence v Intype Libra Ltd* UKEAT 0617/06/2704, following *Tarbuck v Sainsbury's Supermarkets Ltd* [2006] IRLR 664, EAT and *British Gas Services v McCaull* [2001] IRLR 60, EAT and disagreeing with *Mid-Staffordshire General Hospitals NHS Trust v Cambridge* [2003] IRLR 566. That this is the correct approach has been confirmed by the EAT in *Scottish and Southern Energy Plc v Mackay* UKEAT/0075/06/MT, following the *Tarbuck* line of cases for the reasons given in the case of *HM Prison Service v Johnson* UKEAT/0420/06 'unless and until the Court of Appeal rules otherwise'. And see to like effect *London Borough of Camden v Price-Job* UKEAT/0507/06/DM and *EA Gibson Shipbrokers*. This is because the reasonable adjustments duty is a duty to take reasonable steps to prevent the provision (etc) from placing the disabled employee at a comparative substantial disadvantage – but the carrying out of an assessment or the obtaining of a medical report 'does not of itself mitigate or prevent or shield the employee from anything' (*Spence* at 43; see further at 47). (See also *Rowan v Environment Agency* [2008] ICR 218, [2008] IRLR 20, where similar reasoning was applied to a trial period, in that case of homeworking.) The issue is whether the necessary reasonable adjustment has been made: 'whether it is by luck or judgment is immaterial' (*ibid* at 38). The *Spence* principle is, in any event, subject to the following caveats:

(a) a failure to consult with an employee or to assess whether reasonable adjustments are necessary puts the employer at very significant risk of failing to spot that a particular (substantive) adjustment is required and therefore of failing to comply with the reasonable adjustments duty in that respect;

(b) in particular, the mere fact that an employee (or her doctor) has not put forward any particular adjustment for the employer's consideration does not absolve the employer of its reasonable adjustments duty (see *Cosgrove v Caesar & Howie (a firm)* [2001] IRLR 653, EAT, but note that that case predated *Tarbuck v Sainsbury's* and *Spence v Intype Libra*, above, and should be read in the light of those cases);

(c) moreover, a failure to consult prior to dismissal will very often have the consequence of rendering a potentially fair dismissal unfair for the purposes of *Employment Rights Act 1996, s 98*.

3.89 *Reasonableness*

The question for the tribunal (*EqA 2010, s 20*) is whether the step(s) in question is/are step(s) which it is 'reasonable [for the employer] to have to take' in order to avoid the disadvantage. It has been held, in relation to the similar provisions under *DDA 1995, s 4A(1)*, that this is an objective test – the question is what steps it is reasonable for the employer to have to take, not what steps the employer reasonably believes should be taken: see eg *Smith v Churchills Stairlifts plc* [2005] EWCA Civ 1220, [2006] ICR 524 at 44–45 (citing *Collins v Royal National Theatre Board Ltd* [2004] EWCA Civ 144, [2004] IRLR 395 at 20).

3.90 *Factors to be taken into account*

The *EqA 2010* does not list any factors to be taken into account when deciding whether a particular adjustment would be reasonable.

However, *DDA 1995, s 18B(1)* required regard to be had, in particular, to the following in determining whether it is reasonable for an employer to have to take a particular step in order to comply with the reasonable adjustments duty. This list may still provide helpful guidance in a case under the *EqA 2010* and all except (g) are now included in the *EHRC Employment Code* at *section 6.28*:

(a) the extent to which taking the step would prevent the effect in relation to which the duty is imposed (see, eg, *Romec Ltd v Rudham* UKEAT/0069/07/DA (13 July 2007);

(b) the extent to which it is practicable for the employer to take the step;

(c) the financial and other costs which would be incurred by the employer in taking the step and the extent to which taking it would disrupt any of his activities (see, eg, *Murphy v Slough Borough Council* [2005] EWCA Civ 122, [2005] ICR 721);

(d) the extent of the employer's financial and other resources;

(e) the availability to the employer of financial or other assistance with respect to taking the step;

(f) the nature of the employer's activities and the size of his undertaking;

(g) where the step would be taken in relation to a private household, the extent to which taking it would—

    (i) disrupt that household, or

    (ii) disturb any person residing there.

Other factors may additionally be relevant. The *DRC Code of Practice* (*section 5.42*) gave the following additional examples of factors relevant to reasonableness:

- *effect on other employees*. Note in particular that the fact that non-disabled employees would resent the making of adjustments is most unlikely to mean that the employer is not obliged to make them;

- *adjustments made for other disabled employees*. It would often be very difficult to justify a refusal to make an adjustment for one employee when a similar adjustment had previously been made for another working for the same employer;
- *the extent to which the disabled person is willing to co-operate.*

3.91 *Justification*

There is no possibility of justifying a failure to make reasonable adjustments, under either the *EqA 2010* or the *DDA 1995*. (Prior to 1 October 2004, a failure to make reasonable adjustments could be justified under *DDA 1995, s 5(2)(b), (4)*.)

3.92 *Problem areas*

The duty to make reasonable adjustments is a difficult area for employers to deal with, particularly because: (a) it requires more favourable treatment of disabled than non-disabled employees and applicants; and (b) it is unique to disability discrimination. The duty may commonly arise, and cause difficulties, in areas such as:

(a) *Performance-related pay*. See the *EHRC Employment Code* at *section 6.33* (previously *DRC Code*, *section 5.20*), final box, which suggests that a disabled employee paid purely on output should be paid at an agreed rate—eg her average hourly rate—during frequent short additional breaks necessitated by her disability, though whether this is required will ultimately depend (assuming that comparative substantial disadvantage is established) upon whether this is reasonable in all the circumstances. Note that the *DRC* Code stated in the example that it was 'likely' to be a reasonable adjustment, whereas the *EHRC Employment Code* states that it 'may' be a reasonable adjustment. While the courts have not yet grappled with the problem of performance-related pay generally, it seems likely that they will take a fairly robust approach to implementing agreed performance-related pay schemes without modification in individual cases, provided that: (i) all possible reasonable adjustments to enhance the disabled employee's performance level have been made; and (ii) the scheme has been properly applied to the employee's individual circumstances without (for example) the making of any disability-based assumptions. But much will, of course, depend on the particular circumstances of the case and the provisions of the scheme. See, by analogy, the position in relation to sick pay at (c) below.

(b) *Absence monitoring*. See *Royal Liverpool Children's NHS Trust v Dunsby* at **3.60**, where the EAT recognised that it would be rare for an absence procedure to require periods of disability-related absence to be disregarded. As always, the ultimate question will be one of reasonableness in the particular case and once again care should be taken to ensure that: (i) all possible adjustments (eg ensuring adequate rest breaks and/or shorter working hours) have been made to minimise the amount of time off sick taken by the employee; and (ii) that the absence monitoring scheme has been applied to the disabled employee as it is (or would be) applied to non-disabled employees (and without, for example, any assumption that the disabled employee is likely to take more time off or to need closer monitoring).

(c) *Sick pay*. The Court of Appeal in *O'Hanlon v Revenue & Customs Cmrs* (see **3.60**), took a robust approach to this difficult issue, recognising that in many cases an employer will readily be able to justify a refusal to depart from the provisions of an agreed sick pay scheme by making enhanced sick payments to a particular disabled employee.

(d) *Alternative positions for disabled employees*. This issue is particularly likely to arise when an existing employee becomes disabled. As set out above, the duty to make reasonable adjustments may (depending on the facts and circumstances, and subject always to reasonableness) require an employer not only to transfer a disabled employee to an equivalent post but also: (i) to promote her to a higher grade (*Archibald v Fife Council* [2004] UKHL 32, [2004] IRLR 651; see **3.80**); or even (ii) (in particular circumstances, eg when carrying out a re-organisation) to create a post tailored to her needs (*Southampton City College v Randall*; see **3.80**); (iii) the duty may also cover swapping the role of a disabled employee with that of another employee (*Chief Constable of South Yorkshire Police v Jelic* UKEAT/0491/09/CEA).

(e) *Dismissal*: In *Clark v Novacold Ltd* [1999] ICR 951 the Court of Appeal held that dismissal could not amount to a breach of the duty to make reasonable adjustments. Until the decision of the House of Lords in *Malcolm*, this did not have a great impact because claims for disability-related dismissal could be brought as claims for disability-related discrimination. However, the narrowing of disability-related discrimination in *Malcolm* led to a renewed focus on the scope of the duty to make reasonable adjustments. In *Aylott v Stockton-on-Tees Borough Council* [2010] EWCA Civ 910, [2010] IRLR 994 the Court of Appeal expressed the view (although it did not have to decide the point) that in the light of the amendments to the *DDA 1995* to implement the *Framework Directive* the duty to make adjustments under *DDA 1995* had to be read as applying to dismissals (see also *Fareham College Corporation v Walters* [2009] UKEAT/0396/08).

3.93 Harassment

The provisions relating to harassment related to disability are at *EqA 2010, s 26* and *s 40*. These provisions are the same as those relating to harassment related to other protected characteristics, and are therefore discussed at COMMON CONCEPTS **(1)**. Note that *EqA 2010, s 26* is drafted in such a way as to cover any conduct related to disability, whether or not the employee has the disability in question. It therefore covers harassment by association or perception, as well as situations where the unwanted conduct is not directed anyone in particular but nevertheless relates to disability: see the *EHRC Employment Code* at *section 7.10*.

Under the slightly different harassment provisions of *DDA 1995*, an employer subjects a disabled person to harassment where, for a reason which relates to the disabled person's disability, he engages in unwanted conduct which has the purpose or effect of:

(a) violating the disabled person's dignity, or

(b) creating an intimidating, hostile, degrading, humiliating or offensive environment for him (*s 3B(1)*).

By *DDA 1995, s 3B(2)*, conduct is to be regarded as having the effect in (a) or (b) only if, having regard to all the circumstances, including in particular the perception of the disabled person, it should reasonably be considered as having that effect.

Note that the *DDA 1995* should be read so as to cover associative harassment: see *EBR Attridge LLP v Coleman (No 2)* UKEAT/0071/09.

3.94 *Examples*

The following were examples given in the *DRC Code* of behaviour amounting to harassment (see further boxes after *section 4.39*):

- calling a disabled employee by offensive names (whether or not in his presence) with the intention of humiliating him;
- making constant jokes about persons with particular disabilities, or circulating such jokes by e-mail;

- making references to an employee's disability in front of other members of his team, despite his requests not to do so.

3.95 **Compound claims**

The four different claims of discrimination (direct, indirect, discrimination arising from disability and the duty to make reasonable adjustments) are free standing and independent. While it is quite possible for a claimant to bring a disability discrimination claim based on only one type of discrimination, it will be much more common for claims to allege more than one of these (and claims may, of course, additionally allege that there has been harassment (see **3.93**) or victimisation (see **3.96**)).

Historically, direct discrimination has been narrowly interpreted and succeeded relatively infrequently, but the uncertainty over the comparator following the decision of the Court of Appeal in *Aylott v Stockton-on-Tees Borough Council* may lead to the claim being more widely pleaded, given that there is no defence of justification. In addition, discrimination arising from disability is likely to be claimed in all cases where disability-related discrimination was claimed before *Malcolm*. It will also be advisable for a claimant to plead a failure to make reasonable adjustments and in the overwhelming majority of cases under the *EqA 2010*, a claimant will be well advised to plead (and to seek to prove) both indirect discrimination and a failure to make reasonable adjustments. Most cases can be pleaded in both ways (see **3.68**). The only clear exception will be a case where it is plain that the employer did not have (either actual or constructive) knowledge of the employee's disability, so that no reasonable adjustments duty could arise.

It is undoubtedly true that some cases may 'feel' more like indirect discrimination cases, and others more like reasonable adjustments cases. For example, suppose that a disabled employee with arthritis has a slower-than-average typing speed of 20 wpm because of her disability, and consider two cases:

(a) her employer runs a promotion competition for a managerial role but requires applicants to have a typing speed of 50 wpm in order to be eligible;

(b) the employee requires a special keyboard in order to be able to type without suffering pain, and her employer fails to provide this.

Case (a) might be more naturally categorised as an indirect discrimination case and case (b) as a reasonable adjustments case. But:

(i) case (a) could be pleaded as a reasonable adjustments case, on the basis that the 50 wpm requirement placed the employee at a substantial comparative disadvantage and should therefore have been modified in her case;

(ii) in case (b), if the failure to provide the keyboard led to reduced performance and, thus, to a failure to receive performance-related pay or to achieve promotion (or, indeed, to dismissal), then an indirect discrimination claim might be pleaded and proved.

3.96 **OTHER UNLAWFUL ACTS**

Victimisation

As with all of the other discrimination strands, it is unlawful for an employer to subject a person to a detriment because that person performed a 'protected act' or is believed or suspected of doing or intending to do a protected act (*EqA 2010, s 39(3), 39(4)*). For general principles, see **1.100** ff. This replaces similar provisions in *DDA 1995, s 55*.

Unlike protection from disability discrimination and harassment, victimisation applies to both disabled and non-disabled persons. Both groups are also protected against victimisation from a former employer once their employment has come to an end (see COMMON CONCEPTS (1)).

3.97 Discussions about pay

EqA 2010, s 77 makes contractual pay secrecy clauses unenforceable to the extent that they prevent employees from making relevant pay disclosures, that is, a disclosure that is sought or made for the purpose of finding out whether (or to what extent) any difference in pay is related to a protected characteristic (EqA 2010, s 77(3)). Action taken by an employer as a result of an individual making or seeking to make a relevant pay disclosure, or receiving information disclosed in a relevant pay disclosure, may amount to victimisation. (See COMMON CONCEPTS (1).)

3.98 Discriminatory advertisements

Under *DDA 1995, s 16B*, there were express provisions making it unlawful for a person to publish or cause to be published an advertisement inviting applications for (amongst other things) employment, promotion or transfer of employment if it indicates or might reasonably be understood to indicate that an application will or may be determined by reference to:

(a) the applicant not having a disability or any particular disability;

(b) the applicant not having had any disability or any particular disability; or

(c) any reluctance of the persons determining the application to comply with a duty to make reasonable adjustments.

Claims in relation to discriminatory advertisements could not be brought by an individual but only by the EHRC (*EqA 2006, s 25(1)(c)*).

These express provisions were repealed by *EqA 2010*. The government took the view that discriminatory advertisements would be caught by other parts of *EqA 2010*, and so no express provisions were required *(Explanatory Notes to the EqA 2010, note 1024*). The EHRC has broad powers to bring proceedings for contraventions of *EqA 2010* under the amended *EqA 2006* (*s 24A*).

The *EHRC Employment Code, sections 16.19–16.31* sets out detailed guidance with regard to arrangements for advertising and the content of the advertisement. For example, it states that a job advertisement should accurately reflect the requirements of the job and should not include wording which suggests that reasonable adjustments will not be made or that disabled people will be discriminated against, or should not bother applying (*section 16.26*).

Under *EqA 2010, s 13(3)* employers are allowed to positively discriminate in favour of disabled people. Therefore *EqA 2010* does not make it unlawful for an employer to try to attract disabled candidates, and this is supported by *EHRC Employment Code, sections 3.35* and *16.28*. Therefore, a job advertisement can include wording such as that the employer 'would welcome applications from disabled people'. (As set out above, the disability discrimination provisions, unlike other discrimination strands, operate asymmetrically in that they do not prohibit discrimination against non-disabled people—so that an employer may not only advertise for but actually appoint a disabled candidate in preference to a non-disabled candidate, subject always to other legal requirements—see **3.43**.)

3.99 Pre-employment health enquiries

In a provision with no equivalent under *DDA 1995*, *EqA 2010, s 60* makes it unlawful for employers or anyone to whom an application for work is made to ask about the health of the applicant for work either: (i) before offering work to that person; or (ii) where the employer is not in a position to offer work to that person, before including them in a pool of applicants from whom it is intended to select a person to whom to offer work (*EqA 2010, s 60(1)*).

3.100 *What is a question about a person's health?*

In many cases, it will of course be obvious whether a question is about the health of an individual. Sometimes, it might be less clear cut, such as questions about sickness absence in the applicant's current or previous employment. The *EHRC Employment Code* states that questions relating to previous sickness absence are questions that relate to disability or health. It remains to be seen whether employment tribunals will decide that a question about the level of absence *for any reason* will be questions about the applicant's health, although caution should in any case be exercised in asking such a question unless there is a specific relevance to the role to be filled since the answer could encumber the employer with irrelevant information it may later be accused of having unlawfully taken into account.

For the purposes of *EqA 2010, s 60* whether or not a person has a disability is an aspect of that person's health and therefore questions about a whether a person has a disability will be questions about their health.

3.101 *Conditional offers*

It is important to note that it is expressly provided that an offer of work may be a conditional or unconditional offer of employment (*EqA 2010, s 60(10)*). It therefore remains permissible to make an offer of employment which is conditional on the satisfactory completion of a medical or answers to a medical questionnaire. Of course, employers will still need to be careful not to discriminate against disabled persons on the basis of information provided even after an offer has been made. Employers should continue to consider whether it is reasonably necessary, taking into account the demands and importance of the role being filled, to require the completion of a medical or health questionnaire. Employers should also bear in mind their duties under the *Data Protection Act 1998* in deciding what information to collect and what to do with it. Information about an employee's health is likely to be 'sensitive personal data' for these purposes (see Employment Practices Data Protection Code for guidance on collecting and retaining information as part of the recruitment process).

It should be noted that *EqA 2010, s 60* does not specifically provide that the inclusion of a person in a pool from whom the employer intends to select a person to whom to offer work may be conditional although it may be assumed that it is permissible to inform applicants that any subsequent offer of work, once in the pool, may be conditional on satisfactory medical reports or questionnaires.

3.102 *Exceptions*

The general prohibition on questions set out above does not apply to questions which are necessary for one of the following purposes (*EqA 2010, s 60(6)*):

(a) establishing whether the relevant applicant will be able to comply with a requirement to undergo an assessment or establishing whether a duty to make reasonable adjustments is or will be imposed on the employer in relation to the applicant in connection with a requirement to undergo an assessment

It appears that this exception applies only in the context of assessments undertaken for the purposes of the recruitment process and is not of wider application although the answers to the questions may of course provide employers with information from which it may be apparent that reasonable adjustments may be required if the applicant is successful. The *EHRC Employment Code* states that questions about reasonable adjustments needed for the job itself should not be asked until after the offer of employment has been made, unless they relate to a function which is intrinsic to the job (see below).

(b) establishing whether the applicant will be able to carry out a function that is intrinsic to the work concerned

The precise meaning of 'intrinsic' in this context remains to be seen, but it is likely that it will represent a relatively high threshold and that this exception will apply only to functions which are essential elements of the relevant role. Where the employer reasonably believes that it would be subject to a duty to make reasonable adjustments in relation to the applicant in connection with the work, the reference to a 'function that is intrinsic to the work' must be interpreted as a reference to a function that would be intrinsic once the duty to make reasonable adjustments had been complied with (*s 60(7)*). This means that before an enquiry relating to disability or health can be made under this exception, an analysis must be carried out as to whether the function to which the enquiry would be relevant, could be, for example, modified or allocated to another employee.

One approach for an employer which believes that any function applicable to a role to be filled is intrinsic may be to describe the requirements of the relevant intrinsic function and ask the applicant whether they are subject to any disability or other health condition which would mean they are unable to carry out that function, making it clear that any reasonable adjustments will be made. Employers should in general avoid making assumptions that particular disabilities or conditions would prevent an applicant from carrying out any relevant function, unless in the circumstances that fact is beyond doubt.

(c) monitoring diversity in the range of persons applying to A for work,

This means that it remains permissible to ask for information on a voluntary basis for the purpose of monitoring the diversity of those applying for work. The *EHRC Employment Code* contains good practice guidance in *Chapter 18* and *Appendix 2*.

(d) taking positive action permitted under *s 158*:

It is logical that an employer who wishes to implement measures with positive action aims permitted under *EqA 2010, s 158* (see **1.159**) must be able to enquire about whether a particular applicant has a disability. The EHRC Employment Code gives the example of offering guaranteed interviews where a disabled person meets the essential requirements of the job, but also states that the purpose of the question should be made clear before it is asked.

(e) occupational requirements

Assuming that it is an occupational requirement of a particular role for the successful applicant to have a specific impairment the employer may ask about a person's health or disability to establish that the applicant has that impairment.

A general comment in relation to each of the above exceptions is that the question must be 'necessary' for the relevant purpose. Although the meaning of necessary in this context is not entirely clear, it may be expected that it will be given a narrow meaning.

3.103 *Effect of breaching s 60*

An individual who has been asked about their health in breach of the provisions of *EqA 2010, s 60* cannot bring a standalone claim against the relevant employer. There are two main effects of health questions being asked.

First, the breach would be enforceable by the EHRC as an unlawful act under *EqA 2006, Part 1*. An employee can complain to the EHRC, who can exercise their enforcement powers under *EqA 2006, Part 1*. The EHRC has the power to investigate whether an unlawful act has been committed (*EqA 2006, s 20(1)*), and issue an unlawful act notice if it is satisfied an unlawful act has been committed (*EqA 2006, s 216*). The notice may require the employer to prepare an action plan or recommend action to be taken (*EqA 2006, s 21(4)*).

Second, where an applicant for work argues that the potential employer's conduct was 'in reliance on information given in response to' a prohibited health question, the burden of proof will automatically shift to the employer to show that no direct discrimination took place (*EqA 2010, s 60(4), (5)*). It should be noted that this will only have an effect on direct discrimination claims and not other types of disability discrimination claim. Of course, even if the burden of proof shifts, it remains open to the employer to prove that the reason for the conduct complained of was not the disability of the claimant but some other reason, such as having received applications from better qualified individuals. This reinforces the benefit of keeping proper records of the reason for recruitment decisions.

3.104 Instructions and pressure to discriminate

Under *EqA 2010, s 111* it is unlawful for a person to instruct, induce or cause another to do anything which contravenes *EqA 2010*, where the people are in a relationship (eg employment relationship) in which discrimination, harassment or victimisation is prohibited (*s 111(7)*). Such instructions would be unlawful even if they were not acted on. There were similar provisions under *DDA 1995 (s 16C)*.

The EHRC has the right to bring proceedings against the guilty party regardless of whether an individual has actually experienced a detriment (*s 111(5)(c)*). In addition, both the person instructed and the intended victim of the discriminatory instruction can bring proceedings if they suffer a detriment, even where the instruction is not carried out (*s 111(5)(a), (5)(b), (6)*). (See **Common concepts (1)**.)

3.105 Liability of employers and principals for the unlawful acts of others and personal liability of employees and agents

Employees

Anything done by a person during the course of their employment is treated for the purposes of *EqA 2010* as also done by their employer, whether or not it was done with the employer's knowledge or consent (*ss 109(1), 109(3)*). This replaces provisions to similar effect in *DDA 1995, s 58*. 'In the course of employment' has a wide meaning to include acts in the workplace and may extend to circumstances outside of the workplace such as work related social functions, business trips abroad, etc. However, the employer will have a defence if it can show that it took 'all reasonable steps' to prevent such actions (*s 109(4)*). The employee will also be personally liable for their acts, even if the employer can establish the defence unless he reasonably acted in reliance on a statement by his employer that his actions were not a contravention of *EqA 2010*. For further information on liability of employers and principals see **Common concepts (1)**.

3.106 *Agents*

Employers who act through agents are liable for their agents' actions where such actions are done with the authority of the employer (*EqA 2010, s 109(2)*). It does not matter whether the employer knows about or approves of their agent's actions (*EqA 2010, s 109(3)*). 'With the authority of' is to be given a broad meaning, and an agent would be considered to be acting with the employer's authority if the employer consents (whether expressly or impliedly) to the agent acting on their behalf. For example, an employer may be liable for the acts of a contractor or consultant who discriminates or harasses an employee contrary to *EqA 2010*. The agent will also be personally liable for their acts, even if the employer can establish the defence unless he reasonably acted in reliance on a statement by his principal that his actions were not a contravention of *EqA 2010*. This replaces provisions to similar effect in *DDA 1995, s 58(2)*. For further information on liability for unlawful act of an agent, see COMMON CONCEPTS (1).

3.107 Aiding unlawful acts

A person must not knowingly help another person to do an unlawful act under *EqA 2010 (s 112)*. A person who helps another in this way will be treated as having done the unlawful act. The *EHRC Employment Code* (*section 9.27*) gives the example of a junior employee who looks at the HR files of job applicants because his manager wants to know the sex of the applicants so that he can find a pretext to reject the male candidates. In this scenario, in addition to the employer's (and manager's) liability for the unlawful act, the junior employee could be liable for aiding the employer (and manager) to discriminate under *s 112*. See COMMON CONCEPTS (1).

3.108 *False or misleading statements*

An employee or agent who is liable for aiding an unlawful act may have a defence if they can show that they acted in reliance on a statement made by their employer or principal that the act in question was not unlawful, and it was reasonable for them to rely on the statement (*EqA 2010, s 112(2)*, previously in *DDA 1995, s 57(3)*). Where a person knowingly or recklessly makes such a statement that is materially false or misleading they are guilty of a criminal offence and liable on summary conviction to a fine not exceeding level 5 (*s 112(3), (4)*).

3.109 IN PRACTICE

General

The EHRC states on its website that it 'aims to create a society in which all disabled people have real freedom and opportunity to participate fully and contribute to society as equal citizens'.

The potential benefits of avoiding disability discrimination and harassment, aside from legal obligations, may include making an employer's workforce more representative of the community; attracting and keeping able staff; not undervaluing, under-using or losing able staff; and improving staff morale and productivity.

3.110 *Practical steps on how to avoid discrimination*

The *EHRC Employment Code* (like the *DRC Code* before it) has a number of good practice suggestions for avoiding discrimination. Although the aim of these suggestions is to avoid discrimination in the first place, in many instances having undertaken these steps will also aid an employer in defending any discrimination claims. (Note further that in the case of an employer which is also a public authority, the general duty to promote equality and the specific duties, including the duty to prepare and implement a Disability Equality Scheme, in the *Disability Discrimination (Public Authorities) (Statutory Duties) Regulations 2005*, made under *DDA 1995, s 49D*, will in addition be relevant in this area. The duties are to be replaced by *EqA 2010, s 149* which is expected to come into force in April 2011, but the detailed requirements of those duties are beyond the scope of this work).

(a) Implementing equality policies and practice in the workplace: There is no statutory requirement for an employer to put in place an equality policy. However, the implementation of a policy will help to avoid discrimination, is good evidence that an employer is taking its responsibilities seriously and may (in certain circumstances) provide a defence to claims of discrimination against it (see **3.105** and **3.106**). The *EHRC Employment Code, section 18.12* suggests that all employers should take the following steps to implement an equality policy:

(i) audit existing policies and procedures;

(ii) ensure the policy is promoted and communicated to all job applicants and workers and agents of the employer; and

(iii) monitor and review the policy.

The *DRC Code* had set out additional recommendations specifically directed at preventing disability discrimination:

(i) address acts of disability discrimination by employees as part of disciplinary rules and procedures;

(ii) have complaints and grievance procedures which are easy for disabled employees to use and which are designed to resolve issues effectively;

(iii) have clear procedures to prevent and deal with harassment for a reason related to a person's disability;

(iv) establish a policy in relation to disability-related leave, and monitor the implementation and effectiveness of such a policy;

(v) consult with disabled employees about their experiences of working for the organisation;

(vi) regularly review the effectiveness of reasonable adjustments made for disabled people in accordance with *DDA 1995* (and act on the findings of those reviews);

(vii) keep clear records of decisions taken in respect of the above matters.

(b) Promotion and communication of an equality policy: The policy should be promoted and communicated as widely as possible; this will assist the employer in demonstrating that they have taken all reasonable steps to prevent discrimination within the workplace. *EHRC Employment Code* suggests a number of ways of communication to promote the policy including: training; intranet and/or website; team meetings; handbooks; email bulletins; circulars, newsletters; induction packs; annual reports; office notice boards; cascade systems.

The promotion and communication of a policy should not be a one-off event. *EHRC Employment Code, section 18.16* recommends that employers periodically provide reminders and updates to its staff.

EHRC Employment Code, section 18.17 states that the policy should have the explicit backing of people in senior positions. Senior management should ensure that the policy is implemented, resourced, monitored and reviewed and its effectiveness is regularly reported.

Employers should ensure that all workers and agents understand the policy by providing them with regular training. The training should ensure that training on the policy covers: all protected characteristics and prohibited conduct; what is and what is not acceptable conduct; risk of condoning or seeming to approve inappropriate behaviour and personal liability; the equality monitoring process.

(c) Monitoring and reviewing an equality policy: Monitoring the policy allows an employer to ascertain whether its policy is working. The employer should use monitoring to establish whether the policy is effective; analyse the effect of the policy on different groups (eg disabled employees) and highlight inequalities; set targets and timetables for reducing discrepancies.

EHRC Employment Code, section 18.32 recommends that equality policies are kept under regular review (at least annually) and to consider workers' needs as part of the review process. The review process can help employers to consider and anticipate the needs of disabled workers.

3.111 Applicants for employment

It is unlawful for an employer to discriminate against a job applicant on the grounds of the applicant's disability in the following ways:

(a) in the arrangements which he makes for the purpose of determining to whom he should offer employment (*EqA 2010, s 39(1)(a)*);

(b) in the terms on which he offers that person employment (*s 39(1)(b)*); or

(c) by refusing to offer or deliberately not offering the applicant employment (*s 39(1)(c)*).

EqA 2010, s 39, replacing *DDA 1995, s 4.*

3.112 *Arrangements made for the purpose of determining to whom he should make an offer*

For the purposes of *EqA 2010*, 'arrangements' has a wide meaning that covers all aspects of the recruitment process, from specifying the job and advertising it, to the process of assessing candidates, interview and selection. See generally *EHRC Employment Code, Chapter 16.*

(a) *Advertisements*: see **3.98** and *EHRC Employment Code, sections 16.19–16.31.*

(b) *Application forms:* The *EHRC Employment Code, sections 16.32–16.38* explains that an employer must not discriminate through the application process. Best practice is for the employer to take a standard approach to the process, in order that the employer can make an objective assessment of an applicant's ability to do the job. However, a standardised approach does not preclude the employer from making reasonable adjustments or asking whether reasonable adjustments need to be made for the interview process. The *EHRC Employment Code* goes on to explain that where an employer provides information about a job, it is likely to be a reasonable adjustment for it to provide, on request, information in a format accessible to a disabled applicant, eg email, Braille, large print, audio tape or computer disc. It is also likely to be a reasonable adjustment to allow an applicant to submit an application which contains necessary information in alternative accessible formats.

(c) *Qualifications (EHRC Employment Code, section 16.14)*: An employer is entitled to require applicants to have certain qualifications. However, these must be justified and necessary or desirable. The qualification must be relevant and significant for the purposes of the job and the particular applicant and there should be no reasonable adjustment which would change this. An example given under the *DRC Code* is that an employer requiring two GCSEs would be unable to justify rejecting an applicant whose dyslexia precluded this if she could show that she had expertise required for the job in some other way. *EHRC Employment Code* advises that reference is made to 'equivalent qualifications' or to 'equivalent levels of skill or knowledge'.

(d) *Job (or person) specifications (EHRC Employment Code, sections 16.10–16.15*): Including unnecessary or marginal requirements in a job description or person specification can be discriminatory, eg requiring an applicant to be 'energetic' where the job is actually sedentary may unjustifiably exclude applicants whose disabilities result in them tiring more easily (*EHRC Employment Code*, section *16.13*). Clear job descriptions should set out the fundamental elements of the job to be advertised.

Job descriptions should also avoid blanket exclusions, such as would occur (for example) if an employer were to stipulate that candidates must have no history of mental illness, believing that such candidates will have poor attendance. If that employer then rejects an applicant solely because they have had a mental illness, without checking the individual's actual attendance record, this will amount to unlawful direct disability discrimination. However, where possible the description should include all intrinsic/fundamental aspects of the job to demonstrate to the applicant what the requirements of the role are (see **3.102**).

(e) *Short-listing* (*EHRC Employment Code, section 16.50*): The *EHRC Employment Code* recommends guidelines for short-listing candidates to reduce the possibility of unlawful discrimination and avoid adverse inferences being made by an employment tribunal where a claim is brought by an unsuccessful applicant. The guidelines include:

(i) where possible, more than one person should be involved in short listing.

(ii) the marking system should be agreed before applications are assessed and applied consistently,

(iii) those involved in short listing should make applications separately and then compare and agree a final mark.

(iv) selection should be based only on information provided in the application form, CV or, for internal candidates, formal performance assessment reports.

(v) weight given to each criterion should not be changed during short listing.

Some employers use a guaranteed interview scheme, allowing disabled applicants to be automatically short listed for interview if they demonstrate they can meet the minimum criteria for getting the job. *EqA 2010, s 60(6)(d)* allows a question to be asked at the application stage to identify disabled applicants who want to use the scheme (*EHRC Employment Code, section 16.51*).

(f) *Interviews* (*EHRC Employment Code, sections 16.57–16.64*): Where an employer is aware, or could reasonably be expected to be aware, that an applicant or potential applicant has a disability which is likely to place him at a substantial disadvantage in the employer's existing interview practices and procedures, the employer may be required to make reasonable adjustments (*EHRC Employment Code, section 16.59*) to accommodate the applicant. This might include allowing an applicant to bring a helper to an interview to assist when answering questions that are not part of the assessment (*DRC Code, section 7.22*).

The *EHRC Employment Code, section 16.59*, provides that it is good practice to allow an applicant to indicate any relevant effects of a disability and to suggest adjustments to help overcome any disadvantage the disability may cause at interview. This mirrors the guidance given under *DDA 1995*. However, the EAT in *Ridout v TC Group* [1998] IRLR 628, EAT stated that not too great a burden should be placed on the employer to require them to question job applicants in great detail about their disability. In this instance Ridout applied for a position with TC Group indicating on her application form that she had photosensitive epilepsy. At the interview, R said that the lighting in the interview room might cause her a problem, but that if it became an issue, she had her sunglasses with her. She did not put her sunglasses on during the interview and did not complain about the lighting. Her job application failed and she claimed that TC Group had failed to make reasonable adjustments for the interview. The EAT held that the duty to make reasonable adjustments must be assessed on the basis of what employers can reasonably be expected to do when faced with circumstances requiring detailed investigations into the effects of a rare type of disability without help from the individual telling them what her needs were. The EAT went on to say that if Ridout had informed TC Group of her needs prior to the interview, it might have been required to have done more to facilitate her.

EqA 2010 has prohibited employers from asking candidates health related questions during the interview process (*s 60*) (see **3.99** for further details).

(g) *Selection tests, assessment centres and aptitude tests* (*EHRC Employment Code, sections 16.52–16.56*): Such tests should only be used where they're well designed, properly administered and professionally validated and a reliable source for predicting an applicant's performance of a particular job. The test should not be used where it leads to indirect discrimination or discrimination arising from disability unless it can be objectively justified and employers will need to consider whether to make reasonable adjustments to assist disabled applicants.

3.113 *The terms on which he offers that person employment*

A disabled employee should not be offered terms and conditions of employment that are less favourable than those offered to other people (*EqA 2010, s 39(1)(b)*). For example, offering a person with a history of depression a six-month probationary period, even though other employees are only offered a three-month probationary period will amount to direct discrimination (*EHRC Employment Code, section 16.69*).

3.114 *Not offering employment*

It is unlawful for an employer to discriminate against a disabled applicant by not offering employment to them without justification (*EqA 2010, s 39(1)(c)*). This replaces a provision to similar effect in *DDA 1995, s 4(1)(c)*. The employer should not make assumptions about the applicant's capabilities to do the job or its own ability to make reasonable adjustments to accommodate his needs.

3.115 Discrimination against employees

It is unlawful for an employer to discriminate against a disabled employee:

(a) in the terms of employment which the employer affords the employee (*EqA 2010, s 39(2)(a)*);

(b) in the opportunities the employer affords (or does not afford) the employee for promotion, a transfer, training or receiving any other benefit, facility or service (s *39(2)(b)*);

(c) by dismissing the employee (*s 39(2)(c)*); or

(d) by subjecting the employee to any other detriment (*s 39(2)(d)*).

This replaces similar provisions in *DDA 1995, s 4(2)*. In fact, *DDA 1995* also referred to not affording the employee an opportunity of the type referred to in (b) above (*DDA 1995, s 4(2)(c)*) but the removal of this reference is not intended to limit the scope of the protection (see *Explanatory Notes to the EqA 2010, section 39*).

3.116 *Terms and conditions of employment*

Disabled employees should not be discriminated against in relation to their terms and conditions of employment. Employers will need to consider what reasonable adjustments, if any, need to be made to a disabled employee's terms and conditions. These may include, for example, varying the contractual working hours of an employee who cannot travel on public transport during peak hours because of a disability.

Prior to 1 October 2004 the *Disability Discrimination (Employment) Regulations 1996 (SI 1996/1456)* ('*Employment Regulations*') prevented employers from being liable for disability discrimination in relation to most performance-related pay (PRP) schemes. The *Employment*

Regulations provided that as long as a PRP scheme applied to all employees, or to a class of employees which included a disabled person, then disability-related less favourable treatment in relation to the scheme would be deemed to be justified. Further, such schemes would not place disabled people at a substantial disadvantage (so there would be no duty to make reasonable adjustments). The *Employment Regulations* were revoked from 1 October 2004 and the provisions related to PRP schemes were not replaced. As a result, PRP schemes can frequently prove difficult for employers to manage in relation to disabled employees. If, for example, in relation to a performance-related bonus, an employee fails to achieve the targets set for them in the usual manner, but the reason for this failure is disability-related absence, this could give rise to a claim of discrimination arising from disability, indirect discrimination, and failure to make a reasonable adjustment to the scheme. The employer will have to decide whether to pay a bonus and, if so, at what level. The robust approach taken in the sick pay cases under *DDA 1995* (see **3.60**) may provide some comfort to employers in these circumstances, but much will depend on the circumstances of the case and the provisions of the scheme going forward under *EqA 2010*.

3.117 *Induction, training and development*

Employers must ensure that arrangements for induction, training and development do not disadvantage disabled employees. For example, materials provided during induction to new employees may, following discussion with the employee, need to be provided in Braille, or made available via a computer equipped with a voice synthesiser or speech-enabled applications, to a blind employee.

Employers should avoid making assumptions about disabled employees' suitability for, or willingness to attend, training sessions. Reasonable adjustments may need to be made to enable disabled employees to attend. For example, an employee with severe dyslexia may require the trainer to talk them through certain aspects of written training materials, or audio-visual materials may need to be provided with subtitles in the case of a deaf employee.

3.118 *Promotion, transfer and benefits*

Employees must not be treated less favourably on the grounds of a disability, or for a reason related to disability, in relation to decisions on promotions, access to opportunities for promotion, transfers, training and any other benefit, facility or service as well as the practical arrangements made in relation to them (*EqA 2010, s 39(2), (4)*).

An employer should evaluate whether the key skills he has determined as a requirement for a vacancy are really necessary. If a disabled employee applies, but would be unable to carry out a small part of that role due to a disability, it might well be reasonable for the employer to consider whether training would help or whether that part could be reallocated to another employee.

Employers should be careful about making assumptions in respect of a disabled employee's suitability for more senior roles. For example, an employer should not simply assume that an employee suffering from depression would not be capable of carrying out a manager's role without basing this opinion on medical evidence.

3.119 *Benefits*

Benefits, in this context, means any benefits, facilities or services which an employer provides to its employees in connection with their employment and would include items commonly thought of as benefits, such as permanent health insurance, but also car parking spaces and access to a staff restaurant or self-service refreshments. In general, benefits will be widely construed, although in most circumstances it does not include benefits which the employer is in the business of providing to the public (see **Common concepts (1)**).

If a disabled employee is unable to take advantage of a facility provided by an employer to its employees and the reason for this relates to that employee's disability, the employer must consider whether there are any reasonable adjustments which might remove this barrier. For example, an employer may need to make modifications for an employee in a wheelchair to access the staff restaurant.

Assumptions should not be made about disabled employees' willingness to participate in social events connected with work, or client entertainment events.

3.120 *Managing disability*

An employer must not discriminate against an employee who becomes disabled during employment, or whose disability worsens. If the employee's condition alters during employment, the employer may need to re-evaluate the need to make reasonable adjustments and consider whether any adjustments already in place remain appropriate. The primary objective of the employer, at least to begin with, should be to consider whether any adjustments can be made to enable the employee to remain in their original role. If that is not possible, then the employer should first consider alternative roles, including adjustments to such a role, before considering termination of the disabled employee's employment. The employee's eligibility under any benefit schemes, such as permanent health insurance or ill health early retirement, should also be considered before dismissing.

If possible, the employer should discuss the employee's needs with the employee and, in relation to progressive conditions, what the effect on the employee's ability to carry out the role in the future will or may be, so that the employer can consider and plan future reasonable adjustments. An occupational health practitioner or other suitable specialist may need to be involved, particularly where an employee is returning from a period of absence. An employer may need to consider rearranging working methods or allocating any minor parts of the disabled employee's role to another employee.

The *EHRC Employment Code* recommends that when an employer is seeking to determine what reasonable adjustments to put in place to allow the employment of a disabled person, they may want to consider the advice available from Jobcentre Plus through the Access to Work scheme (section 6.36–6.39). The purpose of the Access to Work scheme is the provision of practical support to disabled people in, or entering into, paid employment to help overcome work-related obstacles resulting from disability. The Access to Work scheme can provide a grant towards these additional employment costs, although this is not automatic. It may well be a reasonable step for the employer to assist a disabled person in making an application for assistance from the Access to Work scheme and for the employer to provide ongoing administrative support (by completing claim forms, for example).

The new 'fit notes' allow an employee's GP to recommend reasonable adjustments where an employee is able to return to work. These should be considered carefully by an employer but the employer does not necessarily need to make the adjustments. The employee's GP will not have full information about the work place and the adjustments might not be practicable. Equally, comments on a fit note will not absolve an employer from considering whether other adjustments are also needed.

In appropriate cases, employers should also consider seeking expert advice on the extent of a disabled person's capabilities and what might be done to change premises or working arrangements. Where an employee has been off work, a phased return might be appropriate. In addition, an appropriate specialist will be able to offer an opinion on the employee's fitness to return to work; which of the employee's usual tasks should be avoided and for how long; and what adjustments can be made to the employee's physical workplace and other working conditions to facilitate the employee's return to work.

An employer cannot apply to a medical practitioner who has clinical care of an employee for a copy of a medical report about the employee without the employee's consent (*Access to Medical Reports Act 1988, s 3(1)*). Further, the employee must be informed that he has the right to withhold his consent and request to see the report supplied in response to the employer's application before it is provided to the employer (*s 4(1)*). If the employee exercises his right to see the report, the practitioner must not supply the report to the employer until the employee has provided his consent for that to be done (*s 5(1)*). The employee can also request that amendments are made to parts of the report that the employee considers to be incorrect or misleading (*s 5(2)*), and if the practitioner is not prepared to make such amendments, the employee can require the practitioner to attach to the report a statement of the employee's views in respect of the parts of the report which the practitioner is declining to amend (*s 5(2)(b)*).

The *Access to Medical Reports Act 1988* only applies to medical practitioners who have 'clinical care' of an employee, so might not apply to a report from an occupational health adviser or specialist appointed by the employer to prepare a report. However, the General Medical Counsel ('GMC') guidance on confidentiality, which applies to all practitioners registered with the GMC, requires doctors to have seen written consent before disclosing information to their employer and to give the patient the opportunity to review any report before it is provided to the employer.

Medical information relating to employees will almost certainly constitute sensitive personal data within the meaning of *DPA 1998*, and an employer must therefore ensure that one of the relevant conditions set out in *DPA 1998, Sch 3* is fulfilled. Where the employee has given his specific informed consent this will be sufficient, but employers must be certain that all uses they make of the medical information are covered by the wording of the consent.

Many contracts of employment contain provisions allowing the employer to require that the employee attends a medical examination with a doctor chosen by the employer. This can prove a useful provision for an employer, particularly where an employee is unwilling to co-operate or the employer for whatever reason wishes to obtain a second opinion having received a report from the employee's GP.

3.121 *Termination*

Direct discrimination can occur if an employee is dismissed or selected for redundancy on the ground of their disability. If a dismissal decision is made for a reason that arises in consequence of disabled employee's disability (other than the disability itself) there will be discrimination arising from a disability unless the employer can show that it is objectively justified. The duty to make reasonable adjustments applies to dismissals as to other arrangements and dismissals could give rise to a claim of indirect discrimination in some cases.

Where an employer is required to set redundancy selection criteria, the employer must consider whether any proposed criteria could disadvantage disabled employees. If so, the employer should consider whether any adjustments could reduce or remove that impact. The *EHRC Employment Code* (*section 19.17*) gives the example of a redundancy procedure which uses attendance records as a selection criterion. It may well be a reasonable adjustment to discount disability-related sickness absence under those circumstances.

3.122 Discrimination against former employees

As a result of the House of Lords' finding in *Relaxion Group plc v Rhys-Harper* [2003] UKHL 33, [2003] 4 All ER 1113 that discrimination on the grounds of sex, race or disability can be unlawful where it occurs after the termination, *DDA 1995* was amended with effect from 1 October 2004 to prohibit post-employment discrimination. *EqA 2010 (s 108)* now makes it unlawful for a former employer to discriminate against or harass a former employee on the grounds of his disability if the discrimination or harassment arises out of and is closely connected to the employment. 'Closely connected to' is not defined in *EqA 2010* but will be a matter of degree to be judged on a case by case basis. For example, it would be unlawful to refuse to provide a reference or provide a poor reference for a former employee on the grounds of the person's disability (although a blanket policy of refusing to provide references to former employees could not normally be impugned, unless perhaps an argument could be made that the policy placed a particular person at a comparative substantial disadvantage and thus required adjustment).

A former employer may also be under a duty to make reasonable adjustments where a provision, criterion or practice applied to the disabled person in relation to matters arising out of his former employment; or any physical feature of premises occupied by a former employer, places the disabled ex-employee at a substantial disadvantage compared to those who are not disabled (*EqA 2010, s 108(4)*, previously *DDA 1995, s 16A*). For example, if a former employee is a member of a work social club and that person can no longer access the building because of a disability, once the former employer is aware of this, it will need to consider reasonable adjustments (*EHRC Employment Code, section 10.60*).

However, the duty imposed under *s 108(4)* will not apply if the employer did not know and could not have reasonably known that the disabled person has a disability and is likely to be affected as mentioned above (*EqA 2010, Sch 8, Part 3, para 20*) (see **3.79**).

3.123 **Exceptions**

Individuals excluded from DDA protection

The 2004 amendments to *DDA 1995* to implement the *Framework Directive* significantly increased the scope of the *DDA*'s coverage (not least by abolishing the 'small employers' exception previously found in *s 7*: see the *2003 Regulations, reg 7*) and this broad coverage is continued in *EqA 2010*. Individuals are, however, be excluded from protection in the following cases:

(a) *Overseas Employment*. The prohibition on discrimination by employers in *DDA 1995, s 4* applied 'only in relation to employment at an establishment in Great Britain'. (Similar provision were made in *s 4B(8)* in relation to contract workers; note that other provisions of *Part II* were not explicitly made subject to such territorial limitations.) This express restriction has been removed from *EqA 2010* which does not include any express territorial limitation. It will therefore be left to tribunals to determined who can, in practice, bring a claim. See **1.42**ff for a discussion of the tests under *DDA 1995* and the likely position under *EqA 2010*.

(b) *Armed forces*. Under *EqA 2010, Sch 9, para 4* the provisions of *EqA 2010, Part V ('Work')* do not apply to the armed forces, insofar as they relate to disability discrimination and *EqA 2010, s 55* (which prohibits discrimination by employment service providers) does not apply to work experience in the armed forces. This replaces *DDA 1995, s 64(7)* which provided that *Part II* did not apply to 'service in any of the naval, military or air forces of the Crown' and *s 14C(5)* which provided that the practical work experience provisions of *DDA 1995, ss 14C–14D* did not apply to a work placement undertaken in any of those forces (*s 14C(5)*). See also **1.117**.

3.124 *Occupational requirements*

Under *EqA 2010, Sch 9, para (1)*, the occupational requirements exception applies to disability discrimination. This provides that a person will not contravene *EqA 2010* (in relation to certain aspects of the employment relationship) in applying a requirement that a person has a particular disability, provided: (a) the requirement is an occupational requirement; (b) the application of the requirement is a proportionate means of achieving a legitimate aim; and (c) the person to whom the requirement is applied does not meet the requirement or the person applying the requirement has reasonable grounds for being satisfied that he does not. These provisions consolidate the provisions on genuine occupational requirements and genuine occupational qualifications which were included in the pre-October 2010 discrimination legislation dealing with other protected characteristics. There were no such provisions included in the *DDA 1995*. However, although the exception has now been extended to disability, the fact that it is not unlawful to treat disabled person more favourably (see **3.43**) means that the change is unlikely to make any practical difference to the scope of protection. See **COMMON CONCEPTS (1)**.

3.125 *Positive action*

The provisions permitting positive action (falling short of positive discrimination) to promote under-represented groups in the workplace have now been standardised across all strands of discrimination. See **Common concepts (1)**.

3.126 *Compliance with a statutory provision*

By *EqA 2010, s 191* and *Sch 22* there is an exception to the disability discrimination provisions where a person does something which they must do pursuant to a requirement of an enactment (defined in *s 212* to include Acts of Parliament, Acts of the Scottish Parliament, Acts or Measures of the National Assembly for Wales and subordinate legislation) or a requirement or condition imposed by virtue of an enactment by a Minster of the Crown, a member of the Scottish Executive, the National Assembly for Wales or the Welsh Ministers, First Minster for Wales or the Counsel General to the Welsh Assembly. This replaces similar provisions under *DDA 1995, s 59(1)* and the case law under *DDA* is still likely to be relevant to *EqA 2010*. The exception in *s 59(1)* was narrowly construed; in particular, an act is only done 'in pursuance' of an enactment or instrument if it is specified in and required by that enactment or instrument (*Hampson v Department of Education and Science* [1991] 1 AC 171, HL at 181). The mere fact that an act of discrimination is permitted by the statute is insufficient. In the specific context of the *DDA*, see *Farmiloe v Lane Group plc* [2004] All ER (D) 08 (Mar), where the EAT held (at 52) that:

> 'Health and Safety Legislation takes precedence over the protection against disability discrimination provided that all reasonable steps have been taken to accommodate the particular needs of the individual worker'.

As set out above at **3.50**, the *Framework Directive* (*Article 2(5)*) only allows for exceptions to its non-discrimination provisions in cases where measures are laid down by national law pursuant to a number of set aims and meet a proportionality test (of necessity in a democratic society). If reliance is placed upon a statutory or other requirement requiring disability discrimination by a defendant employer which is an 'emanation of the state' for EC law purposes (see *Foster v British Gas plc: C-188/89* [1990] IRLR 353, ECJ at 20), it may therefore be possible for the claimant employee to place reliance upon any relevant directly effective provisions of the *Framework Directive* in order to override that requirement. In the light of the decision of the ECJ in *Seda Kucukdevici v Swedex GmbH & Co KG: C-555/07* [2010] All ER (EC) 867 employees of purely private sector employers may also be able to disapply the necessary legislation on the basis that the *Framework Directive* gives expression to a general principle of EU law.

3.127 *National security*

By *DDA 1995, s 59(2A)* nothing in *Part II* (the employment field) of the *DDA* made unlawful any act done for the purpose of safeguarding national security 'if the doing of the act was justified by that purpose'. This has now been replaced by *EqA 2010, s 192* which provides that a person does not contravene *EqA 2010* only by doing something for the purpose of safeguarding national security, provided it is proportionate to do the thing for that purpose. See **Common concepts (1)**.

3.128 *Charities*

Under *DDA 1995, s 18C(1)*, nothing in *Part II* (employment) affected any charitable instrument providing for conferring benefits on one or more categories of person determined 'by reference to any physical or mental capacity' or made unlawful any act done by a charity in pursuance of its charitable purposes so far as connected with persons so determined. The exception for conferring benefits is now replicated in *EqA 2010, s 194*, but the exception for acts done in pursuance of charitable purposes has not been replicated.

By *DDA 1995, s 18C(2)*, nothing in *Part II* prevented a person who provided supported employment from treating members of a particular group of disabled persons more favourably than other persons in providing such employment (or the Secretary of State for agreeing to arrangements for the provision of supported employment which will, or may, have that effect). This is now replicated by *EqA 2010, s 193(3)*. See **Common concepts (1)**.

3.129 *Facilities provided to the public*

By *EqA 2010, Sch 19, para 19* (replacing *DDA 1995, s 4(4)*), the prohibition on discrimination by employers against employees (*s 4(2)*) does not apply to benefits, facilities or services of any description if the employer is concerned with the provision (whether or not for payment) of benefits of that description, to the public or to a section of the public which includes the employee in question, unless:

(a) that provision differs in a material respect from the provision of the benefits by the employer to his employees;

(b) the provision of the benefits to the employee in question is regulated by the employees terms of employment; or

(c) the benefits relate to training.

This provision is designed to prevent an overlap between the provisions dealing with discrimination in employment and the provisions dealing with discrimination in the provision of benefits, facilities and services.

3.130 Protection outside employment

Upon implementation of the *Framework Directive*, *DDA 1995, Part II* was considerably expanded (it had originally dealt with employment; contract workers; trade organisations; occupational pensions; and group insurance). In addition to employees and applicants the following groups of individuals and categories of activity were subject to *DDA* protection and are now subject to the protection of the *EqA 2010*: contract workers, office holders, occupational pension schemes, partnerships, barristers and advocates, trade organisations, qualification bodies and employment service providers. The scope of the protection of each category is considered in **Common concepts (1)**.

Crown employees are specifically included within the definition of employment under *EqA 2010, s 83(2)*. They were also protected under *DDA 1995, s 64(2)*. These provisions are necessary because of the theory that civil servants do not enjoy a contract of employment with the Crown. Note though the exception in relation to the armed forces (see above). Special provisions are also included in *EqA 2010, s 42* and previously *DDA 1995, s 64A* to ensure that the police are protected from discrimination and to identify who is treated as their employer.

3.131 ENFORCEMENT

Complaints to employment tribunal

EqA 2010, s 120 (replacing *DDA 1995, s 17A(1)*) provides that a complaint by any person that another person has discriminated against him, or subjected him to harassment or victimisation, may be presented to an employment tribunal.

3.132 *Time limits*

Claims of disability discrimination in the employment tribunal should be brought within three months of the date of the alleged act of discrimination (*EqA 2010, s 123(1)*). Note that this time limit can be extended in the event that the employment tribunal finds that it is just and equitable to do so (*s 123(1)(b)*, replacing *DDA 1995, Sch 3, para 3*). This may include where the employee has been generally reluctant to acknowledge he is or was disabled (*Department of Constitutional Affairs v Jones* [2007] EWCA Civ 894, [2008] All ER (D) 43 (Jan)).

As to the extension of time limits generally, see **Common concepts (1)**.

For the purposes of the time limit, an act (or acts) of discrimination which extend over a period of time is treated as having been done at the end of that period (*EqA 2010, s 123(3)(a)*, replacing *DDA 1995 s 3(3)(b)*). A failure to do something is treated as occurring where the person in question decided upon it (*EqA 2010, s 123(3)(b)*, replacing *DDA 1995, s 3(3)(c)* which related to 'deliberate omissions). In the absence of evidence to the contrary, a failure to act is treated as being done either when the employer does an inconsistent act or (if there is no inconsistent act) on expiry of the period in which the employer might reasonably have been expected to do it.

The legislation does not explicitly state how a failure to make reasonable adjustments is treated. The EAT found that under the DDA a failure to make reasonable adjustments is an omission and not a continuing act (*Humphries v Chevler Packaging* UKEAT/0224/06/2407). In *Matuszowicz v Kingston-upon-Hull City Council* [2009] EWCA Civ 22 the Court of Appeal found that this was also the case where there was no deliberate omission, but an inadvertent failure to make an adjustment. The Court of Appeal held that in those circumstances, where an employer had not done an act inconsistent with its duty to make a reasonable adjustment, the time limit for bringing a claim would start to run at the time when the employer might reasonably have been expected to comply with its duty, acknowledging that this might not always be a straightforward enquiry. These cases are likely to be equally applicable to the provisions of *EqA 2010*.

3.133 *Restricted reporting orders*

A restricted reporting order may be made in any claim under *EqA 2010*, in which evidence of a personal nature is likely to be heard by the employment tribunal or a chairman (*Employment Tribunals (Constitution and Rules of Procedure) Regulations 2004, Sch 1, rule 50*).

3.134 *Remedies*

In the event of a successful claim of disability discrimination, the remedies are the same as under the other discrimination strands (see *EqA 2010, s 124* and **Common concepts (1)**). If the employee is successful, the employment tribunal will make a declaration that the employer has unlawfully discriminated against the employee.

Compensation will be awarded to a successful employee on the basis of statutory torts and is unlimited (*EqA 2010, s 124(6)*). Compensation can therefore be very high in cases where the employee has lost his job, or future earning prospects are poor. Instances of six-figure awards were relatively frequent in *DDA 1995* cases. The possible heads for financial awards are broadly:

(a) loss of earnings and other employment-related benefits to the date of hearing;

(b) future loss of earnings and employment-related benefits (which may include stigma or 'career damage' losses for bringing a claim);

(c) injury to feelings;

(d) personal injury;

(e) aggravated damages;

(f) exemplary damages.

(See **Common concepts (1)**.)

In *Travis v Electronic Data Systems Ltd* [2004] EWCA Civ 1256, 148 Sol Jo LB 1033 an employee with schizophrenia, aged 40, had been discriminated against in a redundancy programme. The employment tribunal awarded compensation based on 50 per cent of salary and benefits which the employee would have earned up to his 65th birthday had he not been made redundant. Factors which the employment tribunal took into account are the fact that prejudice against his illness would make it difficult for him to find another job.

Tribunals may take into account future pay rises, promotions the employee may have achieved and whether the illness has been aggravated by the conduct of the employer.

The Court of Appeal has held that in discrimination cases the appropriate test for deciding whether an employer is liable to pay compensation for psychiatric injury suffered by an employee is simply whether unlawful discrimination caused it (*Essa v Laing Ltd* [2004] EWCA Civ 02, [2004] ICR 746).

Where an employee has been discriminated against but has subsequently been dismissed for a non-discriminatory reason, future loss for failure to make reasonable adjustments during employment will not be recoverable (*Royal Mail Group plc v Sharma* UKEAT/0839/04/ILB).

Where an employee's compensation for discrimination includes compensation for ill-health which is in part caused by the employer and in part caused by other things, compensation can be reduced to take into account those other factors (*Thaine v London School of Economics* (2010) UKEAT/0144/10, [2010] ICR 1422).

3.135 *Injury to feelings*

In *Vento v Chief Constable of West Yorkshire Police* [2002] EWCA Civ 1871, [2003] IRLR 102 (Sex discrimination (8)), the Court of Appeal identified three broad bands for injury to feelings, as distinct from compensation for psychiatric or similar personal injury. Vento outlined the levels of compensation payable under each band, these levels have recently been revisited and increased in *Da'Bell v National Society for Prevention of Cruelty to Children* [2009] UKEAT/0227/09. The bands are now as follows:

(i) the top band should normally be between £18,000 and £30,000. Sums in this range should be awarded in the most serious cases, such as where there has been a lengthy campaign of discriminatory harassment. Only in the most exceptional case should an award of compensation for injury to feelings exceed £30,000;

(ii) the middle band of between £6,000 and £18,000 should be used for serious cases, which do not merit an award in the highest band;

(iii) awards of between £600 and £6,000 are appropriate in less serious cases, such as where the act of discrimination is an isolated or one-off occurrence. In general, awards of less than £600 are to be avoided altogether, as they risk being so low as not to be a proper recognition of injury to feelings.

3.136 Questionnaire process

An employee can request information from an employer through the use of a standard questionnaire, (*EqA 2010, s 138*, previously *DDA 1995, s 56*). See Common concepts (1).

3.137 Other sources of help and advice

Equality and Human Rights Commission

As part of its general duties, the EHRC gives advice and information, not only to disabled people but also employers and service providers. It, like its predecessor body the DRC, will produce policy documents and research on disability issues and organise campaigns. Appropriate tribunal cases, primarily test cases which test the limits of the law, will also supported and funded by the EHRC.

3.138 *ACAS*

ACAS aims to improve organisations and working life through better employment relations. It provides information, independent advice and training and aims to work with employers and employees to solve problems and improve performance. ACAS also has a helpline which will answer employment queries in confidence. In addition, it operates a service called Equality Direct, which is a confidential advice service for small businesses on equality.

3.139 NO CONTRACTING OUT

General

A term of a contract is unenforceable by a person in whose favour it would operate if it purports to exclude or limit the effect of *EqA 2010 (s 144(1))*. Terms which constitute, promote or provide for treatment which is prohibited by *EqA 2010* are also unenforceable in relation to such treatment by virtue of *s 142*.

4 Gender reassignment

4.1 INTRODUCTION

Since 1999, sex discrimination law has been expanded so as to prohibit certain instances of discrimination against those whose gender identity (self-perception in terms of masculinity and femininity) does not accord with their birth sex (the sex which the organs of their bodies match). Such persons are known variously as 'transpersons', 'transgender' or 'transsexuals'.

Prior to 1999, the discrimination law of the United Kingdom provided no direct protection against discrimination on ground of gender reassignment. The *Sex Discrimination Act 1975* ('*SDA 1975*') was generally thought not to apply to such discrimination, since it was considered that discrimination on ground of gender reassignment did not constitute discrimination on ground of a person's sex.

4.2 Pre-EqA 2010: The P v S case

In the case of *P v S* [1996] IRLR 347, a tribunal found that a claimant had been dismissed by reason of gender reassignment, but that this did *not* constitute discrimination on grounds of sex contrary to the *SDA 1975*.

This interpretation of the existing legislation was challenged before the European Court of Justice (ECJ) (*Case C-13/94*) The ECJ, effectively overturning the tribunal's understanding of the law, held that the scope of the *Equal Treatment Directive* (*Council Directive 76/207*) ('the *Directive*') *included* discrimination arising from gender reassignment, since such discrimination was based, essentially if not exclusively, on the sex of the person concerned. This principle continues to be applied by the ECJ today, for instance in a case establishing that a transsexual must be permitted to claim a retirement pension at 60: *Richards v Secretary of State for Work and Pensions: C-423/04* [2006] ECR I-3585, [2006] All ER (EC) 895. Gender reassignment is not a separate protected characteristic under the *Framework Directive*.

4.3 The courts' response

The courts in the United Kingdom responded quickly to the *P v S* decision. In the case of *Chessington World of Adventures Ltd v Reed, ex p News Group Newspapers Ltd* [1998] IRLR 56, which raised the question whether discrimination on ground of gender reassignment was contrary to *SDA 1975*, the English EAT reinterpreted the relevant provisions of *SDA 1975* ' . . . consistently with the ruling of the European Court in *P v S* . . . '. The result of this reinterpretation was that ' . . . where . . . the reason for the unfavourable treatment is sex based, that is a declared intention to undergo gender reassignment, there is no requirement for a male/female comparison to be made', and thus there was discrimination contrary to *SDA 1975*.

4.4 The 1999 amendments

The *Chessington* decision, and a number of post-*P v S* tribunal decisions to similar effect, were, however, felt by the government to be an insufficient response to *P v S*. With regard to *Chessington*, the Department for Education and Employment (DFEE) (as it was then called) observed that 'the re-interpretation places a strain upon the provisions of the Sex Discrimination Act' (DFEE paper, 'Legislation regarding discrimination on the grounds of transsexualism in employment', January 1998). It was felt that there was a need for legislation to clarify the position.

Gender reassignment

After a consultation process, the government introduced the *Sex Discrimination (Gender Reassignment) Regulations 1999 (SI 1999/1102)*. These Regulations made appropriate amendments to the *SDA 1975* so that, in the spheres of employment and vocational training, it was unlawful to discriminate on grounds of gender reassignment.

4.5 The Equality Act 2010

Gender reassignment is now a protected characteristic pursuant to the *Equality Act 2010* ('*EqA 2010*'), *ss 4 and 7*. The definition of gender reassignment in *EqA 2010, s 7(1)* is broader than that in *SDA 1975, s 82* in that the requirement under the *SDA 1975* for the process of reassignment to be carried out under medical supervision has been removed. Further, *EqA 2010* extends the new concepts of discrimination by association and discrimination by perception to gender reassignment and indirect discrimination is now also available as a cause of action. *EqA 2010, s 7(2)* also clarifies the terminology used in this sphere, providing that 'a reference to a transsexual person is a reference to a person who has the protected characteristic of gender reassignment' and, by *s 7(3)* that all those who are at any stage of gender reassignment, as defined, are recognised by *EqA 2010* as being transsexual persons.

Key concepts/glossary

Gender dysphoria: The concept of 'gender dysphoria' underlies much of the academic literature on transgender issues. It describes the anxiety, uncertainty or persistently uncomfortable feelings about one's birth gender which afflict transpersons, often from an early stage in their lives.

Gender reassignment: The definition in *EqA 2010, s 7(1)* states, 'A person has the protected characteristic of gender reassignment if the person is proposing to undergo, is undergoing or has undergone a process (or part of a process) for the purpose of reassigning the person's sex by changing physiological or other attributes of sex.' This is wider than the definition under *SDA 1975* which required a process under medical supervision (see **4.5**).

Transsexual person: *EqA 2010, s 7(2)* provides that 'a reference to a transsexual person is a reference to a person who has the protected characteristic of gender reassignment'.

Treatment: Diagnosis of transsexualism is carried out by a specialist. Where an individual undergoes medical treatment, preliminary diagnosis is followed by hormone therapy. If an individual has not yet changed social gender, they can be expected to start to do so at around this stage. At some point over the next few months the individual will generally start to live full-time as a member of their 'new' sex. The individual then usually proceeds to surgery after one or two years of hormone therapy.

Gender recognition certificates: Under a procedure governed by the *Gender Recognition Act 2004*, it is now open to a person who has undergone gender reassignment to seek legal recognition of their acquired gender. This Act was passed against a background of criticism by the European Court of Human Rights of the United Kingdom's comparative lack of legal recognition or protection for transsexuals: See *Goodwin v United Kingdom (Application 28957/95)* [2002] IRLR 664; *Grant v United Kingdom (Application 32570/03)* [2006] All ER (D) 337 (May). This is achieved by obtaining a gender recognition certificate from a gender recognition panel. Surgery is not necessary in order to fulfil the requirements for making an application. Rather, a person must:

(a) have or have had 'gender dysphoria';

(b) have lived in his or her acquired gender for two years prior to the application; and

(c) intend to live permanently in his or her acquired gender.

The effect of a gender recognition certificate is that, for almost all legal purposes, the person concerned must be treated as if he or she had been born in his or her acquired gender. Consequently, it becomes possible for a transsexual to experience discrimination on the basis of his or her acquired gender, as set out elsewhere in this book. See also *M v Revenue and Customs Comrs* [2010] UKFTT 356 (TC), [2010] SFTD 1141, [2010] STI 2863 for the importance of a Gender Recognition Certificate for National Insurance purposes.

Most recently, the Court of Appeal has held that the *Equal Treatment Directive* had not been properly implemented in that the law prior to the *State Pension Credit Act 2002* was that a transsexual who had obtained a Gender Recognition Certificate as a woman was not entitled to receive a pension at the age of 60, ie at the female age and instead had to wait until the male age of 65; *Timbrell v Secretary of State for Work and Pensions* [2010] EWCA Civ 701, [2010] ICR 1368.

Gender dysphoria as disability: Where a transsexual has suffered from gender dysphoria for twelve months or more, or the condition is likely to last for twelve months or more, it may constitute a disability within the meaning of the *EqA 2010, s 6* (see *EHRC Employment Code* at *section 2.28*). In such circumstances discrimination against a transsexual could conceivably contravene either the provisions on gender reassignment or disability discrimination under *EqA 2010* (or previously the *DDA 1995* and *SDA 1975*). Issues relating to disability are discussed in **Disability discrimination (3)**.

4.6 DISCRIMINATION ON THE GROUNDS OF GENDER REASSIGNMENT

Meaning of gender reassignment

The legal definition of 'gender reassignment' in *SDA 1975, s 82* was ' . . . a process which is undertaken under medical supervision for the purpose of reassigning a person's sex by changing physiological or other characteristics of sex, and includes any part of such a process'. This was a relatively broad definition of a process which, whilst it included reference to 'medical supervision', did not require surgery. Accordingly, hormonal or other types of therapy, so long as undertaken with a view to reassigning a person's sex, fell within the definition.

However, in response to consultation on the proposed *EqA 2010* the government decided to amend the definition to make clear that the reference to gender reassignment being a process under medical supervision did not go so far as to require either ongoing medical supervision or surgery. They therefore removed the reference to medical supervision (see *The Equality Bill—Government Response to Consultation* at para 9.41). The new definition of gender reassignment is set out in the box above. The *EHRC Employment Code* states that gender reassignment is a personal process, that is, moving away from one's birth sex, rather than a medical process.

The government did not intend to cover 'transvestites', ie those who temporarily adopt the appearance of the opposite gender (see *The Equality Bill—Government Response to Consultation* at para 9.42). The *EHRC Employment Code* states at *para 2.26* that protection is provided where, as part of the process, of reassigning their sex, someone is driven by their gender identity to cross-dress, but not where someone chooses to cross-dress for some other reason. However, transvestites may have protection from discrimination by perception if they are perceived to be transsexuals.

4.7 Point at which provisions engaged

Since protection for gender reassignment deals with acquired gender, rather than birth sex it is necessary for the draughtsman to define when a person acquires the characteristic on the basis of which discrimination is prohibited. Under *SDA 1975*, by using the words 'intends to undergo', *s 2A(1)* ensured that the gender-reassignment regime prohibited not merely discrimination on the ground of an *existing* gender reassignment process, but also an *intended* process. An employee or other relevant person therefore acquired the protection of *SDA 1975* as soon as they declared an intention to undergo the process.

EqA 2010, s 7(1) replaces the phrase 'intends to undergo' with the phrase 'proposes to undergo'. The *Explanatory Notes to the EqA 2010* do not suggest that any change from *SDA 1975* is intended by this change in wording but it is submitted that it might be argued that 'proposing' entails a pronouncement, whether in writing or orally, of an intention to undergo gender reassignment whereas 'intends' might be thought to refer only to a thought process, which may not have been pronounced or evinced in any way.

The *EHRC Employment Code* states that the proposal to undergo gender reassignment need not be irrevocable and people who start the gender reassignment process but then decide to stop, still have the protected characteristic of gender reassignment.

4.8 Direct discrimination: definition

Prior to *EqA 2010*, the definition of discrimination on ground of gender reassignment was to be found in *SDA 1975, s 2A(1)*, which provided:

> 'A person ('A') discriminates against another person ('B') . . . if he treats B less favourably than he treats or would treat other persons, and does so on the ground that B intends to undergo, is undergoing or has undergone gender reassignment'.

This provision was drafted in very similar fashion to *SDA 1975, s 1(1)(a)*, which dealt with direct discrimination on ground of sex.

By *EqA 2010, s 13*, the revised definition of direct discrimination applies to gender reassignment:

> 'A person (A) discriminates against another (B) if, because of a protected characteristic, A treats B less favourably than A treats or would treat others'.

For a discussion of direct discrimination, see **1.45**ff.

4.9 *Discrimination by association and discrimination by perception*

Under *SDA 1975* discrimination by association and perception did not explicitly extend to gender reassignment (but see *Coleman v Attridge Law: C-303/06*).

The new definition of direct discrimination at *EqA 2010, s 13(1)* is intended to cover associative discrimination and discrimination based on perception within the provisions on direct discrimination and harassment (but not indirect discrimination). Since all of *s 13* applies to gender reassignment cases, direct discrimination by association (ie discrimination against someone who associates with a transsexual person) and perception (ie discrimination against someone perceived to be a transsexual) are therefore also available as causes of action. See **1.54**.

4.10 *Combined discrimination*

EqA 2010 also contains a new provision enabling an employee to bring a discrimination claim on two (but no more than two) combined protected grounds, although the provision was not implemented on 1 October 2010 and will certainly not be implemented before April 2011. (See **1.57–1.59**.)

4.11 Indirect discrimination: definition

Under *SDA 1975*, discrimination on ground of gender reassignment was prohibited only to the extent that such discrimination was *direct*; there were no indirect discrimination provisions. By *EqA 2010, s 19(1)*, indirect discrimination was extended to gender reassignment cases:

'(1) A person (A) discriminates against another (B) if A applies to B a provision, criterion or practice which is discriminatory in relation to a relevant protected characteristic of B's.

(2) For the purposes of subsection (1), a provision, criterion or practice is discriminatory in relation to a relevant protected characteristic of B's if:

(a) A applies, or would apply, it to persons with whom B does not share the characteristic,

(b) it puts, or would put, persons with whom B shares the characteristic at a particular disadvantage when compared with persons with whom B does not share it,

(c) it puts, or would put, B at that disadvantage, and

(d) A cannot show it to be a proportionate means of achieving a legitimate aim.'

In the gender reassignment context a reference to a person who has a particular protected characteristic is a reference to a transsexual person and a reference to persons who share a protected characteristic is a reference to transsexual persons (*EqA 2010, s 7*).

The *EHRC Employment Code* gives as an example of potential indirect discrimination the situation of an induction session for new staff with an ice-breaker designed to introduce everyone in the room to the others. Each worker is required to provide a picture of themselves as a toddler. One worker is a transsexual woman who does not wish her colleagues to know she was brought up as a boy. When she does not bring her photo she is criticised in front of the group for not joining in.

For a discussion of indirect discrimination, see **1.72**ff.

4.12 Absences for gender reassignment

With regard to the specific issue of gender-reassignment-related absences, *EqA 2010, s 16* provides that a transsexual person will be discriminated against if he is treated less favourably than he would be if the absence was because of: (a) 'sickness or injury'; or (b) 'some other reason and, it is not reasonable for him to be treated less favourably'. For these purposes someone is regarded as absent because of gender-reassignment if their absence is because they are proposing to undergo, are undergoing or have undergone the process (or part of the process) of gender reassignment. These provisions were previously included in *SDA 1975, s 2A(3)*.

The *EHRC Employment Code* gives two examples:

(a) if a worker who takes time off to visit a Gender Identity Clinic as part of the gender reassignment process, his employer cannot treat him less favourably than if he had been absent due to illness or injury, eg by paying him less (see *para 9.31*);

(b) a transsexual worker tells her boss that she intends to undergo gender reassignment and asks to take an afternoon's annual leave to attend counselling. The request is brusquely refused although there are sufficient staff members on duty to cover her absence. This could amount to gender reassignment discrimination (see *para 9.32*).

These provisions are considerably less extensive protection than that afforded in the context of maternity. Less favourable treatment of transsexual persons on grounds of absence, even where the same criteria are applied irrespective of the reason for absence, might now potentially give rise to claims of indirect discrimination.

4.13 Harassment: definition

The definition of harassment on ground of gender reassignment was to be found in *SDA 1975, s 4A(3)*. This provision employed the same terminology as that relating to harassment on ground of sex and, accordingly, those same principles were relevant (see **1.88**). There is now a common definition of harassment applicable to gender reassignment, in *EqA 2010, s 26(5)*, which includes harassment by a third party apply to gender reassignment, but the case law under the *SDA* will continue to be relevant. Protection may also be available under the *Protection from Harassment Act 1997*, irrespective of whether any harassment was related to gender reassignment

For a discussion of harassment, see **1.86–1.97**.

4.14 Victimisation: definition

Under *SDA 1975, s 4* victimisation was a type of discrimination. Under *EqA 2010* it is a free-standing claim (*s 27*) which applies to gender reassignment as it does to other protected characteristics.

For a discussion of victimisation see **1.98–1.108**.

4.15 Discussions about pay

EqA 2010, s 77 makes contractual pay secrecy clauses unenforceable to the extent that they prevent employees from making relevant pay disclosures—that is, a disclosure that is sought or made for the purpose of finding out whether (or to what extent) any difference in pay is related to a protected characteristic (*EqA 2010, s 77(3)*). Action taken by an employer as a result of an individual making or seeking to make a relevant pay disclosure, or receiving information disclosed in a relevant pay disclosure, may amount to victimisation. (See **1.109**.)

4.16 Equal pay

Discrimination against transsexuals in terms of payment for work is prohibited by *Article 157* of Treaty on the Functioning of the EU (formerly *Article 141* of the *EC Treaty*) and the *Equal Pay Directive 75/117*: *KB v National Health Service Pensions Agency: C-117/01* [2004] IRLR 240. Such claims were previously brought under *SDA 1975* rather than the *Equal Pay Act 1970* (see *SDA 1975, s 6(8)*). Claims by transsexuals complaining that they are paid less than someone else, whether male or female, simply because they are a transsexual would now constitute direct discrimination claims under *EqA 2010*. However, if a transsexual claims that they are contractually paid less than someone of the opposite sex to their re-assigned gender on because of their sex they would bring an equal pay claim under *EqA 2010, Part 5, Chapter 3*.

4.17 Comparators

Under *EqA 2010* a comparison for the purposes of direct or indirect discrimination must be with a person who does not have the protected characteristic in question (ie has not undergone gender reassignment) but whose circumstances are otherwise not materially different (*EqA 2010, s 23*). Case law has established that a transsexual is to be regarded in his or her reassigned gender, at least once gender reassignment process is completed and surgery has been undertaken: *A v Chief Constable of West Yorkshire Police* [2004] UKHL 21, [2005] 1 AC 51, para 58 (Baroness Hale; see also *M v Revenue and Customs Comrs* [2010] UKFTT 356 (TC), [2010] SFTD 1141, [2010] STI 2863 at para 25 (Nicholas Paines J). Accordingly, in a gender reassignment claim, although the identification of a comparator will depend on the circumstances of the case, where sex is material the comparator will usually be someone of the claimant's reassigned gender, who has not undergone gender reassignment, at least once the gender reassignment process is completed. If a transsexual is bringing a claim of sex discrimination, the comparison will generally be with someone of their original sex but whose circumstances are not materially different.

4.18 Scope of application

Prior to *EqA 2010* the prohibitions on discrimination and harassment on ground of gender reassignment applied only to discrimination in the fields of employment and vocational training. Unlike discrimination on ground of sex, the prohibitions did *not* apply to discrimination in education, or in the provision of housing, goods, facilities and services. (See *SDA 1975, s 2A(1)–(2)* and *Part III.*) *EqA 2010, s 29* now extends protection for gender reassignment cases to the provision of services and the exercise of public functions.

4.19 DISCRIMINATION IN EMPLOYMENT

In the context of employment and vocational training, *EqA 2010, s 39* prohibits discrimination, harassment or victimisation against applicants for employment and employees in relation to recruitment, terms of employment, access to opportunities for training and benefits and in dismissal. Former employees are protected under *EqA 2010, s 108* although they are not expressly protected from victimisation, which appears to be a drafting error (see **1.107**).

In the context of gender reassignment, there are a number of areas where the cases suggest there is a greater risk of discrimination occurring, or discrimination claims being brought.

- *harassment by his or her colleagues or clients:* see *Chessington World of Adventures Ltd v Reed, ex p News Group Newspapers Ltd* [1998] IRLR 56), where the appellant announced a change of gender identity from male to female and changed her name to Niki by statutory declaration, which led to a concerted course of serious harassment by some of her male colleagues;

- *making inappropriate arrangements for the use of single sex facilities, particularly, toilet facilities:* see *Croft v Royal Mail Group plc* [2003] EWCA Civ 1045, [2003] ICR 1425), which concerned a male-to-female pre-operative transsexual person who claimed she was discriminated against by being required by the employer to use the gender-neutral disabled toilet in the workplace. On the facts of this case both the EAT and the Court of Appeal found that there was no unlawful discrimination under *SDA 1975, s 2A* and it was appropriate for the employer in the particular circumstances to make separate arrangements for a transsexual employee while he or she is in the course of undergoing a gender reassignment. The protection offered in *s 2A* does not extend to giving an employee automatic entitlement to use the facilities of the new gender as soon as they start presenting themselves in that gender;

- *gender-specific roles:* see **4.7**;

- *not permitting adequate time off work for the purposes of undergoing the required surgery*;

- *discriminatory decisions in recruitment and promotion exercises:* see *Baldwin v Brighton and Hove City Council* [2007] IRLR 232, which concerned a female-to-male transsexual person who was asked to apply for an alternative post at the expiry of his existing contract. He alleged that a member of the interview panel was 'transphobic' so did not attend the interview and alleged constructive dismissal. The EAT held that it is not sufficient to show that a respondent 'would have' treated the claimant in a less favourable way—the treatment in question must actually take place;

- *dismissing employees who have transitioned, or intend to transition*

- *withholding work, or changing the nature of someone's role, particularly to keep them away from client-facing roles*;

- *not ensuring that people who transition are treated equally in the provision of benefits.*

For practical advice on how to deal with a member of staff who intends to transition see **4.9** ff.

4.20 Instructing, causing or inducing discrimination

It is unlawful to instruct, cause or induce someone to discriminate against, harass or victimise another person, or to attempt to do so (*EqA 2010, s 111*). A claim can be brought by the 'victim' of the discrimination, the person who was instructed to carry out the discrimination and the EHRC. (See **1.161**.)

4.21 Liability of employees and agents and aiding discrimination

Where employees commit acts of discrimination against fellow employees, their employer will be liable if the acts were committed during the course of employment (*EqA 2010, s 109(1)*). Employers are also liable for the discriminatory acts of their agents if they are acting with the employer's authority (*s 109(4)*). In each case it is irrelevant whether the employer knew or approved of the acts (*s 109(3)*). However, there is a defence for employers in relation to the acts of their employees (but not agents) if they can show that they took all reasonable steps to prevent the employee such steps as were reasonably practicable to prevent the employee from doing the act in question (*s 109(4)*). The employees and agents will also have personal liability for their acts of discrimination (*EqA 2010, s 110*), even if the employer has a defence. See **1.163–1.168**.

It is also unlawful for an individual to knowingly help another to carry out an act which is unlawful under *EqA 2010* (*s 112(1)*). (See **1.62**.)

4.22 GENUINE OCCUPATIONAL QUALIFICATIONS AND OCCUPATIONAL REQUIREMENTS

Pre-*EqA 2010*, there was a limited exception to the general prohibition on direct discrimination for situations where such discrimination arises from a 'genuine occupational qualification' (GOQ). The GOQs which were set out in *SDA 1975, s 7* effectively applied, under *s 7A*, to transitioning transsexuals.

In addition to the 'standard' GOQs, *SDA 1975, s 7B* provided four supplementary GOQs specifically related to gender reassignment, which applied in the case of transsexuals in the course of 'transitioning'. These applied where:

(1) the job involved the holder being liable to be called upon to perform intimate physical searches pursuant to statutory powers;

(2) the job entailed work in a private home in an intimate context and reasonable objection is taken to a transitioning transsexual performing such work;

(3) the nature and location of the establishment is such that it would be impracticable to live elsewhere than premises provided by the employer, reasonable objection is taken to the holder of such a job sharing accommodation and facilities with either sex, and it is not reasonable to expect the employer to alter the premises; and/or

(4) the holder of the job provided vulnerable individuals with personal services and, in the reasonable view of the employer, those services cannot be effectively provided by a transitioning transsexual.

The *s 7B* GOQs were only available to employers whilst an employee was 'transitioning'. Once the transsexual had been registered under their acquired gender under the *Gender Recognition Act 2004* he or she had to be treated on a fully equal basis with those born into his or her acquired gender. This meant that the GOQ position must be assessed as if the person concerned had been born into their acquired gender.

Under *EqA 2010, Sch 9, para 1* the old provisions on GOQs have been replaced. There is now a general exception which, in relation to gender reassignment, allows employers to require certain roles to be carried out by someone who is not a transsexual. To rely on the exception an employer must be able to show that, having regard to the nature or context of the work, not being a transsexual is an occupational requirement and applying the requirement is a proportionate means of achieving a legitimate aim. The *Explanatory Notes to the EqA 2010* give an example that a counsellor working with victims of rape might have to be a woman and not a transsexual person, even if she has a gender recognition certificate, in order to avoid causing them further distress. (See **1.145**ff.)

There is also a specific exception relating to employment for the purpose of an organised religion, which allows transsexual people to be excluded from employment where the exclusion is to comply with the doctrines of the religion or where, because of the nature or context of the employment, employing a transsexual person would conflict with the strongly held religious convictions of a significant number of the religion's followers (*Sch 9, para 2*). The *EHRC Employment Code* at *section 13.13* states that this exception should only be used for a limited number of posts such as ministers of religion and a small number of posts outside religion including those which exist to promote or represent the religion. See **1.145**ff and **9.19**.

Importantly, however, the specific GOQs in *SDA 1975, s 7B* for those in transition have not been replicated in the *EqA 2010* thus providing, in theory, wider protection for transsexuals than has previously existed. However, those specific GOQs from *s 7B* will still be capable of being lawful pursuant to *Sch 9, para 1* if they satisfy the legitimate aim test. In practice, therefore, the position may well be that protection remains much the same, save that specific potential exclusions are not suggested in *EqA 2010*.

4.23 ENFORCEMENT AND REMEDIES

Where a person has been discriminated against in an employment or vocational training context on ground of gender reassignment, he or she may bring a claim to an employment tribunal: *SDA 1975, s 63*. The reversal of the burden of proof which is provided for in *SDA 1975, s 63A* applies in the same way as a claim based on discrimination on ground of sex: *B v BA* [2006] EWCA Civ 132, [2006] IRLR 471.

4.24 GUIDANCE FOR EMPLOYERS

Introduction

This section provides practical guidance for employers on handling issues relating to gender reassignment in the workplace. Para **4.25** sets out advice for all employers, irrespective of whether any of their staff are undergoing or proposing to undergo a gender reassignment process. Para **4.27** addresses the issues to be considered by the employer once it becomes aware that a member of staff proposes to undergo gender reassignment.

4.25 General guidance for all employers

Policies and training

An employer may be liable for any discriminatory act done by an employee in the course of his or her employment, unless it can show that it took such steps as were reasonably practicable to prevent the act from occurring (see *EqA 2010, s 109*). Maintaining adequate policies and holding regular training can assist an employer in demonstrating that it took these preventative steps.

Gender reassignment

All relevant policies and practices should be vetted to ensure they do not directly or indirectly discriminate on the grounds of gender reassignment. Equal opportunities policies should as a matter of best practice, refer explicitly to gender reassignment.

Employers who have specific policies and procedures to cover specific protected characteristics, for example sexual orientation, religion or age, should consider introducing a separate gender identity policy. General HR policies, for example those dealing with confidentiality or harassment, should be checked to ensure that they would adequately cover an employee undergoing or proposing to undergo gender reassignment.

Employers should also include transgender issues in training programmes addressing equal opportunities and harassment.

4.26 *Recruitment, selection and promotion*

The process of recruitment and selection of a new employee should not be affected by an individual's transsexual status (which includes their intention to undergo gender reassignment, see **4.4**). Allowing such status to influence the decision as to whether to recruit will be unlawful unless the rationale falls within the occupational requirement exception referred to at **4.7**.

The normal rules of best practice should be adopted when conducting interviews. Employers should have a job description for each role, together with a prepared set of questions relating to the requirements of the job and which are used consistently for all candidates. Interviewees may not want to disclose their transsexual status at interview and this is not a question that should be asked. Questions about a person's gender dysmorphia could also be unlawful enquiries about a person's health contrary to *EqA 2010, s 60* if asked before an offer of employment is made (see **3.99–3.103**). Interviewers should receive training to ensure that they treat all applicants consistently and do not ask any inappropriate questions.

In terms of career advancement and opportunities for promotion, the employer should ensure that decisions are not influenced in any way by someone's transsexual status.

4.27 Specific guidance for employers of transsexual employees

First approach by the employee and managing the transition

When a manager, supervisor or colleague is first approached by an employee who is suffering from gender dysphoria, or considering gender reassignment, the employer should reassure the individual that the employer will be as supportive as possible through the transition process. The employer should take all appropriate steps to ensure respect for the individual's privacy, dignity at work and confidentiality.

It is helpful if the employer nominates one person to manage the transition from the employer's perspective, with the agreement of the individual. That person should engage at an early stage with the individual to discuss the handling of the transition and the ways in which the employer can support the individual and prepare an action plan for the process. This should be kept strictly confidential.

The whole process should be actively managed and kept under review, including regular meetings throughout the process.

Employers may want to consider agreeing a 'Memorandum of Understanding' with the individual to make clear the measures that will be in place to facilitate the process. The agreement should not represent a binding legal document, but rather a commitment by the employer to engage with and support the employee at all stages of the transition process.

Specific matters to be discussed at the meetings and addressed by the employer are set out below.

Time off for medical treatment

4.28 Employers should discuss with the individual how much time off he or she will need to undergo treatment. During absence for treatment or surgery normal sick pay arrangements apply. *EqA 2010, s 16* makes it unlawful for an employer to treat an individual less favourably, in relation to an absence because of gender reassignment, than someone who is absent for some other medical reason (see **4.5**).

Employers should follow their normal policy for medical appointments. However, employers should try to allow some flexibility so that an employee can, for example, travel the longer distances that may be required to see a qualified professional, or attend follow-up appointments, which may take place outside the individual's home town or overseas. If complications arise from any relevant medical treatment that result in a long-term incapacity for work, then the employee should be treated in the same way as any other person who becomes unfit for duty, including complying with its duties under the disability discrimination provisions where applicable, where the employee has been diagnosed as suffering from gender dysphoria and the condition is likely to last for more than 12 months (see **Disability discrimination (3)**).

Informing colleagues, clients and customers

4.29 There is no general need or requirement to inform colleagues, clients or the public that an employee is undergoing gender reassignment. Indeed, it is not appropriate to inform anybody about this matter without the individual's explicit consent as the information will constitute sensitive personal data under the *Data Protection Act 1998*.

In some circumstances, information may be necessary where the relationship with somebody who knew the person prior to their change of status is to continue. It is usually good practice for employers to agree to take responsibility for informing those who need to know, with the individual's consent, unless the employee would prefer to do this his or herself. If the individual wishes to make personal explanations to some or all of his or her contacts, the employer should ask to know when the disclosure is to take place and offer to assist with the detail of the communication.

Dress codes

4.30 If there is a dress code, it is good practice to allow enough flexibility in the code to accommodate the process of transition from one sex to another. The individual concerned should be given his or her new uniform early on in the process, and before transitioning at work, to allow him or her to become used to wearing it. A new name badge should also be provided, if appropriate.

Single sex facilities

4.31 It will always be preferable for an employer and employee to agree the point at which the use of gender-split facilities such as toilets and changing rooms should change. While it is clearly not acceptable to insist upon a transsexual employee using separate facilities (such as a disabled toilet) in the long term, there is a period during which an employer is entitled to make separate arrangements for those undergoing gender reassignment, particularly when other employees raise objections.

In *Croft v Royal Mail Group plc* [2003] All ER (D) 319 the Court of Appeal held that a formerly male employee could not, by presenting as a female, necessarily and immediately assert the right to use female toilets. On the other hand, the Court of Appeal also held that an employee could not necessarily be required, in relation to toilets, to behave as if they were not undergoing gender reassignment until they reached the post-operative stage. Pill LJ held that the moment at which a person at the pre-operative 'real life test' stage is entitled to use female toilets will depend on all the circumstances:

> 'The employers must take into account the stage reached in treatment, including the employee's own assessment and presentation. They are entitled to take into account, though not to be governed by, the susceptibilities of other members of the workforce'.

In that case, the measures taken by the employers were held to be appropriate ones in the circumstances. They were entitled, for a period of time, to require the employee to use the unisex disabled toilet. The time had not come when they were obliged to permit her to use the female toilets.

Reactions of others

4.32 The employer should take appropriate steps to ensure that all members of staff refer to the transsexual person by their new name and use pronouns appropriate to their new gender role. This may involve having to train the individual's colleagues, but this should only be done with the individual's consent. The employer should consider agreeing in advance with the employee how they would like the situation to be managed if there are colleagues who are hostile to the change, and ensure someone is available to assist the individual if any incidents do arise.

The employer should be prepared to address the concerns of other employees, for example if concerns are raised about sharing single-sex facilities. The employer should try to determine what is at the heart of the concerns and try to resolve issues. It may be the case that issues can be dealt with relatively simply, for example by ensuring that cubicle doors offer sufficient privacy, or through training staff.

Media interest and harassment

4.33 If the gender reassignment attracts media attention, the employer should be prepared to support the employee. A single point of contact should be nominated to liaise with the media, from the press office if there is one. Other staff should be advised to maintain strict confidentiality and not to provide any information in response to media enquiries.

If an employee is being harassed by the media at the workplace or in connection with their work, the employer should try to protect him or her and consider strategies that minimise personal exposure. In extreme cases complaints can also be made to the Press Complaints Commission.

If the employer does not take such steps as are 'reasonably practicable' to prevent employees from being harassed by a third party (whether the press, a client, or other third party) in the course of their employment, the employer is at risk of a claim for harassment pursuant to *EqA 2010, s 40*. There is currently no authority on when harassment will be regarded as taking place 'in the course of employment' in these circumstances or what steps will be 'reasonably practicable' to prevent it.

Records and personnel file and disclosure of gender information

4.34 Employers should ensure that all documents, public references (for example, telephone directories and websites) and employment details reflect the new gender of the employee.

Under *GRA 2004, s 22(1)* it is an offence for any person who has acquired 'protected information' in an official capacity to disclose the information to any other person (subject to certain exceptions). *Section 22(2)* defines 'protected information' as information about:

- a person's application for a gender recognition certificate; or
- the gender history of a successful applicant.

The penalty on conviction can be fine up to level 5 on the standard scale (currently £5,000).

Under *s 22(3)(b)* a person acquires protected information in an official capacity if the person acquires it as an employer, or prospective employer, of the person to whom the protected information relates, or as a person employed by such an employer or prospective employer. *GRA 2004* does provide some exceptions when protected information may be disclosed, for example where the person to whom the protected information relates agrees to the disclosure of the information or where the information does not enable that person to be identified.

If employers require proof of a person's legal gender, then their (new) birth certificate should be sufficient confirmation. The individual must not routinely be asked to produce their gender recognition certificate as evidence of their legal gender, because such a request could compromise the individual's right to privacy.

Pensions and benefits

4.35 Employers registering staff for corporate insurance and benefits policies should be aware of whether their underwriters need to be informed of a transsexual employee's status, since some insurers may automatically invalidate a policy if gender reassignment is not disclosed.

Typical policies which may require the information to be disclosed include, for example:

- life assurance;
- permanent health or income protection;
- private medical insurance;
- personal accident insurance;
- motor vehicle insurance in the case of company cars.

Once a Gender Recognition Certificate has been obtained, an employer will need an employee's consent to disclose 'protected information' to a benefit provider unless one of the exceptions under *GRA 2004* applies. One such exception applies where a disclosure is made for the purposes of the social security system or a pension scheme.

Relocation and redeployment

4.36 The employer should ensure that, to the extent possible, it carries out 'business as usual' in respect of the employee, and so the employee should not be shielded from contact with clients or otherwise have his or her job altered. The employer should not offer to relocate or redeploy the individual unless he or she specifically raises the issue.

However, it is possible that a transsexual employee may wish to be relocated to another workplace during the transition period, or even permanently. The employer should consider this request in the same way as it would consider any other request for relocation. However, it should take into account the particular sensitivities of the situation and possible legal obligations. In particular, if its normal policy puts transsexual persons at a particular disadvantage compared to non-transsexual persons then applying the policy could amount to indirect discrimination, unless it could be objectively justified. Similarly, if the transsexual person suffers from gender dysmorphia, this could amount to a disability and the employer would be under a duty to make reasonable adjustments to the extent that the policy put the employee at a substantial disadvantage over someone who did not have gender dysmorphia. Claims for indirect discrimination could also arise either based on disability (see **3.68–3.74**) or gender reassignment (see **4.5**). Ultimately, a decision should be made in conjunction with the individual employee.

4.37 *Checklist for employers*

In summary, some of the key issues which an employer should consider with an individual who is undergoing or intends to undergo gender transitioning are:

- What is the individual's preferred timetable for the transitioning and the medical procedures?

Gender reassignment

- What time off will be required for this?
- At what point will the employee's name and social gender change?
- Have arrangements been agreed for dress code and use of single-sex facilities?
- Which clients and staff should be informed and when?
- Does the employee wish to tell his or her line manager, colleagues and clients him or herself, or does he or she prefer the employer to do so?
- Have the nature and contents of any communications to clients and staff been agreed?
- What amendments need to be made to the individual's personnel records and the employer's IT systems and other records?
- Does any special training need to be arranged for particular staff or groups of staff?
- What steps have been agreed to handle any harassment, hostile reactions or media interest?

4.38 OTHER SOURCES

There are a number of resources available to employers wishing to address these issues. Examples include:

- The 'Employment Statutory Code of Practice', published by EHRC (which is the formal Code which Employment Tribunals are obliged to take into account when considering claims under the *EqA 2010*).
- 'Legal Protection and Good Practice for Gender Variant, Transsexual and Transgender People in the Workplace' (November 2010), produced by the Gender Identity Research and Education Society (GIRES).
- 'Gender Reassignment—a Guide for Employers' (January 2005), produced by the Women and Equality Unit of the Department for Trade and Industry (now Department for Business, Enterprise and Regulatory Reform).
- 'Gender Reassignment—Guidance for Managers and Supervisors' (May 2006), produced by the Equal Opportunities Commission (now Equality and Human Rights Commission (EHRC)).
- 'Transsexual People in the Workplace: PFC Code of Practice' (December 1998), produced by Press For Change (the pressure group for transsexual people).

5 Marital status and civil partnership

5.1 INTRODUCTION

Discrimination against married persons and civil partners is now dealt with in the *Equality Act 2010* ('*EqA 2010*'), *s 8*, which replaces the *Sex Discrimination Act 1975* ('*SDA 1975*'), *s 3*. A person discriminates against another ('A') in any circumstances relevant for the purposes of any of the provisions relating to employment, where A is either married or a civil partner and:

(1) because of A being married, or being a civil partner, that person treats A less favourably than he treats or would treat others (direct discrimination); or

(2) he applies to A a provision, criterion or practice which is discriminatory in relation to A's characteristic of being married or a civil partner. A provision, criterion or practice is discriminatory if:

   (a) he applies, or would apply, the provision, criterion or practice to persons who are not married or a civil partner;

   (b) the provision, criterion or practice puts, or would put, persons who are married or civil partners at a particular disadvantage when compared with persons who are not married or civil partners;

   (c) the provision, criterion or practice puts, or would put, A at that disadvantage; and

   (d) he cannot show the provision, criterion or practice to be a proportionate means of achieving a legitimate aim (indirect discrimination).

The prohibition on discrimination against married persons appeared in the originally enacted version of *SDA 1975*, and it remains an uncommon subject of discussion in the law reports. This is presumably because it is a relatively unusual distinct ground of discrimination in practice and because, where it does occur, it can sometimes be subsumed within other, more familiar, discrimination provisions.

Marital discrimination is also somewhat unusual in principle, because most forms of anti-discrimination legislation were designed to protect persons who were members of groups which had been disadvantaged by society in the past, and/or which were minority groups. Nevertheless marital status discrimination has a role in anti-discrimination laws for three principal reasons. First, it provides a short cut to exposing a type of sex discrimination which might otherwise be more difficult to expose. For example, the promotion by an employer of single women over married women within an organisation simply because the latter are not perceived as the right 'types' is an obviously suspect practice from the point of view of equality. Stated in those terms, the problem does not in fact (and conceptually it should not necessarily) require any comparison between a man and a woman (cf *EqA 2010, s 11* and *SDA 1975, s 1(1)(a)*). The concept of marital status discrimination allows the married female complainant to compare herself to an unmarried *woman*, rather than to a man (actual or hypothetical). Second, by countering assumptions about how married people will behave at work or will contribute to their work, it has the capacity to provide, albeit in a modest and imperfect way (given the modern prevalence of unmarried families), a conceptual framework which does not focus *solely* on formal or theoretical sexual equality, but which also takes into account the practical, generalised and gendered societal problem of family responsibility versus work. Third, in its recently amended form it provides some further protection for workers in non-heterosexual relationships, albeit only those who have entered into civil partnerships.

Marital status and civil partnership

5.2 Married persons

Who does *EqA 2010, s 8* and previously *SDA 1975, s 3* protect? In the first place, a person who is 'married' (*EqA 2010, s 8(1)* and *SDA 1975, s 3(2)(a)*). In the second place, a person who is 'a civil partner' (*EqA 2010, s 8(1)* and *SDA 1975, s 3(2)(b)*).

It has been held that the dismissal of a woman on the ground that she was *about* to get married was not an act of unlawful discrimination under *SDA 1975, s 3*, because the woman, whilst married by the time of the termination of employment, had not been married at the time she was given notice: *Bick v Royal West of England Residential School for the Deaf* [1976] IRLR 326. In the previous edition of this book, it was submitted that *Bick* (a first instance decision) was wrongly decided. The previous edition noted that the intention behind *SDA 1975, s 3* was to protect people from being subjected to detriment on account of marital status. In principle one would have thought that this form of anti-discrimination law should at least protect people who are *about* to get married and dismissed as a direct result and therefore it seemed unsatisfactory to say that a person in the position of Mrs Bick might have other remedies: eg direct sex discrimination (by comparing herself to a hypothetical male), or unfair dismissal (see *McLean v Paris Travel Service* [1976] IRLR 202 or *Pickering v Kingston Mobile Unit* [1978] IRLR 102). The tribunal's approach in *Bick* exacerbated, instead of ameliorating, the potentially incomplete protection afforded by the section as drafted. Indeed, the tribunal in *Bick* expressed dissatisfaction with their decision and stated that it had not the least doubt that Parliament intended the section to apply to discrimination against a woman who announces her intention of getting married; however, the tribunal concluded that Parliament had not so stated and it could see no way round the interpretation of the *SDA 1975* without rewriting *s 3(1)*. The wording of the *EqA 2010* reflects the wording of the *SDA 1975* and the *Explanatory Notes to the EqA 2010* explain that a person who is engaged to be married is not married and therefore does not have the protected characteristic (see also the *EHRC Employment Code*, *para 2.33*). Accordingly, Parliament's intention is apparent, namely that a person only receives protection under *EqA 2010, s 8* or *SDA 1975, s 3* when they are married or a civil partner. Notwithstanding this fact, the tribunal in *Bick* could have held that a relevant act of discrimination occurred at the date of the termination of the employee's contract (see *Gloucester Working Men's Club and Institute v James* [1986] ICR 603, EAT) by which time the complainant was 'married'.

There is no definition of 'married' in *EqA 2010* and *SDA 1975*. The common law and statutory provisions concerning marriage apply and the *EHRC Employment Code* states that marriage is 'any formal union of a man and woman which is legally recognised in the UK as a marriage'. A person who has previously married, but is now divorced is very unlikely to be regarded as 'married' under *EqA 2010)* (with the consequence that *EqA 2010* does not specifically protect people from prejudice against divorced persons even though the fact of having been divorced might be thought to be a marital 'status'). Indeed, the *Explanatory Notes to the EqA 2010* explain that a divorcee or a person whose civil partnership has been dissolved is not married or in a civil partnership and therefore does not have the relevant protected characteristic (see also *EHRC Employment Code*, *para 2.33*).

5.3 Civil partners

SDA 1975, s 3 was amended with effect from 5 December 2005 by the *Civil Partnerships Act 2004* ('*CPA 2004*'). *CPA 2004* created the civil partnership, a new legal status for relationships between homosexual couples, and it brought to an end certain discriminatory effects of the rule that under English law a marriage can only exist between a man and a woman (see eg *KB v NHS Pensions Agency and Secretary of State for Health* [2004] IRLR 240, ECJ). *CPA 2004, s 251* amended *SDA 1975, s 3* so as to include civil partners as well as married persons within its reach. The *EqA 2010* retains that protection, so, for example, a civil partner who is treated by his employer less favourably than a person who is neither a civil partner nor a married person has a right to make a complaint.

A 'civil partner' is a person who has been registered as the civil partner of a person of the same sex (see *CPA 2004, s 1*).

The inclusion of discrimination on the grounds of civil partnership into *SDA 1975, s 3*, did not reinvigorate marital status discrimination law, which remains a somewhat uncommon concept in the tribunals. For now, it can simply be observed that, just as unmarried heterosexual partners remain unprotected by *EqA 2010, s 8* and *SDA 1975, s 3*, so too do those homosexual partners who have chosen not to enter into a formal civil partnership. They must rely, to the appropriate extent, on the provisions dealing with discrimination on the basis of sexual orientation (see SEXUAL ORIENTATION (9)).

5.4 DIRECT DISCRIMINATION: LESS FAVOURABLE TREATMENT ON GROUNDS OF MARITAL STATUS/CIVIL PARTNERSHIP

The two most obvious examples of direct discrimination under *EqA 2010, ss 8 and 13* (or *SDA 1975, s 3(1)*) might be summarised by the behaviour of two theoretical and paradigmatically unenlightened employers: (1) the 'anti-family employer'; and (2) the 'homophobic employer'. The anti-family employer, for example, does not want to employ anyone who is married, because he feels they will not be sufficiently dedicated to their career. Their priorities will be elsewhere. The employer is treating people less favourably on grounds of their marital status. The homophobic employer, by contrast, gladly accepts married persons, or unmarried persons, but not homosexual employees who are part of a civil partnership. Those employees are being treated less favourably than others on account of their civil partnership status. They too are protected by *EqA 2010, ss 8 and 13* or *SDA 1975, s 3*.

There are relatively few examples in the case law of direct discrimination contrary to *SDA 1975, s 3*, and such examples as exist might prove misleading to the unwary. Take for example, *Chief Constable of Bedfordshire Constabulary v Graham* [2002] IRLR 239, EAT. Here a female police inspector was promoted to the position of area inspector, only to be promptly demoted back to her former position. The reason for the demotion was that she was married to the chief superintendent of the same police force. Her complaints of indirect sex discrimination, and both direct and indirect discrimination contrary to *SDA 1975, s 3*, were upheld by a tribunal and consequently by the EAT. But was Mrs Graham in fact demoted on grounds of *marital status* (ie the fact that she was a married person), or was she demoted because of the *identity of her husband*? The two things are not necessarily the same, and the case is not, in fact, authority for the proposition that a person subjected to a detriment because of her marriage to, or partnership or relationship with, a particular person necessarily has a claim under *s 3*. (It may of course, be unfair to dismiss a person because of her relationship with a particular person, or discriminatory on grounds of sex: see eg *McLean v Paris Travel Service* [1976] IRLR 202.) The EAT in *Graham* explained (at para 58 of its judgment) that the reason why the claim under *s 3* succeeded was that the employer's reason for the treatment of Mrs Graham, in this particular case, was that she would not be a competent and compellable witness against her spouse in any criminal proceedings. That was a reason, thought the EAT, which (being an attempt to apply the law of evidence in relation to married persons) was *marriage-specific* (not spouse-specific), and it was therefore direct discrimination on grounds of marital status within *s 3*.

The principles relating to direct discrimination, developed in detail in the sex and race discrimination case law, will also apply here. One specific question which arises in this context (and has not yet been answered by the courts) relates to the identity of the comparator. Might a civil partner be able to complain of direct discrimination under *EqA 2010, s 8* or *SDA 1975, s 3(1)(a)* by comparing himself to a married person? (For example, an applicant for a job discovers after interview that the employer believes in 'family values' and is looking to take on married persons with or without children, but no single people, or homosexual people, and definitely not people (like him) who have entered into a civil partnership, which the employer believes undermines family values). The wording of the *SDA 1975* suggested that he could not. The complainant needed to satisfy the condition (*s 3(1)*) of being *either* married, *or* being a civil partner, in order to come within the section at all. The person (or hypothetical person) with whom comparison was to be made was someone who did not satisfy that condition, ie someone who is neither a married person nor a civil partner. By contrast, the wording and structure of the *EqA 2010* provides some scope for arguing that a civil partner can compare his treatment to that of a married person. By *EqA 2010, s 8* a person has the protected characteristic if the person is married or is a civil partner. To establish direct discrimination contrary to *EqA 2010, s 13(1)*, a person must show that they were treated less favourably than others, there is no longer a requirement that a person must show that they were treated less favourably than someone who does not fulfil the condition of being married or a civil partner.

Unlike other protected characteristics, direct discrimination because of marital status or civil partnership does not occur where the less favourable treatment is because of the victim's association with someone who is married or a civil partner. *EqA 2010, s 13(4)* provides that direct discrimination because of being married or a civil partner only occurs if the victim of the discrimination is married or a civil partner. Further, the new provision contained in the *EqA 2010* (*s 13(1)*) allowing for a discrimination claim on two combined protected grounds does not apply to the protected ground of marriage/civil partnership. This provision did not come into force in October 2010: see **1.57–1.59**.

5.5 INDIRECT DISCRIMINATION AGAINST MARRIED PERSONS/CIVIL PARTNERS

Here the classic example, no doubt rarer these days than it was when *SDA 1975, s 3* was enacted in its original form, is the employer who firmly believes that any applicant for employment who has a child is 'unreliable' and refuses to recruit such a person, or subjects him or her to other detriments once employed. In *Hurley v Mustoe* [1981] ICR 490, [1981] IRLR 208 it fell to the EAT (Browne-Wilkinson J, as he then was, presiding) to correct the judgment of an industrial tribunal, who had erroneously thought that there was nothing wrong with such an attitude under *SDA 1975*. As the EAT pointed out, even if (which should not have been assumed) there might have been some individuals for whom, in the employer's experience, the very fact of having had children had caused unreliability at work, it obviously did not follow that it was justifiable for him to have excluded from his consideration the entire class of persons with children: 'a condition excluding all members of a class from employment cannot be justified on the ground that some members of that class are undesirable employees'. The practice would indirectly discriminate against married persons and would be disproportionate.

Beyond the straightforward cases, and just as in other claims of indirect sex discrimination, it will be necessary to consider carefully the evidence to be tendered about differential impact, and the correct pool to be assessed. It is no longer wise for a party to expect tribunals to assume that apparently neutral provisions, criteria or practices in fact operate to the disadvantage of married persons or persons in civil partnerships. See, for example, *Kidd v DRG (UK) Ltd* [1985] ICR 405, [1985] IRLR 190, EAT; to be compared with an older, and more relaxed approach in *Thorndyke v Bell Fruit (North Central) Ltd* [1979] IRLR 1.

As to justification and proportionality (*EqA 2010, s 19(3)(d)(iii)* and *SDA 1975, s 3(1)(b)(iii)*), it is likely that the concepts and authorities which are relevant to indirect sex discrimination generally will apply here (see **8.20**).

5.6 FURTHER INDICATIONS OF DISCRIMINATION: STEREOTYPING

Discriminatory attitudes to married persons can take various forms. An employer should not assume that the husband is the breadwinner, and such an assumption will be evidence of sex discrimination if applied detrimentally: see eg *Coleman v Skyrail Oceanic Ltd* [1981] IRLR 398, CA. Similarly, the mere fact that an employee's husband has relocated does not justify an assumption that the couple will necessarily live together and/or that the employee will necessarily follow the husband with no concern for her own career: *Horsey v Dyfed County Council* [1982] IRLR 395, EAT. Such generalised assumptions can constitute direct sex discrimination if they lead to less favourable treatment.

5.7 THE HARASSMENT PROBLEM

Whilst it is unlawful to discriminate on grounds of sex and sexual orientation: *EqA 2010, s 26* (previously *SDA 1975, ss 4A and 6(2A)* and the *Employment Equality (Sexual Orientation) Regulations 2003*, *reg 5*), it is not unlawful to harass a person on grounds that they are married or a civil partner (*EqA 2010, s 26)*. This is because the protected characteristics relevant to the harassment protection at *EqA 2010, s 26* expressly exclude marriage or civil partnership.

Before the inclusion of *SDA 1975, ss 4A* and *6(2A)* into the *SDA 1975* (in force from 1 October 2005) there was a somewhat artificial practice of viewing sexual harassment at work as actionable as a type of 'detriment' under *s 6(2)(b)*, and as a form of 'less favourable treatment' on grounds of sex under *s 1(1)(a)*. Indeed an amendment to *SDA 1975, s 82(1)* (with effect from 1 October 2005) made it clear that harassment was not a type of detriment.

However, there was no equivalent provision to *s 6(2A)*, specifically deeming harassment on the grounds of marital status (or civil partnership) as an unlawful act. The potential answer to the problem was to suggest that *s 4A(1)*, by referring to harassment 'on grounds of sex', was potentially wide enough to include marital status discrimination. After all, the *Equal Treatment Directive (76/2007/EC)* prohibits 'discrimination . . . on grounds of sex either directly or indirectly by reference in particular to marital or family status', and thus arguably views marital status discrimination as a subset of sex discrimination.

But that answer required a very strong Euro-inspired decision from a tribunal or court, since it appeared to go against the grain of the domestic *SDA 1975*, in three respects. First, and unlike the *Equal Treatment Directive*, *SDA 1975* specifically distinguished between 'discrimination' (clearly wide enough to include *s 3* discrimination), and 'sex discrimination' (limited to *ss 1*, *2*, and *3A* discrimination only): see *s 5(1)*. So discrimination on the grounds of marital status was not, according to *SDA 1975* itself, sex discrimination. Second (a similar point), if direct marital status discrimination was discrimination on grounds of sex, then why the need for *s 3* at all? Third, if correct, the argument would leave civil partners stranded, and worse off than married persons: whilst married employees might be able complain about being harassed by reference to the words of the *Equal Treatment Directive*, civil partners probably could not. One was therefore forced to concede that neither the problem as stated, nor the potential answer to it as formulated, are particularly attractive, and that legislative reform could and should make the position clear.

Legislative reform in the shape of the *EqA 2010* has now made the position clear and it is apparent that it is not unlawful to harass a person on grounds that a person is married or a civil partner. However, it may be possible for a claimant in these circumstances to construct a claim of sex or sexual orientation discrimination/harassment (*EHRC Employment Code* at *para 7.5*). A claim under the *Protection from Harassment Act 1997* may also be possible (see **1.96**).

5.8 **Instructing, causing or inducing discrimination**

It is unlawful to instruct, cause or induce someone to discriminate against, or victimise another person, or to attempt to do so (*EqA 2010, s 111*). A claim can be brought by the 'victim' of the discrimination, the person who was instructed to carry out the discrimination and the EHRC. (See **1.60**.)

5.9 **Liability of employees and agents and aiding discrimination**

Where employees commit acts of discrimination against fellow employees, their employer will be liable if the acts were committed during the course of employment (*EqA 2010, s 109(1)*). Employers are also liable for the discriminatory acts of their agents if they are acting with the employer's authority (*s 109(4)*). In each case it is irrelevant whether the employer knew or approved of the acts (*s 109(3)*). However, there is a defence for employers in relation to the acts of their employees (but not agents) if they can show that they took all reasonable steps to prevent the employee from doing the act in question (*s 109(4)*). The employees and agents will also have personal liability for their acts of discrimination (*EqA 2010, s 110*), even if the employer has a defence. See **1.163**ff.

It is also unlawful for an individual to knowingly help another to carry out an act which is unlawful under *EqA 2010* (*s 112(1)*). (See **1.62**.)

5.10 **Former employees**

Former employees are likewise protected against direct and indirect discrimination, provided the detriment complained of 'arises out of or is closely connected to' a previous relationship with the respondent (*EqA 2010, s 108(1)*). (See **1.35**.)

However, there is an unintended lacuna in the *EqA 2010*'s protection for former employees from victimisation. (See **1.107**.)

5.11 **STATUTORY EXCEPTIONS**

By virtue of *EqA 2010, Sch 9* and *s 83* there are a number of statutory exceptions to direct or indirect discrimination against married persons or civil partners.

EqA 2010, s 83 and *Sch 9, para 1* provides a general exception to what would otherwise be unlawful direct discrimination in relation to work. The exception applies where it is a requirement that a person is not married or a civil partner and the person to whom that requirement is applied does not meet the requirement (or does not meet it to the reasonable satisfaction of the person who applied it). To satisfy the exemption and having regard to the nature of or context of the work, the requirement must be an occupational requirement and the application of the requirement must be a proportionate means of achieving a legitimate aim. The *Explanatory Notes to the EqA 2010*, which are likely to be relevant to the interpretation of the exception, state that the requirement must be crucial to the post, and not merely one of several important factors. It also must not be a sham or pretext. The paragraph makes it expressly clear that the burden of showing that the exception applied is on those seeking to rely on it. The exception can be used by employers, principals (as defined in *s 41*) in relation to contract work, partners, members of limited liability partnerships and those with the power to appoint or remove office-holders, or to recommend an appointment to a public office (*EqA 2010, Sch 9, para 1(2)*) (see further **1.145**ff).

The *SDA 1975, s 7(2)(h)* provided one of a number of situations in which sex could be a genuine occupational requirement. *Section 7* as a whole applied to 'sex discrimination' (*s 7(1)*), and therefore marital status discrimination was probably not caught (*s 5(1)(b)*). However, it was worth noting that *s 7(2)(h)* specifically allowed an employer to appoint a husband and wife or civil partnership team to a position without discriminating against other applicants on the grounds of sex.

Where employment is for the purposes of an organised religion, *EqA 2010, Sch 9, para 2* allows an employer to apply a requirement that a person is not married or a civil partner or not married to, or a civil partner of, a person who has a living former spouse or civil partner or a requirement relating to circumstances in which a marriage or civil partnership came to an end if it can be shown that the employment is for the purposes of an organised religion, the application of the requirement engages the compliance or non-compliance principle and the person to whom the requirement is applied does not meet it (or the employer has reasonable grounds for not being satisfied that the person meets it) (*EqA 2010, Sch 9, para 2*). The application of a requirement will engage the compliance principle if the requirement is applied so as to comply with the doctrines of the religion. The application of a requirement will engage the non-compliance principle if, because of the nature or context of the employment, the requirement is applied so as to avoid conflicting with the strongly held religious convictions of a significant number of the religion's followers. Similar exclusions exist for discrimination in the context of office-holders (*EqA 2010, Sch 9, para 2(2)*).

The *Explanatory Notes to the EqA 2010* suggest that this exception is intended to have a much narrower effect than it might appear to have on the face of the legislation. The notes state that the requirement must be '*crucial to the post, and not merely one of several important factors*' and that this specific exception '*is intended to cover a very narrow range of employment: ministers of religion and a small number of lay posts, including those that exist to promote and represent religion*', and applying such a requirement is permissible only where it is '*a proportionate way*' of complying with a religion's doctrine or avoiding conflict with a group of followers. The emphasis placed in the *Explanatory Notes* on proportionality is striking, given the absence of a reference to it in the legislation itself, and it may be anticipated that the courts will soon have to deal with the extent to which the *Explanatory Notes* should influence the interpretation of *Sch 9*, in particular taking into account the guidance of Lord Steyn in *R (on the application of Westminster City Council) v National Asylum and Support Service* [2002] UKHL 38, [2002] 1 WLR 2956 (at paras [5] and [6]). It is likely that *Sch 9, para 2* will be given a narrow construction, since it is a derogation from the principle of equal treatment: see *R (on the application of Amicus – MSF section) v Secretary of State for Trade and Industry* [2004] EWHC 860 (Admin), [2004] IRLR 430.

Pursuant to the *SDA 1975, s 19(1)*, where employment was for the purposes of organised religion an employer was entitled to apply a requirement relating to a person not being either married or a civil partner (*s 19(3)(c)*); or, in relation to a person who is either married or a civil partner, relating to the person or their spouse or civil partner, not having a living former spouse or civil partner, or to how either the person or their spouse or civil partner ceased to be married or a civil partner (*s 19(3)(d)*). However, the requirement must be applied so as to comply with the doctrines of the religion or to avoid conflicting with the strongly held religious convictions of a significant number of the religion's followers (*s 19(1)(c)*).

Neither the occupational requirement exclusion nor the religious requirement exclusions apply to discrimination as to the terms on which a person is offered employment or employed.

In addition, there was an exception found in the *Employment Equality (Sexual Orientation) Regulations 2003 (SI 2003/1661), reg 25* ('*SOR 2003*'), which provided that neither any prevention or restriction of access to benefits by reference to marital status, nor the conferring of a benefit on married persons and civil partners to the exclusion of all others, shall be unlawful (see **9.22**). A similar exclusion can now be found at *EqA 2010, Sch 9, para 18*.

6 Race discrimination

6.1 INTRODUCTION

Legislation

Pre-Race Relations Act 1976

Race discrimination has been outlawed in the UK since the introduction of the *Race Relations Acts* of *1965* and *1968*. Both these pieces of legislation were, however, considerably narrower in scope than the later *Race Relations Act 1976 ('RRA 1976')* which repealed and replaced them. In October 2010 *RRA 1976* was itself repealed and it is now the *Equality Act 2010 ('EqA 2010')* which provides the UK legislative framework for protection from discrimination on grounds of race.

6.2 *Race Relations Act 1976*

Throughout its enactment, the *RRA 1976* was amended by numerous pieces of secondary legislation, the most significant of which was the *Race Relations Act 1976 (Amendment) Regulations 2003 (SI 2003/1626) ('2003 Amendment Regulations*'). The *2003 Amendment Regulations* implemented the *Race Discrimination Framework Directive (Council Directive 2000/43/EC)* ('*Race Directive*') which was issued by the European Council in accordance with its powers under *Article 6* of the *Treaty of Rome* (now *Article 13* of the amended *Treaty*).

Despite strong opposition from the Commission for Racial Equality, the UK government limited the ambit of the *2003 Amendment Regulations* to race, ethnic and national origins, in accordance with the ambit of the *Race Directive*. However, *RRA 1976* also prohibited discrimination on grounds of colour and nationality (the latter of which is expressly excluded from the scope of the *Race Directive* by *Article 3, para 2*). The *2003 Amendment Regulations* therefore gave rise to a disparity in the protection afforded to employees (and others) by the *RRA 1976*, depending upon which racial ground was under consideration.

6.3 *Equality Act 2010*

The *EqA 2010* repealed *RRA 1976* and related legislation with effect from October 2010, and set in place a new legislative structure. The *EqA 2010* harmonised protection across all racial grounds, removing the differential treatment of ethnic and national origins. It also introduced a power for caste to be added as an aspect of race, although the government has not announced whether it intends to exercise the power at this stage. The Act also harmonised much of the law between the different strands of discrimination as well as amending some of the underlying concepts (see **1.4**).

6.4 The CRE and EHRC

The Commission for Racial Equality (CRE) was brought into being by *RRA 1976, s 43*. As discussed at **1.182**, the Equality and Human Rights Commission (EHRC) replaced the CRE in October 2007.

The CRE was granted authority to issue codes of practice in its field by *RRA 1976, s 47*. The EHRC was granted similar power (in respect of all forms of discrimination, not just race) under *Equality Act 2006* (*EqA 2006*)*, s 14(1)*.

6.5 Codes of Practice and Guidance

In addition to the legislative framework described above, employers can also turn to a wide variety of guidance materials. In particular, the EHRC has produced an *Employment Statutory Code of Practice* (*'EHRC Employment Code*') which is in draft form at the time of writing. When it comes into effect it will replace the Commission for Racial Equality's statutory code of practice, which has to date been the principal guidance in place and held similar status to the new *EHRC Employment Code*. The contents of the *EHRC Employment Code* are admissible in evidence in an employment tribunal or court. Further, if any provision of the *EHRC Employment Code* appears to the tribunal or court to be relevant to any question arising in the proceedings before it, it *must* take that provision into account when determining that question. However, failure to observe any provision of the *Code* is not of itself unlawful.

The EHRC has also produced non-statutory guidance for employers and employees, although this does not have any statutory status and tribunals do not have to take it into account.

6.6 RACE AND RACIAL GROUNDS

Introduction

The protected characteristic of race is defined in *EqA 2010, s 9(1)* to include '(a) colour; (b) nationality; (c) ethnic or national origins'. A Minister may, by Order, amend *EqA 2010* to include caste as an aspect of race (*EqA 2010, s 9(5)*).

A reference in *EqA 2010* to a person who has a particular protected characteristic is a reference to a person of a particular racial group. A reference to persons who share the protected characteristic of race is a reference to a person of the same racial group respectively (*EqA 2010, s 9(2)*). A racial group is a group defined by reference to race (*EqA 2010, s 9(3)*) and a particular racial group may comprise two or more distinct racial groups (*EqA 2010, s 9(4)*). The *EHRC Employment Code* gives the following examples of racial groups: 'black Britons' (comprising those people who are both black and who are British citizens); 'South Asian' (including Indians, Pakistanis, Bangladeshis and Sri Lankans); and those of a 'non-British' nationality.

The new definition of race in *EqA 2010* differs from the definition of 'racial grounds' in *RRA 1976, s 3(1)*. The old definition included 'any of the following grounds, namely colour, race, nationality or ethnic or national origins'. Race is no longer treated as a sub-category of racial grounds, but (more logically) as the over-arching concept. Under the old law, the EAT emphasised that the grounds for race discrimination overlap with one another (*Chagger v Abbey National plc* [2009] EWCA Civ 1202, [2010] ICR 397). The old authorities on the common concepts of colour, nationality and ethnic or national origins are likely to remain authoritative and are set out below.

6.7 Colour

This category is self-explanatory and has produced little case law. An employer discriminates against an employee on grounds of their colour if, for example, they treat black employees less favourably than white employees. The EAT has stated that it is very hard to conceive of a case of discrimination on the ground of colour which cannot also properly be characterised as discrimination on the ground of race or ethnic origin (*Chagger*, above). This raises the question of why colour is a separate head of race discrimination at all. The likeliest explanation is that it has been in use since the *Race Relations Act 1965* and, at that time, its use was more prevalent. Colour is not referred to expressly in the *Race Directive*.

6.8 Nationality

'Nationality' did not appear on the list of prohibited grounds in either the 1965 or 1968 predecessors of the *RRA 1976*. This created a gap in protection as revealed by the decision in *Ealing London Borough v Race Relations Board* [1972] AC 342. Ealing adopted the rule that the applicant should be a British subject under the *British Nationality Act 1948* as a condition of appearing on its waiting list for council accommodation. On this basis, a Polish applicant, who was otherwise qualified, was refused council accommodation. The Race Relations Board argued that Ealing had discriminated against the applicant on the ground of his national origins as prohibited by the 1968 Act. The House of Lords held by a majority that the terms national in 'national origins' referred to race and not citizenship. On that basis, Ealing did not discriminate against the applicant on the basis that he was a Polish national and would have treated him the same way of whatever foreign country he was citizen.

RRA 1976 expressly included nationality in the list of prohibited grounds. However, the distinction between citizenship and race remained as is clear from *Tejani v Superintendant Registrar for the District of Peterborough* [1986] IRLR 502. In *Tejani*, the Court of Appeal held that it was not unlawful racial discrimination for the Registrar to require to see the passports of anyone from abroad who wished to be married by him. The Registrar treated all persons from abroad in the same way, regardless of their national or racial origins. This distinction is likely to be maintained under *EqA 2010*. Nationality is distinct from national origins, which is discussed below.

6.9 Ethnic or national origins

Under *RRA 1976*, the concept of 'ethnic origins' was broader than race. In *Mandla v Dowell Lee* [1983] 2 AC 548, the House of Lords held that Sikhs could qualify as an ethnic group, even if they were not a racial group. The case concerned a headmaster's decision to refuse a Sikh boy a place at his school on the ground that the boy wished to wear a turban and refused to cut his hair. The case concerned indirect discrimination (not direct) since there were several Sikh pupils at the school. However, the requirement not to wear a turban clearly had a disproportionate impact upon Sikhs. The Court of Appeal had reasoned that ethnic origins were the same as racial origins and that Sikhs were not a racial group as they were not biologically distinguishable from other inhabitants of the Punjab. The court went on to hold that the complaint was really of religious discrimination (which was not at the time prohibited).

In the House of Lords, Lord Fraser of Tullybelton gave the leading speech and defined an ethnic group as one which regards itself, and is regarded by others, as a distinct community on the basis of certain characteristics. Some of these characteristics are essential and include:

(i) a long-shared history of which the group is conscious as distinguishing it from other groups and which it keeps alive; and

(ii) a cultural tradition of its own, including family and social customs often, but not necessarily, associated with religious observance.

Non-essential characteristics which serve as a useful guide to distinguishing ethnic groups from the broader community include:

(i) a common geographical origin or descent from a small number of common ancestors;

(ii) a common language, although this need not be peculiar to the group;

(iii) a common literature which is peculiar to the group;

(iv) a common religion which is different from that of neighbouring groups or the broader community; and

(v) being a minority or being an oppressed or dominant group within a larger community.

Lord Fraser also emphasised that membership of an ethnic group could occur through adherence.

In *R (on the application of E) v Governing Body of JFS (Secretary of State for Children, Schools and Families, interested parties) (United Synagogue intervening)* [2009] UKSC 15, [2010] 1 AC 278, a 5-4 majority of the Supreme Court found that the reference to ethnic or national origins in *RRA 1976* requires a focus on descent and that a requirement that an applicant to a faith school should be descended from a Jewish woman was discriminatory on the grounds of ethnic origin.

Applying *Mandla*, it has been held that Jews may be members of a racial or ethnic group (*Seide v Gillette Industries* [1980] IRLR 427). The Court of Appeal has also found, again applying *Mandla*, that gipsies could constitute an ethnic group as they had not merged wholly with the majority population (*Commission for Racial Equality v Dutton* [1989] IRLR 8). This was so notwithstanding despite their long presence in the country and the fact that they could no longer claim common racial stock.

By contrast, Rastafarians have been found not to constitute an ethnic group (*Crown Suppliers (PSA) Ltd v Dawkins* [1993] ICR 517). In *Dawkins*, the Court of Appeal found that there were insufficient grounds to distinguish Rastafarians from the rest of the Afro-Caribbean population and the 60-year history of the Rastafarian movement did not amount to a long-shared history. For the same reason, Muslims cannot be regarded as an ethnic group. However, there remains the possibility that a rule which disadvantages Muslims as a class (for example, by disciplining them for taking time off to attend Eid or requiring them not to wear a headscarf) may be found to constitute indirect discrimination against a racial group (*J H Walker Ltd v Hussain* [1996] IRLR 11). Now that there is express provision on religious discrimination (see **Religion and belief (7)**), such actions are less likely under *EqA 2010*. It is a mistake to focus on the single factor of language as sufficient to identify an ethnic group. In *Gwynedd County Council v Jones* [1986] ICR 833, the EAT held that the tribunal had erred in regarding the English-speaking Welsh as a distinct ethnic group from the Welsh-speaking Welsh.

'National origins' has a broader meaning than an individual's legal nationality acquired at birth. Thus, the Inner House has held that the English and Scots have different national origins, although they both share citizenship of the United Kingdom (*BBC Scotland v Souster* [2001] IRLR 150). Mr Souster claimed that his contract as a rugby journalist with BBC Scotland was not renewed on the ground that he was English. He was replaced by a Scottish woman. BBC Scotland sought to defend the proceedings on the basis that the English and the Scots were not different racial groups and so discrimination between them could not be said to be on racial grounds. The Inner House rejected this argument: 'national origins' is a broader term than nationality and could cover differences between the Scots and English.

6.10 TYPES OF RACE DISCRIMINATION

Direct discrimination

EqA 2010, s 13(1) sets out the test for direct discrimination. It provides that a person unlawfully discriminates against another if, because of race, he treats that person less favourably than he treats or would treat others. There is no justification defence to a claim of direct race discrimination (see **1.46**) and so any direct race discrimination will be unlawful unless an occupational requirement applies under *EqA 2010, Sch 9, Part 1* (see **6.54**).

The *EqA 2010* test is very similar to the previous test under *RRA 1976, s 1(1)(a)* but, as discussed in **1.46**, the phrase 'on the grounds of' has been replaced by 'because of'. As the government did not intend to change the legal meaning of the test, tribunals are likely to make use of the pre-October 2010 case law when determining whether direct race discrimination has occurred.

Despite the fact that the test for direct discrimination under the *RRA 1976* required an answer to be given to a single question, the courts, in line with their approach to the other strands of discrimination (see **1.49**ff), historically followed a two-stage approach. It is likely they will continue to do so when interpreting *s 13(1)*. The courts looked first at whether the complainant was treated less favourably than others were treated, or would have been treated in the same circumstances, and then at the reason for that less favourable treatment (see *Glasgow City Council v Zafar* [1998] ICR 120). Originally, *RRA 1976* placed the burden of proving both 'stages' on the claimant. However, the courts recognised the difficulty faced by claimants in producing direct evidence of racial discrimination, since those who discriminate on grounds of race 'do not in general advertise their prejudices' (*Zafar*). Case law established that where there was no direct evidence of race discrimination, the tribunal was entitled to look at all the facts and circumstances of the case and draw appropriate inferences. Furthermore, where a claimant established that he was treated less favourably, and demonstrated a difference in race pointing to the possibility of racial discrimination, the tribunal could look to the alleged discriminator for an explanation. Where the tribunal considered the explanation to be inadequate, it *could* infer that the discrimination was on racial grounds (*King v Great Britain-China Centre* [1992] ICR 516), but was not bound to do so as a matter of law (Zafar).

This approach was in effect codified by the insertion of *s 54A* into *RRA 1976* by the *2003 Amendment Regulations* (which implemented the *Burden of Proof Directive (2000/43/EC)*), although only in relation to race, ethnic or national origin. Where the claimant has proved facts from which the tribunal *could*, in the absence of an adequate explanation by the respondent, conclude that the respondent had committed an act of discrimination, the burden shifts to the respondent to prove that he did not commit that act (see *Madarassy v Nomura International plc* [2007] All ER (D) 226 (Jan) for more detail on what is needed to shift the burden of proof to the respondent). At this second stage, if the respondent is unable to prove that he did not commit the act, then the tribunal *must* uphold the claimant's complaint (for guidance on the application of *s 54A* see *Wong v Igen Ltd (Equal Opportunities Commission intervening)* [2005] EWCA Civ 142, [2005] ICR 931 and *Madarassy*).

The burden of proof provision in *RRA 1976* is replicated in *EqA 2010, s 136* and applies to all aspects of 'race' as defined. There is a slight change to the wording in where the burden of proof shifts to the respondent, the section now provides that the tribunal must find discrimination 'in the absence of any other explanation' (rather than in the absence of an adequate explanation), but it seems likely that this will not affect the application of the section and the pre *EqA 2010* case law will continue to be relevant.

In respect of pre-October 2010 cases of discrimination on grounds of nationality, the approach adopted by pre-*s 54A* case law will continue to apply. In light of *Chagger v Abbey National plc* [2009] EWCA Civ 1202, [2010] ICR 397 it would appear that the 'new' regime under the *RRA 1976* as amended by the 2003 Amendment Regulations applies to claims on grounds of 'colour' (but see also *Okonu v G4S Services (UK) Ltd* [2008] ICR 598). In practice, the distinction in relation to different racial grounds is came into play relatively infrequently, as different grounds are frequently inextricably linked. It has also been suggested by the Court of Appeal that the *s 54A* approach should be followed in any event (see *Adebayo v Dresdner Kleinwort Wasserstein Ltd* [2005] IRLR 514).

It was established prior to the inclusion of *RRA 1976, s 54A* that a two-stage approach may not always be appropriate in every case, as the issues of less favourable treatment and racial grounds may be intertwined, particularly, for example, where the identity of the relevant comparator is a matter of dispute (see *Shamoon v Chief Constable of the Royal Ulster Constabulary* [2003] UKHL 11, [2003] 2 All ER 26 and **1.46**). The Court of Appeal confirmed that this remained the position under *s 54A*, and it is likely that this will continue to be the position under *EqA 2010, s 136*; failure to follow a two-stage test will not automatically mean that a tribunal has erred in law, provided that it placed the burden of explaining the differential treatment on the alleged discriminator (*Brown v Croydon London Borough Council* [2007] All ER (D) 239 (Jan)). For further discussion on burden of proof see **1.128ff.**

6.11 Less favourable treatment

Treatment

Treatment has been interpreted widely, to include not only obvious behaviour (such as failing to promote an employee or dismissing an employee), but also, for example, acts or words of discouragement (in appropriate circumstances) (*Simon v Brimham Associates* [1987] ICR 596; Tower *Hamlets London Borough Council v Rabin* [1989] ICR 693) or a denial of choice (*Birmingham City Council v Equal Opportunities Commission (No 1)* [1989] AC 1155). The less favourable treatment must actually have taken place; it is not enough for a complainant to show that he 'would have' been treated less favourably, for example, if he had attended a job interview (*Baldwin v Brighton and Hove City Council* [2007] ICR 680; EAT decision under *SDA 1975*). A discriminatory public statement (such as that the employer will not employ Moroccans) will amount to less favourable treatment (see the ECJ's decision in *Centrum voor gelijkheid van kansen en voor racismebestrijding v Firma Feryn NV: C-54/07.*

Paying someone who is being less favourably treated extra does not make the treatment lawful (*Jeremiah v Ministry of Defence* [1980] QB 87, per Lord Denning and Brightman LJ in a Court of Appeal decision under *SDA 1975*).

It is the treatment itself rather than the consequences of that treatment that the tribunal must look at (*Balgobin v Tower Hamlets London Borough Council* [1987] ICR 829; EAT decision relating to the *SDA 1975*). *Chief Constable of West Yorkshire v Khan* [2001] UKHL 48, [2001] 1 WLR 1947 (a victimisation case) illustrates the point. In that case, the House of Lords held that the claimant was treated less favourably where his employer refused his request to provide a reference to support his application for a promotion, even though the reference would have been poor and the consequences of providing that reference would have been seriously damaging to his application.

It is less favourable treatment to segregate someone from others because of their race (*EqA 2010, s 13(5)*) and there is no need to identify a comparator in these circumstances. This was also the position taken in *RRA 1976, s 1(2)* (*Furniture, Timber & Allied Trades Union (FTATU) v Modgill* [1980] IRLR 142, EAT); and is the case regardless of whether the facilities are equal for both sets of employees. In other words, the separation on racial grounds is itself less favourable treatment. However, *Modgill* established that it is not discriminatory for an employer to fail to prevent segregation caused by the workers themselves. In this case, only Asian workers were employed in the paint shop, and it was alleged that this was segregation by the employer on racial grounds since the paint shop was considered 'dirty' work which no one else wanted to do. Only Asian people were put forward for these jobs, but, as it turned out, this was not because of any policy of the employer but because when vacancies arose in the shop they were filled by persons introduced by workers already working there, usually relatives. The failure of the employer to enforce a positive policy to remove any possibility of segregation was not unlawful discrimination. Such a recruitment practice, involving 'word of mouth' advertising of roles is, however, not to be recommended and may amount to unlawful indirect discrimination even if it does not amount to direct discrimination. This point was not considered in *Modgill.*

6.12 *Unfavourable and less favourable treatment distinguished*

The requirement in *EqA 2010, s 13(1)* (and previously in *RRA 1976, s 1(1)(a)*) refers to *less* favourable treatment. This requires a comparative element. Thus showing unfavourable or unreasonable treatment will not be enough. The House of Lords has stated:

> '[T]he conduct of a hypothetical reasonable employer is irrelevant. The alleged discriminator may or may not be a reasonable employer. If he is not a reasonable

> employer he might well have treated another employee in just the same unsatisfactory way as he treated the complainant, in which case he would not have treated the complainant "less favourably"' (*Glasgow City Council v Zafar* [1998] ICR 120).

In *Madarassy* (a sex discrimination case) the Court of Appeal held that the claimant had failed to show discrimination at the first stage where there was no *less* favourable treatment as all employees were treated equally badly regardless of gender or level within the company. The tribunal had found that there was 'equality of shouting regardless of gender or level'.

The principle from *Zafar* was applied in *Martins v Marks & Spencer plc* [1998] ICR 1005, where the Court of Appeal held that a tribunal had erred in law in asking whether there had been bias on the part of the employer instead of asking whether the complainant had been treated less favourably than a person of a different racial group (see also *Bradford Hospitals NHS Trust v Al-Shabib* [2003] IRLR 4).

Since *Zafar*, arguments have been raised that it is open to a tribunal to infer discrimination from unreasonable treatment if the alleged discriminator does not show that equally unreasonable treatment was or would have been applied to others (see the *obiter* comment of Sedley LJ in *Anya v University of Oxford* [2001] ICR 847 at 857A). This argument was rejected by the Court of Appeal in *Bahl v The Law Society* [2004] IRLR 799. The court applied *Zafar* and emphasised that showing unreasonable treatment of others is only one way of avoiding an inference of discrimination. However, their Lordships did state that the absence of an explanation for unreasonable treatment (rather than the unreasonable treatment itself) could lead a tribunal to infer racial discrimination which the respondent could then rebut through leading evidence of a genuine reason which is not discriminatory and was the ground of his conduct. *Bahl* was a case on the law before the statutory change to the burden of proof. In *Igen v Wong* [2005] ICR 931 (another sex discrimination case) the Court of Appeal cautioned tribunals from too readily inferring unlawful sex discrimination from unreasonable conduct where there is no evidence of other discriminatory behaviour on such ground, but held that 'it was open to a tribunal to make such an inference'.

6.13 *Comparators*

The test in *EqA 2010, s 13(1)* (and previously in *RRA 1976, s 1(1)(a)*) requires the tribunal to compare the treatment of the complainant to that to which other persons are or would be subjected.

This 'other person', commonly referred to as the 'comparator', has to be someone of a different race whose circumstances are not materially different to those of the complainant (*EqA 2010, s 23(1)*). This test replaces *RRA 1976, s 3(4)*, although the *RRA* test referred to 'relevant circumstances'. It appears from the explanatory notes that this was not intended to effect any change and therefore cases interpreting *RRA 1976, s 3(4)* will be relevant when interpreting *EqA 2010, s 23(1)*. See for example *Shamoon v Chief Constable of the Royal Ulster Constabulary* [2003] ICR 337.

It is for the complainant to choose the comparator(s) with whom he wishes to be compared. Where there is no appropriate actual comparator whose circumstances were the same or not materially different to the complainant, a hypothetical comparator can be used.

The courts interpreted *RRA 1976, s 3(4)* as requiring a comparison of 'like with like' (*Shamoon*; *Dhatt v McDonalds Hamburgers Ltd* [1991] ICR 238). This does not mean that the comparator has to be a clone of the complainant in every respect except race (*Madden v Preferred Technical Group CHA Ltd* [2005] IRLR 46), but the circumstances of the comparator must be the same as the complainant in all material respects apart from in respect of the protected category (*Shamoon*). The circumstances that are important will inevitably depend on the facts of each case. In *Shamoon*, the comparators identified by the tribunal were two male chief inspectors in other regions. They were regarded by the tribunal as suitable comparators because 'they were in the traffic branch, held the same rank and carried out similar responsibilities in their regions to the complainant'. However, the Court of Appeal ultimately held that the two Chief Inspectors were not proper comparators. It held that the tribunal had 'overlooked the fact that Shamoon's superintendent had no authority over [them] . . . and no complaints or representations had been made about them'. In other words, their circumstances were materially different to those of the claimant. The way in which the complainant carries out his/her role is likely to be a significant factor in deciding the suitability of comparators.

The following cases give examples of factors which have led to a finding that the circumstances of a comparator were materially different to those of the complainant. In *Wakeman v Quick Corpn* [1999] IRLR 424, a claim for race discrimination on the basis that secondees from Japan received higher pay than the claimants, who were employed through the UK company, failed as the circumstances of the comparators' terms and conditions (as secondees) were materially different to those of the claimants. As it happened, the secondees were all Japanese, but, in fact, there was no reason why they could not have been of a different race. In *Famy v Hilton UK Hotels Ltd* [2006] All ER (D) 112 (Oct) the supervisor of a bar, who was of Filipino ethnic origin, complained that he had been discriminated against on grounds of race in not being promoted to the position of bar manager over several years, the position having been given to external white job applicants. These external white applicants were found to be inappropriate comparators as, in having formally applied for the position, their circumstances were materially different to those of the claimant, who had not applied for the job. There was therefore no actual comparator. With regard to any hypothetical comparator, the EAT held that the tribunal had rightly concluded that he would have been treated the same as the claimant (ie anyone not applying would not be appointed).

Where a complainant has selected actual comparators whose circumstances the tribunal does not think are sufficiently similar, the Court of Appeal has said that in appropriate cases the tribunal itself should consider the construction of a hypothetical comparator in place of the actual comparator(s) (*Balamoody v United Kingdom Central Council for Nursing, Midwifery and Health Visiting* [2002] IRLR 288, CA; see also *Chief Constable of Cambridgeshire v McLachlan* EAT (14 February 2003, unreported)). The Court of Appeal was mindful of the counter argument (that it was for the claimant to make out his/her case) and Ward LJ was at pains to say (at para 61) 'I am far from saying that in . . . every case the tribunal has to be robustly interventionist and do the task which the applicant is not doing for himself or herself. Every case is different'. The Court of Appeal went on to hold that there was some evidence in this particular case to support an inference that the refusal to restore the applicant to the nursing register was discriminatory on the grounds of race. In the circumstances, and based on the particular facts of this case, it held that it was incumbent on the tribunal chairman to construct a hypothetical comparator and test the case against that benchmark.

To construct a picture of how a hypothetical comparator would have been treated in comparable circumstances, inferences will need to be drawn. As such, it may be appropriate for the tribunal to consider how 'actual unidentical, but not wholly dissimilar, cases' were treated (*Chief Constable of West Yorkshire v Vento (No 1)* [2001] IRLR 124, approved by *Balamoody* (CA) (at para 60)).

For a further discussion of comparators see **1.63–1.71**.

6.14 'Because of race'

To be unlawful race discrimination under the *EqA 2010*, the less favourable treatment must be 'because of race'. Race is defined to include:

(a) colour;

(b) nationality;

(c) ethnic or national origins' (*EqA 2010, s 9 (1)*).

Note that this definition is not exhaustive.

As discussed in **1.46**, the phrase 'because of' has replaced 'on the grounds of'. As the government did not intend to change the legal meaning of the test, tribunals are likely to make use of the pre-October 2010 case law when determining whether direct race discrimination has occurred.

Case law under *RRA 1976* maintained that in most cases where a complainant fails in bringing a claim under one of the racial grounds, he will be precluded through the principle of *res judicata* from bringing a new claim on a different ground (*British Airways plc v Boyce* [2001] IRLR 157). It was acknowledged that there could be exceptions to this for 'special circumstances of a wholly unforeseen nature or for a situation . . . in which the tribunal has made it clear that no final decision was intended'. However, except in such exceptional cases *res judicata* should apply. As Lord Nimmo Smith observed, 'any other approach would leave it open to an applicant to lodge up to five separate applications under each of the five meanings of racial groups . . . ' under *RRA 1976*.

6.15 *Determining whether the treatment was because of race*

The approach in cases determined prior to the implementation of *RRA 1976, s 54A* in July 2003 was to use the 'but for' test, asking, for example, 'but for A's race, would he have been treated less favourably?' If not, then causation was established (see *James v Eastleigh Borough Council* [1990] ICR 554, a sex discrimination case). However, the use of the 'but for' test under *RRA 1976, s 1(1)(a)* was rejected in *Chief Constable of West Yorkshire Police v Khan* [2001] UKHL 48, [2001] 1 WLR 1947, as the House of Lords favoured a factual approach of looking at the reason (whether conscious or subconscious) for the discriminator's acts. The House of Lords held that this factual approach is a subjective test, unlike causation which is a legal conclusion, not a question of fact. In light of the *Khan* decision, tribunals were required not to restrict themselves to the 'but for' test, but to consider the reasons why the alleged discriminator acted as he did. The reversal of the burden of proof by *RRA 1976, s 54A* meant that in most cases it was for the respondent to provide a non-discriminatory reason for the treatment.

Although the case law under *RRA 1976* considered whether less favourable treatment was 'on racial grounds' rather than 'because of race', the two are intended to have the same meaning and so the case law under the *RRA* is likely to continue to be applied. The *EqA 2010* language is used in the text below but the cases cited were decided under *RRA 1976*.

Provided that the tribunal is satisfied that the reason for the less favourable treatment was race, it does not need to identify a discriminatory motive or intention on the part of the alleged discriminator (*Nagarajan v London Regional Transport* [2000] 1 AC 501, HL). While the motive of the alleged discriminator may be relevant, it is not the decisive factor and motives which are well-meaning in nature will not save an act of direct discrimination from being unlawful where less favourable treatment is because of race (*Din v Carrington Viyella Ltd (Jersey Kapwood) Ltd* [1982] ICR 256). In *Din*, the employer refused an employee's application for re-employment after he resigned to visit his native Pakistan, despite reassurances that he would be given favourable consideration for re-employment when he returned. The tribunal had identified that the motive of the employer in not re-employing was to avoid any potential industrial unrest that would be caused. This followed earlier unrest amongst the workforce following the claimant's involvement in an alleged racially motivated dispute with a manager. The EAT held that the motive to avoid industrial unrest was not in itself sufficient to amount to discrimination, but it could amount to such if the *reason* for the original unrest was racially discriminatory conduct. As the tribunal had not given reasons to support its conclusion that the original dispute was racially motivated, the case was remitted to another tribunal for further consideration.

Lack of knowledge of the claimant's racial, ethnic or national origin will not conclusively negate a finding of discrimination, but a lack of such knowledge may support a finding that there has not been less favourable treatment on because of race (*Simon v Brimham Associates* [1987] IRLR 307).

Direct discrimination can be either 'conscious or subconscious on the part of the discriminator' (*Appiah v Bishop Douglass Roman Catholic High School* [2007] EWCA Civ 10, [2007] IRLR 264). In *Appiah*, a fight at school between two white pupils and two pupils of black African ethnicity resulted in the two black pupils being excluded from school. On a claim of racial discrimination, the EAT had concluded that there was no direct, conscious discrimination, but the Court of Appeal acknowledged that 'racial motive' could be both conscious and subconscious. The complainant put forward arguments of a 'racist ethos' at the school, based on statistics that 'the school had a high level of exclusions, particularly among the ethnic minorities' and of teachers 'having problems with black students', but ultimately the court concluded this did not cause any subconscious discrimination.

Race does not have to have been the only reason for the less favourable treatment for there to be unlawful discrimination. So long as race was a 'significant cause of [the] decision to treat the complainant less favourably', discrimination is made out (*Nagarajan*). Where there are a number of reasons for the less favourable treatment, it will be for the tribunal which has seen and heard the evidence to decide whether or not the reason for the treatment was race (*Owen and Briggs v James* [1982] ICR 618). In this case, the Court of Appeal held that where the tribunal had found that 'colour' was 'an important factor in [the employer's] failure to consider the applicant's application further . . . the tribunal were right in deciding that there was a sufficient case of racial discrimination'.

Seide v Gillette Industries Ltd [1980] IRLR 427 is an example of a case where, although the complainant's race was a factor in the factual background to the complaint, the reason for the treatment was not found to be on racial grounds (under the new definition, 'because of race'). Mr Seide, a Jewish toolmaker, had previously suffered race-related comments from one of his co-workers. Therefore, he was moved to a different shift, with a Mr Murray, who complained that Mr Seide was inciting him to join his side in the dispute. As a result, Mr Seide was transferred to a day-shift where he could be better supervised, but this meant that he was paid less. Mr Seide claimed he had been treated less favourably on racial grounds. The EAT found, however, that although the matter had begun as a result of racially offensive comments, the transfer of Mr Seide resulted from the difficulties he was causing in the workplace, not because he was Jewish. Thus, although race had been a factor in the overall circumstances, the treatment complained of was based on the second incident with Mr Murray, and therefore was not on racial grounds. The EAT held that 'it is not sufficient merely to consider whether the fact that the person is of a particular racial group . . . is any part of the background . . . of what happens'.

In considering whether the less favourable treatment was because of race, the tribunal can consider evidence on conduct before and after the act complained of (*Rihal v Ealing London Borough Council* [2004] EWCA Civ 623, [2004] IRLR 642). A tribunal is also entitled to rely on words said after the less favourable treatment as casting light on the actions at the time (*Securicor Custodial Services Ltd v Williams* EAT/0042/02 (29 January 2003, unreported)).

In cases where subconscious discrimination is a possibility, it will be particularly important for the tribunal to look for 'indicators from a time before or after the [alleged discriminatory treatment] which might demonstrate that an ostensibly fair-minded decision was, or was not affected by racial bias' (*Anya v University of Oxford* [2001] EWCA Civ 405, [2001] ICR 847).

See also the discussion of direct discrimination at **1.45–1.53**.

6.16 *Discrimination by association or perception*

In many cases, claims of direct discrimination will involve the complainant alleging that he has been less favourably treated on the grounds of his own race. However, this is not necessarily the case. The new definition of direct discrimination at *EqA 2010, s 13(1)* is intended to cover associative discrimination and discrimination based on perception within the provisions on direct discrimination and harassment (but not indirect discrimination). (See **1.54–1.56.**)

However, in the field of race discrimination it has been well established for some time that associative discrimination (ie discrimination against a person on the grounds of another's race) is unlawful. In *Showboat Entertainment Centre Ltd v Owens* [1984] 1 All ER 836, [1984] 1 WLR 384 the white manager of an amusement centre refused to carry out the instructions of his employer to exclude young black people from the centre and was dismissed as a result. The dismissal was held by the EAT to be 'on racial grounds' under *RRA 1976, s 1(1)(a)*, and Brown-Wilkinson P said in his judgment at para 11, that 'the words 'on racial grounds' are perfectly capable in their ordinary sense of covering any reason for an action based on race, whether it be the race of the person affected by the action or of others'. Notably, *RRA 1976* referred to less favourable treatment being 'on racial grounds' and not 'on grounds of [the employee's/complainant's] race'. Accordingly, Brown-Wilkinson P continues at para 15, 'We can, therefore see nothing in the wording of the Act which makes it clear that the words 'on racial grounds' cover only the race of the complainant'. See also *Zarczynska v Levy* [1979] ICR 184, [1979] 1 WLR 125. This approach was followed in *Weathersfield Ltd (t/a Van & Truck Rentals) v Sargent* [1999] ICR 425, CA where an employee working for a vehicle rental company was told to inform 'any coloureds or Asians' that no vehicles were available for rental. The Court of Appeal held that whilst concluding that 'requiring [Sargent] to operate a racially discriminatory policy was treatment on racial grounds involved giving the expression [on racial grounds] a broad interpretation, it was [an interpretation] which was justified in the circumstances of the case.'

Wide as the protection is, some guidance on its limits may be found in *Redfearn v Serco Ltd (t/a West Yorkshire Transport Service)* [2005] IRLR 744, [2006] ICR 1367, where the EAT held that it was discrimination on 'racial grounds' where an employee working in a predominantly Asian workforce became a member of the BNP and was subsequently dismissed on 'health and safety grounds' in fear of the reaction of the other employees. The Court of Appeal curbed this wide interpretation and reversed the decision of the EAT. Although the court accepted the previous authorities which stated that an employer can be guilty of discriminating against an employee on the grounds of another person's race, this does not extend to a situation where an employer is simply trying to protect against racist abuse or tension in the workplace. The sole reason that the employer dismissed Mr Redfearn was to avoid any such adverse effects that his BNP membership might have; this was not discrimination 'on racial grounds'.

6.17 *Combined discrimination*

EqA 2010 also contains a new provision enabling an employee to bring a discrimination claim on two (but not more than two) combined protected grounds, one of which can be race. However, the provision was not implemented on 1 October 2010 and at the time of writing it is not clear when it will be implemented. (See **1.57–1.59.**)

6.18 INDIRECT DISCRIMINATION

Introduction

The essence of indirect discrimination lies in three elements:

(i) that an employer applies some provision, criterion or practice to his employees;

(ii) that it puts, or would put, members of the claimant's racial group at a particular disadvantage compared to non-members of that group; and

(iii) that the employer cannot show that it is a proportionate means of achieving a legitimate aim.

For example, a rule which prohibits all employees from having beards will disproportionately disadvantage Sikhs whose religion requires them not to shave. However, such a rule may be justified on the grounds of hygiene in certain circumstances (*Singh v Rowntree Mackintosh Ltd* [1979] IRLR 199 and *Panesar v Nestlé Co Ltd* [1980] IRLR 64).

Lady Hale in *R (on the application of E) v Governing Body of JFS (Secretary of State for Children, Schools and Families, interested parties) (United Synagogue intervening)* [2009] UKSC 15, [2010] 1 AC 278 at [56], [57] identified the characteristics of indirect discrimination as being that it looks beyond formal equality towards a more substantive equality of outcome and that, in contrast to direct discrimination (with which it is mutually exclusive), it can be justified.

See **6.59** for an explanation of the special provisions regarding PCPs relating to Sikhs wearing safety helmets on construction sites. See **1.72–1.85** for further discussion of indirect discrimination.

6.19 The test for indirect discrimination

EqA 2010, s 19 provides that a person (A) discriminates against another (B) if A applies to B a provision, criterion or practice ('PCP') which is discriminatory in relation to a relevant protected characteristic of B's. A PCP is discriminatory in relation to a relevant protected characteristic of B's if:

(i) A applies, or would apply, it to persons with whom B does not share the characteristic,

(ii) it puts, or would put, persons with whom B shares the characteristic at a particular disadvantage when compared with persons with whom B does not share it,

(iii) it puts, or would put, B at that disadvantage, and

(iv) A cannot show it to be a proportionate means of achieving a legitimate aim.

EqA 2010 replaces the definition of indirect discrimination in *RRA 1976, s 1(1A)* which was in the same terms. As such, the authorities under *RRA 1976, s 1(1A)* are likely to remain determinative. *RRA 1976* also contained the earlier definition of indirect discrimination in *s 1(1)(b)* which was thought to continue to apply to discrimination on grounds of colour or nationality. Recent decisions of the EAT strongly suggest that *RRA 1976, s 1(1A)* applied to such discrimination even before the entry into force of the EqA 2010 (*Chagger and Edozie v Group 4 Securicor plc and G4S Security Services (UK Ltd)* UKEAT/0124/09).

6.20 Applying the test

Provision, criterion or practice

The first element of the test is that the employer should apply a provision, criterion or practice ('PCP') to the worker. These terms are not defined in *EqA 2010*. However, the *EHRC Employment Code* states that the terms should be widely construed so as to include 'policies, rules, practices, arrangements, criteria, prerequisites, qualifications or provisions' whether they are formal or informal (*EHRC Employment Code, section 4.5*). A provision may be in the individual contract or in a more general policy which does not have legal effect. A criterion is likely to apply to selection, promotion or dismissal. A practice is potentially very broad and will cover general policies and the manner in which they are in reality applied by the employer. In contrast to the law under the old test under *RRA 1976, s 1(1)(b)*, it is no longer necessary for an employee to demonstrate that a PCP operates as a complete bar to the worker obtaining a particular benefit (see below). It is now sufficient that the worker demonstrates that the PCP operates to the disadvantage of members of their racial group even if it is only a desirable, and not a mandatory, element.

6.21 *Particular disadvantage*

Again, this concept is not defined in *EqA 2010*. It is thought that the term particular disadvantage is intended to exclude merely trivial or technical disadvantages. As under the old test, this element requires the claimant and the tribunal to identify a pool of comparison for determining whether members of the relevant racial group are disadvantaged compared to other groups. Although the claimant will be required to identify some pool for comparison, the tribunal will not be bound to adopt the claimant's suggestion where it forms the view that it is arbitrary or artificial (*Abbott v Cheshire and Wirral Partnership NHS Trust* [2006] EWCA Civ 523, [2006] ICR 1267). For a detailed discussion of the appropriate pool for comparison, see **1.78**.

The next question is how great a disparity of treatment is required between the claimant's racial group and that of the comparison group before one can say that the claimant's group is particularly disadvantaged. There is no guidance in *EqA 2010* and little in the cases; the matter is discussed at **1.79**.

6.22 *Personal disadvantage*

The claimant must demonstrate that the application of the PCP has (or would have) disadvantageous consequences for him. It is not sufficient to show that a disproportionate number of members of his racial group cannot comply if, in fact, he can. See also **1.82**.

6.23 *Proportionality*

The final element of the test is that the employer cannot show (the burden being on him) that the PCP is a proportionate means of achieving a legitimate aim. This test is familiar from other areas of EU law and that under the ECHR. It is a three-stage process.

The first stage is to identify a legitimate aim. This is a matter of fact for the tribunal (*Ladele v London Borough of Islington* [2009] EWCA Civ 1357, [2010] IRLR 211). This must be an aim which is not infected by any discriminatory purpose and equates most closely to the idea of the legitimate economic, administrative or other needs of the business. An example would be where an employer can demonstrate that there is a genuine risk to health in a food production business if workers are permitted to wear beards. For reasons outlined previously, such a PCP is potentially racially discriminatory against Sikhs, a racial group whose religion requires them not to shave. By contrast, although considerations of cost are not per se illegitimate, they will not generally provide adequate justification unless combined with other factors (*R (on the application of Elias) v Secretary of State for Defence* [2006] EWCA 1293, [2006] IRLR 934 but see comments in *Woodcock v Cumbria Primary Care Trust* (2010) UKEAT/0489/09/RN, [2011] IRLR 119 and also **1.84**). This decision also held that although it is not necessary for the employer to demonstrate that he carried out a balancing exercise to determine the proportionality of any PCP at the time of its adoption, his failure to do so may make it more difficult to establish justification.

If the employer demonstrates a legitimate aim, he is still required to fulfil the second element of the test, that is, that the PCP is a proportionate means of achieving that aim. The requirement of proportionality contains two distinct elements. The ECJ has set out the classic formulation of the test as requiring that the measures in question 'correspond to a real need . . . are appropriate with a view to achieving the objectives pursued and are necessary to that end' (*Bilka-Kaufhaus GmbH v Weber Von Hartz* (Case 170/84) [1986] IRLR 317). In applying the test of proportionality, the tribunal will apply its own judgment and adopt an objective approach (*Redfearn v Serco Ltd* [2005] IRLR 744 (EAT) applying *Hardy & Hansons plc v Lax* [2005] EWCA Civ 846,[2005] IRLR 726 on SDA 1975 (see SEX DISCRIMINATION (8)). The tribunal will not apply a 'range of reasonable responses' or 'margin of appreciation' test. The tribunal's task has been described as one of 'critical evaluation' of the justification put forward by the employer (*Allonby v Accrington and Rossendale College* [2001] EWCA Civ 529, [2001] IRLR 364 under *EPA 1970* and *SDA 1975*).

First, therefore, the employer must demonstrate that the PCP actually advances the aim. If it does not do so, it cannot be proportionate. Second, there must be a reasonable relationship between the PCP and the aim and the tribunal is entitled to consider whether the legitimate aim could be achieved in a way which has a lesser impact on the affected individuals. *Elias* (above) concerned the government's compensation scheme for those interned by the Japanese in the Second World War. Under the scheme, civilian internees had to show that either they (or a parent or grandparent) were born in the United Kingdom. The government's aim of ensuring that claimants had a strong link with this country was a legitimate one, but there had been no attempt to analyse the impact of the requirement in terms of indirect race discrimination and no assessment of what other criteria could have been devised to establish a link with the UK. As such, the Court of Appeal rejected the Secretary of State's plea of justification.

By contrast, in *Azmi v Kirklees Metropolitan Borough Council* [2007] IRLR 484 (a case on religious discrimination), the EAT affirmed the tribunal's conclusion that the school's decision to prohibit a teaching assistant from wearing a full-face veil when teaching was proportionate in light of the fact that the school had conducted assessments of the claimant's effectiveness as a teacher with and without the veil and permitted her to wear the veil at all other times except when teaching.

In addition to leading factual evidence where appropriate, an employer is entitled to rely on reasoned and rational judgment. What is impermissible is to advance disguised stereotypical assumptions as justification for discriminatory treatment (*Chief Constable of West Yorkshire Police and West Yorkshire Police Authority v Homer* [2009] IRLR 262, [2009] ICR 223 and *Seldon v Clarkson Wright and Jakes* [2009] IRLR 267, [2009] 3 All ER 435).

The tribunal will also consider how serious the impact of the PCP is on the individuals concerned. In certain cases (such as *Elias* above), the tribunal may conclude that the criterion chosen is so closely linked to the prohibited ground (in that case national origins) that it could not be justified.

6.24 *Indirect discrimination and recruitment of non-EEA nationals*

One particular area where indirect race discrimination has caused difficulty for employers is in dealing with non-EEA nationals as part of the recruitment process. Non-EEA nationals do not have the automatic right to work in the UK and must obtain a visa or work permit from the UK Border Agency before commencing employment. However, a practice of automatically rejecting job applications from non-EEA nationals on the grounds of their immigration status could amount to indirect discrimination on the grounds of nationality. *Osborne Clarke Services v Purohit* [2009] IRLR 341 illustrates this point. Osborne Clarke had a blanket practice of automatically rejecting applications from non-EEA nationals for trainee solicitor posts. It was accepted that this practice amounted to indirect race discrimination. However Osborne Clarke argued that its approach could be objectively justified when taking account of matters such as the likelihood of successfully obtaining a work permit and the administrative burden (in terms of costs and time) involved.

The EAT did not agree and pointed to the lack of evidence to support the employer's contention that any applications for work permits were bound to fail. The EAT also made specific reference to the CRE Code of Practice which suggested that recruitment selection should be based purely on merit and that work permit issues should only come into consideration at the final stages of selection. This is echoed in the *EHRC Employment Code* (at *para 16.67*).

The decision highlights the difficulties for employers in seeking to objectively justify recruitment practices which indirectly discriminate against nationals of non-EEA countries. The UK Border Agency has provided a Code of Practice for employers on how to avoid unlawful racial discrimination in this situation.

6.25 VICTIMISATION

Introduction

The aim of the law of victimisation is to protect an employee from being subjected to a detriment by their employer because the employee has sought to rely on *EqA 2010* or has assisted another in doing so (a protected act). The law on victimisation therefore represents a substantial extension of the scope of *EqA 2010* since the detriment suffered is not related to the race (or other protected characteristic) of the claimant. Under *EqA 2010*, victimisation is regarded as other prohibited conduct, rather than falling within scope of discrimination. Unlike under *RRA 1976, s 2* there is no longer any requirement to compare the treatment of the victim with that of another person who has not done a protected act.

The definition of victimisation is in *EqA 2010, s 27(1)* and provides that a person (A) victimises another person (B) if A subjects B to a detriment because:

(i) B does a protected act; or

(ii) A believes that B has done, or may do, a protected act.

6.26 *Protected act*

The protected acts under *EqA 2010, s 27(2)* are:

(i) bringing proceedings under the *EqA 2010*;

(ii) giving evidence or information in connection with proceedings under the *EqA 2010*;

(iii) doing any other thing for the purposes of or in connection with the *EqA 2010*;

(iv) making an allegation (whether or not express) that A or another person has contravened the *EqA 2010*.

The list is similar to that contained in *RRA 1976* and the old cases will continue to apply on the scope of protected acts.

An illustration of the breadth of the definition under *RRA 1976* was *Kirby v National Probation Service* [2006] IRLR 508. Mrs Kirby was interviewed in relation to an allegation of race-based bullying involving two other employees which was raised by way of internal grievance. Mrs Kirby was found to have performed a protected act under (iii) above (and therefore 'by reference to' *RRA 1976*) by giving information in connection with an internal complaint of race discrimination. This was the case even though Mrs Kirby's information was to the effect that there had been no discrimination.

However, the tribunal did not always apply such a broad definition. In *Kirby v Manpower Services Commission* [1980] 3 All ER 334, [1980] 1 WLR 725, Mr Kirby worked as a clerk at a job centre and suspected three employers of discriminating on the grounds of race against potential employees. He reported his suspicions to the CRE and procedures were instituted against one of the employers. The MSC transferred Mr Kirby to less congenial work after discovering his actions. The EAT upheld the MSC's contention that it acted because of Mr Kirby's breach of confidentiality and not because of the substance of the allegations. The EAT held that Mr Kirby's conduct did not qualify under (ii) since no proceedings had been brought at the time of the allegations. Equally, his conduct did not fall within (iii) since he was not acting pursuant to any duty. Finally, Mr Kirby could not rely on (iv) since he did not allege that the employers *had* breached *RRA 1976*, but merely that they *might have* done so.

If the employee complains of actions which would not be unlawful under *EqA 2010*, there is no basis for a claim of victimisation. For example, in *Waters v Metropolitan Police Commissioner* [1997] IRLR 589, the claimant had complained of (sexual) harassment by a fellow officer. However, this was not capable of constituting a breach of *SDA 1975* for which the Commissioner was responsible because it occurred when both officers were off duty. (See **1.101**.)

6.27 *Detriment*

Although defined in *EqA 2010, s 212*, the statutory definition of detriment only excludes 'conduct which amounts to harassment'. As such, the definition from *Shamoon v Chief Constable of the Royal Ulster Constabulary* [2003] UKHL 11, [2003] IRLR 285 and the cases which apply it will remain relevant. See **1.105**.

6.28 *Because of a protected act*

Under *RRA 1976*, the claimant had to establish that the less favourable treatment was caused by ('by reason that') he had performed a protected act. Although *EqA 2010* uses different terminology, the substance of the requirement of causation is likely to remain the same. The *EHRC Employment Code* (*section 9.10*) states that the protected act must be one of the reasons for the treatment, and need not be the only reason for it.

The House of Lords in *Khan* held that *RRA 1976* required the tribunal to consider the state of mind (both conscious and unconscious) of the employer rather than to ask whether 'but for' the protected act the less favourable treatment would not have taken place. Further guidance is provided by *Nagarajan v London Regional Transport* [1999] IRLR 572, in which the claimant alleged that the potential employer had victimised him by denying that they had received a job application from him. The tribunal inferred that the employer had treated Mr Nagarajan less favourably by reason of his protected act as they did not request him to re-apply and this was found to demonstrate a reluctance on their part to employ him. The House of Lords upheld this view. There was no need to show bad faith or consciously racist motivation on the part of the employer: it was enough to show that the reason for the less favourable treatment was the protected act.

Where the employer may have been influenced by a number of factors (including the protected act), it is sufficient for victimisation to be made out that the protected act was a significant (in the sense of not being trivial) part of the employer's reasons for their action (*Wong v Igen Ltd* [2005] EWCA Civ 142, [2005] IRLR 258).

The claimant failed to establish the causal connection between his protected act and the less favourable treatment he received in *Aziz v Trinity Street Taxis Ltd* [1988] IRLR 204. Mr Aziz made allegations of race discrimination against the respondent (an association which protected the interests of taxi drivers) in Tribunal proceedings. In the course of the hearing, it emerged that Mr Aziz had made covert tape recordings of his conversations with a number of members of the association. As a result, Mr Aziz was expelled from the association. There was no doubt that he had suffered less favourable treatment and making the recordings was 'by reference to' *RRA 1976, s 2(1)(c)*. However, the Court of Appeal found that the expulsion did not take place by reason of the protected act, but because Mr Aziz had behaved in an underhand manner and in breach of trust.

As stated above, in *Khan*, the House of Lords held that an employer may still protect their position in pending *RRA 1976* proceedings without being found to have victimised the claimant. However in *St Helens Metropolitan Borough Council v Derbyshire* [2007] UKHL 16, [2007] IRLR 540, the House of Lords set clear limits to how far the employer can go.

In *Derbyshire*, the employer's solicitor wrote to the claimants before their equal pay tribunal proceedings explaining the severe impact on all staff that the proceedings would be likely to have. This letter was also sent to other staff in the claimants' department. The House of Lords was not prepared to interfere with the tribunal's conclusion that the employer here had crossed the line and had not conducted itself like an 'honest and reasonable' employer. The House emphasised that less favourable treatment required more than the ordinary incidents of all litigation. For further discussion see **1.103**.

6.29 *Defence*

As under *RRA 1976*, it is a defence if false evidence or information is given or a false allegation is made in bad faith (*EqA 2010, s 27(3)*). As under the old law, the employer will not necessarily have a defence just because the substantive discrimination action fails (*Garrett v Lidl Ltd* EAT/0541/08; a disability case).

6.30 *Burden of proof*

Despite some doubt under *RRA 1976*, *EqA 2010, s 136* makes clear that the burden of proof provisions apply to victimisation claims as well.

6.31 *Former employees*

There is an unintended lacuna in the *EqA 2010*'s protection for former employees from victimisation as *EqA 2010, s 108(7)* expressly excludes victimisation. This was done on the basis that the provisions on victimisation would make express provisions for former employees. However, the *EqA 2010* fails to do so. (See **1.107**.)

6.32 *Less favourable treatment (pre-EqA cases only)*

Under *RRA 1976*, the claimant had to identify a comparator by reference to whom it is claimed that he has suffered less favourable treatment. The cases demonstrated that the tribunal should not approach this question in an unduly technical manner. In *Chief Constable of West Yorkshire v Khan* [2001] UKHL 48, [2001] IRLR 830, Lord Nicholls held that *RRA 1976* calls for a simple comparison between the treatment afforded to the claimant and that which would be afforded to other employees who have not done a protected act. Khan concerned a police officer who complained that he had been victimised by the Chief Constable's refusal to provide him with a reference. The Chief Constable stated that his refusal was based on his reluctance to prejudice the pending case which the officer had brought before the tribunal for race discrimination. The House of Lords held that the proper comparator was not another officer who had instituted legal proceedings against the Chief Constable under another enactment, but any other officer who requested a reference. In the end, Mr Khan's claim failed because the House found that the reason for the refusal was not that *RRA 1976* proceedings had been issued, but because legal proceedings were still pending. As stated above, there is no such requirement to show less favourable treatment under the *EqA 2010*.

6.33 Discussions about pay

EqA 2010, s 77 makes contractual pay secrecy clauses unenforceable to the extent that they prevent employees from making relevant pay disclosures, ie a disclosure that is sought or made for the purpose of finding out whether (or to what extent) any difference in pay is related to a protected characteristic (*EqA 2010, s 77(3)*). Action taken by an employer as a result of an individual making or seeking to make a relevant pay disclosure, or receiving information disclosed in a relevant pay disclosure, may amount to victimisation. (See **1.109**.)

6.34 HARASSMENT

Before the *2003 Amendment Regulations* came into force in July 2003, an employee who had suffered racial harassment had to bring a claim of direct discrimination under *RRA 1976, s 1(1)(a)*, showing that they had been treated less favourably and that this had caused them a detriment under *RRA 1976, s 4(2)(c)*.

The *2003 Amendment Regulations* implemented the *Race Directive*, implementing the principle of equal treatment between persons irrespective of racial or ethnic origin. *Article 2(3)* of the *Race Directive* defines harassment as being deemed to be discrimination when 'unwanted conduct related to racial or ethnic origin takes place with the purpose or effect of violating the dignity of a person and of creating an intimidating, hostile, degrading, humiliating or offensive environment'.

RRA 1976, s 78, as amended by the *2003 Amendment Regulations*, defined 'detriment' as not including harassment falling within *RRA 1976, s 3A* and introduced a statutory definition of harassment resulting in a free-standing cause of action. *Section 3A* prohibited harassment on the grounds of race, or ethnic or national origin. The *s 3A* definition did not apply to harassment on the grounds of colour or nationality, which continued to be actionable under the head of direct discrimination. However note the position following *Chagger v Abbey National plc* [2009] EWCA Civ 1202, [2010] ICR 397, where the EAT held that the law following amendment of *RRA 1976* by the *2003 Amendment Regulations* applied to race claims based on colour.

EqA 2010, s 26(1) now prohibits harassment related to race, where 'race' includes nationality and colour. The new definition therefore eliminates the inconsistency between different types of racial harassment. However, many elements of definition remain the same, and therefore case law under *RRA 1976, s 3A* is likely to continue to be relevant when interpreting the new provision.

In addition to the civil remedies under *EqA 2010*, harassment on racial grounds (or indeed on other prohibited grounds may amount to a criminal offence or be actionable in the civil courts under other legislation (see **6.41–6.44** ff).

6.35 Harassment under EqA 2010, s 26

Under *EqA 2010, s 26* (replicating *RRA 1976, s 3A* (as inserted by the *2003 Amendment Regulations*)) a person unlawfully harasses another person where he engages in unwanted conduct related to race, which has the purpose or effect of:

(a) violating that other person's dignity; or

(b) creating an intimidating, hostile, degrading, humiliating or offensive environment for that other person.

Conduct will be regarded as having the effect in (b) if, having regard to all the circumstances, including in particular the perception of that other person, it should reasonably be considered as having that effect (*EqA 2010, s 26(4)*).

EqA 2010, s 40(1) makes harassment by employers of a person whom he employs or who has applied to him for employment unlawful. It therefore expressly applies to job applicants.

Harassment also applies to acts outside the employment relationship. For further discussion of harassment see **1.86**ff.

6.36 *Related to race*

The new definition uses the term 'related to' race, which mirrors the wording of *Article 2(3)* of the *Race Directive*. This is a departure from *RRA 1976*, which referred to conduct 'on the grounds of' race and led to concerns that the UK legislation was narrower in scope than the definition in the *Race Directive*. What is clear is that the new wording is intended to be very broad: the *EHRC Employment Code* notes that 'any connection with a protected characteristic' will be sufficient.

The wording of *EqA 2010, s 26* means that it is not necessary for the complainant to have the protected characteristic, and therefore racial harassment based on association and perception will also be unlawful (see also **1.54–1.55**). Significantly, there will also be unlawful harassment where there is unwanted conduct related to a race (or any other relevant protected characteristic) which is neither based on perception nor association: the *EHRC Employment Code* gives the example of homophobic banter by colleagues who know the victim is not gay (*section 7.10* and see also *English v Thomas Sanderson Blinds Ltd* [2008] EWCA Civ 1421) (see also **6.39** below).

In a harassment claim under *EqA 2010, s 26* (as was the case under *RRA 1976, s 3A)*, there is no requirement for the complainant to point to a real or hypothetical comparator as it is unnecessary to show that someone of a different race would have been treated differently. However, the complainant must still prove that there was a discriminatory reason for the conduct in question. Where the conduct is race-specific (such as racist language), it is likely that the complainant will be able to show that the conduct is related to race. Stereotypical assumptions will also be indicative of the particular characteristic.

6.37 *Unwanted conduct*

Under *EqA 2010*, as under *RRA 1976*, the complainant must show that the conduct was unwanted. There are no reported cases that consider in detail when conduct is 'unwanted' in the context of racial harassment. However, guidance can be sought from sexual harassment cases (see **1.90**), and also from the *EHRC Employment Code* which states that unwanted means essentially the same as 'unwelcome' or 'uninvited' (*section 7.8*).

There is no requirement for the complainant to have previously made it clear that the conduct is unwanted. Although there will often be a course of conduct or number of incidents, a one-off incident (eg racist joke) can constitute harassment if sufficiently serious (*Insitu Cleaning Co Ltd v Heads* [1995] IRLR 4). Failure to complain at the time of the conduct or soon after does not automatically preclude a finding that it was unwanted but may have evidential weight. The complainant may feel unable to object because of fear for his job (*Driskel v Peninsula Business Services Ltd* [2000] IRLR 151).

6.38 *Having the purpose or effect of*

Where it is a person's 'purpose' to violate another's dignity or create an intimidating, hostile, degrading or offensive environment for that person, there is no 'reasonableness' requirement. An oversensitive complainant could therefore succeed with a harassment claim where a person deliberately harasses him. However, an alleged harasser will not readily admit to the conduct. A tribunal will therefore have to consider the surrounding circumstances.

For the second limb (*EqA 2010, s 26(1)(b)*, as under *RRA 1976, s 3A(1)(b)*), there is an objective reasonableness test. Conduct will be regarded as having the necessary effect only if it is reasonable for it to do so, having regard to all the circumstances (*EqA 2010, s 26(4)*). There is a subjective element, however, in that the complainant's perception must be taken into account. Nonetheless the conduct must still be such that it could reasonably be considered as having that effect. A claim for harassment will fail if the complainant is being hypersensitive (*Driskel*) (as long as there was no intention to cause offence, in which case the claim would come within the first limb).

It is clear that when considering 'effect', the harasser does not have to have intended to violate the complainant's dignity or cause offence, but a bad motive will make the complainant's case stronger (*Chief Constable of the Kent Constabulary v Kufeji* EAT 1135/00 (4 May 2001, unreported)).

6.39 *Dignity and working environments*

This part of the statutory definition is wider than *Article 2(3)* of the *Race Directive* in that it covers conduct that has the purpose or effect of violating dignity *or* creating an intimidating, hostile, degrading, humiliating or offensive environment, whereas the *Race Directive* requires the conduct to satisfy both elements. On this basis, it should be easier for complainants in the UK to make out a harassment claim than if the wording of the *Race Directive* had been tracked. The reason for this broader definition when it was first enacted under *RRA 1976* was existing case law which had already established this greater protection for UK employees.

As to what could constitute a violation of dignity or an offensive environment, there have been few cases under the *RRA 1976* provision. Cases pre-dating the statutory definition are illustrative.

Often the two elements will overlap. For example, a derogatory or abusive comment, whether directed at the complainant or at a third party, could violate the complainant's dignity at the same time as creating an intolerable environment in which to work.

In *Chin v Post Office* (12 December 1996, unreported), a tribunal held that Mr Chin, who witnessed the taunting of a black colleague (including his being called names such as 'black bastard', 'Zulu warrior' and 'tribes Mandela') could claim harassment on the basis that the abuse of his fellow worker could amount to a detriment to Mr Chin, even though it was not directed at him or on the ground of *his* race.

In a more recent tribunal case, an employee (a Maltese national) who overheard her supervisor saying 'I hate foreigners' and 'I am against immigration' was awarded compensation against the supervisor and her employer, even though the comment was not directed at her (*Ruby Schembri v HSBC* ET/330/361/05 (14 July 2006, unreported). The chairman commented that *RRA 1976, s 3A* did not require the alleged harasser to have used racist language or other overtly race-specific behaviour. The comments made by her supervisor were 'specific unwarranted and by any objective assessment signalling at the very least she disliked immigrants coming to Britain and being employed and at worst a racist comment intended for or directed at the claimant'.

A one-off incident may be sufficient to violate dignity if it is sufficiently serious, but a series of acts, which individually would be insufficient by themselves to amount to harassment, could create an offensive environment.

A case on the *RRA 1976* definition held that racist text messages sent by a colleague could amount to harassment by creating an offensive environment for an employee *Gravell v London Borough of Bexley* UKEAT/0587/06/CEA (2 March 2007, unreported). The fact that the text messages were sent to the claimant outside the ordinary scope of employment did not prevent the employer being fixed with responsibility for the act of harassment (see **1.163** ff for more detail on liability of employer for acts of employee). Further, although the comments made were not on grounds of Ms Gravell's race, they were on grounds of someone else's race and created an offensive environment for Ms Gravell.

Gravell also established that an employer's practice or policy of not challenging racist comments or behaviour by clients is capable itself of having the effect of creating an offensive environment for an employee (a move away from the findings in *Macdonald v Advocate for Scotland*; *Pearce v Governing Body of Mayfield School* [2003] UKHL 34.

See also **6.47–6.51** on liability for acts of third parties including liability for harassment by third parties.

6.40 *Nationality and colour prior to EqA 2010*

Nationality and colour were not covered by the *2003 Amendment Regulations* (or the *Race Directive*). An employee wishing to claim harassment on the grounds of nationality and/or colour therefore had to bring a claim for direct discrimination. This required him to establish that he had been treated less favourably on racial grounds under *RRA 1976, s 1(1)(a)* and that this was unlawful under *s 4(2)*. Harassment was most likely to made out where the employee was able to show that he had been 'subjected to any other detriment' under *s 4(2)(c)* (although note that this section did not apply to job applicants).

Establishing less favourable treatment required identifying a suitable comparator, one of the key differences prior to *EqA 2010* between claims based on nationality and colour and those based on race, ethnic or national origins. Key cases are *Burton v De Vere Hotels Ltd* [1996]

IRLR 596; *Macdonald v Advocate for Scotland; Pearce v Governing Body of Mayfield School* [2003] UKHL 34; *Smith v Gardner Merchant Ltd* [1998] 3 All ER 852, [1999] ICR 134 and *Hussain v Elonex plc* UKEAT/80/95 (25 April 1996, unreported) (subsequently upheld by the Court of Appeal ([1999] IRLR 420)).

The employee also had to show that his employer had 'subjected him to any other detriment'. There had been a considerable amount of case law on what amounted to a 'detriment' as well as when the employer will be liable for harassment. Key cases are *De Souza v Automobile Association* [1986] ICR 514; *Youri v Glaxo Wellcome Operations UK Ltd (1) and Smith (2)* EAT/448/99 (3 August 1999, unreported); *Thomas v London Borough of Hackney* UKEAT 461/95 (13 March 1996, unreported); *Thomas v Robinson* [2003] IRLR 7; *Olasehinde v Panther Securities plc; Kufeji* (see **6.38**) and *Driskel* (see **6.37**).

6.41 Other legal remedies

Racial harassment may also be actionable under other legislation. In addition to the victim being able to take action in the civil courts, some statutes make it a criminal offence to harass another person.

6.42 *Protection from Harassment Act 1997*

The *Protection from Harassment Act 1997* ('*PHA 1997*') makes harassment both a civil tort and a criminal offence. Initially introduced to protect victims from stalking, it has been used by complainants in harassment claims. Employers can also be found vicariously liable where the harassment occurs in the course of employment (*Majrowski v Guy's and St Thomas's NHS Trust* [2006] UKHL 34, [2006] 4 All ER 395). See **1.96** for further discussion of the impact of *PHA 1997* in the employment field.

6.43 *Public Order Act 1986*

The *Criminal Justice and Public Order Act 1994* amended the *Public Order Act 1986* so as to include a new *s 4A* which created an offence of causing intentional harassment, alarm or distress, where a person uses threatening, abusive or insulting language or behaviour, or disorderly behaviour, or displays any writing, sign or other visible representation which is threatening abusive or insulting, which causes that or another person harassment, alarm or distress. As specified in the preamble to the Act, the offence was originally introduced to deal with racial harassment cases and to control the 'stirring up of racial hatred'.

The maximum penalties under this section are six months imprisonment and/or a fine of £5,000.

6.44 *Crime and Disorder Act 1998*

The *Crime and Disorder Act 1998* ('*CDA 1998*') created 'racially aggravated offences' which cover serious offences such as assault, grievous bodily harm and criminal damages and also include harassment. These carry significantly higher penalties with imprisonment of up to two years when convicted on indictment. If a person is convicted on indictment of putting a victim in fear of violence and the offence was racially aggravated (under *CDA 1998, s 32(1)(b)*), the maximum penalty is imprisonment for up to seven years, and/or a fine.

6.45 OTHER UNLAWFUL ACTS

Discriminatory practices

Under *RRA 1976* the Commission for Racial Equality ('CRE') had the right to issue an enforcement notice against any person operating a discriminatory practice which amounts or could amount to indirect discrimination under *RRA 1976, s 1(1)(b)* or *s 1(1A)* (*RRA 1976, s 28*). When the CRE was dissolved in 2007, the Equality and Human Rights Commission (EHRC) took on this power under *EqA 2006, s 21* (unlawful act notice). The EHRC retains this notification power under *EqA 2010*. The *Explanatory Notes to the EqA 2010* note that direct and indirect discrimination are covered under this power (*note 1024*).

As was the case under *RRA 1976, s 28* this power is broad enough to cover practices the application of which has not, as a matter of fact, caused detriment to any particular individual and in respect of which no claim could therefore be brought in the employment tribunal. So, for example, a strict requirement that all applicants have five GCSEs, grade A–C (which requirement would exclude those who were schooled outside the UK) might be the subject of an enforcement notice even if, in practice, all interested candidates have to date been able to satisfy that requirement.

6.46 Discriminatory advertisements

Under *RRA 1976* and *EqA 2006* there were express provisions making it unlawful to publish (or cause to be published) an advertisement which indicates, or might reasonably be understood to indicate, an intention by a person to do an act of discrimination (*RRA 1976, s 29(1)*), and the EHRC (formerly the CRE) has the power to bring proceedings for contravention of this provision.

These express provisions were repealed by *EqA 2010*. The government took the view that discriminatory advertisements would be caught by other parts of *EqA 2010*, and so no express provisions were required (*Explanatory Notes to the EqA 2010, note 1024*). The EHRC has broad powers to bring proceedings for contraventions of *EqA 2010* under the amended *EqA 2006* (*s 24A*).

6.47 Instructing, causing or inducing discrimination

Under *EqA 2010, s 111* it is unlawful for a person (A) to instruct, cause or induce another person (B) to do anything to a third person (C) which contravenes *EqA 2010*, where A and B are in a relationship (such as an employment relationship) where it would be unlawful for A to discriminate against B (*s 111(7)*). Attempting to cause or induce such conduct is also unlawful (*s 111(8)*). Claims for breach of these provisions can be brought by either B or C, if they suffer a detriment, irrespective of whether the discrimination actually occurs. Proceedings can also be brought by the EHRC.

These provisions replace similar provisions under *RRA 1976, s 30* ('instructions to commit unlawful acts') and *s 31* (pressure to commit unlawful acts). However, under the *RRA 1976* provisions only the EHRC could bring proceedings, not the individuals affected. However, an individual employee who is dismissed for failing to comply with such an instruction, or who resigns and claims constructive dismissal, could bring proceedings for direct discrimination, in accordance with a line of authorities dating back to *Showboat Entertainment Centre Ltd v Owens* [1984] IRLR 7, where 'on racial grounds' in *RRA 1976, s 1(1)(a)* was held to include action based upon the race of someone other than the affected employee. So, for example, white bar staff who were dismissed for refusing to obey an instruction not to serve 'coloured' customers had been discriminated against (*Zarczynska v Levy* [1979] 1 All ER 814, [1979] ICR 184). Similarly, a receptionist who resigned after having been told by a car rental company not to hire vehicles to 'coloureds or Asians' was entitled to claim direct discrimination in respect of her constructive dismissal (*Weathersfield Ltd v Sargent (t/a Van & Truck Rentals)* [1999] ICR 425).

In the context of *RRA 1976, s 31(1)*, 'to induce' has been held to mean 'to persuade' or 'to prevail upon' (see *Commission for Racial Equality v Imperial Society of Teachers of Dancing* [1983] ICR 473 in which the society was found to be in contravention of *RRA 1976, s 31* when it sought applicants for a filing clerk role from a local school, but informed the head of careers at the school that it would rather not be sent any 'coloured' candidates as they were likely to feel out of place).

6.48 Employer's liability for unlawful acts of employees

In common with the other discrimination strands, anything done by an employee in the course of his employment is treated for the purposes of *EqA 2010* as done by his employer as well as by him. This will be the case whether or not the unlawful act was done with the employer's knowledge or approval (*EqA 2010, s 109(1), (3)* replicating *RRA 1976, s 32(1)*).

It is a defence for an employer to show it took such steps as were reasonably practicable to prevent the employee from doing that act, or from doing during the course of his employment acts of that description (*EqA 2010, s 109(4)*). This replicates *RRA 1976, s 32(3)* and is commonly known as the 'employer's defence' or the 'statutory defence'. Note, however, that the employment tribunal will rarely accept the mere existence of an equal opportunities policy prohibiting discrimination on grounds of race to be sufficient for an employer to successfully rely upon the employer's defence. Employers will need to be able to demonstrate that the employee(s) in question have themselves received equal opportunities training (including, where relevant, updates/refreshers) and that the employer has taken active steps to prohibit discrimination in the workplace and to stamp out race discrimination whenever it has arisen (see *Explanatory Notes to the EqA 2010, note 366*). Evidence of steps taken to comply with the *EHRC Employment Code* may also be required. Where *EqA 2010 s 109(4)* is pleaded in defence of a claim, employees will often seek to have individual employees named as co-respondents to prevent that section from depriving them of a remedy (see **6.51**).

For further information on the vicarious liability of employers, see **1.163ff**.

6.49 Liability for unlawful acts of agents

Anything done by a person as agent for another person (the principal) with that other person's express or implied authority is treated as done by the principal as well as by him (*EqA 2010, s 109(2)*). Note that vicarious liability of principals does not extend to offences under *EqA 2010* (other than those related to transport for disabled persons under *Part 12*).

Under *RRA 1976* there was a similar provision—*s 32(2)*. For the purposes of *EqA 2010, s 109(2)* case law concerning *RRA 1976, s 32(2)* will be relevant. For the purposes of *s 32(2)* it was irrelevant whether the authority was given by the principal before or after the act was committed by the agent. Nor did the principal need to have given the agent specific authority to discriminate. It was sufficient if the agent had authority to do an act which was equally capable of being done in both a lawful and a discriminatory manner (see *Lana v Positive Action Training in Housing (London) Ltd* [2001] IRLR 501, a case considering the similar provisions in the *SDA 1975, s 41(2)*). So, for example, an employer would potentially be liable for the actions of a recruitment consultant which operates a policy of not putting forward ethnic minority candidates.

As was the case under *RRA 1976, s 32(2)*, no employer's defence exists in relation to claims under *EqA 2010, s 109(2)*. For this reason, employers should continue to ensure that the terms upon which they engage agents contain appropriate drafting to prohibit unlawful discrimination and provide for an indemnity in the event of such discrimination in the performance of the agency.

6.50 Liability for acts of other third parties

Under the *RRA* 1976, where an employee suffered race discrimination at the hands of a third party, an employer would not be liable unless the employer's failure to prevent that discrimination was, itself, an act of discrimination under (*Macdonald v Advocate for Scotland*; *Pearce v Governing Body of Mayfield School* [2003] UKHL 34 in which the House of Lords disapproved the broader approach taken by the EAT in *Burton v De Vere Hotels Ltd* [1996] IRLR 596).

Under *EqA 2010, s 40* an employer will now be liable under statute for harassment of its employees by third parties over whom the employer does not have direct control, for example customers and clients. Liability will only arise when harassment has occurred on at least two previous occasions *(s 40(3))*, the employer is aware that it has taken place (*s 40(3)*) and has not taken reasonable steps to prevent it happening again (*s 40(2)(b)*).

For further discussion on this point, also see **1.95**.

6.51 Personal liability of employees, agents and others who aid an unlawful act

By virtue of *EqA 2010, s 112* (replicating *RRA 1976, s 33(1)*), knowingly helping someone to commit an unlawful act of discrimination, victimisation, or harassment is, itself, a separate breach of the *EqA 2010* for which the person 'helping' will be liable.

In addition, employees will be liable for acts done in the course of their employment which is treated as unlawful discrimination by his employer (even if the employer has a defence to a claim against it under *EqA 2010, s 109(4)*) (see **6.48**). Similarly, agents will be liable for acts done with the authority of the principal, which would amount to unlawful discrimination by the principal (*EqA 2010, s 110)*. Again, this replaces similar provisions in *RRA 1976, s 33(2)*.

It is a defence for an employee or agent or a person accused of aiding an unlawful act to show that:

(a) he acted in reliance upon a statement made to him by the employer/principal that that act would not be unlawful; and

(b) it was reasonable for him to rely on that statement (*EqA 2010, s 110(3)* and *s 112(2)*).

An employee acting with his employer's assurance that his act will not amount to race discrimination will not therefore be personally liable, unless his reliance upon the employer's statement was unreasonable.

It is an offence to knowingly or recklessly make a false or misleading statement of the type described at (a) above (*EqA 2010, s 110(4)* and *s 112(4)*).

See also **1.62** on aiding an unlawful act.

6.52 Liability of Chief Police Officer

Members of the police force are, strictly speaking, office holders rather than employees working under a contract of employment. This obviously would have a knock-on effect upon the protection afforded to police officers and the ambit of the vicarious liability provisions contained in *EqA 2010, s 109* (see **6.48**) which applies only to acts done in the course of employment. *EqA 2010* therefore makes specific provision for this by providing that police officers are to be treated as employees for all material purposes (*s 42*) and providing who their employer is deemed to be (usually the Chief Officer). This mirrors *RRA 1976, s 76A* which was introduced by the *2003 Amendment Regulations* as a result of the Court of Appeal's decision in *Chief Constable of Bedfordshire Police v Liversidge* [2002] ICR 1135.

6.53 EXCEPTIONS, DEFENCES AND NON-EMPLOYEES COVERED BY THE EMPLOYMENT PROVISIONS

This section sets out the miscellaneous exceptions and defences to discrimination claims in the employment sphere brought under the race discrimination provisions of *EqA 2010*.

6.54 Occupational requirements

EqA 2010, Sch 9 contains exceptions to the prohibition on discrimination and other prohibited conduct and *Part 1* deals with occupational requirements. These have been harmonised across the different strands of discrimination.

Paragraph 1 is of general application and provides a defence for an employer if (in the race context) he can demonstrate that, having regard to the nature and context of the work, belonging to a particular racial group:

(a) is an occupational requirement;

(b) the application of the requirement is a proportionate means of achieving a legitimate aim; and

(c) the person to whom the employer applies the requirement does not meet it (or the employer has reasonable grounds for not being satisfied that the person meets it).

Where these conditions are met, the existence of an occupational requirement creates an exception to those parts of *EqA 2010, s 39* which make it unlawful to discriminate in relation to:

(a) the arrangements made to determine to whom employment should be offered;

(b) the refusal to offer that employment;

(c) the way access to opportunities for promotion, transfer or training or receiving any other benefit, facility or service are offered; and

(d) dismissal from employment

(*EqA 2010, Sch 9, para 2*).

It follows that the existence of an occupational requirement is no defence to a claim brought in relation to discrimination in the terms on which employment is offered, the terms of employment themselves and subjecting an individual to any other detriment. This paragraph contains other specific exemptions in relation to the provisions on contract workers, partnerships (including LLPs) and personal and public offices.

The old law distinguished between genuine occupational requirements and genuine occupational qualifications (*RRA 1976, ss 4A and 5*). *EqA 2010, Sch 9* replaces both provisions. The provisions on genuine occupational requirements (GOR) were similar to the provisions on occupational requirements under *EqA 2010* but applied only to discrimination on grounds of race or ethnic or national origin.

In cases involving discrimination on grounds of colour or nationality, or which occurred before 19 July 2003 (when *s 4A* entered into force), the defence of genuine occupational qualification (GOQ) was available (*s 5*). A GOQ arose in limited circumstances where:

(a) the job involved participation in a dramatic performance or other entertainment where authenticity demands a person of that racial group;

(b) the job involved being an artist's or photographic model in the production of a work of art, visual image or sequence of visual images where a person of that racial group is required for authenticity;

(c) the job was in a public restaurant, bar or similar establishment where the setting is such that authenticity demands that that particular job be filled by a person of a particular racial group; or

(d) the job involved providing personal welfare services which can be most effectively provided by someone of a particular racial group (*s 5(2)*).

The old authorities are likely to remain relevant. The scope of the genuine occupational qualification under *RRA 1976, s 5(2)(d)* was interpreted broadly in *Tottenham Green Under-Fives' Centre v Marshall* [1989] ICR 214, [1989] IRLR 147. In that case, a day care centre catering for an ethnically diverse group of children was entitled to advertise for an Afro-Caribbean worker to replace an employee of the same ethnic origin. The personal welfare services in question were found to be maintaining the children's cultural links, dealing with parents, reading and speaking in dialect and looking after the children's skin and hair. However, the EAT did emphasise in a related decision that the personal services concerned must not be trivial and must not be inserted in the job description as a sham (*Tottenham Green Under-Fives' Centre v Marshall (No 2)* [1991] ICR 320, [1991] IRLR 162).

In *Lambeth London Borough Council v Commission of Racial Equality* [1990] ICR 768, [1990] IRLR 231, the Court of Appeal adopted a narrower definition of personal services. As an exception to the general prohibition on discrimination, a genuine occupational qualification for personal services would usually require that they were provided directly (often face-to-face) where knowledge and understanding of language and cultural or religious issues were material. Balcombe LJ also held that the use of the word 'personal' in category (d) referred to both the identity of the provider of the services and the recipient. As such, the defence was not made out in relation to an advertisement for managerial and supervisory posts in the respondent's housing department.

6.55 Exceptions

Skills to be exercised outside Great Britain

Prior to the *2003 Amendment Regulations*, *RRA 1976* differentiated between training in skills to be exercised within Great Britain and those which it appeared to the employer were to be exercised by the employee wholly outside Great Britain, permitting discrimination on grounds of race in relation to the latter. Since 2003, this exception (*RRA 1976, s 6*) applied only in respect of discrimination on grounds of colour or nationality.

EqA 2010 eliminated the distinction between colour and nationality and other forms of race. However, there is a general exception under *Schedule 23*, which allows a person (A) to discriminate based on nationality when offering training to a non-EEA resident (B), provided that A 'thinks that' B will not exercise the skills gained in Great Britain (*para 4)*. This provision is to enable people from developing countries to acquire vital skills which may not be available in their country of residence (*Explanatory Notes to the EqA 2010, note 1014*).

6.56 *Private households*

RRA 1976 contained the only remaining vestige of a historical exemption applied across the discrimination legislation and relating to employment for the purposes of a private household: it remained lawful to discriminate on grounds of colour or nationality in respect of such employment (although this exception did not apply to victimisation).

EqA 2010 has eliminated the distinction between colour and nationality and other forms of race (*s 9*) and this exception no longer applies.

6.57 *Seamen recruited abroad*

Section 9 of the *RRA 1976*, which allows employers to discriminate against seafarers on the ground of nationality in relation to pay, has not been repealed by the *EqA 2010*, pending regulations under *EqA 2010, s 81* setting out the way in which the employment provisions under the *EqA 2010* will apply to seafarers and hovercraft crew (*Equality Act 2010 (Commencement No 4, Savings, Consequential, Transitional, Transitory and Incidental Provisions and Revocation) Order 2010 (SI 2010/2317), art 11*).

Under *RRA 1976* seamen recruited or engaged (whether as employees or contract workers) outside Great Britain may lawfully be discriminated against in relation to their employment on any ship, to the extent that the discrimination:

(a) relates to pay (which includes retirement and death benefits); and

(b) is on grounds of nationality only (*RRA 1976, ss 9(1), (2)*).

A person brought to Great Britain with a view to his entering into an agreement in Great Britain to be employed on a ship was also covered by the exception (*s 9(4)*).

EqA 2010, s 81 states that the employment provisions will only apply to seafarers and hovercraft crew in the way set out in an order or regulations made by a minister.

Offshore workers are subject to separate orders or regulations under *EqA 2010, s 82* (*The Equality Act 2010 (Offshore Work) Order 2010 (SI 2010/1835)*).

6.58 *Sports and competitions*

It is not unlawful to discriminate on grounds of nationality, place of birth or the length of time for which a person has been resident in a particular area or place, when selecting a person to represent a country, place or area, or any related association in any sport or game, or in pursuance of the rules of any competition relating to eligibility to compete in any sport or game (*EqA 2010, s 195*, replicating *RRA 1976, s 39*).

6.59 *Sikhs and safety helmets*

Under the *Employment Act 1989, s 11* (the '*EA 1989*'), a specific exemption was introduced for turban-wearing Sikhs working on construction sites. Such individuals are exempt from any provision which would otherwise require them to wear a safety helmet on that site. That section goes on to provide that where a Sikh who is wearing a turban on a construction site suffers injury, loss or damage, his recovery against any third party is limited to such sum as would have been recoverable had he been wearing a safety helmet.

The *EA 1989, s 12* provides that an employer who applies a PCP to a Sikh relating to wearing a safety helmet on a construction site, where there are no reasonable grounds to believe that he would not wear a turban at all times whilst on the site, is guilty of indirect race discrimination which is not capable of justification. The *EA 1989, s 12(2)* makes clear that any special treatment accorded to Sikhs by virtue of these provisions cannot be used by non-Sikhs to mount a claim of discrimination under *EqA 2010*.

6.60 *Employment outside Great Britain*

Position from October 2010

EqA 2010 does not include any express territorial limit and it will therefore be left to tribunals to determine who can in practice bring a claim (see **1.43**).

Pre October 2010 position

RRA 1976 contained similar limits upon the scope of its jurisdiction as the other discrimination legislation (see **1.42**). The jurisdiction test was more restrictive in respect of discrimination on grounds of colour or nationality. For an employee to be protected by the provisions of *RRA 1976* in respect of discrimination on grounds of his colour or nationality, that employee must work wholly or partly in Great Britain (*RRA 1976, s 8(1)*). Employees working abroad were able to bring a claim for discrimination on grounds of colour or nationality if their employment when viewed as a whole was classed as partly in Great Britain. The tribunal is not entitled to limit its consideration to the time at which the discrimination took place (*Saggar v Ministry of Defence* [2005] EWCA Civ 413, [2005] ICR 1073).

EU nationals were able to bring a claim of discrimination under *RRA 1976* on grounds of nationality only if their job was within the EU and the act of discrimination (which occurred in the UK) restricted their freedom of movement as workers within the EU. See, in particular, *Van Duyn v Home Office* [1975] Ch 358 and *Bossa v Nordstress Ltd* [1998] IRLR 284. Where an employee is posted to another Member State temporarily, national non-discrimination laws will apply by virtue of the *Posted Workers Directive (96/71/EC)*.

RRA 1976 also differed from the other strands of discrimination in that it did not contain specific provision for employment on aircraft or hovercraft being covered by the provisions of the act in certain circumstances.

6.61 *Employment under an illegal contract*

In discrimination cases brought under *RRA 1976* the fact that an individual was employed pursuant to an illegal contract did not automatically exclude the tribunal's jurisdiction. So, in *Hall v Woolston Hall Leisure Ltd* [2001] ICR 99 (which approved the EAT's decision in *Leighton v Michael* [1995] ICR 1091) the Court of Appeal found that an employee's knowledge that her employer was paying her in cash, and thereby defrauding the Revenue, did not prevent her recovering damages (in that case under the *SDA 1975*). Jurisdiction would, however, be excluded where the employee's claim was so clearly connected or inextricably bound up or linked with their illegal conduct that the tribunal could not permit the employee to recover compensation without appearing to condone that conduct (*per* Peter Gibson LJ in *Hall*). The position will remain unchanged under *EqA 2010*. Also see **1.127**.

6.62 *Benefits provided to the public*

Replicating the position under the *RRA 1976*, protection extended to employees under the race elements of *EqA 2010* does not apply to benefits, facilities or services provided by their employer which they receive as a member of the public, rather than as an employee (for example, a current account provided to an employee of a high street bank) (*Sch 9, para 19)*. Where the benefits are materially different to those provided to members of the public, are regulated by the contract of employment or relate to training, the anti-discrimination provisions will have effect (*EqA 2010*, replicating *RRA 1976, s 39*).

6.63 *Discrimination in compliance with the law*

EqA 2010, Sch 23, para 1(1) contains an exception for direct and indirect discrimination based on nationality for anything done:

(a) in pursuance of an enactment;

(b) in pursuance of an instrument made by a member of the executive under an enactment;

(c) to comply with a requirement imposed by a member of the executive by virtue of an enactment;

(d) in pursuance of arrangements made by or with the approval of, or for the time being approved by, a Minister of the Crown;

(e) to comply with a condition imposed by a Minister of the Crown.

In addition, *Sch 23, para 1(3)* provides an exception for indirect discrimination in relation to any type of race discrimination by applying a PCP relating to a persons place of ordinary residence or the amount of time they have been present or resident inside or outside the UK or an area within it, where the application of the PCP falls within (a) to (e) above.

RRA 1976 originally contained wider exceptions. Before the *2003 Amendment Regulations* were implemented, *RRA 1976* included a blanket exception where the discrimination was carried out pursuant to any enactment.

The exception in the amended *RRA 1976, s 41* broadly mirrored that under *EqA 2010, Sch 23, para 1* save that the exception for direct discrimination was applicable to discrimination on grounds of colour as well as nationality.

In the context of *RRA 1976 t*he words 'in pursuance of' have been held by the House of Lords to be much more restrictive than 'by virtue of', such that the application of *RRA 1976, s 41(1)* was limited to acts done in necessary performance of an express obligation contained in the act or other instrument (*Hampson v Department of Education and Science* [1990] ICR 511).

See also the case of *R (on the application of Mohammed) v Secretary of State for Defence* (2007) 104(20) LSG 32 for consideration of the application of *s 41(2)* to a government scheme for the making of ex gratia payments to ex-servicemen who had been Japanese prisoners of war.

6.64 *National security*

Discriminatory acts relating to any element of race done for the purpose of safeguarding national security are not unlawful, provided that those acts are proportionate to do for that purpose (*EqA 2010, s 192* replicating *RRA 1976, s 42*).

6.65 *Employees working for those with State immunity*

The *State Immunity Act 1978* applies equally to claims of race discrimination as it does to the other forms of discrimination in the UK.

6.66 NON-EMPLOYEES AND NON-EMPLOYERS

EqA 2010, Part 5 (replacing *RRA 1976, Part II*) sets out provisions relating to discrimination in the employment field. In certain circumstances the provisions of *EqA 2010, Part 5* are extended to apply to non-employees and non-employers. These circumstances are, for the most part, common to the other strands of discrimination law in the UK. The below sections identify where the provisions relating to race differ from the norm. For further information on the generally applicable rules, see **1.15**ff.

6.67 Contract workers

It is not unlawful for a principal to act in a discriminatory manner (relating to nationality only) for the benefit of a contract worker not ordinarily resident in Great Britain in, or in connection with, allowing that worker to do contract work, where the purpose of allowing him to do that work is to provide him with training in skills which it appears to the principal the contractor intends to exercise wholly outside Great Britain (*EqA 2010, Sch 23, para 4*, replacing *RRA 1976, s 7(4)*).

6.68 Office holders

In the public sector

Holders of public offices are protected from discrimination, victimisation, and harassment by virtue of *EqA 2010, s 50* (replicating *RRA 1976, s 76*) as though they were employees and the Crown their employer. However, it is not unlawful to apply rules relating to birth, nationality, descent or residence to such offices (*EqA 2010, Sch 22, para 5(2)*).

6.69 *Other office holders*

Other office holders come within the ambit of the employment provisions set out in *EqA 2010, Part 5* by virtue of *s 49*. To be entitled to protection, the post must be one which is to be discharged personally by one person under the direction of another, and one in respect of which remuneration is payable (*s 49(2)*). Political offices and posts are excluded (*Sch 6, para 2*), as are posts to which an individual has been elected (*s 52(5)*).

6.70 Crown employees

Crown employees were protected under *RRA 1976* in broadly the same way as private sector employees by virtue of *ss 75, 75A* and *75B*. *EqA 2010, Part 5 (Work)* applies to Crown employees by virtue of the extended definition of 'employment' in *s 83(2)*. However, as was the case under *RRA 1976*, nothing in *EqA 2010* will invalidate any rules restricting employment in the service of the Crown, or by any prescribed public body, to persons of particular birth, nationality, descent or residence. A specific exception also exists in relation to the publication, display or implementation of such rules, or the publication of the gist of them (*Sch 22, para 5(1)*).

6.71 *Armed forces*

Members of the armed forces are specifically included within the ambit of *EqA, Part 5* by virtue of *s 83(3)* (although there are some specific exceptions in relation to eg disability). However, generally speaking, no complaint in respect of an act of discrimination under *Part 5* may be brought by a member of the armed forces where it relates to service in those forces and has not first been presented internally to the appropriate authorities (*s 121(1)*).

6.72 The police and barristers and advocates

Police officers and barristers and advocates are included within *Part 5* by virtue of *ss 42* (police officers), *47* (barristers) and *48* (advocates). See **1.29** and **1.32**.

6.73 Partnerships

Under *RRA 1976* the provisions relating to partnerships were in common with the other discrimination legislation, save that:

(a) for discrimination on grounds of colour and nationality, *RRA 1976* only applied to firms with six or more partners (*s 10(1A)*); and

(b) under *RRA 1976*, the genuine occupation requirement/qualification provisions set out in *ss 4A* and *5* only applied to discrimination in the arrangements made for the purposes of determining who to offer a position as a partner or a refusal to offer a position as a partner.

These inconsistencies have not been replicated in *EqA 2010* (see **1.19**).

6.74 Other categories

Replicating the position under the *RRA 1976*, the employment provisions are extended in certain circumstances to trade organisations (*EqA 2010, s 57 (RRA 1976, s 11)*), qualifications bodies (*EqA 2010, s 53, RRA 1976, s 12*), and employment service-providers (*EqA 2010, s 55 (RRA 1976, s 14)*). Each of these is for practical purposes dealt with in the same way as for all other forms of discrimination legislation (see **1.15**ff).

6.75 The duty to promote race equality

RRA 1976 imposed a duty on public authorities a general duty to promote race equality in carrying out their functions. There were similar duties in relation to sex and disability discrimination. The duties are to be replaced by *EqA 2010, s 149* which applies across all strands of discrimination and is expected to come into force in April 2011. The detailed requirements of those duties are beyond the scope of this work.

7 Religion and belief

7.1 INTRODUCTION

Protection from discrimination on the grounds of religion or belief in employment and related fields has now been consolidated in the *EqA 2010*, substantially coming into force on 1 October 2010. In respect of religion and belief, *EqA 2010* gives effect to, *but* in some respects goes beyond, *Directive 2000/78/EC* ('the *Framework Directive*'), issued by the Council on 27 November 2000 and establishing a general framework for equal treatment in employment and occupation, insofar as it requires Member States to regulate discrimination in certain fields where it is connected to religion and belief. Prior to the enactment of the *EqA 2010*, the Framework Convention's religion and belief provisions were given effect to in Great Britain by the *Employment Equality (Religion and Belief) Regulations 2003 (SI 2003/1660)* ('*RBR 2003*'), which came into force on 2 December 2003. The *EqA 2010* effectively re-enacts the main provisions of *RBR 2003*, although with some significant changes. The religion and belief provisions of the *EqA 2010* do not extend to Northern Ireland (*s 270)*), which has its own legislation dealing with employment discrimination on the grounds of religion or belief (primarily the *Fair Employment and Treatment (Northern Ireland) Order 1998*) and which is outside the scope of this book.

7.2 Pre-existing protection

Prior to *RBR 2003* coming into force, protection from discrimination on the grounds of religion or belief could be found under two legislative schemes.

The first legislative scheme was the *Race Relations Act 1976* ('*RRA 1976*'); however, only members of religious groups that could also claim to belong to a particular racial group as defined in *RRA 1976, s 3(1)* were protected from discrimination. The resulting protection was unequal as between different faiths: Sikhs and Jews were protected, but Muslims were not (compare *R (on the application of E) v Governing Body of JFS (Secretary of State for Children, Schools and Families, interested parties) (United Synagogue intervening)* [2009] UKSC 15, [2010] 1 AC 278; *R (on the application of Watkins-Singh) v Governing Body of Aberdare Girls' High School* [2008] EWHC 1865 (Admin), [2008] 3 FCR 203; *Mandla v Dowell Lee* [1983] 2 AC 548, [1983] 2 WLR 620, [1983] 1 All ER 1062, [1983] ICR 385, [1983] IRLR 209, CA and *Seide v Gillette Industries Ltd* [1980] IRLR 427, EAT with *JH Walker v Hussain* [1996] ICR 291, [1996] IRLR 11, EAT). Even those members of faiths that were protected as ethnic groups found themselves unprotected where the less favourable treatment in question was not attributable to their membership of the ethnic group synonymous with their faith, but to their adherence to the tenets of the faith in question.

The second legislative scheme was the *European Convention on Human Rights* ('*ECHR*') and the *Human Rights Act 1998* ('*HRA 1998*'). *Article 9(1)* of the *ECHR* guarantees freedom of thought, conscience and religion. These freedoms are subject to the limitations set out in *Article 9(2)* which provides that they shall be subject to such limitations as are prescribed by law and are necessary in a democratic society for the protection of, amongst other things, the rights and freedoms of others. Moreover, *Article 14* prohibits discrimination in the enjoyment of these rights. However, these provisions have been relied on with limited success by claimants in the United Kingdom, Strasbourg case law having placed considerable weight on *Article 9(2)* to balance the right to religious expression against other interests, including the contractual and *Article 9(1)* rights of others (*Ahmad v United Kingdom* (1981) 4 EHRR 126; *Stedman v United Kingdom* (1997) 23 EHRR CD 168). The protections in the *ECHR* have been made somewhat more accessible by *HRA 1998*; but *s 6(1)* of the Act only imposes direct obligations on 'public authorities' so that the availability of protection remains dependent upon the status of the relevant employer. Even in cases where protection has been available, the rights protected by *Article 9(1)* have been interpreted narrowly, particularly as regards what constitutes a protected 'manifestation' of religion, and the limitations provided by *Article 9(2)* broadly (see, for example, *Dogru v France (Application 27058/05)* (2008) 49 EHRR 179; *R (on the application of Begum) v Headteacher and Governors of Denbigh High School* [2006] UKHL 15, [2006] 2 All ER 487; *R (on the application of Playfoot) v Governing Body of Millais School* [2007] EWHC 1698 (Admin), [2007] LGR 851; *R (on the application of X) v The Headteacher of Y School* [2007] EWHC 298 (Admin), [2008] 1 All ER 249; *R (on the application of Williamson) v Secretary of State for Education and Employment* [2005] UKHL 15, [2005] 2 AC 246, [2005] 2 WLR 590, [2005] 2 All ER 1; *Pretty v United Kingdom (Application 2346/02)* (2002) 35 EHRR 1 and *R v Taylor* [2001] EWCA Crim 2263, [2002] 1 Cr App Rep 519).

7.3 Legislative history

The origins of the religion and belief provisions of *EqA 2010* lie in *RBR 2003*, which in turn lie in the consultation that was initiated by the government on the implementation of the *Framework Directive*: *Towards Equality and Diversity, Implementing the Employment and Race Directives: Consultation Documents* (2001) Department of Trade and Industry and Cabinet Office ('the Consultation Paper'). There followed lengthy debates, particularly in the House of Lords, on the content of the draft Regulations and specifically the definition of 'religion and belief'. *RBR 2003* as enacted following those debates were soon amended, principally to provide for discrimination in respect of occupational pension schemes and in institutions of further and higher education (see *Employment Equality (Religion or Belief) (Amendment) Regulations 2003 (SI 2003/2828)*, *Employment Equality (Religion or Belief) (Amendment) Regulations 2004 (SI 2004/437)*, but also *Employment Equality (Religion or Belief) Regulations 2003 (Amendment) (No 2) Regulations 2004 (SI 2004/2520)*); they were amended again, in various respects, by the *Equality Act 2006* ('*EqA 2006*') and the *Employment Equality (Sexual Orientation) (Religion or Belief) (Amendment) Regulations 2007 (SI 2007/2269)*. *EqA 2006*, in particular, extended the protection found in *RBR 2003* to the provision of goods, facilities and services.

7.4 Guidance

Apart from case law, the principal source of guidance on the interpretation of the provisions of the *EqA 2010* is the *EHRC Employment Code*. There is also guidance from ACAS: *Religion or Belief and the Workplace: a Guide for Employers and Employees* (2010, ACAS) ('the ACAS Guidance'), at http://www.acas.org.uk/CHttpHandler.ashx?id=107&p=0. In addition, the *Explanatory Notes to the EqA 2010* are a useful point of reference.

7.5 THE EQUALITY ACT 2010

The religion and belief provisions of *EqA 2010* follow a similar structure to the provisions of the Act regarding other protected characteristics.

As explained in **1.1** certain 'characteristics' are 'protected' (*s 4*). These include the 'characteristic' of 'religion or belief'. Subsequent provisions in the *EqA 2010* protect these characteristics by providing that in certain situations, such as employment, certain persons, such as employers, may not discriminate against other persons, such as employees, on the basis of these characteristics. 'Discrimination' in this context includes both direct and indirect discrimination. The material and personal scope of the provisions prohibiting discrimination are generally similar for each of the protected characteristics. In addition, 'harassment' is prohibited (*s 26*), but with regard to the characteristic of religion and belief, such harassment is made unlawful primarily in the context of employment. These provisions are explored in COMMON CONCEPTS (1). As a result, what follows focuses on provisions that are particular to the religion and belief provisions of the *EqA 2010*.

7.6 **Definition of 'religion or belief'**

'Religion or belief' is now defined in *EqA 2010, s 10*. There is no prescriptive list in respect of what is a 'religion' or 'belief'; given the wide variety of different faiths and beliefs in the country, this was felt to be unduly restrictive and it has been left to courts and tribunals to decide how far protection extends. However, both terms require the relevant opinions to be held as a matter of principle rather than logic or consideration of an evidence base (*McClintock v Department of Constitutional Affairs* [2008] IRLR 29, EAT at [45]). Lack of religion or belief is expressly protected (*EqA 2010, s 10(1) and (2)*).

The *Explanatory Notes to the EqA 2010* at *para 71* state that the definition of religion and belief: 'is a broad definition in line with the freedom of thought, conscience and religion guaranteed by *Article 9* of the *European Convention on Human Rights* (which guarantees such freedoms). The main limitation for the purposes of *Article 9* is that the religion or belief must have a clear structure and belief system. Denominations or sects within a religion can be considered to be a religion or belief, such as Protestants and Catholics within Christianity.' This is reflected in the *EHRC Employment Code* (*para 2.52*).

Thus the interpretive exercise of what is and what is not a religion or belief does not take place in a vacuum, but has regard to the jurisprudence of *Article 9* of the *ECHR*, given the references to that provision in recitals (1) and (4) of the *Framework Directive* and the requirements of *HRA 1998, s 3*. There may be interesting issues to resolve here, *Article 9(1)* being broader than the *EqA 2010* in protecting freedom of 'thought' and 'conscience' (rather than belief), together with religion and including within that protection the right to 'manifest' religion or belief, subject to the limitations of *Article 9(2)*.

7.7 *Meaning of 'religion'*

'Religion' means any religion and includes lack of religion. The *EHRC Employment Code* states that it includes those religions recognised in this country, together with the branches and sects within them (*paras 2.53–2.54*). The Code gives the following as examples of religions for the purposes of the *EqA 2010*: the Baha'i faith, Buddhism, Christianity, Hinduism, Islam, Jainism, Judaism, Rastafarianism, Sikhism and Zoroastrianism. According to *Article 9* jurisprudence, the reference might include more controversial 'religions' such as Scientology (*X and Church of Scientology v Sweden* 16 DR 68 (1979)). The main limitation is that the 'religion' must have a clear structure and belief system (*X v United Kingdom* 11 DR 55 (1977); *EHRC Employment Code, para 2.54*). *Moore v Hartlepool Borough Council* (16 Sep 2009, ET/2501537/09) distinguished between matters of religion and ethical or morality issues; the latter were not included. Hypnotism does not appear to fall within the statutory definition (*Sethi v Accord Operations Ltd* (19 July 2007; ET/3201823/06)).

7.8 *Meaning of 'belief'*

'Belief' means 'any religious or philosophical belief and a reference to belief includes a reference to a lack of belief.' Examples suggested by the *Explanatory Notes to the EqA 2010* of 'beliefs' for the purpose of this provision include such beliefs as humanism and atheism, but not adherence to a particular football team. The *EHRC Employment Code* provides further guidance on the meaning of 'religious belief', and 'philosophical belief' (*paras 2.56–2.59*, considered below).

7.9 *Meaning of 'religious belief'*

A 'religious belief', according to the *EHRC Employment Code* 'goes beyond beliefs about and adherence to a religion or its central articles of faith and may vary from person to person within the same religion' (*para 2.56*). A belief 'need not include faith or worship of a God or Gods but must affect how a person lives their lives or perceives the world' (*para 2.58*). *EqA 2010* distinguishes between 'religion' and 'religious belief'. It is arguable that religious beliefs, for the purposes of *EqA 2010* may warrant protection only where they attain a serious level of cogency, seriousness, cohesion and importance, and provided they are worthy of respect in a democratic society and are not incompatible with human dignity (*Campbell and Cosans v United Kingdom* (1982) 4 EHRR 293 at [36]).

7.10 *Meaning of 'philosophical belief'*

Prior to the amendments introduced by *EqA 2006*, in order to be protected under *RBR 2003*, a philosophical belief had to be 'similar' to a religious belief. This requirement was removed by the *EqA 2006* amendments, and the requirement is also omitted from the *EqA 2010*. The change was not intended to be significant, only to remove a word which does not appear in *Article 1* of the *Framework Directive* and was considered to be redundant, in the sense that a 'philosophical belief' in the context of *RBR 2003* must always be of a similar nature to religious belief (Hansard, HL, Vol 673, Col 1109–10 (13 July 2005)). Examples of 'philosophical beliefs' are Rastafarianism (*Harris v NKL Automotive* EAT/134/07/DM, 3 October 2007), spiritualism and the philosophical belief in life after death and psychic powers (*Greater Manchester Police Authority v Power* [2009] EAT 0434/09/DA (12 November 2009)), belief in man-made climate change and the alleged resulting moral imperatives (*Nicholson v Grainger plc* [2010] 2 All ER 253, [2010] ICR 360, EAT), and perhaps paganism and humanism (*ACAS Guidance, para 1.1*).

Under *ECHR, Article 9*, philosophical beliefs must attain a level of cogency, seriousness, cohesion and importance, be worthy of respect in a democratic society and must not be incompatible with human dignity (*Campbell and Cosans* at [36]). The *Employment Code* specifies various criteria that a philosophical belief must satisfy in order to be protected under the Act (*para 2.59*):

'• it must be genuinely held;
• it must be a belief and not an opinion or viewpoint based on the present state of information available;
• it must be a belief as to a weighty and substantial aspect of human life and behaviour;
• it must attain a certain level of cogency, seriousness, cohesion and importance;
• it must be worthy of respect in a democratic society, not incompatible with human dignity and not conflict with the fundamental rights of others.'

These criteria derive from the judgment of Burton J in *Nicholson v Grainger plc* [2010] 2 All ER 253, [2010] ICR 360, EAT.

The *EHRC Employment Code* (*para 2.59*) gives an example to illustrate how the last criterion on this list could operate to limit the scope of what constitutes a protected philosophical belief:

> 'A woman believes in a philosophy of racial superiority for a particular racial group. It is a belief around which she centres the important decisions in her life. This is not compatible with human dignity and conflicts with the fundamental rights of others. It would therefore not constitute a "belief" for the purposes of the Act'.

It may be noteworthy that the *EHRC Employment Code* applies this list only to 'philosophical beliefs' and not to 'religious beliefs'. This appears to be based on a narrow reading of the *ECHR Article 9* jurisprudence, in which the last criterion was developed and has so far been explicitly applied only in the context of 'philosophical beliefs' and not, so far, to 'religious beliefs'. This being the case, it is arguable that religious beliefs are subject to less stringent interrogation than philosophical beliefs; a belief claimed to be religious will always potentially qualify for protection, a philosophical belief in the same end may not.

The remaining area of controversy over this provision relates to whether philosophical beliefs include political beliefs. It seems clear that *RBR 2003*, as originally enacted, were not intended to protect such beliefs, at least unless they are similar to a religious belief. Supporting the British National Party would not therefore qualify (*Baggs v Fudge* ET/1400114/05). But this leaves a grey area regarding ideologies that are akin to religious beliefs in terms of the coherence of their structure and belief system and the conviction with which they are held; and the area has arguably been widened by the removal of the word 'similar' following *EqA 2006* amendments. In *Kelly v Unison* (28 Jan 2010, ET/2203854-57/08) the employment tribunal in this case concluded that 'political beliefs' are not included, nor were the particular political beliefs of the claimants, based on Marxism/Trotskyism and the Socialist Party.

7.11 *Lack of 'religion' or 'belief'*

The definition of 'religion' and 'belief' in *EqA 2010, s 10(1)* and *(2)* includes the absence of such a belief, eg in *Khan v Ghafoor t/a Go Go Real Estate* (2 July 2010; case no1809595/09) the tribunal found that the claimant's refusal to wear a headscarf, which led to her dismissal, was due to the absence of belief that her Muslim religion obliged her to and upheld her direct religious discrimination claim.

Article 9 jurisprudence is similar in this respect, such as *Kokkinakis v Greece* (1993) 17 EHRR 397.

7.12 *Manifestation of a religion or belief*

Prior to the enactment of the *EqA 2010*, it was unclear whether or not the definition of religion or belief included the manifestation of, or conduct based on or expressing, a religion or belief. The point was significant because if the answer was in the affirmative, then the manifestation of religion or belief might have given rise to direct discrimination), which, unlike indirect discrimination, was not capable of justification under *RBR 2003*. This result would have been potentially broader than that provided for by the *ECHR*.

Article 9 of the *ECHR* expressly protects the right to manifest religion and belief, albeit in a qualified fashion, and the jurisprudence on this topic indicates that freedom of religion implies freedom to manifest that religion and to bear witness in words and deeds (*Kokkinakis* at [31]). Moreover, the courts have held that direct discrimination on the basis of sexual orientation does not distinguish sexual orientation and the manifestation of that orientation (*R (Amicus) v Secretary of State for Trade and Industry* [2004] EWHC 860 (Admin), [2007] ICR 1176, [2004] IRLR 430). The EAT declined to express a view on the issue in the context of religion and belief (*Azmi v Kirklees Metropolitan Borough Council* [2007] ICR 1154, [2007] IRLR 484 at [75]). However, in *McConkey v Simon Community, Northern Ireland* [2009] UKHL 24, [2009] ICR 787, Lord Rodger (in interpreting the *Fair Employment and Treatment (Northern Ireland) Order 1998*) distinguished between discrimination against a person for holding a belief and discriminating against a person for manifesting it. 'So, for instance, if someone belonged to a religious sect which favoured wife beating, it would be unlawful for me to discriminate against him, simply because of religious belief. But I would be quite entitled to refuse to employ him if he actually gave effect to his beliefs by helping a friend to beat his wife.'

Following the enactment of the *EqA 2010*, however, the *EHRC Employment Code* (*paras 2.60–2.61*) draws attention to the distinction in *ECHR, Article 9* case law between the right to hold a belief, and the right to 'manifest' that belief, with only the former being guaranteed absolutely, and the latter being subject to limits. What could constitute a 'manifestation' of a religion or belief is set out in *para 2.61*:

> 'Manifestations of a religion or belief could include treating certain days as days for worship or rest; following a certain dress code; following a particular diet; or carrying out or avoiding certain practices. There is not always a clear line between holding a religion or belief and the manifestation of that religion or belief'.

The relevance of the distinction for the purpose of the *EqA 2010*, according to the *Code*, is that:

> 'Placing limitations on a person's right to manifest their religion or belief may amount to unlawful discrimination; this would usually amount to *indirect* discrimination' (emphasis added).

The *EHRC Employment Code* provides the following example:

> 'An employer has a "no headwear" policy for its staff. Unless this policy can be objectively justified, this will be indirect discrimination against Sikh men who wear the turban, Muslim women who wear a headscarf and observant Jewish men who wear a skullcap as manifestations of their religion'.

Thus, the *EHRC Employment Code*, like many commentators on the *RBR 2003*, appears to regard the issue as one of indirect, rather than direct discrimination.

7.13 Definition of discrimination

EqA 2010 outlaws both direct (*s 13* and *s 14)*) and indirect (*s 19)*) discrimination, and specifies the characteristics of the relevant comparator for the purposes of establishing less favourable treatment (*EqA 2010, s 23(1)*): on a comparison of cases for the purposes of *s 13, 14 or 19* there must be 'no material difference between the circumstances relating to each case'. The key distinction between the two forms of discrimination, as elsewhere in anti-discrimination legislation, is that direct discrimination cannot be justified; although an 'occupational requirement' can be applied to direct discrimination, it provides a much narrower defence than that available for indirect discrimination (see further **1.145**ff).

7.14 *Direct discrimination*

The less favourable treatment must arise 'because of" religion or belief (see further **1.49**ff). Direct discrimination can take place 'because of' of religion or belief even though the employer and the worker share the same protected characteristic that gives rise to the less favourable treatment. For the purposes of *RBR 2003*, the discriminator must have been aware of interference with the religious or other similar philosophical belief in order for the less favourable treatment to be conferred *on grounds of religion or belief* (*McClintock* at [46]) and it is likely that this interpretation will continue to be applied despite the change in definition of direct discrimination from 'on the grounds of' to 'because of'.

It is also significant that direct discrimination on the grounds of religion or belief includes:

- discrimination against a person based on a religion or belief to which he is perceived to belong or subscribe (*Explanatory Notes to the EqA 2010, para 59*);
- discrimination against a person by reason of the religion or belief of someone with whom the person associates (*Explanatory Notes to the EqA 2010, para 59*), and *Saini v All Saints Haque Centre* (UKEAT/00227/08) (24 October 2008); and
- discrimination against a person by reason of a refusal to follow an instruction to discriminate against another person on the grounds of religion or belief (*EqA 2010, s 111*).

The *EHRC Employment Code* provides several examples of potential direct discrimination:

- work breaks: 'An observant Muslim requests two additional 10-minute breaks every day to allow him to pray at work. The employer allows other workers to take additional smoking breaks of similar lengths. Refusing this request could amount to direct discrimination because of religion or belief' (*para 17.14*);

- provision of prayer rooms: 'A large employer has one meeting room which is generally unused. There is also a separate rest room, and the employer has made provision for smokers by permitting them to use an open porch by the back entrance. A group of Muslim workers has asked the employer to convert the small meeting room into a quiet room. Refusing this request may amount to direct discrimination if the Muslim workers have been treated less favourably because of religion or belief, compared to non-Muslim workers' (*para 17.59*);
- customer preferences: 'A Muslim businessman decides not to recruit a Muslim woman as his personal assistant, even though she is the best qualified candidate. Instead he recruits a woman who has no particular religious or non-religious belief. He believes that this will create a better impression with clients and colleagues, who are mostly Christian or have no particular religious or non-religious belief. This could amount to direct discrimination because of religion or belief . . . ' (*para 3.10*).

7.15 *Combined discrimination*

EqA 2010 also contains a new provision enabling an employee to bring a discrimination claim on two combined protected grounds, although the provision was not implemented on 1 October 2010 and will certainly not be implemented before April 2011. *Section 14* provides that a person can allege direct discrimination on the basis of a combination of two relevant protected characteristics. The protected characteristics that may be combined are age, disability, gender reassignment, race, religion or belief, sex and sexual orientation. One of the examples given by the *Explanatory Notes to the EqA 2010* illustrates how this may work in practice, in a context where religion or belief is involved:

> 'A bus driver does not allow a Muslim man onto her bus, claiming that he could be a "terrorist". While it might not be possible for the man to demonstrate less favourable treatment because of either protected characteristic if considered separately, a dual discrimination claim will succeed if the reason for his treatment was the specific combination of sex and religion or belief, which resulted in him being stereotyped as a potential terrorist'.

For a fuller discussion of the concept of dual discrimination see **1.57–1.59**.

7.16 *Indirect discrimination*

The *EHRC Employment Code* provides several examples of potential indirect discrimination:

- dietary needs: 'An all-day assessment that involves a social dinner may amount to indirect discrimination if the employer has not taken account of dietary needs relating to an applicant's religion—unless the arrangements can be objectively justified' (*para 16.48*);
- leave arrangements: 'Last year, a Sikh worker took annual leave on 1 and 2 March to celebrate Hola Mohalla. This year, he requests annual leave on 6 and 7 March to celebrate the same holiday. No other staff members in his department have requested leave on these dates. The employer refuses the request but says that the worker can take off the same days as he did last year. Festivals in Sikhism are based on the lunar calendar, so the dates on which they fall differ every year. It could be indirect discrimination for the employer to expect the worker to take annual leave on the same days every year, unless this can be objectively justified (*para 17.37*);
- dress codes: 'An employer introduces a "no jewellery" policy in the workplace. This is not for health and safety reasons but because the employer does not like body piercings. A Sikh worker who wears a Kara bracelet as an integral part of her religion has complained about the rule. To avoid a claim of indirect discrimination, the employer should consider allowing an exception to this rule. A blanket ban on jewellery would probably not be considered a proportionate means of achieving a legitimate aim in these circumstances' (*para 17.40*);

- personal grooming: 'A food manufacturer has a rule that beards are forbidden for people working on the factory floor. Unless it can be objectively justified, this rule may amount to indirect religion or belief discrimination against the Sikh and Muslim workers in the factory. If the aim of the rule is to meet food hygiene or health and safety requirements, this would be legitimate. However, the employer would need to show that the ban on beards is a proportionate means of achieving this aim. When considering whether this policy is justified, the employment tribunal is likely to examine closely the reasons given by the employer as to why they cannot fulfil the same food hygiene or health and safety obligations by less discriminatory means, for example by providing a beard mask or snood' (*para 4.32*).

In determining whether a 'provision, criterion or practice' (PCP) puts or would put persons of the same religion or belief as B at a particular 'disadvantage' when compared with other persons, care must be taken in identifying the appropriate group of persons of the same religion or belief and otherwise in not materially different relevant circumstances (see *s 23*). For example, for the purposes of a complaint by a Sabbath-observant Jew about a PCP requiring him to work a full-time week, including the Sabbath, the relevant group would be other Sabbath-observant Jews, notwithstanding that this may be only 5–10% of Jews overall (*Wetstein v Misprestige Management Services* EAT/523/91). It must also be shown that B, the individual, is put, or would be put, at a disadvantage (*Haye v London Borough of Lewisham* (16 June 2010; case no 2301852/09)). But disadvantage to a single individual is not sufficient. In *Eweida v British Airways* [2010] EWCA Civ 80 (a case under *RBR 2003*), the Court of Appeal held inconvenience to a single individual did not constitute a disadvantage that 'puts or would put *persons* of the same religion or belief as B at a particular disadvantage when compared with other persons. In that case, Sedley LJ held that 'some identifiable section of a workforce, quite possibly a small one, must be shown to suffer a particular disadvantage which the claimant shares.' Sedley LJ's judgment leaves open the question of whether the workforce relevant for these purposes is the individual employer's or the British workforce more generally.

On the question of whether a PCP is a proportionate means of achieving a legitimate aim, likely legitimate aims might be business efficacy or health and safety, for example, in the context of work patterns and dress codes respectively; and a PCP will be proportionate where it strikes a balance between the importance of that aim and its otherwise discriminatory effect. On this reasoning, a prohibition on the wearing of a veil while teaching young children in the company of a male teacher has been held to be justified since it is intended to prevent the teacher's communication being obscured, and since alternative ways of accommodating the individual's belief were unduly onerous (*Azmi*). Similarly, it has been suggested that the requirement to abide by the judicial oath, requiring Justices of the Peace to apply the laws of the land 'without fear or favour, affection or ill-will', including placing children for adoption with same-sex couples when this conflicts with their religious or philosophical beliefs, would be justified by the need to uphold good administration of justice (*McClintock* at [49]–[57]). In *Lillian Ladele v London Borough of Islington* [2009] EWCA Civ 1357, the Court of Appeal decided that RBR 2003 did not give a registrar the right on religious grounds to refuse to have civil partnership duties assigned to her, because to permit her to do so would mean allowing her to discriminate on the basis of sexual orientation. Islington Council's aim of ensuring adherence by all employees to its 'Dignity for All' policy was objectively justified and an argument that it was not proportionate to uphold such a policy if it offended Ms Ladele's religious beliefs was not accepted. The court also noted, interestingly and following intervention by the human rights organisation Liberty, that once Ms Ladele has been designated a civil partnership registrar (in common with all other registrars) Islington may well have been in breach of its obligations as a service provider under the *Equality Act (Sexual Orientation) Regulations 2007* if it had allowed Ms Ladele a dispensation on grounds of her religious views. In *Edge v Visual Security Services* [2006] ET Case No 1301365/06, the employer's failure to find alternative solutions because they were 'simply too much trouble' meant that it could not demonstrate proportionality.

Special provisions apply to the wearing of safety helmets on construction sites. The *Employment Act 1989, s 12(1)* is amended to provide that a PCP that relates to a Sikh wearing a safety helmet while on a construction site, applied when the employer has no reasonable grounds for believing that the Sikh would not wear a turban at all times while on the site, is incapable of justification for the purposes of *EqA 2010, s 19 (indirect discrimination)*. This provision is restricted to employees on construction sites (*Dhanjal v British Steel plc* IT/50740/91).

7.17 Victimisation and harassment

EqA 2010, s 26 and s 27 govern harassment and victimisation. The material and personal scope of the provisions prohibiting discrimination are generally very similar for each of the protected characteristics (see **1.86–1.108**). However, with regard to the characteristic of religion and belief, harassment is made unlawful primarily in the context of employment only. Examples of such harassment are offensive comments relating to the religion of the claimant (*Bhatti and Dar v Pontiac Coils Europe Ltd* (Nottingham, 4 Dec 2007; ET/2600837/07 and ET/2600824/07)), and inappropriate 'joking', including offering pork to Muslim colleagues during Ramadan (*Taj v GBM Services Ltd* (Watford, 9 Dec 2008; ET/3301281/07 and ET/3302910/07)).

7.18 Protection from Harassment Act 1997

The *Protection from Harassment Act 1997* ('*PHA 1997*') makes harassment both a civil tort and a criminal offence. Initially introduced to protect victims from stalking, the Act has been used by complainants in harassment claims. Employers can also be found vicariously liable where the harassment occurs in the course of employment (*Majrowski v Guy's and St Thomas's NHS Trust* [2006] UKHL 34, [2006] 4 All ER 395). See **1.96** for further discussion of the impact of *PHA 1997* in the employment field.

7.19 Instructing, causing or inducing discrimination

It is unlawful to instruct, cause or induce someone to discriminate against, harass or victimise another person, or to attempt to do so (*EqA 2010, s 111*). A claim can be brought by the 'victim' of the discrimination, the person who was instructed to carry out the discrimination and the EHRC. (See **1.61**.)

7.20 Liability of employees and agents and aiding discrimination

Where employees commit acts of discrimination against fellow employees, their employer will be liable if the acts were committed during the course of employment (*EqA 2010, s 109(1)*). Employers are also liable for the discriminatory acts of their agents if they are acting with the employer's authority (*s 109(4)*). In each case it is irrelevant whether the employer knew or approved of the acts (*s 109(3)*). However, there is a defence for employers in relation to the acts of their employees (but not agents) if they can show that they took all reasonable steps to prevent the employee from doing the act in question (*s 109(4)*). The employees and agents will also have personal liability for their acts of discrimination (*EqA 2010, s 110*), even if the employer has a defence. See **1.163**ff.

It is also unlawful for an individual to knowingly help another to carry out an act which is unlawful under *EqA 2010* (*s 112(1)*). (See **1.162**.)

7.21 Discussions about pay

EqA 2010, s 77 makes contractual pay secrecy clauses unenforceable to the extent that they prevent employees from making relevant pay disclosures - that is, a disclosure that is sought or made for the purpose of finding out whether (or to what extent) any difference in pay is related to a protected characteristic (*EqA 2010, s 77(3)*). Action taken by an employer as a result of an individual making or seeking to make a relevant pay disclosure, or receiving information disclosed in a relevant pay disclosure, may amount to victimisation. (See **1.109**.)

7.22 Discrimination in employment

RBR 2003 (and other previous legislation) prohibited employers from discriminating 'at an establishment in Great Britain' in various circumstances. This is no longer the case, and it will be up to the courts to determine whether there is a sufficient connection with Great Britain for the legislation to bite (see further **1.43**).

The term 'employment' is defined in *s 83(2)* as 'employment under a contract of employment, a contract of apprenticeship or a contract personally to do work'. A proposal for an artistic display which contains no specification of personal service, and which is made to a rolling open-tender programme, is not a response to an offer of employment; it is a response to an offer to listen to a proposal which may, or may not, lead to an offer of employment (*Padgett v Serota and the Board of Trustees of the Tate Gallery* EAT/97/07 and EAT/99/07). As in other areas of equality legislation, the definition of 'employment' is broader than that in *ERA 1996, s 230*. In *Jivraj v Hashwani* [2010] EWCA Civ 712 a clause in an arbitration agreement requiring the arbitrators to be from the Ismaili community was struck out by the Court of Appeal on the grounds that an arbitrator fell within the extended definition of employment because he would be undertaking work personally under a contract. (The Supreme Court has granted leave to appeal, with the appeal due to be heard in late 2011.) See also *Masih v AWAZ FM Ltd* (26 Aug 2009, ET/S/116403/08), where an employment tribunal made a reference to the ECJ on the issue of whether a volunteer, in the circumstances of this particular case, is covered by the *Framework Employment Equality Directive*. The decision to make a reference has been appealed. Discrimination against contract workers by those to whom their employer contracts to supply their services, rather than by the employer himself, is covered by *s 41* (see **1.17**).

7.23 Former employees

Former employees are likewise protected against direct and indirect discrimination and harassment, provided the detriment complained of 'arises out of or is closely connected to' a previous relationship with the respondent (*EqA 2010, s 108(1)*). (See **1.35**.)

However, there is an unintended lacuna in the *EqA 2010's* protection for former employees from victimisation. (See **1.107**).

7.24 Occupational requirements

In the employment context, there is a general exception from the requirement not to discriminate (including by reference to religion or belief), allowing certain 'occupational requirements' to be adopted that would otherwise be unlawful provided that the employer can show that the requirement is a justified, ie a proportionate means of achieving a legitimate aim (*EqA 2010, Sch 9, Part 1, para 1*) (see further **1.145**ff).

EqA 2010, Sch 9, Part 1, para 3 also provides, more specifically, that an employer with an ethos based on religion or belief does not contravene the same provisions by applying in relation to work a requirement to be of a particular religion or belief. To rely on this exception, therefore, the employer must be able to show that its ethos is based on a religion or belief. The *EHRC Employment Code* (*para 13.17*) provides further:

> 'an "ethos" is the important character or spirit of the religion or belief. It may also be the underlying sentiment, conviction or outlook than informs the behaviours, customs, practices or attitudes of followers of the religion or belief.'

An example, according to the Employment Code, would be where 'a Humanist organisation which promotes Humanist philosophy and principles [applies] an occupational requirement for their chief executive to be a Humanist.' The provision has the potential to apply to a broad category of organisations, such as faith schools or care homes with a religious ethos; but it seems it will not apply to local authorities that merely maintain such organisations. In *Glasgow City Council v McNab* [2007] IRLR 476, EAT), the local education authority was not entitled to have recourse to the occupational requirement exception in *RBR 2003* in respect of a teaching post in a maintained Roman Catholic school because they could not show that it was the local authority employer itself which maintained a religious ethos.

Both with regard to the general exception, and with regard to the more specific ethos-based exception, three conditions must be satisfied, having regard to the nature or context of the work (in the case of the religion or belief requirement, also having regard to the 'ethos based on religion or belief'). First, the requirement must be an 'occupational' requirement. In contrast with the previous legislation, there is no requirement that being of a particular religion or belief is a 'genuine and determining occupational requirement' (*RBR 2003, reg 7(2)(a)*). (See also *Jivraj v Hashwani*.) Second, the application of the requirement must be 'a proportionate means of achieving a legitimate aim'. Third, the person to whom the requirement is applied does not meet it (or there are reasonable grounds for not being satisfied that the person meets it). In *Muhammed v The Leprosy Mission International* (16 Dec 2009, ET/2303459/09) the tribunal upheld a requirement for a finance administrator to be a Christian due to the context in which the job was carried out.

The *EHRC Employment Code* suggests (*para 13.19*) that 'an employer may wish to consider' some of the following issues when addressing the question of whether the application of an occupational requirement is proportionate to a legitimate aim:

'• Do any or all of the duties of the job need to be performed by a person with a particular characteristic?
• Could the employer use the skills of an existing worker with the required protected characteristic to do that aspect of the job?'

The *EHRC Employment Code* also stresses (*para 13.20*) that employers 'should not have a blanket policy of applying an occupational requirement exception, such as a policy that all staff of a certain grade should have a particular belief.' In *Hender & Sheridan v Prospects for People with Learning Difficulties* [2008] ET Case No 2902090/2006 (13 May 2008), it was held that there could be no assumption that, as a matter of principle, every job in a Christian organisation should be done by Christians; each job needed to be assessed separately. In addition, employers 'should also re-assess the job whenever it becomes vacant to ensure that the statutory conditions for applying the occupational requirement exception still apply.'

As well as these exceptions, *EqA 2010, Sch 9, Part 1, para 2* provides an additional specific exception where employment is for the purposes of an organised religion. Under this exception, an employer (or a person who makes, recommends or approves appointments of office holders) does not discriminate if it applies one of a set of specified requirements. These are: a requirement to be of a particular sex; a requirement not to be a transsexual person; a requirement not to be married or a civil partner; a requirement not to be married to, or the civil partner of, a person who has a living former spouse or civil partner; a requirement relating to circumstances in which a marriage or civil partnership came to an end; a requirement related to sexual orientation. This occupational exception may be used in the context of the arrangement made for making job offers, the job offer itself, the provision of access to opportunities for promotion, transfer or training, and dismissal and termination.

The use of these requirements is permitted, however, only if three conditions are satisfied. One of these is the same as those set out in the previous paragraphs: the person to whom the requirement is applied does not meet that requirement (or there are reasonable grounds for not being satisfied that the person meets it). The remaining two requirements differ significantly from those considered above: the employment to which the requirement applies must be for the purposes of an 'organised religion'; and the application of the requirement is one that 'engages the compliance or non-conflict principle'. The application of a requirement 'engages the compliance principle' if the requirement is applied so as to comply with the doctrines of the religion. The application of a requirement engages the 'non-conflict principle' if, because of the nature or context of the employment, the requirement is applied so as to avoid conflicting with the strongly held religious convictions of a significant number of the religion's followers.

The *EHRC Employment Code* (*para 13.12*) provides two examples where these requirements may be satisfied: where an 'orthodox synagogue could apply a requirement for its rabbi to be a man', and where an 'evangelical church could require its ministers to be married or heterosexual if this enables the church to avoid a conflict with the strongly held religious convictions of its congregation.' The requirement must, according to the *EHRC Employment Code* (*para 13.13*), also be, a proportionate way of meeting the 'compliance' or 'non-conflict' principle: 'The occupational requirement exception should only be used for a limited number of posts, such as ministers of religion and a small number of posts outside the clergy including those which exist to promote or represent the religion'. The *EHRC Employment Code* (*para 13.15*) also provides an example of where the use of this occupational requirement would not be regarded as satisfying the 'compliance' or 'non-conflict' principle:

> 'The trustees of a Mosque want to employ two youth workers, one who will provide guidance on the teachings of the Koran and the other purely to organize sporting activities not involving promoting or representing the religion. The trustees apply an occupational requirement for both workers to be heterosexual. It might be lawful to apply the occupational requirement exception to the first post but not the second post because the second post does not engage the "compliance" or the "non-conflict" principle'.

The statutory provisions will need to be read in a way that as far as possible fulfils the requirements of the ECHR (see, eg *Schüth v Germany* [2010] ECtHR (No 1620/03) (23 September 2010), regarding the possible relevance of *ECHR, Article 8*).

The statutory provisions must also be read together with the equivalent, if somewhat differently drafted, provisions in the Framework Directive (see **1.149**).

7.25 Other exceptions

Schedule 22 allows differential treatment that would otherwise be made unlawful by specific parts of the Bill, where that is required by law. More specifically, it allows people of particular religions or beliefs to be appointed to specified educational posts. *Schedule 22, para 3* provides that a person does not contravene the employment provisions of the *EqA 2010* (Part 5 (work)) by doing an act that is necessary in order to comply with a requirement of an instrument relating to an educational establishment that the head teacher or principal of the educational establishment must be a member of a particular religious order. Para 3 also provides that a person does not contravene the provisions in Part 5 by doing an act that is necessary in order to comply with a requirement of an act or instrument relating to the appointment to a canon professorship in a university, or to a professorship to which a canonry is annexed. A Minister may by order provide that these exceptions do not have effect in relation to a specified educational establishment or university, or a specified description of educational establishments. *Schedule 22, para 4* provides that a person does not contravene the *EqA 2010* by doing anything that the School Standards and Framework Act permits for the purposes of dismissing a teacher because of a failure to give religious education efficiently, or having regard to religious considerations relating to certain appointments, or preferring certain teachers at independent schools of a religious character.

7.26 Discrimination outside employment

EqA 2010 prohibits discrimination in a variety of areas outside employment, such as within barristers' chambers (*s 47*), trade organisations (*s 57*), qualifications bodies (*s 96*), providers of vocational training (*s 55*), employment agencies (*s 55*) and institutions of further and higher education (*chapter 2*). *EqA 2010* provides this protection in a number of other areas, including the provision of goods, facilities and services (*Part 3*) and the disposal of premises (*Part 4*).

7.27 PRACTICAL CONSIDERATIONS

Particular issues that are likely to arise under *EqA 2010* include complaints about recruitment, working time and dress codes. Guidance on these issues is set out below, together with advice on monitoring and drafting suitable policies. Although the case law under *RBR 2003*, and *EA 2006* is limited, assistance can be found in UK and ECJ sex discrimination, and more particularly, race discrimination, law, as well as under the *ECHR* and *HRA 1998*; however, care should be taken in drawing analogies.

7.28 Recruitment

Advertising for positions should reach as diverse an audience as possible. Making use of religious press is acceptable provided that multiple faiths are targeted, unless an occupational requirement applies. If an occupational requirement does apply, this should be identified at the beginning of the recruitment process (bearing in mind the duties of the role and its profile within the organisation), made clear in any advertisements for the position and reiterated in the selection process.

Organisations should recruit based on the qualifications needed for the job in question, irrespective of religion or belief, and interview questions should be framed accordingly. However, some positive action is justifiable under *EqA 2010, ss 158–159*, when these provisions are brought into force in April 2011 (see **1.154–1.162**).

7.29 Working time

Employers are not legally obliged to provide time and facilities for religious or belief observance in the workplace or elsewhere. Employers should, however, try to accommodate requests for time off where possible by approving annual leave, time off in lieu, unpaid leave, use of flexi-time and/or flexible working arrangements. Failure to do so may lead to claims of indirect discrimination.

Some religions or beliefs require their followers to pray at specific times during the day. Employees should use what facilities are already available, and may request time off where this is necessary (*Mansoor v Andrews Estate Agents Ltd* (30 Jun 2009, ET/232807/08)). Workers may also request access to an appropriate quiet place (or prayer room) to undertake their religious observance. While employers are not legally obliged to provide a prayer room, the *EHRC Employment Code* notes that 'if a quiet place is available and allowing its use for prayer and contemplation does not cause problems for the business or for other workers, an employer with sufficient resources may be discriminating because of religion or belief by refusing such a request—especially if comparable facilities are provided for other reasons' (*para 17.58*). Employers 'should be careful to avoid creating a disadvantage for workers who do not need a quiet room (for example, by converting the only rest room), as this might amount to indirect religion or belief discrimination' (*para 17.59*). It would be good practice 'to consult with all workers before designating a room for prayer and contemplation and to discuss policies for using it, such as the wearing of shoes' (*para 17.59*).

Where a worker seeks to opt out of regular working on a day which has religious significance for them, employers should consider whether working on that day can be justified as a legitimate aim and whether it is proportionate to apply that justification to the individual.

Specific provisions apply to workers in the retail or betting trades who seek to opt out of Sunday working in the *Employment Rights Act 1996, ss 36–43*. Complaints of indirect discrimination by a Jew refused leave on the Sabbath (*Fugler v Macmillan-London Hair Studios Ltd* ET 2205090/04 (15 July 2005)) and a Christian given shift patterns that included Sundays (*Williams-Drabble v Pathway Care Solutions* ET 2601718/04 (10 January 2005)) have been upheld, especially where instructions were given without discussing the matter with other employees to find ways of avoiding the claimant having to work Sundays (*Estorninho v Zoran Jokic t/a Zorans Delicatessen* [2006] Employment Tribunal Case No 23014871/06). In contrast, indirect discrimination has been found to be justified where a Muslim teacher was refused Friday afternoon leave because of the disruptive effect on students that would follow from granting the leave (*Mayuff v (1) The Governing Body of Bishop Challoner Catholic Collegiate School and (2) The Mayor and Burgesses of the London Borough of Tower Hamlets* ET 3202398/04 (21 December 2005)) and where Saturday working was accepted as standard practice in the tourism industry (*James v MSC Cruises Ltd* ET 2203173/05 (12 April 2006)). Working time claims made under human rights law have met with little success. The European Commission on Human Rights has also held there to be no breach of *Article 9* where a Muslim teacher was refused Friday afternoon leave; the employee had entered freely into his contract of employment, which stipulated Friday working, and the employer had not, in relying on that contract, arbitrarily disregarded his freedom of religion (*Ahmad*).

Where workers request holiday in order to celebrate festival or spiritual observance periods, the *EHRC Employment Code* recommends that employers 'should seek to accommodate the request—provided the worker has sufficient holiday due to them and it is reasonable for them to be absent from work during the period requested' (*para 17.36*). Failure to consider requests can in itself be held to be discriminatory (*Khan v G and J Spencer Group t/a NIC Hygiene Ltd* ET 1803250/04 (9 January 2005)). Refusals of religious holiday have been held to indirectly discriminate in the context of Eid (*JH Walker*).

Requests/representations from people with less well known religions or beliefs—and those with no religion or belief—should be treated in the same way as those from followers of better known religions or beliefs. The logical result of the extension of the definition of religion to include a reference to lack of religion and of belief (see **7.11**) is the possibility of direct and/or indirect discrimination claims from those who do not hold the same belief or share the same religion as the comparator and those who have no religion or belief. Such claims could arise in connection with leave arrangements if they are seen as disproportionately favourable to adherents of particular religions.

Employers that operate or alter shift patterns should:

- make work patterns clear at recruitment;
- when changing work patterns review whether religious issues might be an issue and include in any consultation process;
- offer alternative solutions where practicable; and
- give the business reasons for any refusal to work required shifts.

7.30 Dress codes and uniform requirements

Many employers impose uniform requirements and/or dress codes, whether contractual or non-contractual, precise/prescriptive or imprecise/descriptive, eg 'business dress', 'smart casual'. Those which conflict with the dress requirement of a particular religion or faith may constitute indirect discrimination unless they can be justified as a proportionate means of achieving a legitimate aim such as health and safety considerations (*EHRC Employment Code, para 17.39*). Any which are targeted at particular religious practices and requirements may discriminate directly. It is 'good practice for employers to consult with workers as to how a dress code may impact on different religious or belief groups, and whether any exceptions should be allowed, for example, for religious jewellery' (*para 17.40*).

Dress codes may be easier to justify where there are health and safety concerns or where employees work directly with the public. For example, a complaint of indirect discrimination was upheld where a Muslim female shop assistant was required to wear an overall over a skirt for image purposes, because the detriment caused to her outweighed any benefit to the employer (*Malik v British Home Stores* (ET 29014/79)); but a Sikh woman's complaint regarding her employer's prohibition on trousers, following the dress regulations laid down by the General Nursing Council, which led to the withdrawal of her training place, was dismissed on the basis of justification (*Kingston and Richmond Area Health Authority v Kaur* [1981] ICR 631, [1981] IRLR 337, EAT). Similarly, both refusals to employ and dismissals of Sikhs for failing to cut their hair or shave their beards have been held to be justified on the grounds of hygiene (*Singh v RHM Bakeries (Southern) Ltd* EAT 818/77 and *Singh v Rowntree Mackintosh Ltd* [1979] ICR 554, [1979] IRLR 199, EAT respectively). A nurse who refused on religious grounds to stop wearing a crucifix with her uniform contrary to the Trust's health and safety policy and who, as a consequence, was redeployed had not been subjected to direct or indirect religious discrimination (*Chaplin v Royal Devon & Exeter Hospital NHS Foundation Trust* [2010] ET 1702886/2009 (21 April 2010). See also *Eweida v British Airways plc* [2010] EWCA Civ 80, [2010] ICR 890).

But where there are no clear justifications presented for the restriction (*Watkins-Singh*, prohibiting a Sikh girl from wearing a Kara), or the grounds for justification, such as safety requirements, are implausible (*Bhakerd v Famous Names Ltd*, ET 19289/87, where a turban was not plausibly any less suitable than the prescribed company hat), where there is no evidence supporting the respondent's allegation of adverse effect on achieving the legitimate aim if the restriction is not maintained (*Noah v Desrosiers t/a Wedge* (13 Jun 2008; ET/2201867/07)), or where the restriction is not enforced consistently, a provision, criterion or practice will be difficult to justify (*Hussain v Midland Cosmetic Sales plc*, EAT 915/00. The employer did not allow Ms Hussain to wear a headscarf as well as protective headgear, but had permitted eight other Pakistani women employees to do so).

As to the jurisprudence under *Article 9* of the *ECHR*, domestic courts have been slow to find interferences with the right to manifest religious beliefs in the context of uniform policies that perform valid functions. In *R (on the application of Begum) v Headteacher and Governors of Denbigh High School* [2006] UKHL 15, [2007] 1 AC 100, [2006] 2 WLR 719, [2006] 2 All ER 487 the House of Lords found that a school uniform policy, which was acceptable to mainstream Muslim opinion but did not permit the wearing of a jilbab, did not interfere with a Muslim schoolgirl's *Article 9* rights; the girl's parents had chosen the school with knowledge of its uniform requirements, and anyway her right to manifest her religion did not extend to any time and place of her choosing. Similarly, in *R (on the application of Playfoot) v Governing Body of Millais School* [2007] EWHC 1698 (Admin), [2007] 3 FCR 754, a school uniform policy which forbade the wearing of jewellery did not infringe *Article 9* by preventing a pupil from wearing a chastity ring; the girl had voluntarily accepted the school's uniform policy, which was both a legitimate and proportionate means of fostering the school identity and an atmosphere of allegiance, discipline, equality and cohesion which was conducive to learning.

When instituting dress codes, employers should consider whether:

- any part of an existing or proposed dress code is likely to conflict with religious or other genuinely held beliefs;
- any such elements are strictly necessary and, if not, whether they can be objectively justified;
- to seek workplace validation of the dress code (for example, by means of employee survey or consultation with worker representatives);

- to seek external expert advice from, say, representatives of a particular faith groups.

It should be made clear to employees that if any elements of a dress code cause them personal difficulty, problems should first be discussed in confidence with HR/line managers. Ideally, dress codes should be neutrally worded, flexible and minimal.

7.31 Special treatment

In policies which are as accommodating as possible for individuals from a variety of faiths, employers must also be careful not to accord special treatment to individuals from any one faith. Even if this is intended to avoid discriminating directly or indirectly against them, it may constitute unlawful direct or indirect discrimination if it amounts to less favourable treatment of others on the grounds of their religion or belief, unless there is a specific exception permitting it. Examples of possible direct or indirect discrimination might be giving a Jewish employee extra paid holiday to mark a religious festival or paying employees extra to work on Sundays, to the disadvantage of Christians who observe Sunday as a day of rest, or permitting a registrar to refuse to have civil partnership duties assigned to her on religious grounds to the disadvantage of those wishing to enter into civil partnerships (*Ladele*), or a psychosexual counsellor to refuse to counsel same-sex couples about sexual matters, to the disadvantage of those couples (*McFarlane v Relate Avon Ltd* [2010] EWCA Civ 880), or where halal meat was served at work functions to the disadvantage of Sikhs, who objected to such meat (*Singh-Thaper v HFC Bank Ltd* (23 Apr 2009, ET/1302319/07)). Where an employer takes steps to accommodate the needs of one particular religion, it needs to ensure it takes account of the potential disadvantages of this accommodation for other religious groups as well as those with no religion or belief.

7.32 Monitoring and information-gathering

In Great Britain, there is no legal obligation to include religion or belief in any equal opportunities monitoring processes (although this may arise indirectly for public sector employers under the public sector equality duty), nor are job applicants or employees obliged to respond to any such enquiries, and there may, indeed, be human rights problems if this were attempted: a requirement to disclose one's religion may in certain circumstances violate *ECHR, Article 9* (*Dimitras v Greece (Applications Nos 42837/06, 3269/07, 35793/07 and 6099/08)* (3 June 2010, unreported); *Sinan Isik v Turkey* [2010] ECtHR (No 21924/05) (2 February 2010)).

However, monitoring can assist employers in ensuring that their equality policy is working to the benefit of all concerned. The *EHRC Employment Code* recommends that all employers carry out equality monitoring (*para 18.25*).

Before opting to monitor, employers should consider how information could be obtained, how accurate it might be, and what should be done with it. Without a clear purpose and, in particular, the willingness and ability to act where appropriate, monitoring on the basis of this protected characteristic could be counter-productive. Staff should be told why information is being collected, how it will be used and whether or not it will be kept confidential and anonymous. A named and trained individual should have responsibility for the collation and storage of such information, which will constitute sensitive personal data under the *Data Protection Act 1998*.

Some employers that monitor invite staff to classify themselves under the categories used in the 2001 census: Christian, Buddhist, Hindu, Jewish, Muslim, Sikh, any other religion, no religion or religion not stated. Given the breadth of the definition of 'religion or belief' in *EqA 2010*, however, it is unlikely that questions could be devised which would dovetail with the full range of potential claims or satisfy any genuine requests for such information.

In the face of potential difficulties with formal monitoring processes, anonymous surveys and information from other sources such as exit interviews or grievance meetings may provide useful information, but these can create difficulties if the information, supplied in confidence and/or anonymously, reveals specific problems which require resolution, eg complaints about specific people. Alternatively, information can be collated from the workforce by enquiring whether any changes are necessary or desirable to specific rules or practices to accommodate particular religions or beliefs. This approach may be better tailored towards ensuring compliance with *EqA 2010*, whilst also acknowledging that people manifest their religion or belief in a range of ways, even amongst those who affiliate themselves with a particular religious denomination. If from this data there appears to be a substantial number of people who consider a particular working practice such as shift arrangements, staff food facilities or the dress code to be disadvantageous on the grounds of religion or belief, then consideration should be given to reviewing and adjusting those arrangements. However, it should be explained at the outset that it may not be reasonable, or possible, to remedy all perceived disadvantages.

7.33 Drafting suitable policies

Whilst employers do not have to have an equality policy in place, doing so is a commonplace means of demonstrating that an employer has taken reasonably practicable steps to prevent employees discriminating against or harassing other employees. The *EHRC Employment Code* recommends, 'as a matter of good practice, that [employers] draw up an equality policy (also known as an equal opportunities policy or equality and diversity policy) and put this policy into practice' (*para 18.1*). Employers may also be able to rely on a defence of having taken reasonable steps to prevent discrimination where they have a 'dynamic regime' of monitoring of and training on equality policies (*Ali v Sitel* (11 November 2009, ET/2801037/09)).

Either the equality policy or other policies of the employer should provide guidance on how to resolve conflicts between either the equality policy and other policies on working time or dress codes, or between protection from discrimination on the grounds of religion and belief and discrimination on other grounds. An obvious example of the latter sort of conflict is where a fundamentalist Christian refuses to work with a gay colleague. Any such guidance should be formulated neutrally. Similarly, when considering whether adjustments need to be made to standard company rules or practices, care should be taken not to create specific formal exemptions only available to people of a particular religion or belief. The aim should be minimal procedures, maximum flexibility and regular review of all practices and procedures.

The *Azmi, Eweida, Ladele* and *Noah* cases (see **7.16** and **7.30–7.31**) all indicate for the present that the tribunals consider that treating any consequent claims as indirect rather than direct discrimination, where that is possible, is the better approach (although not the only one). As a matter of principle, the employer should have the opportunity of showing that provisions, criteria and practices that are genuinely neutral, are justifiable. This will not be possible where a rule or practice, even if well intentioned, is directed at adherents of a particular religion or a particular manifestation of that belief. For example, a policy which specifically permits (and/or delimits) time off for religious observance (particularly if it is especially beneficial) may conceivably give rise to claims of direct discrimination from atheists or agnostics, whereas the better course might be to refer instead to a general policy on the treatment of time off for purposes not expressly covered by the *Employment Rights Act 1996*.

7.34 Further sources of information

Further information is available from:

- the BBC website: which contains information on many religions or beliefs, including their history, beliefs, ethics and customs: http://www.bbc.co.uk/religion/religions;

Religion and belief

- a five-year religious calendar can be found at http://www.interfaithcalendar.org;
- the ACAS Guidance, Appendix 2 contains useful information on 'commonly practised religions'. This covers food, clothing and bereavement requirements.

8 Sex discrimination

8.1 INTRODUCTION

The *Sex Discrimination Act 1975* ('*SDA 1975*') made gender discrimination unlawful in the field of employment (*Part II*) and in other fields such as education and the provision of goods, facilities and services (*Part III*). On 1 October 2010 the *SDA 1975* was repealed and the *Equality Act 2010* ('*EqA 2010*') came into force. It is now the *EqA 2010* which provides the UK legislative framework for protection from discrimination on the ground of sex, and indeed across all other forms of discrimination. It is a consolidating Act and the language used is intended to make the legislation easier to understand, although it does introduce some new features (see **1.4**).

Much of this chapter focuses on pregnancy and maternity-related matters. While this is, of course, not the only context in which sex discrimination can arise, it is an area on which a great deal of law—legislation and case law, domestic and European—has been generated. These, and the assertion of other 'family-friendly' rights which are often significant in the context of sex discrimination claims, therefore provide the primary focus for this chapter.

8.2 Unlawful discrimination

Types of discrimination

Unlawful discrimination takes four different forms. *EqA 2010* categorises the different types of discrimination as follows:

(a) direct discrimination (*s 13*);

(b) indirect discrimination(*s 19*);

(c) discrimination by way of victimisation (*s 27*); and

(d) harassment, including sexual harassment (*s 26*).

See **1.45** for more detailed commentary, and **8.3** ff for specific commentary with reference to sex.

8.3 *Specific provisions for gender*

There are specific provisions for certain types of gender discrimination:

(a) gender reassignment discrimination (*s 7*) (see **Gender reassignment (4)**);

(b) marriage and civil partnership discrimination (*s 8*) (see **Marital status and civil partnerships (5)**); and

(c) pregnancy and maternity discrimination (*ss 17–18*) (see **8.55** ff).

In addition, and uniquely in the field of discrimination law, there are specific provisions with respect to discrimination in relation to pay and other terms of the employment contract. These are contained within *EqA 2010, Pt 5, Chapter 3*, which is the successor to the *Equal Pay Act 1970*. These provisions are the subject of **Equal pay (11)** and are not considered in this chapter.

Although more commonly relied upon by women who experience discriminatory treatment, the prohibition on sex discrimination applies equally to discrimination against men: *EqA 2010, s 11(a)*.

8.4 *Limitations in scope*

Discrimination is unlawful only in so far as it is prohibited by the terms of *EqA 2010* (subject to compliance with EU law: see **8.6** ff). There is no common law rule against gender discrimination. Therefore, it is essential to identify at the outset of every case whether a claimant comes within the scope of one or more of the anti-discrimination provisions in *EqA 2010*. Those provisions relating to employment are primarily found in *EqA 2010, Part 5* (Work) and are described at **1.15**ff.

8.5 **Family-friendly provisions**

In response to EU Directives and developing social policy in the UK, a raft of 'family-friendly' provisions has been introduced in recent years. In summary, they are:

(a) the right to be absent from work to care for young children (*Maternity and Parental Leave etc Regulations 1999 (SI 1999/3312)*);

(b) the right to take time off work to care for dependants in the event of family emergencies (*Employment Rights Act 1996* (*ERA 1996*), *ss 57A* and *57B*);

(c) the right to paternity and adoption leave and pay (*ERA 1996, ss 75A–75D, 80A–80E*; *Paternity and Adoption Leave Regulations 2002 (SI 2002/2788)*; and more recently the *Additional Paternity Leave Regulations 2010 (SI 2010/1055)* and *Additional Statutory Paternity Pay Regulations (SI 2010/1056)*); and

(d) flexible working arrangements to care for children and adults (*ERA 1996, Part VIIIA*; *Flexible Working (Eligibility, Complaints and Remedies) Regulations 2002 (SI 2002/3236)*; *Flexible Working (Procedural Requirements) Regulations 2002 (SI 2002/3207)*; *Flexible Working (Eligibility, Complaints and Remediation) (Amendment) Regulations 2009 (SI 2009/595)*).

These family-friendly provisions are considered in their own right at **8.86** ff. In addition, it should be borne in mind that a failure to comply with the relevant requirements may in itself give rise to a valid complaint of discrimination, particularly in the field of maternity rights and flexible working.

8.6 **EU law**

EU law has had a significant impact on the development of gender discrimination law in the UK.

8.7 *Treaty on the Functioning of the European Union*

Article 157 of the *Treaty on the Functioning of the European Union* ('*TFEU*', previously the *Treaty of Rome 1957, Article 119* and then *Article 141* of the *Treaty of Maastricht 1992*), initially only contained express provision in relation to the right to equal pay, not other forms of gender discrimination. However it was subsequently amended to add an obligation on the Council to 'adopt measures to ensure the application of the principle of equal opportunities and equal treatment of men and women in matters of employment and occupation'. This falls short of a directly enforceable right under the *TFEU*.

8.8 *Equal Treatment Directive*

The *Equal Treatment Directive* (*76/207/EEC*) required Member States to put into effect the principle of equal treatment for men and women in respect of access to employment, training and working conditions. The *Equal Pay Directive* (*75/117/EEC*) and the *Equal Treatment (Social Security) Directive (79/7/EEC)* imposed similar requirements in those areas. In the seminal case of *Defrenne v Sabena: 149/77* [1978] ECR 1365, the European Court of Justice (ECJ) at paras 26–27 held that:

'. . . respect for fundamental personal human rights is one of the general principles of community law . . . There can be no doubt that the elimination of discrimination based on sex forms part of those fundamental rights'.

8.9 *Further Directives*

Important amendments were introduced by the *Equal Treatment Amendment Directive (2002/73/EC)*. In addition, directives on occupational social security (*86/378/EEC*), pregnant workers (*92/85/EEC*), parental leave (*96/34/EC*), the burden of proof (*97/80/EC*), part-time work (*97/81/EC*) and the *Framework Directive* (*2000/78/EC*) made further changes to UK law. *Directive 2006/54/EC* ('*2006 Directive*') consolidates and updates the major Directives on equal opportunities and equal treatment.

Directives may be relied upon:

(a) directly, in a claim against an 'emanation of the State' but not against a private individual or organisation;

(b) to interpret the scope and meaning of domestic law in conformity with the directive, eg *Webb v EMO Air Cargo (UK) Ltd (No 2)* [1995] 4 All ER 577, [1995] 1 WLR 1454; and

(c) to set aside conflicting domestic law where it derogates from a general principle of community law, eg *Mangold v Helm* [2006] All ER (EC) 383, [2006] IRLR 143.

Proceedings may be brought against a Member State for failure to implement a directive (for example, *Equal Opportunities Commission v Secretary of State for Trade and Industry* [2007] EWHC 483 (Admin), [2007] 2 CMLR 1351) and, where appropriate, damages may be awarded for loss suffered (*Francovich and Bonifaci v Italy: C-6/90 and C-9/90* [1991] ECR I-5357).

8.10 *Charter of Fundamental Rights*

The preamble to the *2006 Directive* makes express reference to The Charter of Fundamental Rights of the European Union ('Charter'), which enshrines the right to equal treatment between men and women in all areas, including employment, work and pay. The Charter is now expressly recognised by *Article 6(1)* of the *Treaty on European Union* ('*TEU*'), which provides that it has the 'same legal value' as *TEU* and *TFEU*, while not extending the competences of the EU as defined in the Treaties. It is expected that the Charter will be used largely as an aid to interpretation, and indeed a protocol to the Charter negotiated by the UK, Czech and Polish Governments is intended to ensure that it does not create new rights in those countries.

8.11 *Court of Justice of the European Union*

Judgments of the Court of Justice of the European Union (formerly the European Court of Justice, 'ECJ') have played an important part in shaping UK law on gender discrimination, by identifying aspects of UK law which are incompatible with EU law. A notable example is *Marshall v Southampton and South West Hampshire Area Health Authority (No 2)* [1994] QB 126, [1993] 4 All ER 586, in which the ECJ held that the statutory cap on compensation for sex discrimination was in breach of the *Equal Treatment Directive*. As Miss Marshall's employer was an 'emanation of the State', the Directive had direct effect, so enabling her to rely on it before the UK courts.

8.12 *European Commission*

The European Commission also has the power to make recommendations to Member States. It has previously made a recommendation regarding the protection of dignity of men and women at work, which includes a Code of Practice on sexual harassment. The Commission recommendations and code are not legally binding, but will be taken into account by courts and tribunals (Recommendation *92/131/EEC*).

8.13 Equality and Human Rights Commission

The Equal Opportunities Commission (EOC) was established by the *SDA 1975*. It had a wide range of powers in the field of sex discrimination. It, together with the Commission for Racial Equality and the Disability Rights Commission, was replaced by a single equality body, the Equality and Human Rights Commission (EHRC), under the *Equality Act 2006*. The EHRC has duties to promote awareness and understanding and encourage good practice in relation to equality, as well as a power to provide advice and guidance on the law. It also has powers to enforce discrimination law in some circumstances.

8.14 Code of Practice and Guidance

There is a wide variety of guidance materials available to assist with the interpretation of *EqA 2010*. In particular, the EHRC has produced both: (a) a Statutory Code of Practice on Employment ('*EHRC Employment Code*'); and (b) non-statutory guidance for employers and employees.

Various Codes of Practice were issued by the EHRC's predecessor bodies, most notably in the field of sex the EOC's Code of Practice on Sex Discrimination (1985). This will be revoked with effect from 6 April 2011, although it will continue to apply to proceedings arising from alleged contraventions of the *SDA 1975* and in certain other circumstances (see COMMON CONCEPTS at **1.5**). In all other cases, the new *EHRC Employment Code* will apply. The *EHRC Employment Code* therefore forms the focus of the examples given in this chapter.

For a discussion of the legal status of the *EHRC Employment Code*, see **1.7**.

The EHRC's non-statutory guidance is not designed to be used in legal proceedings, and tribunals do not have to take it into account.

8.15 THE EQUALITY ACT 2010 AND SEX DISCRIMINATION

Sex as a protected characteristic

Sex is a 'protected characteristic' under the *EqA 2010, s 4*. It is defined in *s 11*, which provides:

> 'In relation to the protected characteristic of sex:
>
> (a) a reference to a person who has a particular protected characteristic is a reference to a man or to a woman;
>
> (b) a reference to persons who share a protected characteristic is a reference to persons of the same sex'.

'Man' and 'woman' are expressly defined to include men and women of any age: *EqA 2010, s 212(1)* (General interpretation).

A man or woman may bring a claim of discrimination on the basis of sex only if the discriminatory conduct falls within one or more of the types of discrimination which are prohibited under *EqA 2010*. The same concepts are used in other areas of discrimination and therefore they are analysed fully in **1.45**ff. Below is a brief summary of the legislation and commentary on its specific implications in relation to gender.

8.16 Direct discrimination

EqA 2010, s 13 sets out the test for direct discrimination. It provides that:

> '(1) A person (A) discriminates against another (B) if, because of a protected characteristic, A treats B less favourably than A treats or would treat others.

. . .

(6) If the protected characteristic is sex:

(a) less favourable treatment of a woman includes less favourable treatment of her because she is breast-feeding;

(b) in a case where B is a man, no account is to be taken of special treatment afforded to a woman in connection with pregnancy or childbirth.

(7) Subsection (6)(a) does not apply for the purposes of Part 5 (work)'.

There is no justification defence to a claim of direct sex discrimination (see **1.46**) and so any direct sex discrimination will be unlawful unless an exception applies (see 'occupational requirements' and 'positive action' below).

The *EqA 2010* test is very similar to the previous test under *SDA 1975, s 1(1)(a)* but, as discussed at **1.46**, the phrase 'on the ground of' has been replaced by 'because of'. As the government did not intend to change the legal meaning of the test, tribunals are likely to make use of the pre-October 2010 case law when determining whether direct sex discrimination has occurred.

The meaning of 'special treatment afforded to a woman in connection with pregnancy or childbirth' is one of the more hotly-disputed issues specific to sex discrimination cases, and is considered further at **8.60**.

There have been a number of relatively high profile direct sex discrimination cases—not all successful—which relate to 'City' institutions, typically involving female employees who allege that they have not been paid bonuses or received promotions because they are women: see, for example, *Barton v Investec Henderson Crosthwaite Securities Ltd* [2003] IRLR 332 and *Madarassy v Nomura International plc* [2007] ICR 867.

8.17 *Comparators*

The *EqA 2010*, like the *SDA 1975*, requires the making of a comparison. *EqA 2010, s 23* (comparison by reference to circumstances) provides: 'On a comparison of cases . . . there must be no material difference between the circumstances relating to each case'. The comparator can be actual or hypothetical.

There is, however, no requirement for a comparator in pregnancy or maternity cases: this is considered further at **8.55**.

8.18 *Discrimination by association or perception*

The new definition of direct discrimination at *EqA 2010, s 13(1)* is intended to cover associative discrimination and discrimination based on perception within the provisions on direct discrimination and harassment (but not indirect discrimination). (See **1.53–1.55**.) Protection for discrimination by association did not apply to sex prior to *EqA 2010*, but the protection should be straightforward in this field, avoiding the uncertainties which apply to other strands (see **3.45**). However, one exception to this is in the treatment of complaints of discrimination by association with women who are pregnant or on maternity leave. This is considered further at **8.62**.

8.19 *Combined discrimination*

EqA 2010 also contains a new provision enabling an employee to bring a discrimination claim on two combined protected grounds, although the provision was not implemented on 1 October 2010. (See **1.57–1.59**.)

The purpose of the new provision is to make it easier for a claimant to succeed in a claim of discrimination where she considers that she has been treated less favourably because, for example, she is an 'older woman', but may have difficulty succeeding in a claim of either age or sex discrimination because of the comparator issue. The *Explanatory Notes to the EqA 2010* give the following specific example:

'A black woman has been passed over for promotion to work on reception because her employer thinks black women do not perform well in customer service roles. Because the employer can point to a white woman of equivalent qualifications and experience who has been appointed to the role in question, as well as a black man of equivalent qualifications and experience in a similar role, the woman may need to be able to compare her treatment because of race and sex combined to demonstrate that she has been subjected to less favourable treatment because of her employer's prejudice against black women'.

8.20 Indirect discrimination

EqA 2010, s 19 prohibits indirect discrimination. It provides:

'(1) A person (A) discriminates against another (B) if A applies to B a provision, criterion or practice which is discriminatory in relation to a relevant protected characteristic of B's.

(2) For the purposes of subsection (1), a provision, criterion or practice is discriminatory in relation to a relevant protected characteristic of B's if:

(a) A applies, or would apply, it to persons with whom B does not share the characteristic,

(b) it puts, or would put, persons with whom B shares the characteristic at a particular disadvantage when compared with persons with whom B does not share it,

(c) it puts, or would put, B at a that disadvantage, and

(d) A cannot show it to be a proportionate means of achieving a legitimate aim'.

Thus the essence of indirect discrimination lies in three elements:

(i) that an employer applies some provision, criterion or practice (PCP) to his employees;

(ii) that it puts, or would put, members of the claimant's sex at a particular disadvantage compared to non-members of that group; and

(iii) that the employer cannot show that it is a proportionate means of achieving a legitimate aim—in other words, that it is 'objectively justified'.

Indirect discrimination is considered in more detail at **1.72**ff.

Pregnancy and maternity cannot be included as relevant characteristics in an indirect discrimination claim, under *EqA 2010, s 25(5)*. However, in the field of work, wide protection applies under s 18 (see **8.58** ff below).

In the field of sex discrimination, the refusal of flexible working requests is a common cause of complaint and may amount to indirect discrimination unless justified, as most employees making such requests are female. Examples of this are considered further at **8.137**. It is also long established that PCPs which disadvantage part-time employees may provide women with a basis for a successful indirect discrimination claim, as the majority of part-timers are female.

8.21 *Objective justification*

Arguments on objective justification in relation to sex discrimination often involve a consideration of whether the reasons put forward by an employer for refusing a flexible working request amount to the application of proportionate means of achieving one or more legitimate aims of the employer. The employer must have this in mind, in addition to ensuring that the reasons given fall within the valid grounds for doing so as set out in *ERA 1996, s 80G*. Indirect discrimination and objective justification in relation to flexible working is considered further at **8.137**.

See **1.83–1.85**.

8.22 **Instructing, causing or inducing discrimination**

It is unlawful to instruct, cause or induce someone to discriminate against, harass or victimise another person, or to attempt to do so (*EqA 2010, s 111*). A claim can be brought by the 'victim' of the discrimination, the person who was instructed to carry out the discrimination, and the EHRC. (See **1.61**.)

8.23 **Liability of employees and agents and aiding discrimination**

Where employees commit acts of discrimination against fellow employees, their employer will be liable if the acts were committed during the course of employment (*EqA 2010, s 109(1)*). Employers are also liable for the discriminatory acts of their agents if they are acting with the employer's authority (*s 109(4)*). In each case it is irrelevant whether the employer knew or approved of the acts (*s 109(3)*). However, there is a defence for employers in relation to the acts of their employees (but not agents) if they can show that they took all reasonable steps to prevent the employee from doing the act in question (*s 109(4)*). The employees and agents will also have personal liability for their acts of discrimination (*EqA 2010, s 110*), even if the employer has a defence. See **1.163**ff.

8.24 **Harassment and sexual harassment**

EqA 2010, s 40 expressly protects employees (and applicants for employment) from being subjected to harassment. Harassment is defined by *EqA 2010, s 26*. A person (A) will harass another (B) if A engages in unwanted conduct related to a relevant protected characteristic, including sex, and the conduct has the purpose or effect of either: (i) violating B's dignity; or (ii) creating an intimidating, hostile, degrading, humiliating or offensive environment for B. Harassment under *EqA 2010* is unlawful where it is 'related to' the protected characteristic. See **1.87**ff. This mirrors the wording of *SDA 1975, s 41(1)(a)*, amended from 'on the ground of sex' by the *Sex Discrimination Act 1975 (Amendment) Regulations 2008 (SI 2008/656)* after the High Court held in *Equal Opportunities Commission v Secretary of State for Trade and Industry* [2007] EWHC 483 that the *SDA* failed to implement the *Equal Treatment Directive* correctly by including the words 'on the ground of her sex' (implying that causation was required).

There are also a couple of specific extensions to the concept of harassment which relate to sex. *EqA 2010*, *s 26(2)* extends harassment to encompass circumstances where A engages in unwanted conduct of a sexual nature, and this has the purpose or effect of either: (i) violating B's dignity; or (ii) creating an intimidating, hostile, degrading, humiliating or offensive environment for B.

There is a further extension in *s 26(3)(b)*, encompassing engaging in unwanted conduct of a sexual nature that is related to gender reassignment or sex, which has the purpose of effect of either: (i) violating B's dignity; or (ii) creating an intimidating, hostile, degrading, humiliating or offensive environment for B, and because of B's rejection of or submission to the conduct, A treats B less favourably than A would treat B if B had not rejected or submitted to such conduct. The purpose of this provision is to provide protection against less favourable treatment which is caused by the victim's decision either to 'reject' or 'submit to' conduct such as sexual advances.

The protected characteristic of pregnancy/maternity (also marriage and civil partnership) is excluded from the harassment provisions (*EqA 2010, s 26(5)*). However, the *EHRC Employment Code* specifically states that pregnancy and maternity harassment would amount to harassment related to sex.

8.25 Third party harassment

EqA 2010, s 40(2) also provides that A will be treated as harassing B where: (a) a third party harasses B in the course of B's employment; and (b) A failed to take such steps as would have been reasonably practicable to prevent the third party from doing so. A third party is someone other than A, or an employee of A's (*s 40(4)*). However, this will not apply unless A knows that B has been harassed during the course of B's employment on at least two other occasions by a third party (whether the same or a different third party on each occasion).

There were equivalent provisions in relation to sex discrimination under *SDA 1975, s 4A*. These provisions followed the High Court decision in *Equal Opportunities Commission v Secretary of State for Trade and Industry* [2007] EWHC 483, where it was found that by omitting to provide for claims that an employer failed to protect an employee from repetitive harassment by a third party such as a supplier or customer, the legislation did not implement the *Equal Treatment Directive* correctly. However, it has now been extended to all protected characteristics. See **1.95**.

8.26 Victimisation

EqA 2010, s 27 prohibits victimisation because of sex and other protected characteristics. It provides:

'(1) A person (A) victimises another person (B) if A subjects B to a detriment because:
- (a) B does a protected act, or
- (b) A believes that B has done, or may do, a protected act.

(2) Each of the following is a protected act:
- (a) bringing proceedings under this Act;
- (b) giving evidence or information in connection with proceedings under this Act;
- (c) doing any other thing for the purposes or in connection with this Act;
- (d) making an allegation (whether or not express) that A or another person has contravened this Act.

(3) Giving false information, or making a false allegation, is not a protected act if the evidence or information is given, or the allegation is made, in bad faith.

(4) This section applies only where the person subjected to a detriment is an individual.

(5) The reference to contravening this Act includes a reference to committing a breach of an equality clause or rule'.

Honest and reasonable steps taken in the course of litigation are unlikely to amount to victimisation: *Chief Constable of West Yorkshire Police* [2001] ICR 1065, *St Helen's Metropolitan Borough Council v Derbyshire* [2007] IRLR 540 and *Bird v Sylvester* [2008] IRLR 232. See **1.98ff**.

8.27 Discrimination on the ground of pregnancy or maternity leave

See below at **8.55** ff.

8.28 Gender reassignment discrimination

See **Gender reassignment (4)**.

8.29 Marital status and civil partnership discrimination

See **Marital status and civil partnerships (5)**.

8.30 **Burden of proof**

The *Burden of Proof Directive 97/80/EC*, as amended by *Directive 98/52/EC*, was implemented into domestic law by the *Sex Discrimination (Indirect Discrimination and Burden of Proof) Regulations 2001 (SI 2001/2660)* and *SDA 1975, s 63A(2)*. The burden of proof provision in the *EqA 2010* is *s 136*. Its wording is different from that in the *SDA 1975* but it is intended to have the same effect as its predecessors. *EqA 2010, s 136* provides:

> '(2) If there are facts from which the court could decide, in the absence of any other explanation, that a person (A) contravened the provision concerned, the court must hold that the contravention occurred.
>
> (3) But subsection (2) does not apply if A shows that A did not contravene the provision.
>
> (4) The reference to a contravention of this Act includes a reference to a breach of an equality clause or rule'.

The *SDA 1975* said 'if the complainant proves facts' rather than the 'if there are facts' formulation in the *EqA 2010*. Further, the *SDA* required 'an adequate explanation' rather than 'any other explanation'. However, the draft Employment Statutory Code of Practice (paras 15.32–15.35) and the *Explanatory Notes to the EqA 2010* both proceed on the basis that the application of the burden of proof under the *EqA 2010* is the same as that under the *SDA 1975*.

This shifting burden of proof has generated much case law, which is analysed in **1.128**ff.

8.31 WHO IS PROTECTED BY EQA 2010?

Territorial scope

Before the *EqA 2010* came into force, the *SDA 1975* (like most of the other discrimination legislation) applied to 'employment at an establishment in Great Britain'. In contrast, the *EqA 2010* does not include any express territorial limit and it will therefore be left to tribunals to determine who can in practice bring a claim.

8.32 *Pre-October 2010 position*

SDA 1975 only applied to employment at establishments in Great Britain. Employment was to be regarded as being at an establishment in Great Britain if (per *SDA 1975, s 10*):

(a) the employee did her work wholly or partly in Great Britain; or

(b) the employee did her work wholly or partly outside Great Britain but the employer had a place of business at an establishment in Great Britain, the employee's work was for the purpose of that business at that establishment, and the employee was ordinarily resident in Great Britain either when she applied for the job, or was offered it or at any time during the course of her employment.

There were specific provisions for ships, aircraft and oil rigs (see *s 10(2)–(6)*).

In applying *s 10*, the tribunal was to consider the whole period of employment, not just the position at the date of the alleged discriminatory act (*Saggar v Ministry of Defence* [2005] EWCA Civ 413, [2005] ICR 1073).

8.33 *Position from October 2010*

As already noted, unlike the previous single strand legislation, the *EqA 2010* does not include any express territorial limitation.

The *Explanatory Notes to EqA 2010, para 15* states:

> 'As far as territorial application is concerned, in relation to Part 5 (work) and following the precedent of the Employment Rights Act 1996, the Act leaves it to tribunals to determine whether the law applies, depending for example on the connection between the employment relationship and Great Britain'.

The *EqA 2010* contains a power to specify territorial application of *Part 5* in relation to ships and hovercraft (*s 81*) and offshore work (*s 82*).

It is not yet known how, in practice, tribunals will approach the question of whether there is a sufficient connection with Great Britain.

This issue is discussed in more depth in **1.42–1.44**.

8.34 Employees—meaning of 'employment'

EqA 2010, s 83(2) defines 'employment' as:

> '(a) employment under a contract of employment, a contract of apprenticeship or a contract personally to do work;
> (b) Crown employment;
> (c) employment as a relevant member of the House of Commons staff;
> (d) employment as a relevant member of the House of Lords staff'.

See further **1.16**.

8.35 Contract workers

It is unlawful for a principal (the end user who contracts with another person for the supply of contract workers) to discriminate against those workers in the work he provides to them (*EqA 2010, s 41* which effectively replicates *SDA 1975, s 9*). The principal is treated as if it were the employer for the purposes of the non-discrimination provisions in each of the statutes, extending the protection, for example, to a prohibition on harassment and victimisation.

In *BP Chemicals v Gillick* [1995] IRLR 128, the EAT held that the old *s 9* test applied where a principal had refused to allow an agency worker to return to her old job after maternity leave, even though at the date of the refusal she was no longer working for BP; see **8.107**.

As in the case of employees, cases of occupational requirement where a worker is not allowed to do, or to continue to do, the work are excepted from liability (*EqA 2010, Sch 9, Part 1(1)(2)(b)*). See **8.44** and also see further **1.17**.

8.36 Partnerships

The *EqA 2010* (like the *SDA 1975*) makes specific provision for the protection of partners (and applicants for partnership) from discrimination.

EqA 2010, s 44(1) provides:

> 'A firm or proposed firm must not discriminate against a person:
> (a) in the arrangements it makes for deciding to whom to offer a position as a partner;
> (b) as to the terms on which it offers the person a position as a partner;
> (c) by not offering the person a position as a partner'.

EqA 2010, s 44(2) provides:

> 'A firm (A) must not discriminate against a partner (B):
> (a) as to the terms on which B is a partner;

(b) in the way A affords B access, or by not affording B access, to opportunities for promotion, transfer or training or for receiving any other benefit, facility or service;
(c) by expelling B;
(d) by subjecting him to any other detriment.

Various other provisions prohibit harassment and victimisation of partners and applicants for partnership, and extend the protection to LLPs as well as partnerships (see *ss 44(3)–(6)* and *45*). See further at **1.19**

8.37 UNLAWFUL DISCRIMINATION IN EMPLOYMENT

Job applicants

Under *EqA 2010, s 39(1)* (which effectively replaces *SDA 1975, s 6(1)*), an employer (A) must not discriminate against a person (B) (an applicant for employment):

(a) in the arrangements he makes for deciding to whom to offer employment (eg recruitment procedures);

(b) as to the terms on which A offers B that employment (eg lower pay, fewer benefits); or

(c) by not offering B employment.

Under *EqA 2010, s 40(1)* (which replaces *SDA 1975, s 6(2A)*), it is unlawful for an employer to harass a person who has applied to him for employment. See **1.18**.

Under *SDA 1975, s 38(1)*, it was unlawful to publish an advertisement which indicated an intention to discriminate. The publishing of unlawful advertisements was a criminal offence under *SDA 1975, s 38(5)*. Use of a job description with a sexual connotation, such as 'waiter', 'salesgirl', 'postman' or 'stewardess' was taken to indicate an intention to discriminate, unless the advertisement indicated to the contrary (*s 38(2)*). The publisher of an advertisement could rely, as a defence, on placing reasonable reliance on a statement by the author that the publication was not contrary to the *SDA 1975* (*s 38(4)*). Proceedings could only be brought by the EHRC (*s 38(6)*).

This requirement not to publish an advertisement which indicates an intention to discriminate has been repealed by *EqA 2010* (*Sch 27, Part 1*) and no equivalent provision brought in to replace it, on the basis that discriminatory advertisements are considered to be sufficiently prohibited by *EqA 2010, s 39* (employees and applicants). In this regard, Chapter 16 of the *EHRC Employment Code* provides guidance on 'Avoiding discrimination in recruitment'. It cautions against advertising for a 'waiter' or 'waitress' instead of 'waiting staff', and against the use of job titles showing a predetermined bias for the recruitment of those with a particular characteristic, such as 'shop girl' or 'office boy'. It also warns against advertising for a full-time position unless the employer has considered whether the post actually needs to be performed full time, because of the risk of indirect discrimination against women who may only be able to work part-time hours. As noted above, tribunals can take breaches of the Codes of Practice into account in determining discrimination claims.

The *EHRC Employment Code* also recommends that employers be flexible about the time of job interviews, noting that women with childcare responsibilities may have difficulty attending early morning interviews. It reminds employers that questions about marriage plans or family intentions should not be asked (but see *Saunders v Richmond-upon-Thames London Borough Council* [1977] IRLR 362 where the EAT held it was not automatically unlawful to ask questions of a woman which would not be asked of a man; it depended on the purposes for which the questions were asked, and whether the woman had been treated less favourably. However, it must be questioned whether a tribunal today would take this approach).

Action to favour a particular gender in the recruitment process is permitted in certain respects: see **8.52** regarding *EqA 2010, s 159* (positive action: recruitment and promotion), which is due to be brought into force in April 2011.

8.38 Employees

Under *EqA 2010, s 39(2)* an employer (A) must not discriminate against an employee of A's (B):

(a) as to B's terms of employment,

(b) in the way A affords B access, or by not affording B access, to opportunities for:

  (i) promotion, transfer or training; or

  (ii) for receiving any other benefits facilities or services,

(c) by dismissing B;

(d) by subjecting B to any other detriment.

These provisions replace *SDA 1975, s 6(2)* and are intended to have the same effect. Accordingly the case law decided under the *SDA 1975* is likely to apply. See **1.13**ff.

8.39 *Promotion, training or transfer*

Chapter 17 of the *EHRC Employment Code* provides guidance on 'Avoiding discrimination in employment'. This includes (at *para 6.82* ff) guidance on promotions and transfers.

Promotion decisions will be open to challenge where there is a failure to follow transparent and objective procedures and where opportunities are made known by 'word of mouth' or recommendation, rather than advertising. See *Watches of Switzerland v Savell* [1983] IRLR 141, where the EAT held that promotion procedures indirectly discriminated on grounds of sex.

Past practices may have a discriminatory impact on promotions and transfers. In *Steel v Post Office (No 2)* [1978] IRLR 198, transfers to popular delivery rounds were allocated on basis of seniority. Seniority was based on length of service as permanent employees but women were not eligible for permanent status prior to 1975. Mrs Steel had 16 years' service but only two years' seniority. The seniority condition was held to be discriminatory and unjustifiable.

Assumptions made on the basis of a person's sex are likely to be discriminatory. In *Horsey v Dyfed County Council* [1982] IRLR 395 the EAT held that the employer had discriminated against the female claimant by refusing her secondment to a two-year training course closer to where her husband was based. Her employer made the discriminatory assumption that married women normally move jobs to follow their husbands and therefore she would not return to her original job after completing the period of secondment.

Part-time workers and employees who are on a fixed-term contract have the right to be treated no less favourably than comparable full-time and permanent employees. See FIXED-TERM AND PART-TIME WORKERS (**10**). Discrimination against part-time and/or fixed-term workers may also amount to unlawful indirect sex discrimination.

Similarly, a failure to inform women on maternity leave of any jobs that become available, and to enable them to apply if they wish to do so, may be unfavourable treatment which could amount to discrimination because of pregnancy and maternity.

8.40 *Benefits, facilities or services*

Under the old regime, *EqPA 1970* prohibited discrimination in relation to any contractual terms, not just those relating to pay, while *SDA 1975* applied in relation to any matter not included in the contract terms, even if it was concerned with pay or financial benefits. While both sets of provisions are now consolidated in *EqA 2010*, employees must still make a decision on whether a claim in respect of benefits falls under *Part 5, Chapter 3* (the successor equal pay provisions), or the broader sex discrimination provisions, or plead in the alternative.

A woman should claim under *Part 5, Chapter 3* about matters relating to the payment of money if this is regulated by her contract of employment. In *Hoyland v ASDA Stores Ltd* [2006] IRLR 468, the Court of Session (Scotland) held that a claim about a discretionary bonus was 'regulated' by the contract of employment and therefore came within *EqPA 1970*, even though the entitlement was not part of the formal contract of employment (see also **8.101**). The *EqA 2010* contains a similar provision: *s 39(6)*. The same logic should apply to other financial benefits, for example cash allowances.

The *EC Treaty, Article 141(1)*, which confers a directly enforceable right to equal pay for equal work or work of equal value, applies to pay which is defined in *Article 141(2)* as 'the ordinary basic or minimum wage or salary and any other consideration, whether in cash or in kind, which the worker receives directly or indirectly, in respect of his employment, from his employer'. This definition is wide enough to include a claim in respect of non-contractual pay, and therefore may be relied upon in a claim under the broader sex discrimination provisions.

A claim may only be made in respect of benefits, facilities or services which are already in existence, but are being denied to a particular employee. In *Clymo v Wandsworth London Borough Council* [1989] IRLR 241, the EAT held that a refusal to allow a woman to job share was not a refusal to allow access to a 'facility' under *SDA 1975, s 6(2)(a)*, since job sharing was not available to any workers in her grade; however, it is unlikely that this case would be decided the same way today because of different social and legal norms.

A trivial advantage in treatment, such as allowing women to leave five minutes early to avoid the peak hour 'crush', was held not to be a sufficient benefit to amount to discrimination against men in *Peak v Automotive Products Ltd* [1977] IRLR 365, CA, although it is questionable whether the case would be decided on the same basis today.

8.41 *Dismissal or any other detriment*

In many cases, a sex discrimination claim under *EqA 2010* will be combined with a claim for unfair dismissal. The absence of any cap on the award of compensation and the lack of any qualifying period of employment makes a discrimination claim the preferred choice for many claimants.

The definition of 'dismissal' in *EqA 2010, s 39(7)* includes non-renewal of a fixed-term contract or constructive dismissal.

Chapter 19 of the draft Employment Statutory Code of Practice provides guidance on 'Termination of employment', and makes a number of recommendations on how to avoid discrimination in decisions to dismiss and in procedures for dismissal. This includes a reminder that, in redundancy situations, a requirement for 'flexibility'—for example, willingness to relocate or to work unsocial hours—may amount to indirect sex discrimination, and therefore require objective justification.

Maternity and family leave dismissals are dealt with at **8.64–8.67**.

It is not necessary to demonstrate physical disadvantage or financial loss if arguing that the employee has been subject to a detriment: *Shamoon v Chief Constable of Royal Ulster Constabulary* [2003] ICR 337 (see **1.14**). An employee does not suffer a 'detriment' if she is denied a benefit which is not provided to others in the same grade of employment.

Dress codes which impose different rules on male and female employees have generally been held not to be discriminatory on the grounds that, if the codes are different but equal, then less favourable treatment is not established. See **1.47**. However, a dress code which was less favourable to one sex could constitute a 'detriment'.

8.42 Ex-employees

EqA 2010, s 108 replicates the position under the *SDA 1975, s 20A* and provides that where an (employment) relationship has come to an end, discrimination or harassment on the ground of sex is unlawful where it 'arises out of and is closely connected with' a previous relationship with the respondent and would have been unlawful if it had occurred during the relationship. The uncertainty stemming from the House of Lords decision in *Relaxion Group plc v Rhys-Harper* [2003] UKHL 33, [2003] 4 All ER 1113 (which pre-dated *SDA 1975, s 20A* coming into force) has therefore largely been resolved. However, note that *EqA 2010, s 108(7)* seemingly unintentionally excludes former employees from protection against victimisation (see **Common concepts (1)**).

8.43 Unlawful discrimination by other bodies

See **1.20**ff for protection against discrimination by trade organisations, qualifications bodies, vocational training bodies and employment service-providers.

8.44 Occupational requirements

EqA 2010 has created a unified occupational requirement exception across all protected characteristics (*EqA 2010, Sch 9, Part 1, paras 1–6*). This unified exception absorbs the pre-October 2010 law on genuine occupational qualifications (GOQs) (*SDA 1975, ss 7–7B*). See **1.145**ff.

Under *EqA 2010, Sch 9, Part 1(1)* provides that a person will not contravene *EqA 2010* (in relation to certain aspects of the employment relationship) in applying a requirement that a person has a particular protected characteristic provided: (a) the requirement is an occupational requirement; (b) the application of the requirement is a proportionate means of achieving a legitimate aim; and (c) the person to whom the requirement is applied does not meet the requirement or the person applying the requirement has reasonable grounds for being satisfied that he does not. The words from '(or' to the end are omitted in the case of the requirement to be of a particular sex. An example of when the occupational requirement may be used is if a women's refuge, which lawfully provides services to women only, applies a requirement for all of its staff members to be women. This job requires women workers for reasons of privacy or decency, or because personal services are being provided.

Employers can use the occupational requirement exception in relation to: arrangements for deciding who to offer employment to; an offer of employment; and the provision of access to opportunities for promotion, transfer or training. Employers are not permitted to apply the occupational requirement exception in relation to sex to dismissals, expulsions or terminations. An employer is not permitted to rely on an occupational requirement to prevent a worker of a particular sex from continuing to work.

The domestic legislation insofar as it applies to gender reflects *Article 14(2)* of the *Equal Treatment Directive*, which provides that a difference in treatment based on a characteristic related to sex shall not constitute discrimination in access to employment and training where by reason of the particular occupational activities or the context in which they are carried out, the characteristic constitutes a genuine and determining occupational requirement, providing that the objective is legitimate and the requirement is proportionate. *SDA 1975, s 7(2)* previously set out an exhaustive list of circumstances in which being of a particular gender would be considered a GOQ, and reasons which did not fit any of the statutory categories could not be relied upon. *EqA 2010, Sch 9* provides for a broader list of occupational requirements where differential treatment may be justified, which contains a number of differences when compared to *SDA 1975*. Nevertheless, the old *s 7(2)* list may continue to be influential, for example under the general exception at *EqA 2010, Sch 9, para 1*, particularly as there were a number of decisions on occupational qualifications in the sex context. However, employers will now have to frame their arguments in the language of legitimate aims and proportionality. The old list included:

- a job where its essential nature calls for a man for reasons of physiology (excluding physical strength or stamina) or, in dramatic performance or other entertainment, for reasons of authenticity, so that the essential nature of the job would be materially different if carried out by a woman;
- a job which needs to be held by a man to preserve decency or privacy because:

  (a) it is likely to involve physical contact with men in circumstances where they might reasonably object to its being carried out by a woman; or

  (b) the holder of the job is likely to do her work in circumstances where men might reasonably object to the presence of a woman because they are in a state of undress or are using sanitary facilities; or

  (c) the job is likely to involve work in a private home and objection might reasonably be taken to allowing a woman:

    (i) the degree of physical or social contact with a person living in the home; and

    (ii) the knowledge of intimate details of such a person's life.

  Illustrations of the application of this occupational requirement may be found in *Wylie v Dee & Co (Menswear) Ltd* [1978] IRLR 103; *Etam plc v Rowan* [1989] IRLR 150 (both sales assistants in clothing stores); *Timex Corpn v Hodgson* [1981] IRLR 530 (female first aid and toilet duties); *Lasertop Ltd v Webster* [1997] IRLR 498 (access to changing rooms and sauna in women-only leisure club); *Sisley v Britannia Security Systems Ltd* [1983] IRLR 404 (female security staff slept in underwear to avoid crumpling uniforms). Chapter 13 of the draft Employment Statutory Code of Practice notes that the *EqA 2010* occupational requirement may still apply where privacy or decency are an issue, or personal services are being provided;
- where the nature of the job, or its location, makes it impracticable for the employees to live away from the employer's premises, the only premises available do not have separate sleeping accommodation and sanitary facilities for men and women, and it is not reasonable for the employer to provide them. See *Sisley v Britannia Security Systems Ltd* [1983] IRLR 404 (all female security staff in sleeping accommodation on premises, not practical to provide accommodation separately for one male employee);
- where the nature of the establishment requires the job to be held by a man because it is in a hospital, prison or other establishment giving special care, supervision or attention to only one sex and it is reasonable that the job should not be held by someone of the opposite sex;
- the holder of the job provides individuals with personal services promoting their welfare or education, or similar personal services, and those services can most effectively be provided by a man;

- the job needs to be held by a man because it is likely to involve the performance of duties outside the UK in a country whose laws or customs are such that the duties could not effectively be performed by a woman. Employers posting employees to Middle Eastern countries where significant restrictions are placed on women's employment have previously sought to make use of this argument.

SDA 1975 case law established that employers should look to reorganise work between employees of different genders, where reasonable, before refusing work to one sex. In *Wylie v Dee & Co (Menswear) Ltd* [1978] IRLR 103, where there were seven other male shop assistants who could assist in measuring a male customer's inside leg, the need for this task to be performed was not a valid reason to refuse the female claimant a job in a menswear store. Similarly *Etam plc v Rowan* [1989] IRLR 150 held in a male shop assistant's favour where female employees could assist female customers in changing rooms. In both cases it was held to be reasonable and not unduly inconvenient to expect the employer's existing male employees, who were capable of carrying out the duties within the statutory list, to do so. A similar conclusion would likely be reached under the new test, where a tribunal would need to consider whether or not it was proportionate to require that the vacancy be filled by a man.

8.45 Specific exceptions

Requirements of organised religion or organisations with a 'religious ethos'

EqA 2010, Sch 9, para 2 largely replicates *SDA 1975, s 19(1), (2)* in permitting gender, marriage and civil partnership discrimination in relation to employment, authorisation or qualification for an organised religion either:

(a) so as to comply with the doctrines of the religion ('the compliance principle'), or

(b) to avoid conflicting with the strongly-held religious convictions of a significant number of the religion's followers ('the non-conflict principle').

The use of these requirements is permitted, however, only if three conditions are satisfied: (1) that the person to whom the requirement is applied does not meet that requirement (or there are reasonable grounds for not being satisfied that the person meets it); (2) that the employment to which the requirement applies is for the purposes of an 'organised religion'; and (3) that the application of the requirement is one that 'engages the compliance or non-conflict principle'. The application of a requirement 'engages the compliance principle' if the requirement is applied so as to comply with the doctrines of the religion. The application of a requirement engages the 'non-conflict principle' if, because of the nature or context of the employment, the requirement is applied so as to avoid conflicting with the strongly-held religious convictions of a significant number of the religion's followers.

EqA 2010, Sch 9, para 3 provides a separate exception, to permit an employer with an ethos based on religion or belief to discriminate against a person with any protected characteristic. To rely on this exception, the employer must show that its ethos is based on a religion or belief. It must also show: (1) that the requirement genuinely applies to the role in question, ie it is an 'occupational' requirement; (2) that the application of the requirement is 'a proportionate means of achieving a legitimate aim'; and (3) that the person to whom the requirement is applied does not meet it (or there are reasonable grounds for not being satisfied that the person meets it).

Schedule 22 contains a further exception, at *para 3*, for people of particular religions or beliefs to be appointed to specified educational posts, which can include a requirement that the holder of a position is a woman, or that they comply with a requirement of an act or instrument relating to the appointment to a canon professorship in a university, or to a professorship to which a canonry is annexed (*Sch 9, para 3(3)(b), (c)*).

For further commentary see **7.24**.

8.46 *Armed forces*

EqA 2010, Sch 9, para 4 permits the armed forces to refuse a woman employment or access to opportunities for promotion, transfer or training if this is a proportionate way of ensuring that the armed forces have combat effectiveness. This exception only applies to service personnel; non-service personnel are covered by the *EqA 2010* provisions on employees.

8.47 *Police officers and prison officers*

The former specific exceptions in the *SDA 1975* relating to police officers (height, uniform and equipment requirements, and uniform and equipment allowances (*SDA 1975, s 17*)), and prison officers (height requirements (*SDA 1975, s 18*)), have not been replicated in the *EqA 2010*.

8.48 *Communal accommodation*

Employers will not be guilty of sex discrimination by refusing to admit persons to communal accommodation if, for reasons of privacy, the accommodation should only be used by persons of the same sex (*EqA 2010, Sch 23, para 3*). This exception reflects case law under the *SDA 1975*. Employers will also not fall foul of sex discrimination provisions by providing any benefit, facility or service linked to that accommodation if it cannot properly and effectively be provided except for those using the accommodation. As far as is reasonable, alternative arrangements must be made to compensate a worker who has been refused accommodation or a linked benefit, facility or service. When refusing a person access to communal accommodation or a linked benefit, facility or service, the employer must consider if it would be reasonable to alter or extend the accommodation so that it can be provided to the worker, and the relative frequency of demand for the accommodation by persons of each sex.

8.49 *Educational appointments*

The *Employment Act 1989, s 5(3)* previously exempted the application of *SDA 1975* to appointments of staff at women-only colleges which were established before *SDA 1975* came into force. This has now been repealed by *EqA 2010*. A broader occupational requirement applies under *EqA 2010, Sch 22, paras 3–4*. This allows schools and further and higher education institutions to reserve certain academic posts for women where the governing instrument provides for this and that governing instrument was made before 16 January 1990.

8.50 *National security*

EqA 2010, s 192 replicates the effect of *SDA 1975, s 52* in providing that 'A person does not contravene this Act only by doing, for the purpose of safeguarding national security, anything it is proportionate to do for that purpose'.

In *Johnston v The Chief Constable of the Royal Ulster Constabulary* [1987] QB 129, [1986] 3 All ER 135, a woman was prevented from taking on a full-time permanent post because this would require her to carry firearms. In considering equivalent Northern Ireland provisions, the ECJ rejected the submission that *EC Treaty, Article 224*, on public security, entitled the government to disregard EU anti-discrimination measures. It also disapproved of the procedure under *SDA 1975, s 53(2)* entitling a Minister to certify that an act was done for the purpose of safeguarding national security (that provision was subsequently repealed in relation to *Part II* and vocational training in *Part III: Sex Discrimination (Amendment) Order 1988 (SI 1988/249)*). The ECJ held that the RUC was entitled to rely on *Equal Treatment Directive, Article 2(2)* (now replaced by *Article 2(6)*) permitting Member States to exclude occupational activities where the sex of the worker is a determining factor, provided that the principle of proportionality was observed. This principle is key to the *EqA 2010* occupational requirements.

8.51 POSITIVE DISCRIMINATION AND POSITIVE ACTION

The *EqA 2010* contains more-wide ranging provisions in respect of positive action than the *SDA 1975*. To understand the current position it is necessary to consider the position under the previous legislation.

The principal purpose of *SDA 1975* was to prohibit discrimination between men and women. Positive discrimination (ie discrimination in favour of women to the detriment of men) was unlawful. However, positive action (ie action to overcome historical inequalities between men and women) was permitted and indeed encouraged under EU law, and still is. The *TFEU* provides:

> 'In all its activities, the Union shall aim to eliminate inequalities and to promote equality, between men and women' (*Article 8*, formerly *Article 3 of the EC Treaty*).
>
> With a view to ensuring full equality in practice between men and women in working life, the principle of equal treatment shall not prevent any Member State from maintaining or adopting measures providing for specific advantages in order to make it easier for the under-represented sex to pursue a vocational activity or to prevent or compensate for disadvantages in professional careers' (*Article 157(4)*, formerly *Article 141(4)* of the *EC Treaty*).

The *Equal Treatment Directive 2006/54/EC* (the successor to *Directive 76/207*/EEC) provides:

> 'Member States may maintain or adopt measures within the meaning of *Article 141(4)* of the *Treaty* with a view to ensuring full equality in practice between men and women' (*Article 3*).

The distinction between lawful positive action and unlawful positive discrimination was considered by the ECJ in *Kalanke v Freie Hanestadt Bremen* [1995] ECR I-3051, [1996] All ER (EC) 66; *Marschall v Land Nordrhein-Westfalen* [1998] IRLR 39; *Re Georg Badeck* [2000] IRLR 432; *Abrahamsson and Anderson v Fogelgvist* [2000] IRLR 732; *Lommers v Minister Van Landbouw, Natuurbeheer en Visserij* [2002] ECR I-2891, [2004] 2 CMLR 1141. The case law was reviewed in *Briheche v Ministre for the Interior, Internal Security and Local Freedoms* [2004] ECR 1-8807, the ECJ stating (at para 23):

> 'A measure which is intended to give priority in promotion to women in sectors of the public service must be regarded as compatible with Community law if it does not automatically and unconditionally give priority to women when women and men are equally qualified, and the candidatures are the subject of an objective assessment which takes account of the specific personal situations of all candidates'.

UK domestic law only permitted positive action in very limited circumstances. For example, *SDA 1975, s 47* permitted positive action to redress gender imbalance in certain industries. Where it reasonably appeared that, at any time within the previous 12 months there were no persons of the gender in question doing a particular type of work, or the number was comparatively small, *s 47* permitted provision of facilities for the training of the minority gender or encouragement to take up that work. The comparison of the number of men and women carrying out the work in question had to be in the whole of Great Britain or in an area of Great Britain. Where the comparison was confined to an area, the minority gender had to appear likely to take up that work in that area.

Section 47(3) permitted training for employment directed at those who had been out of work because they had been discharging family responsibilities, even though this may be discriminatory.

SDA 1975, s 48(1) permitted positive action by employers to redress gender imbalance among employees. Where at any time within the previous 12 months there were no persons of the gender in question doing particular work, or the number was comparatively small, *s 48(1)* permitted provision of facilities for the training of the minority gender or encouragement to take up that work.

The EOC's 1985 Code of Practice suggested positive action measures for employers.

8.52 Positive action

The provisions in the *SDA 1975* have now been replaced by the general positive action provisions contained in *EqA 2010, s 158*. These permit the use of positive action measures to alleviate disadvantage experienced by people who share a protected characteristic, reduce their under-representation in relation to particular activities, and meet their particular needs. It will, for example, allow measures to be targeted to particular groups, including training to enable them to gain employment. Any such measures must be a proportionate way of achieving a legitimate aim.

The extent to which it is proportionate to take positive action measures which may result in people not having the relevant characteristic being treated less favourably will depend, among other things, on the seriousness of the relevant disadvantage, the extremity of need or under-representation and the availability of other means of countering them. This provision will need to be interpreted in accordance with European law, which limits the extent to which the kind of action it permits will be allowed.

Chapter 12 of the *EHRC Employment Code*, which is based on the new positive action provisions in the *EqA 2010*, provides the following specific examples of positive measures which would be permitted in the case of sex:

(a) a partnership between employers in an industry sector such as engineering in which women are under-represented and an equalities organisation which offers opportunities exclusively to girls and women to learn more about the career choices through a careers fair attended by women working in the profession;

(b) a national labour force survey shows women are under-represented at board level in the financial services sector. An employer could take positive action to increase their representation in the sector.

A controversial new provision in the, *EqA 2010, s 159*, will (when it comes into force in April 2011) allow employers to treat persons more favourably in connection with recruitment or promotion on account of their possession of a particular protected characteristic if they reasonably think that persons with the characteristic suffer a disadvantage connected to the characteristic, and participation in an activity by persons with the characteristic is disproportionately low. Their aim must be to enable such persons to overcome or minimise that disadvantage, or encourage them to take part in the activity. However, such action is only permitted if two candidates are 'as qualified', and the employer does not have a policy or practice of automatically treating people who share the protected characteristic more favourably than those who do not have it in these circumstances; each case must be considered on its merits. The action must also be a proportionate means of achieving the required end. In principle this could be used by an employer to prefer a woman over an equally-qualified man if women are particularly under-represented in its workforce. See **1.160** for further details.

8.53 Elections

SDA 1975, s 42A excluded from the scope of *SDA 1975, Parts II–IV* arrangements made by registered political parties to regulate the selection of the party's candidates for the purpose of reducing inequality in the number of men and women elected as candidates in parliamentary, local government and European elections. This provision was added as an amendment to reverse the effect of *Jepson and Dyas-Elliott v Labour Party* [1996] IRLR 116, in which a tribunal held that all-women shortlists were unlawful. It is now included within the *EqA 2010*, and extended to other protected characteristics, at *s 104*.

8.54 Public sector equality duty

The new single public sector equality duty (PSED) is contained in *EqA 2010, s 149*. This replaced *SDA 1975, s 76A*, which imposed a general (but more limited) duty on public authorities to have due regard to the need to eliminate unlawful discrimination and harassment and promote equality of opportunity between men and women. The public sector equality duty is outside the scope of this book.

8.55 DISCRIMINATION ON THE GROUNDS OF PREGNANCY AND MATERNITY

An overview of the position prior to 1 October 2005

Prior to 1 October 2005, a woman who claimed discrimination on the grounds of pregnancy or maternity had to bring her complaint under the general prohibition on sex discrimination under *SDA 1975, s 2*. This meant that she had to identify an appropriate male comparator (whether actual or hypothetical) to demonstrate that she has suffered less favourable treatment.

However, in the case of discrimination on the ground of pregnancy, the requirement for a comparator raised difficulties, since only women are capable of childbirth. The UK courts initially agreed that a pregnant employee should be compared to a male employee who was unavailable for work for medical reasons; however, the ECJ rejected this approach (see *Dekker v Stichting Vormingscentrum Voor Jong Volwassen (VJV – Centrum) Plus* [1990] ECR I-3941, [1992] ICR 325 and *Webb v EMO Air Cargo (UK) Ltd* [1995] IRLR 645, [1995] 1 WLR 1454). The ECJ made it clear that less favourable treatment on the grounds of pregnancy was gender-specific and so a male comparator was not required. In addition, in *Gillespie v Northern Health and Social Services Board* [1996] ECR I-475, [1996] All ER (EC) 284 the ECJ (at 513) referred to pregnant women as being in a '. . . special position which requires them to be afforded special protection, but which is not comparable either with that of a man or that of a woman actually at work'. As a result of the ECJ jurisprudence, the UK courts disapplied the statutory requirement for a comparator in pregnancy and maternity cases.

8.56 *SDA 1975, s 3A*

The Government sought to codify the position in respect of discrimination on the grounds of pregnancy and maternity by the insertion of *s 3A* into *SDA 1975* by the *Employment Equality (Sex Discrimination) Regulations 2005* (*SI 2005/2467*). *Section 3A* came into force on 1 October 2005 and specifically prohibited discrimination on the grounds of pregnancy and maternity where:

(a) at a time in a 'protected period' and on the grounds of the woman's pregnancy, she was treated less favourably than if she were not pregnant (*s 3A(1)(a)*); or

(b) she exercised, or sought to exercise, or had exercised, or had sought to exercise, a statutory right to maternity leave and she was treated less favourably than if she were not seeking to exercise that right (*s 3A(1)(b)*).

Section 3A(2) also provided that a woman was discriminated against if she was treated less favourably on the ground that she was not permitted to work during the compulsory maternity leave (CML) period than she would have been if the CML provision did not apply to her. *Section 3A* applied to all those individuals protected by *SDA 1975, Part II*.

8.57 *Judicial review of s 3A*

In March 2007 the EOC successfully brought an application for judicial review before the High Court in respect of *SDA 1975, s 3A* (see *Equal Opportunities Commission v Secretary of State for Trade and Industry* [2007] IRLR 327).

The EOC contended that *s 3A* did not comply with the UK's obligations under the *Equal Treatment Directive*, as the wording of *s 3A* still required a comparator, albeit not a male comparator. This was because *s 3A* required the woman to show that she had been treated less favourably than she would have been had she not been pregnant or not taken maternity leave. The High Court was persuaded by the argument that this was inconsistent with the ECJ's case law and held that *s 3A* should be recast so as to eliminate the statutory requirement for a comparator who was not pregnant or was not on maternity leave. As a result, the government issued the *Sex Discrimination Act 1975 (Amendment) Regulations 2008 (SI 2008/656)*, which removed the reference to a comparator who was not pregnant (or seeking to exercise a right to statutory or compulsory maternity leave) in *s 3A*. Therefore, from 6 April 2008, *s 3A* simply protected women from being treated 'less favourably' on the grounds of pregnancy or maternity leave.

8.58 *EqA 2010*

EqA 2010, which came into force on 1 October 2010, repealed *SDA 1975*. The main pregnancy and maternity provision is now *EqA 2010, s 18:*

> '(2) A person (A) discriminates against a woman if, in the protected period in relation to a pregnancy of hers, A treats her unfavourably:
> (a) because of the pregnancy, or
> (b) because of illness suffered by her as a result of it.
> (3) A person (A) discriminates against a woman if A treats her unfavourably because she is on compulsory maternity leave.
> (4) A person (A) discriminates against a woman if A treats her unfavourably because she is exercising or seeking to exercise or has exercised or sought to exercise, the right to ordinary or additional maternity leave.'

The use of the term 'unfavourable' in place of 'less favourable' seems to be an attempt to make it clear that no comparator is required: the *Explanatory Notes to the Equality Act 2010* state that *s 18* 'is designed to replicate the effect of similar provisions' in *SDA 1975 (note 76)*. At first sight 'unfavourable treatment' seems to be an unfamiliar concept in English discrimination law. However, commentators have suggested that tribunals are likely to treat it in a similar way to the more familiar concept of 'detriment' which requires that 'a reasonable worker would or might take the view that he or she had been disadvantaged' (see *Shamoon v Chief Constable of the Royal Ulster Constabulary* [2003] ICR 337).

The replacement of 'less favourably' with 'unfavourably' does not mean that comparator evidence will never be relevant in pregnancy and maternity discrimination cases. Identifying a comparator (male or female) may help to determine whether in fact the unfavourable treatment in question was related to the woman's pregnancy or maternity leave.

8.59 *Protected period*

For the purposes of *s 18(2)* the protected period is defined as any time during which the woman is pregnant or on maternity leave. If the woman is not entitled to maternity leave, then the protected period ends two weeks after the end of the pregnancy (*s 18(6)*).

In addition, the provision makes it clear that a person's treatment of a woman on the ground of her pregnancy-related illness is to be equated with treatment on the ground of the pregnancy itself (*s 18(2)(b)*).

The special protection for pregnancy-related discrimination ends at the end of the protected period. After this point, a woman must compare her unfavourable treatment with the treatment of a real or hypothetical man in similar circumstances. However, *s 18(5)* provides for an extension of the protected period in limited circumstances. If a woman experiences unfavourable treatment after the end of the protected period, but which results from a decision made during it (eg in relation to bonus payments, or redundancies), that treatment is regarding as occurring during the protected period, even if the decision is not actually implemented until the protected period has ended. This is a codification of the principle expressed by the ECJ in *Paquay v Societe d'architectes Hoet & Minne SPRL: C-460/06* [2007] ECR I-8511, [2007] All ER (D) 137 (see **8.64**).

8.60 Discrimination against men

With regard to sex discrimination against men, no account shall be taken of special treatment afforded to women in connection with pregnancy or childbirth (*EqA 2010, s 13(6)(b)*).

The scope of 'special treatment' is the subject of much debate, and there is limited case law guidance. Some commentators take the view that it is limited to specific statutory protections conferred on women, for example, the right to receive a bonus in respect of a period of compulsory maternity leave, or the right to be preferred for suitable alternative vacancies in redundancy situations. Others argue for a more expansive definition.

Such case law as there is supports the more limited approach. The cases include *Alvarez v Sesa Start Espana ETT SA: C-104/09* [2011] All ER (EC) 253, [2011] 1 CMLR 861 in the ECJ (discussed further at **8.125**), and a recent employment tribunal decision, *De Belin v Eversheds Legal Services Ltd* ET1804069/09 (a case decided under the equivalent provisions of *SDA 1975*). In *De Belin*, the tribunal held that the statute does not permit 'blanket special treatment'. The case concerned a male employee who was made redundant after the redundancy selection score of his female colleague on maternity leave was artificially inflated. He succeeded in his claim for sex discrimination and unfair dismissal. This is, however, only a first instance decision, and subject to an appeal at the time of publication; it is hoped that the EAT may clarify the position.

8.61 Pregnancy and maternity-related dismissals: discrimination claims

Prior to the specific unfair dismissal and discrimination protection introduced by *ERA 1996, s 99* and *SDA 1975, s 3A* (now *EqA 2010, s 18*), it was well established that dismissing an employee because of her pregnancy amounted to direct discrimination on the grounds of sex (*Dekker* and *Webb v EMO*) and that no comparator was required; see **8.55**.

In *Tele Danmark A/S v Handels-og Kontorfunktionærernes Forbund i Danmark (HK)* [2001] ECR I-6993, [2001] All ER (EC) 941, the ECJ confirmed that this was the case whether a woman was employed on an indefinite or fixed-term basis and notwithstanding any failure by the woman to inform the employer of her pregnancy. In this case, the employee was dismissed one month into a six-month contract when she told her employer she was pregnant and due to give birth almost two months prior to the expiry of the contract. The ECJ held, at para 31, that:

> 'Since the dismissal of a worker on account of pregnancy constitutes direct discrimination on grounds of sex, whatever the nature and extent of the economic loss incurred by the employer as a result of her absence because of pregnancy, whether the contract of employment was concluded for a fixed or an indefinite period has no bearing on the discriminatory character of the dismissal. In either case, the employee's inability to perform her contract of employment is due to pregnancy'.

As set out at **8.58**, *EqA 2010, s 18* now provides that pregnancy and maternity leave are specific grounds on which to bring a discrimination claim under the *SDA 1975* and so are no longer merely facets of sex discrimination. The direct sex discrimination provisions under *EqA 2010, s* 13 will not apply to claims of pregnancy or maternity discrimination during the protected period (*EqA 2010, s 18(7)*).

The following examples of pregnancy-related dismissals both amounted to sex discrimination prior to *SDA 1975, s 3A* and would no doubt also amount to discrimination under *EqA 2010*:

(a) in *O'Neill v (1) Governors of St Thomas More RCVA Upper School, (2) Bedfordshire County Council* [1997] ICR 33, Mrs O'Neill was a religious education teacher at a Roman Catholic school. She became pregnant as a result of a relationship with a Roman Catholic priest and was constructively dismissed. The EAT held that she had been discriminated against on the ground of her sex, as the pregnancy precipitated and permeated the decision to dismiss her. The respondents had sought to distinguish the case where an employee was dismissed for pregnancy per se (which they acknowledged would be discriminatory) and dismissal as a result of the pregnancy in these particular circumstances. The EAT did not accept this distinction and found the concept of pregnancy per se is misleading, because it suggests pregnancy as a sole ground of dismissal whereas, in fact, pregnancy always has surrounding circumstances which cannot be viewed in isolation from the pregnancy itself;

(b) in *Abbey National plc v Formoso* [1999] IRLR 222, Ms Formoso was dismissed for gross misconduct but had been unable to attend the relevant disciplinary interview due to a combination of her being 28 weeks' pregnant and suffering from anxiety. Ms Formoso's doctor certified that she was emotionally unfit to attend the disciplinary meeting and would remain so until after her pregnancy was over. The EAT upheld the employment tribunal's decision that the disadvantage she suffered as a result of her pregnancy amounted to direct sex discrimination. The EAT accepted that the pregnancy need not be the sole cause of the dismissal.

8.62 *Associative discrimination*

EqA 2010, s 13, provides that (save in the case of marriage and civil partnership) those who are associated with someone who has a protected characteristic are themselves protected from less favourable treatment because of that characteristic. This would suggest that a man whose wife/partner is pregnant could bring a claim for discrimination on the grounds of pregnancy or maternity. An example of a scenario where such a claim might arise is where both parents are employed by the same employer and the father complains to the employer that his partner has not been allowed to take paid time off for an antenatal appointment, and is subjected to disciplinary action as a result. A question arises, however, since *s 13* does not expressly exclude the protected characteristic of pregnancy/maternity, although see also *s 25(5)*.

It is clearly not the intention of the legislation that pregnancy discrimination falls within *s 13*. The *EHRC Employment Code* suggests that, since *EqA 2010, s 18* requires unfavourable treatment to be because of the woman's own pregnancy, an associative pregnancy/maternity discrimination claim by a third party would not be possible. Someone treated less favourably because of his/her association with a pregnant woman would nonetheless be able to bring a direct sex discrimination claim. This contrasts with the position under *SDA 1975*, as shown by the case of *Kulikaoskas v MacDuff Shellfish* EATS/0062/09/BI. Here the EAT held that *SDA 1975, s 3A* clearly relates to discrimination against 'a woman' on the ground of 'the woman's pregnancy', distinguishing the ECJ's decision establishing associative disability discrimination in *Coleman v Attridge Law: C-303/06* [2007] ICR 654 on the basis that *Coleman* dealt with disability discrimination (which derives from the *Framework Directive (2000/78/EC)*), whereas the right not to be discriminated against on the grounds of pregnancy derives from the *Pregnant Workers Directive (92/85/EC)* and the recast *Equal Treatment Directive (2006/54/EC)*.

For further details on discrimination by association, see **1.54**.

8.63 *Pregnancy-related illness*

SDA 1975, s 3A(1) codified the case law in relation to dismissal for maternity-related absence, and *EqA 2010, s 18(2)* contains similar provisions. The case law itself was clear that an employer must ignore any absence caused by pregnancy or childbirth-related illness which occurs either during pregnancy or maternity leave (this period is referred to as the protected period). In *Brown v Rentokil Ltd* [1998] ECR I-4185, [1998] All ER (EC) 791, the ECJ held it was directly discriminatory on the ground of sex to dismiss a woman during her pregnancy for pregnancy-related illness absence. The ECJ went on to state that illness relating to pregnancy or childbirth which occurs during pregnancy or the maternity leave period cannot be taken into account by an employer to justify a dismissal, but that absence arising after maternity leave can be taken into account in the same way as a man's absence.

The combined effect of the *Brown* decision and the requirement for a pregnancy discrimination claim to arise during the protected period (as well as the similar provision in the context of an automatically unfair dismissal connected to childbirth, see **8.64**) means, however, that it would be extremely unlikely that a woman could succeed in claiming either discrimination or automatically unfair dismissal if she was dismissed solely on the basis of absence occurring after the protected period but by reason of a maternity-related illness (as was the case in *Caledonia Bureau Investment & Property v Caffrey* [1998] ICR 603).

The *EHRC Employment Code* states that sickness absence associated with a miscarriage should be treated in the same way as absence due to pregnancy-related illness.

8.64 Pregnancy and maternity-related dismissals: automatic unfair dismissal

Pursuant to *ERA 1996, s 99* and the *Maternity and Parental Leave Regulations 1999 (SI 1999/3312)* (*MPL Regulations*), *reg 20*, a woman will automatically be regarded as being unfairly dismissed in certain redundancy situations (see **8.65**) or if the reason or principal reason for her dismissal is connected to:

(a) her pregnancy;

(b) the fact that she has given birth and the dismissal brings her ordinary maternity leave (OML) or additional maternity leave (AML) to an end;

(c) her taking or seeking to take OML or AML;

(d) her availing herself of the benefits of OML (as provided for by *ERA 1996, s 71* and *MPL Regulations, reg 9*);

(e) her failure to return from OML or AML in circumstances where her employer did not give her the proper notice of when her maternity leave was to end and she reasonably believed her maternity leave had not ended;

(f) her failure to return from OML or AML in circumstances where her employer gave her less than 28 days' notice of the date on which her maternity leave was to end and it was not reasonably practicable for her to return on that date; or

(g) the fact that she undertook, considered undertaking or refused to work on a keeping in touch day (KIT days are dealt with at **8.104**).

There is no qualifying period applicable to a claim of automatically unfair dismissal.

The employer must know of the employee's pregnancy, the fact that she has given birth or the other factors listed above; in *Ramdoolar v Bycity Ltd* [2005] ICR 368, the EAT held that it is generally not enough that the employer, for example, ought to have known that the employee was pregnant. It did, however, qualify this by recognising there may be an automatically unfair dismissal if an employer who merely suspects an employee may be pregnant dismisses her before his suspicion can be proved correct. This is reiterated in the draft EHRC Employment Statutory Code of Practice, which states that, in order to treat an employee unfavourably because of her pregnancy or a related illness, the employer must know, believe, or suspect (whether through formal notification or through the grapevine) that she is pregnant.

The words 'connected to' in *reg 20* should be interpreted widely to give full protection against the mischief envisaged by the legislation (*Clayton v Vigers* [1989] ICR 713, dealing with the precursor to the current provision).

In the case of *Paquay v Societe d'architectes Hoet & Minne SPRL: C-460/06* [2007] All ER (D) 137 (Oct), the ECJ held that the protection against dismissal on the grounds of pregnancy and maternity contained in the *Pregnant Workers Directive* does extend beyond the protected period (ie pregnancy and maternity leave) to the extent that any preparatory steps relating to a dismissal took place during the protected period even though the dismissal itself was not notified to the employee until after the end of the protected period. As referred to at **8.58** above, this is now expressly stated in the legislation in *EqA 2010, s 18(5)*.

8.65 Pregnancy and maternity-related dismissals: redundancy

It is possible for an employer to make an employee redundant while she is on maternity leave. However, there are two situations when doing so may result in an automatically unfair dismissal.

First, there will be an automatically unfair dismissal if the reason or principal reason for selecting an employee for redundancy is one of the reasons set out at (a)–(g) of **8.64**. This is the effect of *MPL Regulations, reg 20(2)*, which deals with a redundancy situation which applies equally to one or more employees in an undertaking holding similar positions to the employee in question but who has not been dismissed.

Second, there will also be an automatically unfair dismissal if a dismissal brings the maternity leave to an end, the reason or principal reason for the dismissal is redundancy and the *reg 10* requirements have not been complied with (*MPL Regulations, reg 20(1)(b)*). *Regulation 20(1)(b)* does not apply where a woman either accepts or unreasonably refuses an offer by an associated employer of a suitable alternative job which is appropriate for her to do in the circumstances.

MPL Regulations, reg 10 gives a woman who is made redundant while on maternity leave the right to any suitable available job. It is generally accepted that this puts the woman in a better position than other potentially redundant employees; the employer cannot select a better qualified candidate if the work is a suitable alternative for the woman (see, for example, the employment tribunal's decision in *Bentley v Body Shop International plc* 3100348/00 (unreported)). This is the case notwithstanding the EAT's comment in *Bellamy v American Airlines* UKEAT/0542/05 (unreported)) that the policy behind the *MPL Regulations* is to ensure that women returning from maternity leave are not disadvantaged, rather than providing them with a positive advantage over other employees.

Regulation 10 stipulates that if it is not practicable for an employer to continue to employ a woman on maternity leave by reason of redundancy, then she must be offered any suitable available vacancy. The suitable alternative role may be with the employer, his successor or an associated employer and must:

(a) be offered before the end of her employment;

(b) start immediately on the ending of her employment;

(c) be suitable in relation to the employee and appropriate for her in the circumstances; and

(d) be not on substantially less favourable terms (including as to capacity and place of work) as her previous employment.

In a decision dealing with the precursor to *reg 10*, the EAT upheld an employment tribunal's decision that a vacancy was available even though the post was funded by a third party whose rules rendered the claimant ineligible for the post (*Community Task Force v Rimmer* [1986] ICR 491).

MPL Regulations, reg 10 has not been the subject of many appellate decisions. The EAT has, however, held that:

(a) where a woman's position becomes redundant prior to her maternity leave, *reg 10* will still apply where the redundancy situation and matter of alternative roles is not resolved before the maternity leave starts (*The Secretary of State for Justice v Slee* UKEAT/10349/106 (20 July 2007, unreported));

(b) redundancy in this context has the same meaning as under the *ERA 1996* (*Slee*);

(c) *reg 10* does not mean that the consultation period must be extended until after maternity leave; the reference to the impracticability of continuing to employ a woman on maternity leave due to redundancy merely means that the employer must satisfy the employment tribunal that it needed to implement the redundancy during the period of maternity leave (*Calor Gas Ltd v Mrs D Bray* UKEAT/10633/04 (unreported));

(d) where an employer has more than one suitable alternative vacancy, the employer can decide which one to offer to the employee in fulfilment of its *MPL Regulations, reg 10* obligation (*Bellamy v American Airlines*); and

(e) both limbs of the test set out in *MPL Regulations, reg 10(3)* must be satisfied: where the work to be done in the alternative position is suitable in relation to the employee and appropriate for her to do in the circumstances (*MPL Regulations, reg 10(3)(a)*), but the terms and conditions are substantially less favourable than those of her previous position (*MPL Regulations, reg 10(3)(b)*), the position will not amount to a suitable alternative vacancy (*Simpson v Endsleigh Insurance Services Ltd* EAT/0544/09).

8.66 Pregnancy and maternity-related dismissals: notice of termination

As set out at **8.98**, a woman's right to contractual notice of termination is preserved during both OML and AML. Once her entitlement to SMP or contractual maternity pay has expired, however, she is not entitled to be paid during any period of contractual notice, although she may be entitled to a payment in lieu of notice or to payment pursuant to *ERA 1996, ss 86–91*.

8.67 Pregnancy and maternity-related dismissals: written statement of reasons for dismissal

As a general rule, an employee with one year's service is entitled to a written statement of the reasons for his dismissal if he makes a request for this to his employer.

Article 10(2) of the *Pregnant Workers Directive* requires employers to 'cite duly substantiated grounds for her dismissal in writing' if they dismiss a woman during the protected period. *ERA 1996, s 92(4)* therefore amends the general position for women in this situation and provides that they are entitled to the written statement of reasons for dismissal whatever their length of service and whether or not they have requested it.

If the employer unreasonably fails to provide the statement or if the reasons are inadequate or untrue, the employee can seek a declaration of the reasons and an award of two weeks' pay. (A 'week's pay' is not subject to the statutory maximum for this purpose.)

8.68 Pregnancy or maternity-related detriment

Women are protected from being subjected to a detriment as a result of pregnancy, childbirth and maternity leave by *ERA 1996, s 47C* and *MPL Regulations, reg 19*. The facts which give rise to a detriment claim are also likely to amount to discrimination under *EqA 2010, s 18* and employees are likely to bring both claims in the alternative.

MPL Regulations, reg 19 provides that an employee is not to be subjected to any detriment by any act, or deliberate failure to act, by her employer for any of the following reasons:

(a) her pregnancy;

(b) the fact that she has given birth and the detriment takes place during OML or AML;

(c) her taking or seeking to take OML or AML;

(d) her availing herself of the benefit of OML provided for by *ERA 1996, s 71* and *MPL Regulations, reg 9*;

(e) her failure to return from OML or AML in circumstances where her employer did not give her the proper notice of when her maternity leave was to end and she reasonably believed her maternity leave had not ended;

(f) her failure to return from OML or AML in circumstances where her employer gave her less than 28 days' notice of the date on which her maternity leave was to end and it was not reasonably practicable for her to return on that date; or

(g) the application of a legislative requirement or recommendation under a Code of Practice that she be suspended from work on the grounds of her pregnancy, her having recently given birth or her breastfeeding (ie as defined in *ERA 1996, s 66(2)*).

If the detriment amounts to a dismissal, however, the employee must bring a claim of automatic unfair dismissal or discrimination and the detriment provisions do not apply.

An employee who has suffered a detriment is able to bring a complaint under *ERA 1996, s 48* within three months, beginning with the act or failure complained of or the last in a series of acts or failures. The time limit can be extended by a tribunal if it was not reasonably practicable for the claimant to bring a claim within the time limit.

If the tribunal finds that the complaint was well-founded, it can make a declaration to that effect and make an award of compensation which it considers to be just and equitable in all the circumstances and will take into account the loss attributable to the act or omission, any reasonable expenses incurred in consequence of the act or omission and any benefit that the employee may have been expected to have but for the act or omission (*ERA 1996, s 49*).

The following are examples of situations where employees have succeeded in discrimination or detriment claims:

(a) an employee did not qualify for a performance assessment which was a pre-condition for a pay rise because of her absence on maternity leave. The ECJ held that the denial of the assessment amounted to discrimination on the grounds of sex as, but for her maternity leave, the employee would automatically have had the assessment (*Caisse Nationale d'Assurance Vieillesse Des Travailleurs Salaries v Thibault* [1998] ECR I-2011, [1998] All ER (EC) 385);

(b) an employee was not informed of a new role which arose during her pregnancy. She considered she was well suited to the new role (a view supported by one of her ex-colleagues), although the employment tribunal accepted that the employer was entitled to its view that she was not suitable for the job. The EAT upheld the employment tribunal's decision that the failure to inform the employee of the vacancy amounted to maternity-related detriment and discrimination on the grounds of sex (*Visa International Service Association v Mrs O L Paul* [2004] IRLR 42);

(c) an employee on maternity leave was appointed to a new role with her employer and successfully argued that it would be discrimination on the grounds of sex for continuous service in the new job to run from the date she started working in that role as opposed to the date of her appointment (*Herrero v Instituto Madrileno de la Salud (Imsalud): C-294/04* [2006] IRLR 296);

(d) promotion to a higher salary grade was dependent on length of service. Only eight of the twenty weeks spent by Mrs Sass on maternity leave counted as qualifying service as these were equivalent to the then West German maternity leave; the other twelve weeks of the then East German statutory maternity leave entitlement did not count. The ECJ held that the failure to recognise this additional period of statutory maternity leave would amount to sex discrimination if its purpose was the same as the West German eight-week compulsory leave. They stated that taking such leave should interrupt neither the employment relationship nor the application of the rights derived from it. The ECJ left it to the national courts to decide whether the purpose of the additional leave was in fact the same, but made it clear that neither the compulsory nature of the West German maternity leave nor the question of whether the leave was paid could be decisive factors in this assessment (*Land Brandenburg v Sass: C-284/02* [2005] IRLR 147). If an employer has a policy of promoting (or considering for promotion) employees purely on the basis of time served, the discounting of time spent both on OML and AML may well be held to be discriminatory.

Interestingly, in the case of *Ojinnaka v Sheffield College* UKEAT/0201/00 (2001, unreported), an employee failed in her claim that the failure of her maternity cover to keep her informed of what was going on while she was on maternity leave (and, in particular, potential changes to the course she taught) amounted to discrimination on the ground of sex. The EAT accepted there was no detriment as there was nothing of sufficient importance to discuss with the employee and that she would have been consulted had any concrete changes been proposed to her course or otherwise to her status or job description.

8.69 PREGNANCY AND MATERNITY RIGHTS

Paid time off for ante-natal appointments

If a registered medical practitioner, registered midwife or registered nurse has advised a pregnant employee to attend ante-natal care, the employee is entitled to take time off during the employer's working hours to keep this appointment (*ERA 1996, s 55(1)*). The employee is also entitled to be paid for this period of absence at the appropriate hourly rate (*ERA 1996, s 56(1)*) and this includes any travel and waiting time.

With effect from 1 October 2011, agency workers will enjoy the same rights as employees to take reasonable time off to attend ante-natal appointments once they have completed 12 weeks on assignment with an end user (*ERA 1996, s 57ZA*). Time at the appointments is paid at their usual rate by the agency (*ERA 1996, s 57ZB*).

8.70 *What is ante-natal care?*

Guidance from DBERR (now BIS) refers to ante-natal care as including medical examinations, tests for the likelihood of any genetic conditions or abnormalities, parentcraft classes and relaxation classes where medically advised (see also *Gregory v Tudsbury Ltd* [1982] IRLR 267).

8.71 *Eligibility requirements*

There is no length of service eligibility requirement and this right is available to both full-time and part-time employees. With the exception of the employee's first appointment, however, the employer can request:

(a) a certificate from a registered medical practitioner, registered midwife or registered nurse stating the employee is pregnant; and

(b) an appointment card or other document showing that the appointment has been made,

and if the employee does not provide this information to the employer, she is not entitled to take paid time off for that ante-natal appointment (*ERA 1996, s 55(2)*).

8.72 *Unreasonable refusal*

An employer cannot unreasonably refuse to permit an employee to take such time off work; however, there may be circumstances where an employer could reasonably expect an employee to make appointments outside of working hours (*Gregory v Tudsbury Ltd* [1982] IRLR 267). This is more likely to arise in situations where the employee works relatively few hours each week, although the BIS reminds employers in its guidance (which is not binding) that they should bear in mind that there is often little flexibility as to when appointments can be arranged.

8.73 *Appropriate hourly rate*

The employee is entitled to be paid for the period of absence at the appropriate hourly rate, calculated in accordance with *ERA 1996, s 56*.

The employee's statutory right to remuneration does not affect any contractual right that the employee may have to remuneration, although any contractual remuneration will discharge the relevant portion of statutory entitlement and vice versa (*s 56(6)*).

8.74 *Complaint*

An employee may present a complaint to an employment tribunal within three months from the date of the act complained of where:

(a) the employer has unreasonably refused to permit the employee to take time off (*ERA 1996, s 57(1)(a)*); or

(b) the employer has failed to pay (in whole or part) any amount to which the employee is entitled in respect of the period of absence for ante-natal care (*s 57(1)(b)*).

This time period can be extended by a tribunal if it was not reasonably practicable for the employee to bring the claim within time. If the complaint is upheld, a tribunal can make a declaration to that effect and where relevant, order the employer to pay the employee the remuneration she would have been entitled to and that is due (*s 57(3), (4)*).

8.75 *The expectant father's rights*

There is no right for the expectant father to take paid time off work to accompany the employee to the ante-natal appointments. However, the BIS and EHRC encourage employers to take a flexible approach where practicable and suggest that it is considered best practice to either allow the expectant father to take paid time off or make up this time.

8.76 Health and safety, suspension from work

The TUC states that every year there are around 1,500 potential tribunal cases involving pregnancy and maternity-related discrimination and of these the vast majority (over 90%) involved a breach of health and safety legislation.

The *Pregnant Workers Directive* (*Council Directive 92/85/EEC*) has been implemented into UK law under the *Management of Health and Safety at Work Regulations 1999* (*SI 1999/3242*) (*'HSW Regs'*). This legislation states that:

(a) subject to certain requirements, an employer should conduct a risk assessment in respect of new and expectant mothers as part of its general risk assessment (see **8.77**); and

(b) subject to certain requirements, an employer should carry out a specific risk assessment in respect of an individual employee who has informed her employer that she is a new or expectant mother (see **8.78**).

8.77 The general risk assessment

Where an employer has:

(a) persons working in the undertaking of a childbearing age; and

(b) the work is of a kind that could involve risk, by reason of her condition, to the health and safety of a new or expectant mother or to that of her baby, from any processes or working conditions, or physical, biological or chemical agents that are listed in *Annexes I* and *II* of the *Pregnant Workers Directive*,

an employer is required to undertake an assessment that considers that risk as part of its general risk assessment (*HSW Regs, reg 16(1)*). If the employer has more than five employees, this assessment must be recorded in writing. If risks are identified, the employer should inform both the concerned employees of the risk and their employee representatives.

As part of the risk assessment hazards such as physical, chemical and biological agents; industrial processes; movements and postures; mental and physical fatigue and other physical and mental burdens should be identified. Such hazards may arise in connection with work materials, equipment, methods and practices. The potential for harm and the possible extent of the harm should be assessed in terms of its nature, intensity and duration. In assessing this, the employer should take into account all relevant information, including information from new or expectant mothers and their advisers. For example, early shift work and nauseating smells may be likely to have an effect on sickness and headaches, or if the employee has to stand for long period of time this may increase the risk of varicose veins. The Health and Safety Executive gives useful guidance on these types of considerations.

8.78 A risk assessment for an individual new or expectant mother

Where an employee has notified the employer in writing that she is a new or expectant mother, an employer is subject to further health and safety obligations in respect of that individual employee (*HSW Regs, reg 18(1)*).

A 'new or expectant mother' is an employee who is either pregnant, has given birth in the past six months, or who is breastfeeding. 'Given birth' means a woman who has delivered a living child, or miscarried after at least 24 weeks of pregnancy. The protection of the *HSW Regs* only extends for six months after the birth if the employee is still breastfeeding. For these definitions and others, see *HSW Regs, reg 1(2)*.

8.79 *Notification*

There is no prescribed form of notification that the employee must give to her employer. The only requirement is that the notification must be in writing and indicate pregnancy. For example, the EAT found that a medical certificate stating an employee suffered from 'hyperemesis gravidarum' (severe sickness associated with pregnancy) constituted written notification of pregnancy and the employer was unable to show that this was an inadequate notification (*Day v T Pickles Farm Ltd* [1999] IRLR 217).

The employer is able to request that the employee produces for its inspection a certificate from a registered medical practitioner or midwife showing that she is pregnant (such as a form MAT B1). If the employee fails to provide such evidence within a reasonable time, the employer will not be required to 'maintain action in relation to the employee' such as undertake an individual risk assessment or implement its recommendation (*HSW Regs, reg 18(2)(a)(ii)*).

8.80 *The individual risk assessment*

The employer must identify the risks that are applicable to that specific new or expectant mother. These may be risks that it has identified in the general risk assessment and also risks that the employer has identified from taking into account all other relevant information, such as information from the new or expectant mother and her adviser, including any medical advice, reports and certificates. Any information provided should be dealt with in the strictest confidence.

The employer must record the findings of the risk assessment, but there is no requirement that a written record must be provided to the employee when information about the risks is given orally (*Stevenson v JM Skinner & Co* UKEAT/0584/07).

A single individual risk assessment may not be sufficient since during the various stages of pregnancy and after birth, the risks affecting the mother and her unborn or newborn child may change and so should be continually monitored.

8.81 *Duty to take action to avoid the risks*

The employer has a duty to take action in respect of the risks that are applicable to that individual employee and the employer should consult with the employee and any health and safety representatives regarding this. The action taken by the employer should 'avoid' the risk; however, the EAT has stated that this does not mean that the employer must eliminate the risk entirely but instead should reduce the risks to 'its lowest acceptable level' (*New Southern Railway Ltd v Quinn* [2006] IRLR 266) (see also the general obligations on employers in relation to health and safety set out in *Article 6* of the *Framework Directive*).

The employer must do the following:

(a) take action to avoid the risk; for example, if a risk is connected with manual handling it may be reduced by providing physical aids (*HSW Regs, reg 16(2)*);

(b) if taking action would not avoid the risk, if it is reasonable to do so and this would avoid such risks, the employee's working conditions or hours of work should be altered (*reg 16(2)*). For example, providing that the employee no longer has to work early shifts when she is suffering from morning sickness;

(c) if it is not reasonable to alter the working conditions or hours of work, or if it would not avoid such risk, the employee has a right to be offered 'suitable alternative work' (*reg 16(3)* and *ERA 1996, s 67*) (see **8.82**); and

(d) if suitable alternative work cannot be offered, the employer must suspend the employee for so long as necessary to avoid such a risk (*reg 16(3)*). Such suspension would be paid (*ERA 1996, ss 66* and *68*) (see **8.83**).

Employers and end users are already under an obligation to carry out a risk assessment for agency workers who are new or expectant mothers. For agency workers who have been assigned for 12 weeks or more, end users will now be required to make adjustments to address any risks identified (*HSW Regs, reg 16A*). If the adjustments will not remove the risk, the end user must notify the employment agency, which will be required to place on her any new assignment which is available, on no less favourable terms for the duration of the assignment, or if that is not feasible, to instead pay her for the period (*ERA 1996, ss 68B, 68C*).

8.82 *'Suitable alternative work'*

Care must be taken by an employer that the work offered is 'suitable alternative work', being:

(a) work of a kind which is both suitable in relation to her and appropriate for her to do in the circumstances; and

(b) the terms and conditions applicable to her for performing the work, if they differ from the corresponding terms and conditions applicable to her for performing the work she normally performs under her contract of employment, must not be substantially less favourable to her than those corresponding terms and conditions (*ERA 1996, s 67*).

In *New Southern Railway Ltd v Quinn* [2006] IRLR 266, an employee was demoted from her position as a railway station duty manager to a personal assistant, and her salary was reduced accordingly to reflect the lower rate of pay for that role. The EAT upheld complaints of sex discrimination, constructive dismissal and unlawful deductions from wages on the basis that the risks identified were small and it was not necessary for the employer to demote Mrs Quinn or reduce her salary in order to comply with the *HSW Regs*.

In *British Airways (European Operations at Gatwick) Ltd v Moore and Botterill* [2000] IRLR 296, an employee was removed from flying duties to ground duties. The loss of her cabin crew member's flying allowance meant that the alternate role was on terms substantially less favourable than her previous terms (regarding pay and benefits). This meant that the transfer to ground duties did not constitute suitable alternative work within the meaning of *ERA 1996, s 67*. The claimants were therefore entitled to receive the remuneration due to them calculated in accordance with *s 67* and the principles set out in *S and U Stores Ltd v Wilkes* [1974] 3 All ER 401.

8.83 *Suspension from work*

To justify the suspension of a pregnant employee an employer must first assess the risk; second, take appropriate measures to avoid the risk; and third (if the risks cannot be avoided or it is unreasonable to alter her hours or conditions), offer suitable alternative work. Only once these three steps have been pursued can the employee be suspended (see *New Southern Railway Ltd v Quinn*).

In addition, where a new or expectant mother normally works at night and a certificate from a registered medical practitioner or midwife shows that it is necessary for her health and safety that she should not be at work for any period, then the employer must suspend the employee from work for as long as is necessary for her health and safety (*HSW Regs, reg 17*).

In either case, an employee is entitled to be paid during the period of suspension (*ERA 1996, s 68*).

8.84 Exemptions to pregnant worker's risk assessment

Whilst there are no exemptions in relation to the general risk assessment for employees of a childbearing age, an employer is not required to take any action in relation to a new or expectant mother until she has notified her employer in writing that she is pregnant, or has given birth during the past six months, or is breastfeeding (*HSW Regs, reg 18(1)*).

In addition, *reg 18* provides that an employer is not required to 'maintain action' in respect of an employee:

(a) if, following a request by the employer, the employee fails to provide evidence of her pregnancy within a reasonable time; or

(b) once the employer knows that the employee is no longer a new or expectant mother; or

(c) if the employer cannot establish whether she remains a new or expectant mother.

8.85 Failure to carry out a specific risk assessment

In *Hardman v Mallon (t/a Orchard Lodge Nursing Home)* [2002] 2 CMLR 1467 a failure to carry out a risk assessment amounted to sex discrimination as the new or expectant mother's work involved heavy lifting. It was thereafter thought that any failure to carry out a risk assessment in respect of a new or expectant mother is capable of constituting sex discrimination. However, the Court of Appeal has confirmed that the duty to conduct a risk assessment under *HSW Regs, reg 16* only arises where the work is of a nature that could involve potential risk for a new or expectant mother. In *Madarassy v Nomura International plc* [2007] EWCA Civ 33, [2007] ICR 867, the employee had a desk-based role and although she complained of radiation from her computer, this was not enough to trigger the obligation to conduct a specific risk assessment. *Madarassy* was applied in *O'Neill v Buckinghamshire County Council* UKEAT/0200/09, where the EAT held that the 'stressful nature of [teaching] in general terms' did not oblige the employer to carry out a specific risk assessment. This is in contrast to the case of *Queen Victoria Seamen's Rest Ltd (QVSR) v Ward* UKEAT/0465/08, where a failure to carry out a risk assessment contributed to a finding of sex discrimination in circumstances where there was a risk of violence from residents at the premises and potentially from nightworking, and the employer failed to carry out a risk assessment even after the pregnant employee was assaulted.

Although the mere possibility of discrimination is not enough to shift the burden of proof onto the employer (see **8.30**), it is considered safer and best practice to carry out a risk assessment rather than rely on the narrow interpretation of *reg 16* in *Madarassy v Nomura International plc*, given that damages for sex discrimination are unlimited and failure to carry out a risk assessment could result in a negligence claim in the event of the mother or the baby suffering a detriment (such as an injury which would have been identified had a risk assessment been carried out).

The Health and Safety Executive is able to serve an improvement notice on the employer to require it to carry out the risk assessment or a prohibition notice (prohibiting an activity until remedial action has been taken). In addition, the *Health and Safety at Work etc Act 1974, s 33(1)(a)* provides that it is an offence for a person to contravene the general duties of employers to their employees (such as providing a safe system of work) and *s 33(1)(c)* provides that it is an offence to contravene any health and safety regulations. The offender can be liable on conviction to a fine (depending on the various breaches and whether conviction is a summary conviction or on indictment, the fines may not be capped). Any action that the Health and Safety Executive takes should be proportionate, consistent and in the public interest (see the Health and Safety Commission's Enforcement Policy Statement published by the Health and Safety Executive (HSC41, reprinted 02/09)).

8.86 MATERNITY LEAVE AND PAY

Maternity leave

Most of the law relating to maternity leave is set out in the *MPL Regulations* and *ERA 1996, ss 71–75* (provisions relating to pay are elsewhere).

8.87 *Eligibility*

Subject to the notification requirements set out below, all employees are entitled to 52 weeks of maternity leave, regardless of their length of service; but not all employees are entitled to maternity pay (see **8.92**). Individuals who are not employees—such as contractors/consultants—are not entitled to maternity leave, but in many cases are entitled to protection from discrimination.

8.88 *EWC and notification*

Under the *MPL Regulations, reg 4(1)(a)*, to receive maternity leave, the employee must notify the employer no later than the end of the 15th week before the expected week of childbirth (the 'EWC'). This is the week beginning with midnight between Saturday and Sunday when childbirth is expected to occur, and 'childbirth' includes still birth after 24 weeks of pregnancy. Under *MPL Regulations, reg 2(1)* the employee must notify the employer of the following:

(a) that she is pregnant;

(b) the EWC;

(c) the date she intends her leave to start. This date cannot be earlier than the start of the eleventh week before the EWC.

If it is not reasonably practicable to give notice by then, the employee must do so as soon as it is reasonably practicable. In the case of *St Alphonsus RC Primary School v Blenkinsop* [2009] All ER (D) 54 (Aug) the EAT held that it was not reasonably practicable for a teaching assistant to comply with the notice requirement where she simply did not know she was entitled to either maternity leave or pay. The notification does not have to be in writing unless the employer asks for it (*MPL Regulations, reg 4(2)(a)*). The employer may also ask for a medical certificate—a MAT B1—confirming the EWC (*reg 4(1)(b)*), but this certificate cannot be signed before the 20th week before the EWC (*Statutory Maternity Pay (Medical Evidence) Regulations 1987 (SI 1987/235), reg 2*). Upon receiving this notice, the employer must, within 28 days, notify the employee of the date on which her maternity leave will end (*reg 7(6)* and *7(7)(a)*). Where the notification is not made within 28 days, the employee is exempted from the obligation to notify her intention to return to work early (*reg 11(5)*), and is protected from detriment or dismissal arising out of her failure to return to work on time, provided it was not reasonably practicable for her to return at that time (*regs 19* and *20*). Where the employer gives no notice at all, the employee is protected from detriment/dismissal so long as she reasonably believed her maternity leave had not ended (*regs 19* and *20*).

8.89 *Starting maternity leave*

Under the *MPL Regulations, reg 6*, maternity leave will start on the earliest of:

(a) the date notified by the employee;

(b) automatically the day after birth;

(c) the day after absence due wholly or partly to a pregnancy-related reason after the beginning of the fourth week before the EWC.

An employee may change their notified start date, but must give at least 28 days' notice of the change, that is at least 28 days' notice before the original date if it is to be postponed, or 28 days before the new date if leave is being started earlier (*MPL Regulations, reg 4(1A)*).

8.90 *Duration and characteristics of maternity leave*

Maternity leave is a maximum of 52 weeks. It is split into two periods of 26 weeks. The first is ordinary maternity leave (OML) (*ERA 1996, s 71*). The second is additional maternity leave (AML) (*ERA 1996, s 73*). Historically some employees were entitled to OML but not

AML, but the length of service requirement for AML was removed by amendments to the *MPL Regulations* under the *Work and Families Act 2006* and now all employees are eligible for both OML and AML. The position changed again in 2008 when almost all the differences between OML and AML were removed (see **8.98** below). The only remaining distinction is the formulation of the right to return.

It is up to the employee to decide how much maternity leave she takes, save that the first two weeks of OML—referred to as compulsory maternity leave (CML)—must be taken and the employee is not permitted to work (*ERA 1996, s 72* and *MPL Regulations, reg 8*). CML is extended to four weeks for women employed in factories; it is a criminal offence to allow an employee to work in a factory at such time, punishable by a fine of up to £200 (*Public Health Act 1936, ss 205* and *343* and *Factories Act 1961, s 175*). More generally, allowing an employee to work during any period of CML is a criminal offence under health and safety law, punishable by a fine not exceeding level 2 on the standard scale, currently up to £500 (*ERA 1996, s 72*).

8.91 **Statutory maternity pay**

The relevant legislation is mainly set out in the *Social Security Contributions and Benefits Act 1992* (*SSCBA 1992*), *Part VII* and the *Statutory Maternity Pay (General) Regulations 1986 (SI 1986/1960)* ('*SMP Regulations*').

Key terms:

(a) as for maternity leave, the expected week of confinement (or childbirth) (EWC) is the week in which the child is expected to be born. More precisely, confinement is defined as labour resulting in the issue of a living child or labour after 24 weeks of pregnancy resulting in the issue of a child whether alive or dead (*SSCBA, s 171(1)*);

(b) the 'qualifying week' is the 15th week before the EWC;

(c) the reference or qualifying period for calculating eligibility for and the amount of statutory maternity pay (SMP) is, broadly speaking, the eight-week period ending with the qualifying week.

8.92 *Eligibility*

The eligibility criteria for SMP differ from those for maternity leave. Once she has qualified for SMP, a woman will be entitled to receive it notwithstanding any subsequent dismissal (see (c) below if the dismissal is in order to avoid paying SMP). If she is not eligible to receive SMP, a woman may be entitled to maternity allowance. A woman who is absent from work is entitled to SMP if:

(a) she is pregnant at the beginning of the 11th week before the EWC (or has given birth at this point);

(b) she has been employed for a continuous period of 26 weeks ending with the 15th week before the EWC (*Part III* of the *SMP Regulations* sets out the rules on continuous employment and these are similar to the rules contained in *ERA 1996*);

(c) her normal weekly earnings during the qualifying period are higher than or equivalent to the lower earnings limit at the rate applicable at the end of the qualifying week;

(d) she has given the required notice to her employer (see **8.93**).

In this context, 'employed' means a woman who is employed in Great Britain either under a contract of service or as an office-holder and whose earnings are subject to income tax under the *Income Tax (Earnings and Pensions) Act 2003, s 7* and *SSCBA 1992, s 17(1)*.

In addition:

(a) *SSCBA 1992, s 17* provides that anyone who is treated as an employed earner for National Insurance purposes by virtue of the *Social Security (Categorisation of Earners) Regulations 1978 (SI 1978/1689)* will also be entitled to SMP. The most significant of these are agency workers who will qualify for SMP if the agency retains an ongoing role in paying them;

(b) the *Statutory Maternity Pay (Persons Abroad and Mariners) Regulations 1987 (SI 1987/418)* provide for an employee who is based abroad to be entitled to SMP if her employer is liable to pay secondary Class 1 NI contributions in respect of her, or if she is working in an EU Member State and deemed to be subject to UK social security legislation by virtue of *EC Regulation 1408/71*;

(c) if an employer brings an employee's employment to an end solely or mainly for the purpose of avoiding liability for SMP, the employer will be liable to make SMP payments if the employee was employed by him for a continuous period of at least eight weeks (*SMP Regulations, reg 3(1), (2)* sets out how such SMP is calculated).

Employers who do not have a liability to pay secondary Class 1 NICs will not be required to pay SMP.

A woman will not be entitled to SMP in respect of any week that she works during maternity leave other than a keeping in touch day (KIT days are dealt with at **8.104**). There is also no liability to pay SMP in respect of a week when a woman is in legal custody or imprisoned, or if she dies.

8.93 *Notice requirements*

A woman is required to give her employer at least 28 days' notice of the date that she wants her SMP to begin or, if that is not reasonably practicable, she must give notice as soon as is reasonably practicable. The notice only has to be in writing if the employee requests it (*SMP Regulations, reg 23*).

As for maternity leave, a woman must also give her employer evidence of when the EWC is (or evidence of the date of birth if it has already occurred). The evidence must be provided by the end of the third week of the maternity pay period or, if there is good cause for the evidence to be submitted later, by the end of the thirteenth week of the maternity pay period (*reg 22*). This evidence is usually provided by giving the employer the MAT B1 certificate in accordance with the requirements of the *Statutory Maternity Pay (Medical Evidence) Regulations 1987 (SI 1987/235)* (see **8.88**).

8.94 *Period of SMP*

SMP is payable for a maximum period of 39 consecutive weeks. In common with maternity leave itself, this period starts either on the date:

(a) notified;

(b) that the employee gives birth, if that is before the notified date;

(c) after the first day of absence if the employee is absent from work partly or wholly due to pregnancy or confinement at any time after the beginning of the fourth week before the EWC. In the case of *North Yorkshire Police and Mrs Deborah Wade* Case TC 00186 [2009] UKFTT 237CTF, the first-tier tax tribunal confirmed that any pregnancy-related absence is sufficient to start the SMP period. The absence does not need to be due to pregnancy-related illness; in this case, the employee had already started maternity leave under her employer's scheme;

In addition, the payment of SMP starts after the date the employee's employment terminates if it terminates at any time after the beginning of the 11th week before the EWC.

8.95 *Amount, calculation and payment of SMP*

SMP is paid at a higher rate of 90% of a woman's normal weekly earnings during the eight-week reference period for the first six weeks and at a lower flat rate for the remaining period of up to 33 weeks. The flat rate with effect from 3 April 2011 is £128.73 (or continues at the rate of 90% of normal weekly earnings if that amount is lower). The flat rate is typically increased by regulation in April of each year.

The eight-week reference period and the method of calculating normal weekly earnings for this purpose are governed by the *SMP Regulations, reg 21*. Normal weekly earnings include any remuneration or profit derived from a woman's employment and so in addition to wages and salary, payments such as overtime pay, holiday pay, commission and bonuses must be included in the calculation. It is therefore possible for the higher rate of SMP to exceed a woman's normal weekly pay if, for example, a significant annual bonus is paid during the eight-week reference period.

As a result of the ECJ's decision in *Alabaster v Woolwich plc* [2004] ECR I-3101, [2005] All ER (EC) 490, which is considered at **8.97**, *reg 21(7)* provides that where a woman is awarded a pay increase (or would have been awarded such an increase had she not been absent on statutory maternity leave) and the pay increase applies to the whole or any part of the period between the beginning of the eight-week reference period and the end of her maternity leave, the normal weekly earnings must be calculated as if the pay increase applied in each week of the eight-week reference period. The period from the beginning of the reference period until the end of statutory maternity leave could extend to 17 months if a woman takes her full entitlement to maternity leave. This provision can result in women on maternity leave being treated more favourably than their colleagues. For example, if the pay rise is awarded at the end of maternity leave, it will affect payments of SMP for earlier weeks.

Regulation 27 provides that SMP should be paid in a like manner to normal pay and so monthly paid employees are typically paid SMP on a monthly basis. SMP can also be paid in a lump sum, which is an option often used in case of redundancy.

8.96 **Contractual or enhanced maternity pay**

Many employers provide maternity pay in excess of SMP. Payments of SMP can be set off against any such enhanced payments and vice versa. The ECJ judgment in *Alabaster* was couched in wide enough terms to apply to contractual or enhanced pay if the enhanced pay is based on pay received by the employee prior to her maternity (for example, if a contractual scheme used the same reference period as for SMP).

This position was then codified in the *SDA 1975*, and the *EqPA 1970* with the relevant provisions now being found in *EqA 2010, s 74* and *Sch 9*.

Where the terms of a woman's work do not already provide for this, *s 74* provides that maternity pay which is calculated by reference to her pay at a particular time must be subject to any pay increases which arise (or which would have arisen had the woman not been on maternity leave) after the rate of maternity pay has been calculated and before the end of the protected period.

There is a similar provision for maternity pay which is not regulated by the contract of employment in *Sch 9, Pt 3, para 17*. This paragraph generally carves out non-contractual pay from the pregnancy discrimination protection. However, it specifically preserves a woman's ability to bring a pregnancy discrimination claim in circumstances where her non-contractual maternity pay is not increased by reference to pay increases which she would have received had she not been on maternity leave.

In relation to agency workers, the 'equal treatment' principle set out in the *Agency Worker Regulations 2010* does not extend to contractual or enhanced maternity pay (*reg 6(3)*). The Regulations do not affect an agency worker's statutory entitlements.

8.97 Maternity pay and discrimination

Various challenges have been made to the SMP scheme and to enhanced maternity pay schemes on the basis that they are discriminatory on the grounds of sex.

(a) In *Gillespie v Northern Health and Social Services Board* [1996] ECR I-475, [1996] All ER (EC) 284, the employees were entitled to an enhanced maternity pay scheme and sought to argue that it was directly discriminatory on the grounds of sex for:

(i) their pay to be reduced at all while on maternity leave; and

(ii) for them not to receive the benefit of a backdated pay rise which was awarded after the rate of their maternity pay had been calculated.

The ECJ held that, while women on maternity leave require special protection, there was no requirement that they should continue to receive full pay during maternity leave. The only requirement is that the amount of maternity pay cannot be so low as to undermine the purpose of maternity leave, namely the protection of women before and after giving birth. Without much analysis, they also held that a woman on maternity leave should, however, receive a pay rise awarded before or during the maternity leave period. This is on the basis that the principle of non-discrimination requires that a woman on maternity leave must, like any other worker, benefit from any pay rise awarded between the beginning of the period covered by the reference pay and the end of the maternity leave. The ECJ held that to deny such an increase to a woman on maternity leave would discriminate against her purely in her capacity as a worker since, had she not been pregnant, she would have received a pay rise.

It was as a result of the *Gillespie* case that the government amended the *SMP Regulations* to provide that if a woman receives a pay rise backdated to a time within the reference period, SMP must be recalculated to take the increase into account.

(b) This change then led to the challenge in *Alabaster v Woolwich plc* [2004] ECR I-3101, [2005] All ER (EC) 490, as it did not fully implement the ECJ's decision in *Gillespie*. Before going on maternity leave, Mrs Alabaster received a pay rise which, although backdated, still fell outside the reference period for calculating SMP. Under the *Gillespie* form of the Regulations, Mrs Alabaster's SMP was not affected by the pay rise and she brought a claim of sex discrimination. The ECJ held, following *Gillespie*, that any pay rise having effect during the reference period or the entire period of maternity leave should be included in the calculation for SMP.

(c) In *Boyle v Equal Opportunities Commission: C-411/96* [1999] ICR 360 the EOC provided enhanced maternity pay if the employee agreed to return to work after maternity leave and to repay the enhanced element if she did not return. The ECJ held that it was not discriminatory on the ground of sex to provide an enhanced rate of maternity pay only on the basis that the woman returns to work after maternity leave, and nor did such a provision infringe the *Pregnant Workers Directive*.

(d) In *Banks v Tesco Stores Ltd* [1999] ICR 1141, an employee challenged the lower earnings limit eligibility requirement for SMP, relying on the ECJ's statement in *Gillespie* that the level of maternity pay should not be so low as to undermine the purpose of maternity leave. The EAT held it was not discriminatory to impose eligibility requirements of this sort.

(e) In *North Western Health Board v McKenna* [2006] All ER (EC) 455, [2006] ICR 477, the employee claimed that a sick pay scheme which went down to half pay after a set period and was subject to an overall maximum period of payment was discriminatory on the ground of sex when applied to a pregnancy-related illness. The ECJ held that employers are not required to pay full pay to women absent from work because of pregnancy-related illness. The ECJ drew an important distinction between dismissals and pay, explaining that while the only way to accommodate 'the special nature of pregnancy-related illness' is to prevent employers from dismissing women for this reason; the situation is different as far as pay or sick pay is concerned as accommodations can be made in other ways, such as a reduced level of pay, provided that this is not so low as to undermine the objective of protecting pregnant workers. The ECJ also held that offsetting pregnancy-related absences against a maximum total of days of paid sick leave was not discriminatory. Again, as in relation to the level of pay, there was a twist to this; the rules as to the offsetting of absences cannot result in a woman receiving less than this protective minimum level of pay in a subsequent period of illness. This minimum level should be satisfied as long as the employee is receiving statutory sick pay or incapacity benefit.

(f) Some company schemes provide that if an employee does not return from maternity leave, or returns within a certain period of time, the employee must repay some or all of the enhanced maternity pay she received. The ECJ concluded that such provisions were not unlawfully discriminatory (*Boyle*). Requiring repayment may, however, depending on the circumstances, amount to victimisation or whistleblowing detriment (*Visa International Service Association v Paul* [2004] IRLR 42).

It is not always possible to reconcile the ECJ cases in this area. Women are accorded special protection in recognition of the fact that pregnancy and maternity are unique to them and so their position cannot be compared with that of someone at work. This special protection has extended to many non-monetary matters such as dismissals (*Webb, Dekker* and *Tele Danmark*), performance assessments (*Thibault*) and promotions (*Sass*), but not to full pay, sick pay or bonuses (*Gillespie*, *McKenna* and *Lewen v Denda*; see **8.101**). The distinction drawn by the ECJ in *McKenna* in between dismissals and pay does help to reconcile these decisions to some extent but still does not account for the difference in the treatment of pay itself (which does not come within the special protection) and pay rises (which do: *Gillespie*, *Alabaster*).

8.98 Benefits during maternity leave

Ordinary and additional maternity leave

During maternity leave, an employee is entitled to the benefit of:

(a) all the terms and conditions of employment, other than those relating to remuneration (*ERA 1996, s 71(4)–(5)* and *MPL Regulations, reg 9*);

(b) any contractual rights regarding maternity leave which are more favourable than the statutory right (*MPL Regulations, reg 21*);

(c) 'matters connected with . . . employment, whether or not they arise under her contract of employment' (*ERA 1996, s 71(5)*); and

(d) pension contributions to an occupational pension scheme during paid maternity leave (see **8.103**).

Remuneration is defined as a payment by way of wages and salary (*MPL Regulations, reg 21*) and is considered further in the context of bonuses (see **8.101**) and childcare vouchers (see **8.102**).

If a woman is unlawfully deprived of these terms, she has a number of possible claims:

(a) pregnancy detriment under *MPL Regulations, reg 19*;

(b) pregnancy or maternity discrimination (*EqA 2010, s 18*);

(c) unlawful deduction from wages (*ERA 1996, s 13*).

Prior to October 2008, there was a key distinction between OML and AML. Whereas all terms and conditions and non-contractual matters (excepting remuneration) continued during OML, employees were only entitled to benefit from specified implied and express terms during AML (namely mutual trust and confidence, notice, redundancy compensation and disciplinary or grievance procedures). This distinction was replicated when pregnancy and maternity was included as a specific ground of discrimination in the *SDA 1975* in 2005. For example, employees could only bring a pregnancy/maternity discrimination claim in respect of AML in respect of the specified terms listed above.

The government abolished this distinction as a result of the ECJ decision in *Land Brandenburg v Sass: C-284/02* [2005] IRLR 147 and the High Court decision in *Equal Opportunities Commission v Secretary of State for Trade and Industry*. Sass suggested that the suspension of contractual terms during AML amounted to unlawful discrimination. The ECJ held that the purpose of the leave should be considered and if it is the protection of women as regards pregnancy and maternity:

> 'Community law requires that taking such statutory protective leave should interrupt neither the employment relationship . . . nor the application of the rights derived from it and cannot lead to discrimination against that woman'.
>
> (para 48)

The government subsequently conceded in *Equal Opportunities Commission v Secretary of State for Trade and Industry* (at 57) that the purpose of AML is the same as that of OML. The High Court held that the government must make amendments to the *SDA 1975* so as expressly to permit claims of the type referred to in a certain fact sheet (eg to give an appraisal or consult about a reorganisation). The government therefore removed the distinction between OML and AML and the changes came into effect for women whose expected week of childbirth started on or after 5 October 2008. Now all terms and conditions (other than those relating to remuneration) continue during OML and AML.

8.99 *Notice*

A woman's right to notice is preserved during OML and AML. This period of notice may be unpaid if she is not receiving pay at the relevant time, but an employee on maternity leave would be entitled to paid notice periods or pay in lieu of notice in certain circumstances, including:

(a) employees at work are paid in lieu of notice ('PILON'). A failure to make a PILON to the employee on maternity leave is because of her pregnancy/maternity leave, and therefore unlawful discrimination. If there is some other (non-discriminatory) reason for the failure to pay a PILON, that is a potential defence to the claim;

(b) if the employee's contractual notice period is *not* one week longer than their statutory notice period. *ERA 1996, ss 86–91* provide that where an employee's contractual notice is not one week longer than statutory minimum notice, then if she is absent from work because of sickness or pregnancy or on adoption, parental or paternity leave, the employee is entitled to her usual pay in respect of her statutory notice period.

In all cases, there would be credit for maternity pay received. While there is no double recovery, there would be an obligation to top-up notice pay in those circumstances.

8.100 *Holidays*

Employees on maternity leave accrue contractual holiday entitlement and are entitled to statutory holiday under the *Working Time Regulations 1998* ('*WTR 1998*'). Despite the fact that the *WTR 1998* do not allow the majority of WTR leave to be carried over, a woman on maternity leave must be able to take her holiday entitlement at a time other than maternity leave (*Gómez v Continental Industrias del Caucho SA: C-342/01* [2004] ECR I–2605).

This position was reinforced by the ECJ's subsequent decision in *Stringer*, which held that where holiday cannot be taken at the same time as another type of leave (as is the case for maternity leave) the employee must be able to carry it over and take it another time. Employers should therefore allow employees to carry over holiday (whether statutory or contractual) that they have accrued during maternity leave if they would otherwise be unable to take it. In practice, many employees choose to take some or all of their accrued holiday entitlement just before or just after their maternity leave.

8.101 *Payment of bonuses*

Bonuses which reflect performance or contribution to the business in any way must be awarded to women in respect of any time spent at work in the relevant bonus year (*EqA 2010, s 74* and the combined effect of *s 18* and *Sch 9, Pt 3, para 17*). Employers must assess performance for women who are only at work for a part of the relevant bonus year and should, for example, make allowances in situations where targets cannot be met because of lead-in times etc; a failure to do so is likely to be contrary to *EqA 2010, s 18* and may also constitute indirect sex discrimination under *s 19*.

Employees are entitled to receive bonus payments in respect of the two-week period of compulsory maternity leave. This principle was established by the ECJ in *Lewen v Denda* [1999] ECR I-7243, [2000] All ER (EC) 261 and followed in the UK in *Hoyland v Asda Stores Ltd* [2006] CSIH 21, [2006] IRLR 468. This position is now enshrined in statute (*EqA 2010, s 74* and *s 18/Sch 9, Pt 3, para 17*). Prior to there being specific statutory provision, it was accepted in *Hoyland v Asda Stores Ltd* that such a claim could be brought as an unlawful deduction from wages claim under the *ERA 1996*.

Under maternity legislation, employees are *not* entitled to bonuses in respect of the remainder of maternity leave if the bonus is a sum payable by way of wages or salary (see **8.98**). A bonus is more likely to be regarded as a payment by way of wages or salary if it is a reward for performance (whether individual or company), part and parcel of the salary system, contractual, a structured discretionary scheme or pensionable. A bonus is less likely to be treated as wages or salary if it is a one-off bonus unrelated to performance, designed to promote retention or future motivation or truly discretionary with employees having very little idea of whether they will get a bonus or even a rough idea of the size of their bonus (see *Connolly v HSBC Bank plc* May 2004, Employment Tribunal Case No 3202622/2001 and *Hoyland v Asda Stores Ltd*).

This position is reflected in the *EqA 2010*. *Section 74* prevents a woman from bringing a pregnancy and maternity discrimination claim in respect of a term of her work which relates to pay. Similarly, *Sch 9, Pt 3, para 17* is a specific exception from the pregnancy and maternity discrimination provisions for payments of money which are by way of wages or salary and which are not regulated by the contract of employment to women on maternity leave.

These provisions are consistent with the (earlier) ECJ decision in *Lewen v Denda*, which provided that it will not be discriminatory to withhold a one-off bonus in respect of maternity leave if the bonus is subject to the sole condition that employees are in active employment at the time of payment. If the purpose of the bonus is to reward performance or contribution to the business, then employers must pay it in respect of any period of compulsory maternity leave, but it will not be discriminatory to withhold the bonus in relation to any other maternity or parental leave. In the UK, this aspect of *Lewen v Denda* was followed by the EAT in *Hoyland v Asda*. (*Hoyland v Asda* was appealed to the Court of Session on a different and more limited point.)

The scope for women to bring a claim for bonus is therefore broadly limited to cases where they can show it is not payable by way of wages or salary. This may be possible where, for example, the bonus is designed to promote retention or future motivation. In *GUS Home*

Shopping Ltd v Green [2001] IRLR 75, it was held that a loyalty bonus which was not linked to performance or actual attendance at work could not be withheld from a woman on maternity leave. However, such facts are relatively uncommon in practice.

In this regard, it should be noted that the exact formulation of the exception dealing with payments varies slightly, with the *MPL Regulations* referring to sums payable by way of wages and salary and the *EqA 2010* referring to payments of money by way of wages and salary (in the non-contractual context) and terms relating to pay (in the contractual context). This may broaden the scope for a woman to bring a claim for a non-contractual bonus which is paid other than in cash.

8.102 *Childcare vouchers*

In May 2008, HM Revenue & Customs (HMRC) issued guidance entitled '*Statutory Maternity leave—salary sacrifice and non-cash benefits*' which expressed the view that any benefits which have a transferable cash value amount to a payment by way of wages and salary and therefore do not need to be continued during maternity leave. The examples of cash benefits given included cash allowances (for example, car allowance, housing allowance and fuel allowance) and vouchers which have a transferable cash value (for example, luncheon vouchers, retail vouchers or certain vouchers for recreational benefits like membership of a sports club).

Conversely, what were described as non-cash benefits were not considered by HMRC to be payments by way of wages and salary, and so must be continued.

HMRC's view is that the provision of childcare vouchers, whether or not via a salary sacrifice arrangement, is a non-cash benefit. It is the case that the vouchers are not payable to the employee, and cannot be freely spent by the employee. The situation is not completely clear, however, as in practice, most employees treat vouchers as part of their salary, albeit used to pay for a particular portion of fixed outgoings.

In the absence of any judicial guidance, the safest option is to continue to provide the vouchers even though the employee is receiving no salary from which deductions can be made. Where an employee only receives statutory maternity pay, the cost of providing this benefit could therefore be significant.

8.103 *Pensions*

The status of occupational pension schemes during maternity leave is now regulated by the *EqA 2010, s 75*. This was previously dealt with by the *Social Security Act 1989, Sch 5, para 5* ('*Schedule 5(5)*') which was repealed by the *EqA 2010*.

EqA 2010, s 75 largely replicates the previous position. It requires employers to maintain pension benefits during any period of ordinary maternity leave (whether paid or unpaid) and any period of additional maternity leave when the employee is being paid (whether SMP or otherwise). In a defined contribution scheme, the employer's contribution must be calculated in the same way as if the woman was at work whereas the woman can only be required to make contributions based on the amount of pay she is actually receiving. In a defined benefit scheme, the woman will be entitled to accrue rights in a scheme as if she were paid her usual salary, but she will only be required to make contributions based on her actual pay. The scheme meets the balance of the cost.

The *MPL Regulations* are designed to reflect this position by providing that the obligation in *reg 9* for employers to continue an employee's terms and conditions of employment (with the exception of payments by way of wages and salary) does not require employers to go further than as outlined above as regards pension benefits. However, the *MPL Regulations* have not yet been updated and still refer to the now repealed *Sch 5(5)*. It is nevertheless likely that an employment tribunal would interpret the Regulations as now referring to *s 75*.

Schedule 5(5) was wider than *EqA 2010, s 75* as it applied to 'employment-related benefits' which included 'benefits, in the form of pensions or otherwise, payable in money or money's worth in respect of: (i) termination of service; (ii) retirement, old age or death; (iii) interruptions of service by reason of sickness or invalidity; (iv) accidents, injuries or diseases connected with employment; (v) unemployment; or (vi) expenses . . . in connection with children or dependants . . . '. *Section 75* clearly only applies to membership, accrual of rights and entitlement to benefits under an occupational pension scheme as defined in *Pension Schemes Act 1993, s 1*.

Contributions to personal pension schemes are not covered by *EqA 2010, s 75* and current government guidance in the form of the BIS publication 'Pregnancy and Work; What You Need to Know as an Employer' simply does not deal with personal pension contributions. At the time the maternity regime was changed as a result of the ECJ decision in *Land Brandenburg v Sass: C-284/02* [2005] IRLR 147 and the High Court decision in *Equal Opportunities Commission v Secretary of State for Trade and Industry* (see **8.98**), the government indicated in the relevant explanatory memorandum that the abolition of the distinction between OML and AML did not affect the position in relation to pensions. It is arguable however that personal pension contributions should not be categorised as payments by way of wages and salary under the *MPL Regulations* and so (subject to the uncertainty posed by the yet to be updated *reg 9* as noted above) should be continued during both OML and AML.

8.104 Keeping in touch days and reasonable contact

KIT days

An employee can agree to work for her employer during her period of maternity (or adoption) leave on 'keeping in touch days' ('KIT days') without that work bringing the period of leave to an end and without losing entitlement to SMP (*MPL Regulations, reg 12A(1)* and *Statutory Maternity Pay (General) Regulations 1986 (SI 1986/1960), reg 9A*). A maximum of ten days' or part-days' work for the employer during the leave period is permitted without impacting upon maternity entitlements (work done on any day counts as a whole KIT day; in other words, if an employee works one hour a day on ten days that would exhaust the ten KIT days in the same way as working eight hours a day on ten different days) (*MPL Regulations, reg 12A(2)*). This applies to all periods of maternity leave with the exception of the two-week compulsory leave period (*MPL Regulations, reg 12A(5)*) when she is prohibited from working. Any work carried out as a result of these provisions shall not have the effect of extending the total duration of the statutory maternity (or adoption) leave period (*reg 12A(7)*).

During consultation on the new KIT day provisions, activities such as training, attendance at conferences, appraisals and team meetings were suggested as occasions where employees and employers may wish to take advantage of the KIT days.

KIT days may be taken either as a single block or separately. This will be a matter for agreement between employer and employee. Neither can be forced to allow or take a KIT day (*reg 12A(6)*). The employee is protected from dismissal or detriment because she undertook, considered undertaking or refused to undertake work in respect of a KIT day (*regs 19(2)(eee)* and *20(3)(eee)*).

The legislation does not specify whether KIT days should be paid and the government guidance suggested that it was a matter to be agreed between employer and employee. However, there may be National Minimum Wage issues if an employee agrees to work for nothing on a KIT day, or for a very low amount. If she has received little or no pay in the National Minimum Wage reference period (usually the preceding month), then that would be a breach of National Minimum Wage legislation. In addition, it will be discriminatory not to provide pay for a KIT day.

The same analysis applies to benefits; a failure to provide benefits to a woman on a KIT day would amount to unlawful discrimination, although in practice the administrative burden of stopping and re-starting pension contributions and other benefits may outweigh the cost of any successful claims for not providing these benefits.

Although it has not been addressed in legislation or case law, the authors believe that maternity pay paid to the employee should be offset against pay which she may be entitled to for a KIT day: in other words, the employer must 'top up' maternity pay for a KIT day, not pay both normal pay and maternity pay.

8.105 *Reasonable contact*

In addition to KIT days, 'reasonable contact from time to time' between employer and employee during both maternity and adoption leave is permitted (*MPL Regulations, reg 12A(4)*).

This was not a change to the law per se—such contact was almost certainly permitted prior to *MPL Regulations, reg 12A(4)*—but it is a useful clarification of the law.

According to the government, this is designed to enhance communication and may include, for example, discussing plans regarding a return to work or keeping an employee updated with developments. DBERR (now BIS) has advised that the frequency and nature of 'reasonable contact' will depend on a number of factors, such as the nature of the work and the employee's post, any agreement that the employer and employee might have reached before maternity leave began as to contact, and whether either party needs to communicate important information to the other, for example news of changes at the workplace that might affect the employee on her return. We believe that this approach is likely to be adopted by tribunals; what is reasonable will vary between employees, and depending on what is happening at the workplace at any given time.

If an employer does not keep an employee on maternity leave up to date on important matters in the workplace such as vacancies and restructurings, there is a high risk of a successful claim for pregnancy/maternity discrimination and/or pregnancy detriment (eg *Visa International v Paul*).

8.106 Return to work

Return after maternity or parental leave

An employee who returns to work after a period of OML only, or parental leave of four weeks or less, is entitled to return to the 'job in which she was employed before her absence'. An employee who returns to work after a period of AML or parental leave of more than four weeks is entitled to return to the 'job in which she was employed before her absence, or if it is not reasonably practicable for the employer to permit her to return to that job, to another job which is both suitable for her and appropriate for her to do in the circumstances' (*MPL Regulations, reg 18*). The job 'before her absence' is defined as that she was doing immediately before the leave (or before the first period of consecutive periods of statutory leave) (*reg 18(3)*).

Upon return, the employee is entitled to seniority, pension and similar rights as if she had not been absent, but effectively excluding any period of AML (subject to the equal treatment provisions of the *EqA 2010, s* 75) and on terms and conditions (under the wider *ERA 1996, s 71* definition, ie including non-contractual items) no less favourable than if she had not been absent (*reg 18A*).

The practical question is what 'job' she returns to. 'Job' is defined as 'the nature of the work which she is employed to do in accordance with her contract and the capacity and place in which she is so employed' (*reg 1*). The only appellate decision on the meaning of this is *Blundell v Governing Body of St Andrews Roman Catholic Primary School* [2007] IRLR 652. It is a question of fact for the tribunal, but in *Blundell* the teacher's job was held to be that of a teacher at the school generally and not that of the particular reception class she taught before she went on maternity leave, although the background to this was that the school reserved the right to—and frequently did—change the classes which teachers taught.

A refusal to allow an employee to return because her replacement is more efficient or preferable has been found to be direct sex discrimination (*Rees v Apollo Watch Repairs plc* [1996] ICR 466) (and may now also be caught by *EqA 2010, s 18(5)*). Even though the employee is not at work, the employer's conduct (or indications of actions at the time the employee returns) can constitute a constructive dismissal through anticipatory repudiation (*Nelson v Kingston Cables Distributors Ltd* [2000] All ER (D) 606).

8.107 *Temporary workers: right to return*

The definition of 'employee' contained in the *MPL Regulations* limits the rights afforded by the *MPL Regulations* (including the right to return to work following maternity leave) to 'an individual who has entered into or works under . . . a contract of employment'. This definition operates to exclude temporary workers. However, *EqA 2010, s 83* contains a broader definition of individuals protected from discrimination (see **1.16**). Under *s 83(2)(a)*, employment means 'employment under a contract of employment, a contract of apprenticeship or a contract personally to do work', and related expressions (such as 'employee') are to be construed accordingly. Therefore, although the *MPL Regulations* do not afford temporary workers the right to return to work following a period of maternity leave, a failure to allow them to do so may be a breach of *EqA 2010, s 18*.

The protection contained in *s 18* against discrimination on the grounds of pregnancy or maternity leave is extended to contract (agency) workers by virtue of *s 41*, which affords protection to individuals doing 'work for a principal where the individual is employed by another person, and supplied by that other person in furtherance of a contract to which the principal is a party' (see further **1.17**).

The effect is that an employee 'employed' (within the meaning of *EqA 2010*) by an agency is protected against sex discrimination by both the agency itself, and the 'principal' (ie end-user) to whom the services are provided.

It has previously been held that an agency worker may be entitled to return to her original position after a period of maternity leave (*BP Chemicals Ltd v Gillick and Roevin Management Services Ltd* [1995] IRLR 128 and Patefield v Belfast City Council [2000] IRLR 664, a decision of the Northern Irish Court of Appeal); note that these cases were decided prior to the introduction of *SDA 1975, s 3A* (now *EqA 2010, s 18*) (and the equivalent legislation in Northern Ireland) and were therefore based on general principles of sex discrimination. As a result of the fact that both Ms Gillick and Ms Patefield were engaged through agencies, the *Gillick* decision was made in reliance on *SDA 1975, s 9* (and in *Patefield*, the equivalent legislation, being *Article 12* of the *Sex Discrimination (Northern Ireland) Order 1976*).

Although the *EqA 2010* may afford some temporary workers a right to return following a period of maternity leave, it cannot be assumed that *all* temporary workers will possess such a right. First, *s 41* only applies to contract workers that are employed (using the *EqA 2010* definition which, as explained, goes beyond employment in the strict legal sense; see above and **1.16**) by a person other than the end-user organisation that they are working for. There are some categories of worker, such as where there is a right of substitution, which may not be caught by *s 41* or the definition of employee. Second, even if a temporary worker falls within the ambit of *EqA 2010*, in order to claim a right to return to her old position, a worker must demonstrate that were it not for her pregnancy, she would have continued to work for the end-user. In *Patefield*, for example, at the time of commencing her maternity leave, Ms Patefield had three years' service, and was the longest serving member of staff in her office. This enabled the Court of Appeal to conclude that she would have remained in her post were it not for her taking maternity leave. This may not always be the case, for example in circumstances where the employee has a shorter length of service and/or the end-user is able to demonstrate that she would not have been retained in her role regardless of her pregnancy.

Section 18 also affords temporary workers who fall within the *EqA 2010* definition of 'employee' or 'contract worker' the right not to be discriminated against on grounds of pregnancy during the recruitment process, even where the role for which they are applying is for a fixed-term, to cover a period of maternity leave being taken by an existing employee.

8.108 Pregnancy or maternity-related dismissals

A woman who is dismissed because of pregnancy, childbirth or maternity leave may be able to bring a claim of discrimination under *EqA 2010, s 18* and of automatic unfair dismissal (*ERA 1996, s 99* and *MPL Regulations, reg 20*). However, *EqA 2010, s 18(7)* operates to exclude direct sex discrimination claims where a woman falls under the pregnancy and maternity provisions (see **8.55**ff).

8.109 Remedy

For a general discussion on remedies available in discrimination cases, see **1.172** ff. The approach taken to assessing the remedy for sex discrimination is the same as that taken in relation to other types of discrimination.

Some specific issues have been raised, particularly in circumstances when a pregnant employee is dismissed in a discriminatory manner, and the employment tribunal must assess the losses which flow from this. One such question is whether, had the employee not been unlawfully dismissed, she would have returned to work following her maternity leave, and, if so, for how long she would have continued to have been employed by the same employer. The key cases on this point appear to place a burden on the woman to demonstrate that she would have returned to work, and also encourage the use of statistics to assess the chances that she would have done so. These cases are now over ten years old and it may be that tribunals would now apply the usual principles relevant to the determination of compensation for discrimination without giving special consideration as to the likelihood of a female employee returning to the workplace after a period of maternity leave (unless the particular facts of the case meant that this was in issue). An analysis of these cases is set out below in any event.

According to *Ministry of Defence v Cannock* [1995] 2 All ER 449, [1994] ICR 918, the questions which the tribunal must ask itself in assessing a pregnant employee's loss of earnings suffered as a result of being unlawfully dismissed are:

(a) What are the chances that, had she been given maternity leave and an opportunity to return to work, the employee would have returned?

(b) What are the chances that the woman would have been in a position to return to work, had she been given the opportunity?

(c) How long would she have remained employed by the employer for?

The EAT made it clear that a determination of these matters involves an assessment of chance, rather than fact. Usually, there will be different percentage chances at each of these stages. For example, there may be an 80% chance that the employee would have returned to work, had she been given the opportunity, but only a 60% chance that she would have worked until retirement (or some relevant earlier date, such as the end date of a fixed-term contract). The tribunal would then calculate her earnings until retirement (or the relevant date), deduct any amount actually earned (or to be earned) by the employee through alternative employment, then multiply this figure by 80%, and then multiply the resulting figure by 60% (see *Ministry of Defence v Hunt* [1996] IRLR 139).

The starting point in the MOD cases were the statistics showing the percentage of servicewomen who, given the option, return to work after childbirth. What actually happened after the woman gave birth is also relevant. For example, a woman who has made little or no effort to find suitable employment with another employer will struggle to show that there was a high percentage chance that she would have returned to work following maternity leave, had she not been dismissed. The question of searching for alternative employment will also be relevant to the employee's obligation to mitigate loss (see below and **1.172** ff for further detail on this).

In determining whether the woman would have been in a position to return to work, the tribunal will consider the demands placed on her by the job in question, as well as what the woman (and her partner, where relevant) actually did after the child was born. In *Cannock*, the point was made that if the woman's partner was also in the armed services and the couple had decided to remain together as a unit, the tribunal would have to consider the chances of him or her giving up work in order for them to remain together. If the chances were that she would have given up her work, the award would be reduced accordingly.

According to *Cannock*, the starting point for the third question of for how long the woman would have remained employed would again be statistics demonstrating how long, on average, employees would be likely to remain employed by the same employer in the industry in question. Having said this, a claimant is likely to argue that, regardless of these statistics, there is a good chance that she would have been employed by the same employer up until retirement, or some earlier relevant date. *Vento v Chief Constable of West Yorkshire Police (No 2)* [2002] IRLR 177, EAT provides an example of this argument succeeding. The respondent employer will likely suggest that intervening events subsequent to the employee's dismissal mean that the employee would not have remained employed until that date. For example, in *Brash-Hall v Getty Images Ltd* [2006] EWCA Civ 531, [2006] All ER (D) 111 (May), it was held that although Mrs Brash-Hall would have returned to work had she not been unlawfully dismissed, her employment would have terminated shortly after her return, owing to a restructuring exercise which meant her role would have been redundant. On this basis, the Court of Appeal held that she was only entitled to recover her losses up until the date of the restructuring.

Similarly, a tribunal may find that an employee would only have remained employed by her original employer for a limited period before resigning to take up another job. In *Fletcher-Cooke v Board of Governors of Hampton School* [2007] WL 504753 (a disability discrimination case), the EAT upheld such a finding. In doing so, it referred to the fact that the employee in question had a history of short periods of employment, and the fact that, at the time of her dismissal, the employee was already looking for alternative employment. In most cases, such evidence of a probable/actual intervening event such as this will exist to refute a claimant's suggestion that had she not been dismissed, she would have remained employed by the same employer until retirement. The exceptions to this, such as in *Vento* and the Ministry of Defence cases (in which the relevant date was not retirement, but the expiry of the term of engagement) appear to occur in occupations where employees often expect to have a 'job for life' and are therefore able to argue that, had they not been unlawfully dismissed, their jobs would have remained in existence and that they would not have left to take up an alternative position. Even in these cases, the tribunal will still have to assess the percentage chance that the employee would have worked until retirement (in *Vento*, this was assessed at 75%).

Notwithstanding that the test is one of probabilities rather than a determination of the facts, a tribunal may conclude that there was a 100% chance that had she been given the opportunity, a woman would have returned to work following maternity leave and, in 'exceptional and unusual' circumstances, that she would have remained employed for an extended period. In *Hunt*, it was held that there was a 100% chance that the claimant would have remained employed for sixteen years were it not for her employment having been terminated unlawfully. The factors which justified such a conclusion included Mrs Hunt's achievements during her employment, the fact that her mother had also always worked outside the home and was regarded as a role model by Mrs Hunt, and the fact that

Mrs Hunt had previously had an abortion in order to continue working for her employer. The EAT emphasised in this case that statistics as to the probability of women returning to work had their limitations and should be used as a starting point only. Despite its assertions to the contrary, it would appear that the EAT was actually making a finding of fact that, based on her personal circumstances, Mrs Hunt would have returned to work. Therefore, although the EAT claimed to be following the decision in *Cannock*, *Hunt* may indicate a move away from an objective assessment of a woman's percentage chances of returning to work (which, arguably, is based on discriminatory stereotypes) and towards a finding based on the facts of the case.

A tribunal will also consider the extent to which an employee has attempted to mitigate her loss by seeking alternative employment. In *Hunt*, it was said that the tribunal was entitled to consider the difficulties in finding employment encountered by women with young children, which arose out of 'gender-based assumptions' made by employers at the time. See **1.172** ff for further detail on the duty to mitigate.

It is also noteworthy that once a tribunal has assessed the likelihood of a woman returning to work, and the period for which she would have remained employed by the employer in question, it will deduct childcare costs from the compensation payable, on the basis that had the woman remained employed, she would have had to pay these. The fact that a woman's partner would have paid for half of these costs is not relevant for these purposes (*Ministry of Defence v Cannock*).

8.110 OTHER FAMILY RIGHTS

Adoption leave

Entitlement to adoption leave

The entitlement to adoption leave generally mirrors the entitlement to maternity leave. For discussion in relation to bonuses, annual leave and the applicability of terms and conditions during a period of leave, see **8.98** ff.

Under the *Paternity and Adoption Leave Regulations 2002 (SI 2002/2788)* ('*PAL Regulations*'), an employee is entitled to adoption leave in respect of a child if he:

(a) is the child's adopter (ie has been matched with the child for adoption by a UK adoption agency);

(b) has notified the agency that he has agreed that the child should be placed with him and agreed the date of placement;

(c) has been continuously employed by the same employer for at least 26 weeks ending with the week in which he is notified of having been matched with the child; and

(d) has notified the employer of when the employee would like to take his adoption leave, no more than seven days after he was notified that he has been matched with a child.

An employer may request that the employee provides evidence of the adoption by way of a document issued by the agency matching the employee with the child, the name and address of the agency, the date on which the employee was notified he had been matched with the child and the date on which the agency expects to place the child.

Ordinary adoption leave (OAL) may commence on the date of placement or on an alternative date which is no earlier than 14 days prior to the date of placement, provided this has been notified to the employer.

An employee may take 52 weeks of adoption leave, comprising 26 weeks of OAL followed by 26 weeks of additional adoption leave (AAL). The leave period is the same regardless of the number of children placed as part of the same arrangement.

As with AML, an employee who wishes to return to work earlier than the end of his AAL must give at least eight weeks' notice of the date he intends to return. Employees on adoption leave are also entitled to up to ten 'keeping in touch' days whereby the employee may attend work by agreement with his employer—these mirror the entitlement on maternity leave, on which see **8.104**.

The *PAL Regulations, regs 19–27* set out terms relating to the right to return from adoption leave and the application of terms and conditions during OAL and AAL. These mirror the provisions relating to employees on maternity leave and, like the provisions relating to maternity leave, they were amended by the *Maternity and Parental Leave etc and the Paternity and Adoption Leave (Amendment) Regulations 2008 (SI 2008/1966)* so as to abolish the distinction between OAL and AAL in respect of the application of terms and conditions. Employees retain their entitlement to statutory annual leave throughout OAL and AAL. If the employee is also entitled to contractual annual leave, this will also now accrue during both OAL and AAL.

8.111 *Adoption pay*

To qualify for statutory adoption pay (SAP) an employee must:

(a) be an 'employed earner' (ie someone who is liable to pay the employee's share of their Class 1 National Insurance Contributions, such as agency workers, as detailed in the *Social Security (Categorisation of Earners) Regulations 1978 (SI 1978/1689)*);

(b) earn at least the lower earnings limit;

(c) have been matched with a child to be placed with him by a UK adoption agency;

(d) have notified the agency that he agrees that the child should be placed with him and agree on a date of placement;

(e) have been in employed earner's employment with the same employer continuously for at least 26 weeks ending with the week in which he is notified of having been matched with the child;

(f) notify the employer of when he wants to receive SAP at least 28 days before the date he wants it to begin or as soon as reasonably practicable.

(*Social Security Contributions and Benefits Act 1992, s 171ZL*; *Statutory Paternity Pay and Adoption Pay (General) Regulations 2002 (SI 2002/2822) ('SPP Regulations'), regs 23–24*).

If an employee meets these qualifying conditions, he is entitled to 39 weeks' SAP, which is paid by employers and mostly or completely refunded by the government. Where one partner takes adoption leave and pay, the other may take paternity leave and pay (*PAL Regulations*, *reg 8* and *SPP Regulations*, *reg 11*); see further at **8.115** ff.

The right to adoption leave and SAP only arises where a new child is adopted into the family. It does not cover instances where a step-parent or foster carer adopts a child already under their care. The guidance from DBERR (now BIS) states that where foster carers are fostering a child that has not been matched and placed with them for adoption by an adoption agency, but they have applied to the court for an adoption order to be made, they will not be eligible for statutory adoption leave or pay. This is because adoption leave is intended to support the care of a child during the initial stages of the placement. Adoption leave and pay is similarly not available to special guardians, although they may take parental leave. A person becomes a special guardian when a court makes a special guardianship order (SGO). This gives them parental responsibility for the child to the exclusion of others, such as the birth parents. Unlike adoption, however, under a SGO, the parents remain the child's parents and retain parental responsibility, although their ability to exercise this responsibility is extremely limited.

Even where adoptive parents or special guardians do not qualify for adoption leave or pay, they may be entitled to parental leave because they will have 'parental responsibility' when they adopt. 'Parental responsibility' is defined in the *MPL Regulations, reg 2* and the *Children Act 1989, s 3*, as the rights, duties, powers, responsibilities and authority which, by law, a parent of a child has in relation to the child and his property.

8.112 *Protection from unfair dismissal/detriment*

The *PAL Regulations, regs 28* and *29* provide that an employee may not be subjected to any detriment or dismissed by reason of their taking adoption leave or seeking to take such leave. A dismissal is therefore automatically unfair if it is by reason of the employee's taking or seeking to take adoption leave.

The employment tribunal case of *Anna Coulombeau v Enterprise Rent-A-Car (UK) Ltd* ET 2600296/06 (19 February 2007, unreported) is one of the few cases concerning adoption leave. In this case, an employee brought a claim against her employer on various grounds, including automatic unfair dismissal, namely the reason or principal reason for her dismissal was connected with the fact she took, or sought to take, or the employer believed it was likely she would take, adoption leave. The tribunal explained that the burden of proof required Ms Coulombeau to produce evidence to create a presumption of law that the dismissal was for an inadmissible reason under *ERA 1996, s 99*. The respondent then had to show the real reason for the dismissal was by reason of the claimant's conduct.

Ms Coulombeau had learned she would not be able to bear children and undertook various meetings with social workers to gain approval for eligibility to adopt. The claimant was subsequently subject to disciplinary investigations regarding three separate allegations of misconduct. These matters were investigated and the claimant was subsequently dismissed. The tribunal established that the investigations were inadequate and the dismissal unfair. It considered the reason for the dismissal by looking simultaneously at the issues of sex discrimination and adoption leave. The two male comparators put forward by the claimant had committed the same or more serious offences but were only given written warnings. The tribunal held that there was clear evidence of less favourable treatment of women in comparison with men as, on the balance of probabilities, a man would not have been dismissed for similar offences. They found that the reason for the dismissal was that the respondent considered that, as a woman, the claimant would be likely to need time off for adoption purposes including, ultimately, adoption leave.

8.113 *Disrupted placement*

A period of adoption leave may be disrupted if the child dies or is returned to the agency, or if the employee is simply notified that the placement will not go ahead. In such circumstances, the adoption leave comes to an end eight weeks after the end of the relevant week. The relevant week is the week the employee is notified that the placement will not be made or the week the child dies or is returned to the agency. Where the employee's period of OAL comes to an end within those eight weeks, the employee may take the unexpired remainder of the eight weeks as AAL. However, where the employee's period of AAL comes to an end within those eight weeks, the employee must return to work at the end of the AAL as the eight weeks will not extend AAL beyond the date it would originally have expired.

8.114 *Overseas adoption*

The entitlement for employees who are adopting a child from outside the UK is essentially the same as for UK adoptions, save for some minor differences in relation to eligibility criteria, notice and evidential requirements and when leave and pay may begin. The relevant provisions are included in the *Paternity and Adoption Leave (Adoption from Overseas) Regulations 2003 (SI 2003/921)*, *Statutory Paternity Pay (Adoption) and Statutory Adoption Pay (Adoptions from Overseas) (No 2) Regulation 2003 (SI 2003/1194)* and *Social Security Contributions and Benefits Act 1992 (Application of Parts 12ZA and 12ZB to Adoptions from Overseas) Regulations 2003 (SI 2003/499)*.

Rather than receiving a notification of matching, for overseas adoptions, the employee will receive an 'official notification'. The service requirement for adoption pay is 26 weeks ending with the week in which the adopter is notified of the match for UK adoptions, whereas, for overseas adoptions, the period is 26 weeks either ending with the week in which the notification was received, or from the start of their employment.

For the purposes of assessing and calculating eligibility to adoption leave and SAP, the relevant date in overseas adoptions is the date of the child's entry into Great Britain, or a fixed date no later than 28 days after entry. This contrasts with UK adoptions where the critical date when an employee can commence adoption leave and receive SAP is on or up to 14 days prior to the date of the placement. There are additional notification requirements in overseas adoptions, which require the employee to give his employer notice of the date he received an official notification, the date the child is expected to enter Great Britain, the date his adoption leave should begin and the actual date the child enters Great Britain.

8.115 Paternity leave

The entitlement to two weeks' ordinary paternity leave ('OPL') was introduced by the *Employment Act 2002* which sets out the basic rights and amends *ERA 1996* and the *Social Security Contributions and Benefits Act 1992*. The detail of this entitlement is in the *PAL Regulations* and the *SPP Regulations*.

In March 2010 the *Additional Paternity Leave Regulations 2010 (SI 2010/1055)* were passed, creating a new right for employees to take up to 26 weeks of additional paternity leave ('APL') by 'swapping' it for any unused part of the mother's maternity leave. The right to take APL applies in respect of babies whose EWC is on or after 3 April 2011.

The right to OPL and APL also applies, in substantially the same terms, to the partners of persons taking adoption leave, where the adopted child is matched with an adopter on or after 3 April 2011. For ease of comprehension, and in view of the comparative rarity of adoption leave, we will refer in this section only to a person taking OPL or APL following natural childbirth, but it can be assumed that the same broad principles apply to the partner of a person taking adoption leave unless expressly stated otherwise. In a similar vein, for ease of reading we refer as appropriate to the 'father' and 'mother' of the child, but note that the relevant rights extend to, for example, the female partner of a male employee taking adoption leave, to the same-sex partner of an individual giving birth or taking adoption leave, or to an individual who is not the father of the child being adopted but is the partner of (or married to/the civil partner of) the mother and expects to have primary responsibility for the care of the child.

8.116 *Entitlement to ordinary paternity leave*

An employee is entitled to OPL if he or she will be caring for a child or supporting the child's mother. These concepts are not defined and there are no reported cases concerning them. This right is available to employees who have 26 weeks' continuous service ending with the 15th week before the EWC or ending with the week in which the adopter is notified of having been matched with the child. The employee must also be either the father of the child or married to, or the civil partner or partner of, the child's mother or adopter, and he or she must have or expect to have responsibility for the upbringing of the child.

The employee must give his or her employer notice of intention to take OPL in or before the 15th week before the EWC specifying the expected week of birth, the length of leave and the date when the employee expects the leave will begin. An employer is entitled to request the employee provides a signed declaration confirming the purpose of the absence and stating that he or she satisfies the conditions of entitlement. Where an employee is the husband, partner or civil partner of the child's adopter, he or she will be entitled to OPL provided he gives notice within seven days of receiving notification of the match, giving the date the adopter was notified of a match and the expected date of placement.

8.117 *Length of leave*

An employee may take either one week's leave or two consecutive weeks' leave and this leave must be taken within 56 days of the child's birth or placement. During OPL, an employee is entitled to the benefit of all of his terms and conditions of employment, including the accrual of holiday, but with the exception of remuneration. The employee is similarly bound by his obligations under those terms and conditions.

At the end of the period of OPL, the employee is entitled to return to the same job in which he was employed prior to the leave. However, if the paternity leave was not an isolated period of absence and followed another period of statutory leave, namely parental leave of more than four weeks or additional maternity or adoption leave, then the employee's right to return is to the same job or, if that is not reasonably practicable, to a similar job which is suitable and appropriate in the circumstances.

8.118 *Entitlement to additional paternity leave*

The basic eligibility requirements for APL (service, and relationship to the child) are the same as for OPL (see **8.116**). However, importantly, the child's mother must also return to work after her maternity leave, although she does not have to do so at exactly the same time as APL commences. Alternatively, an employee also qualifies for APL if the mother ceases to be entitled to maternity allowance or SMP, thus allowing employees to take APL if (for example) the mother falls below the threshold at which SMP is payable, or loses her job while on maternity leave.

The leave may be taken at any time within the period which begins 20 weeks after the date on which the child is born, and ends 12 months after that date. The minimum period of leave that may be taken is two weeks, and the maximum period 26 weeks. The leave must be taken in a single block.

An employee wishing to take APL must comply with certain notification requirements. These are that, not less than eight weeks before the date the employee wishes the leave to start, he must provide his employer with:

(a) a 'leave notice', specifying the EWC, the actual date of birth, and the period the employee has chosen as the start and end dates for the leave;

(b) an 'employee declaration' stating that the purpose of the leave is to care for the child, that the employee is the father or is married to or is the partner or civil partner of the mother, and has or expects to have the main responsibility (apart from the mother) for the upbringing of the child; and

(c) a 'mother declaration' signed by the mother and stating her name and address, the date she intends to work, her National Insurance number, that the employee claiming APL is the father or is married to or is the partner or civil partner of the mother, and has or expects to have the main responsibility (apart from the mother) for the upbringing of the child. It must also state that the employee is the only person (to the mother's knowledge) exercising the entitlement to APL, and that the mother consents to the processing of her personal data as contained in the declaration.

The father's employer also has a right to ask for a copy of the child's birth certificate, and the name and address of the mother's employer (or, if she is self-employed, her business address). The employee must then provide this within 28 days. It is, however, left to the father's employer's discretion as to whether it runs checks with the mother's employer: there is no obligation to do so. Reasons for doing so include to confirm the veracity of the employee's claim, and also to be able to provide evidence to HMRC in the event of a challenge as to the validity of a claim for repayment of statutory paternity pay. There is though no legislative mechanism by which the mother's employer can be compelled to comply with a request, and any such employer would need to ensure that compliance did not involve any breach of its own data protection obligations towards the mother, for example by obtaining her consent to pass her data to the father's employer.

Withdrawal and variation of APL requests

8.119 The father may cancel his APL notice, or vary his start and end dates, by giving at least six weeks' notice or, if it is not reasonably practicable to do this, by giving notice as soon as is reasonably practicable. If the father fails to comply with these requirements, and it is not reasonably practicable for the employer to accommodate the change, the employer can require him to take a period of up to six weeks' APL in any event, starting on the start date most recently notified.

The father *must* withdraw his request for APL if he ceases to be married to or the civil partner of the mother when he is not the child's father, or ceases to have or expect to have the main responsibility apart from the mother for the upbringing of the child, or if the mother ceases to be entitled to maternity leave, SMP or maternity allowance, or does not return to work at the end of maternity leave. In such circumstances, the employer may again require the father to take up to six weeks' APL in any event if the withdrawal notice is submitted less than six weeks before the notified APL start date, or to remain on APL for up to a further six weeks if it has already started, and it is not reasonably practicable to accommodate the change in the employee's arrangements.

Once APL has begun, the father can also request to return to work early by giving six weeks' notice. If the father tries to return to work without complying with this obligation, the employer can postpone his return until such time as six weeks' notice have been given, and is under no obligation to pay him in the meantime.

Employer's notice

8.120 The father's employer is required to confirm the start and end dates of the father's APL to him in writing within 28 days of receiving the leave notice, or within 28 days of receiving any subsequent notice of variation. The employer must also notify the employee as soon as reasonably practicable of any requirement to take APL where the employee has varied or cancelled their leave notice in the circumstances described above, or in any event before the start of the leave.

Death of mother

8.121 *Regulations 10–13* of the *Additional Paternity Leave Regulations* contain specific provisions which apply in the event of the mother's death during the twelve-month period beginning with the date of the child's birth. The father can take from two weeks to 52 weeks of APL at any time within the period beginning with the date of death and ending on the child's first birthday. If, however, the father has already taken a period of APL at the time of the mother's death, he is not entitled to a further period. If APL has started but not ended at the time of death, he can extend the leave provided that it does not exceed 52 weeks in total or end after the child's first birthday.

Slightly varied notification requirements apply to leave in these circumstances, including in particular a requirement to notify the father's employer as soon as reasonably practicable after the mother's death. There are also provisions relating to the variation or cancellation of leave which are similar to those which apply to APL in other circumstances.

KIT days

8.122 Employees taking APL are entitled to take up to ten 'keeping in touch' or KIT days. These operate in the same way as KIT days during maternity leave: see **8.104** above.

8.123 *Statutory paternity pay and additional statutory paternity pay*

Statutory paternity pay

Statutory paternity pay (SPP) is available in respect of the (maximum) two week OPL period to employees who meet the following conditions: 26 weeks' continuous service with their employer ending with the end of the 15th week before the EWC or ending with the week in which the adopter is notified of having been matched with the child, and continuous service from that week up to the child's birth or placement; a defined relationship with the child and mother; has given appropriate notification (of the EWC, the date from which SPP will be payable and the duration of the period during which it will be payable); and whose average weekly earnings are equal to or above the lower earnings limit.

Employees who satisfy these qualifying conditions are entitled to the lesser of £128.73 or 90% of the employee's average weekly earnings (from 3 April 2011). The flat rate is typically increased by Regulation in April of each year.

Additional statutory paternity pay

8.124 Under amendments made in 2010 to the *Social Security Contributions and Benefits Act 1992*, and the related *Additional Statutory Paternity (General) Pay Regulations 2010 (SI 2010/1056)*, employees taking APL who meet certain qualifying requirements are entitled to additional statutory paternity pay (ASPP). The basic service requirements are the same as for SPP. In addition the mother must be entitled to SMP or maternity allowance, and have returned to work with at least two weeks of her SMP or maternity allowance remaining unexpired.

From 3 April 2011, employees who satisfy these qualifying conditions are entitled to the lesser of £128.73 or 90% of the employee's average weekly earnings for a period which:

(a) begins on the date on which the mother returns to work, as long as this is no earlier than 20 weeks after the child's date of birth; and

(b) ends no later than the date on which the mother's SMP or maternity allowance period would have ended, had she returned to work.

Slightly different provisions apply in circumstances where the mother dies, in which event a maximum of 26 weeks' ASPP can be claimed, ending no later than the first anniversary of the child's birth.

Employees wishing to claim ASPP must also meet certain notification requirements which are broadly the same as those for APL, save that the employee must also provide details of the date on which they expect the employer's ASPP liability to start and end, and the mother's declaration must specify the start date of her SMP/maternity allowance period, and confirm that the employee claiming ASPP is, to her knowledge, the sole applicant for ASPP in relation to the child. It is generally assumed that employees will use the same standard notification forms to meet both the APL and ASPP notification requirements.

Enhanced paternity pay, and possible discrimination issues

8.125 Some employers elect, at their discretion, to offer enhanced paternity pay for the two week OPL period. This typically involves simply carrying on paying the employee their salary as normal. It is, however, highly unlikely that a failure to provide enhanced pay for the OPL period amounts to sex discrimination, given the provisions of *EqA 2010, s 13(6)* and that ECJ case law emphasises the special protection of pregnant women (*Gillespie v Northern Health and Social Services Board* [1996] ECR I-475, [1996] All ER (EC) 284).

A much more interesting, and as yet unanswered, question is whether an employer is at risk of a successful sex discrimination claim from a man if it does not offer benefits equivalent to enhanced maternity pay in respect of (at least part of) a period of APL. Unlike OPL, APL, and the associated right to ASPP, can in many respects be seen as directly analogous to (part of) a period of maternity leave. For example:

(a) a father's right to APL is directly in place of a mother's right to (continued) maternity leave;

(b) a father has a right to ASPP which is of the same amount as SMP, and continues for as long as SMP would have continued had the mother stayed off work; and

(c) a father's right to return, to KIT days, and to protection in redundancy situations, is essentially the same as a mother's while on maternity leave.

There is therefore a strong prima facie argument that an employer which fails to offer enhanced paternity pay to a male employee in respect of a period in which a female employee would have received enhanced maternity pay is culpable of sex discrimination. Against this, the employer can point to *EqA 2010, s 13(6)* as affording it a defence on the basis that all it is doing when paying enhanced maternity pay is conferring on a woman 'special treatment . . . in connection with pregnancy or childbirth'. It is arguable, however, that 'special treatment' should properly be confined to such matters as the woman's right to extended time off work, protection from redundancy and rights on return, and right to benefit from pay reviews in her absence, and should not extend as far as a benefit which the employer at its discretion elects to confer (see further at **8.60**).

The argument for a more limited definition of 'special treatment' is supported by the European Court of Justice's decision in *Alvarez v Sesa Start Espana ETT SA: C-104/09* [2011] All ER (EC) 253, [2011] 1 CMLR 861. The ECJ held that a Spanish law which (insofar as is relevant) permitted women, but not men, to take up to an hour off work each day during the first nine months of their baby's life for the purpose of breastfeeding or bottlefeeding breached the *Equal Treatment Directive*. The claim was brought by a man who wished to bottlefeed. The law had been extended to bottlefeeding as well as breastfeeding in 2007, and the ECJ considered that in doing this the law had become detached from the biological fact of breastfeeding, taking it outside the scope of a measure ensuring the protection of a woman's biological condition following pregnancy (the equivalent of the 'special treatment' defence under the relevant directive). It also expressed concern that, by precluding men from taking the leave, the law actively risked perpetuating gender stereotypes by making men less likely to involve themselves with child care: the same could be said of not paying men for a period of APL which is analogous to a period of paid maternity leave. So while *Alvarez* is not directly on point, and may be capable of being distinguished, it has shifted the balance in employees' favour.

In practice, the consequences of this issue may be fairly limited. It seems likely that, at best, fathers could only claim enhanced paternity pay in respect of a period during which a mother, had she been working, would have received enhanced maternity pay, and not for the whole period of APL. Many—perhaps most—employers enhance maternity pay for a period of either 18 weeks (reflecting the 'old' law on maternity leave) or 26 weeks. The former group will not be impacted at all, and the latter group will only be required to pay enhanced paternity pay for a maximum of six weeks from the earliest date on which APL can start (20 weeks after the birth). Only the minority of employers who pay enhanced maternity pay for more than 26 weeks face a more significant (and costly) impact. Finally, and for the avoidance of doubt, it is generally assumed that any claim to enhanced paternity pay by the father would be to pay equivalent to the enhanced maternity pay offered by his employer, and that there would be no basis for claiming the pay offered by the mother's employer.

8.126 *Return to work, and protection from unfair dismissal/detriment*

OPL

An employee entitled to OPL is protected against detriment or dismissal as a result of taking or seeking to take OPL. A dismissal is automatically unfair if it is by reason of the employee's taking or seeking to take OPL and extends to selection for redundancy on grounds associated with the taking of OPL. Despite the 26 weeks' eligibility requirement, an employee can bring a claim on such grounds, regardless of their length of service.

APL

8.127 During APL, an employee is entitled to the benefit of all the terms and conditions of employment which would have applied had he not been absent, with the exception of terms and conditions about remuneration—exactly the same position as that which prevails during OML and AML. See **8.98** for discussion of the issues around this. He is also entitled, under *Additional Paternity Leave Regulations, reg 28*, to protection in redundancy situations which is the same as that afforded to women on maternity leave under *MPL Regulations, reg 10*, namely to the first call on any suitable alternative vacancies even if there are better qualified candidates: see **8.65** for further discussion.

Under *reg 31* of the *Additional Paternity Leave Regulations*, employees are entitled upon returning from a period of APL which does not exceed 26 weeks (plus other periods of statutory leave but not including AML or AAL or a period of parental leave of more than four weeks) to return to the same job in which they were employed before their absence. If the employee takes a period of APL which exceeds 26 weeks, for example, following the death of the mother, his right is to return to the same job or, if it is not reasonably practicable to permit this, to another job which is both suitable for him and appropriate for him to do in the circumstances. In other words, the right to return mirrors the right to return at the end of OML as long as APL does not exceed 26 weeks, and otherwise mirrors the right to return at the end of AML. The right is to return with the same 'seniority, pension rights and similar rights' as would have applied if the employee had not been absent, again, mirroring the position after maternity leave.

An employee is also entitled to protection against detriment or dismissal as a result of taking or seeking to take APL, and a dismissal is automatically unfair if it is by reason of the employee's taking or seeking to take APL. A redundancy dismissal will also be automatically unfair if the *reg 28* protection has not been applied.

8.128 **Parental leave**

Entitlement to parental leave

Employees who have at least one year's continuous employment, and have or expect to have responsibility for a child, are entitled to parental leave. An employee has responsibility for a child if he has parental responsibility or has been registered as the child's parent. This right was introduced by the *MPL Regulations* and is included at *ERA 1996, ss 76–80*. 'Parental responsibility' is defined in the *Children Act 1989, s 3*, as the rights, duties, powers, responsibilities and authority which, by law, a parent of a child has in relation to the child and his property.

Pursuant to *ERA 1996, s 78(7)* and the *MPL Regulations, reg 16*, parties may make their own agreements about how parental leave is to be taken within a particular workplace. This can be done by a collective agreement, workforce agreement, or individual agreement with the employee. Where no such agreement has been reached, the default provisions in *Sch 2* to the Regulations will apply. Where an employee has a contractual right to parental leave, he may not exercise both the statutory right and the contractual right but may take advantage of the more favourable of the two.

Employees may take up to 13 weeks' unpaid leave in respect of any individual child up until that child's fifth birthday or, in the case of an adopted child, the earlier of the fifth anniversary of the date of placement or the child's eighteenth birthday. Employees are entitled to 18 weeks' unpaid leave for a child who is entitled to a disability living allowance, up until the child's 18th birthday. This leave can be taken by both parents in relation to each child. As with the other family-friendly rights, one week's leave is calculated to be the amount an employee is normally required to work in a week and, where this is irregular, an average should be calculated using a 12-week reference period.

Under the default scheme, leave must be taken in multiples of one week. The only exception to this is in relation to children who are entitled to a disability living allowance, when parents can take parental leave in multiples of one day. In *New Southern Railways Ltd (formerly South Central Trains) v Rodway* [2005] EWCA Civ 443, [2005] ICR 1162, where an employer refused an employee's request to take one day's parental leave to look after his (non-disabled) son on the ground that his job could not be covered on that day, the employee went ahead and took the day off and was given a written warning for his unauthorised absence from work. The employee claimed that he had been subjected to a detriment for a reason relating to parental leave. The EAT and Court of Appeal, which allowed the employer's appeal, held that where no workplace agreement provides otherwise, the default position is that leave can only be taken in weekly blocks.

The employee must give his employer 21 days' notice, specifying the proposed dates of leave. The *MPL Regulations, Sch 2* sets out the conditions of entitlement and provides that an employer may request proof of an employee's entitlement to parental leave. Evidence of entitlement may include proof of the child's date of birth or placement for adoption, and evidence of a child's entitlement to a disability living allowance. An employer may also postpone the period of leave where the employer considers that the operation of the business would be unduly disrupted by that period of leave. Such a postponement is possible on condition that the employer allows the employee to take a period of leave of the same duration within the following six months and provides written notice to the employee of the reason for the postponement and the dates of the rescheduled leave. An employer may not postpone leave when the employee has requested to take it immediately after the birth or placement of a child.

The ECJ case of *Kiiski v Tempereen Kaupunki: C-116/06* [2007] All ER (D) 120 (Sep) is authority for the extent to which employers may be required to reschedule parental leave at the employee's request. In this case, which concerned an employee in Finland, the ECJ held that an employer's refusal to allow the employee to change the dates of her unpaid parental leave so as to enable her to take paid maternity leave constituted direct sex discrimination. The relevant collective agreement, which provided that a new pregnancy was not a good reason to change the dates of parental leave once agreed, was contrary to both the *Equal Treatment Directive* and the *Pregnant Workers Directive*.

During parental leave, an employee is entitled to the benefit of the implied term of trust and confidence and terms relating to notice, compensation and disciplinary and grievance procedures; she is also bound by terms relating to notice, confidential information, acceptance of gifts and participation in other businesses (see *Maternity and Parental Leave etc Regs 1999 (SI 1999/3312), reg 17*).

8.129 *Protection from unfair dismissal/detriment*

The *Rodway* case is also authority for the proposition that treatment by an employer is only victimisation it if is 'done for a prescribed reason'. In this case, the employee could not lawfully take one day of parental leave and therefore the disciplinary warning was not for a prescribed reason and was therefore not victimisation.

8.130 *Right to return to work*

Pursuant to the *MPL Regulations, reg 18*, where an employee has taken parental leave of four weeks or less and the leave is not taken immediately after a period of AML or AAL, he will be entitled to return to the same job. Otherwise, the employee's right to return is the same as after AML, being the same job unless it is not reasonably practicable, in which case he is entitled to another job which is suitable and appropriate in the circumstances.

8.131 **Time off for dependants**

Entitlement to time off for dependants

Pursuant to *ERA 1996, s 57A*, an employee is entitled to take a reasonable amount of time off in order to take action which is necessary for one of the following events:

(a) to provide assistance when a dependant falls ill, gives birth or is injured or assaulted;

(b) to make arrangements for the provision of care for a dependant who is ill or injured;

(c) in consequence of the death of a dependant;

(d) because of the unexpected disruption or termination of arrangements for the care of a dependant; or

(e) to deal with an incident which involves a child of the employee's and which occurs unexpectedly in a period during which an educational establishment which the child attends is responsible for him.

A 'dependant' is a spouse or civil partner, a child, parent or person who lives in the same household as the employee, other than by reason of being his employee, tenant, lodger or boarder. A dependant also includes any person who reasonably relies on the employee for assistance or to make arrangements for the provision of care.

In *Harrison v Royal Bank of Scotland plc* [2009] IRLR 28, the EAT indicated that the scope of the right to time off may be somewhat broader than had previously been thought. The case concerned an employee who was told on 8 December that her childminder would be unavailable on 22 December. She used all her contacts but by 12 December had failed to find a substitute. On 13 December, she informed her supervisor that she would take 22 December off. On 20 December RBS told her that they could not cover for her on the 22nd and that, if she took that day off, it would be treated as an unauthorised absence. She did, and was subsequently disciplined.

The tribunal found that the employee had been subjected to a detriment for taking time off, and the employer's appeal was dismissed. The EAT held that there was no warrant for inserting the words 'sudden and' or 'in emergency' alongside the requirement for an 'unexpected' disruption in *s 57A(1)(d)*. The passage of time between the employee's discovery of the need to make alternative arrangements and the taking of time off was dealt with by the requirement that the action be 'necessary' for the purposes specified in the section. The consequence of *Harrison* is that employees may be entitled to benefit from *s 57A* even where there is quite a lengthy delay between the unexpected event coming to their notice and the taking of the time off, although the longer the period, the more the employee can expect to be put to proof on whether the arrangements are 'necessary', for example by showing they have taken all steps possible to locate alternative cover.

Harrison considered and distinguished the earlier case of *Qua v John Ford Morrison Solicitors* [2003] IRLR 184, in which the EAT also gave guidance as to the scope of the right to time off. Ms Qua had been dismissed because of a high level of absences to look after her child. She claimed she had been unfairly dismissed for exercising her right to time off but this was dismissed by the tribunal on the basis that Ms Qua had failed to tell the employer the reason for and duration of her absences as soon as reasonably practicable.

The EAT held that the tribunal had erred in how it approached the duty to inform the employer and remitted the matter to the tribunal. The EAT also clarified the purpose and limitations of the right to time off. It explained that the right was to 'reasonable' time off to take action which is 'necessary', and explained that, in determining whether the action was necessary, the disruption and inconvenience to the employer are irrelevant. The factors to consider include the nature of the incident, the closeness of the relationship between employee and dependant, and the extent to which anyone else was available to assist.

The entitlement is conditional upon the employee telling the employer the reason and the expected duration for the absence. In *Truelove v Safeways Stores plc* [2005] ICR 589, the EAT held that there must be:

> 'a communication that imparted an understanding into the employer's mind that something had happened to cause the breakdown of what would otherwise be a stable arrangement affecting, in the present case, a child and making it necessary, urgently, for the employee to be absent from work.'

The EAT held that the employee telling his employer that he might need leave on the following day because his partner had to attend a meeting and he had to look after their young child was sufficient communication, even though the employee had not disclosed that there had been an unexpected disruption to the arrangements. This case is authority that when considering the reasonableness of an employee's request, an employer should consider how often it has happened before, whether or not there is another way of solving the problem, and the business needs of the employer.

The case of *Forster v Cartwright Black* [2004] ICR 1728 clarified that this provision does not cover the right to compassionate leave as a result of a bereavement, but rather is triggered by the need to take action which is necessary in consequence of the death, including registering the death and, where necessary, applying for probate. It appears, therefore, that the leave is for practical rather than emotional needs.

8.132 *Complaint to a tribunal*

ERA 1996, s 57B provides that an employee is entitled to make a complaint to the tribunal that his employer has unreasonably refused him the right to take time off, within three months of the refusal or such further period as the tribunal decides is reasonable. Where such a complaint is found to be well-founded, an employee is entitled to compensation which is just and equitable in the light of the employer's default in refusing to permit time off to be taken by the employees, and any loss sustained by the employee which is attributable to the matters complained of.

8.133 In vitro fertilisation (IVF)

The ECJ considered the position of women undergoing IVF treatment in *Mayr v Bäckerei und Konditorei Gerhard Flöckner OHG: C-506/06* [2008] IRLR 387. The case concerned an Austrian employee who was dismissed at a point in her treatment which was after ova had been collected from her and fertilised with her partner's sperm, but before the fertilised ova had been planted in her uterus. The ECJ held that the employee was not protected by the *Pregnant Workers Directive*, noting that fertilised ova could be kept for an indeterminate period—sometimes years—and it would therefore be inconsistent with the principle of legal certainty to apply the protection against dismissal afforded by that Directive to women in these circumstances. However, and crucially, the ECJ also found that, as certain medical treatment related to IVF, namely a follicular puncture immediately after fertilisation, only affected women, it would be direct discrimination on grounds of sex under the *Equal Treatment Directive* to dismiss a woman essentially based on the fact that she was absent from work undergoing this important stage of IVF treatment.

Mayr was followed domestically by the EAT in *Sahota v Home Office* (2009) UKEAT/342/09, [2010] ICR 772. *Sahota* involved an employee who was dismissed following a series of sickness absences, some (but not all) of which were for IVF treatment. The Home Office's sickness absence policy treated all absences the same for the purpose of determining whether certain triggers had been reached, at which point action would be taken. The employee argued that to compare a woman undergoing IVF with a man undergoing some other form of medical treatment amounted, following *Mayr*, to direct sex discrimination, because only women were affected by IVF.

The EAT disagreed. It held that *Mayr* should be interpreted narrowly, and that the ECJ had only intended to confer sex discrimination protection in relation to the important advanced stage of IVF between follicular puncture and the immediate transfer of the in vitro fertilised ova into the uterus, and not to the whole of IVF treatment including circumstances where ova were frozen with a view to implementation a number of years later.

Partly in response to *Mayr* and *Sahota*, it has become increasingly common for employers to put in place policies setting out the principles to be applied to absences for the purpose of undergoing IVF treatment. Typically, such a policy includes an agreement to a limited period of paid leave for IVF (such as one or two weeks), and a specification that any additional time must be taken as sick leave or annual leave. It also includes a limitation on the number of periods of such leave that can be taken, for example only one in any rolling 12-month period. The advantage of such a policy is that it reduces the risk of a claim of direct discrimination in relation to the period between follicular puncture and implantation into the uterus, which in most cases where eggs are not frozen will be quite limited, while helping to ensure consistency of treatment and capping the cost to employers of IVF absence. While there is no legal requirement for such a policy, and there is still scope for employers to take the position that absence for IVF should be taken under either a holiday or a sickness absence policy, there is a risk that an employer could fall foul of direct sex discrimination laws if, for example, it then disciplines an employee for sickness absence and that absence directly relates to the latter stages of IVF treatment (unlike in *Sahota*).

8.134 Surrogacy

Surrogacy is the practice whereby one woman carries a child for another with the intention that the child be handed over at birth to the intended parents and raised as their child. In a surrogacy situation, there may be up to four parties: the surrogate mother who is carrying the child and her husband or civil partner, as well as the woman who intends to take maternal responsibility for the child after birth, and her spouse or civil partner/partner who intends to take parental responsibility.

There are several ways surrogacy can occur, depending on whether the intended mother has donated an egg and also whether the sperm of the intended father is used.

If an embryo is created using gametes of two anonymous donors (ie from neither of the intended parents) this is not seen as surrogacy. Because neither of the intended parents would be genetically related to the child, they would have to adopt the child in any case.

8.135 *Taking responsibility for the child*

The surrogate mother is always treated in law as the mother of the child in the first instance, even if she is not genetically related to the child (*Human Fertilisation and Embryology Act 2008* ('*HFEA 2008*'), *s 33(1)*). Thereafter, the intended mother can take responsibility for the child by obtaining a parental order from the courts or by adopting the child. Adoption is necessary where the conditions for obtaining a parental order are not fulfilled.

Under *HFEA 2008, s 54* the conditions of obtaining a parental order are:

(a) the child is genetically related to at least one of the intended parents;

(b) the surrogate parents have consented to the making of the order (unless untraceable or incapable of giving consent), and in the case of the mother no earlier than six weeks after the birth of the child;

(c) the intended parents are aged 18 or over;

(d) the intended parents are married or civil partners or living as partners in an enduring family relationship;

(e) the intended parents apply for the Parental Order within six months of the birth of the child;

(f) no money, other than expenses, has been paid in respect of the surrogacy, unless authorised by a court;

(g) the child is living with the intended parents; and

(h) the intended parents are domiciled in a part of the United Kingdom or the Channel Islands or Isle of Man.

The default position is that the surrogate mother's husband or civil partner will be named on the birth certificate as the father/other parent (*HFEA 2008, ss 35, 42*). However, if the surrogate mother is unmarried, or if the surrogate mother's husband/civil partner states that he or she has not given permission for the surrogacy, then the intended father/other parent can be registered on the birth certificate as the father/other parent if certain preconditions are met (see *ss 36–37* and *42–43*). It will not then be necessary for the intended father/other parent to obtain a parental order or to adopt the child.

8.136 *Leave available for the intended parents*

There are various types of leave which surrogate parents may potentially, depending on the circumstances, be eligible for:

(a) *adoption leave.* The intended parents will not usually be eligible for adoption leave or pay, as they have not been matched with the child through an agency. It is unclear whether a Parental Order is equivalent to adoption for the purposes of adoption leave (and paternity leave, since this is available to the partner of the adopter). However, this will only be relevant where an adoption agency is used, an unlikely situation in surrogacy;

(b) *paternity leave.* In a surrogacy situation, the intended father/other parent may be entitled to paternity leave even where his or her partner does not qualify for adoption leave under *PAL Regulations, reg 2(a)(i)*, if he or she is the child's 'father'. This would seem to entitle the intended father/other parent who is genetically related to the child to paternity leave, whether or not he is named on the birth certificate;

(c) *parental leave.* Where a parental order is made or adoption, through an agency or otherwise, occurs, the intended parents will be eligible for parental leave as they will have 'parental responsibility' for the child under the law (*MPL Regulations, reg 13*). A parental order cannot be made within six weeks of the child's birth (*HFEA 2008, s 54(7)*). However, parental leave will be available even before the parental order is made (or adoption occurs) since an employee who 'expects to have' responsibility for a child is eligible for such leave (*MPL Regulations, reg 13(1)(b)*).

8.137 FLEXIBLE WORKING

The *Employment Act 2002* ('*EA 2002*') creates a right for employees to make a flexible working request. This can be a request to a change in the number of working hours worked by the employee, when those hours are worked, and/or where he or she works (ie from home or at the employer's place of business). The legislation was originally targeted at those who are responsible for caring for a young or disabled child, but in April 2007 the right was extended to carers of adults over the age of eighteen, and in April 2009 to those responsible for any child under the age of 17. The coalition government has stated that it will consult on proposals to extend the right to request flexible working to all employees. The planned extension of the flexible working legislation to parents of all children under the age of 18 in April 2011 will not now go ahead.

8.138 Who can apply?

Under the *Flexible Working (Eligibility, Complaints and Remedies) Regulations 2002 (SI 2002/3236), reg 3*, in order to qualify for the right to make a flexible working request, an employee must:

(a) have at least 26 weeks' continuous service; and be:

- (i) the mother, father, adopter, guardian, or foster parent of the child; or
- (ii) married to, the civil partner or the partner of the child's mother, father, adopter, guardian or foster parent; and

(b) have, or expect to have, responsibility for the upbringing of a child under the age of 17, or eighteen if the child is disabled; or

(c) care or expect to be caring for a person over the age of 18 who is either:

- (i) married to, the civil partner, or the partner of the employee;
- (ii) a relative of the employee; or
- (iii) living at the same address as the employee.

Under the *Flexible Working (Eligibility, Complaints and Remedies) Regulations 2002*, from 1 October 2007, private foster carers (and the spouse, partner or civil partner of such a person) and those in whose favour a residence order is in force in respect of a child (and the spouse, partner or civil partner of such a person) have been entitled to request flexible working. Additionally, the definition of 'adopter' has been extended to those who are adopting a child which has not been placed through a UK adoption agency.

The purpose of the application must be to enable the employee to care for the child or adult for whom he or she is responsible, although some employers have voluntarily extended the right to all staff. Agency workers and military personnel are not entitled to make statutory requests.

8.139 How a request is made

The *Flexible Working (Procedural Requirements) Regulations 2002 (SI 2002/3207*) and *ERA 1996, ss 80F–80I* create a very specific procedure that must be followed by employer and employee. Employees are entitled to make one request every 12 months. The request must be in writing and must state the following:

(a) that the application is being made under the statutory right to request a flexible working pattern;

(b) the basis of the employee's eligibility, for example that he is a parent of a child under 17, or a carer of an adult;

(c) what working arrangements the employee is requesting;

(d) what effect the employee thinks the arrangements might have on the employer's business, and how this could be addressed;

(e) when the employee would like the new arrangements to take effect;

(f) whether any previous requests have been made, and if so, when; and

(g) the date of the application.

8.140 What an employer must do on receipt of a request

The process

Upon receipt of an application, an employer should first check its content. If the request is missing any of the details set out in **8.139**, or does not meet the eligibility criteria, it is not valid (although refusing to consider it may give rise to claims of sex discrimination (see **8.144** ff), or perhaps breach of the implied term of mutual trust and confidence. If the request is valid, the employer must hold a meeting within 28 days of receipt at which the employee and employer can discuss the application. The employee is entitled to be accompanied to this meeting by a colleague. However, if the request is to be accepted in full, no meeting is necessary, provided that the employee is notified of the decision and the date upon which it will take effect in writing within the 28-day period.

Within 14 days after the date of the meeting, the employer must given written notification of its decision, including, if the application is refused, a 'sufficient explanation' of the reason(s). If the request is refused, the employer must notify the employee of his right to appeal, and explain that any request must be received within 14 days, as well as what the appeal procedure will be. Again, the employee should be given the right to be accompanied.

In the event that the employee appeals against the decision, the employer must hold an appeal meeting within 14 days of receiving the notice of appeal. (No meeting is necessary in the event that the employer upholds the appeal and notifies the employee of this within the 14-day period.) The employer must then give its final decision within 14 days after the appeal meeting. As with the original decision, the appeal decision must give a 'sufficient explanation' in the event that the application is refused. If the request is approved, the resulting changes to the employee's working arrangement will constitute a permanent change to his terms and conditions of employment.

Employer and employee may agree to extend any of the above timescales. If such an agreement is reached, the employer should write to the employee confirming the new timescales.

8.141 *Considering a request*

Employers are under no obligation to agree to a request for a flexible working pattern. However, such a request may only be refused for certain prescribed business reasons (*ERA 1996, s 80G*). These are as follows:

(a) burden of additional costs;

(b) detrimental effect on ability to meet customer demand;

(c) inability to reorganise work amongst existing staff;

(d) inability to recruit additional staff;

(e) detrimental impact upon quality or performance;

(f) insufficiency of work during periods the employee proposes to work; or

(g) planned structural changes.

In refusing a request, employers must explain why they consider that one or more of the above reasons applies.

An employee whose request is refused may subsequently bring a claim against the employer. The types of possible claim are discussed at **8.142** ff. In considering a complaint that an employer has failed to comply with its obligations under the right to request legislation, a tribunal will not consider whether the reason given by the employer was fair or reasonable; however, it will assess whether the reason is 'factually correct'. For example, in *Commotion Ltd v Rutty* [2006] ICR 290, Mrs Rutty, a warehouse assistant, made an application to work three days a week, which was refused on the grounds that such an arrangement would have a detrimental impact on the performance of the warehouse, would affect staff morale, and would put a strain on resources. In a decision upheld by the EAT, the tribunal found, at para 11 of its judgment, that these were:

> 'really outdated responses to requests for part-time working; they are off the cuff and made without research'.

On this basis, the tribunal held that there had been a breach of the *ERA 1996, s 80G*. Employers should therefore be prepared to substantiate any reasons they give. Crucially, even if the reason given is found to be 'factually correct', if the refusal is found to be indirectly discriminatory, the employer will have to go one step further and show that the discriminatory treatment is justified in order to successfully defend the claim. This involves balancing the commercial reasons behind the decision against its discriminatory effect. Indirect discrimination in the context of flexible working is discussed in more detail at **8.144**.

8.142 **Remedies available to an employee where a request is refused**

In the event that an employee's request for flexible working is refused, there are number of claims potentially available to him.

8.143 *Complaint under the ERA 1996*

ERA 1996, s 80H confers a right of complaint to a tribunal in circumstances where an employee's flexible working request has been refused and the internal procedure has been exhausted. The grounds for the complaint are either that the employer has failed to follow the prescribed procedure, or that the rejection was based on incorrect facts. If the tribunal upholds the claim under *ERA 1996, s 80I*, it can make a declaration to that effect, and may make an award of up to eight weeks' pay (capped at the statutory maximum (see *ERA 1996, s 227(1)(za)*) or order the employer to reconsider the request. It cannot, however, require the employer to implement a new flexible working arrangement. For this reason, the remedies available to an employee under *s 80I* are generally regarded as somewhat limited, resulting in frequent claims for indirect sex discrimination, and sometimes unfair dismissal.

8.144 *Indirect sex discrimination*

Many claims under *ERA 1996, s 80H* will be made in conjunction with a claim for indirect sex discrimination, and prior to the introduction of the right to request legislation, this was the main cause of action available to an employee whose flexible working application had been refused. Successfully defending a claim for indirect sex discrimination is more of a challenge for employers than defending a *s 80H* claim, and the stakes are higher. However, an indirect sex discrimination claim may not always be as effective a remedy for men or for carers (of either sex) of adults.

In considering a discrimination claim, the tribunal will first consider whether the refusal of the flexible working request constitutes or forms part of a provision, criterion or practice which places women (or men) at a particular disadvantage. If it is held that it does, the tribunal will then consider the reasons for the refusal to allow flexible working and will balance these against the discriminatory effect, to decide whether the discrimination is justified. Demonstrating justification is manifestly more difficult than simply showing that the reasons given for the refusals are factually correct (which is all that is required by *s 80H*, assuming that the procedure is complied with).

An example of this principle in action is *Chief Constable of Avon and Somerset Constabulary v Chew* EAT/503/00. Ms Chew was a police officer who made an application to work part-time. This was refused because it did not comply with the department's part-time working policy, which required staff to work a shift pattern. The tribunal found that this rule constituted a provision, criterion or practice which had a disparate impact on women, who were less likely to be able to comply because of childcare obligations (the claimant had adduced evidence to this effect). The tribunal then went on to consider whether this discriminatory policy was justified. The reasons given by the Constabulary for the policy were that there would be operational problems were it not strictly enforced, staff morale would be affected were some officers to work atypical hours, and any change would lead to large numbers of applications from other officers to work different hours. These reasons were rejected by the tribunal, partly because of a lack of evidence to support them, and the tribunal noted that the argument about large numbers of new applications was 'double-edged', since it assumed that there were many other workers who were also having difficulty in working the required shift pattern. The claim of indirect discrimination was upheld by the tribunal and the EAT on appeal.

A more recent example of a finding of indirect sex discrimination is the case of *Shaw v CCL Ltd* [2008] IRLR 284. Mrs Shaw (a sales executive) submitted a request to work flexibly on her return from maternity leave, asking to return on a part-time basis. This request was refused by CCL on the basis that Mrs Shaw working part-time would create difficulties for its business, including the need to employ another part-time member of staff to work on Mrs Shaw's days off. The employment tribunal found that CCL's insistence that Mrs Shaw should return to work full-time constituted indirect sex discrimination which CCL could not objectively justify. The EAT also found that the acts of discrimination suffered by Mrs Shaw amounted to a fundamental breach of contract entitling her to resign and claim constructive unfair dismissal.

An example of a case where the tribunal found in the employer's favour is *Georgiou v Colman Coyle* [2002] EAT/535/00. The EAT held that a refusal to allow a solicitor to work flexibly was justified: the office was small; there was a need for two full-time solicitors; commercial clients expected a prompt and efficient service; the need to consult files and to be supervised meant that the complainant had to attend the respondent's premises; and reduced fee income would have affected the profitability of the firm.

For more information on indirect sex discrimination, see **8.20**.

8.145 *Other forms of discrimination*

Employers should also ensure that requests are considered equally seriously regardless of the applicant's personal circumstances. For example, in the Scottish case *Walkinshaw v The John Martin Group* S/401126/00 (15 November 2001), which was decided prior to the introduction of the right to make a flexible working request, Mr Walkinshaw applied to work part-time to look after his newborn son. His employer refused on the basis that it would be 'too complicated' to arrange a job share, but the tribunal found that the employer had always accepted requests by women to work part-time. On this basis, Mr Walkinshaw's claim of direct sex discrimination was upheld. One can also envisage circumstances in which an inconsistent and/or subjective approach to flexible working requests could lead to other claims of discrimination, eg on grounds of race or sexual orientation.

It should also be noted that in circumstances where a request has been made in order to allow an employee to care for a disabled relative, and that request is refused, the refusal could constitute discrimination by association even though the employee making the request is not disabled (see **1.54**).

8.146 *Unfair dismissal and detriment*

Employees who are sufficiently adversely affected by a refusal of their request may resign and claim constructive unfair dismissal (see *Commotion Ltd v Rutty*). The dismissal of an employee because he has made a flexible working application will also be automatically unfair (*ERA 1996, s 104C*). An employee may also claim that he has suffered detriment (other than dismissal) because he made/proposed to make a request or exercised rights or brought or threatened proceedings (*ERA 1996, s 47E*).

As an alternative to litigation, there is a special ACAS arbitration scheme which employers and employees can use to resolve a dispute arising out of a flexible working request (see the *ACAS (Flexible Working) Arbitration Scheme (Great Britain) Order 2004 (SI 2004/2333)*). However, it cannot be employed in the event that any other claims, apart from unfair dismissal, are being brought, which has limited its use.

For information on the rights of part-time workers not to be discriminated against, see FIXED-TERM AND PART-TIME WORKERS **(10)**.

9 Sexual orientation

9.1 INTRODUCTION

Directive 2000/78/EC ('the *Framework Directive*') was implemented in the UK, in relation to sexual orientation discrimination, by the *Employment Equality (Sexual Orientation) Regulations 2003 (SI 2003/1661)* ('*SOR 2003*'). *SOR 2003* came into force on 1 December 2003 and prohibited direct and indirect discrimination, as well as victimisation and harassment, on grounds of sexual orientation. *SOR 2003* were revoked by the *Equality Act 2010* ('*EqA 2010*'), which came into force on 1 October 2010, but many of their provisions were replicated in the new legislation, and therefore much of the pre-existing guidance and case law will continue to be relevant. Accordingly, *SOR 2003* is the governing legislation for acts of discrimination which occurred between 1 December 2003 and 30 September 2010 and did not continue after that date, while the *EqA 2010* governs those acts occurring from 1 October 2010 onwards or continuing after that date. Both are discussed below.

9.2 Protection prior to 1 December 2003

Before *SOR 2003* came into force, there was little protection for workers who were discriminated against because of their sexual orientation. The House of Lords rejected a claim brought by a member of the Royal Air Force who was dismissed for being gay, and by a teacher who was subject to harassment by pupils because she was a lesbian (*Macdonald v Advocate General for Scotland* and *Pearce v Governing Body of Mayfield School* [2003] UKHL 34, [2003] IRLR 512). Both employees argued that they had been discriminated against on grounds of their sex. However, the court decided that the prohibition of discrimination on grounds of sex under *SDA 1975* did not include discrimination on grounds of sexual orientation. The treatment complained of by both employees was treatment on grounds of sexual orientation, not sex, and the law only recognised the latter as actionable discrimination, not the former.

The other potential complaint was that of a violation of human rights. See, eg, *Smith and Grady v United Kingdom* (1999) 29 EHRR 493. From 2 October 2000, claims could be brought under the *Human Rights Act 1998*, relying in particular upon the *European Convention on Human Rights* ('*ECHR*'), *Article 8*, which provides a (qualified) right to respect for private and family life, and *Article 14*, which prohibits discrimination in relation to other Convention rights. Such claims remain an option, although not a simple one, especially where the employer is not a public authority: see *XXX v YYY* [2004] EWCA Civ 231, [2004] IRLR 471.

9.3 Guidance on SOR 2003 and EqA 2010

Useful guidance on *SOR 2003* is provided by the Explanatory Notes issued by the DTI (as it was then called), 'Explanation of the Provisions of the Employment Equality (Sexual Orientation) Regulations 2003 and Employment Equality (Religion or Belief) Regulations 2003', the ACAS Guide 'Sexual orientation and the workplace—a guide for employers and employees' (April 2004) and the TUC's 'Guide for Union Negotiators'. Whilst these documents did not have legal force, they are useful guidance, especially in light of the fact that there are very few authorities from the higher courts about the correct interpretation of *SOR 2003*.

Useful guidance on *EqA 2010* is provided by the *Explanatory Notes to the EqA 2010*, and the *EHRC's Employment Statutory Code of Practice* ('*EHRC Employment Code*'), which is admissible in proceedings (see **1.7**). The EHRC has also published non-statutory guidance for employers and employees.

The ACAS Guide 'Sexual orientation and the workplace' (October 2010) may also provide assistance, although, like the EHRC's non-statutory guidance, it does not have any legal force.

9.4 DEFINITION OF 'SEXUAL ORIENTATION'

EqA 2010, s 12(1) defines 'sexual orientation' as a person's sexual orientation towards:

(a) persons of the same sex;

(b) persons of the opposite sex; or

(c) persons of either sex.

This definition is slightly different from that in *SOR 2003, reg 2(1)* which, instead of 'persons of either sex', referred to 'persons of the same sex and of the opposite sex'. However, the change is unlikely to have any effect in practice.

The definition of 'sexual orientation' will clearly include protection for homosexual, heterosexual and bisexual people. It does not, however, cover the absence of an orientation, or celibacy, nor does it provide protection on grounds that a person actually engages in any particular sexual practice. The protection given is in respect of a sexual orientation, expressly defined, rather than by reference to a looser concept of, say, sexual activities. The *EHRC Employment Code* states that sexual orientation 'relates to how people feel as well as their actions' (*para 2.65*).

Transsexuals are not covered under these provisions, but have separate protection under the gender reassignment provisions of *EqA 2010* (and previously under *SDA 1975*) (see **GENDER REASSIGNMENT (4)**).

9.5 DIRECT DISCRIMINATION

EqA 2010, s 13(1) provides that direct sexual orientation discrimination occurs where A treats B less favourably than he treats or would treat other persons because of the protected characteristic of sexual orientation. Direct discrimination, unlike indirect discrimination, cannot be justified.

This is the same in substance as under *SOR 2003, reg (3)(1)(a)*, which provided that discrimination on the grounds of sexual orientation occurred where 'on the grounds of sexual orientation, A treats B less favourably than he treats or would treat other persons'.

The change from the term 'on the grounds of' in *SOR 2003* to 'because of' in the *EqA 2010* definition of direct discrimination is not intended to alter the legal scope of direct discrimination. Rather, the government's intention in making this change was simply to make the definition more accessible to the 'ordinary user' (see **1.46**).

9.6 Discrimination by association or perception

The definition of direct discrimination under *EqA 2010* is intended to cover cases where the victim is treated less favourably because of his or her association with someone who has a particular sexual orientation ('associative discrimination') or because he or she is incorrectly thought to be of a particular sexual orientation ('discrimination by perception').

Case law on race discrimination suggested that this was already the position under *SOR 2003*, which referred to less favourable treatment 'on grounds of sexual orientation' (*reg 3(1)(a)*). See by analogy the principle explained in *Showboat Entertainment Centre Ltd v Owens* [1984] IRLR 7; although see also *Redfearn v Serco Ltd (t/a West Yorkshire Transport Service)* [2006] EWCA Civ 659, [2006] ICR 1367 (stressing the importance of the need to show that the relevant treatment is truly on the prohibited 'grounds'). Discrimination by association was also contrary to the *Framework Directive* (see *Coleman v Attridge Law: C-303/06* [2007] ICR 654).

Therefore, dismissing a person for having homosexual friends will constitute direct discrimination under *EqA 2010*. Similarly, the dismissal of a person in the (mistaken) belief that that person is himself homosexual will be covered. Indeed, in the harassment context, under *SOR 2003*, the courts have gone one step further and have held that 'homophobic banter' can be unlawful even where the victim was not homosexual, his discriminators did not believe him to be homosexual and the victim was aware of this (see *English v Thomas Sanderson Blinds Ltd* [2008] EWCA Civ 1421, [2009] 2 All ER 468 at **9.15** below).

The *EHRC Employment Code* gives an example of a heterosexual worker who is less favourably treated because she has been seen out with a person who is gay. This could be direct discrimination against the worker because of her association with the gay person.

For a more detailed discussion of discrimination by association and perception see **1.53–1.55**.

9.7 What will constitute direct discrimination?

Direct discrimination will occur, in this context, whenever there is less favourable treatment of a person because of the sexual orientation (or perceived sexual orientation) of that person (or a person associated with them). For example, and in relation to offers of employment, a refusal to employ a homosexual person to work in a pub because of his sexuality will constitute direct discrimination, and the employer will not be able to attempt to justify such refusal (for example) by reference to an asserted adverse impact on his business. The *EHRC Employment Code* at *para 3.4* gives the example of an applicant who mentions at interview that she has a same-sex partner and is turned down for the role in favour of a heterosexual woman despite being the best qualified. If the treatment is because of her sexual orientation, this will be direct discrimination. In relation to terms of employment, the provision of less favourable pay or conditions to an employee because of sexual orientation will constitute direct discrimination. A refusal to provide equivalent training to an employee because of sexual orientation will also be covered. Dismissing a person because of their sexual orientation is also an act of direct discrimination under *EqA 2010* (as it was previously under *SOR 2003*).

In *HM Land Registry v Grant* UKEAT/0232/09/DA, decided under *SOR 2003*, the EAT observed that if a gay person is 'outed' against his wishes, to those whom he would rather not know of his orientation, that fact alone may well constitute an act of direct discrimination (or harassment), but all will depend on the context. In that case, the fact that the claimant had been open about his sexual orientation in a previous role with the same employer (at a different workplace) and the question of whether the alleged discriminator had intended to discriminate against him were relevant to the question of whether there had been direct discrimination. This is because those factors could affect the analysis of whether the claimant had been treated differently than a heterosexual man would have been treated and whether he had suffered a detriment. The EAT observed that although intention to discriminate is not necessary in law for there to be discrimination or harassment, it is highly relevant to an assessment of whether conduct which is not inherently and self-evidently discriminatory is or is not unlawful.

In *Secretary of State for Work and Pensions (Jobcentre Plus) v Mr B Whyment McCarthy* UKEAT/0419/09/JOJ, also decided under *SOR 2003*, the tribunal upheld a claim for direct discrimination by a gay man who claimed that he had been less favourably treated in a disciplinary investigation into a suggestion that he may have had an inappropriate relationship with a job centre client. The tribunal held that his treatment was because the employer knew of his sexual orientation and made stereotypical assumptions about the likely behaviour of the claimant and gay men generally. The EAT held that this decision was not perverse on the facts of the case.

9.8 The appropriate comparator

A complainant must typically show that he has been treated less favourably than another person whose circumstances are not materially different (*EqA 2010, s 23(1)* which replaced *SOR 2003, reg 3(2)*).

So, for example, an unsuccessful homosexual applicant for a post cannot simply point to a successful heterosexual applicant for the same post and thereby demonstrate discrimination. He must also demonstrate that, apart from sexual orientation, his case was materially the same as the person who was treated more favourably.

In relation to sexual orientation discrimination specifically, *EqA 2010, s 23(3)* (replacing *SOR 2003, reg 3(3)*) provides that the fact that one person in the comparison exercise is a civil partner while another is married is not a material difference between the circumstances relating to each case. This means that a gay employee in a civil partnership should not be treated differently from a heterosexual employee who is married but whose material circumstances are otherwise the same, because the fact that one is married and the other is in a civil partnership will not be a material difference between them (see example in the *EHRC Employment Code, para 3.31*). This will be relevant, for example, in the provision of benefits which provide cover for spouses.

The use of the words 'would treat' in *EqA 2010, s 13(1)* (and previously in *SOR 2003, reg 3(1)(a)*) means (as in other discrimination strands) that the use of a hypothetical comparator is also permitted. For sexual orientation cases in which hypothetical comparators were considered, see *Secretary of State for Work and Pensions (Jobcentre Plus) v Mr B Whyment McCarthy* and *HM Land Registry v Grant.*

For a discussion of direct discrimination in more detail see **1.45**ff.

9.9 Combined discrimination

EqA 2010 also contains a new provision enabling an employee to bring a discrimination claim on two (but no more than two) combined protected grounds, although the provision was not implemented on 1 October 2010 and will certainly not be implemented before April 2011. (See **1.57**.)

9.10 INDIRECT DISCRIMINATION

Indirect discrimination (described in *EqA 2010, s 19*) occurs where a person (A) applies to a person (B) a provision, criterion or practice ('PCP') which:

(a) A applies or would apply to persons not of the same sexual orientation as B;

(b) puts or would put persons of the same sexual orientation as B at a particular disadvantage when compared with other persons;

(c) puts or would put B at that disadvantage; and

(d) A cannot show to be a proportionate means of achieving a legitimate aim.

This wording is very similar to that contained in *SOR 2003, reg 3(1)(b)*, save that it has been widened slightly in that the PCP no longer has to actually put B at the relevant disadvantage, it is sufficient if it 'would put' B in this position.

An example of indirect discrimination in the sexual orientation context would be where a childless, and homosexual, man or woman wishes to apply for a teaching job at a nursery whose recruitment policy expressly promotes applicants who are themselves biological parents over all other applicants. The nursery would in that situation be applying a criterion or practice, ie a preference for employees who are biological parents, which would put homosexual applicants at a particular disadvantage when compared with heterosexual applicants. This would constitute discrimination unless the nursery could show the discriminatory policy to be a proportionate means of achieving a legitimate aim.

9.11 The concept of 'disadvantage'

The *EHRC Employment Code, para 4.13* (and see the DTI Guidance, 3.99) recognises that, in certain cases, the question whether persons who share the same protected characteristic as the claimant are put at a particular disadvantage is likely to apply to small groups. In such cases statistical evidence will not always be required to show particular disadvantage, and reliance may instead be placed on expert evidence to show that a requirement disadvantages a particular group.

9.12 A proportionate means of achieving a legitimate aim

In determining what constitutes 'proportionate means' it is for the courts to balance the needs of the employer in applying the provision, criterion or practice against its discriminatory effect. This will involve a careful consideration of the facts in each case.

In order for a practice to be proportionate it must be an appropriate and necessary means of achieving a legitimate aim (see *Bilka-Kaufhaus GmbH v Weber von Hartz: 170/84* [1986] ECR 1607, [1986] IRLR 317) (see **1.83–1.85**). 'Necessary' means something that is more than merely convenient, but it does not have to be the only possible way of achieving the legitimate aim (*EHRC Employment Code, para 4.31* and DTI Guidance at 3.109). However, the measure taken must be a proportionate means of achieving the objective in question: if it can be shown that there is some other way of achieving the stated objective, in a manner that has a significantly less discriminatory effect, then this requirement is unlikely to be satisfied.

What amounts to a legitimate aim will depend on the circumstances. They typically include business efficacy, or health and safety objectives. The EAT has held in the context of sex discrimination that while cost alone cannot amount to a legitimate aim, cost considerations could be included where another legitimate aim exists (*Cross v British Airways plc* [2005] IRLR 423). However, this has been questioned by the EAT in an age discrimination case (*Woodcock v Cumbria Primary Care Trust* (2010) UKEAT/0489/09/RN, [2011] IRLR 119) where the EAT suggested (obiter) that there may be no good reason why cost alone could not be a legitimate aim in an appropriate case. A legitimate aim cannot itself be discriminatory.

For further commentary on indirect discrimination see **1.72**.

9.13 VICTIMISATION

The concept of discrimination under *SOR 2003* included discrimination by way of victimisation. Under EqA 2010 victimisation is not technically a form of discrimination, but a free-standing claim. The reasoning underlying all prohibitions on victimisation is that a person who complains (or who is about to complain) of being discriminated against or who supports such a claim should be protected from suffering the imposition of detriments in consequence. Otherwise the protection provided by the law against discrimination on prohibited grounds would be devalued.

Sexual orientation

Under *SOR 2003*, discrimination by way of victimisation in the context of sexual orientation was defined as occurring where a person (A) treats another (B) less favourably than he treats or would treat other persons in the same circumstances, and does so 'by reason that' B has done one of the four protected acts set out in *SOR 2003, reg 4(1)*, or by reason that A knows that B intends to do any of those protected acts, suspects that he has done any of those acts, or suspects that B intends to do one of those acts.

The protected acts set out in *reg 4(1)* were described very broadly. They were that:

(a) B has brought proceedings against A (or any other person) under *SOR 2003*; or

(b) B has given evidence or information in connection with proceedings brought by any person against A (or any other person) under *SOR 2003*; or

(c) B has done something under or by reference to *SOR 2003* in relation to A or any other person; or

(d) B has alleged that A (or any other person) has contravened *SOR 2003*. Note that the relevant allegation made by B does not have to state in terms that the conduct was a contravention of *SOR 2003*.

As part of the harmonisation of protection against various forms of discrimination, *EqA 2010* has introduced a common concept of victimisation (*s 27*), which is concerned with giving protection to persons carrying out certain 'protected acts' related to the exercise of rights under *EqA 2010*, and does not vary according to the particular protected characteristics an act of victimisation may concern. The test is set out and discussed at **1.99**ff.

The definition in *EqA 2010* broadly follows the definition under *SDA 1975*, but there are two differences:

(a) under *EqA 2010* B does not need to show that he is treated less favourably than someone else in the same circumstances (ie he does not need to identify a comparator); he just needs to show that he was subjected to a detriment;

(b) in addition, under *EqA 2010* if B has not actually done a protected act, A must believe that B has done or may do a protected act. Under *SOR 2003*, the equivalent test was whether A knew or suspected that B had done or intended to do a protected act. It remains to be seen whether this change in wording will give rise to any substantive change to the law, but the Explanatory Notes suggest that it was not intended to.

In practice, under either *EqA 2010* or *SOR 2003*, if an employee is dismissed by his employer because his employer suspects that he is about to complain that a colleague, on grounds of sexual orientation, was demoted, the dismissal would potentially be an act of victimisation, with the protected (imminent) act falling within *EqA 2010, s 27(2)(b)* or *(c)* (and previously *SOR 2003, reg 4(1)(c)* or *(d)*). Similarly, if an employer rejected an application for employment because he knew that the applicant had sued a former employer under *SOR 2003*, that would also amount to victimisation, with the protected act falling within *s 27(2)(a)* (*reg 4(1)(a)*).

Individuals will not gain protection against victimisation where the evidence, information or allegations that they make are both false *and* not given in good faith (*EqA 2010, s 27(3)*, and previously *SOR 2003, reg 4(2)*). The wording of this provision is potentially important, because it means that a person who alleges a contravention of *EqA 2010*, honestly believing such allegation to be correct, is protected from suffering detriments at the hands of his employer as a result, even if the alleged contravention turns out to be false.

9.14 DISCUSSIONS ABOUT PAY

EqA 2010, s 77 makes contractual pay secrecy clauses unenforceable to the extent that they prevent employees from making relevant pay disclosures—that is, a disclosure that is sought or made for the purpose of finding out whether (or to what extent) any difference in pay is related to a protected characteristic (EqA 2010, s 77(3)). Action taken by an employer as a result of an individual making or seeking to make a relevant pay disclosure, or receiving information disclosed in a relevant pay disclosure, may amount to victimisation. (See **1.109**.)

9.15 HARASSMENT

EqA 2010, s 40 expressly protects employees (and applicants for employment) from being subjected to harassment. Harassment is defined by *EqA 2010, s 26*. A person (A) will harass another (B) if A engages in unwanted conduct related to sexual orientation, and the conduct has the purpose or effect of either: (i) violating B's dignity; or (ii) creating an intimidating, hostile, degrading, humiliating or offensive environment for B. Harassment was similarly defined in *SOR 2003, reg 6(3)*.

EqA 2010, s 40(2) also provides that A will be treated as harassing B where: (a) a third party harasses B in the course of B's employment; and (b) A failed to take such steps as would have been reasonably practicable to prevent the third party from doing so. A third party is someone other than A, or an employee of A's (*s 40(4)*). However, this will not apply unless A knows that B has been harassed during the course of B's employment on at least two other occasions by a third party (whether the same or a different third party on each occasion). There was no equivalent provision relating to third party harassment under *SOR 2003*, although there were equivalent provisions in relation to sex discrimination under *SDA 1975*.

Harassment is an unlawful act which is discrete from the concept of unlawful 'discrimination' as separately defined. Thus, it is not necessary, for example, for a person complaining of harassment to show less favourable treatment. It follows that it is not a defence to a claim of harassment on grounds of sexual orientation for a person to say that he would have treated a person of a different sexual orientation equally badly, as long as the harassment complained of is in fact on grounds of sexual orientation.

The wording of *EqA 2010, s 26(1)(b)* (previously *SOR 2003, reg 5(1))* ('purpose or effect') demonstrates that a person cannot escape liability for harassment merely because he did not intend to violate a person's dignity (where his conduct in fact had that effect). As in other strands of discrimination law, this is likely to be significant. The fact that one person believes he is engaging in what he might see as light-hearted banter with another does not necessarily mean that he is not harassing the other person. Nor will the alleged harasser have a defence where his purpose was violating a person's dignity but, in fact, his conduct did not have that effect, even though it was unwanted.

In determining whether conduct has the relevant 'effect', regard must be had under *s 26(4)* to: (a) the perception of B; (b) other circumstances of the case; and (c) whether it is reasonable for the conduct to have that effect. This is similar to the position under *SOR 2003, reg 5(2)*, which provided that conduct shall only be regarded as having the relevant 'effect' if, having regard to all the circumstances, including in particular the perception of B, it should reasonably be considered as having that effect. This means that the subjective impact on B is on the one hand highly relevant, but on the other not determinative. B must show that the conduct of A and of which he complains was (subjectively) 'unwanted', otherwise he will fail to satisfy *EqA 2010, s 26(1)(a)* (*SOR 2003, reg 5(1))*. But an assertion that A violated B's dignity, or created an intimidating, hostile, degrading, humiliating or offensive environment for B, must also be one that (objectively) could reasonably be considered as having such effect, otherwise B will fail to satisfy *EqA 2010, s 26(1)(b)* (*SOR 2003, reg 5(2)*).

As noted above at **9.6**, it was held in *English v Thomas Sanderson Blinds Ltd* [2008] EWCA Civ 1421, [2009] 2 All ER 468 that 'homophobic banter' can be unlawful even where the victim was not homosexual, his discriminators did not believe him to be homosexual and the victim was aware of this. What matters is whether (in this context) his sexual orientation, real or imagined, forms the basis of the relevant unwanted conduct.

The word 'unwanted' describes the conduct, and makes no logical requirement about the previous behaviour of the victim. It does not follow that simply because the victim has not previously objected to a particular type of conduct, such conduct is not unwanted (*Reed v Stedman* [1999] IRLR 299). If a single act is sufficiently serious it can amount to harassment even though notice that it is unwanted has not been given.

Protection may also be available under the *Protection from Harassment Act 1997*, irrespective of whether any harassment was related to sexual orientation.

The concept of harassment under *EqA 2010* is discussed in more detail at **1.87**.

9.16 UNLAWFUL DISCRIMINATION

In the context of employment, *EqA 2010, s 39* prohibits an employer from discriminating against applicants for employment and against employees. This is in similar terms to *SOR 2003, reg 6*. With regard to recruitment decisions, an employer must not discriminate against a person in the arrangements it makes for determining to whom to offer employment or in determining whether and on what terms it should offer a person employment (*EqA 2010, s 39(1)*; *SOR 2003, reg 6(1)*). With regard to acts during the course of a person's employment, an employer must not discriminate against its employee as to the terms of employment (*EqA 2010, s 39(2)(a)*; *SOR 2003, reg 6(2)(a)*), access to opportunities for promotion, transfer or training or other benefits, facilities or services (*EqA 2010, s 39(2)(b)*; *SOR 2003, reg 6(2)(b) and (c)*); or in terms of dismissal or other detriments (*EqA 2010, s 39(2)(c) and (d)*; *SOR 2003, reg 6(2)(d)*).

Dismissal in this context includes constructive dismissal (*EqA 2010, s 39(7)(b)*; *SOR 2003, reg 6(5)(b)*). So, for example, where an employee resigns because of acts of harassment (or an employer's failure to prevent them), and it is shown that those acts (or omissions) constitute a constructive dismissal, the dismissal may itself be an unlawful act within *EqA 2010, s 39(2)* (*SOR 2003, reg 6(2)(d)*).

It is not only employees that are protected. *EqA 2010, s 83(2)* defines an employment as 'employment under a contract of employment, a contract of apprenticeship or a contract personally to do work', giving *s 39* a similar scope to *SOR 2003, reg 2(3)*, which defined employment as 'employment under a contract of service or of apprenticeship or a contract personally to do any work'. Note, though, that certain context specific protection against discrimination is given to contract workers (*EqA 2010, s 41*), police officers (*s 42*), partners (*s 44*), members of LLPs (*s 45*) and barristers (*s 47*); see **1.15**ff.

Note that ex-employees are protected under *EqA 2010, s 108*, which makes it unlawful for a person (A) to discriminate against another (B) or to harass him, where the discrimination or harassment arises out of and is closely connected to a relationship which used to exist between them, and discrimination or harassment by A of B would have contravened the *EqA 2010* had it occurred during the relationship. Similar provision was made under *SOR 2003, reg 21*. *EqA 2010* does not expressly protect former employees from victimisation, which appears to be a drafting oversight (see **1.35**).

9.17 Instructing, causing or inducing discrimination

It is unlawful to instruct, cause or induce someone to discriminate against, harass or victimise another person, or to attempt to do so (*EqA 2010, s 111*). A claim can be brought by the 'victim' of the discrimination, the person who was instructed to carry out the discrimination and the EHRC. There were no equivalent provisions under *SOR 2003*. (See **1.61**.)

9.18 Liability of employees and agents and aiding discrimination

Where employees commit acts of discrimination against fellow employees, their employer will be liable if the acts were committed during the course of employment (*EqA 2010, s 109(1)*). Employers are also liable for the discriminatory acts of their agents if they are acting with the employer's authority (*s 109(4)*). In each case it is irrelevant whether the employer knew or approved of the acts (*s 109(3)*). However, there is a defence for employers in relation to the acts of their employees (but not agents) if they can show that they took such steps as were reasonably practicable to prevent the employee from doing the act in question (*s 109(4)*). The employees and agents will also have personal liability for their acts of discrimination (*EqA 2010, s 110*), even if the employer has a defence. These provisions replace provisions to similar effect under *SOR 2003, regs 22, 23*) and are discussed further at **1.164**ff.

It is also unlawful for an individual to knowingly help another to carry out an act which is unlawful under *EqA 2010* (*s 112(1)*). (See **1.62**.)

9.19 OCCUPATIONAL REQUIREMENTS

The *EqA 2010* has harmonised the provisions which were previously contained in *SOR 2003* and other legislation relating to genuine occupational requirements (GOR) and genuine occupational qualifications, which provide a defence to what would otherwise generally be direct discrimination. The exceptions are perhaps particularly controversial in their application to religious belief and sexual orientation discrimination. Under what circumstances might it be acceptable to discriminate against people at work on the basis of their sexual orientation?

EqA 2010 provides two exceptions which are relevant to sexual orientation. There is a general exception for occupational requirements, which applies for all employments and all protected characteristics (*Sch 9, para 1*) and a specific exception relating to employment for the purposes of an organised religion (*Sch 9, para 2*). Both exceptions provide a defence to the provisions relating to recruitment (*s 39(1)(a) or (c)*), opportunities for training, promotion, transfer or any other benefit, facility or service (*s 2(b)*) and dismissal (*s 2(c)*). However, it is important to note that these exceptions do not apply to provisions relating to the terms on which people are employed or are offered employment, or which protect against harassment in the course of employment or against victimisation in the recruitment or employment of any person.

The general occupational requirement exception permits an employer to apply in relation to work a requirement to have a relevant protected characteristic (which includes a 'particular sexual orientation', *s 12(2)(a)*) provided three conditions are satisfied. They are that the employer must be able to show that, having regard to the nature and context of the work: (a) the requirement is an occupational requirement; (b) its application is a proportionate means of achieving a legitimate aim; (c) the person to whom the requirement is applied does not meet it (or the employer has reasonable grounds for believing that he does not meet it). This replaces the previous exception for 'genuine occupational requirements' under *SOR 2003, reg 7(2)*.

The *EHRC Employment Code* emphasises that as an exception to the prohibition on discrimination, the occupational requirement test should be interpreted narrowly and these conditions are likely to constitute a demanding test. It will not be satisfied, for example, where a bar which is popular with homosexuals subjects its heterosexual employees to detriments, or is only interested in employing homosexual people. That is because being homosexual is not a 'requirement' for the occupation of serving drinks. Nor will it necessarily be satisfied even in the rare situation where an employer reasonably needs an employee who will desist from homosexual conduct (eg sending a representative to a country where all non-heterosexual activity is criminalised). That is because an employer should not assume that simply because a person has a sexual orientation, he will necessarily engage in a particular sexual activity.

The specific exception in relation to employment for the purposes of an organised religion allows a person (A) to apply in relation to employment a 'requirement related to sexual orientation' if he can show that: (a) the employment is for the purposes of an organised religion; (b) the application of the requirement engages the compliance or non-conflict principle; and (c) the person to whom A applies the requirement does not meet it (or A has reasonable grounds for not being satisfied that the person meets it). The application of a requirement engages the compliance principle if it is applied so as to comply with the doctrines of the religion (*Sch 9, para 2(5)*). The application of a requirement engages the non-conflict principle if, because of the nature of the employment, the requirement is applied so as to avoid conflicting with the strongly held religious convictions of a significant number of the religion's followers (*Sch 9, para 2(6)*).

The Explanatory Notes suggest that this exception is intended to have a much narrower effect than it might appear to have on the face of the legislation. They state that the requirement must be 'crucial to the post, and not merely one of several important factors' and that this specific exception 'is intended to cover a very narrow range of employment: ministers of religion and a small number of lay posts, including those that exist to promote and represent religion', and applying such a requirement is permissible only where it is 'a proportionate way' of complying with a religion's doctrine or avoiding conflict with a group of followers. The *EHRC Employment Code* also states that the requirement must be a proportionate way of meeting the compliance or non-conflict principle and that the exception should only be used for '*a limited number of posts, such as ministers of religion and a small number of posts outside the clergy including those which exist to promote or represent the religion*'.

The emphasis placed in the notes and the *EHRC Employment Code* on proportionality is striking, given the absence of a reference to it in the legislation itself. Tribunals will be required to have regard to the Code where it is relevant and it may be that the courts will soon have to deal with the extent to which the *Explanatory Notes* should influence the interpretation of *EqA 2010, Sch 9*, in particular taking into account the guidance of Lord Steyn in *R (on the application of Westminster City Council) v National Asylum and Support Service* [2002] UKHL 38, [2002] 1 WLR 2956 (at [5] and [6]). What is clear is that *Sch 9, para 2* will be given a narrow construction, since it is a derogation from the principle of equal treatment: see *R (on the application of Amicus – MSF section) v Secretary of State for Trade and Industry* [2004] EWHC 860 (Admin), [2004] IRLR 430, discussed below, in particular at [115]–[117], [121] and [122].

Both the general occupational requirement exception and the specific exception in relation to employment for the purposes of an organised religion replace equivalent provisions which were previously included in *SOR 2003, reg 7(2)* and *(3)*. Although there have been some changes to the wording, these do not appear to have been intended to change the effect of the exceptions as they were interpreted under *SOR 2003*. In *R (on the application of Amicus – MSF section) v Secretary of State for Trade and Industry* [2004] EWHC 860 (Admin), [2004] IRLR 430 various unions challenged the lawfulness of the genuine occupational requirement provisions contained in *SOR 2003*. It was said that they were insufficiently reflective of the right to be protected against discrimination on the grounds of sexual orientation, and therefore incompatible with both the *Framework Directive* and with *Articles 8* and/or *14* of *ECHR*. The challenge failed. The Administrative Court held that the Regulations needed to be construed purposively, and having done so, they survived scrutiny. In relation to the requirement for a genuine occupational requirement to be proportionate, which was set out in *reg 7(2)(b)*, for example, a requirement would have to pursue a 'legitimate objective' in order to qualify as proportionate (a condition which is expressly included in *EqA 2010*). In relation to the requirement that the person to whom the requirement is applied must either be of the relevant sexual orientation, or the employer must be reasonably satisfied that he was (*reg 7(2)(c)(ii)*), the concept of reasonableness would prevent an employer from stereotyping or making unjustified assumptions. And the exception for organised religion set out in *reg 7(3)* (replaced by *EqA 2010, Sch 9, para 2*) was intended, and was to be treated, as a very narrow one (and narrower than the corresponding provision in *RBR 2003*), importing a demanding objective test. Employment as a teacher in a faith school, for example, would be unlikely to fall within it. This case is likely to remain relevant to interpretation of the equivalent provisions under *EqA 2010*.

See also the discussion in **1.145**ff.

9.20 OTHER EXCEPTIONS

National security

EqA 2010, s 192 provides as a general exception that '[a] person does not contravene this Act only by doing, for the purpose of safeguarding national security, anything it is proportionate to do for that purpose'. Similarly, under *SOR 2003*, discriminatory acts done 'for the purpose of safeguarding national security' will not be unlawful, if the doing of the act was justified for that purpose (*reg 24*). These provisions reflect a specific provision in the *Framework Directive* providing that the non-discrimination measures shall be 'without prejudice' to measures laid down by national law, relating to (among other things) national security. See **1.111**.

9.21 Positive action

Under *EqA 2010, s 158* the provisions in relation to positive action in relation to various different characteristics are harmonised. These are discussed at **1.152–1.164**.

In relation to *SOR 2003*, there was a positive action exception which could apply where an act was done in connection with affording persons of a particular sexual orientation access to facilities for training which would help fit them for particular work, or encouraging them to take advantage of opportunities for doing particular work. In order for the exception to apply, the person doing the act in question must reasonably think that it prevents, or compensates for, disadvantages linked to sexual orientation suffered by persons of that sexual orientation doing that work or likely to take up that work (*reg 26(1)*).

9.22 Marital status

Discrimination on grounds of marital or civil partnership status is covered in **Marital status and civil partnership (5)**. For present purposes, it suffices to note that it is not unlawful discrimination on the basis of sexual orientation to prevent or restrict access to a benefit by reference to marital status where the right to the benefit accrued or the benefit is payable in respect of periods of service prior to the coming into force of the *Civil Partnership Act 2004*, as set out in *EqA 2010, Sch 9, para 18* (and previously *SOR 2003, reg 25*). This provision (in its original form) was one of those unsuccessfully challenged in the *Amicus* judicial review (see **9.19**).

9.23 CONFLICTS WITH RELIGION OR BELIEF

One interesting question is how the courts should resolve the apparent tension or conflict between the protection provided by *EqA 2010* in respect of, on the one hand, sexual orientation and, on the other hand, religion or belief. Some of the beliefs protected by the religion or belief provisions of *EqA 2010* (and previously *RBR 2003*), especially traditional religious beliefs, will themselves be inconsistent with the principles of equality in relation to sexual orientation upon which *EqA 2010* (and previously *SOR 2003*) is based.

The question that might need to be answered is whether sexual orientation discrimination rights trump religious non-discrimination rights in the event of any apparent conflict, because discrimination on the grounds of sexual orientation is recognised as one of the categories inherently worthy of protection (see *R (on the application of Carson) v Secretary of State for Work and Pensions* [2005] UKHL 37, [2006] 1 AC 173 at para 17). There might need to be consideration of cases from other jurisdictions which touch on similar issues (see eg the USA case of *Peterson v Hewlett-Packard*, USA Court of Appeals, 9th Circuit, January 2004). Alternatively, the tribunals and the courts might strain to find a more subtle question to ask. One issue is whether the right to manifest or conduct oneself in line with religious beliefs is to be treated as a protected characteristic or not. If it is not (as the *EHRC Employment Code* suggests), then less favourable treatment of someone because of a manifestation of their belief will not be direct discrimination but only indirect discrimination, which is capable of justification (see **7.12**). But the wider conceptual problem—the tension between respect for equality and respect for beliefs—is one that arises out of constitutional values based on liberalism and individual rights, and is already one that is exercising the courts, outside of the employment context.

While the matter may not have been finally determined, the strong indications from the case law so far suggest that employees will not be permitted to act in a way which amounts to sexual orientation discrimination even where this is in line with their religious beliefs. In the context of the *Equality Act (Sexual Orientation) Regulations 2007 (SI 2007/1263)* ('*the 2007 Regulations*', which *EqA 2010* also replaces) which prohibited discrimination in the provision of services on grounds of sexual orientation, the courts have held that the rights contained in these provisions will apply in spite of apparent conflict with those in the *RBR 2003*. In the case of *Ladele v London Borough of Islington* [2009] EWCA Civ 1357, [2010] IRLR 211 the Court of Appeal held that the local authority was entitled to require a registrar to conduct civil partnerships, even though this conflicted with her religious beliefs and to discipline her for failing to do so. This did not amount to direct discrimination, because it was based on her behaviour rather than her belief. Nor did it amount to indirect discrimination because, although the local authority's policy did put persons with Ms Ladele's religious belief at a particular disadvantage, it could be objectively justified in the light of the authority's commitment to equal opportunities and indeed was required by the *2007 Regulations*. In *McFarlane v Relate Avon Ltd* [2010] EWCA Civ 880, [2010] IRLR 872, Laws LJ refused permission to appeal to the Court of Appeal to a man employed as a relationship counsellor who had been dismissed for refusing to counsel a homosexual couple because of his religious beliefs, holding that this did not amount to discrimination under *RBR 2003, reg 3(1)(a)*. Laws LJ considered that no distinction in principle could be drawn between the case before him and *Ladele*, which he accordingly applied. As part of his ruling, he also opined that society does not protect a person's right to act on the content of a religious belief merely because of its religious provenance. Although, at an academic level, striking the balance may not, with respect, be as easy as this reasoning suggests (while clearly unbridled protection for the acting out of all religious belief cannot be countenanced, nevertheless a right to hold and express beliefs may lose a lot of its value if one is not also permitted to act on them), where there is a balance to be struck a decision must be taken, and this view does appear to reflect the scheme of the legislation. There is good reason to think this same position will hold under *EqA 2010*.

9.24 ENFORCEMENT AND REMEDIES

Questionnaire procedure

EqA 2010, s 138 permits a person who believes that he has been discriminated against (or subject to harassment) to seek information from the employer by serving a questionnaire.

9.25 Compensation

The principles relating to compensation for unlawful discrimination on grounds of sexual orientation are the same as for other protected characteristics. The issue of appropriate compensation was considered in the context of *SOR 2003* in *Ministry of Defence v Fletcher*

UKEAT/044/09/JOJ. Ms Fletcher joined the Army in October 1996. Between 2004 and 2006 she suffered serious sexual harassment and extensive victimisation. The employment tribunal found that the Ministry of Defence had unlawfully discriminated against Ms Fletcher on the grounds of her sex and sexual orientation and awarded her injury to feelings of £30,000, aggravated damages of £20,000 and exemplary damages of £50,000. On appeal, the EAT reduced the aggravated damages element to £8,000 and completely overturned the award of exemplary damages.

For further information see **1.172–1.181**.

9.26 DISCRIMINATION OUTSIDE EMPLOYMENT

EqA 2010 and the *2007 Regulations* contain prohibitions on discrimination related to sexual orientation which fall outside of the employment context. Unlike *SOR 2003*, which was enacted under powers conferred by the *European Communities Act 1972, s 2(2)* (ie by transposing the *Framework Directive*, which relates to employment, into domestic law), the *2007 Regulations* required primary domestic legislation: see the *Equality Act 2006, Part 3*.

The provisions of the *EqA 2010* in this regard and of the *2007 Regulations* go beyond the scope of this book and are not considered in any detail here. Briefly, they prohibit discrimination on grounds of sexual orientation in the provision of goods, facilities and services to the public, the exercise of public functions, in education, the management and disposal of premises, and in other areas.

10 Fixed-term and part-time workers

10.1 FIXED-TERM EMPLOYEES

Introduction

The *Fixed-term Employees (Prevention of Less Favourable Treatment) Regulations 2002* ('*FTR 2002*') came into force on 1 October 2002.

They were made pursuant to the *Employment Act 2002* ('*EA 2002*'), *s 45* to give effect to *Directive 99/70/EC* ('the Directive') concerning the framework agreement on fixed-term work.

FTR 2002 gives fixed-term employees the right in principle not to be treated less favourably than permanent employees of the same employer doing similar work. The right, exercisable by complaint to an employment tribunal, applies where the less favourable treatment is on the ground that the employee is working under a fixed-term contract and the less favourable treatment in question is not justified on objective grounds.

10.2 *The Directive*

Article 1 of the Directive states that its purpose is to put into effect the framework agreement on fixed-term contracts concluded on 18 March 1999 between general cross-industry organisations.

Article 2 states that Member States should bring into force the laws, regulations and administrative provisions necessary to comply with the Directive.

The framework agreement, to which the Directive gives effect, is intended (as stated in *clause 1*) to:

(a) improve the quality of fixed-term work by ensuring the application of the principle of non-discrimination;

(b) establish a framework to prevent abuse arising from the use of successive fixed-term contracts or relationships.

To this end, *clause 4* sets out the principle of non-discrimination: that is that fixed-term workers should not be treated in a less favourable manner than comparable permanent workers solely because they have a fixed-term contract, unless justified on objective grounds. In *Impact v Minister for Agriculture and Food: C-268/06* [2008] 2 CMLR 47 (at [59]–[68]) the ECJ held that the prohibition of discrimination in *clause 4(1)* enjoys direct effect in national courts.

Further, under *clause 5*, Member States shall introduce one or more measures to prevent abuse of successive fixed-term contracts, such measures being the need for an objective reason to justify such renewals, the maximum total duration of successive fixed-term contracts and/or the number of renewals of such contracts. It is also open for Member States to rely on equivalent legal measures previously in existence. The discretion enjoyed by Member States under *clause 5* led the ECJ to hold that clause incapable of enjoying direct effect (*Impact v Minister for Agriculture* at [76]–[79]).

10.3 *Pre-existing protection*

Prior to the coming into force of *FTR 2002*, there was protection for fixed-term employees only in certain situations.

For example, a claim of indirect sex discrimination (see **8.20**) could be brought under the *Sex Discrimination Act 1975, s 1(1)(b)* (prior to the amendments made pursuant to the *Burden of Proof Directive (97/80/EC)* if the facts supported a claim that a requirement or condition, when applied equally to both men and women, had a disproportionate impact on one gender. So in *Whiffen v Milham Ford Girls' School* [2001] EWCA Civ 385, [2001] LGR 309, a teacher working under repeated fixed-term contracts was successful in showing that the failure to renew her final fixed-term contract was indirect discrimination since the proportion of the women who could comply with the requirement to work under a permanent contract (for the purpose of being included in a model redundancy process) was considerably smaller than the proportion of men, and the school had failed to put forward any relevant justification.

In relation to acts occurring or continuing past 1 October 2010, claims for indirect sex discrimination should now be brought under the *Equality Act 2010* ('*EqA 2010*'), *ss 11, 19* and *39*.

Alternatively, a complainant could bring a claim under the *Equal Pay Act 1970* ('*EqPA 1970*') on the basis that she was paid less than a man for like work (or work of equal value). There remain some advantages to an equal pay claim, compared with a claim under *FTR 2002*:

(a) *FTR 2002* applies only to employees whereas *EqPA 1970* includes self-employed workers (as long as they work under a contract);

(b) the range of comparators is wider (it not being possible to compare with a predecessor under *FTR 2002*);

(c) the *EqPA 1970* limits the comparison to a term-by-term approach, whereas *FTR 2002* allows for a less favourable term to be balanced by a more favourable term.

However, there are advantages to a claim under *FTR 2002*:

(i) a comparison can be made with a worker of the same sex;

(ii) *FTR 2002* applies to contractual and non-contractual terms;

(iii) *FTR 2002* gives an employment tribunal the power to make a recommendation.

In relation to acts occurring or continuing past 1 October 2010, equal pay claims should now be brought using the new sex equality clause in the *EqA 2010, s 66*. If the matter relates to an occupational pension scheme, the claim should be brought using the new sex equality rule in *EqA 2010, s 67*.

10.4 *Introduction of FTR 2002*

FTR 2002 was brought into force to give effect to the Directive in exercise of the powers granted to the Secretary of State under *EA 2002, ss 45* and *51(1)*.

According to the Explanatory Note to *FTR 2002*, in addition to giving positive rights, they:

> '. . . make a number of amendments to primary legislation to remove discrimination in statutory rights between fixed-term employees (or certain types of fixed-term employees) and permanent employees'.

Guidance, which does not have statutory force, is available from the Department for Business, Innovation and Skills (via http://www.businesslink.gov). Its stated purpose is 'to explain how fixed-term employees are classified and how [employers] must treat them'. This Guidance is referred to in this chapter where relevant.

FTR 2002 do not specifically address the question of territorial scope. However, in *Duncombe v Secretary of State for Children, Schools and Families* [2009] EWCA Civ 1355, [2010] IRLR 331, the Court of Appeal applied the *Bleuse* principle and said that the *FTR*

2002 could apply to a fixed-term employee working in another EU country as the *FTR 2002* should be construed in a way not to deny rights derived from that EU legislation (for further detail see **1.42**). In *Duncombe* the claimant was a teacher on a fixed-term contract who had worked solely in Karlsruhe, Germany. See further **1.43**.

10.5 *Impact of FTR 2002*

It must be assumed that *FTR 2002* has had only limited impact since the employment tribunal statistics for 1 April 2009 to 31 March 2010 (and for the previous four years) have not included cases based on *FTR 2002* as a separate category. (The 'others' heading included 8,100 cases in 2009–10, but no information as to what constitutes 'others' is given, except that it includes unfair dismissal claims from transfers of undertakings.) This is in contrast to the *Part-Time Workers Regulations* (see **10.22**), which are recorded as a separate category.

There have been several cases concerning fixed-term contracts in the EAT (eg *Allen v National Australia Group Europe Ltd* [2004] IRLR 847 and *Cure v Coutts & Co plc* [2005] ICR 298); two in the Court of Appeal (*Webley v Department for Work and Pensions* [2004] EWCA Civ 1745, [2005] ICR 577 and *Duncombe v Secretary of State for Children, Schools and Families* [2009] EWCA Civ 1355, [2010] IRLR 331), and four in the European Court of Justice (*Adeneler v Ellinikos Organismos Galaktos: C-212/04* [2006] IRLR 716; *Impact v Minister for Agriculture and Food: C-268/06* [2008] CMLR 47; *Angelidaki v Organismos Nomarkhiaki Aftodiikisi Rethimnis: C-378/07 to C-380/07* [2009] 3 CMLR 15 and *Zentralbetirebsrat der Landeskrankenhauser Tirols v Land Tirol: C-486/08* [2010] IRLR 631).

10.6 What is a fixed-term contract?

FTR 2002, reg 1(2) states that a fixed-term contract means a contract of employment that, under its provisions determining how it will terminate in the normal course, will terminate:

(a) on the expiry of a specific term;

(b) on completion of a particular task; or

(c) on the occurrence or non-occurrence of any other specific event (other than the attainment by an employee of any normal and bona-fide retiring age).

These definitions would cover: employees doing seasonal or casual work; cover for maternity, paternity, parental or sick leave, and those undertaking a specific task like painting a house.

A contract is for a fixed-term even when it includes a notice provision (*Allen v National Australia Group Europe Ltd* [2004] IRLR 847). The ability of the parties to bring the contract to an end at an earlier date does not make a contract anything other than one for a fixed-term. What is envisaged by the *FTR 2002* is a provision relating to the termination of the relationship 'in the normal course'. Provision for earlier notice does not destroy the original intention of such a contract that the parties would see out the fixed-term, unless and until some event which was not in the normal course occurs.

10.7 *Who is covered?*

Under *reg 2(1)*, a fixed-term employee can compare himself to a comparable permanent employee if, at the time when the treatment that is alleged to be less favourable takes place, both employees are:

(a) employed by the same employer; and

(b) engaged in the same or broadly similar work having regard, where relevant, to whether they have a similar level of qualification and skills.

The permanent employee must work or be based at the same establishment as the fixed-term employee or, where there is no such comparable permanent employee, must work or be based at a different establishment (while still satisfying the requirements above).

As the Guidance makes clear, a fixed-term employee cannot compare conditions with an employee at an associated employer's establishment.

Special classes of people included under *FTR 2002* are set out in *regs 13–17*. They are:

(a) those employed by the Crown (*reg 13*);

(b) those employed by an establishment for the purposes of the *Reserve Forces Act 1996, Part XI* (but not members of the naval, military or air forces) (*reg 14*);

(c) House of Lords staff (*reg 15*);

(d) House of Commons staff (*reg 16*); and

(e) police officers and cadets (*reg 17*).

Those who are excluded from *FTR 2002* are set out in *regs 18–20*. They are:

(a) those employed on schemes designed to provide training or work experience where the schemes are provided under arrangements made by the government or are funded in whole or in part by an institution of the European Community (*reg 18(1)*);

(b) fixed-term employees whose employment consists in a period of work experience not exceeding one year as part of a higher education course (*reg 18(2)*);

(c) agency workers (*reg 19*); and

(d) apprentices (*reg 20*).

10.8 *Comparator*

A fixed-term employee can compare his treatment to the treatment of a comparable permanent employee.

Where a fixed-term employee does the same work as several permanent employees whose contractual terms are different, the fixed-term employee may select a comparator.

Although the comparator may be of the same sex, a comparison cannot be made with:

(a) a hypothetical comparator;

(b) a comparator employed by an associated employer;

(c) a comparator whose employment has ceased (*reg 2(2)*).

As stated above, only if there is no comparator in the establishment can a comparison be made with a similar permanent employee working for the same employer in a different establishment.

In *Hart v Secretary of State for Education and Skills* (ET/2304973/2004) (8 September 2005, unreported), it was necessary to consider whether the claimant education advisers could compare themselves with a particular individual in order to show that they were excluded from redundancy and early retirement benefits payable under the Civil Service Compensation Scheme because of their status as fixed-term employees.

In order to determine this, the employment tribunal fastened on the word 'broadly' in *reg 2(1)(a)(ii)*, which suggested a 'reasonably ample approach' to any comparison. Further, a claimant must establish not only broad similarity in the nature and subject matter of the work but also approximate equivalence in the level of expertise and responsibility at which it is undertaken.

The employment tribunal considered that this approach was fortified by the Court of Appeal in *Matthews v Kent and Medway Towns Fire Authority* [2004] EWCA Civ 844, [2004] 3 All ER 620, [2005] ICR 84, which took a similar view in a case concerning the *Part-time Workers Regulations* (see **10.25**), which are in almost identical terms to *reg 2(1)*. Following the Court of Appeal decision, the *Matthews* case did progress to the House of Lords (see **10.25**) where Lord Hope, who was in a majority on this issue, cautioned that the question as to whether two kinds of workers had similar levels of skill and experience was relevant only so far as it bore on the exercise of assessing whether the work engaged in was the same or broadly similar.

In *Hart*, the particular individual was considered to be an appropriate comparator, the tribunal stating:

> 'We are quite satisfied that the Claimants are entitled to succeed on the Comparator Issue. Their essential function, to advise, was the same. The broad subject matter on which they were required to advise was the same and the fund of experience on which they were expected to call, while diverse, was similarly rooted in long experience in the education sector. The categories of individuals and bodies to whom their advice was directed were the same although there were minor differences in balance as between the recipients of the advice. The fact that [the particular individual's] work tended to focus on a particular problem (failing schools) whereas the Claimants' responsibilities tended to be arranged on a regional basis does not, to our minds, detract from the proposition that the work being undertaken was broadly similar. Nor does the modest difference in balance between the amount of time committed to "policy" and "field work" . . . it seems to us self-evident that two jobs may be broadly similar despite the fact that one is somewhat more "operational" and the other has a rather higher "policy" content.'

It was not disputed that the claimants and the particular individual had similar levels of qualification and skills and, accordingly, the rider to *reg 2(1)(a)(ii)* was satisfied.

For a general discussion of the comparator concept see **1.63–1.71**.

10.9 Less favourable treatment

Less favourable treatment is defined by *reg 3*. A fixed-term employee has the right not to be treated less favourably by his employer as regards the terms of his contract (*reg 3(1)(a)*) or by being subjected to any other detriment by any act, or deliberate failure to act (*reg 3(1)(b)*).

The right conferred by *reg 3(1)* includes, in particular, the right of the fixed-term employee not to be treated less favourably than a permanent employee (*reg 3(2)*) in relation to:

(a) any period of service qualification relating to any particular condition of service;

(b) the opportunity to receive training; or

(c) the opportunity to secure any permanent position in the establishment.

However, the right conferred by *reg 3(1)* applies only if the treatment is on the ground that the employee is a fixed-term employee (*reg 3(a)*) and the treatment is not justified on objective grounds (*reg 3(b)*) (as defined in *reg 4*; see **10.11**).

Further, in determining whether a fixed-term employee has been treated less favourably than a comparable permanent employee, the pro rata principles 'shall be applied unless it is inappropriate' (*reg 3(4)*).

The Guidance sets out examples of less favourable treatment, including:

(a) fixed-term employees being offered less paid holiday (see the ECJ decision in *Zentralbetirebsrat der Landeskrankenhauser Tirols v Land Tirol: C-486/08* [2010] IRLR 631), or not being paid for bank holidays;

(b) fixed-term employees being excluded from non-contractual bonuses, or training; and

(c) fixed-term employees being selected for redundancy purely because they are fixed-term (see, for example, *Whiffen v Milham Ford Girls' School*).

When considering whether there is less favourable treatment a term-by-term approach is required (*Hart v Secretary of State for Education and Skills*). That approach was also adopted in *Matthews v Kent and Medway Towns Fire Authority* in the EAT in the context of the *Part-time Workers Regulations* (reported at [2003] IRLR 732, and not appealed to the Court of Appeal). His Honour Judge Birtles said:

> 'In our view it will be practically impossible to achieve proper and effective equality between part-time and full-time workers if a broad brush approach is adopted . . . Furthermore [cases concerning equal pay] . . . provide strong judicial support from the House of Lords and the European Court of Justice for the specific term by term analysis contended for by [Counsel for the Claimants] and agreed by the Employment Tribunal to be the correct approach.'

There is no less favourable treatment if an employer simply fails to renew a fixed-term contract: *Webley v Department for Work and Pensions* [2004] EWCA Civ 1745, [2005] ICR 577, [2005] IRLR 288. Lord Justice Wall stated (para 36):

> ' . . . it seems to me inexorably to follow that the termination of such a contract by the simple effluxion of time cannot, of itself, constitute less favourable treatment by comparison with a permanent employee. It is of the essence of a fixed-term contract that it comes to an end at the expiry of the fixed-term. Thus unless it can be said that . . . entering into a fixed-term contract is of itself less favourable treatment, the expiry of a fixed-term contract resulting in the dismissal of the fixed-term employee cannot, in my judgment, be said to fall within *regulation 3(1)*.
>
> '37. Similarly, the fact that the termination of the contract by effluxion of time results in the dismissal of the fixed-term employee cannot, of itself, represent a detriment within *regulation 3(1)(b)*. The same argument applies. The termination of the contract is an inevitable consequence of it being for a fixed term.'

10.10 *'On the ground that'*

Regulation 3(3) states that the less favourable treatment must be 'on the ground that' an employee is a fixed-term employee.

It is interesting to note that this is a more favourable test for the employee than the principle as stated in the Directive (*clause 4*) which is that:

> ' . . . fixed-term workers shall not be treated in a less favourable manner than comparative permanent workers *solely* because they have a fixed-term contract or relation unless justified on objective grounds' (emphasis added).

In *Chief Constable of West Yorkshire Police v Khan* [2001] UKHL 48, [2001] 1 WLR 1947, [2001] ICR 1065, a case involving direct race discrimination and victimisation, the House of Lords stated that phrases such as 'on racial grounds' and 'by reason that' require an investigation as to why the discriminator did what he did. Lord Scott of Foscote put it in this way (para 77):

> 'The words "by reason that" suggest, to my mind, that it is the real reason, the core reason, the causa causans, the motive, for the treatment complained of that must be identified'.

(For further detail see **1.49ff.**) In *Cure v Coutts & Co plc* (17 September 2004, unreported), EAT, it was contended that the employees were not treated less favourably on the grounds of being on fixed-term contracts, for the exclusion from the bonus applied to all non-permanent staff (para 18). Although being a fixed-term employee may have been a contributory cause to their exclusion, it was only one of the causes. However, it was accepted in argument that the proper approach to 'on the ground that' in *FTR 2002* was that outlined in *Khan* (para 34) (see **10.31**). On the facts, the EAT rejected the contention that the less favourable treatment was not 'on the ground that the employee is a fixed-term employee' (para 50):

> ' . . . the reason why the Respondents decided to provide no bonus to the [employees] was because they were members of an employee group which consisted of fixed-term contractors. The fact that the Respondent excluded other employee groups, or other business groups, is not relevant . . . Once an employee is within scope of a relevant anti-discrimination measure, and suffers a detriment because he is in that category, it is not relevant to know whether the Respondent discriminates against other employees who may or may not be within the scope of that or another anti-discrimination measure. The Tribunal did not err when it found that the reason for the exclusion of the [employees] from the bonus was that they were in the group of fixed-term employees. As such they were protected by the Regulations, subject to any defence of justification.'

10.11 *Justification*

Under *reg 4(1)*, less favourable treatment of a fixed-term worker shall be treated as justified on objective grounds if the terms of the fixed-term employee's contract of employment, taken as a whole, are at least as favourable as the terms of the comparable permanent contract of employment.

This justification is in addition to the justification specified in *reg 3(3)(b)*.

Hence, there are two ways of justifying under the Regulations:

(a) on a term-by-term basis (*reg 3(3)(b)*);

(b) a 'package approach' peculiar to the *FTR 2002* (*reg 4*) (for example, such an approach in not available in *EqPA 1970* or in relation to cases of part-time discrimination).

The normal test of justification, available under *reg 3(3)(b)* (and *reg 4*, but by reference to the package approach rather than term by term) is as follows:

(a) Does the measure achieve a legitimate objective, for example a genuine business objective?

(b) Is the measure necessary to achieve that objective?

(c) Is the measure an appropriate way to achieve that objective?

See, for example, *Bilka-Kaufhaus GmbH v Webber Von Hartz* [1986] IRLR 317, para 36 (see **11.27**). A shorter definition is more commonly used: Is the measure a proportionate means of achieving a legitimate aim?

Applying the test of justification to a term-by-term approach is straightforward. The only question is whether the less favourable treatment in relation to the term in question can be justified.

Applying the test of justification to the package approach is a novel concept (since it is not available elsewhere in discrimination law). In determining the success of any trade-off in terms, the value of benefits should be assessed on the basis of their objective monetary worth, rather than the value that the employer or employee perceives them to have.

In *Hart v Secretary of State for Education and Skills*, the tribunal described the alternative routes to justification as follows:

> 'It seems to us that [Regulation] *3(3)(b)* read in conjunction with [Regulation] *4* provides the employer with two alternative routes to proving justification. The first . . . requires a narrow focus on the specific treatment complained of by the Claimant and any justification argument directed specifically to that treatment. The second . . . deems the justification defence under [Regulation] *3(3)(b)* to be made out if the employer can establish, on a "compendious" approach, overall comparability between the terms of the claimant's contract and that of his comparator.'

Justifications must refer to 'precise and concrete circumstances', such as the specific nature of the tasks to be performed under the fixed term contract or the pursuit of a legitimate social policy objective (*Adeneler v Ellinikos Organismos Galaktos*). 'Abstract national norms' will not suffice (*Zentralbetirebsrat der Landeskrankenhauser Tirols v Land Tirol: C-486/08* [2010] IRLR 631).

10.12 Written statements

FTR 2002, reg 5 provides that, if an employee considers his employer may have treated him in a manner which infringes a right conferred on him by *reg 3*, he may request a written statement giving particulars of the reasons for the treatment. The employee is entitled to be provided with such a statement within 21 days of his request.

Such a written statement is admissible as evidence in any proceedings under *FTR 2002*. Further, if it appears to the employment tribunal in such proceedings that an employer deliberately, and without reasonable excuse, omitted to provide such a statement, or that the statement was evasive or equivocal, it may draw inferences (including that the employer has infringed the right in question).

However, *reg 5* does not apply where the treatment complained of is dismissal, the employee then being entitled to a written statement of reasons under *Employment Rights Act 1996* (*ERA 1996*), *s 92*.

FTR 2002, reg 9 provides that an employee who considers himself to be a permanent employee by virtue of *reg 8* is able to request in writing from his employer a written statement confirming that his contract is no longer fixed-term. Such a statement must, again, be provided within 21 days. Alternatively, the employer should give a statement giving reasons why the contract remains fixed-term (*reg 9(1)(b)*). With regard to the latter, this should include any assertion that there were objective grounds for engagement under a fixed-term contract, or the renewal of such a contract.

Such statements are admissible as evidence in any proceedings before a court, an employment tribunal and the Commissioners of the HM Revenue and Customs. Inferences may be drawn if the employer deliberately, and without reasonable excuse, omits to provide a statement or if the statement is evasive or equivocal.

If an employer fails to provide a statement, or has given a statement of reasons under *reg 9(1)(b)* (above), and the employee is still employed, the employee may present an application to an employment tribunal under *reg 9(5)* for a declaration that he is, in fact, a permanent employee.

10.13 Right to be informed of vacancies

Regulation 3(6) provides that, in order to ensure that an employee is able to exercise the right conferred by *reg 3(1)*, the employee also has the right to be informed by his employer of available vacancies in the establishment.

Reg 3(7) makes it clear that an employee is so informed only if the vacancy is contained in an advertisement which the employee has a reasonable opportunity of reading in the course of his employment, or if the employee is given reasonable notification of the vacancy in some other way.

10.14 Unfair dismissal or other detriment

Regulation 6(1) states that an employee who is dismissed shall be regarded as unfairly dismissed for the purposes of *ERA 1996, Part 10* if the reason—or, if more than one, the principal reason—is a reason specified in *reg 6(3)*.

Further, under *reg 6(2)* an employee has the right not to be subjected to any detriment by any act, or deliberate failure to act, of his employer done on a ground specified in *reg 6(3)*.

The reasons, or grounds, in *reg 6(3)* are that the employee:

(a) brought proceedings against the employer under *FTR 2002*;

(b) requested from his employer a written statement under *reg 5* or *9*;

(c) gave evidence or information in connection with such proceedings brought by any employee;

(d) otherwise did anything under *FTR 2002* in relation to the employer or any other person;

(e) alleged that the employer had infringed *FTR 2002*;

(f) refused (or proposed to refuse) to forgo a right conferred on him by *FTR 2002*.

(g) declined to sign a workforce agreement under *FTR 2002*;

(h) was a representative of members of the workforce of *Sch 1* to *FTR 2002* (concerning workforce agreements), or was a candidate to become such a representative.

Similarly, an employee is protected by *reg 6(3)* if the employer believes or suspects that the employee has done or intends to do any of these things.

As is usual with such provisions, there will be no unfair dismissal or detriment if any allegation made by the employee is false and not made in good faith (*reg 6(4)*).

Of course, by *ERA 1996, s 95(1)(b)* (substituted by *FTR 2002* as from 1 October 2002) an employee is dismissed by his employer if he is employed under a limited-term contract and that contract terminates because of the limiting event and is not renewed. (See also *ERA 1996, s 136(1)(b)*, in relation to dismissal by reason of redundancy.)

Hence any fixed-term contract which comes to an end requires an employer to follow the statutory dismissal procedure and, if relevant, to pay a statutory redundancy payment; the provisions enabling fixed-term employees to waive their rights have been removed by *FTR 2002*. Hence, fixed-term employees on task contracts of two years or more will now have a right to statutory redundancy payments if they are made redundant at the end of their contracts. They cannot be excluded from the statutory payments scheme, even where it may appear objectively justified. However, they may be excluded from contractual schemes if this may be objectively justified.

It should be noted, too, that even if it would have been futile to consult with employees who have completed a task (assuming there were sufficient numbers of employees to bring the *Trade Union and Labour Relations (Consolidation) Act 1992, s 188* into play) such consultation is still necessary (*GMB v Susie Radin Ltd* [2004] EWCA Civ 180, [2004] IRLR 400).

10.15 Complaint to an employment tribunal

Under *reg 7*, an employee may present a complaint to an employment tribunal that his employer has infringed a right conferred on him by *reg 3*.

Regulation 7(2) provides that the employment tribunal shall not consider a complaint unless it is presented before the end of the period of three months beginning with the date of the less favourable treatment or detriment or, where an act or failure to act is part of a series of similar acts or failures, the last of them. If the alleged infringement relates to the right under *reg 3(6)* to be informed of a vacancy, then the three months runs from the date, or if more than one the last date, on which other individuals (whether or not employees of the employer) were informed of the vacancy.

In *Cure v Coutts & Co plc* the date of the act complained of (being the non-payment of a contractual bonus) was not the date on which an intention in principle was enunciated, but when the employer decided on the date, detail and application to relevant employees of the bonus.

A complaint may be considered out of time if, in all the circumstances of the case, the employment tribunal considers that it is just and equitable to do so.

The remedies available to an employment tribunal are specified in *reg 7(7)*. If an employment tribunal considers that a case is well-founded it can:

(a) make a declaration as to the rights of the complainant and the employer;

(b) order the employer to pay compensation to the complainant; and/or

(c) recommend that the employer take, within a specified period, reasonable action to reduce the adverse effect on the complainant.

10.16 Fixed-term to permanent

Regulation 8 provides that, where an employee is employed under a purported fixed-term contract, and such contract has previously been renewed (or the employee has previously been employed on a fixed-term contract), the employee shall be a permanent employee if he has been continuously employed for a period of four years or more and the use of a fixed-term contract was not justified on objective grounds. The justification must be judged as at the time when the contract was last renewed, or if it has not been renewed, at the time of entering into the contract.

Regulation 8 does not require that the fixed term should be a false pretence or that the contract is pretending to be something it is not. It applies even in cases where the use of successive fixed-term contracts was not an abuse (*Duncombe v Secretary of State for Children, Schools and Families* [2009] EWCA Civ 1355, [2010] IRLR 331).

The operation of *reg 8* can be modified by a collective or workforce agreement which specifies a maximum total period for fixed-term work, or a maximum number of fixed-term contracts, or objective grounds for such contracts.

It should be noted that there is no limit on the duration of a first fixed-term contract. However, if a first fixed-term contract for four years or more is renewed, the second will be regarded as permanent (unless the second contract is objectively justified).

The limitation on successive fixed-term contracts will apply only where the employee has been continuously employed for the whole period. An employee may be continuously employed even where there is a gap between successive contracts. The relevant test for continuity is that in *ERA 1996, Part 14, Chapter 1, ss 210–219.*

10.17 Minimum notice

Employees on task contracts expected to last three months or less have the right to a minimum notice period of one week if their contracts are terminated (other than by completion) after they have one month or more of continuous service. (This change is a result of the Regulations amending *ERA 1996, s 86.*) This means employees must also give their employers one week's notice of the termination of their contracts if they have one month or more of continuous service.

10.18 Liability of employers and principals

Liability for employers and agents under *FTR 2002* follows that in *EqA 2010* (see **1.163**ff).

10.19 Redundancy

Employers must justify making staff on fixed-term contracts redundant before any permanent employee although, insofar as such a claim constitutes indirect sex discrimination (see **1.80**; justification in such circumstances has always been necessary (*Whiffen v Milham Ford Girls' School* (see **10.3**)).

Justification will equally be necessary where a fixed-term employee is precluded from obtaining an enhanced redundancy payment (*Hart v Secretary of State for Education and Skills*).

It is impermissible for national legislation to exclude fixed-term employees for the purpose of calculating thresholds for collective redundancies (*Confederation Generale du Travail v Premiere ministre: C-385/05* [2007] ECR I–611.

10.20 PART-TIME WORKERS

Derivation of UK Legislation

The *Part-time Workers (Prevention of Less Favourable Treatment) Regulations 2000 (SI 2000/1551)* ('*PTWR 2000*') came into force on 1 July 2000, provision having been made for their introduction by *ERA 1999, ss 19–21.* They were introduced to implement *Directive 1997/81/EC* (the '*Part-Time Directive*'), which was adopted on 15 December 1997 (and which applied to the UK as a result of the provisions of *Directive 1998/23/EC*) concerning the Framework Agreement on Part-Time Work, which was concluded by cross-industry organisations in June 1997. *PTWR 2000* were subsequently amended by the *Part-time Workers (Prevention of Less Favourable Treatment) Regulations 2000 (Amendment) Regulations 2002 (SI 2002/2035)* (the '*PTWR (Amendment) 2002*'), in relation to comparators and access to pension schemes.

10.21 Pre-existing protection

Prior to the implementation of the *PTWR 2000* part-time workers could only bring a claim under discrimination legislation, generally an indirect sex discrimination claim or equal pay claim (see Sex discrimination (8) and Equal pay (11)) in appropriate circumstances. The *PTWR 2000* give rights to part-timers because of their status as part-timers and so provide a remedy for male part-timers who have been disadvantaged because of their part-time status.

In practice, many women will continue to bring a sex discrimination or an equal pay claim in addition to a claim under *PTWR 2000* (see SEX DISCRIMINATION (8) and EQUAL PAY (11)).

10.22 Why were the PTWR 2000 introduced and what has been their impact?

Part-time working is a very common form of atypical work in the UK. In 2009, there were approximately 6.5 million part-timers (5.1 million of whom were women) (*Labour Force Survey 2009*). The stated aim of the *Part-Time Directive* was to end the less favourable treatment of part-timers and support the development of a flexible labour market. This would be done, the *Part-Time Directive* envisaged, by encouraging the greater use of part-time employment, and increasing the quality and range of jobs that are considered suitable for part-time working or job-sharing. *PTWR 2000* were introduced in order to implement the Directive. The more aspirational aims of the *Part-Time Directive* are not directly addressed in the *PTWR 2000*, but are to be found in the Department for Business, Innovation and Skills ('BIS') Best Practice Guide, eg in respect of widening access to part-time work at the recruitment stage or maximising opportunities, career progression and mobility for part-timers, (see further below).

The *PTWR 2000* create no right to work part-time.

Relatively few cases have been brought under the *PTWR 2000*. For example, only 530 claims were brought in the year from April 2009 to March 2010 which compares with 57,400 unfair dismissal claims and 18,200 sex discrimination claims in the same period (*Employment Tribunal and EAT Statistics (GB) 1 April 2009 to 31 March 2010*). In guidance that was published in 2002, BIS (then the DTI) expressed the view that *'less-favourable treatment of part-time workers is not widespread in the UK'* ('Part-time Workers. The law and best practice—a detailed guide for employers and part-timers' URN No: 02/1710).

10.23 Guidance on the PTWR 2000

The *Employment Relations Act 1999, ss 20–21* anticipates publication of a Code of Practice. This has not been produced, but the former EOC's Code of Practice on Sex Discrimination included guidance on part-timers (recommending that employers consider whether certain jobs can be carried out on a part-time basis). This Code has, however, been replaced by the Employment Code that accompanies the *EqA 2010*, which makes no specific mention of part-time workers.

BIS (then the DTI) produced a useful guide for employers in 2002 entitled 'Part-time Workers. The law and best practice'. This is broken down into 'Compliance Guidance' and 'Best Practice Guidance'. The Best Practice Guidance provides examples of the ways in which employers can widen the access to part-time work, for example, by making a wider range of jobs available part-time, by operating job-sharing arrangements and by improving the flow of information to workers.

The ACAS guide 'Flexible working and work-life balance' (April 2009) also deals with issues concerning part-time working.

10.24 Who is covered?

The legislation protects 'part-time workers'. A part-time worker is defined as a person who is 'paid wholly or in part by reference to the time he works and, having regard to the custom and practice of the employer in relation to workers employed by the worker's employer under the same type of contract is not identifiable as a full-time worker' (*reg 2(2)*). This definition affords some flexibility: any worker who works and is paid in respect of less than full-time work may qualify.

A worker is defined as:

'an individual who has entered into or works under or (except where a provision of these Regulations otherwise requires) where the employment has ceased, worked under:

(a) a contract of employment; or
(b) any other contract, whether express or implied and (if it is express) whether oral or in writing, whereby the individual undertakes to do or perform personally any work or services for another party to the contract whose status is not by virtue of the contract that of a client or customer of any profession or business undertaking carried on by the individual' (*PTWR 2000, reg 1(2)*).

The *PTWR 2000* cover those in Crown employment, as well as House of Lords and House of Commons staff, together with members of police forces, special constables and those police cadets who are treated as being employed under a contract of employment. They also apply to members of the armed forces, but not necessarily to members of the reserve forces (*R (on the application of Manson) v Ministry of Defence* [2005] EWHC 427 (Admin), [2005] All ER (D) 270 (Feb)). They do not apply to any holder of a judicial office if paid on a daily-fee basis (as opposed to salaried part-time judges, who are covered). However, following a challenge by a fee-paid judicial office holder in respect of access to a pension, the Supreme Court has referred to the ECJ the question of whether fee-paid judicial office holders can be excluded under the PWTR 2000 (*O'Brien v Ministry of Defence* [2010] UKSC 34, [2010] 4 All ER 62). It therefore remains to be seen if this exclusion will continue.

Unlike, for example, in the case of sex discrimination under *EqA 2010*, job applicants are not protected. This means that an employer may advertise for a full-time position and reject any candidate who is only prepared to work part-time (although the rejected candidate may nevertheless have a valid indirect sex discrimination claim (see **8.37**).

There is no minimum qualifying period.

Under the *EA 2002* employees have a separate statutory right to request flexible working, which can include part-time working (see **8.137ff**).

In a slightly unusual case, *Hudson v University of Oxford* [2007] EWCA Civ 336, [2007] All ER (D) 356 (Feb), the Court of Appeal decided that an employee who worked full-time hours but under two separate part-time contracts could in theory contend that he is a part-timer in respect of each contract (although ultimately this will of course always depend on the facts). (This case should, however, be treated with some caution because the decision was made in the context of an appeal against a strike out of the worker's claim, where the employee had only to show that he had a reasonable prospect of success.)

10.25 Comparator

An actual comparator

The *PTWR 2000* set out the conditions that must be met by the part-timer and the full-time comparator.

The *PTWR 2000* require that (with the exception of circumstances explained in **10.26**) the worker must choose an appropriate full-time worker with whom to compare himself. The option of using a hypothetical comparator is not permitted. The *Part-time Directive* is not so restrictive, as it provides that where there is no comparable full-time worker at the same establishment, a comparison can be made by reference to national law, a collective agreement or 'practice'. This arguably provides scope for the use of a hypothetical comparator in certain circumstances.

However, in *Carl v University of Sheffield* [2009] UKEAT 0261/08 the EAT found, unequivocally, that the 'plain effect' of the *PTWR 2000* is that an actual comparator must be identified. Accordingly, it was not permissible, on the facts, for a part-time teacher of shorthand to compare herself to a hypothetical, 'generic', full-time teacher.

Regulation 2 of the PTWR 2000 requires that:

- both the part-time worker and the full-time comparator must be employed by the same employer (*reg 2(4)(a)(i)*). There is no provision for a part-timer to compare his treatment with that of a full-timer at an associated company. In theory, it appears that a business could set up a separate company to employ all its part-timers. However, if this were to be done solely to avoid claims under *PTWR 2000*, it is possible that a tribunal may take a purposive approach to the legislation and look beyond the corporate structure.
- both workers must be employed under the same type of contract (*reg 2(4)(a)(i)*). *Regulation 2(3)* identifies four categories of contract under which both workers must be engaged. These categories are mutually exclusive and are: employees working under a contract of employment that is not a contract of apprenticeship (*reg 2(3)(a)*); employees working under an apprenticeship contract (*reg 2(3)(b)*); workers who are not employees (*reg 2(3)(c)*); and 'any other description of worker that it is reasonable for the employer to treat differently from other workers, on the ground that workers of that description have a different type of contract' (*reg 2(3)(d)*).

  The requirement, however, that a permanent part-timer had to compare himself with a permanent full-timer (and a fixed-term part-timer had to compare himself with a fixed-term full-timer) was removed by the *PTWR (Amendment) 2002*.

  In *Matthews v Kent and Medway Towns Fire Authority* [2006] UKHL 8, [2006] ICR 365, it was acknowledged that although there were structural differences between the contracts that both part- and full-time firefighters worked under, for example in relation to the calculation of pay and working patterns, these did not mean that the types of contract were different. The House of Lords decided that both part-time and full-time firefighters were employed under a contract of employment that, in the language of the *PTWR 2000*, was not a contract of apprenticeship. Although the tribunal and the EAT had found that the part-time firefighters were employed on contracts that fell within the 'any other description of worker' type of contract, this was viewed by the House of Lords as a residual category that was only included in the *PTWR 2000* in case an employer adopted an unusual contract that was not covered by any of the other three categories. The House of Lords said it could not envisage any such contract being agreed.

  A more restrictive approach was taken by the ECJ in *Wippel v Peek & Cloppenburg GmbH and Co Kg: C-313/02* [2005] IRLR 211. An employee working under a part-time 'zero hours' contract could refuse work and had no fixed hours. The employee argued that the absence of a contractual provision stipulating a fixed period of weekly working time, plus the lack of a guaranteed salary, amounted to less favourable treatment on the grounds of her part-time status. The ECJ held, however, that her claim could not succeed as she could not compare herself with either full-time or part-time workers working for the same employer whose contracts identified working hours.
- both workers must be engaged in the same or broadly similar work (*reg 2(4)(a)(ii)*), having regard to whether they have similar levels of qualification, skill and experience.

  In *Matthews*, the House of Lords held (by a 4:1 majority on this issue) that the main purpose of both the part-time and full-time firefighters jobs was the same (putting out fires) and that most of their duties and responsibilities were the same. The

House of Lords decided that more weight should be given to the extent that both jobs are the same, rather than emphasising their differences, as it will commonly be the case that part-timers will be given different work from that of full-timers.

On remission from the House of Lords, the tribunal found, as a matter of fact, that the part-time firefighters were, indeed, carrying out the same or broadly similar work to their full-time counterparts. The 'central duties' were the same for both roles (London South Employment Tribunal, 6100000/2001).

If a worker who has two part-time contracts can bring a claim under the *PTWR 2000* in relation to either contract (see *Hudson*), his employer may argue that only a full-timer doing two comparable jobs can be considered to do broadly similar work—an impossibility. However, tribunals may be reluctant to uphold such a narrow approach and might conceivably permit the employee to compare himself with a full-timer doing only one of the jobs.

- both workers must be based at the same establishment. If, however, no full-time worker works or is based at the same establishment as the part-timer, the comparator can be based at a different establishment operated by the same employer (*reg 2(4)(b)*).
- both workers must be paid by reference to the time that they work (*reg 2(1), (2)*).
- the part-time worker must be identifiable as a part-time worker, and the full-time worker must be identifiable as a full-time worker. In each case, regard should be had to the employer's custom and practice in relation to workers employed by the employer under the same type of contract (*reg 2(1), (2)*).

A part-time employee at a school was unable to compare herself with two workers in the same department who worked 35 hours per week during term time only. This was because the employer's contractual documents stipulated that full-timers work 37 hours per week and the applicant had produced no evidence that the school had treated the workers who worked 35 hours as full-timers. It was noted, though, that if the employer, by custom and practice, had treated these workers as full-timers then a comparison could be made (*England v Governing Body of Turnford School* [2003] All ER (D) 105 (May)).

For a general discussion of the comparator concept see **1.63–1.71**.

10.26 *Comparison with a worker's previous contract*

Using another worker as a comparator is not necessary in certain limited circumstances, where a comparison can be made with the same worker's previous contract. *Regulation 3* permits a worker who switches from full-time to part-time work to compare his terms with those that he enjoyed immediately before the change, even if the new contract is of a different type from the previous one.

Regulation 4 provides that this comparison can be made even if there is a break in employment, provided that this break lasts for less than 12 months and the worker returns either to the same job, or to a job at the same level. This means that, for example, a woman who meets these conditions after taking maternity leave or workers who take a career break, can compare themselves with the treatment or the terms that applied prior to the break. If the employer can show that the worker's original contract would have been varied during the period of absence, then the comparison must be made with that varied contract.

10.27 Less favourable treatment

A part-time worker has the right not to be treated less favourably by his employer than a comparable full-time worker (*reg 5(1)*). The right covers the terms of a worker's contract, which the BIS Guide explains includes:

(a) the reorganisation of working hours;

(b) seeking promotion;

(c) rates of pay, including enhanced pay, overtime, profit-sharing, share option schemes and contractual sick and maternity pay;

(d) access to occupational pensions;

(e) access to training;

(f) benefits, such as health insurance;

(g) annual leave, maternity and parental leave and career breaks; and

(h) public and bank holidays.

The right to protection from less favourable treatment in the *Part-time Directive* relates to employment conditions and other detriment arising from any act, or deliberate failure to act, by the employer. In this regard, the BIS Guide refers specifically to selection for redundancy of part-time workers before full-time workers. It is likely that 'detriment' will be construed as in other discrimination legislation (see **1.14**). In *Pipe v Hendrickson Europe Ltd* [2003] All ER (D) 280 (Apr) it was accepted that dismissal amounted to a detriment under *reg 5(1)(b)*. (The employer abandoned the contrary argument which seems to have been based on the premise that dismissals were only caught by the Regulations to the extent they came within the automatically unfair dismissal provision of *reg 7*.)

Whilst lower remuneration and benefits are often straightforward to identify, some less favourable treatment may be less so. For example, will promotion of a comparable full-time worker be less favourable treatment where the full-timer is promoted to manage a team of full-time workers? Arguably yes, but there may be good counter-arguments to say that it is objectively justifiable. Would it make any difference if the employer were to interview the part-timer, to confirm his/her suitability and willingness to work full-time? The BIS Guide says that employers should be open to workers' willingness to work full-time. In practice there may be other considerations and it may not be possible for an employer to justify preferring a full-timer, eg where no absolute requirement for the manager to manage full-time can be made out.

The question whether less favourable treatment may be counterbalanced by more favourable treatment in relation to other terms and conditions such that there would be a finding of no less favourable treatment overall was considered in *Matthews*. Baroness Hale (with whom Lord Hope and Lord Nicholls agreed), while considering this as a 'subsidiary question', did not wish to rule out the possibility. On remission from the House of Lords, however, the tribunal followed a 'term-by-term' approach, holding that each term was capable of being pro-rated and should therefore be considered separately (*London* South Employment Tribunal, 6100000/2001). This approach seems to be similar to comparison of terms under *EqPA 1970* (now *EqA 2010*) (also see **10.32**). The Tribunal's approach in this case is consistent with the BIS Guide which does not anticipate that an off-setting exercise will take place. The approach is one of a term-by-term analysis of less favourable treatment. For example, it states that part-time workers must receive the same basic rate of pay as comparable full-time workers, unless objectively justifiable. Subject to the pro rata principle, the same goes for other remuneration and benefits. There may be greater scope to argue that a package approach may be taken when considering justification (see **10.32**). (*FTR 2002*, on the other hand, provide expressly that less favourable treatment is justified where the fixed-term employee's overall package is no less favourable (*reg 4(1)*).)

10.28 *Pro rata principle*

Regulation 5(3) introduces the pro rata principle to be used when determining whether there has been less favourable treatment, unless it is inappropriate. The pro rata principle derives from the *Part-time Directive, Article 4(2)* and is defined at *reg 1(2)*. It is limited to pay or any other benefits. The definition read in isolation provides that part-timers are entitled to receive proportionate pay and benefits. This was raised in *McMenemy v Capita Business Services Ltd* [2007] IRLR 400, and the court confirmed that *PTWR 2000* do not provide a free-standing right to pro rata pay and benefits. The pro rata principle acts as a tool to enable a valid comparison to be made between part-time and full-time remuneration.

If it is appropriate to use the pro rata principle, it will be necessary to consider how it should be applied. For example, where a monthly wage is made up of component parts, should each part be analysed separately or should the wages as a whole be pro-rated? The BIS Guide suggests a term-by-term approach; however, this may not always produce a valid comparison. For example, in order to avoid a 'completely unreal and impractical' outcome, whereby part-time workers would be paid at a higher hourly rate than their full-time counterparts, *James v Great North Eastern Railways* [2005] All ER (D) 15 (Mar) held that the pro rata principle should be applied to the employees' average hourly wage. In this way, the composite hourly rate of full-timers who received an additional hourly allowance could be compared against the hourly rate of part-timers who did not.

Matthews is an example of where the pro rata principle may not be appropriate. The tribunal in the first instance held that it was inappropriate to apply the pro rata principle to the entire financial package claimed by the fire fighters, which included pension benefit, sick pay and pay for additional duties. This was not challenged in the EAT. That is not to say that such terms were capable in principle of being pro-rated individually (see **10.27** above).

Benefits such as health care or a company car are further examples of where applying the pro rata principle may not be appropriate. To provide no benefit would, however, be likely to be difficult to justify. It may therefore be that a pro rated car allowance, based on the cost of the car, or a contribution to health care cover, should be provided (see BIS Guide).

10.29 *Overtime*

Overtime is dealt with specifically in the *PTWR 2000. Regulation 5(4)* reflects the principle laid down in *Stadt Lengerich v Helmig* [1995] IRLR 216, that part-timers are not entitled to pro rata overtime payments until they have worked the same number of hours as their comparators.

This principle was tested in *James*. The case turned on the pay structure for GNER staff. The EAT held that the 'additional hours allowance', which formed part of contractual, rostered hours, did not amount to overtime in the *reg 5(4)* sense. The EAT's application of the pro rata principle, however, reflected its concern that part-timers should not benefit disproportionately from a pay structure originally implemented for full-time staff. In assessing the less favourable treatment, the EAT considered that the comparison should be between the average hourly rate of basic pay and additional hours allowance earned by full-timers, as against the basic pay (but no 'additional hours allowance') earned by part-timers.

The ECJ has also decided, in *Voss v Land Berlin: C-300/06*, [2007] All ER (D) 87, ECJ, that a female part-timer suffered a detriment compared with a male full-time employee where she was paid overtime at a lesser rate than that which applied during her normal working hours. This was the case even though the full-timer would also be paid for overtime at the same lesser rate. The decision was based on the fact that the part-timer's rate of pay for overtime would be less than the full-timer's rate of pay for normal work. The ECJ decided that this difference in treatment would be contrary to the *EC Treaty, Article 141(3)* where a considerably higher percentage of women would be affected as compared with the percentage of men so affected, and the difference in treatment could not be objectively justified (see **8.144**). In the absence of justification, any disparate impact could be remedied by paying the part-timer for overtime, for the period until the part-timer has worked the equivalent of the full-timer's normal working hours, at the same rate as a full-timer's normal working hours. The case emphasises that employers should carefully assess the impact on part-time workers when making and implementing their arrangements for overtime.

10.30 *Statutory holidays*

The risk of less favourable treatment arising for part-time workers in respect of Monday public holidays is identified in the BIS (then DTI) Guide. It provides,

> '. . . because most bank and public holidays fall on Monday, those who do not work Mondays will be entitled to proportionately fewer days off. In many workplaces, these workers will predominantly be part-timers. In such cases, it may be necessary to remove the disadvantage suffered . . . for example by giving all workers a pro rata entitlement of days off in lieu according to the number of hours they work'.

The government has now taken steps to reduce the risk of less favourable treatment for part-timers in respect of statutory holidays. Minimum annual holiday entitlement for full-time workers under the *Working Time Regulations 1998* increased from 24 days to 28 days from 1 April 2009. This is said to benefit 2.5 million men and 3.5 million women, equating to 31% of part-time workers, and 14% of full-time workers. Where employers' holiday entitlement exactly mirrors the new statutory entitlements, the question of less favourable treatment under the *PTWR 2000* has reduced because there is a requirement under the amended *Working Time Regulations 1998* to provide 5.6 weeks' holiday per year to all workers regardless of the days on which workers may be required to work. There is still scope for inequality, for example if employers offer bank and public holidays in addition to the 5.6 weeks minimum, or indeed for part-time workers required to take bank or public holidays, leaving them with less relative flexibility as to when they may take holiday. This disadvantage can be mitigated by offering unpaid leave.

There have been two Scottish decisions on statutory holidays, *Gibson v Scottish Ambulance Service* UKEATS/0052/04 and *McMenemy* (see **10.28**). Both hinged on the reason for the less favourable treatment, and both found in favour of the employer, that the reason was not part-time status, rather that the employees did not work on Mondays. However, following an English EAT decision (*Sharma v Manchester City Council* [2008] IRLR 336 (see **10.31**)), it appears that employers may no longer be able to rely on this argument and in both Scottish cases it was accepted that there had been less favourable treatment.

10.31 Less favourable treatment on the ground that the worker is a part-time worker

Regulation 5(2)(a) limits the scope of the *PTWR 2000* to less favourable treatment 'on the ground that' the worker is a part-time worker. This reflects, but does not precisely mirror, the *Part-Time Directive 1997/81/EC, Article 4*, which prohibits less favourable treatment 'solely' because of working part-time.

There is currently a conflict between English and Scottish authority as to whether part-time status must be the *only* reason for the less favourable treatment.

In *Gibson* the Scottish EAT focused on the 'sole' reason for the treatment. In *McMenemy v Capita Business Services Ltd* [2007] IRLR 400 the Scottish Court of Session approved *Gibson* and took a similar approach. However in *Sharma v Manchester City Council* [2008] IRLR 336 the then President of the EAT, Elias J, categorically disagreed, finding that the *Gibson* approach was not a 'legitimate construction' of the *PTWR 2000.* The EAT found that the protection afforded by the *PTWR 2000* was triggered where part-time status was 'one of the reasons' for the less favourable treatment. Similarly, in *Carl v University of Sheffield* [2009] UKEAT 0261/08 the EAT held that part-time status need not be the sole reason for the less favourable treatment but must be the 'effective and predominant cause'. While *Sharma* and *Carl* bring the test of causation under the *PTWR 2000* more into line with that for other direct discrimination claims, (see **1.49**ff), it is clearly unsatisfactory that there is currently a North-South divide in the authorities on this point.

Notwithstanding the above uncertainty, case law has provided clarification of other issues related to the way in which 'on the ground that' should be interpreted under the *PTWR 2000*:

(a) the test is a subjective, factual one, looking at the motive operating in the mind of the employer, rather than a causative, 'but for' test (*Chief Constable of West Yorkshire Police v Khan* [2001] IRLR 830, [2001] UKHL 48; *Gibson*, *McMenemy*);

(b) dismissal will be on the grounds of part-time work and not redundancy where business needs require full-time, rather than part-time staff (*Hendrickson*);

(c) unlike the type of comparator with whom a part-time worker must compare himself under the *PTWR 2000* (see **10.25**), a tribunal may consider a *hypothetical* full-time comparator when deciding on the motive of the employer (*McMenemy*);

(d) pressure to work full-time for employment to continue will be less favourable treatment on the grounds of part-time status (*Hendrickson*);

(e) a tribunal may conclude that the less favourable treatment has not been on the ground of part-time status, despite the fact that no full-time worker has been so disadvantaged (*McMenemy*).

The analysis of the reason why the treatment occurred provides the tribunal with a broad discretion to make its decision based on the evidence in each particular case. Guidance on this analysis may be drawn from other areas of discrimination law (see **1.49**ff).

Where less favourable treatment is a likely outcome of a particular practice, it follows that it may assist employers to put in place clear contractual and policy wording indicating the reasons for the practice. The disparate impact of the practice should be monitored, to avoid any adverse impact on part-timers. An example of this is access to training for part-time workers who do not work particular days. Whilst, on the *McMenemy* reasoning, the reason for the less favourable treatment would not be part-time status, but the fact that part-timers do not work on a particular day, the BIS Guidance recommends that steps be taken to minimise the less favourable treatment, for example, by paying part-timers for the extra hours worked to attend training, or by offering other training methods such as distance learning courses.

10.32 Justification

Neither *PTWR 2000* nor the *Part-Time Directive* give any guidance on objective justification. However, as with the *FTR 2002* (see **10.11**), it is expected that this will be assessed in the same way as in other discrimination legislation (see **1.83**ff), ie it can only be justified if the treatment aims to achieve a legitimate business objective and it is necessary and appropriate to achieve that objective.

Baroness Hale's judgment in *Matthews* considered whether less favourable elements contained in a part-timer's pay and benefits may be justified by other, more favourable elements contained elsewhere in the package. Baroness Hale said that it may be an appropriate route to take in certain cases; however, the House of Lords upheld the tribunal's conclusion that it was difficult for the employer objectively to justify the differences. Baroness Hale believed that it would be difficult to see how the differently configured pay package could justify part-timers' exclusion from the employer's pension or sick pay schemes.

It is significant, however, that the *PTWR 2000* do not contain the equivalent of *FTR 2002, reg 4(1)*, which require the terms of the employment contract as a whole, to be at least as favourable. The analogy, therefore, would more naturally be with the term-by-term analysis under *EqPA 1970* (now *EqA 2010*). The status of fixed-term employees, where more favourable terms may, in practice, be agreed, lends itself more naturally to a consideration of the 'package' approach (see **10.11**). However, in appropriate circumstances, there should not be any reason why such an argument objectively to justify less favourable treatment should not succeed.

The pro rata principle, whilst not a free-standing right, limits the scope of the justification defence. There is a presumption that proportionate remuneration or benefits will be provided, and a failure to do so will need to be justified on objective grounds which do not include financial constraints (*Hill v Revenue Comrs: C-243/95* [1998] ECR I-3739, [1998] All ER (EC) 722, [1999] ICR 48), but which may include demand (*Gibson*).

10.33 Right to a written statement

Pursuant to a provision designed to reduce the number of tribunal claims, a part-timer who believes that he has been treated less favourably than a comparable full-timer, can write to his employer and ask for written reasons for the different treatment (*reg 6(1)*). The employer must respond in writing within 21 days, and the statement can be used in evidence in proceedings under *PTWR 2000*. The tribunal can infer that the worker was discriminated against on the ground of his part-time status if the employer does not provide a written statement, or if the reasons given are evasive or equivocal.

If an employee is dismissed, this specific right to receive a written statement under *PTWR 2000* will not apply. However, the employee will be entitled to receive a written statement of the reasons for his dismissal in accordance with *ERA 1996, s 92(1)*, within 14 days of making a written request. This statement can then be used in evidence in any proceedings (*ERA 1996, s 92(5)*). The tribunal can award two weeks' pay should the employer unreasonably refuse to provide the statement, or if it is inadequate or untrue.

10.34 Unfair dismissal or other detriment

Regulation 7(1) provides that dismissing an employee will be automatically unfair if the reason or principal reason for the dismissal is that the employee has done (or the employer believes or suspects that he has done or intends to do) one of a number of protected acts. Workers also have the right not to be subjected to any detriment by any act, or any failure to act, on the same protected grounds (*reg 7(2)*). Protected status arises where a worker has:

- brought proceedings against the employer under *PTWR 2000*;
- requested from his employer a written statement of reasons (under *PTWR 2000, reg 6*);
- given evidence or information in connection with such proceedings brought by any worker;
- otherwise done anything under *PTWR 2000* in relation to the employer or any other person;
- alleged that the employer has infringed *PTWR 2000* (but if such an allegation is false and not made in good faith there is no protection);
- refused (or proposed to refuse) to forgo a right conferred on him by *PTWR 2000*.

An automatic unfair dismissal claim means that the employee will not need a minimum qualifying period of employment as is usual for unfair dismissal claims (*ERA 1996, s 108*).

In addition to a *reg 5* claim, following general unfair dismissal protection, if the sole or principal reason for the dismissal is that the employee is a part-time worker, this will not be a fair reason in accordance with *ERA 1996, s 98(1)*.

10.35 Tribunal claims

Claims of less favourable treatment or unfair dismissal must ordinarily be presented to an employment tribunal within three months from the date of the less favourable treatment or detriment, or where an act or failure to act is part of a series, the last of them.

10.36 Tribunal remedies

Less favourable treatment

Where the tribunal finds less favourable treatment or detriment, it can make a declaration, order the employer to pay compensation and make a recommendation that the employer, within a specified period, takes specified measures and/or reduces the adverse effect on the worker (see **1.171**ff).

10.37 *Unfair dismissal*

Regulation 8(11) of the *PTWR 2000* expressly precludes a part-timer from obtaining an injury to feelings award if he is treated less favourably than a full-timer, and *Dunnachie v Kingston-upon-Hull City Council* [2004] EWCA Civ 84, [2004] 2 All ER 501 established that such an award cannot be made in unfair dismissal cases. However, following *Virgo Fidelis Senior School v Boyle* [2004] ICR 1210, where an injury to feelings award was made for subjecting a worker to a detriment for making a protected disclosure, it is possible that a worker may obtain such an award if he is subjected to a *reg 7(2)* detriment, since this is not expressly excluded by *reg 8(11)*.

10.38 Employer's liability

Liability for employers and agents under *PTWR 2000* follows that in *EqA 2010* (see **1.163**ff).

11 Equal pay

11.1 INTRODUCTION

There is no separate legislative regime to address pay-related discrimination on prohibited grounds other than sex. Claims must be brought under the general legislation which applies to the relevant ground. However, a different approach is taken as regards differences in pay between men and women. Those differences are thought to be systemic and structural rather than resulting from individual acts of irrationality, and thus to require a very different regime to deal with them.

The right to equal pay for men and women has now been brought within the *Equality Act 2010* ('*EqA 2010*'). However, that right continues to be treated as a self-contained area of law to which the general anti-discrimination model does not apply. The government considered it to be inappropriate to expose employers to potential liability for aggravated or exemplary damages, damages for injury to feelings and any other injury suffered by the claimant as a result of the discrimination, since '[i]n many cases, structural differences in pay may have evolved over a long period, with no deliberate discriminatory intent' ('Discrimination Law Review: A Framework for Fairness: Proposals for a Single Equality Bill for Great Britain—A Consultation Paper' (Department for Communities and Local Government, June 2007), Chapter 3). The government further defended the retention of the distinct approach to equal pay on the basis that 'the implied contractual equality provision provides a valuable guarantee to women in the workforce of their right to be employed on the same terms as men' ('The Equality Bill—Government response to the Consultation' (Cm 7454; June 2008), para 7.58).

The gender pay gap remains deeply entrenched in the United Kingdom. Based on median hourly earnings, women in full-time work earn 13% less than men; based on mean hourly earnings, they earn 17% less. Women who work part-time earn 38% less per hour than the median hourly pay of women who work full-time and 41% less per hour than men who work full-time ('Shaping a Fairer Future' (Women and Work Commission, February 2006)). The underlying causes of the gender pay gap are thought to be 'related to differences between men and women in their experience of education, training and the workplace, and also in the roles men and women play in the family' ('Towards a Fairer Future: Implementing the Women and Work Commission recommendations' (Department for Communities and Local Government, April 2007)).

However, the limitations inherent in the legislative regime may also be partly to blame. The absence of any positive obligation on employers to introduce or maintain non-discriminatory pay systems is thought by many to be most significant in this regard. Reliance is instead placed on individual complaints and litigation, which is frequently expensive, time-consuming and unpredictable in outcome. Positive duties to make pay systems transparent or to audit pay have been imposed in other jurisdictions, notably Ontario and Quebec. Despite the recommendation in 2001 of an Equal Pay Task Force set up by the Equal Opportunities Commission (EOC), the government has to date resisted the introduction of similar statutory duties in this country.

EqA 2010 creates a power to make regulations requiring larger private and voluntary sector employers to publish information on what they pay their male and female employees, but the intention of the outgoing Labour government was to encourage voluntary publication in the first instance, with the power to compel publication only to be used after April 2013 if sufficient progress on reporting had not by then been made (*Explanatory Notes to the EqA 2010, para 278*). In December 2010, the new Conservative-Liberal Democrat coalition government indicated that it, too, proposes to develop a scheme for voluntary gender pay reporting, aimed in particular at companies with 150 or more employees. It will review progress on an annual basis in order to assess whether it is necessary to use the mandatory approach provided for in *EqA 2010*.

11.2 OVERVIEW OF THE STATUTORY FRAMEWORK

There are two separate but overlapping legal regimes which regulate equal pay in the United Kingdom: domestic law and EC law.

First, the domestic law. Until 1 October 2010 this was contained in the *Equal Pay Act 1970* (*EqPA 1970*). Overlap with the *Sex Discrimination Act 1975* (*SDA 1975*) was avoided since the latter had no application to 'benefits consisting of the payment of money when the provision of those benefits is regulated by the [employee's] contract of employment' (*SDA 1975, s 6(6)*). The rights conferred by the two statutes were mutually exclusive and led to different remedies (*Peake v Automotive Products Ltd* [1977] QB 780, EAT). However, they were designed to be complementary and should be construed as far as possible 'so as to form a harmonious code' (*Steel v Union of Post Office Workers* [1978] 1 WLR 64, EAT at 69). Indeed, several provisions of *SDA 1975* applied to claims under *EqPA 1970*, such as *s 4* on discrimination by way of victimisation (see **1.98**) and *s 10* on the meaning of employment at an establishment in Great Britain.

As from 1 October 2010, *EqA 2010* has repealed and replaced the material provisions of both *EqPA 1970* and *SDA 1975* (see the *Equality Act 2010 (Commencement No 4, Savings, Consequential, Transitional, Transitory and Incidental Provisions and Revocation) Order 2010 (SI 2010/2317)*). In general, the equal pay provisions in *EqA 2010* replicate those in *EqPA 1970*, but there are some notable differences which are examined in this chapter.

Second, the EU regime is found in *Article 157* of the Treaty on the Functioning of the European Union ('*TFEU*') (formerly *Article 119* of the Treaty of Rome and *Article 141* of the Treaty of Amsterdam); these provisions are directly effective. Accordingly, individuals can rely upon their rights under *Article 141* in domestic employment tribunals and courts (*Defrenne v Sabena: 43/75* [1976] ECR 455). A claim under *Article 157* is not 'free-standing' insofar as, absent detailed EC law rules, the procedural rules of *EqPA 1970* (concerning such matters as time limits) apply. However, EC law can be relied upon to disapply barriers to a claim which are incompatible with EC law (*Biggs v Somerset County Council* [1996] 2 All ER 734, [1996] 2 CMLR 292, [1996] ICR 364; *Barber v Staffordshire County Council* [1996] ICR 379).

In effect, claimants can choose to pursue claims under whichever regime is more advantageous to them. Although domestic law and EC law seek to give effect to the same basic principle, they sometimes produce different results. The extent to which this occurs has diminished since, where possible, *EqPA 1970* has been construed in a way that accords with *Article 157*, and the *EqA 2010* has been drafted with the ECJ's case law in mind. Nevertheless, it remains the case that the domestic and EC equal pay regimes approach the same task in quite different ways, which must be outlined before a detailed examination of each regime can be conducted.

11.3 EqPA 1970 and EqA 2010

EqPA 1970 was a highly technical piece of legislation, whose complexity has attracted criticism since its enactment. Some of the same criticisms can be levelled at *EqA 2010*, whose approach to equal pay in *Part 5, Chapter 3* largely mirrors that in *EqPA 1970*, albeit that it is drafted in a more accessible style. However, the essential mechanism of both statutes can be summarised thus: *EqA 2010, s 66(1)* (formerly *EqPA 1970, s 1(1)*) implies into every contract of employment an 'equality clause', whose operation is set out in *s 66(2)* (formerly *EqPA 1970, s 1(2)*). The clause takes effect where the claimant and an individual of the opposite sex (the 'comparator') are employed in the same employment (see further *EqA 2010, s 79*) on like work, work rated as equivalent under a job evaluation scheme, or work of equal value (*EqA 2010, ss 64–65*). If any term of the claimant's contract (whether or not it is concerned with pay) is less favourable than a term of a similar kind in her comparator's contract, the claimant's contractual term shall be modified so that it is no less favourable, unless the employer can establish that the difference in pay is genuinely due to a material factor which is not the difference of sex (*EqA 2010, s 69*). If the claimant's contract does not contain a term corresponding to a beneficial term in the comparator's contract, the claimant's contract is treated as including such a term.

11.4 TFEU, Article 157

In contrast to the narrow, contractual approach of *EqPA 1970* and now *EqA 2010*, *Article 157* sets out the basic principle in general terms, while leaving it to the EC legislature and the European Court of Justice (ECJ) to provide a detailed scheme for implementing the principle. *Article 157* provides:

> '1. Each Member State shall ensure that the principle of equal pay for male and female workers for equal work or work of equal value is applied.
>
> '2. For the purpose of this Article, 'pay' means the ordinary basic or minimum wage or salary and any other consideration, whether in cash or in kind, which the worker receives directly or indirectly, in respect of his employment, from his employer.
>
> 'Equal pay without discrimination based on sex means:
>
> (a) that pay for the same work at piece rates shall be calculated on the basis of the same unit of measurement;
>
> (b) that pay for work at time rates shall be the same for the same job.'

The express reference in *Article 157(1)* to the principle of 'equal pay for work of equal value' was inserted by the *Treaty of Amsterdam*. However, that principle had previously been referred to in *Article 1* of *Directive 75/117/EEC* on equal pay for male and female workers ('the *Equal Pay Directive*') and the ECJ has held that it was implicit in the original *Article 119* in any event (*Brunnhofer v Bank der Österreichischen Postsparkasse AG: C-381/99* [2001] ECR I-4961). Other amendments effected by the *Treaty of Amsterdam* were the additions of *Article 157(3)*, which gives the Council an express legal basis for equal pay legislation, and *Article 157(4)*, which enables Member States to adopt or maintain positive-action measures for the under-represented sex in respect of professional careers.

11.5 EHRC Code of Practice on Equal Pay

The EHRC is empowered by *Equality Act 2006*, *s 14* to issue a code of practice in connection with any matter addressed by the *EqA 2010*, which must contain provision designed to ensure or facilitate compliance with that Act and to promote equality of opportunity. The employment tribunals must take into account any such code where it is relevant to matters in issue (cf. the similar power previously conferred on the EOC by *SDA 1975, s 56A*). The EHRC Code of Practice on Equal Pay was laid before Parliament on 12 October 2010. Like its EOC predecessor, the Code summarises the law on equal pay in non-technical language and provides guidance on good practice in matters of pay equality. The EHRC has also, in conjunction with the British Chambers of Commerce, produced a 'Quick-start guide to providing equal pay', which is designed to help small and medium-sized businesses examine their pay systems to ensure compliance with the law on equal pay.

11.6 THE KEY ISSUES

Six key issues arise under both domestic law and EC law, all of which have been the subject of important recent decisions by the courts:

(1) Who can bring an equal pay claim?

(2) With whom may a claimant compare herself?

(3) What can be compared?

(4) How is the comparison conducted?

(5) When can a difference in pay be justified?

(6) What remedies are available?

A further issue concerns the mechanics of bringing an equal pay claim (see **11.42** ff).

11.7 WHO CAN BRING AN EQUAL PAY CLAIM?

Categories of workers

EqPA 1970 gave rights to individuals who are 'employed', which was defined as meaning 'employed under a contract of service or of apprenticeship or a contract personally to execute any work or labour' (*s 1(6)(a)*). This is wider than the definition of 'employee' used in relation to many employment law rights, such as the right to claim unfair dismissal. Even the self-employed were covered if they worked under a contract personally to execute work (*Quinnen v Hovells* [1984] ICR 525, EAT).

EqPA 1970 also made express provision concerning specific categories of potential claimants. Thus, those employed by or for the purposes of the Crown were covered, with any reference to a contract of employment being construed as a reference to the terms of service (*s 1(8)*). There were two excluded sub-categories: those holding a 'statutory office' (meaning an office set up by or in pursuance of any enactment: *s 1(10)*) and government ministers listed in the *House of Commons Disqualification Act 1975, Sch 2* (*s 1(10)*). However, *ss 1(6A)* and *1(6B)*, inserted by the *Employment Equality (Sex Discrimination) Regulations 2005 (SI 2005/2467)*, extended *EqPA 1970* to those appointed (as opposed to elected) to statutory office other than political office. Specific provision was made for the application of the Act to House of Commons staff (*s 1(10A)*) and House of Lords staff (*s 1(10B)*). The Act also applied to members of the armed forces (*s 7A*), although they must make a service complaint under the *Armed Forces Act 2006, s 334* before they could pursue a tribunal claim (*s 7A(5)*).

An issue of increasing importance is whether an agency worker (whose contractual relationship is with the agency, not the end user of her services) can bring an equal pay claim. This issue arose in *Allonby v Accrington and Rossendale College* [2001] EWCA Civ 529, [2001] ICR 1189. The claimants were teachers formerly employed directly by the college on fixed-term contracts, but who were subsequently engaged by an agency, ELS. The claimants worked on specific assignments at the college agreed by them with ELS. The college agreed the fee they were to receive for each assignment and set the conditions under which they were to work. The Court of Appeal held that the claimants' contracts with the agency qualified under *EqPA 1970, s 1(6)(a)*.

The position is broadly the same under *EqA 2010*, which gives rights to individuals who are 'employed' or 'holding a personal or public office' (*s 64(1)*). 'Employment' is defined as employment under a contract of employment, a contract of apprenticeship or a contract personally to do work, Crown employment, and employment as a relevant member of the

House of Commons or House of Lords staff (*s 83(2)*). 'Crown employment' and 'relevant member' bear the same meaning as in the Employment Rights Act 1996 (*s 83(5), (6) and (9)*). 'Personal or public office' is to be construed in accordance with *s 52* (*s 83(8)*), which gives effect to the definitions in *ss 49–50*. Service in the armed forces is deemed to be employment (*s 83(3)*).

Unlike *EqPA 1970* and *EqA 2010*, *Article 157* does not expressly address the question of what type of individual can bring a claim. The ECJ has for some time referred in this regard to 'workers', but until recently had not provided a detailed definition of that term. However, when the agency worker question was referred to the ECJ in *Allonby: C-256/01* [2004] ECR I-873, it ruled that the concept of 'worker' cannot be defined by reference to national legislation but instead has an EC law meaning, namely 'a person who, for a certain period of time, performs services for and under the direction of another person in return for which he receives remuneration' (para 67). The court justified this broad definition by reference to the fact that *Article 144 (now 157)* 'constitutes a specific expression of the principle of equality for men and women, which forms part of the fundamental principles protected by the Community legal order' (para 65). However, the court went on to observe that, given the definition of 'pay' in *Article 144(2) (now 157(2))*, the term 'worker' cannot cover 'independent providers of services who are not in a relationship of subordination with the person who receives the services' (para 68).

The question of whether such a relationship exists is one of substance rather than form, and is inevitably highly fact-sensitive. As regards the claimants in *Allonby* itself, the court observed that 'it is necessary in particular to consider the extent of any limitation on their freedom to choose their timetable, and the place and content of their work' and that '[t]he fact that no obligation is imposed on them to accept an assignment is of no consequence in that context' (para 72).

11.8 Territorial scope

EqPA 1970 gave rights to individuals who were employed 'at an establishment in Great Britain' (see **1.42**).

By contrast, *EqA 2010* does not make detailed provision on its geographical scope. The *Explanatory Notes to the EqA 2010* state (*para 15*): 'As far as territorial application is concerned, in relation to Part 5 (work) and following the precedent of the Employment Rights Act 1996, the Act leaves it to tribunals to determine whether the law applies, depending for example on the connection between the employment relationship and Great Britain'. However, the Act contains a power to specify territorial application of Part 5 in relation to ships and hovercraft (*s 81*) and offshore work (*s 82*) (see **1.43**).

11.9 THE COMPARATOR

By definition, the concept of 'equal pay' requires a claimant to allege his or her pay to be unequal to that received by another individual of the opposite sex. There is often protracted litigation on the question of whether the claimant's chosen comparator is a legitimate one. A number of sub-issues arise under this head.

11.10 Hypothetical comparators

Most domestic anti-discrimination legislation permits the use of hypothetical comparators, by prohibiting an employer from treating an employee less favourably, on discriminatory grounds, than it 'treats or would treat' other persons. *EqPA 1970* did not: a real comparator had to be identified. This was problematic as it could prevent claims from succeeding even where the claimant could prove that the reason why her employer did not pay her more was that she was a woman. An alternative claim under *SDA 1975* was expressly excluded by *s 6(6)* of that Act.

Prior to the enactment of *EqA 2010*, the government indicated that it did not favour permitting hypothetical comparators, on the basis that this would create undue uncertainty as to whether pay arrangements were lawful or not, while at the same time claimants would in practice find it difficult to prove that a hypothetical comparator would have been employed under more favourable contractual terms. See 'Discrimination Law Review' (above), paras 3.25–3.29.

However, Parliament recognised the strong arguments in favour of allowing claims by individuals who can prove direct sex discrimination in relation to contractual pay. Under *EqA 2010, ss 70–71*, the applicability of the equal pay provisions excludes the applicability of the other relevant sex discrimination provisions but not where treatment of the individual amounts to a contravention of the provision by virtue of *s 13* (direct discrimination) or *s 14* (combined discrimination) in relation to terms '*to which a sex equality clause or rule has no effect*'. See the *Explanatory Notes to the EqA 2010, paras 249–250*. The net effect of this somewhat opaque drafting is that employees who are unable to identify a 'flesh and blood' comparator, but consider that their pay would be more if they were of the opposite sex, may alternatively assert a claim under the direct sex discrimination provisions. It is likely such claims will become a common alternative pleading in any case where the appropriateness of the identified comparator is challenged. It is unclear, however, how parties will deal with the obvious evidential difficulties that such claims may pose.

EU law on this issue may also be in a state of flux. In *Macarthys Ltd v Smith: 129/79* [1981] QB 180, the ECJ held that hypothetical comparators are not permitted under *Article 141 (now 157)*. However, this is arguably no longer the case following the amendment of the *Equal Treatment Directive* (*Directive 76/207/EEC*, amended by *Directive 2002/73/EC*), which extends the general definition of discrimination to equal pay. Moreover, there is some indication that the ECJ may be becoming more amenable to hypothetical comparators. As noted above, in *Allonby* the court held that agency workers in principle have rights under *Article 141 (now 157)*. The claimant's remaining problem was identifying an available comparator (because of the 'single source' test, examined below). However, the court held that because she sought to challenge the discriminatory effect of a pension scheme rule derived from national law, she did not need to identify a comparator, but could simply rely upon statistical evidence to show that the rule had a disproportionate impact on female workers.

Nevertheless, it remains to be seen whether EC law will take a similar approach in cases where the claim does not concern the impact of discriminatory legislation. In *Shaikh v Department for Constitutional Affairs* UKEAT/0234/05 (31 August 2005), the EAT indicated that it will not. It further held that a rule embodied in statute must 'apply across the whole of the labour force' in order to trigger the *Allonby* principle, and that the principle requires a finding or a concession that there are workers of the opposite sex engaged in like work or work of equal value (para 25). *Shaikh* thus treats *Allonby* not as sanctioning the use of hypothetical comparators, but as merely relieving claimants of the need to point to a specific actual comparator where it is obvious that many actual comparators do exist.

11.11 The temporal nexus

Although an actual comparator must be identified under *EqPA 1970*, he did not need to be still employed at the time of the claim. If there was a point in time when the claimant met the conditions of *EqPA 1970*, then the equality clause will have operated to vary her contract, and the contract as varied remained in force notwithstanding the comparator's subsequent departure (*Sorbie v Trust House Forte Hotels Ltd* [1977] QB 931).

Under *Article 157*, the comparator can be a predecessor of the claimant (*Macarthys Ltd v Smith*, above). EC law was until recently thought to be more generous than domestic law in this regard. However, in *Kells v Pilkington plc* [2002] IRLR 693, the EAT cast doubt on whether, in light of EC law developments, *EqPA 1970* required contemporaneous employment. This contradicted the decision of the Court of Appeal in *Macarthys Ltd v Smith* [1979] 1 WLR 1189. That the ECJ's decision in that case could lead to a new interpretation of the *EqPA 1970* itself (as distinct from permitting a non-contemporaneous comparator in a direct *Article 157* claim) illustrates the interplay between domestic and EC law.

However, even under *Article 157*, the comparator cannot be a successor of the claimant. The EAT so held in *Walton Centre for Neurology and Neurosurgery NHS Trust v Bewley* [2008] ICR 1047, overruling its previous decision in *Hallam Diocese Trustee v Connaughton* [1996] ICR 860. Elias P took the view that the exercise of comparing with a successor is too hypothetical, since it requires asking what would have happened in the past, as opposed to the question in *Macarthys Ltd v Smith*, which is what did happen in the past (para 52). However, Elias P notably did not dispute that there are cogent arguments which can be advanced in favour of permitting hypothetical comparisons in equal pay cases, and that '[t]he justification for refusing hypothetical comparisons with respect to pay but permitting it for other forms of discriminatory conduct is not self evident' (para 57).

As explained at **11.10**, Parliament has now recognised the cogency of those arguments by changing the law so that a claimant can succeed by proving direct sex discrimination in relation to contractual pay without identifying a real comparator. *EqA 2010* also expressly provides that the relevant comparison is not restricted to work done by the comparator contemporaneously with work done by the claimant (*s 64(2)*). The *Explanatory Notes to the EqA 2010* state (*para 223*) that this provision is 'intended to ensure the effect of pre-existing case law', namely the ECJ's decision in *Macarthys Ltd v Smith*, so that a predecessor can be used as a comparator. Arguably, however, it also reverses the EAT's decision in *Bewley*, so as to allow the use of successors as comparators.

11.12 The work nexus

Having selected a comparator, how does a claimant show that the two of them do work which should be equally well remunerated? There were three routes under *EqPA 1970* and now under *EqA 2010*, the first and third of which are mirrored in *Article 157*.

11.13 *'Like work'*

The 'like work' route under *EqPA 1970, s 1(2)(a)* required the claimant to show two things. First, her work had to be 'of the same or a broadly similar nature' to the comparator's. Second, any differences in the duties they undertook must 'not [be] of practical importance in relation to terms and conditions of employment', having regard to 'the frequency or otherwise with which any such differences occur in practice as well as to the nature and extent of the differences' (*s 1(4)*). This provision is reproduced in materially identical terms in *EqA 2010, s 65(2)–(3)*.

Tribunals should consider these two questions of fact separately, but are not required 'to undertake too minute an examination' (*Capper Pass Ltd v Lawton* [1977] QB 852, EAT at 857). The first question 'can be answered by a general consideration of the type of work involved, and of the skill and knowledge required to do it'. As to the second question, 'trivial differences, or differences not likely in the real world to be reflected in the terms and conditions of employment, ought to be disregarded' (*ibid*).

As Lord Denning noted, '[t]he employer should not be able to avoid the principle by introducing comparatively small differences in "job content" between men and women: nor by giving the work a different "job description"' (*Shields v E Coomes (Holdings) Ltd* [1978] 1 WLR 1408 at 1417). However, substantial differences in the duties undertaken cannot be ignored, save perhaps in extreme cases where 'part of the work, although subsumed under the general description of the tasks of the employee, is in effect a separate and distinct job'

(*Maidment v Cooper & Co (Birmingham) Ltd* [1978] ICR 1094 at 1098, giving the example that if two cleaners, one male and one female, do identical work during the week, 'it might be right to ignore work of a quite different kind done by the man coming in, say on Saturdays, in order to cut the grass').

The key consideration is the work actually done as opposed to the work that might be done under the claimant's and comparator's particular contractual terms, although it is only work done *pursuant to those terms* that is relevant. Thus, an employer who prays in aid the comparator's additional contractual obligations may fail to defeat the claimant's assertion that she does like work if those obligations are rarely enforced (*Electrolux Ltd v Hutchinson* [1977] ICR 252; *Redland Roof Tiles Ltd v Harper* [1977] ICR 349; *Dorothy Perkins Ltd v Dance* [1978] ICR 760). Equally, a like work claim should not be defeated on the basis that the comparator is particularly diligent or talented and does more than he is contractually required to do. As Lord Denning put it, *s 1(4)* 'involves a comparison of the two jobs—the woman's job and the man's job—and making an evaluation of each job as a job irrespective of the sex of the worker and of any special personal skill or merit that he or she may have' (*Shields*, above, at 1417).

While the focus is on the physical acts done by the claimant and the comparator, regard may also be had to the circumstances in which each does the work, and in particular to the degree of responsibility upon each of them. This might be decisive 'where it can be seen to put one into a different grade from the other' (*Eaton Ltd v Nuttall* [1977] 3 All ER 1131, [1977] 1 WLR 549, [1977] ICR 2; see also *Waddington v Leicester Council for Voluntary Services* [1977] 1 WLR 544, EAT).

The fact that the claimant and the comparator do the same work at different times of the day cannot justify a difference in their basic rates of pay: '[t]he only legitimate way of dealing with night work or work for longer hours is by paying a night shift premium or overtime rate assessed at a reasonable figure' (*Shields*, above, at 1418). The same principle applies to work done on Sundays. However, difference of practical importance may exist as between the duties of those working at different times, such as the added responsibility of working alone and unsupervised at night, which may defeat a 'like work' claim (*Thomas v National Coal Board* [1987] ICR 757).

The ECJ has interpreted the equivalent concept in *Article 157*—'same work'—in broadly the same way as the domestic courts. Thus, it has said that the terms 'the same work', 'the same job' and 'work of equal value' in *Article 157* and the *Equal Pay Directive* 'are entirely qualitative in character in that they are exclusively concerned with the nature of the work actually performed' and that 'in order to determine whether employees perform the same work or work to which equal value can be attributed, it is necessary to ascertain whether, taking account of a number of factors such as the nature of the work, the training requirements and the working conditions, those persons can be considered to be in a comparable situation' (*Brunnhofer v Bank der Österreichischen Postsparkasse AG: C-381/99* [2001] ECR I-4961 at 42–43).

11.14 *'Work rated as equivalent'*

The 'work rated as equivalent' route under *EqPA 1970, s 1(2)(b)* could only be used where an analytical, non-discriminatory job evaluation study (JES) had already been undertaken by the employer and had attributed equal value to the jobs of the claimant and her comparator (*s 1(5)*). Where such a scheme had given different values to the two jobs, any attempt to bring an 'equal value' claim under *s 1(2)(c)* would have failed unless the JES was made on a system which discriminated on grounds of sex or was otherwise unsuitable to be relied upon, for example if the work of one of them had changed since the date of the evaluation (*s 2A(2), (2A)*). There is no obligation on an employer to undertake a JES, although an employer who sets pay levels without first conducting some form of job evaluation leaves itself vulnerable to 'equal value' claims (see below).

The *Explanatory Notes to the EqA 2010* indicate that it was intended to replicate the substance of *EqPA 1970* in this regard (*para 225*). That has been achieved so far as the basic mechanism of a 'work rated as equivalent' comparison is concerned by *s 65(4)–(5)*. Further, the ability of an employer to defend an equal value claim by pointing to a JES which gave different values to the claimant's and comparator's jobs is preserved by *s 131(5)–(7)*, again with the possibility of a claimant defeating the defence by arguing that the JES was itself discriminatory or is otherwise unreliable.

The key issues are whether any particular JES is analytical and non-discriminatory.

An *analytical* JES is one which assesses the content of jobs in terms of objective criteria which reflect the demands placed upon employees, such as skill, effort and decision-making (factors specific to individual employees, such as productivity and length of service, are irrelevant). Points are awarded for each criterion according to a predetermined scale and the total points determine a job's place in the overall ranking order. If the jobs of the claimant and the comparator obtain the same total scores, or having obtained similar scores are placed in the same 'band' or 'grade' (*Springboard Sunderland Trust v Robson* [1992] ICR 554), their work is rated as equivalent.

However, the EAT held in *Home Office v Bailey* [2005] IRLR 757 that if a claimant's job scores slightly lower than the comparator's and they are not then banded together, it is not open to the tribunal to hear evidence as to what would be regarded as a significant difference or to find that the jobs are of equal value. The EAT stressed that the formula used is 'if, but only if' the jobs have been given equal value in the JES and stated that 'the *s 1(2)(b)* gateway is precise when read with *s 1(5)*' (para 33). The difficulty with this approach is that *s 1(5)* referred to 'equal value', not 'equal scores', and JESs will usually treat different scores as indicating equal value where the difference is not regarded as significant. The EAT's decision may have been influenced by a desire to preclude claimants from attempting to unpick JESs and thereby lengthen tribunal proceedings. However, given that an 'equal value' claim under *s 1(2)(c)* was not open to a claimant where a JES was already in place, this ruling could produce unjust results.

The importance of a JES being *non-discriminatory* is that decisions as to how many points should be awarded to particular factors may themselves be influenced by discriminatory attitudes. In particular, there is a danger that qualities traditionally viewed as 'female' or as pertaining to 'women's work' will be undervalued. Consequently, it is only a JES which avoids such discrimination which could be invoked for the purposes of *s 1(2)(b)*. There is one exception: *s 1(5)* provides that a woman's job will be rated as equivalent to her comparator's if they have been accorded equal value by a JES or 'would have been given an equal value but for the evaluation being made on a system setting different values for men and women on the same demand under any heading'. An evaluation in a JES will be regarded as discriminatory where a difference, or coincidence, between values set by the JES on different demands under the same or different headings is not justifiable irrespective of the sex of the person on whom those demands are made (*s 2A(3)*).

A JES which has been completed but not yet implemented may be relied upon (*O'Brien v Sim-Chem Ltd* [1980] 3 All ER 132, [1980] 1 WLR 1011). However, it is not possible to 'backdate' a JES. In *Redcar and Cleveland Borough Council v Bainbridge* [2007] EWCA Civ 929, [2007] IRLR 494, the claimants argued that, having had their jobs rated under a JES, they could rely upon that JES to pursue claims under *s 1(2)(b)* in respect of a period up to six years preceding its implementation. The EAT rejected this argument, primarily on the basis that '[i]t is simply wrong to say that somebody in the period prior to the job evaluation study coming into effect has had their job rated as equivalent under a job evaluation study' (para 36). Significantly, the EAT further rejected the argument that when jobs are related as equivalent under *s 1(2)(b)*, that is the same as jobs being of equal value under *s 1(2)(c)*, since '[i]t is not uncommon for jobs to be fitted into grades where there may be real distinctions in the value of the jobs' (para 41). The Court of Appeal upheld that approach: [2008] EWCA Civ 885, [2009] ICR 133 at paras 277–284.

Finally, it should be noted that changes in job content occurring after a JES has rated two jobs as equivalent may support an argument that the jobs should no longer be regarded as rated as equivalent.

11.15 *'Work of equal value'*

The 'work of equal value' route under *s 1(2)(c)* was inserted into *EqPA 1970* in order to ensure compliance with the UK's obligations under the *Equal Pay Directive*. The importance of this route is that it can remedy pay discrimination even where there is gender segregation as between different jobs. Thus, a woman who is performing what might traditionally be viewed as 'women's work', such as a cleaner, might succeed in claiming pay parity with a man whose job sounds more valuable but on analysis is not. *Section 1(2)(c)* is reproduced in *EqA 2010, s 65(6)*, which refers to work being of equal value in terms of the demands made on the claimant under such headings as effort, skill and decision-making.

The 'work of equal value' route is only available where the 'like work' and 'work rated as equivalent' routes are not: *EqA 2010, s 65(6)(a)* (*EqPA 1970 s 1(2)(c)*). However, this limitation only applies in respect of any given comparator; it does not have the effect that a woman is bound to treat as the proper comparator a man who happens to be employed on like work or work rated as equivalent, in preference to any other man. As Lord Keith observed in *Pickstone v Freemans plc* [1989] AC 66 at 111, such a rule 'would leave a large gap in the equal work provision, enabling an employer to evade it by employing one token man on the same work as a group of potential women claimants who were deliberately paid less than a group of men employed on work of equal value with that of the women'. This case illustrates the purposive approach which the courts have generally adopted when construing *EqPA 1970*.

An analytical and non-discriminatory JES which rates the claimant's job as less valuable than that of the chosen comparator will defeat an equal value claim regardless of when the JES was carried out, provided that it evaluated the jobs done on the date when proceedings were issued (*Dibro Ltd v Hore* [1990] ICR 370). However, the JES must have properly evaluated the jobs in terms of demand made on the worker under various headings, as opposed to merely slotting those jobs into a ranking order produced using duly-evaluated 'benchmark' jobs (*Bromley v H & J Quick Ltd* [1988] ICR 623).

Where a JES places two different jobs into the same pay band so that, for the future, the jobs are 'rated as equivalent' under *EqA 2010, s 65(4) (EqPA 1970, s 1(2)(b))*, an employee in the job which was previously in a lower pay band may bring a claim seeking equal pay for the period before the JES took effect, on the basis that the two jobs were 'work of equal value'. The fact that the two jobs have now been rated as equivalent is not determinative in the claimant's favour (see **11.14**). Equally, however, the fact that the claimant's job scored fewer points in the JES than that of her comparator is not fatal to the claim. However, the claimant will have to set the difference in the context of the particular JES and explain why the difference should be ignored: *Hovell v Ashford and St Peter's Hospital NHS Trust* [2009] EWCA Civ 670, [2009] ICR 1545.

The burden of proving that the work is of equal value is on the claimant. Equal value claims are notorious for giving rise to extremely complex factual investigation and argument, resulting in lengthy litigation. This has led to a specific set of procedural rules being created, the *Employment Tribunals (Equal Value) Rules of Procedure* (see **11.54**).

11.16 Beyond equal pay?

Can a claimant claim pay proportionate to that of an individual who does unlike work or work of unequal value? This may seem right as a matter of principle, but it was not permitted at all under *EqPA 1970*. Thus, a woman could not allege that, because her work is worth 70% of a man's, she should receive 70% of his pay rather than 60%. Nor could she claim to do work worth 120% of the man's and therefore demand 120% of his pay. For example, in *Pointon v University of Sussex* [1979] IRLR 119, a claimant who was paid more than her comparator but thought she should be paid yet more failed in her claim since she had not shown that her contract was less favourable than his. Nor can a woman whose work is of equal value to that of her comparator claim higher pay by reason of her greater seniority. As Roch LJ stated in *Evesham v North Hertfordshire Health Authority* [2000] ICR 612 at 628, 'neither the obligation to modify terms in the applicant's contract nor the obligation to include a term found in the comparator's contract in the applicant's contract require the employer to modify a term or to include a term so that the term in the applicant's contract becomes more favourable than the term in the comparator's contract'. As he observed, '[t]he title to the Act of 1970 is "Equal Pay Act"'.

The EAT's decision in *Llewellyn v Hartlepool Borough Council* [2009] ICR 1426 concerning 'piggyback' claims could arguably be seen as a movement towards the *EqPA 1970* being used to achieve 'fair pay', although others will view it simply as an orthodox application of the statutory provisions. The decision establishes that a male claimant is entitled to the benefit of a contractual term enjoyed by a female comparator even where the comparator herself has only acquired the benefit of that term as a result of the operation of the *EqPA 1970*. The EAT gave the example of a case where the woman (F1) and the man (M1) are working alongside one another on the same work, but the man is being paid £9 per hour whereas the woman—by virtue of a previous successful claim by reference to the pay of a man doing a different job (M2)—is receiving £10 (para 15). The statutory presumption that the equality clause will operate so as to modify M1's terms applies under *s 1(2)(a)(i)* (para 17). Moreover, the *s 1(3)* defence does not apply, since M1 is a victim of direct sex discrimination: 'but for' his sex, he would be entitled to the same pay as F1, since he too would have been able to bring an equal pay claim invoking M2 as the comparator (para 22).

The ECJ has also shied away from moving beyond equal pay to fair pay. However, it has held that a woman doing work of greater value than a man but being paid less than him may claim equal pay (eg she does work worth 120% of his work and is allowed to claim 100% of his pay) (*Murphy v Bord Telecom Eireann: 157/86* [1988] ECR 673). The English courts have held that this analysis applies not only to claims under *EqPA 1970, s 1(2)(c)*, but also to those under *s 1(2)(a)* (*SITA UK Ltd v Hope* UKEAT/0787/04 (8 March 2005) and *s 1(2)(b)* (*Redcar and Cleveland Borough Council v Bainbridge* [2007] EWCA Civ 929, [2008] ICR 238).

The position in this regard has changed under *EqA 2010*. As explained at **11.10**, it is now possible for a claimant to succeed by proving direct sex discrimination in relation to contractual pay without identifying a real comparator who does work equal to hers. In order to succeed in such a claim, it will plainly assist the claimant to identify male employees who, although not doing work equal to hers, are being paid at rates which seem out of line with her own salary. Thus, a tribunal might be persuaded to infer direct discrimination if it accepts that her work is worth 70% of a man's but she receives only 60% of his pay, or that her work is worth 120% of another man's but she is only paid at the same level as him.

11.17 The institutional nexus

What link must there be between claimant and comparator aside from the fact that they do work which should be equally well remunerated? This issue has been of importance in recent years, as organisational structures and working patterns have become increasing diversified.

Under *EqPA 1970, s 1(2)*, claimant and comparator had to be in 'the same employment'. As set out in *s 1(6)*, this required not simply that they did the same type of work, but that they were employed by the same employer (or associated employers), either at the same establishment or at different establishments belonging to that employer (or those associated employers) where common terms and conditions of employment were laid down for the two establishments. These requirements are replicated in *EqA 2010, s 79(3)–(4)*.

The 'same employment' test is inherently somewhat restrictive. The courts have generally resisted attempts to narrow it further still, in particular on the question of what terms and conditions are 'common'. In *Leverton v Clwyd County Council* [1989] AC 706, the House of Lords overruled the EAT and Court of Appeal in holding that 'the concept of common terms and conditions of employment observed generally at different establishments necessarily contemplates terms and conditions applicable to a wide range of employees whose individual terms will vary greatly inter se' (Lord Bridge at 745). Accordingly, the claimant could use a comparator at a different establishment, even though there were significant differences between her terms and his in relation to the actual number of hours worked and holiday entitlements. A similarly broad and purposive approach to construing *EqPA 1970* was taken in *British Coal Corpn v Smith* [1996] 3 All ER 97, [1996] ICR 515. The House of Lords held that to require terms that are 'common in the sense of identical' would be 'far too restrictive a test'; instead, only 'broadly similar terms' are required (Lord Slynn at 527). Whether terms are sufficiently similar for a broad comparison to be made 'is a matter of factual judgment for the employment tribunal' (*South Tyneside Metropolitan Borough Council v Anderson* [2007] ICR 1581 at para 21, per Sedley LJ). Moreover, at first instance in *Villalba v Merrill Lynch & Co Inc* [2007] ICR 469, the tribunal held that the territorial restriction in *s 1(6)* to employment at two different establishments 'in Great Britain' was 'an artificial bar to the elimination of sex discrimination in pay' (para 270) which should be disapplied and *Article 157* relied on directly, allowing the claimant to use a comparator based abroad.

More recently, a purposive approach has led the EAT to hold that it may be unduly restrictive to compare the concept of 'establishment' to circumstances where employees work at a single geographical location, and that the relevant question is whether it is fair and reasonable to regard a particular group of employees as being a single establishment for comparison purposes in an equal pay claim, which requires that the group have a clear identity such as would be discernible if, for instance, they worked together to achieve a common purpose: *Edinburgh City Council v Wilkinson* [2010] IRLR 756 at para 68. Furthermore, a claimant can satisfy *s 1(6)* (now *EqA 2010, s 83(2)*) by showing that men in her comparator's class and any man employed, or who might be employed, to do the same job at her establishment would be employed on common terms and conditions, which can in principle be done by carrying out a hypothetical exercise, although it should only be done where there was a real possibility of a man being employed there to perform the comparator's job or a broadly similar job: *Dumfries and Galloway Council v North* [2009] ICR 1363 at paras 20–27 and 54–59.

The restrictive nature of the 'same employment' test under *EqPA 1970* has prompted many claimants to bring claims under *Article 157* instead. The parameters of permissible comparison under *Article 157* were previously somewhat unclear, but the ECJ set out its preferred approach in the leading case of *Lawrence v Regent Office Care Ltd: C-320/00* [2002] ECR I-7325. It held that, although the applicability of *Article 157* is not limited to situations in which claimant and comparator work for the same employer, the differences in their pay must be attributable to a single source. Otherwise, there would be no body which was responsible for the inequality and which could restore equal treatment.

The single source test has not proved an unqualified victory for claimants. It was interpreted in *Allonby v Accrington and Rossendale College* [2001] EWCA Civ 529, [2001] ICR 1189 to prevent the agency worker from using one of the end user's employees as a comparator. This was despite the fact that they worked in the same establishment and were both ultimately paid by the end user. The fact that the claimant's level of pay was influenced by the amount which the end user paid the agency was held not to be a sufficient basis for concluding that the end user and the agency constituted a single source to which the differences in pay could be attributed. Nor did it matter that the claimant had originally been employed by the end user directly and that the contracting out of her services was openly designed to reduce the end user's costs (see paras 41–50).

Concerns have been expressed that employers can now manipulate employment arrangements to deprive workers of equal pay rights by effecting changes of form rather than substance. This concern is enhanced by a Court of Appeal decision in *Robertson v Department for Environment, Food and Rural Affairs* [2005] EWCA Civ 138, [2005] ICR 750. The single source test was held to preclude the use of a comparator who has the same employer as the claimant (in both the legal and factual sense) where they work in different departments which are individually responsible for negotiating and setting staff pay levels.

This interpretation arguably goes beyond what the ECJ envisaged in *Lawrence* and gives rise to serious questions as to whether employers are now able to avoid the application of *Article 157* by departmentalising the negotiating and setting of pay levels. Such departmentalisation is institutionally less disruptive than contracting out of the type found in *Allonby* and is therefore even more likely to be used as a cost-cutting measure. On the other hand, judicial acknowledgement that any large, complex organisation which delegates responsibility for setting pay levels to lower tiers of management will inevitably have numerous 'sources' of differences in pay will be viewed by some as a sensible recognition of industrial relations reality.

The Court of Appeal applied *Robertson* in *Armstrong v Newcastle upon Tyne NHS Hospital Trust* [2005] EWCA Civ 1608, [2006] IRLR 124, holding that female hospital ancillary staff could not use male porters as comparators even though at the time of the claim they were all employed by the same hospital trust, on the basis that the porters had previously been employed by a different trust which was responsible for introducing the bonus pay which was the subject of the claim. The Court of Appeal has, however, proved willing to pursue this line of reasoning only so far. In *South Tyneside MBC v Anderson* (above), the council argued that the claimants (cooks and cleaners at local authority schools) and their comparators (who included drivers, street cleaners and refuse collectors) were not in the same employment because it was open to each school governing body to decide what an individual worker's terms and conditions of employment should be. The Court found that this discretion was 'largely illusory', and that it would be both unrealistic and arguably perverse for the governors to try to depart from the collectively agreed terms. The claimants and the comparators were, therefore, working under common terms and conditions of employment. Moreover, the scope for employers to avoid liability by invoking the single source test has been narrowed following the EAT's decision that identifying the 'single source' is not a matter of inquiring as to who was responsible for creating the inequality, but rather who is 'responsible' in the sense of perpetuating the inequality (or who was perpetuating it when the claimant last worked) and who is able to put it right: *North Cumbria Acute Hospitals NHS Trust v Potter* [2009] IRLR 176 at paras 107–108, followed in *Wilkinson* at paras 78–80.

Ironically, it may prove more difficult to avoid domestic equal pay law. Had the claimants in *Robertson* and their comparators of choice been employed at the same establishment, comparison would have been permitted under *EqPA 1970* despite departmentalisation. There may therefore now be some situations in which domestic law is more generous to claimants than EC law, yet others where it is less so. The proposition that the single source test does not apply when considering *EqPA 1970, s 1(6)* (now *EqA 2010, s 83(2)*) was approved by the EAT in *Potter* at paras 80–87.

11.18 Pregnancy

As in sex discrimination law generally, *EqPA 1970* disapplied the equal treatment principle where special treatment was accorded to pregnant women. *Section 6(1)(b)* provided that the equality clause will not operate in relation to terms affording special treatment to women in connection with pregnancy or childbirth. This is replicated in *EqA 2010, Sch 7, para 2.*

Under *EqPA 1970, s 6(1AA), s 6(1)(b)* did not affect the operation of an equality clause falling within *s 1(2)(d), (e)* or *(f)*, which makes specific provision addressing discrimination in pay related to pregnancy and maternity leave. These provisions were inserted into *EqPA 1970* in order to give effect to the ECJ's decisions in *Gillespie v Northern Health and Social Services Board: C-342/93* [1996] ECR I-475 and *Alabaster v Woolwich plc: C-147/02* [2004] ECR I-3101. They are broadly replicated by *EqA 2010, ss 72–76.*

The overall effect of these provisions is that, where a woman is arguing that she receives lower pay or less favourable contractual terms on grounds of her pregnancy or maternity leave, she need not rely on a comparator. Thus, a pay increase which a woman would have received but for pregnancy or maternity leave must be taken into account when calculating any earnings-related maternity pay and pay on her return to work. Further, the equality clause guarantees the right to the benefit of any pay increase or bonus referable to periods before or after maternity leave and during the two weeks of compulsory leave (under the *Employment Rights Act 1996, s 72(1)*) at the time they would ordinarily fall due for payment.

11.19 WHAT CAN BE COMPARED?

The equality clause inserted into every employment contract by *EqA 2010* affects *all* contractual terms, not merely those governing pay. The Act thus regulates contractual terms such as those governing sick leave, holiday entitlement and health insurance. However, where a claimant seeks to allege discrimination in the provision of payments or benefits which are not regulated by the contract, the claim had to be brought under *SDA 1975* or now under the general discrimination provisions of *EqA 2010* (see **8.101**). In principle this should include discretionary bonuses, although there is Scottish authority to the effect that even where a bonus scheme is described as 'discretionary', a claim should be brought under *EqPA 1970* where the bonus is regulated by the contract of employment and depends on the satisfaction of (unchanging) qualifying requirements (*Hoyland v Asda Stores Ltd* [2006] IRLR 468 (Court of Session)). *EqPA 1970* did not cover state pensions, while equal treatment in occupational pensions was addressed by the *Pensions Act 1995. EqA 2010* addresses equal treatment in occupational pensions alongside equal treatment in pay in Part 5, Chapter 3: see in particular *s 67* (sex equality rule).

In contrast, *Article 157* focuses more clearly on 'pay' but is not restricted to contractual entitlements. Despite the extensive definition now provided in *Article 157(2)*, the ECJ has continued to produce a voluminous case law on the meaning of 'pay'. Much of the underlying litigation has been prompted by claimants' desire to bring their claims within *Article 157* as opposed to the separate social security Directives (*79/7/EEC* and *86/378/EEC*), which contain additional limitations on the equal treatment principle.

The trend has been for the definition of 'pay' to be extended beyond the core meaning of wages and salary. 'Pay' includes benefits which employers provide voluntarily or are required by legislation to provide. It can be 'immediate or future' provided that the employee receives it, albeit indirectly, in respect of his employment from his employer. Thus, the definition includes sick pay, redundancy pay, unfair dismissal compensation, occupational pensions, survivors' benefits, bridging pensions, maternity benefits paid under legislation or collective agreements, and concessionary travel facilities granted voluntarily to ex-employees (see, respectively, *Rinner-Kuhn v FWW Spezial-Gebaudereinigung GmbH & Co KG: 171/88* [1989] ECR 2743; *Barber v Guardian Royal Exchange Assurance Group: C-262/88*

[1990] ECR I-1889; *R v Secretary of State for Employment, ex p Seymour-Smith: C-167/97* [1999] ECR I-623; *Bilka-Kaufhaus GmbH v Weber von Hartz: 170/84* [1986] ECR 1607; *Ten Oever v Stichting Bedrijfspensioenfonds voor het Glazenwassers- en Schoonmaakbedrijf: C-109/91* [1993] ECR I-4879; *Birds Eye Walls Ltd v Roberts: C-132/92* [1993] ECR I-5579; *Gillespie v Northern Health and Social Services Board: C-342/93* [1996] ECR I-475; *Garland v British Rail Engineering Ltd: 12/81* [1982] ECR 359).

However, 'pay' does not include social security schemes or retirement pensions which are directly governed by legislation without any element of agreement and which are obligatorily applicable to general categories of workers (*Defrenne v Belgium: 80/70* [1971] ECR 445). Moreover, not every employment-related benefit is caught by *Article 157*. The ECJ stressed in *Lommers v Minister van Landbouw, Natuurbeheer en Visserji: C-476/99* [2002] ECR I-2891 that '[t]he fact that the fixing of certain working conditions may have pecuniary consequences is not sufficient to bring such conditions within the scope of *Article 157*, which is a provision based on the close connection existing between the nature of the work done and the amount of pay' (para 28). The Court held that a scheme under which an employer made nursery places available on advantageous terms to employees was not governed by *Article 157*. Sex discrimination claims concerning working conditions which fall outside *Article 157* must be brought under the *Equal Treatment Directive (76/207/EEC)*.

11.20 HOW IS THE COMPARISON CONDUCTED?

Once it has been established that the claimant has selected an appropriate comparator, each term of the claimant's contract (in domestic law) or each element of his or her 'pay' (in EC law) must be compared separately with the equivalent aspect of the comparator's contract or pay. Equality is required in respect of each individual element of the consideration received by the two employees in return for working. It is therefore no defence for an employer to argue that, when looked at as a whole, the claimant's contract or pay is no less favourable than the comparator's because the claimant is entitled to certain benefits (eg free meals, car allowance, etc) to which the comparator is not entitled.

In the leading domestic case of *Hayward v Cammell Laird Shipbuilders Ltd* [1988] AC 894, the House of Lords justified this rule by reference to the wording of *EqPA 1970*. In contrast, in the leading EC case of *Barber v Guardian Royal Exchange Assurance Group: C-262/88* [1990] ECR I-1889, the ECJ—which does not have a detailed legislative scheme to interpret and apply—referred to the underlying policy reasons. Without such a rule, the courts would have to ascribe a monetary value to every element of the consideration received by claimant and comparator in order that overall figures could be calculated and compared. This would render judicial review difficult and thereby diminish the effectiveness of *Article 157* (paras 33–34).

Although the rule requiring term-by-term comparison is established by authority of the highest standing, it has recently come under a degree of pressure in the context of high-profile equal pay claims by local government employees in the North East of England. In *Redcar and Cleveland Borough Council v Degnan* [2005] IRLR 179, EAT), the female claimants were respectively employed by the council as a cleaner, a supervisory cleaner and a supervisory assistant in schools and a home help in social services. Their male comparators (who the council accepted were employed on work rated as equivalent) were employed as gardeners, refuse workers and drivers and road workers. The claimants and their comparators were all paid at the same basic hourly rate. However, there were differences in relation to the rates for attendance allowances and bonuses. The gardeners received a fixed bonus of 40%. The refuse workers and drivers received a 36% bonus and an attendance allowance of between £33.81 and £34.88 per week. The road workers received a fixed bonus of 33% and an attendance allowance of between £13.91 and £14.61 per week.

Each claimant sought to compare herself with the male comparator most advantageous to her for the purpose of the bonus element of his pay and with the most advantageous comparator for the purpose of the attendance allowance element. The tribunal held that this was permissible, but the EAT disagreed, holding that the attendance allowance related to the same subject matter as basic hourly pay and the bonus and was an *element* of a distinct part of the contract rather than itself being a distinct part. As such, the contractual 'terms' that fell to be compared were the provisions for monetary payment for performance of the contracts, by attending at work and working during normal working hours. The Court of Appeal upheld this approach ([2005] IRLR 615).

The EAT was evidently influenced by the grave financial consequences of allowing the claimants to cherry-pick the best contractual benefits from a range of comparators. It felt that to allow this would 'impose an inequitable burden, surely not intended by Parliament, on the current generation of council tax payers and general tax payers' (para 30). However, it must be doubted whether the decision truly accords with *Hayward*, where Lord Goff expressly stated, at 907, that a construction of the word 'term' which collectively embraced basic pay, benefits in kind such as the use of a car, cash bonuses and sickness benefits would do 'unacceptable violence to the words of the statute'. Perhaps for this reason, *Degnan* has subsequently been treated as turning on its specific facts, in particular the claimants' concession that the fixed bonus was part of basic pay and the finding that the attendance allowance was a benefit paid merely for turning up to work and was therefore part of the basic pay received for doing simply what was contractually required: *Brownbill v St Helens and Knowsley Hospital NHS Trust* EAT/0074/10 (6 August 2010, unreported) at paras 75–78.

Whereas the Court of Appeal has sanctioned an apparent departure from the strictness of the term-by-term rule, the ECJ recently reaffirmed that rule in its full rigour in *Elsner-Lakeberg v Land Nordrhein-Westfalen: C-285/02* [2004] ECR I-5861, stressing the need for a separate comparison in respect of the pay for regular hours and the pay for additional hours.

11.21 WHEN CAN A DIFFERENCE IN PAY BE JUSTIFIED?

Once a woman establishes that she is engaged on like work, work rated as equivalent, or work of equal value to a better paid comparator, the burden of proof shifts to the employer to make out a 'material factor' defence on the balance of probabilities. As the EAT put it in *Villalba v Merrill Lynch & Co Inc* [2007] ICR 469, 'the principle is that once a woman demonstrates that her job is either like work or work of equal value to that of her male chosen comparator, there is a presumption of discrimination on grounds of sex [and it] is then for the employer to rebut that presumption' (para 104). The employer must establish that the reason for the difference in their pay is not tainted with sex, which requires him to establish that there has been no sex discrimination, direct or indirect: *Glasgow City Council v Marshall* [2000] 1 WLR 333 at 339 (Lord Nicholls).

The statutory mechanism pursuant to which the employer must rebut the presumption of unlawful discrimination is by demonstrating that the difference between the employee and her male comparator is due to a *material factor*, reliance on which does not involve treating her less favourably due to her sex (*EqA 2010, s 69*). A similar defence is present under *TFEU, Article 157* (formerly *EC Treaty, Article 141*).

Where the factor relied on puts the claimant and persons of her sex doing equal work at a particular disadvantage compared to persons of the opposite sex, the employer must also demonstrate that reliance on that factor is a proportionate means of achieving a legitimate aim (*EqA 2010, s 69(1)(b) and (2)*) (see further **1.83–1.85**).

Note that the precursor to *EqA 2010, s 69(1)* (*EqPA 1970, s 1(3)*) referred to a '*genuine* material factor'. The word 'genuine' was removed from the equivalent section in *EqA 2010*, the government taking the view that it 'added nothing to the meaning of the requirement, which is that the employer's obligation is to show that the reason for the difference is genuine and not a sham' (*Explanatory Notes to the EqA 2010, para 243*). A sham or non-genuine explanation is a false one, designed to disguise the true reason for the difference in pay, itself tainted by sex (see eg *Dolphin v Hartlepool Borough Council* [2009] IRLR 168).

11.22 Burden of proof

In *Armstrong v Newcastle upon Tyne NHS Hospital Trust* [2005] EWCA Civ 1608, [2006] IRLR 124, the Court of Appeal appeared to impose a high threshold before the burden of proof will shift to the employer to make out its material factor defence. Arden LJ indicated (para 32) that it is only if the employee produces a gender-based comparison showing that women doing equivalent work were being paid less than men that the burden of proof shifts to the employer.

However, a differently constituted Court of Appeal has since confirmed in *Gibson v Sheffield City Council* [2010] EWCA Civ 63, [2010] ICR 708 that that element of Arden LJ's judgment is erroneous. In fact, all that is required to shift the burden of proof to the employer is for the employee to show that she was being paid less than a comparable male employee (Smith LJ, para 72). She will only need to provide evidence of the kind of adverse impact referred to by Arden LJ if she wishes to allege that the employer's material factor is indirectly discriminatory. This approach is now enshrined in *EqA 2010, s 69(2)*, which places the burden on the employee to demonstrate prima facie indirect discrimination before the employer is required to demonstrate objective justification pursuant to *s 69(1)(b)*.

If, as is often the case, the employer's pay system is not transparent, the burden of proof may be difficult to discharge, since the tribunal will be entitled to draw inferences from the lack of transparency (*Barton v Investec Henderson Crosthwaite Securities Ltd* [2003] ICR 1205). For that reason, employers should exercise caution when responding to questions from an employee or their representative regarding the rates of pay of other employees. There is a careful balance to be struck between protecting the comparator employee's confidentiality and disclosing sufficient detail to ensure that there is no prejudice to any subsequent defence put forward by the employer (see **11.41** ff).

11.23 *Material factor—multiple uses?*

Employers may rely on the same factor both:

(i) in seeking to demonstrate a difference between the woman's work and the man's work in denying that work is like work or work of equal value; and

(ii) in support of an *EqA 2010, s 69(1)* (*EqPA 1970, s 1(3)*) defence if that similarity is made out (*Davies v McCartneys* [1989] ICR 705).

In fact, even where the factor has been taken into account by the tribunal in its determination that the work is like work or work of equal value, that same factor may be relied on under *s 69(1)* (*Christie v John E Haith Ltd* [2003] IRLR 670). This gives rise to the possibility of a difference in, say, the level of skill not being sufficiently important to make two jobs of unequal value, yet being treated as sufficient to defeat the equal pay claims of a claimant in one job vis-à-vis a comparator in the other.

11.24 Material difference

How, then, does an employer establish a material difference between the claimant and her comparator? In *Rainey v Greater Glasgow Health Board* [1987] AC 224 the House of Lords provided the following guidance on the matters that may be taken into account in determining whether the employer has made out a 'material difference' for the purpose of *EqPA 1970, s 1(3)* (now *EqA 2010, s 69(1)*):

> 'The difference must be "material", which I would construe as meaning "significant and relevant", and it must be between "her case and his". Consideration of a person's case must necessarily involve consideration of all the circumstances of that case. These may well go beyond what is not very happily described as "the personal equation", ie the personal qualities by way of skill, experience or training which the individual brings to the job. Some circumstances may on examination prove to be not significant or not relevant, but others may do so, though not relating to the personal qualities of the employee. In particular, where there is no question of intentional sex discrimination whether direct or indirect (and there is none here) a difference which is connected with economic factors affecting the efficient carrying on of the employer's business or other activity may well be relevant'.
>
> (Lord Keith at 235)

Lord Keith also approved the view expressed by Browne-Wilkinson J in *Jenkins v Kingsgate (Clothing Production)* [1981] 1 WLR 1485 that the defence afforded to employers under *EqPA 1970,s 1(3)* (now *EqA 2010, s 69)* is equivalent in scope to the justification defence available under *TFEU, Article 157*, as set out by the ECJ in *Bilka-Kaufhaus GmbH v Weber von Hartz: 170/84* [1986] ECR 1607.

11.25 *Direct discrimination*

Historically, doubts were raised as to whether the distinction between direct and indirect discrimination is relevant in the field of equal pay (see in particular the speech of Lord Slynn in *Ratcliffe v North Yorkshire County Council* [1995] ICR 833). However, in *Strathclyde Regional Council v Wallace* [1998] 1 WLR 259 the House of Lords confirmed the need to construe *EqPA 1970* so far as possible to work harmoniously with *SDA 1975* and what is now *TFEU, Article 157*, both of which address direct and indirect discrimination. An employer could not demonstrate that a factor is 'not the difference of sex' under *EqPA 1970, s 1(3)* if the factor relied on is sexually discriminatory, whether directly or indirectly.

Recent decisions, both domestic (eg *Armstrong* and *Gibson*) and European (eg *Cadman v Health and Safety Executive: C-17/05* [2006] ICR 1623), have adopted the conceptual distinction between direct and indirect discrimination in the context of *EqPA 1970*. The relevance of both concepts is even clearer following the enactment of *EqA 2010*, under which the concepts of direct discrimination and indirect discrimination are encapsulated within *s 69(1)(a)* and *s 69(2)* respectively.

Despite previous suggestions to the contrary (in particular by Lord Browne Wilkinson in *Wallace* and Elias P (as he then was) in his judgments in the EAT in *Villalba*, *Middlesbrough Borough Council v Surtees* [2007] ICR 1644, *Cumbria County Council v Dow* [2008] IRLR 91 and *Chief Constable of West Midlands Police v Blackburn & Manley* [2008] ICR 505) it is now settled law that an employer cannot seek to defend a claim under *EpA 1970* by reference to a material factor that is directly discriminatory. For recent reference to this principle, see para 60 of the Court of Appeal's decision in *Gibson* and para 48 of the Court of Appeal's decision in the conjoined cases of *Redcar and Cleveland Borough Council v Bainbridge* and *Middlesbrough Borough Council v Surtees* [2008] EWCA Civ 885, [2009] ICR 133.

The same is certainly true under *EqA 2010. Section 69(1)(a)* requires that the material factor relied on by the employer 'does not involve treating [the employee] less favourably because of [her] sex than the responsible person treats [her comparator]'. Unlike in respect of indirect discrimination, there is no possibility of objectively justifying reliance on a directly discriminatory factor under *s 69(2)*. The *EHRC Equal Pay Code* confirms the inability to rely on a directly discriminatory factor as a defence (para 82).

11.26 Establishing prima facie indirect sex discrimination

In accordance with the Court of Appeal's decision in *Nelson v Carillion Services Ltd* [2003] ICR 1256, the burden lies with the claimant to demonstrate a prima facie case of indirect discrimination. This is consistent with the requirements of the *Burden of Proof Directive (97/80/EC)*, which applies to equal pay claims. However, the rule has been criticised: see in particular Waller LJ in *Bailey v Home Office* [2005] ICR 1057 at paras 37–38, suggesting that the rule results in cases 'get[ting] into an unnecessary evidential tangle', and Smith LJ in *Gibson* at para 67, noting that 'there are powerful arguments for saying that *Nelson* was wrongly decided' but that 'it is binding unless and until the Supreme Court says otherwise'.

Under *EqPA 1970*, there were two ways in which the material factor relied on might be shown to be prima facie indirectly discriminatory:

(i) by identification of a seemingly gender-neutral provision, criterion or practice that puts persons of one sex at a disadvantage compared with persons of the other sex (see, for example, the *Equal Treatment Directive (2006/54/EC), Article 2(1)(b)*);

(ii) by demonstrating 'significant statistics [which] disclose an appreciable difference in pay between two jobs of equal value, one of which is carried out almost exclusively by women and the other predominantly by men' (*Enderby v Frenchay Health Authority: C-127/92* [1993] ECR I-5535, para 19). That approach does not require the identification of some provision, criterion or practice. It simply requires 'cogent, relevant and sufficiently compelling statistics' to demonstrate that one sex suffers a disparate impact, even if it is not possible to identify from where that disparate impact derives: *Villalba* (see **11.22**; para 117).

Approach (i) is, of course, consistent with the concept of indirect discrimination as it is used in the wider group of protected characteristics (now enshrined in *EqA 2010, s 19(1)*). The classic example of this type of prima facie indirect discrimination is the less favourable treatment of part-time workers (see, for example, *Voss v Land Berlin: C-300/06* [2007] ECR I-10573 in which, for an equal number of hours worked, part-time teachers were paid less than full-time teachers).

In contrast, the *Enderby* principle is specific only to the field of equal pay. That principle was well-established by the time *EqA* 2010 was being drafted. It is perhaps surprising, then, that the principle is arguably omitted from the relevant section of the legislation. *EqA 2010, s 69* provides as follows:

> **'69 Defence of material factor**
>
> (1) The sex equality clause in A's terms has no effect in relation to a difference between A's terms and B's terms if the responsible person shows that the difference is because of a material factor reliance on which–
>
> (a) does not involve treating A less favourably because of A's sex than the responsible person treats B, and
>
> (b) if the factor is within subsection (2), is a proportionate means of achieving a legitimate aim.
>
> (2) A factor is within this subsection if A shows that, as a result of the factor, A and persons of the same sex doing work equal to A's are put at a particular disadvantage when compared with persons of the opposite sex doing work equal to A's'.

On the face of that section, there is no reference to the *Enderby* statistical approach to establishing a prima facie indirect sex discrimination. *Section 69(2)* appears to reflect the concept of demonstrating that there exists a 'provision, criterion or practice' which puts one gender at a disadvantage. In contrast, in an *Enderby* scenario, there is no need to show that such a provision, criterion or practice exists.

The government has taken the view that *s 69* adequately 'incorporates the effect of EU law in respect of objective justification of indirectly discriminatory factors' (*Explanatory Notes to the EqA 2010, note 243*). It is also likely that *EqA 2010, s 69* will be given the purposive interpretation necessary to give full effect to *Enderby*. What impact *s 69* will have on the various interpretative difficulties to which *Enderby* has given rise (in particular the *Armstrong* issue referred to at **11.27**) remains to be seen.

11.27 Objective justification

The issue of in what circumstances the material factor relied on must be objectively justified has given rise to more appellate court authority than any other aspect of *EqPA 1970*. Notwithstanding this repeated judicial consideration, the issue of objective justification continues to be controversial, reflecting a tension between the views of different courts as to the purpose and correct impact of equal pay law more generally. To illustrate the difficulties that have arisen, and the current position on the issue, some examination of historical case law is required.

The starting point for most tribunals when considering objective justification in the context of *EqPA 1970, s 1(3)* was the ECJ's decision in *Bilka-Kaufhaus* (see **11.24**). That case considered a potential infringement of what is now *TFEU, Article 157* in the exclusion of part-time employees from certain occupational pension scheme benefits. The ECJ was asked to address whether *Article 157* extended to indirect discrimination, and if so, whether such discrimination was capable of objective justification. It was held that *Article 157* did extend to indirect discrimination (which is now expressly provided in the *Equal Treatment Directive (2006/54/EC)*) and that the employer could potentially justify indirect discrimination where the means chosen for achieving a legitimate objective:

(a) correspond to a real need on the part of the undertaking;

(b) are appropriate with a view to achieving the objective in question; and

(c) are necessary to achieve that end. Note that, in establishing whether the means are 'necessary', the focus is on proportionality; there is no requirement to demonstrate absolute necessity (see *Hardys & Hansons plc v Lax* [2005] ICR 1565 at para 32, per Pill LJ) (and see **1.85**).

The application of this objective justification requirement to indirect discrimination arising from a 'provision, criterion or practice' is uncontroversial. More controversial, however, is the application of the objective justification requirement to *Enderby* cases.

As noted above, in *Enderby* the ECJ held that, when a measure has an adverse impact on substantially more members of one sex, that gives rise to prima facie indirect discrimination (para 14). Controversy has arisen over whether, once an *Enderby* disparate impact is established, the employer is then automatically required to provide an objective justification, or whether there is an intervening stage whereby the employer can avoid the need to establish objective justification by demonstrating that the pay differential arose from factors that are completely unrelated to sex.

The first tentative steps towards the current law were taken in *Tyldesley v TML Plastics Ltd* [1996] ICR 356. In that case, the claimant argued that, following *Enderby*, any material factor relied on by the employer must be objectively justified, even if there was no suggestion that the application of that material factor defence gave rise to indirect discrimination. The EAT (Mummery P) disagreed, holding that it was not necessary objectively to justify the material factor unless it was 'tainted by gender', either on the 'provision, criterion or practice' basis, or because it adversely impacted on one sex as in *Enderby*. In that case, the comparator's commitment to 'total quality management' was a material factor untainted by gender, and so it was not necessary for the employer to provide objective justification.

Tyldesley was approved by the House of Lords in *Wallace* and *Glasgow City Council v Marshall* [2000] 1 WLR 333. In *Marshall* at 339, Lord Nicholls set out the following guidance on the application of *EqPA 1970, s 1(3)*:

> 'The scheme of the Act is that a rebuttable presumption of sex discrimination arises once the gender-based comparison shows that a woman, doing like work or work rated as equivalent or work of equal value to that of a man, is being paid or treated less favourably than the man. The variation between her contract and the man's contract is presumed to be due to the difference of sex. The burden passes to the employer to show that the explanation for the variation is not tainted with sex. In order to discharge this burden the employer must satisfy the tribunal on several matters. First, that the proffered explanation, or reason, is genuine, and not a sham or pretence. Second, that the less favourable treatment is due to this reason. The factor relied upon must be the cause of the disparity. In this regard, and in this sense, the factor must be a "material" factor, that is, a significant and relevant factor. Third, that the reason is not "the difference of sex" This phrase is apt to embrace any form of sex discrimination, whether direct or indirect. Fourth, that the factor relied upon is or, in a case within section 1(2)(c), may be a "material" difference, that is, a significant and relevant difference, between the woman's case and the man's case.
>
> 'When section 1 is thus analysed, it is apparent that an employer who satisfies the third of these requirements is under no obligation to prove a "good" reason for the pay disparity. In order to fulfil the third requirement he must prove the absence of sex discrimination, direct or indirect. If there is any evidence of sex discrimination, such as evidence that the difference in pay has a disparately adverse impact on women, the employer will be called upon to satisfy the tribunal that the difference in pay is objectively justifiable. But if the employer proves the absence of sex discrimination he is not obliged to justify the pay disparity.'

However, the ECJ's subsequent decision in *Brunnhofer v Bank der Österreichischen Postsparkasse AG: C-381/99* [2001] ECR I-4961 cast some doubt on the correctness of that approach. The court emphasised that, whatever the mechanism that produced unequal pay as between men and women, unequal pay was prohibited by *Article 157* unless justified by objective factors unrelated to discrimination linked to the difference in sex (para 30). Further, 'an employer may validly explain the difference in pay . . . in so far as they constitute objectively justified reasons unrelated to any discrimination based on sex and in conformity with the principle of proportionality' (para 68). The implication therefore appeared to be that objective justification was always required where an *Enderby* disparate impact had been demonstrated, irrespective of the cause of that disparity.

In reliance on *Brunnhofer*, the claimant in *Parliamentary Commissioner for Administration v Fernandez* [2004] ICR 123 submitted that *Marshall* was no longer good law and that, following *Brunnhofer*, *Article 157* requires an employer to justify the difference in pay between a woman and her comparator even where there is no prima facie discrimination. The EAT (HHJ Peter Clark) had little hesitation in rejecting that argument, however, stating that it did not understand the ECJ in *Brunnhofer* to be laying down a requirement to objectively justify the factor relied on where there is no suggestion of discrimination (para 33).

A differently constituted EAT (HHJ Ansell) in *Sharp v Caledonia Group Services Ltd* [2006] ICR 218 declined to follow *Fernandez*, suggesting instead that *Brunnhofer* provides clear guidelines as to the need for objective justification in *all* cases where the material factor relied on gives rise to disparate impact.

In *Armstrong*, the Court of Appeal attempted to reconcile the authorities whilst reaffirming the *Marshall* approach. Arden LJ summarised the speech of Lord Nicholls as setting out the following step-by-step guide (para 32):

'1. The complainant must produce a gender-based comparison showing that women doing like work, or work rated as equivalent, or work of equal value to that of men, are being paid or treated less favourably than men. If the complainant can produce a gender-based comparison of this kind, a rebuttable presumption of sex discrimination arises.

2. The employer must then show that the variation between the woman's contract and the man's contract is not tainted with sex, that is, that it is genuinely due to a material factor which is not the difference of sex. To do this, the employer must show each of the following matters:
   (a) that the explanation for the variation is genuine,
   (b) that the more favourable treatment of the man is due to that reason,
   (c) that the reason is not the difference of sex.

3. If, but only if, the employer cannot show that the reason was not due to the difference of sex, he must show objective justification for the disparity between the woman's contract and the man's contract.'

In effect, therefore, the Court of Appeal was satisfied that, even where there is adverse disparate impact, the employer can avoid liability without requiring objective justification by demonstrating that the difference is caused by a reason other than sex. However, the Court of Appeal did not address the fact that step 2 of the above analysis appears to be inconsistent with *Enderby*, which suggests that, once prima facie indirect discrimination is established, the employer must proceed directly to the question of objective justification.

The EAT (Elias P) in *Villalba* questioned whether the decision of the Court of Appeal in *Armstrong* was correct in the light of *Enderby* (para 131). However, shortly thereafter, in *Middlesbrough Borough Council v Surtees* [2007] ICR 1644, the EAT (Elias P) reconsidered the position and accepted that, even where the claimant has demonstrated disparate adverse impact by reference to sufficiently cogent statistics, it is still open to the employer to demonstrate that that disparate impact is in no way attributed to any sex-tainted act, and thereby avoid the need to provide objective justification (para 46). The EAT (Elias P again) subsequently took the same approach in *Redcar and Cleveland Borough Council v Bainbridge* [2007] IRLR 91 and *Surtees*, emphasising that it runs contrary to logic to require objective justification even where there is no hint of sex discrimination.

Meanwhile, however, the ECJ in *Cadman* repeated the statement relied on by the claimants in *Fernandez* and *Sharp*, that the principle of equal pay for equal work or work of equal value enshrined in *Article 157* prohibits comparable situations from being treated differently unless the difference is objectively justified (para 28), apparently without limiting that requirement to cases where there is a prima facie case of indirect discrimination (although *Cadman* was itself a case involving indirect discrimination).

The claimants reargued the *Brunnhofer* point in the conjoined appeals in *Bainbridge* and *Surtees*. The Court of Appeal did not expressly address the argument in its judgment but plainly did not accept it. There was no further attempt to reargue the point before the Court of Appeal in *Gibson*. However, the Court did re-examine the *Armstrong* issue. In *Gibson*, female carers brought equal pay claims using as their comparators street cleaners and gardeners. The work of the groups had been rated as equivalent, but the street cleaners and gardeners received higher basic pay than the carers. The disparity arose because the street cleaners and gardeners had, historically, received a performance bonus, which had since been consolidated into their basic pay. The tribunal (whose decision was upheld by the EAT) held that the bonuses were genuinely linked to productivity, which was a criterion that could not be applied to the carers' work as their work was not an objectively measurable task. Accordingly, there was no 'taint' of sex discrimination (since the criterion of productivity was unrelated to sex) and therefore, following *Armstrong*, no obligation for the Council to objectively justify its reliance on that material factor.

The Court of Appeal unanimously upheld the claimants' appeals, holding that the *Armstrong* analysis did not apply on the facts of the case, given the clear and compelling statistics which demonstrated that the pay difference disadvantaged a substantially higher proportion of women (para 51). The impossibility of applying the productivity bonus to women's work was genuine enough, but that did not remove the sexual taint from the operation of the scheme. Objective justification was required and the matter was remitted to the tribunal for this issue to be considered. However, while the judges agreed on the disposal of the appeal, they expressed different views on the *Armstrong* issue. Pill LJ noted that *Armstrong* 'is not an easy case' (para 33). Although he rejected the claimants' submission that it was decided *per incuriam* (para 42), he found the approach in *Armstrong* 'very difficult to reconcile' with *Enderby* and *Marshall* (para 49). By contrast, Smith LJ concluded that *Armstrong* was correctly decided (paras 59–72) and Maurice Kay LJ stated that, subject to the same caveat noted by Smith LJ regarding step 1 in Arden LJ's analysis (see **11.22**), he was convinced that *Armstrong* was correct (para 74).

Importantly, Smith LJ noted (para 68) that the *Armstrong* line of defence is of very limited practical application. Whilst it is always open to an employer to demonstrate 'that the particular disadvantage apparently demonstrated is nothing to do with gender...' that defence would almost always require the employer to adduce some historical evidence of how the pay differential came to arise. The tribunal must be satisfied that that explanation is not *in any way* due to the difference of sex. Where, as in *Gibson*, the disadvantaged group is predominantly female and the advantaged group predominantly male, the tribunal will readily be able to draw an inference of a sex taint, and it will be very difficult for an employer to rebut that inference.

In *Armstrong (No 2)* [2010] UKEAT/0069/09, the EAT (Underhill P) adopted a broadly similar approach to the *Armstrong* issue to Smith LJ's (para 70), again holding that it is unnecessary to objectively justify reliance on the material factor in an *Enderby* case where the employer can show that it is genuinely not the result of any form of sex discrimination. Where the statistical disparity is marked, and there is evidence that cultural and economic factors have depressed women's wages, it may be difficult for an employer to discharge that burden. Where the disparity is less marked, however, a more careful analysis will be required.

It is with *Gibson* and *Armstrong (No 2)* that the law currently stands, in a reasonably settled state whereby employers (at least in theory, but perhaps seldom in practice) may demonstrate that notwithstanding *Enderby* statistics the disparity in pay is in no way 'tainted' by sex. There remains scope for further development on the *Armstrong* front, however, both in the Supreme Court (since permission to appeal has been given in *Gibson*) and because of the enactment of *EqA 2010*.

The most immediate difficulty posed by *EqA 2010, s 69* is whether it provides for the *Armstrong* principle at all. If the purposive interpretation of *EqA 2010, s 69(2)* contended for above (see **11.26**) is adopted in order to give effect to the *Enderby* principle, it would appear to follow that *s 69(1)(b)* reverses the effect of *Armstrong* by requiring objective justification in all cases. The use of the present tense in *s 69(2)* (' . . . are put at a particular disadvantage . . . ') suggests that reliance on an historical explanation for a pay disparity will no longer absolve the employer of an obligation to demonstrate that that factor is objectively justified. On one view, that more accurately reflects the intention of the ECJ in *Enderby*, since the 'output'-based *Enderby* approach to establishing prima facie indirect discrimination (as opposed to the 'input'-based concept of a provision, criterion or practice) would appear to suggest a requirement for objective justification without consideration of the historical reason for the relevant statistical disparity.

Ultimately, however, no clear intention to reverse the effect of *Armstrong* emerges either from the text of *s 69* or from the pre-legislative materials or the Explanatory Notes to the Act. As a result, further judicial consideration of the *Armstrong* principle is likely.

11.28 Disadvantage/disparate impact

In circumstances where disparate impact can be discerned from the tribunal's knowledge of the prevailing social or industrial climate (for example where the relevant criterion adversely affects those with childcare responsibilities), it may not be necessary to refer to statistical evidence of disadvantage or disparate impact (see *London Underground Ltd v Edwards (No 2)* [1999] ICR 494, at para 24 and *Chief Constable of West Midlands Police v Blackburn & Manley* [2008] ICR 505 at para 26)). In other cases, however, it is necessary to consider how stark the disparate impact must be in order to demonstrate a prima facie case of indirect discrimination.

Attempts have been made to distinguish the approach to *Enderby* cases from 'provision, criterion or practice' cases when considering the issue of disadvantage/disparate impact, and thereby limit the application of *Enderby* to only those cases where the disadvantaged group are almost exclusively of one sex. However, the Court of Appeal in *Bailey v Home Office* [2005] ICR 1057 has suggested that there is no difference between the statistical analysis in *Enderby* cases and those where some provision, criterion or practice is relied on (although that aspect of the decision has been doubted by the EAT in *Villalba* (para 123)).

In *R v Secretary of State for Employment, ex p Seymour-Smith and Perez: C-167/97* [1999] 2 AC 554, the issue arose in the context of the then two-year qualifying period of service at 16 hours or more per week before an individual was entitled to claim unfair dismissal. The claimants argued that that qualifying period of service constituted prima facie indirect sex discrimination against women. When the two-year qualifying requirement was introduced in 1985, 77.4% of men met the requirement, compared with 68.9% of women. The Divisional Court held that the claimants had failed to demonstrate prima facie discrimination, because the proportion of women who could qualify was not 'considerably smaller' than the proportion of men who could qualify. The House of Lords referred to the ECJ the question of what degree of disparate effect is sufficient to amount to indirect discrimination unless objectively justified.

The ECJ suggested (para 60) that the national court should determine whether the statistics suggested that a 'considerably smaller' percentage of women than men could satisfy the impugned requirement. It suggested that the figures in that case did not suggest that a sufficient disparity existed in 1985 to establish prima facie indirect discrimination. However, it also suggested (para 61) that a small but persistent disparity may be sufficient to establish discrimination. Applying that latter test, the House of Lords held ([2000] 1 WLR 435) by a 3:2 majority that a prima facie case of indirect discrimination had been established, on the basis of a persistent difference between 1985 and 1991 (as opposed to a sufficient disparity in 1985).

Perhaps unsurprisingly, there is commonly dispute as to how statistical evidence should be interpreted. Much of the debate centres around whether the tribunal should focus on the proportion of men and women who *can* comply with the impugned requirement, or the proportion who *cannot* comply. In *Barry v Midland Bank plc* [1999] 1 WLR 1465, Lord Nicholls suggested that the correct approach was to compare the proportion of men who are not disadvantaged with the proportion who are, and to compare those proportions with the equivalent proportions of women who can and cannot comply. However, he also noted that such comparisons could be misleading, since they would be affected by the size of the comparator groups. It was suggested that expressing the proportions in the disadvantaged group as a ratio of each other (for example, nine disadvantaged women for every disadvantaged man) would provide a better guide.

In *Rutherford v Secretary of State for Trade and Industry* [2005] ICR 119, Mummery LJ suggested that reliance on the disadvantaged groups (ie those who could not comply) alone could produce 'seriously misleading' results. It was held that the tribunal had erred when focusing solely on the disadvantaged group, and should instead have considered the respective proportions of men and women who could comply with the relevant requirement (namely the prohibition then in force on individuals aged 65 or over bringing unfair dismissal claims).

On appeal ([2006] ICR 785), a majority of the House of Lords considered that a statistical analysis was unnecessary, since the age limit of 65 applied equally as between men and women. However, Lords Nicholls and Walker did apply a statistical approach, and unlike the Court of Appeal reviewed both the proportions of advantaged and disadvantaged of each sex. Both of their Lordships emphasised the resulting proportions (1.4% of men versus 1% of women disadvantaged) were insufficient to demonstrate an adverse impact on a substantially higher proportion of men than women.

In *Grundy v British Airways plc* [2007] EWCA Civ 1020, [2008] IRLR 74, the tribunal had again focused on the smaller, disadvantaged group in concluding that there was disparate adverse impact. The EAT overturned that decision (prior to the decision of the House of Lords in *Rutherford*), but it was later reinstated by the Court of Appeal, which noted Lord Nicholls' statement in *Marshall* that the tribunal's choice of pool was primarily a finding of fact. It concluded that there is no single suitable pool for every case. The key determinant is the nature of the issue that the claimant has elected to pose. The tribunal's task is simply to find a pool which suitably tests the discrimination complained of. Provided it does so, the tribunal cannot be said to have erred if a different pool, with a different outcome, could equally legitimately have been chosen.

Following *Rutherford*, it seems that the proportions of both advantaged and disadvantaged groups may be relevant. However, it appears from *Grundy* that the tribunal is relatively unburdened (or unassisted, depending on your point of view) by legal principle in choosing the comparator group on which it wishes to focus, irrespective of the fact that a different choice may result in a wholly different finding on the issue of disparate impact. Unfortunately, that approach necessarily results in significant uncertainty for claimants and respondents alike.

11.29 Example material factors

Length of service

Employers may commonly have pay scales related to length of service, perhaps simply to reward loyalty, but perhaps also to reward better performance on the basis that there is often a correlation between length of service and ability to do the job well. That latter defence would seem to be flawed, since the two do not necessarily go hand in hand. However, in *Handels-og Kontorfunktionaerernes Forbund I Danmark v Dansk Arbejdsgiverforening, acting on behalf of Danfoss: 109/88* [1989] ECR 3199, the ECJ was happy to base its decision on that assumption. It stated that the criterion of seniority did not require specific justification, since it generally placed the worker in a better position to carry out his duties and was therefore justified as a means of achieving that legitimate objective.

That decision was called into question by subsequent ECJ decisions in *Nimz v Freie und Hansestadt Hamburg: C-184/89* [1991] ECR I-297, *Gerster v Freistaat Bayern: C-1/95* [1997] ECR I-5253, and *Hill v Revenue Comrs: C-243/95* [1998] ECR I-3739. In all three cases, the ECJ stated that the national courts should determine whether there was sufficient proof of a link between length of service and acquisition of a certain level of knowledge or ability objectively to justify the lesser pay received by part-timers.

In light of the apparent contradiction, the Court of Appeal referred the case of *Cadman v Health and Safety Executive: C-17/05* [2006] ECR I-9583 to the ECJ. In that case, the claimant female employee was paid less than four male comparators of the same grade, each of whom had longer service with the HSE than she did. The employers relied on the claimant's length of service as their material factor defence under *EqPA 1970, s 1(3)*. The Court of Appeal asked the ECJ whether, where the use of length of service had a disparate impact as between men and women, *Article 157* required the employer to provide special justification for the use of that criterion as its defence to an equal pay claim.

The ECJ clarified its previous decisions by stating that, as a general rule, the criterion of length of service is appropriate to attain the legitimate objective of enabling the employee to perform his duties better. However, where the employee provides evidence capable of giving rise to 'serious doubts' as to whether there is a link between that objective and the criterion of length of service, it the employer will be required to objectively justify the use of that criterion.

In the recent case of *Wilson v Health and Safety Executive (Equality and Human Rights Commission intervening)* [2009] EWCA Civ 1074, [2010] ICR 302, the Court of Appeal considered the impact of *Cadman* in the context of an incremental pay scale linked to length of service over 10 years. In that case, the tribunal held that the 10-year period was not legitimate, since all relevant employees had achieved the necessary degree of skill to undertake the relevant job. However, it distinguished between the adoption of a length of service criterion and the period over which it was applied, holding that, if the length of service criterion could be legitimately applied for some period, the 'serious doubts' test could not be satisfied, even if the criterion had been applied over a longer period than was legitimate in the circumstances. Therefore, the employer was not required to justify the use of length of service as its material factor defence.

The Court of Appeal rejected that approach, holding that there was nothing in *Cadman* to suggest a distinction between adoption and application of the length of service criterion. The 'serious doubts' test did not operate to shift the burden of proof to the employee (indeed, that would be inconsistent with the fact that the burden of proof lay with the employer to demonstrate justification), but rather was 'merely a sensible evidential requirement to ensure that the complaint has some prospect of success' (per Arden LJ, para 71).

11.30 *Market forces/financial considerations*

Market forces may constitute a potential material factor defence (*Rainey v Greater Glasgow Health Board* [1987] AC 224). However, an employer cannot pay women less than men for equal work just because a competitor does so (*EHRC Equal Pay Code*, para 81). Naturally, therefore, this defence is certain to fail where, as in *Ratcliffe v North Yorkshire County Council* [1995] ICR 833, the wider market forces were themselves tainted by discrimination. In that case, the claimants were dinner ladies who claimed equal pay with road sweepers and gardeners. The council argued that it had had to reduce its labour costs because of its need to tender for work at a commercially competitive rate following the introduction of compulsory competitive tendering. However, the tribunal (subsequently upheld by the House of Lords) found that that was insufficient to establish a defence under *EqPA 1970, s 1(3)* (now *EqA 2010, s 69(1)*). It held that the need to compete with competitors employing women on less favourable terms was a factor which was due to the difference of sex, because it arose out of the general perception that women should stay at home to look after the children and any work must fit in with that domestic responsibility.

It was suggested by the Court of Appeal in *Armstrong v Newcastle upon Tyne NHS Hospital Trust* [2005] EWCA Civ 1608, [2006] IRLR 124 (para 121), that *Ratcliffe* is an exceptional case that turns on the findings of the tribunal in that case. It is not, it was said, authority for the proposition that the adjustment of wages in order to compete in a predominantly female labour market is necessarily discriminatory—rather, something more is required.

Following remission to the tribunal, the EAT (in *Armstrong (No 2)* UKEAT/0069/09) grappled with the question of what that additional something was. In the *Armstrong* cases, the claimants were female domestic workers whose comparators were male porters. The comparators received bonus payments which the claimants had also historically received, but which were removed as part of the process of compulsory competitive tendering in order to ensure that the NHS Trust was operating on a basis which was on a par with private sector providers of domestic services. Domestic workers were predominantly female, and the tribunal found that the market rates were depressed by social and economic factors that were particular to women, and hence the market rate was 'gender-tainted'.

The EAT examined the Court of Appeal's decision in *Armstrong (No 1)* and held that the ratio of *Ratcliffe*, as interpreted by the Court of Appeal, was that in order to find that an employer's reliance on market forces was discriminatory, not only must the market rates be sex-tainted, but the employer must have known and taken advantage of that fact. The EAT interpreted the (somewhat sparse) reasoning of the tribunal as indicating that that had been the case in *Armstrong*. Accordingly, the case was on all fours with *Ratcliffe* and objective justification was required. The EAT further upheld the tribunal's decision that the difference in pay could not be objectively justified, since there had been no consideration of whether women were disproportionately affected when the bonus was removed, and the bonuses that the male comparators continued to receive, although considered 'performance' bonuses, were no longer linked to productivity, and so ceased to serve any business need.

The ECJ has suggested in *Schönheit v Stadt Frankfurt am Main: C-4/02* [2003] ECR I-12575 that an employer's budgetary considerations cannot be used as justification for treatment that would otherwise constitute indirect discrimination (paras 84–85). However, the EAT (Burton P) clarified in *Cross v British Airways plc* [2005] IRLR 423 that, although indirect discrimination cannot be justified *solely* on the basis of the employer's budgetary considerations, such considerations can constitute a justification if combined with other reasons. The exception to this principle, according to the EAT, is where the party attempting to rely on financial considerations is an emanation of the state, in which case the fact that it effectively has a 'bottomless purse' precludes it from relying on budgetary considerations as providing any element of its objective justification—although query whether this has been undermined by the EAT's subsequent comments in a different context in *O'Hanlon v Commissioners for HM Revenue and Customs* [2006] ICR 1579 (upheld [2007] IRLR 404). The EAT has also cast some doubt on the principle in *Cross* in the case of *Woodcock v Cumbria Primary Care Trust UK* EAT/OLL89/09 where it commented (obiter) that increased cost alone ought to be sufficient to amount to a legitimate aim if it is disproportionate to the discriminatory effect (see **1.84**).

In order to evidence the importance of the relevant market forces or other financial considerations, the employer may refer to the fact that pay arrangements were collectively agreed. In *Specialarbejderforbundet I Danmark v Dansk Industri, acting for Royal Copenhagen A/S: C-400/93* [1995] ECR I-1275, the ECJ noted that, although the principle of equal pay applies where elements of pay are determined by collective bargaining, the national court may take that fact into account in assessing whether the difference in pay is objectively justified (para 46). In *Cumbria County Council v Dow* EAT/0148/06 (12 November 2007, unreported), the EAT noted that the tribunal was wrong not to attach any significance to the fact that the relevant union was a party to an agreed deterioration in terms, particularly given that the tribunal had stated that there was no connivance by the trade unions in any deliberate discrimination (para 157).

11.31 *Union involvement*

Conversely, however, a union's refusal to consent to new pay structures will not constitute a material factor defence in and of itself. In *Coventry City Council v Nicholls* [2009] IRLR 345 the employer council attempted to reach agreement on the implementation of a single status agreement which was intended to eradicate gender pay discrimination. Ultimately, having failed to reach agreement, the council imposed that change unilaterally. When it was then faced with equal pay claims in respect of past pay inequality from women whose pay had been levelled up, the council argued that the union's intransigence to implementing the single status agreement constituted a material factor defence. It was a 'supervening cause' of the pay disparity, which was unrelated to sex, since had the union not resisted single status for so long, the gender pay discrimination would have been removed much earlier.

The EAT (Elias P) rejected this argument, holding that the union's intransigence did not replace sex as the ultimate cause of the inequality. Whilst the EAT had sympathy for the council's predicament—facing as it was the choice between ongoing gender inequality or a real possibility of industrial action—it doubted whether the threat of industrial action could ever justify a continuation of a discriminatory pay practice (para 31). On similar lines, the Court of Appeal in the conjoined cases of *Redcar and Cleveland Borough Council v Bainbridge* and *Surtees v Middlesbrough Council* [2008] EWCA Civ 885, [2009] ICR 133 was faced with the argument that the existence of separate collective bargaining for the claimant and comparator groups might constitute a material factor which is not tainted by sex. However, the tribunal had in that case concluded that the difference in pay was sex-tainted, and was not explained by the separate collective bargaining arrangements. The Court of Appeal concluded that that decision could not be said to be perverse. The door to a material factor defence based on separate collective bargaining machinery is not entirely closed, therefore, but it is clear that it may be difficult to avoid the inference that a discriminatory result of such separate negotiation is tainted with sex.

11.32 *Performance*

A difference in the levels of performance of two comparable employees clearly constitutes a potential material factor. A good example would be a bonus based on an employee's performance during the preceding year of her employment (as in *Villalba v Merrill Lynch & Co Inc* [2007] ICR 469). However, a difference in performance levels that becomes clear during the employee's employment will not constitute a valid material factor defence for differences in pay which existed from the commencement of the employee's employment, or which otherwise pre-date the difference in performance levels (*Brunnhofer v Bank der Österreichischen Postsparkasse AG: C-381/99* [2001] ECR I-4961 at 76).

11.33 *Red circling*

'Red circling' often occurs following restructuring or a redundancy exercise. If an employee loses his job but obtains another within the employer's business, the employer will sometimes guarantee that additional payments will be made (often for a fixed period of time) in order to cushion the blow of a reduction in salary.

Red circling is also sometimes used in the context of job evaluation schemes. The natural result of a JES is that the pay of some employees will go down, and the pay of others will go up. In such scenarios, this type of pay protection arrangement effectively prolongs at least some element of the unequal pay. On its face, that would appear to breach the principle in *Smith v Avdel Systems Ltd: C-408/92* [1995] ICR 596 that, once discrimination is established, it must be eradicated immediately rather than phased out gradually.

However, red circling is not impermissible in principle. That was true under *EqPA 1970* (see *Farthing v Ministry of Defence* [1980] ICR 705) and is confirmed by *EqA 2010, s 69(3)*, which provides that the long-term objective of reducing inequality between men's and women's pay will always constitute a legitimate aim, thereby satisfying the first requirement of the objective justification test in *s 69(1)(b)*. Nevertheless, as will be seen, it is the second requirement of that test, namely that the factor relied upon must be a proportionate means of achieving the legitimate aim, which has proved the more significant barrier to the use of such structures as a valid material factor defence.

The leading decision on the issue is that of the Court of Appeal in the conjoined cases of *Redcar and Cleveland Borough Council v Bainbridge* and *Surtees v Middlesbrough Council* [2008] EWCA Civ 885, [2009] ICR 133. Both cases considered the impact of a pay protection scheme implemented following a re-grading exercise intended to eradicate historic pay inequality. The natural result of that re-grading process was that the pay of some staff increased, and that of others reduced. To cushion against the impact of pay cuts, the councils agreed with the relevant employees' trade unions that the pay cut would be implemented in stages over two or three years. The claimants were female employees who were employed in equal work with those employees who benefited from the pay protection arrangements.

The Court of Appeal considered *Smith v Avdel Systems Ltd*, but noted that that case concerned direct discrimination, and hence the rule that discrimination must be corrected immediately applies only in cases of direct discrimination. In this case, the pay protection arrangements were prima facie indirectly discriminatory, since they were put in place to cushion against measures which were taken to correct historical indirectly discriminatory pay scales. It was thus necessary to consider objective justification.

The Court of Appeal considered that the councils' objectives of replacing discriminatory pay practices and cushioning against pay cuts were legitimate objectives. However, in both cases, it considered that the requirement of proportionality was not satisfied. In particular, in both cases a key element appears to have been the degree of consideration given to the possibility of including the claimants within the ambit of the pay protection scheme. In *Redcar*, there had been no consideration of the discriminatory impact of excluding the claimants from the ambit of the scheme, and even after the event there had been no evidence as to why the claimants could not be included within it (in particular the costs of doing so). Furthermore, there was no evidence that, when the scheme was negotiated with representatives of employees, the views of the claimants (as to the discriminatory effect of the scheme) had been taken into account.

Similarly, in *Surtees* the council had failed to give material consideration to the question of whether it might include the claimants in the pay protection scheme. The sole differentiating factor in *Surtees* was that, in contrast to *Redcar*, the council had not conceded that its prior pay schemes were unlawfully discriminatory, and so in effect did not know that the pay protection scheme would prolong inequality when it was implemented. However, the Court of Appeal noted the tribunal's view that it would not have been difficult to identify the various claimant groups which might succeed and calculate the cost of including such individuals in the pay protection scheme. Having failed to do so, the council could not demonstrate that the pay protection scheme was justified.

The Court of Appeal left open the possibility that, in an appropriate case, an employer may be able to demonstrate that the constraints on its finances are so serious that it is justified in placing the cushioning of pay cuts ahead of the need to eradicate discriminatory pay practices. However, there was no such evidence in either of these cases.

The net result of *Bainbridge/Surtees* is that it will be very difficult for an employer to justify the use of a pay protection scheme which does not give both the men facing pay cuts and the disadvantaged women the same level of pay during even short transitional periods. Furthermore, whilst the employer's lack of awareness of a pay inequality will be relevant to the question of justification, it will not be sufficient to absolve the employer from the requirement to consider the potentially discriminatory impact of the scheme.

That finding would appear to be consistent with the decision of the EAT in *Llewellyn v Hartlepool Borough Council* [2009] ICR 1426 concerning 'piggybacking'. In that case, a number of female claimants made equal pay claims arising from a bonus payment scheme which was available to their male comparators but not to the claimants. At the same time, a number of male claimants who worked alongside the female claimants brought contingent claims arguing that, if the women's claims succeeded, they too should be entitled to the benefit of the relevant bonus payments, since the equality clause had effect as between them and the claimants in the same way as it would between the claimants and their comparators, if their claims were successful. The EAT had little difficulty in accepting that such claims were, in principle, permissible, even though they rested on a contingency which had not yet been resolved at the date on which the claims were brought. Effectively, at the point at which the claims were brought, the council would not know whether a pay inequality existed at all, but that did not preclude the male employees from bringing their claims.

11.34 *Mistake*

A material factor defence may be founded upon a genuine yet mistaken belief that there is some material factor which is not the difference in sex. In *King's College London v Clark* [2003] All ER (D) 118 (Oct), the EAT (HHJ Peter Clark) held that an employer who had genuinely but mistakenly concluded that the employee was correctly graded could rely on *EqPA 1970, s 1(3)*. Even a careless mistake, which could not possibly be objectively justified, can found a material factor defence (*Tyldesley v TML Plastics Ltd* [1996] ICR 356, EAT at 362).

11.35 *Historical differences*

In order to maintain a successful material factor defence the factor relied on must constitute a material difference in relation to the entire period for which the employer relies on it. For example, if an employer pays a premium to hire a member of staff at a time when such staff are scarce, that may constitute a valid material factor for the purposes of *s 69(1)* (see *Enderby*). However, should that factor cease to be relevant, for example because it is some years and many pay reviews since that pay premium was applied, the employer may not be able to rely on it (*Benveniste v University of Southampton* [1989] ICR 617). (See also *EHRC Equal Pay Code*, para 90.)

A good example is *Bailey v Home Office* [2005] IRLR 757. A pension benefit for prison officers was discontinued for those who joined from 1987 onwards, but red circled for those whose service commenced prior to 1987. The EAT held that, although the red circling would have amounted to a material factor defence when it was introduced, that did not justify a continuing disparity in treatment in 1999 when the equal pay claim was brought. See also *Fearnon v Smurfit Corrugated Cases (Lurgan) Ltd* [2008] NICA 45, [2009] IRLR 132, where the Northern Ireland Court of Appeal confirmed that the length of time that a discrepancy in salary has endured because of red-circling is relevant to the question of whether it can continue to be a material factor and that it is therefore incumbent on the tribunal to examine not only the motive for the introduction of red-circling, but also the reasons why it has been continued.

Similarly in *Buchanan v Skills Development Scotland* S/113105/08 (3 June 2010, unreported) an employer was unable to rely on the protection afforded to the comparator's more beneficial contractual terms on a TUPE transfer as a material factor defence when the relevant transfer took place many years before and no steps had been taken in the intervening years to correct the inequality. In that case, the employer had identified the pay inequality, and had put in place provisions for red-circling where inequality was identified, but had taken no steps in the particular case to address the ongoing inequality, and indeed had compounded it by applying across the board pay rises to both the claimants and their comparator,

11.36 *'After the event' justification*

Conversely, both the ECJ (in *Schönheit*; see **11.30**) and the Court of Appeal (in *Cadman*; see **11.25**) have stated that the employer may rely on a material factor which did not enter its mind at the time at which the impugned pay decision was made, or which is different from the factor relied on at that time. Although 'after the event' rationalisation may appear unattractive, the question is whether a justification in fact exists, not whether the employer appreciated this all along. However, as the EAT made clear in *Cumbria County Council v Dow* EAT/0148/06 (12 November 2007, unreported), the tribunal is entitled to take into account the fact that the justification relied on at tribunal was not a justification relied on at the time the pay decision was made in determining whether a material factor defence is made out (para 105).

11.37 DISCUSSIONS ABOUT PAY

One of the most considerable practical difficulties faced by claimants in equal pay claims is obtaining accurate comparator pay data. This problem is particularly acute in the private sector, where pay tends to be less transparent. Indeed, in some cases employers even impose rules prohibiting employees from discussing their pay with others.

In an attempt to address this difficulty, *EqA 2010, s 77* renders unenforceable any rule or contractual provision which prevents or restricts employees from discussing their pay with other colleagues for the purpose of identifying 'a connection between pay and having (or not having) a particular protected characteristic'. Providing, obtaining or seeking pay information for that purpose is a protected act (*s 77(4)*) and victimisation for having committed such an act in unlawful (as to victimisation more generally, see **1.98ff**).

11.38 REMEDIES

Enforcing the equality clause

The primary remedy for a successful claimant who remains employed by the respondent is the enforcement of the equality clause. The tribunal will modify the less favourable term in the claimant's contract so that it becomes no less favourable than the term of a similar kind in the contract of the male comparator with whom she has been found to have been performing equal work (or where the claimant's contract does not contain a term of a similar kind to the male comparator's, the claimant's contract will be treated as including such a term). In future, they will have to be paid at the same rate.

As noted above, enforcement is on a clause-by-clause basis. It is no answer for an employer found to have been paying a woman a lower salary than an appropriate male comparator to say that she had more days of holiday, or better sick pay provisions. The tribunal will still increase the woman's salary to the man's level. From a practical point of view, it is then likely to be necessary for the employer to 'level up' the comparator's sick pay and holiday entitlements as well, or face possible claims from him.

11.39 Arrears of pay

Enforcement of the equality clause provides a forward-looking remedy for the claimant, but what of the historical disparity? Since the employer has been in breach of the contractual 'equality clause' since the difference in pay began or since any previous justification for it ceased, the obvious remedy is one in debt for arrears of wages.

The original *EqPA 1970, s 2(5)* limited claims to arrears or damages in respect of the two years immediately preceding the commencement of proceedings. However, in *Levez v TH Jennings (Harlow Pools) Ltd: C-326/96* [1998] ECR I-7835, the ECJ held that that limitation was incompatible with Community law.

EqPA 1970 was therefore amended to provide that the period in respect of which arrears of pay may be recovered is six years prior to commencement of proceedings in England and Wales (*ss 2(5), 2ZB(3)*) and five years in Scotland (*s 2ZC*), which reflects the limitation period for actions for breach of contract in the two jurisdictions, thereby satisfying the EC law requirement that domestic law procedural and remedial rules for breach of *Article 141* must be no less favourable than those governing similar domestic law claims (the principle of 'equivalence'). These limitation periods have been replicated in *EqA 2010, s 132(4) and (5)*

Different rules apply in 'concealment' and 'incapacity' cases (see **11.44**). In such cases, arrears can be claimed for the whole period since the date of the contravention to which the proceedings relate in England and Wales (*EqA 2010, s 132(4)*), and 20 years prior to commencement of proceedings in Scotland (*EqA 2010, s 132(5)*).

Where the equal pay claim includes a claim for non-monetary contractual benefits, the tribunal will award a sum equal to the monetary value of those benefits for the relevant period.

11.40 Injury to feelings

The EAT has confirmed the contractual nature of remedies under *EqPA 1970* in holding that an equal pay claimant cannot be awarded compensation for non-economic loss, such as for injury to feelings or aggravated or exemplary damages (*Allan v Newcastle upon Tyne City Council* [2005] ICR 1170). The EAT contrasted *EqPA 1970* with other domestic discrimination statutes, under which compensation claims are for a statutory tort and which specifically provide that damages may include compensation for injury to feelings. This approach is also likely to be taken under *EqA 2010*: the *EHRC Equal Pay Code* specifically states that a tribunal cannot make an award of injury to feelings for breach of an equality clause (para 148).

However, it could be argued that since unequal pay is a species of sex discrimination, such compensation should in principle be available. Moreover, *EqA 2010* itself, by its reference (in *ss 130* and *135*) to cases where the employer has 'concealed' an inequality, acknowledges circumstances where an award of aggravated or exemplary damages would seem to be appropriate (similar provisions were found in *EqPA 1970, ss 2ZA, 2ZB, 7AA* and *7AB*). In any event, an equal pay claim will often be combined with a sex discrimination claim, for which an injury to feelings award can be made.

A further example of the differential treatment given to equal pay claims compared with the other discrimination strands is the express carve out at *EqA 2010, s 113(6)* of equal pay claims from the tribunal's power to make recommendations to an employer to take specified steps to obviate or reduce the impact of any adverse discriminatory effect.

11.41 Declaration

An employee may seek a declaration that they have been paid unequally, although in most cases this will be deemed unnecessary because of the automatic operation of the equality clause. An exception to this is where the claimant is a 'test case' for a class of employees, in which case a declaration may be considered desirable in order that it may be relied upon by other claimants.

11.42 PRACTICALITIES

Questionnaires

As in other discrimination strands, there is a statutory procedure for an individual with cause for concern regarding equal pay to ask questions of her employer or former employer and template forms for this purpose (*EqA 2010, s 138*, see **1.183** and the *Equality Act (Obtaining Information) Order 2010 (SI 2010/2194), Sch 2*).

A claimant who submits an equal pay questionnaire before proceedings have commenced should ask for details of the pay and benefits of her proposed comparators. Unless the claimant already has verifiable information from some other source—unlikely, unless her employer has an unusually transparent pay system—she will need it both to form a view on whether a particular comparator is appropriate at all (anyone who has earned the same as, or less than, her throughout the relevant period will not be), and to assess, having regard to the extent of the disparity, how valuable the claim may be. This may determine whether she pursues the claim at all.

Receipt of such a request leaves the employer to perform a balancing act between, on the one hand, the desire to avoid adverse inferences being made against it through the absence of a response, or the provision of an evasive or equivocal response, and, on the other hand, the need to avoid breaching obligations it owes to the comparators under the *Data Protection Act 1998* (‘*DPA 1998*’) and the law on trust and confidence. However, once litigation is underway, it is likely that the employer will have to disclose the pay details anyway—*DPA 1998, s 35* exempts disclosures of personal data that are required by law or made in connection with legal proceedings.

The employer may take the view that some comparators are so clearly not employed on like work/equal value work/work rated as equivalent, or that its material factor defence is so solid, that it is willing to accept the risk of not providing any pay details—the risk being that a tribunal will subsequently take a different view, and draw adverse inferences. This risk can be minimised to some extent by the employer stating clearly in the questionnaire response its explanation for not providing the information.

For comparators where the claimant has a more arguable case, the employer could simply state that the comparator is earning the same as, less or more than the claimant. The difficulty, however, with only stating that the comparator is earning ‘more than’ the claimant is that not only does this (arguably) fall into the ‘evasive’ category, but strategically it is unhelpful for all concerned. It gives the claimant no indication as to the value of pursuing a particular comparator, which in turn makes it more likely for both parties that litigation will be pursued at least for some period of time before a resolution can be reached.

An employer could consider, therefore, approaching each comparator and requesting their written consent to the disclosure of their remuneration details at the questionnaire stage. If the claimant is still employed, this should be accompanied by a clear statement that the claimant should not be victimised by any comparator as a result (particularly in light of the provisions of *EqA 2010, s 77*, as to which see **11.37**). The request will lead either to the details being provided, or to the employer being able to explain (supported by an appropriate paper trail) their non-provision for a reason that is unlikely to lead to adverse inferences being drawn.

11.43 Time limits

An individual who is still employed can bring an equal pay claim against her employer at any time. The position once employment has terminated is less straightforward.

The original *EqPA 1970, s 2(4)* provided: ‘No claim in respect of the operation of an equal pay clause relating to a woman’s employment shall be referred to an [employment tribunal] if she has not been employed in the employment within the six months preceding the date of the reference’. In *Preston v Wolverhampton Healthcare NHS Trust and Secretary of State for Health* [1998] 1 WLR 280, the House of Lords held that, as far as domestic law was concerned, the time limit ran from the end of each contract under which an employee was employed—not from the end of any employment consisting of a succession of different contracts of employment with the same employer. However, the ECJ (*C-78/98* [2001] 2 AC 415) held that it was incompatible with EC law for a woman to have to make a claim in respect of each contract in these circumstances.

When the case returned to the House of Lords ([2001] 2 AC 455), Lord Slynn stated that ‘it is clear that where there are intermittent contracts of service without a stable employment relationship, the period of six months runs from the end of each contract of service, but where such contracts are concluded at regular intervals in respect of the same employment regularly in a stable employment relationship, the period runs from the end of the last contract forming part of that relationship' (para 33). The effect was that the time limit would run from the end of the last contract forming part of that stable employment relationship, and not from the end of the stable employment relationship itself insofar as that might identify a different point in time (*Jeffery v Secretary of State for Education* [2006] ICR 1062).

However, *EqPA 1970* was then amended in 2003 to produce the latter result, which has been retained by *EqA 2010*. *EqA 2010, s 129(2)* provides that proceedings may not be brought in a tribunal after the end of the 'qualifying period'. The 'qualifying period' in a standard case is 'the period of 6 months beginning with the last day of the employment or appointment'. However, in a 'stable work case' (defined as 'a case where the proceedings relate to a period during which there was a stable working relationship between the worker and the responsible person (including any time after the terms of work had expired)' (*EqA 2010, s 130(3)*) it is the period of six months beginning with the day on which the stable working relationship ended.

The Court of Appeal has recently suggested that a 'stable employment relationship' (the pre-*EqA 2010* equivalent of a 'stable working relationship') can also apply in a case where the claimant was employed on a succession of continuous contracts which were not separated by any breaks in work; the variation to terms did not affect the 'employment' even though the original contract had been superseded (*Slack v Cumbria County Council (Equality and Human Rights Commission intervening)* [2009] EWCA Civ 293, [2009] ICR 1217). The test that should be applied is whether or not the 'nature of the work, rather than the legal terms under which it is carried out', has been interrupted (*North Cumbria University Hospitals NHS Trust v Fox* [2010] EWCA Civ 729, [2010] IRLR 804 at para 32).

11.44 *Concealment/incapacity*

Unlike discrimination claims, there is no power for the tribunal to permit an equal pay claim to proceed out of time on the basis that it would be 'just and equitable' to allow this. However, *EqA 2010, s 129* extends the time limit in 'concealment' and 'incapacity' cases by specifying a different 'qualifying period' for such cases.

A 'concealment case' is a case where the employer deliberately concealed from the claimant any fact which is relevant to the claimant, and without knowledge of which the claimant could not reasonably have been expected to bring the proceedings, and the claimant did not discover the fact (or could not with reasonable diligence have discovered it) until after either the last day on which she was employed in the employment or the day on which the stable working relationship ended. The qualifying period is the period of six months beginning with the date on which the claimant discovered the qualifying fact in question (or could with reasonable diligence have discovered it).

An 'incapacity case' is a case where the claimant had an incapacity at any time during the six months after the last day on which she was employed in the employment, or the day on which the stable working relationship ended, or (if it is later) the day on which she discovered (or could with reasonable diligence have discovered) the qualifying concealed fact. The qualifying period is the period of six months beginning with the date on which the claimant ceased to have the incapacity or (if the case is also a concealment case) the later of that date and the 'concealment case' qualifying date.

11.45 *Transfer of undertaking*

The House of Lords held in *Powerhouse Retail Ltd v Burroughs* [2006] ICR 606 that an employee who transfers to a new employer under the *Transfer of Undertakings (Protection of Employment) Regulations 2006 (SI 2006/246)* ('*TUPE*') must bring an equal pay claim against the transferor (eg a claim relating to occupational pensions) within six months of the date of the transfer. This is because *EqPA 1970, s 2(4)* (now *EqA 2010, s 129(2)*) requires a claim to be brought within six months of the end of the employment to which the claim relates, and that employment ends upon the transfer. The House of Lords rejected the employees' argument that time runs from the date on which her employment with the transferee ends. See further *UNISON v Allen* [2007] IRLR 975.

Where an employee's employment automatically transfers to a new employer under TUPE, she remains entitled to bring an equal pay claim that exists at the date of transfer against the transferee, even where the comparator remains in the transferor's employment (*Gutridge v Sodexo Ltd* [2009] EWCA Civ 729, [2009] ICR 1486). However, as her employment with the transferor is deemed to have ended at the date of the transfer, the claim will need to be brought within six months of that date to ensure that she does not have any greater rights against the transferee than she would have had against the transferor. Any claims that the claimant has relating to the post-transfer period can be brought at any time up to six months after her employment with the transferee has ended.

A recent decision of the High Court has opened up the possibility that equal pay claims might be brought outside the 6-month time limit referred to in *EqPA 1970, s 2(4)*. In *Abdulla v Birmingham City Council* [2010] EWHC 3303 (QB), the High Court held that it had jurisdiction to hear an equal pay claim pursuant to *EqPA 1970, s 2(3)* (which is broadly replicated at *EqA 2010, s 128*) where the claimants' claim was outside the 6-month time limit under *EqPA 1970, s 2(3)* but within the six-year time limit for a simple breach of contract claim. Colin Edelman QC (sitting as a Deputy High Court Judge) recognised that this interpretation of *s 2(3)* could result in 'forum shopping' for a more favourable time limit, but stated that it would be wrong for the court to turn an employee's option of bringing an equal pay claim in the employment tribunal into an obligation by preventing her from pursuing a claim in the courts after the time limit for presentation of a complaint to the tribunal had expired (para 38). He concluded that '[o]n the true construction of *Section 2(3)*, it cannot be more convenient for a claim to be disposed of separately by an employment tribunal in circumstances where the employment tribunal could not determine the claim on its merits but would be bound to refuse jurisdiction to deal with the claim because it was time barred' (para 39).

Interestingly, however, the county court in *Ashby v Birmingham City Council* (unreported, 13 October 2009) reached the opposite conclusion on the same point. At the time of writing, the appeal in that case has been heard and judgment is awaited.

11.46 Pleadings

Key elements of an ET1 will include the following.

11.47 *Choice of comparators*

There is no limit on the number of comparators a claimant may name. It is desirable that she should identify all the comparators she wishes to pursue in her ET1. While the EAT held in *Bainbridge v Redcar and Cleveland Borough Council* [2007] IRLR 494 that a claimant is not estopped from bringing an equal pay claim in relation to one comparator when she has already failed in respect of the same period of time in relation to another comparator—on the basis that each claim is a separate and distinct cause of action for breach of contract—it did caution that such an approach may amount to an abuse of process, exposing the claimant to costs penalties. Further, a claimant should also note that any modification to her terms will be limited to those equal to her identified comparators. In *Leverton v Clwyd County Council* [1989] AC 706, Lord Bridge warned that a claimant who had identified comparators in her claim who had different terms as between themselves 'could hardly complain if an Industrial Tribunal concluded that her claim of equality with A itself demonstrated that there were no reasonable grounds for her claim of equality with B'.

Where there is any doubt as to the appropriateness of an identified comparator, a claimant may be advised to bring an alternative claim of direct sex discrimination in relation to contractual pay under *EqA 2010, s 71* which enables a claimant to use a hypothetical comparator where the equality clause provides no remedy. See also **11.10**.

11.48 *Basis of comparison*

For each comparator, the claimant should specify whether she considers that she is employed on like work, work rated as equivalent or work of equal value. It is common for claimants to plead like work or, in the alternative, work of equal value. A plea of equal value work will add significantly to the cost, length and complexity of proceedings. A claimant with a strong like-work claim will therefore need to consider carefully whether the benefits of adding an equal value claim are outweighed by these disadvantages.

11.49 *Period compared*

Particularly where more than one comparator is identified, the claimant should identify the time periods she is seeking to compare, for example 'Mr X for the period January 2003 to December 2005, then Mr Y who replaced Mr X for the period January 2006 to the present day'. Overlapping comparisons are permitted, although a claimant who makes such comparisons should be wary of the danger of losing focus.

11.50 *Remedy*

If it is intended that the claimant should stand as a 'test case' for a group of employees (which may even have been agreed with the employer), the ET1 should specify that a declaration is sought.

The employer should include the following in its ET3.

11.51 *Are comparators employed on equal work?*

The employer must consider whether to dispute the claimant's allegation that she is employed on like work/work rated as equivalent/work of equal value. While the employer's natural instinct may be to dispute it, concessions may be advantageous strategically if the employer has a strong material factor defence. It can then focus on this defence and avoid becoming embroiled in a protracted and costly dispute about (in particular) whether two jobs are of equal value.

11.52 *The 'material factor' defence*

Even if it does dispute that the claimant is employed on equal work with her comparators, the employer will normally argue in the alternative that there are one or more material factors which do not involve less favourable treatment because of the claimant's sex and which justify the difference in pay. Different material factors may apply as between different comparators, and indeed for the same comparator in different time periods. An employer should nevertheless select its material factor with care: any material factors that are inconsistent with an earlier questionnaire response, or that are unsupported by contemporaneous evidence, could undermine an otherwise strong case. If there is, or may be, any suggestion that the material factor is tainted by indirect discrimination, the employer should provide an explanation as to why this is objectively justified.

11.53 *Jurisdictional issues*

Depending on the circumstances, the employer may be able to raise jurisdictional points in its ET3, for example that the claim is out of time, or that there has been a TUPE transfer and liability has not transferred, such that she is suing the wrong respondent.

While most equal pay claims will be brought in tribunal proceedings, not least because of the expertise and experience that the tribunal has in dealing with the complexity of such claims, an employee may choose to bring her claim in the civil courts instead. As noted above at **11.45**, this is the likely course of action where the 6-month time limit for commencement of employment tribunal proceedings has expired, and the employee wishes instead to avail herself of the six-year time limit for a simple breach of contract claim.

EqA 2010, s 128(1) (formerly *EqPA 1970, s 2(3)*) gives the High Court or county court discretion to strike out the claim or counter-claim where it considers that it could be disposed of 'more conveniently' by an employment tribunal. The High Court has held that this discretion is an '*unfettered*' one (*Abdulla v Birmingham City Council* [2010] EWHC 3303 (QB), para 35). In addition, where the court considers that the tribunal is not the more convenient forum to dispose of the claim, it can nevertheless refer certain questions to it for determination (*EqA 2010, s 128(2)*).

11.54 Case management

In principle, the case management directions and orders that a tribunal may make regarding matters such as disclosure, witness statements, agreed statements of facts and chronologies are no different in an equal pay case than in any other discrimination proceedings. Where there is a plea of equal value, however, the tribunal must also grapple with the *Employment Tribunals (Equal Value) Rules of Procedure* ('*Equal Value Rules*') found in the *Employment Tribunals (Constitution and Rules of Procedure) Regulations 2004 (SI 2004/1861), Sch 6*.

The tribunal will often wish to consider the employer's material factor defence first, at a preliminary hearing. If the material factor defence succeeds, the claim fails; if the material factor defence fails, the claim proceeds to a full hearing on whether the claimant is employed on equal work, although the employer may come under pressure in the meantime to negotiate a settlement. The parties will have the opportunity to make submissions on whether the material factor should be dealt with first, which will be shaped by their respective views of its merits. The EAT has recently reaffirmed that there is nothing in the legislation which prevents the material factor issue being taken as a preliminary point: *Sunderland City Council v Brennan* UKEAT/0219/08 (20 June 2008, unreported) at paras 43–46.

An issue which often arises at the interlocutory stage in equal pay cases is the extent of disclosure that an employer must provide about its pay processes. In *Villalba v Merrill Lynch & Co Inc* UKEAT/0461/04 (1 July 2004, unreported), the EAT upheld a tribunal decision to refuse an application by Ms Villalba for the disclosure of pay data for over 120 employees. The application was made on the basis that the employer's pay system was not transparent, that it was shown statistically that the average pay of a group of women was lower than the average pay of a group of men, and that this meant the employer was obliged to objectively justify that differential. The EAT found that the tribunal was entitled to bear in mind that there had been a lengthy equal pay questionnaire responded to at length by the respondent, that the disclosure which had been sought in relation to the claimant's pleadings had been given, and that the disclosure now sought was very wide ranging. The tribunal did, however, criticise the employer for refusing to provide pay data about the comparators until a very late stage in the proceedings.

11.55 Equal value claims and experts

As noted at **11.54**, the *Equal Value Rules* apply to any proceedings 'involving' an equal value claim. This includes claims where like work or work rated as equivalent is pleaded in the alternative, as well as claims that involve entirely separate causes of action from equal pay.

The *Rules* require the tribunal to conduct a 'stage 1 equal value hearing' (*Rule 4*). At the hearing, and assuming the tribunal does not strike the claim out because the claimant and her comparators have been graded differently in an analytical and non-discriminatory JES (*Rule 4(3)(a)*), the tribunal must decide either to determine the equal value question itself, or to require a member of the panel of independent experts to prepare a report on the matter.

Details of the duties and powers of the independent expert are set out in *Rule 10*, and rules on the use of expert evidence generally in *Rule 11*. *Rule 11(1)* states that expert evidence is 'to be restricted to that which, in the opinion of the tribunal, is reasonably required to resolve the proceedings'. If the claim involves a comparison of jobs requiring easily comprehensible, and readily comparable, skills and responsibilities, the tribunal may decide to determine the equal value question on the basis of its own industrial relations experience. Conversely, if the jobs are highly specialised, or the comparators numerous, expert evidence is likely to be required.

Tribunals at stage 1 hearings (which are unlikely to have any great familiarity with the issues at this stage) generally give considerable weight to parties' submissions on the appropriate course to adopt. Each party should therefore decide in advance which approach they would prefer. This should include consideration of whether they wish to ask for permission to instruct their own experts (permission is required: *Rule 11(3)*). The tribunal is more likely to give permission if both parties are legally represented and each proposes to instruct an expert, and if the tribunal has decided to determine the equal value question itself without the assistance of an independent expert.

For a party, the advantage of its 'own' expert is that, while experts owe an overriding duty to the tribunal (*Rule 11(2)*), the party will nevertheless be able to make an informed choice of an expert with (say) knowledge of the relevant industry and/or the requirements of jobs within that industry. The degree of chance involved in relying on a member of the independent panel, or on the tribunal itself, is accordingly reduced. The disadvantages include cost—the parties must each pay for their own expert, whereas the costs of a member of the panel of independent experts are paid out of central funds—and the fact that the field of equal value experts is a relatively limited one, making selection decisions difficult.

Rule 5 sets out 'standard orders' that the tribunal must make at the stage 1 hearing unless it considers it inappropriate to do so. These essentially require each side to clarify its case. If the tribunal decides to appoint an independent expert, it must fix a date for a 'stage 2 equal value hearing'. *Rule 6(2)* allows the tribunal to order the independent expert to assist it in establishing the facts on which the expert may rely in preparing his report. The circumstances in which it may do so are specified in *Rule 6(3)*. The extent to which the tribunal makes use of these interventionist powers will normally depend on how successful the parties have been in complying with orders made under *Rule 5*.

At any stage 2 equal value hearing, the tribunal must make a determination of facts on which the parties cannot agree which relate to the equal value question, and require the independent expert to prepare his report on the basis of facts agreed between the parties or determined by the tribunal (*Rule 7(3)*). These facts then become the only facts relating to the equal value question on which the tribunal may rely at the full hearing (*Rule 7(5)*), unless the expert applies to the tribunal for some or all of the facts relating to the question to be amended, supplemented or omitted (*Rule 7(6)*). The tribunal must, unless it considers it inappropriate to do so, order the expert to prepare his report on the equal value question by a specified date and send copies to the parties and the tribunal (*Rule 8(1)(a)*). It must also fix a date for the full hearing (*Rule 7(4)(c)*).

Once an expert—independent or otherwise—has prepared a report, any party or other expert involved in the proceedings may write to her and ask her questions about the report (*Rule 12(1)*). This provides an opportunity for 'damage limitation' for whichever party's case has been adversely impacted by the expert report(s), although both parties are likely to have some points that they wish to clarify. The expert's answers are treated as part of their report.

The final stage is, of course, the full hearing. The *Equal Value Rules* include an 'indicative timetable' under which it is envisaged that claims not involving an independent expert will proceed to a full hearing within 25 weeks of a claim being filed, and claims involving an independent expert within 37 weeks. It is the authors' experience, however, that these timelines are more often honoured in the breach than the observance, given the complexity of the typical equal value claim.

The question whether the claimant's work and that of her comparators was of equal value must be considered in respect of every part of the claim period, and where it is claimed that the facts were materially different in different parts of the claim period they must be stated on a distinct basis in respect of the different parts of the period. This should be done either, where the differences are great, by two distinct statements of facts, or otherwise at a given base date, typically the date at which the claim was presented, identifying the variations throughout the period (*Potter v North Cumbria Acute Hospitals NHS Trust* [2008] ICR 910).

11.56 Equal pay reviews and audits

Despite the best endeavours of the EOC (now EHRC), it remains comparatively rare for employers, at least in the private sector, to have undertaken an equal pay review/audit. The five step equal pay review model recommended by the EHRC in the *EHRC Equal Pay Code* (*paras 171–185*) consists of the following:

Step 1: Deciding the scope of the review and identifying the data required. The EHRC recommends that all employees in the same employment or whose pay can be attributed to a single source should be included.

Step 2: Determining where men and women are doing equal work. This is, in essence, a process of job evaluation.

Step 3: Collecting pay data to identify equal pay gaps. This involves matching the job evaluation undertaken at step 2 to the pay data collected.

Step 4: Establishing the causes of any significant pay gaps and assessing the reasons for these. This involves the employer assessing the robustness of any prospective material factor defence.

Step 5: Developing an equal pay action plan and/or reviewing and monitoring. This involves taking steps—or example, awarding pay increases and paying back pay—to put right any issues that have been identified, and to keep the organisation's pay policies under review in the future.

At each stage the obstacles facing the employer can be daunting, particularly for large, decentralised organisations. In a company with thousands of employees based in numerous different locations, simply assembling accurate, up-to-date pay data broken down by gender can be a significant logistical challenge. As roles within the modern economy become ever more specialised, the process of evaluating and comparing jobs can be complex and open to challenge. Once the final stage is reached, the employer is not only likely to face a substantial bill to 'level up' those employees whom it is found are being underpaid (as 'levelling down' is rarely a palatable option), but also runs the risk of alerting those same employees to the fact that they may have a strong equal pay claim for arrears of pay for a period of up to six years.

Unless equal pay reviews are made compulsory, or a moratorium is imposed on equal pay claims for earlier periods where an employer has undertaken a review, or (as is increasingly becoming the case) having undertaken a review is made a requirement of undertaking work for public bodies, it seems likely that most employers will continue to abstain from the exercise.

11.57 Gender reporting provisions

The previous Labour government included a power in *EqA, s 78* to make future regulations requiring private sector employers with over 250 employees to publish information about the differences in pay between male and female employees. The new Conservative-Liberal

Democrat coalition government has confirmed that it is not currently proposing to commence, amend or repeal that provision, but instead will develop a voluntary gender pay reporting scheme for all businesses in the private and voluntary sector, with a particular focus on businesses employing 150 or more employees. The number of companies releasing information and the quality of the information will be subject to annual review of whether further steps are necessary (including, in principle, the use of the mandatory approach envisaged by *EqA 2010, s 78*).

Index

Index

B

Index

Index

E

Q